THE NATIONAL TRUST GUIDE

TO HISTORIC BED & BREAKFASTS,

INNS AND SMALL HOTELS

THE NATIONAL TRUST GUIDE TO HISTORIC

BED & BREAKFASTS

INNS AND SMALL HOTELS

FOURTH EDITION

SUZANNE G. DANE

PRESERVATION PRESS

JOHN WILEY & SONS, INC.
New York • Chichester • Brisbane • Toronto • Singapore

Designed and typeset by Marilyn Appleby, Arnold, Maryland

The National Trust for Historic Preservation is the only private, nonprofit organization chartered by Congress to encourage public participation in the preservation of sites, buildings, and objects significant in American history and culture. Support is provided by membership dues, endowment funds, contributions, and grants from federal agencies under provisions of the National Historic Preservation Act of 1966. For information about membership in the National Trust, write to the Membership Office, 1785 Massachusetts Avenue, N.W., Washington, D.C. 20036.

This text is printed on acid-free paper.

Copyright © 1996 by John Wiley & Sons, Inc.

All rights reserved. Published simultaneously in Canada.
Reproduction or translation of any part of this work beyond
that permitted by Section 107 or 108 of the 1976 United
States Copyright Act without the permission of the copyright
owner is unlawful. Requests for permission or further
information should be addressed to the Permissions Department,
John Wiley & Sons, Inc., 605 Third Avenue, New York, NY
10158-0012.

This publication is designed to provide accurate and
authoritative information in regard to the subject
matter covered. It is sold with the understanding that
the publisher is not engaged in rendering legal, accounting,
or other professional services. If legal advice or other
expert assistance is required, the services of a competent
professional person should be sought.

Library of Congress Cataloging in Publication Data:
Dane, Suzanne G.
    The National Trust guide to historic bed & breakfasts, inns &
        small hotels / Suzanne G. Dane. — 4th ed.
                p.   cm.
        ISBN 0-471-14973-X (pbk. : alk. paper)
            1. Bed and breakfast accommodations—United States—Guidebooks.
    2. Hotels—United States—Guidebooks. 3. Historic buildings—United
    States—Guidebooks. 4. United States—Guidebooks. I. National
    Trust for Historic Preservation in the United States. II. Title.
    TX907.2.D36 1996   96-908
    647.9473'03—dc20

Printed in the United States of America

10 9 8 7 6 5 4 3 2 1

CONTENTS

INTRODUCTION

THE NATIONAL TRUST GUIDE TO HISTORIC BED & BREAKFASTS, INNS, AND SMALL HOTELS lists more than 700 historic lodgings across the United States. America's diverse history is reflected in these buildings. The City Hotel in Columbia, California, was built during the state's gold rush era to house in splendor those who had made fortunes from the local mines. *Gone with the Wind* author Margaret Mitchell interviewed Civil War veterans at the Veranda in Senoia, Georgia. Former President Gerald Ford, as a college student, spent some time at the Green Mountain Inn, Stowe, Vermont, to participate in a modeling assignment for *Look* magazine. The first president of the United States was a guest at Tulpehocken Manor in Myerstown, Pennsylvania. The first baseball game was organized by Abner Doubleday at Ängelholm in Cooperstown, New York.

Our colonial days are represented by an "ordinary," or tavern, in Middletown, Virginia, that has welcomed travelers for two centuries. Religious freedom is expressed in dwellings that once housed parsons, monks, and bishops. The course of America's economy is traced in the homes of great inventors and in commercial buildings such as mills, bakeries, and breweries. From the East Brother Light Station in San Francisco Bay to the Big Bay Point Lighthouse in Big Bay, Michigan, from a pineapple-plantation house in Hawaii to a cotton-plantation house in Mississippi, this book provides options for overnight stays that span the country and the centuries.

ABOUT THE INNS

To qualify for listing in this guidebook, an inn must be 50 or more years old and must retain its architectural integrity. Homes and inns that have undergone dramatic remodeling that obliterated original structures or historic additions have been excluded.

Descriptions of the inns, compiled from materials supplied by the innkeepers, include information about each building's architecture, construction, and craftsmanship. They describe the importance of the structure to the community, historic events that occurred there, or maybe a note about the not-so-famous people who were once residents. These bits of information set the historic inns apart from their more anonymous modern counterparts; they are the fragments of the past that catch a traveler's imagination.

ABOUT THE GUIDE

The listing that follows each description summarizes room rates and amenities. It also tells you when the establishment is open for business, how many guest rooms are available, whether or not there are private baths, and if the room rate includes meals. The notation "MAP," which stands for modified American Plan, means that both breakfast and dinner are included in the rate. **Room rates**, unless otherwise stated, are for double occupancy and are exclusive of taxes. The listing also notes those establishments that offer discounted rates to National Trust members and National Trust Visa cardholders.

Credit cards have been abbreviated as follows: AmEx, American Express; MC, Master Card; CB, Carte Blanche; DC, Diners Club. Other credit cards are spelled out.

Some bed and breakfasts cannot accommodate very young **children**. Such restrictions, including an age limit for children, are noted.

Many establishments prohibit cigarette and cigar **smoking** anywhere indoors. "No smoking" will indicate this restriction, even if outside smoking is allowed; "limited" means that smoking is permissible only in certain rooms.

The **Activities** section highlights things to do or see *on the premises*. This category most often includes recreational activities but also may list interesting collections, libraries, or just plain peace and quiet, if that's what an establishment specializes in.

Nearby attractions, listed under town or city names (rather than the names of specific establishments), include historic sites and other points of interest around which you may want to plan your trip. Places for sightseeing, shopping, and outdoor recreation within an hour's driving time all are listed in this category. Frequently, the attractions are within walking distance of the inn.

Some bed and breakfasts in high-tourism areas have minimum-stay requirements on weekends or in peak seasons. If you are headed to a known tourist region at peak season, be sure to ask about possible restrictions.

The owners and managers of these historic bed and breakfasts, inns, and small hotels have proven their dedication to enriching the present and future by preserving the best of the past. With this guide to historic accommodations you too can take part in the adventure and history offered by these one-of-a-kind establishments.

ALABAMA

ANNISTON

Nearby attractions: Mt. Cheaha, Anniston Museum of Natural History, Talladega Super Speedway, historic district walking tours, antique hunting

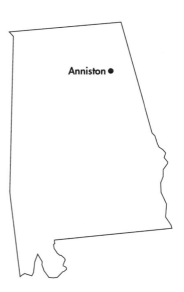

THE VICTORIA, A COUNTRY INN AND RESTAURANT

1604 Quintard Avenue
P.O. Box 2213
Anniston, Alabama 36202
205/236-0503 or 800/260-8781
205/236-1138 Fax
Proprietors: Betty and Earlon McWorter
Innkeepers: Beth and Fain Casey

Built in 1888 by John M. McKleroy, a Civil War veteran and attorney, the Victoria is listed in the National Register of Historic Places. A shining example of the Queen Anne style, it is notable for a three-story turret, a mixture of wavy, square, and incised shingles, stained- and etched-glass windows, and colonnaded verandas. The interior boasts oak detailing rich in ornamentation. The inn consists of the original home, which accommodates a full-service restaurant and three suites, plus a recently constructed annex that wraps around a brick courtyard and swimming pool. Each guest room is decorated with brass, wicker, pine, or mahogany furnishings. Amenities include turn-down service, valet parking, complimentary newspaper, welcoming cocktail, and attentive service. The Victoria sits grandly on a hill surrounded by trees and well-groomed flower beds.

Open: year round **Accommodations:** 48 guest rooms with private baths; 4 are suites **Meals:** continental breakfast included; complimentary refreshments; restaurant on premises **Wheelchair access:** some guest rooms, dining room **Rates:** $64 to $150 **Payment:** AmEx, Visa, MC, CB, DC, Discover, personal and traveler's checks **Restrictions:** no pets **Activities:** swimming pool, gazebos, Wren's Nest art gallery

ALASKA

ESTER

Nearby attractions: Riverboat Discovery, University of Alaska Museum, Alaskaland, gold dredge no. 8

ESTER GOLD CAMP
3660 Main Street
P.O. Box 109
Ester, Alaska 99725
907/479-2500
907/474-1780 Fax
Proprietor: Brenda Winther **Operations Manager:** Nancy Scholl

At the turn of the century, the discovery of gold on Ester, Cripple, and Eva creeks drew prospectors. The town of Ester sprang up to meet their needs, boasting numerous hotels, saloons, and shops. Eventually, the pick and pan gave way to partnerships with steam hoists. Those gave way to the hydraulic cannon and gold dredge. The Fairbanks Exploration Company opened Ester Gold Camp to support a large-scale dredge operation in 1936. A bunkhouse and dining hall, homes, offices, and shops were built. The days of the dredge are gone, but Ester Gold Camp still provides overnight accommodations and delicious buffet dinners in the bunkhouse. The camp's 11 buildings have been listed in the National Register and are open to visitors. The blacksmith shop now sells gifts and souvenirs.

Open: May to September **Accommodations:** 20 guest rooms with sinks; every 2 rooms share a shower and toilet **Meals:** continental breakfast included; restaurant on premises **Rates:** $50 to $80 **Payment:** Visa, MC, Discover, personal and traveler's checks **Restrictions:** no smoking; no pets **Activities:** Malemute Saloon with nightly entertainment, Northern Lights Photosymphony, gift shop

KETCHIKAN
Nearby attractions: historic Creek Street, Southeast Alaska Visitors Center, totem parks, rain forest, museums, salmon hatchery, restaurants and nightclubs, fjords, harbor cruises, fishing for salmon and freshwater trout

GILMORE HOTEL
326 Front Street
Ketchikan, Alaska 99901
907/225-9423
Proprietors: Terry Wanzer and Kay Sims

Built in 1927 of solid concrete, the Gilmore Hotel sits in the center of downtown, affording guests a delightful view of Alaska's busiest waterfront. Here, commercial fishing boats, luxury cruise liners, freighters, and seaplanes come and go regularly. The hotel, listed in the National Register of Historic Places, provides modern conveniences such as private baths, color television, telephones, and room service. Along with friendly Alaskan hospitality, the Gilmore Hotel offers fishing-vacation packages, freezer space for fish caught by guests, and a courtesy van. The Gilmore Hotel is the home of Annabelle's Famous Keg and Chowder House, which is decorated in a style reminiscent of Ketchikan's earlier days. Ketchikan, Alaska's fourth-largest city, offers a remarkable blend of modern and frontier ways of life and offers a variety of activities within walking distance.

Open: year round **Accommodations:** 40 guest rooms (38 have private baths) **Meals:** restaurant on premises **Rates:** $64 to $88; 10% discount to National Trust members and National Trust Visa cardholders **Payment:** AmEx, Visa, MC, DC, Discover

ARIZONA

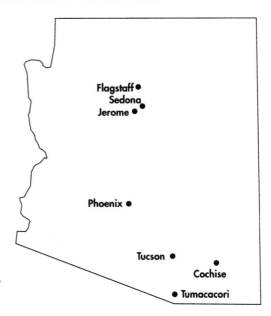

COCHISE

Nearby attractions: Amerind Foundation Museum, Chiricahua National Monument, Rex Allen Museum, town of Tombstone

COCHISE HOTEL AND GIFT SHOP
P.O. Box 27
Cochise, Arizona 85606
602/384-3038 or 602/384-3156
Proprietor: Elizabeth Husband
Manager: Lillie W. Harrington
Location: 15 miles west of Willcox, 85 miles east of Tucson

Built in 1882 as a rooming house at the junction of the Southern Pacific and old Arizona Eastern railways, the Cochise Hotel also housed the town's first post office and a Wells Fargo freight office. Guests visiting the adobe-and-wood-siding structure today can catch a glimpse of turn-of-the-century Arizona in the hotel's authentic furnishings—a wind-up phonograph, heavy walnut tables and chairs, a velvet sofa that was reputedly Jenny Lind's, and a wardrobe with mirrored doors—all formally arranged around an oriental carpet. Guest rooms, refurbished with modern baths and heating, retain their Old West flavor. Behind the hotel, the Cochise Gift Shop is housed in what was once an old harness shop.

Open: year round **Accommodations:** 5 guest rooms with private baths; 2 are suites **Meals:** restaurant on premises serves breakfast, lunch, and dinner **Wheelchair access:** guest rooms, bathrooms, dining facilities **Rates:** $25 single to $30 double; $35 suites **Payment:** personal and traveler's checks **Restrictions:** no smoking **Activities:** piano, card games, gift shop

FLAGSTAFF

Nearby attractions: Grand Canyon, Hopi and Navajo Indian reservations, Indian ruins, Meteor Crater, Oak Creek Canyon, San Francisco Peaks, Coconino National Forest, hiking, mountain biking, bird-watching, cross-country skiing, Museum of Northern Arizona, Lowell Observatory, Northern Arizona University, Flagstaff Arboretum, Native American art galleries, antiques hunting

THE INN AT 410 BED AND BREAKFAST
410 North Leroux Street
Flagstaff, Arizona 86001
602/774-0088 or 800/774-2008
Proprietors: Howard and Sally Krueger

This 1907 Craftsman house was first the residence of a wealthy banker, businessman, and cattle rancher. Now, fully renovated and elegantly decorated, the Inn at 410 offers eight guest rooms filled with a blend of antique and contemporary furnishings in a variety of styles. Rooms include the Southwest, with its Santa Fe decor; Sunflower Fields, in a vibrant country motif; and Dakota, with rustic twig furniture and a cowboy decor. Three rooms offer fireplaces, two have whirlpool tubs. Stained glass, lace curtains, and local antiques fill the remainder of the inn, where fresh home-baked cookies are offered each afternoon. Located just blocks from downtown Flagstaff, the inn is a perfect base from which to visit the natural spendors of northern Arizona.

Open: year round **Accommodations:** 8 guest rooms with private baths; 6 are suites **Meals:** full breakfast included; complimentary refreshments; restaurants nearby **Wheelchair access:** 1 guest room **Rates:** $100 to $150 **Payment:** AmEx, Visa, MC, personal and traveler's checks **Restrictions:** no smoking; no pets **Activities:** books, board games

JEROME
Nearby attractions: Tuzigoot National Monument, Jerome Historic State Park, Douglas Mining Museum, Verde River Canyon Railroad, Montezuma's Castle and Well, galleries, boutiques, hiking, Jeep tours, horseback riding, exploring mine sites, gold panning, antiques hunting, hot-air ballooning

GHOST CITY INN BED AND BREAKFAST
541 North Main Street
P.O. Box 382
Jerome, Arizona 86331
520/63GHOST (520/634-4678)
Proprietors: Don and Carla Hopkins and Rick and Dione Cozens

Guests at the Ghost City Inn can step onto a veranda from their rooms to take in the breathtaking views of the Verde Valley and the terraced red rocks of Sedona. The inn was built in 1898 when Jerome was a thriving copper mining town. Today, guests at the inn can stroll to the nearby historic town to enjoy its colorful history and many art galleries, jewelry boutiques, and restaurants. Guest rooms contain an artful blend of Victorian and early American antiques and contemporary comforts such as ceiling fans and television. The innkeepers provide a full breakfast and afternoon tea, turn-down service with chocolates, and assistance with recreational plans.

Open: year round **Accommodations:** 5 guest rooms (1 has a private bath) **Meals:** full breakfast included; complimentary refreshments; restaurants nearby **Rates:** $75 to $95; 10% discount to National Trust members and National Trust Visa cardholders **Payment:** AmEx, Visa, MC, Discover, personal and traveler's checks **Restrictions:** no smoking; no pets **Activities:** whirlpool tub, bicycling, croquet

INN AT JEROME
309 Main Street
P.O. Box 901
Jerome, Arizona 86331
520/634-5094
Proprietors: Don and Carla Hopkins and Mark Butler

This 1899 Victorian structure sits on Cleopatra Hill in the once-booming copper mining town of Jerome. From its vantage point, the inn offers guests magnificent vistas of the Verde Valley and the Red Rock country of Sedona. The inn has been restored to reflect the mining era and is filled with Victorian antiques. The parlor provides a warming fireplace while distinctively styled guest rooms brim with details for comfort, including terrycloth robes, ceiling fans, evaporative cooling systems, and television. Guests receive complimentary morning coffee. The inn's dining room, the Jerome Grill, specializes in Southwest fare.

Open: year round **Accommodations:** 8 guest rooms (2 have private baths) **Meals:** complimentary refreshments; restaurant on premises **Rates:** $65 to $95; 10% discount to National Trust members and National Trust Visa cardholders **Payment:** AmEx, Visa, MC, Discover, personal and traveler's checks **Restrictions:** no smoking; no pets **Activities:** relaxing in parlor with fireplace

---

PHOENIX
Nearby attractions: art museum, Biltmore Fashion Park, theaters, convention center, Capitol Complex, golfing, tennis, horseback riding

MARICOPA MANOR BED AND BREAKFAST INN
15 West Pasadena Avenue
Phoenix, Arizona 85013-2001
602/274-6302
602/266-3904 Fax
Proprietors: Mary Ellen and Paul Kelley

Maricopa Manor was built in 1928 as a summer home by Byron J. and Neomi Showers, who were early settlers in the Arizona Territory. It was designed in a Spanish Revival style. Guests are invited to share in the use of the spacious gathering room with outside deck, the formal living, dining, and music rooms, the patio, and the gazebo spa. Guest suites are luxuriously furnished in various motifs from the blue-and-white Library Suite, with canopied king bed, to the Victorian Suite, outfitted in satin, lace, antiques, and king bed. The guest house, built on the property in the 1940s, contains two suites—one nostalgic and one modern. All suites have color television and telephones. The one-acre estate sits amid lush gardens, palm and citrus trees, fountains, courtyards, and patios.

Open: year round **Accommodations:** 6 guest suites with private baths **Meals:** continental-plus breakfast included; restaurants nearby **Wheelchair access:** 1 room **Rates:** $89 to $159; 10% discount to National Trust members and National Trust Visa cardholders **Payment:** AmEx, Visa, MC, Discover, personal and traveler's checks **Restrictions:** smoking limited; no pets **Activities:** swimming pool, spa

SEDONA

Nearby attractions: Hopi mesas, Tlaquepaque, national forests, shops and galleries, horseback riding, golfing, tennis, fishing

BED AND BREAKFAST AT SADDLE ROCK RANCH
255 Rock Ridge Drive
Sedona, Arizona 86336
520/282-7640
520/282-6829 Fax
Proprietors: Fran and Dan Bruno

Saddle Rock Ranch is a country estate nestled on three acres of hillside overlooking the town of Sedona. It is surrounded on all sides by breathtaking red rock vistas. The 1926 homestead has native rock and adobe walls, massive-beamed ceilings, and wood and flagstone floors. The spacious parlor, exclusively for guest use, has an 1850s pump organ, fireplace, and Native American artifacts. In the sunny breakfast room works by renowned local artists adorn the rock walls. Each guest room is decorated in romantic themes, enhanced by wood-burning rock fireplaces. Guests are welcome in the courtyard garden to enjoy its deck, lounges, swimming pool, spa, and magnificent views. A guest refrigerator, freezer, and microwave are available.

Open: year round **Accommodations:** 3 guest rooms with private baths; 1 is a suite **Meals:** full breakfast included; complimentary refreshments; restaurants nearby **Rates:** $110 to $140 **Payment:** personal and traveler's checks **Restrictions:** children over 14 welcome; no smoking; no pets **Activities:** swimming, hiking, Jeep tours

TUCSON

Nearby attractions: University of Arizona, Arizona Sonora Desert Museum, Tucson Convention Center, planetarium, observatories, zoo, state and local parks, golfing, tennis, jogging and hiking trails

CASA ALEGRE BED AND BREAKFAST INN

316 East Speedway
Tucson, Arizona 85705
602/628-1800
602/792-1880 Fax
Proprietor: Phyllis Florek

Located in the West University Historic District, this distinguished Craftsman bungalow was built in 1915 for Tucson pharmacist Arthur McNeal. The house features built-in mahogany and leaded-glass cabinetry and hardwood floors. The four guest rooms, each with private bath, are uniquely furnished to reflect Tucson's history: the Saguaro Room, named for the indigenous giant cactus, contains natural saguaro ribs; the Spanish Room features a headboard originally made for a Mexican priest; the Rose Quartz Room holds mining memorabilia; and the Amethyst Room boasts turn-of-the-century antiques and the house's original claw-foot tub. A wall stuccoed to match the house encloses the swimming pool and serene patio where guests enjoy a full breakfast. Casa Alegre allows easy access to Tucson's major attractions and business centers.

Open: year round **Accommodations:** 4 guest rooms with private baths **Meals:** full breakfast included; complimentary refreshments; restaurants nearby **Rates:** $80 to $95; 10% discount to National Trust members and National Trust Visa cardholders **Payment:** Visa, MC, Discover, personal and traveler's checks **Restrictions:** inquire about children; no smoking; no pets **Activities:** swimming pool, hot tub, television room

LA POSADA DEL VALLE

1640 North Campbell Avenue
Tucson, Arizona 85719
602/795-3840
Proprietors: Tom and Karin Dennen

This home, designed by renowned Tucson architect Josias T. Joesler, was built in 1929. Constructed of adobe and stucco, La Posada del Valle is a fine example of the Spanish Colonial Revival, or Santa Fe, style of architecture. Each of the five guest accommodations has a private outside entrance and private bath. Room decors range from Victorian in Sophie's Room to Art Deco in Pola's Room. Karin's Cottage, a charming cottage with private entrance from the courtyard and kitchenette, is dressed in an early 1900s African motif. Breakfast is served in the dining room or on the sunporch overlooking the landscaped yard and orange trees. The living room, where afternoon tea is served, is appointed with fine Art Deco furnishings. Located in one of Tucson's finest neighborhoods, La Posada del Valle is central to the city's attractions.

Open: year round **Accommodations:** 5 guest rooms with private baths; 1 is a cottage **Meals:** full breakfast included on weekends; continental-plus breakfast included on weekdays; restaurants nearby **Rates:** $90 to $125; 10% discount to National Trust members and National Trust Visa cardholders **Payment:** Visa, MC, personal and traveler's checks **Restrictions:** no smoking; no pets **Activities:** patio sitting

TUMACACORI

Nearby attractions: Tumacacori National Historic Park; de Mano Gallery of Contemporary Crafts; Anza Trail Nature Walk; Tubac arts colony; Nogales, Mexico

OLD MISSION STORE BED AND BREAKFAST
1908 East Frontage Road
Tumacacori, Arizona 85640
Mailing address:
P.O. Box 1471
Tubac, Arizona 85646
520/398-9583
Proprietors: Kim and David Yubeta

Tumacacori is three miles south of Tubac, a thriving artist's community, and 21 miles north of the international border city of Nogales, Arizona/Mexico. Tumacacori's bed and breakfast is located in the 1926 building that was once the area grocery store, post office, and gathering place. In the 1960s the building was converted to a private residence. Today, the building's south wing is a bed-and-breakfast facility consisting of a breakfast–sitting room, bedroom, bathroom, additional sleeping area, and patio. Guests enter through a private entrance. Across the street from the inn is Tumacacori National Historic Park, the ruins of a Spanish colonial mission community.

Open: year round **Accommodations:** 1 guest wing sleeps up to 4 in one party **Meals:** full breakfast included; complimentary refreshments; restaurants nearby **Rates:** $65 double, $20 per additional person **Payment:** personal and traveler's checks **Restrictions:** no smoking **Activities:** patio lounging

ARKANSAS

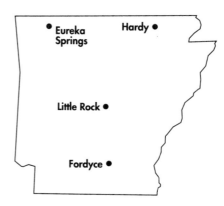

EUREKA SPRINGS

Nearby attractions: historic district, museums, Passion Play of the Ozarks, Silver Dollar City, Lake Beaver, Inspiration Point artists' colony, swimming, fishing, boating, September jazz festival, shopping, antiques hunting

DAIRY HOLLOW HOUSE
515 Spring Street
Eureka Springs, Arkansas 72632
501/253-7444 or 800/562-8650
501/253-7223 Fax
Proprietors: Ned Shank and Crescent Dragonwagon

Dairy Hollow House relieves visitors of their jangled nerves with such pleasures as the smell of hot apple cider, or a quilt-covered, canopied bed and a stack of wood by an antique fireplace, or a jug of tulips and books to read in a sunny nook or on a rocker-filled porch. Guest rooms are in either the 1888 farmhouse or the 1940s main house just up the gravel road. In the farmhouse the Tulip Room has a whirlpool tub for two and potbellied stove; the Rose Room and Iris Room feature antiques and fireplaces. Suites in the main house are individually decorated, but all have fireplaces. Breakfast is brought to bedroom doors. The inn features an acclaimed restaurant serving what the innkeepers call "Nouveau 'Zarks" cuisine. Dairy Hollow House has been praised by the *New York Times*, *USA Today*, *Christian Science Monitor*, *Glamour*, and *Chocolatier*, and is a three-time winner of Uncle Ben's Inn of Distinction award.

Open: February 1 through December 31 **Accommodations:** 6 guest rooms with private baths; 2 are suites **Rates:** $125 to $175 **Payment:** AmEx, Visa, MC, CB, DC, Discover, personal and traveler's checks **Restrictions:** children welcome in suites; no smoking; no pets **Activities:** outdoor hot tub in the woods, porch rocking, bird-watching, reading

SINGLETON HOUSE
11 Singleton
Eureka Springs, Arkansas 72632
501/253-9111 or 800/833-3394
Proprietor: Barbara Gavron

This 1890s two-story bay-front Queen Anne Victorian is located on a ridge above historic Sweet Springs, one of more than 60 springs in the area. Built by a local barber, the house contains many original pieces of furniture, including a barber's cabinet. The present owner, trained as an interior designer, has furnished the light and airy guest rooms with an eclectic collection of treasures and antiques. Full breakfast is served on the balcony overlooking a garden and goldfish pond. Guests can ride an old-fashioned trolley to town or take a short stroll down a wooded footpath to shops and cafes. For a very private retreat, ask about the Gardener's Cottage—a 100-year-old cabin filled with country antiques, yet offering the most modern amenities, including a whirlpool tub for two. The innkeeper, who is beginning her twelfth season, offers a hands-on apprenticeship program for aspiring bed-and-breakfast owners.

Open: year round **Accommodations:** 5 guest rooms with private baths; separately located guest cottage **Meals:** full breakfast included (no breakfast served at cottage); complimentary refreshments; restaurants nearby **Rates:** $65 to $95; cottage $95; 10% discount to National Trust members and National Trust Visa cardholders on midweek stays of two or more nights **Payment:** AmEx, Visa, MC, Discover, personal and traveler's checks **Restrictions:** well-behaved children welcome; no smoking; no pets **Activities:** nature trail, porches with swings and rockers, bird-watching, small library

FORDYCE

Nearby attractions: Civil War battlefield, tennis, hunting, Fordyce on the Cotton Belt Festival

WYNNE PHILLIPS HOUSE
412 West Fourth Street
Fordyce, Arkansas 71742
501/352-7202
Proprietors: Jim and Agnes Phillips

Colonel Thomas Duncan Wynne, three-time mayor and prominent attorney, and his wife, Agnes, lived in this 1905 Neoclassical home and raised their seven children: Annette, Thomas, Hal, Douglas, Frank, French, and Agnes. Agnes and her husband, Colonel James H. Phillips, are the current owners of Wynne Phillips House. They devoted three years to its very careful restoration, using old photographs, newspaper articles, and memories of family and friends to recreate an ambiance true to the period of the house. It is furnished with family antiques, oriental rugs, original paintings, and unique souvenirs and collections from the Phillips' travels. Breakfast is a traditional southern meal, complete with country sausage and grits. Wynne Phillips House is ideally suited to bridal showers, receptions, and formal dinners.

Open: year round **Accommodations:** 5 guest rooms with private baths **Meals:** full breakfast included; complimentary refreshments; restaurants nearby **Rates:** $55 to $65 **Payment:** AmEx, Visa, MC, personal and traveler's checks **Restrictions:** smoking limited; no pets **Activities:** swimming pool, croquet, porch rockers, piano

---

HARDY

Nearby attractions: Spring River, country music theaters, Veteran's Museum, Mammoth Spring State Park, Cherokee Village, Ozark Jubilee Theater, boating, swimming, horseback riding, golfing, antiques hunting, crafts shops, bicycling

OLDE STONEHOUSE BED AND BREAKFAST INN
511 Main Street
Hardy, Arkansas 72542
501/856-2983 or 800/514-2983
501/856-4036 Fax
Proprietors: Peggy and David Johnson

This two-story native stone house was built in 1929 by Hardy's banker. Stone archways define the long front porch, and a large stone chimney rests at the intersection of the house's two wings. Its state is nearly original, except for the modern additions of private baths and central air conditioning. The house is furnished with antiques and reproduction pieces; bedrooms sport decors ranging from romantic Victorian to Depression-era "modern." The living room with fireplace, upstairs sitting area, and porches with rockers are open to guests. Breakfast, featuring homemade breads and hot entrees, is served in the oak-furnished dining room. The inn stocks a supply of current magazines, newspapers, games, and music for guests' entertainment. Old Hardy Town's quaint shops and the Spring River are a comfortable walk from the inn.

Open: year round **Accommodations:** 9 guest rooms with private baths; 2 are suites **Meals:** full breakfast included; complimentary refreshments; restaurants nearby **Rates:** $59 to $95; 10% discount to National Trust members and National Trust Visa cardholders **Payment:** Visa, MC, Discover, personal and traveler's checks **Restrictions:** children over 13 welcome; no smoking; no pets **Activities:** library, magazines, musical instruments, bicycles, croquet

LITTLE ROCK
Nearby attractions: Robinson Center Music Hall, War Memorial Stadium, State House Convention Center, golfing, shopping, museums

HOTZE HOUSE
1619 Louisiana Street
Little Rock, Arkansas 72206
501/376-6563
Proprietors: Suzanne and Steven Gates and Peggy Tooker

Hotze House was built by prominent businessman Peter Hotze in 1900 as a gift to his three children. When built, the elegant Neoclassical mansion was considered to be the finest and most expensive house in Arkansas. Recently restored, the house now offers elegant overnight accommodations. Each room is individually appointed with an attractive and comfortable mixture of antique and traditional furnishings and offers a private bath, telephone, television, individual climate control, and a king- or queen-size bed. Guests may have breakfast in the formal dining room or in the sunny conservatory. Located in the Governor's Mansion District, Hotze House is a downtown landmark and is listed in the National Register of Historic Places.

Open: year round **Accommodations:** 5 guest rooms with private baths; 4 have fireplaces **Meals:** full breakfast included; complimentary refreshments; restaurants nearby **Rates:** $80 to $100; 10% discount to National Trust members and National Trust Visa cardholders **Payment:** AmEx, Visa, MC, personal and traveler's checks **Restrictions:** children over 5 welcome; no smoking; no pets

CALIFORNIA

- McCloud
- Eureka
- Ferndale
- Westport
- Fort Bragg
- Mendocino
- Elk
- Ukiah
- Grass Valley
- Healdsburg
- Calistoga
- St. Helena
- Auburn
- Georgetown
- Santa Rosa
- Napa
- Sacramento
- Sonoma
- Ione
- San Francisco
- Murphys
- Half Moon Bay
- Columbia
- Soquel
- Groveland
- Santa Cruz
- Aptos
- Jamestown
- Carmel
- Pacific Grove
- San Luis Obispo
- Santa Barbara
- Lake Arrowhead
- Los Angeles
- Palm Springs
- Seal Beach
- Avalon
- La Jolla

APTOS

(see also **Santa Cruz***)*

Nearby attractions: redwood and state
parks; watching whales, elephant seals, and monarch butterflies (in winter);
classical music and Shakespeare festivals (in summer); tennis, golfing, water sports,
fishing; antiques hunting

BAYVIEW HOTEL COUNTRY INN
8041 Soquel Drive
Aptos, California 95003
408/688-8654 or 800/4-BAYVIEW (800/422-9843)
Proprietors: Tom and Pat O'Brien **Innkeeper:** Gwen Burkard

This vintage Victorian hotel, built in 1878 by Joseph Arano, was, like so many other western hotels, a product of the rails. As Aptos grew as a trading center, so did the hotel's role and reputation. In time, the trains, rushing out of town carrying local lumber and produce, sped back carrying tourists from around the world. Soon the hotel was doubling as the town's community center, post office, and general store. The establishment quickly became known for its warmth, hospitality, and culinary excellence. Today, Aptos continues to serve as a favorite getaway for California residents as well as a destination for visitors from greater distances. Fully renovated in 1989, the inn provides antique-furnished guest rooms and an elegant restaurant, which has received a four-star rating from the *San Jose Mercury News.*

Open: year round **Accommodations:** 11 guest rooms with private baths; 1 is a suite **Meals:** full breakfast included; restaurant on premises; restaurants nearby **Wheelchair access:** restaurant only **Rates:** $90 to $150 **Payment:** AmEx, Visa, MC, personal check **Restrictions:** children over 5 welcome; smoking limited; no pets

---

AUBURN
Nearby attractions: Old Town Auburn, Gold Country, antiques hunting; hiking, horseback riding, snow skiing, hot-air ballooning, hunting, lakes and rivers for fishing, boating, water skiing, wind surfing, and swimming

POWER'S MANSION INN
164 Cleveland Avenue
Auburn, California 95603
Mailing address:
1910 Rockwood Drive
Sacramento, California 95864
916/885-1166
916/885-1386 Fax
Proprietors: Arno and Jean Lejnieks **Innkeepers:** Tony and Tina Verhaart

Covering a full city block in downtown Auburn, this Queen Anne Victorian house was the turn-of-the-century home of Harold and Mary Power and their six children. The Powers built their home in 1900 with the fortune they had made in gold mining, and spared no expense in making it an elegant showplace. Harold

Power was a state assemblyman, and in 1900 he served as a delegate to the Republican National Convention. The Powers often entertained prominent guests in their home, including Senator (later Governor) Hiram Johnson and young mining engineer Herbert Hoover. As the Power's Mansion Inn, the house's 13 rooms are lavishly decorated with Victorian antiques, including an ornate piano in the parlor. Four-poster and brass beds are complemented by satin and lace comforters and curtains. The inn is located less than a block from Main Street.

Open: year round **Accommodations:** 11 guest rooms with private baths; 2 are suites **Meals:** full breakfast included; catering for meetings and weddings available; restaurants nearby **Rates:** $79 to $160; 10% discount to National Trust members and National Trust Visa cardholders **Payment:** AmEx, Visa, MC, personal and traveler's checks **Restrictions:** smoking limited; no pets **Activities:** patio and garden

---

AVALON

Nearby attractions: museum, tours, botanical garden, water sports, tennis, golfing, horseback riding, shopping

INN ON MT. ADA
398 Wrigley Road
Avalon, California 90704
310/510-2030
Proprietors: Susie Griffin and Marlene McAdam
Location: on Santa Catalina Island

Perched high atop a hill overlooking Catalina Island and the Pacific Ocean, the Inn on Mt. Ada is a Colonial Revival home built in 1920 by William Wrigley, Jr., of the Wrigley chewing-gum family. Here the Wrigleys hosted presidents Calvin Coolidge and Woodrow Wilson. Listed in the National Register of Historic Places, the inn offers fine accommodations in an elegant setting with antiques dating from 1850 to 1920. Guests are pampered with thick terrycloth

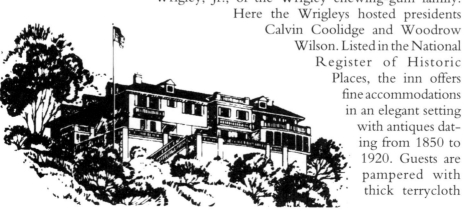

robes, bubble bath, and bottled water in their rooms. At the end of the day, they can indulge in hors d'oeuvres, complimented by sherry, wine, or beer, and a butler's pantry full of freshly baked goods, nuts, fruit, coffees, and teas. A sundeck and a terrace provide views of Avalon Harbor. A golf cart or taxicab is provided for getting around the island. The Inn on Mt. Ada has been lauded by *Vogue, Los Angeles Magazine*, and the *Chicago Tribune*.

Open: year round **Accommodations:** 6 guest rooms with private baths; 2 are suites **Meals:** full breakfast, lunch, and dinner included; complimentary refreshments; restaurant on premises **Rates:** $250 to $620 **Payment:** Visa, MC, personal and traveler's checks **Restrictions:** children over 14 welcome; no smoking; no pets **Activities:** games, library, telescope, television

CALISTOGA
Nearby attractions: Napa Valley wineries, golfing, tennis, bicycling, spas, hot-air ballooning and glider rides, fishing, water skiing

SCARLETT'S COUNTRY INN
3918 Silverado Trail
Calistoga, California 94515
707/942-6669
707/942-6669 Fax
Proprietor: Scarlett Dwyer

This 1900 two-story farmhouse was built on the former site of a Wappo campground, to which these Native Americans migrated when winter cold and snow made hunting poor in the nearby mountains. Their obsidian arrowheads can still be found in the ground around the inn. The farmhouse is set among green lawns and tall pines overlooking nearby vineyards. Guest rooms have private entrances, queen-size beds, air conditioning, mini-refrigerators, microwaves, and private baths with toiletries. Guests will also find bathrobes in the closets and fresh flowers on the tables. Each room offers a special touch: French doors, a wood-burning stove, a wet bar, a claw-foot tub, or Indian artifacts. Breakfast is served on the deck, under the apple trees, next to the swimming pool, or in guest rooms.

Open: year round **Accommodations:** 3 guest rooms with private baths; 2 are suites **Meals:** full breakfast included; complimentary refreshments; restaurants nearby **Rates:** $95 to $150; 10% discount to National Trust members and National Trust Visa cardholders **Payment:** personal check **Restrictions:** no smoking; no pets **Activities:** swimming, sunbathing, hiking, bicycling

CARMEL

Nearby attractions: Old Carmel Mission, Point Lobos State Reserve, 17-Mile Drive, Pebble Beach Golf Course, tennis, fine dining, boutiques, art galleries, beachcombing, Big Sur

HAPPY LANDING

Monte Verde between Fifth and Sixth Streets
P.O. Box 2619
Carmel, California 93921
408/624-7917
Proprietor: Dick Stewart **Manager:** Robert Ballard

Built in 1925 as a family retreat, the Happy Landing is a quaint inn offering antique-filled rooms with cathedral ceilings. Its cottage style, featuring small-paned windows, a balcony, and a round tower, gives it a Hansel-and-Gretel-like appearance. Three separate buildings surround a lush central garden with a gazebo, pond, and flagstone paths. Some rooms have fireplaces; many provide ocean views. Many personal touches, including breakfast served in guests' rooms, make the Happy Landing a quiet and romantic place to stay near town and beach.

Open: year round **Accommodations:** 7 guest rooms with private baths; 2 are suites **Meals:** continental-plus breakfast included; restaurants nearby **Rates:** $90 to $155 **Payment:** Visa, MC, personal check **Restrictions:** children over 12 welcome; no smoking; no pets

---

COLUMBIA

Nearby attractions: boating, swimming, fishing, stagecoach rides, panning for gold, tennis, golfing

CITY HOTEL

Main Street, Box 1870
Columbia State Historic Park
Columbia, California 95310
209/532-1479
Proprietor: Tom Bender
Location: 4 miles north of Sonora

An antique-filled bed-and-breakfast inn, the City Hotel is located in a restored gold rush town that is part of the Columbia State Historic Park. Constructed of brick in 1856, the stately building has survived two major fires and 130 years of continuous service. Wrought-iron shutters cover doors and windows for fire protection, a wrought-iron balcony adorns the second floor, and an authentic wooden sidewalk stretches past the front door. Originally called the "What Cheer House," the hotel was a luxury establishment serving wealthy patrons. The City Hotel still pampers today's guests by providing them with robes, slippers, and toiletries. Guest rooms boast museum-quality antiques, and the hotel's restaurant is nationally acclaimed. Automobiles are not permitted on Main Street in Columbia; their absence lends to the town an authentic nineteenth-century atmosphere.

Open: year round **Accommodations:** 10 guest rooms with private half-baths; showers are shared **Meals:** continental-plus breakfast included; complimentary sherry; restaurant on premises **Wheelchair access:** public bathrooms and dining room **Rates:** $65 to $95; 10% discount offered to National Trust members and National Trust Visa cardholders **Payment:** AmEx, Visa, MC, personal and traveler's checks **Restrictions:** smoking limited; no pets **Activities:** live theater, walking tours, parlor games, wine tastings, gold panning

---

ELK

Nearby attractions: Pacific Ocean and coast, redwood forests, art galleries, wineries, hiking, Mendocino, shopping, whale-watching

ELK COVE INN
6300 South Highway 1
P.O. Box 367
Elk, California 95432
707/877-3321 or 800/275-2967
707/877-1808 Fax
Proprietor: Elaine Bryant

Elk Cove Inn is an 1883 lumber baron's oceanfront guest house nestled atop a bluff on the Mendocino coast, surrounded by more than an acre of flower and herb gardens. Guest accommodations are in the main house, where upstairs rooms have large dormer windows from which to take in panoramic ocean views. A second-story common parlor lets through French doors to an ocean-view roof deck. Behind the main house, four cabins perch on the edge of the bluff, overlooking the ocean. Some guest rooms have fireplaces, some have canopy beds. All rooms have coffeemakers, bathrobes, private baths, and bedtime port and chocolates. A multicourse breakfast, incorporating fresh local produce, is served in the oceanfront dining room. For outdoor enjoyment there is a front porch, a cliff-top gazebo, and private steps down to the one-mile-long driftwood-strewn beach.

Open: year round **Accommodations:** 10 guest rooms with private baths **Meals:** full breakfast included; complimentary refreshments; restaurants nearby **Wheelchair access:** yes **Rates:** $98 to $198; 10% discount to National Trust members and National Trust Visa cardholders, except weekends and holidays **Payment:** AmEx, Visa, MC, personal and traveler's checks **Restrictions:** children over 12 welcome; no smoking; no pets **Activities:** beach, kayaking, gardens

HARBOR HOUSE – INN BY THE SEA
5600 South Highway 1
Elk, California 95432
707/877-3203
Proprietors: Dean and Helen Turner
Location: 15 miles south of Mendocino

Harbor House sits on a bluff overlooking Greenwood Landing, once a busy port for lumber schooners. The main building was built in 1916 by the Goodyear Redwood Lumber Company as an executive residence and guest lodge. The construction is entirely of virgin redwood from the nearby Albion forest. The house is an enlarged version of the "Home of Redwood" designed by Louis Christian Mullgardt and exhibited at the 1915 Panama-Pacific International Exposition in San Francisco. Rooms in the main building and adjacent cottages have wood-burning fireplaces. Some accommodations have sundecks. A garden path descends the bluff, leading to a private beach below. Harbor House's dinners and full breakfasts are designed around home-grown vegetables, naturally raised meats and cheeses from nearby farms, and fresh fish caught just offshore.

Open: year round **Accommodations:** 10 guest rooms with private baths **Meals:** dinner and full breakfast included in rate; restaurant on premises **Rates:** $170 to $255 for two, including dinner and breakfast; rates lower in winter **Payment:** personal and traveler's checks **Restrictions:** no smoking; no pets **Activities:** piano, gardens, private beach, whale watching

EUREKA

Nearby attractions: Old Town Eureka, architectural driving tour, Maritime Museum, Clark Museum, Fort Humboldt Logging Museum, Victorian Ferndale, redwood forests, rugged beaches, Humboldt Bay cruises on historic ferry boat, fishing, hiking, golfing, carriage rides, antiques hunting, specialty shops

"AN ELEGANT VICTORIAN MANSION" BED AND BREAKFAST INN

1406 C Street
Eureka, California 95501
707/444-3144
Proprietors: Doug and Lily Vieyra

Replete with ornate vergeboards at the gables, decorative cornice brackets, bay windows, spindlework, and metal roof cresting, this elaborate Victorian house was built in 1888 for Eureka's two-term mayor, William S. Clark. A local newspaper at the time called it "an elegant Victorian mansion." More recently, the New York Times called it "easily the most elegant house in Eureka," while Architectural Review described it as "the best preserved and restored house in Eureka." Listed in the National Register of Historic Places, the mansion offers guests two parlors, a library, and a sitting room. Guest rooms—some of them named for past guests such as Lily Langtry and Leland Stanford—provide city, mountain, or bay views as well as elegant period furnishings, writing desks, sitting areas, and all modern comforts. The inn has been given three diamonds by AAA.

Open: year round **Accommodations:** 4 guest rooms (2 have private baths); 1 is a suite **Meals:** full breakfast included; complimentary refreshments; restaurants nearby **Rates:** $85 to $155 **Payment:** Visa, MC, travelers check **Restrictions:** children over 15 welcome; no smoking; no pets **Activities:** croquet, bicycles, silent and classic film shows, classical concerts, Finnish sauna, Swedish massage, game room with Victorian games, mystery weekends, antique automobiles

CARTER HOUSE—THE COTTAGE
301 L Street
Eureka, California 95501
707/444-8062 or 707/445-1390
Proprietors: Mark and Christi Carter

With a front facade only 20 feet wide, the Carter House Cottage gives an unpretentious appearance from the street. But the one-story hip-roofed Victorian cottage is saved from simplicity by tall bay windows and decorative cornice brackets. Built in 1888, the house has recently been renovated to accommodate overnight guests. The interior is decorated in an intriguing blend of new and old: whitewashed walls and original works of art combine with black leather chairs and halogen lighting. Contemporary furniture sits side-by-side with European pine antiques. There are three fireplaces in the house; two are bedside in the guest rooms, the other is in a common area. The Cottage provides a fully equipped black marble kitchen for guests' use. Additional amenities include television and VCR, stereo system, and telephones. The Cottage is owned and operated by the Carter House Inn across the street.

Open: year round **Accommodations:** 3 guest rooms with private baths **Meals:** full breakfast included; complimentary refreshments; restaurant on premises for dinner **Wheelchair access:** guest rooms, bathrooms, dining room **Rates:** $125 to $185; $522.50 for full use of the three-bedroom cottage; 10% discount to National Trust members and National Trust Visa cardholders **Payment:** AmEx, Visa, MC, CB, DC, Discover, personal and traveler's checks **Restrictions:** no smoking; no pets **Activities:** reading, conversation, art viewing

FERNDALE

Nearby attractions: historic village, museum, galleries, craft studios, playhouse, hiking trails, redwood forests, ocean, beaches

GINGERBREAD MANSION INN
400 Berding Street
Ferndale, California 95536
707/786-4000
Proprietor: Ken Torbert

Well known as one of northern California's most photographed homes, and honored as one of the 10 best inns in California by *San Francisco Focus* magazine, Gingerbread Mansion Inn is an extravaganza of spindlework, bay windows, turrets, and gables trimmed in peach and yellow and surrounded by English gardens. Built as a doctor's residence in 1899, the striking Queen Anne was expanded to twice its original size by the 1920s. It has been used as a hospital, a rest home, an American Legion hall, and an apartment house. Completely restored, the inn pampers guests with luxuriously appointed baths (including his-and-her claw-foot bathtubs), bathrobes, turn-down service, and bedside chocolates. Four guest rooms have fireplaces. Bicycles are available, painted in colors to match the inn, and umbrellas are offered if it rains. Ferndale is California's best preserved Victorian village and has been designated a State Historic Landmark. The inn has been given a four-diamond rating by AAA.

Open: year round **Accommodations:** 9 guest rooms with private baths; 4 are suites **Meals:** full breakfast included; complimentary refreshments; restaurants nearby **Rates:** $100 to $205 **Payment:** AmEx, Visa, MC, personal and traveler's checks **Restrictions:** children over 10 welcome; no smoking; no pets **Activities:** formal English gardens; bicycles; four parlors (two with fireplaces) offering games, books, and puzzles

FORT BRAGG

Nearby attractions: Skunk Train, whale-watching, beaches, state parks, hiking, bicycling, tennis, fishing party boats, galleries, theater

AVALON HOUSE
561 Stewart Street
Fort Bragg, California 95437
707/964-5555 or 800/964-5556
Proprietor: Anne Sorrells

Avalon House was built in 1905 by Horace Weller, a founder of Fort Bragg, as a wedding gift to his son. The redwood building has been restored, preserving the details of its California Craftsman style. Avalon House and its furnishings may be antique, but not at the expense of modern conveniences. In a quiet residential neighborhood three blocks from the ocean, Avalon House offers guest rooms with private baths, fireplaces, whirlpool tubs, down comforters, and ocean views. Rooms also are equipped with individual heat controls, lighted shaving or makeup mirrors, reading lamps, and extra-thick towels. Guest room individuality is expressed through furnishings and the use of stained-glass windows or private decks in some rooms.

Open: year round **Accommodations:** 6 guest rooms with private baths **Meals:** full breakfast included; complimentary refreshments; restaurants nearby **Rates:** $70 to $135 **Payment:** AmEx, Visa, MC, Discover, personal and traveler's checks **Restrictions:** no smoking; no pets

GEORGETOWN

Nearby attractions: Gold Discovery Park, Tahoe Wilderness Area, fishing, hiking, golfing, tennis, hot-air ballooning

AMERICAN RIVER INN

Main at Orleans Street
P.O. Box 43
Georgetown, California 95634
916/333-4499 or
800/245-6566
916/333-9253 Fax
Proprietors: Will and Maria Collin
Location: 18 miles south of Auburn

This three-story wooden inn and stagecoach stop was built in 1853 in the mining camp known as Growlersburg. When the building was severely damaged by fire in 1899, the town, which had become known as Georgetown, demanded its resurrection, and the American River Inn was created. Guest rooms sport turn-of-the-century decor, featuring country antiques and brass and iron beds. Breakfast is served in the dining room or on the patio. Nestled in the foothills of the Sierra Nevada, the American River Inn boasts clean mountain air and clear lakes and streams for strolling, hiking, swimming, and bicycling. For those who wish to stay closer to home, there is a Victorian garden, a dove aviary, a spa, and award-winning local wines served in the parlor.

Open: year round **Accommodations:** 6 guest rooms with private baths; 2 are suites **Meals:** full breakfast included; complimentary refreshments; restaurants nearby **Wheelchair access:** 2 rooms **Rates:** $85 to $115; 10% discount to National Trust members and National Trust Visa cardholders **Payment:** AmEx, Visa, MC, DC, Discover, personal and traveler's checks **Restrictions:** inquire about children, no pets **Activities:** croquet, putting green, badminton, table tennis, swimming pool, whirlpool spa, mountain bicycles

GRASS VALLEY
Nearby attractions: Empire Mine State Park, gold rush sites, state parks, historic landmarks

SWAN–LEVINE HOUSE
328 South Church Street
Grass Valley, California 95945
916/272-1873
916/272-5720 Fax
Proprietors: Howard and Peggy Levine

The Swan–Levine House was built in 1880 by William Campbell, a local merchant who made his fortune selling mining equipment. He remodeled the house in 1895 to its present Queen Anne style. Doctors John and Carl Jones, brothers, bought the house from Campbell and converted it to a hospital in 1906. The Levine family has been renovating the building since 1975 and offers unique accommodations that reflect the building's previous use as a medical center. One guest room has a sitting room and fireplace; another, a private entrance and small kitchen. The Levines developed their guest house around their interest in printmaking. The house is a gallery full of their work, and the adjoining Carriage House printmaking studio is available to printmakers on a daily or monthly basis. The inn's eclectic Victorian decor has been featured in *Country Living*.

Open: year round **Accommodations:** 4 guest rooms with private baths; 2 are suites **Meals:** full breakfast included; restaurants nearby **Rates:** $75 to $90; 10% discount to National Trust members and National Trust Visa cardholders **Payment:** AmEx, Visa, MC, Discover, personal and traveler's checks **Restrictions:** no smoking **Activities:** printmaking studio, small pool, badminton court

GROVELAND
Nearby attractions: Yosemite National Park, Tuolumne River, horseback riding, hiking, bicycling, mountain climbing, downhill skiing, fishing, whitewater rafting, swimming, tennis, golfing

GROVELAND HOTEL
18767 Main Street
P.O. Box 481
Groveland, California 95321
209/962-4000 or 800/273-3314
209/962-6674 Fax
Proprietors: Peggy A. and Grover C. Mosley
Location: 23 miles west of Yosemite National Park

The Groveland Hotel, belived to have been built by Joshua D. Crippen in 1849, is the largest adobe building in Groveland and one of the oldest buildings in Tuolumne County. The adobe structure with two-story wraparound Monterey-style porches served the community first as a trading post, then as a residence until 1865. After that date the building was dedicated exclusively to hotel or boarding house use. Very little alteration has occurred over the years, leaving the hotel with a high degree of architectural integrity. A two-story frame annex that was built next to the hotel in 1914 is considered to be one of the finest examples of the Neoclassical style in Tuolumne County. Today, the Groveland Hotel and Annex offer 17 guest rooms with private baths.

Open: year round **Accommodations:** 17 guest rooms with private baths; 3 are suites **Meals:** continental-plus breakfast included; complimentary refreshments; restaurant on premises **Rates:** $95 to $175 **Payment:** AmEx, Visa, MC, CB, DC, Discover, personal and traveler's checks **Restrictions:** no smoking; inquire about pets

HALF MOON BAY

Nearby attractions: beaches, hiking, tide pooling, fishing, golfing, art galleries, winery tours, whale-watching, National Trust's Filoli

OLD THYME INN
779 Main Street
Half Moon Bay, California 94019
415/726-1616
Proprietors: George and Marcia Dempsey

Occupying a prominent position on Main Street, the Old Thyme Inn was built in 1899. Its Queen Anne styling is highlighted by decorative fish-scale shingles on the exterior walls. Guest rooms are all decorated with antiques and offer whirlpool or claw-foot tubs. Some rooms contain fireplaces; one room has a stained-glass window, another a skylight. The guest rooms are named for some of the 80 varieties of herbs grown in the inn's bountiful herb garden. Guests are invited to smell the fragrances and take cuttings home. The Garden Suite has its own private entrance, a four-poster bed, fireplace, and complimentary wine in the refrigerator. Every morning the English-style breakfast includes fresh herbs, as well as homemade scones, cold meats, and English cheeses.

Open: year round **Accommodations:** 7 guest rooms with private baths; 1 is a suite **Meals:** full breakfast included; complimentary refreshments; restaurants nearby **Rates:** $65 to $210; 10% discount offered to National Trust members and National Trust Visa cardholders **Payment:** Visa, MC, personal check **Restrictions:** no smoking; no pets **Activities:** herb gardens, whirlpool tubs

HEALDSBURG

Nearby attractions: winery tours and tastings, Luther Burbank gardens, historic house tours, canoeing, golfing, hot-air ballooning, river rafting, swimming, fishing, sailing

CAMELLIA INN
211 North Street
Healdsburg, California 95448
707/433-8182 or 800/727-8182
Proprietors: Ray, Del, and Lucy Lewand

More than 50 varieties of camellias bloom on the landscaped grounds of the Camellia Inn and around its terraced swimming pool. The house, built in 1869 by Ransome Powell, is Italianate in design, and its simple facade is made elegant by arched windows and a round-arched doorway and porch. The home was purchased by Dr. J. Walter Seawell in 1892 to serve as his home and offices, and then as the town's first hospital. Heavily carved crown molding, double parlors with twin marble fireplaces, inlaid hardwood floors, and ceiling medallions are just some of the extant architectural features of the historic home. Guest rooms are decorated individually with antiques, such as a half-testered bed made of tiger maple, which was brought from Scotland. Special amenities may include a gas fireplace or whirlpool bath. Breakfast includes a hearty main dish and freshly baked nut breads.

Open: year round **Accommodations:** 9 guest rooms with private baths **Meals:** full breakfast included; complimentary refreshments; restaurants nearby **Wheelchair access:** 1 guest room **Rates:** $70 to $135; 10% discount to National Trust members and National Trust Visa cardholders **Payment:** AmEx, Visa, MC, personal check **Restrictions:** no smoking; no pets **Activities:** swimming pool, landscaped gardens

HEALDSBURG INN ON THE PLAZA
110 Matheson Street
Healdsburg, California 95448
707/433-6991
Proprietor: Genny Jenkins

Located on the plaza in downtown Healdsburg, the building known as the Healdsburg Inn first served as the Wells-Fargo Express building, its architecture deemed "modern renaissance" by the *Healdsburg Tribune* in 1901. A grand, paneled staircase leads to the second floor, which once served as the town's center for professional services. The doctors' and dentists' offices and photography studio are now spacious guest rooms. All are furnished with antiques and unique collectibles. Central air and heat, fluffy towels, and rubber duckies are standards. Most rooms have fireplaces and claw-foot tubs. Fine art—for viewing and for sale—is displayed in the reception area and throughout the inn. The first floor also boasts antiques and gift shops. A solarium overlooks the village and provides a comfortable common area.

Open: year round **Accommodations:** 9 guest rooms with private baths **Meals:** full breakfast included; complimentary refreshments; restaurants nearby **Rates:** $75 to $175; 10% discount to National Trust members and National Trust Visa cardholders midweek only **Payment:** Visa, MC, personal and traveler's checks **Restrictions:** smoking limited; no pets **Activities:** listening to music, games and puzzles, reading, television and VCR, solarium sitting, art gallery, gift shops

---

IONE
Nearby attractions: museums, historic sites, antiques hunting, wineries, art galleries, river, lakes, fishing, swimming, boating

THE HEIRLOOM
214 Shakeley Lane
Ione, California 95640
209/274-4468
Proprietors: Melisande Hubbs and Patricia Cross

Nestled among the foothills of the great Sierras lies the small village of Ione and the home of one of the earliest settlers in the valley when it served as a supply center for the rich gold fields nearby. Built in 1863, the two-story brick home adorned by classical columns supporting front and rear porches and balconies is today an inn furnished in family heirlooms and antiques. One of the most remarkable is the square grand piano once owned by gold rush entertainer Lola

Montez. Guests are treated to fruit, candy, and flowers in the bedrooms, which are decorated with handmade quilts. Breakfast is served in guest rooms, on private verandas, in the garden, or fireside in the dining room.

Open: year round **Accommodations:** 6 guest rooms (4 have private baths) **Meals:** full breakfast included; complimentary refreshments; restaurants nearby **Wheelchair access:** limited **Rates:** $65 to $100 **Payment:** AmEx, Visa, MC, personal and traveler's checks **Restrictions:** children over 8 welcome; no smoking; no pets **Activities:** croquet, horseshoe pitching, hammock, glider, piano, games, puzzles, books

---

JAMESTOWN

Nearby attractions: Railtown 1897 State Historic Park, gold panning and prospecting, antiques hunting, Moaning Cave and Mercer Caverns, Columbia State Park, Calaveras Big Trees State Park, downhill and cross-country skiing, wineries, golfing, white-water rafting, horseback riding, fishing, hiking, back-packing

HISTORIC NATIONAL HOTEL, BED AND BREAKFAST
77 Main Street
P.O. Box 502
Jamestown, California 95327
209/984-3446
Proprietors: Stephen and Pamela Willey

In the center of Jamestown, in the heart of California's Gold Country, stands the Historic National Hotel, built in 1859 when Jamestown was at its pinnacle as a gold rush town. The National Hotel has offered overnight accommodations continuously for more than 130 years. Quaint bedrooms are authentically decorated, containing most of their original furnishings, including brass beds. Patchwork quilts and lace curtains add to the charming atmosphere. The hotel's dining room is renowned for creative cuisine, and the Gold Rush Saloon, with its original nineteenth-century redwood bar, provides a relaxing place to sample some of the Gold Country's many wines. The dining room will prepare picnic baskets for those wishing to spend their days exploring the region.

Open: year round **Accommodations:** 11 guest rooms (5 have private baths) **Meals:** continental-plus breakfast included; restaurant on premises **Rates:** $65 to $80; 10% discount to National Trust members and National Trust Visa cardholders midweek only **Payment:** AmEx, Visa, MC, DC, Discover, personal and traveler's checks **Restrictions:** children over 10 welcome; smoking limited; pets by arrangement **Activities:** saloon, antiques hunting, theater and ski packages

LA JOLLA

Nearby attractions: San Diego Zoo, Sea World, Museum of Contemporary Art, Old Town San Diego, Scripps Institution of Oceanography, University of California–San Diego, Cove Beach, ocean, golfing, tennis, swimming, surfing, snorkeling

BED AND BREAKFAST INN AT LA JOLLA

7753 Draper Avenue
La Jolla, California 92037
619/456-2066 or 800/582-2466
Proprietor: Ron Ramos

The Bed and Breakfast Inn at La Jolla offers deluxe accommodations in the building listed as Historical Site 179 on the San Diego Register of Historic Places. The inn is one of architect Irving Gill's finest examples of Cubism. Built in 1913 for George Kautz, the house was home to the John Philip Sousa family during the 1920s. Fireplaces and ocean views are featured in many guest rooms, all of which are decorated in a style that evokes elegant country cottages and contain fresh fruit, sherry, cut flowers, and terrycloth robes for guests. Some rooms also contain refrigerators and hair dryers. Guests are invited to relax in the garden, enjoy the view from the deck, or browse in the library–sitting room. Wine and cheese are served daily. The inn is surrounded by lush gardens originally planned by renowned horticulturist Kate Sessions.

Open: year round **Accommodations:** 16 guest rooms (15 have private baths) **Meals:** continental-plus breakfast included; restaurants nearby **Rates:** $85 to $225; 10% discount offered to National Trust members or National Trust Visa cardholders September through June, midweek only **Payment:** Visa, MC, personal and traveler's checks **Restrictions:** children allowed by prior arrangement; no smoking; no pets

LAKE ARROWHEAD

Nearby attractions: snow and water skiing, boating, swimming, hiking, fishing, horseback riding, antiques hunting

STORYBOOK INN
28717 Highway 18
P.O. Box 362
Skyforest, California 92385
909/336-1483
Proprietors: Kathleen and John Wooley
Location: 3 miles south of Lake Arrowhead

Located 6000 feet up in the San Bernardino Mountains along the historic Rim of the World Highway is the Storybook Inn. A man named Foutch (designer of the original Lake Arrowhead Village) built this private estate between 1930 and 1942 for his bride, Mabel. Their romance still prevails throughout the inn, from the mahogany paneling, which was bleached to match the color of Mabel's hair, to the adjoining honeymoon cabin, now used as guest accommodations. The three-story building features glass-enclosed solariums for viewing snow-capped mountains and vistas reaching to the Pacific Ocean. A 2500-square-foot lobby is set off by two massive brick fireplaces and mahogany paneling. Guest rooms are furnished with simple antiques; some offer private solariums. The rustic cabin combines knotty pine paneling and a stone fireplace with a king-size bed and private deck.

Open: year round **Accommodations:** 10 guest rooms with private baths; 5 are suites; 1 is a 3-bedroom, 2-bath cabin with kitchen **Meals:** full breakfast included; evening social hour; restaurants nearby **Rates:** $79 to $200; 10% discount offered to National Trust members and National Trust Visa cardholders **Payment:** AmEx, Visa, MC, Discover, personal and traveler's checks **Restrictions:** children over 6 welcome; no smoking; no pets **Activities:** hot tub, hiking, bicycling, reading

LOS ANGELES

Nearby attractions: Beverly Hills, Hollywood, Universal Studios, downtown Los Angeles, theaters, civic center, museums, UCLA, beaches

SALISBURY HOUSE BED AND BREAKFAST

2273 West 20th Street
Los Angeles, California 90018
213/737-7817 or 800/373-1778
213/737-7817 Fax
Proprietor: Susan German

A classic California Craftsman home designed by noted architect Frank M. Tyler, the Salisbury House was built in 1909 in the then-western suburbs of Los Angeles. Converted to a bed and breakfast in 1982, much of the original workmanship survives—stained, leaded, and beveled glass, built-in cabinets, lighting fixtures, wood paneling, and tilework. With its original design intact and restored, Salisbury House has been used as a location for numerous motion picture productions. Antiques, down comforters, cut flowers, and lace curtains grace the large guest rooms, along with many conveniences, including refrigerators, telephones, television, irons and boards, hair-care appliances, and toiletries. Guests often gather around the fireplace or on the full-length front porch for complimentary refreshments.

Open: year round **Accommodations:** 5 guest rooms (3 have private baths); 2 are suites **Meals:** full breakfast included; complimentary refreshments; restaurants nearby **Rates:** $75 to $100 **Payment:** AmEx, Visa, MC, Discover, personal and traveler's checks **Restrictions:** no smoking; no pets

McCLOUD

Nearby attractions: Mt. Shasta Ski Park, McCloud River and lake, McCloud River Railroad, Dance Country, historic district

McCLOUD HOTEL
408 Main Street
P.O. Box 730
McCloud, California 96057
916/964-2822 or 800/964-2823
916/964-2844 Fax
Proprietors: Lee and Marilyn Ogden

Large center and end gables and many gabled dormers define this three-story hotel. Built in 1916 to replace an earlier hotel on the site, the McCloud Hotel provided housing for mill workers and teachers, as well as accommodations for visitors. In the 1960s the hotel entered a period of decline until the Ogdens purchased and recently rehabilitated it. In the lobby, guests are greeted at the original registration desk and will find comfortable seating before the fireplace and book-lined shelves. Guest rooms are appointed with original hotel furniture (rescued and restored), combined with four-poster beds, antique trunks gathered from the area, antique vanities, coordinated decorator fabrics, and private baths. Four suites feature canopied beds, and whirlpool tubs for two. Afternoon tea and scones are offered daily.

Open: year round **Accommodations:** 18 guest rooms with private baths; 4 are suites **Meals:** continental-plus breakfast included; complimentary refreshments; restaurants nearby **Wheelchair access:** lobby and 1 guest room **Rates:** $60 to $130; 10% discount to National Trust members and National Trust Visa cardholders **Payment:** Visa, MC, personal check **Restrictions:** not suitable for children; no smoking; no pets **Activities:** reading, puzzles, board games

MENDOCINO

Nearby attractions: historic village, shops, art galleries, theater, wineries, redwood forests, four state parks, botanical gardens, horseback riding, canoeing, hiking, bicycling, tennis, golfing, fishing, whale-watching, July music festival

HEADLANDS INN
Corner of Howard and Albion Streets
P.O. Box 132
Mendocino, California 95460
707/937-4431 or 800/354-4431
Proprietors: David and Sharon Hyman

Centrally located in Mendocino Village's historic district, the Headlands Inn was built as the town barbershop in 1868 in a style reflecting New England's Victorian architecture. A second story was added in 1873, and in 1884 the dormered, clapboard building became a restaurant. In 1893 it was relocated and converted to a private residence. Today, the inn offers ocean views across an English garden and an antique-filled parlor in which to relax and unwind. A recent restoration has preserved the historic charm of the last century while adding modern comforts. All guest rooms have featherbeds, wood-burning fireplaces, and private baths. A full breakfast is served in the privacy of guests' rooms, one of which is located in a charming cottage. At Christmas each room features a small tree.

Open: year round **Accommodations:** 6 guest rooms with private baths **Meals:** full breakfast included; complimentary afternoon high tea; restaurants nearby **Wheelchair access:** cottage **Rates:** $95 to $189 **Payment:** Visa, MC, personal and traveler's checks **Restrictions:** children over 12 welcome; no smoking; no pets **Activities:** reading, board games, piano playing

JOHN DOUGHERTY HOUSE
571 Ukiah Street
P.O. Box 817
Mendocino, California 95460
707/937-5266
Proprietors: David and Marion Wells

One of the oldest houses in Mendocino, this historic saltbox home was built in 1867. The main house is furnished with early American antiques and its walls are decorated with stenciling. The guest accommodations range from simple, charming rooms to garden cottages and a unique water tower with an 18-foot-high beamed ceiling, four-poster bed, private bath, sitting room, and wood-burning fireplace. Located in the center of the town's National Register historic district, the inn has some of the best ocean and bay views in the village. John Dougherty House is years removed from twentieth-century bustle but just steps away from great restaurants and shopping.

Open: year round **Accommodations:** 6 guest rooms with private baths; 4 are suites **Meals:** continental-plus breakfast included; complimentary refreshments; restaurants nearby **Rates:** $85 to $165; 10% discount offered to National Trust members and National Trust Visa cardholders **Payment:** Visa, MC, personal and traveler's checks **Restrictions:** children over 12 preferred; no smoking; no pets **Activities:** ocean viewing, gardens, whale-watching, television, relaxing on verandas

MENDOCINO HOTEL
45080 Main Street
P.O. Box 587
Mendocino, California 95460
707/937-0511 or 800/548-0513
Proprietor: Dale Standfast, general manager

Built in 1878 and named the best small hotel in northern California by *San Francisco Focus* magazine in 1992, the Mendocino Hotel overlooks the rugged cliffs of the northern California coast. Twenty-five modern guest suites located in landscaped gardens combine with the historic structure to comprise the Mendocino Hotel's accommodations. All of the rooms are decorated with Victorian antiques, reproductions, and artifacts. In each of the hotel's suites, family-donated memorabilia and photographs depict the lives of the courageous pioneers who settled the town and logged and milled the redwood forests. The hotel's dining rooms and lounges are popular gathering places with residents and visitors alike, serving local specialties and premium wines from the Anderson, Napa, and Sonoma valleys.

Open: year round **Accommodations:** 51 guest rooms (37 have private baths); 6 are suites **Meals:** restaurant on premises **Wheelchair access:** guest rooms, baths, dining facilities **Rates:** $60 to $225 **Payment:** AmEx, Visa, MC, traveler's checks **Restrictions:** smoking limited; no pets

WHITEGATE INN
499 Howard Street
P.O. Box 150
Mendocino, California 95460
707/937-4892 or 800/531-7282
707/937-1131 Fax
Proprietors: Carol and George Bechtloff

Built in 1883 and described by a local journalist as "one of the most elegant and best appointed residences in town," the Whitegate Inn stands today much as it did then. The first floor is still graced with large double parlors separated by 10-foot-high pocket doors, and the original crystal chandeliers hang as they have for more than a century. The front parlor fireplace still provides warmth. Guest rooms are charming with fireplaces, brass and iron beds, Victorian antiques, and glimpses of the Pacific Ocean. Full breakfasts feature homemade muffins and cinnamon raisin rounds, and delicious entrees such as caramel-apple French toast or eggs Florentine. After a day exploring Mendocino's shops and sites, guests are greeted by the innkeepers with light hors d'oeuvres and a glass of wine.

Open: year round **Accommodations:** 7 guest rooms with private baths **Meals:** full breakfast included; complimentary refreshments; restaurants nearby **Rates:** $99 to $185; 10% discount to National Trust members and National Trust Visa cardholders **Payment:** AmEx, Visa, MC, Discover, personal and traveler's checks **Restrictions:** no smoking; no pets **Activities:** relaxing, reading

MURPHYS

Nearby attractions: historic Main Street (with shops, galleries, and museum), Calaveras Big Trees State Park, Columbia State Park, winery tours, skiing, river rafting, golfing, seasonal festivals, antiques hunting, museums, art galleries

DUNBAR HOUSE, 1880
271 Jones Street
Murphys, California 95247
209/728-2897 or 800/225-3764, ext. # 321
209/728-1451 Fax
Proprietors: Barbara and Bob Costa

An Italianate home built in 1880 by Willis Dunbar for his bride, Ellen Roberts, this charming bed and breakfast has won acclaim from such publications as *Victorian Homes, Sunset, Gourmet,* and the *Los Angeles Times.* Located in the historic Gold Country of California, Dunbar House offers fine accommodations accented with antiques, lace, claw-foot tubs, and wood-burning stoves. Service is attentive; the innkeepers will make dinner reservations, turn down beds, and leave chocolates at the bedside. Guest rooms come equipped with a refrigerator stocked with ice and a complimentary bottle of local wine. Each room contains a television, VCR, and a classic video library hidden discreetly in an armoire. Reading lights, makeup mirrors, and hair dryers also are provided. Home-baked goods are part of the full breakfast served by the dining room fire, in the garden, or in guest rooms.

Open: year round **Accommodations:** 4 guest rooms with private baths; 1 is a suite **Meals:** full breakfast included; complimentary refreshments; restaurants nearby **Rates:** $105 to $155; 10% discount offered to National Trust members and National Trust Visa cardholders midweek only, excluding holidays **Payment:** Visa, MC, personal and traveler's checks **Restrictions:** children over 10 welcome; no smoking; no pets **Activities:** reading, gardens, classic videos, music

NAPA

Nearby attractions: winery tours and tastings, Napa Valley Wine Train, hot-air ballooning, glider rides, mud baths, opera house, tennis, golfing, hiking, bicycling, horseback riding

BEAZLEY HOUSE
1910 First Street
Napa, California 94559
707/257-1649 or 800/559-1649
707/257-1518 Fax
Proprietors: Carol and Jim Beazley

Beazley House opened in 1981 as Napa's first bed and breakfast, and is the only inn in Napa still owned and operated by its founders. Built in 1902, the house was designed by Napa architect Luther Turton for Dr. Adolf Kahn, a local surgeon and politician. The chocolate brown Shingle Style mansion with white trim remains in nearly original condition today. Large, individually decorated guest rooms are appointed with antiques, queen-size beds, and private baths. Guest rooms are also found in the reconstructed carriage house behind the mansion, nestled among gardens and trees. In it, five charming rooms with private spas, baths, and fireplaces are available. A full breakfast buffet and afternoon tea are served. Sitting on half an acre of lawns and gardens, Beazley House is a short stroll from old Napa's shops and restaurants.

Open: year round **Accommodations:** 11 guest rooms with private baths; 4 are suites **Meals:** full breakfast included; complimentary refreshments; restaurants nearby **Wheelchair access:** 1 room **Rates:** $125 to $185; 10% discount to National Trust members and National Trust Visa cardholders **Payment:** AmEx, Visa, MC, personal and traveler's checks **Restrictions:** no smoking; no pets (resident cats) **Activities:** wine tastings, gardens

CHURCHILL MANOR BED AND BREAKFAST
485 Brown Street
Napa, California 94559
707/253-7733
Proprietors: Joanna Guidotti and Brian Jensen

Built in 1889 for local banker Edward Churchill, the 10,000-square-foot mansion was a showcase for visitors sailing from San Francisco. An expansive veranda supported by 20 fluted Ionic and Doric columns surround the three-story Second Empire mansion. Following Churchill's death in 1903, his daughter Dorothy resided here until 1956, opening the home to boarders and weddings. The first floor boasts a mosaic marble-floored solarium and four spacious parlors separated by massive redwood pocket doors. Each parlor features a fireplace with an ornate mantel and 17 layers of ceiling moldings. American and European antiques fill the luxurious guest rooms. Pedestal sinks, claw-foot tubs, brass fixtures, and hand-painted and gold-laced tiles adorn the private baths. Evenings at Churchill Manor begin with a Napa Valley varietal wine and cheese reception.

Open: year round **Accommodations:** 10 guest rooms with private baths; 4 are suites **Meals:** full breakfast included; complimentary wine and cheese and freshly baked cookies; restaurants nearby **Rates:** $75 to $145; 10% discount to National Trust members and National Trust Visa cardholders midweek only **Payment:** AmEx, Visa, MC, Discover, personal and traveler's checks **Restrictions:** children over 12 welcome; no smoking; no pets; two-night minimum with Saturday night booking **Activities:** croquet, tandem bicycling, grand piano, library, puzzles, games, television and VCR

LA BELLE EPOQUE BED AND BREAKFAST INN
1386 Calistoga Avenue
Napa, California 94559
707/257-2161
Proprietors: Merlin and Claudia Wedepohl

In 1893, Herman Schwarz, the successful owner of the largest hardware firm in Napa County, commissioned the house at Calistoga and Seminary streets as a wedding gift for his daughter Minnie. This city landmark, designed by respected Bay Area architect Luther

Turton, is an extravagant example of Queen Anne styling. Decorative flat and molded carvings can be seen in the gables and bays, and original stained-glass windows remain in the transoms and semicircular windows. Several historic church windows, which predate the house, have been artfully added to the front of the building. The finely crafted and decorated interiors are graced by an exceptional collection of Victorian antiques. Tucked away in the basement is a wine cellar and tasting room. For further investigation, guests can take a short walk to the Napa Valley Wine Train.

Open: year round **Accommodations:** 6 guest rooms with private baths, 2 have fireplaces **Meals:** full breakfast included; complimentary wine and appetizers; restaurants nearby **Rates:** $115 to $150; 10% discount to National Trust members and National Trust Visa cardholders midweek only **Payment:** AmEx, Visa, MC, Discover, personal and traveler's checks **Restrictions:** no smoking; no pets **Activities:** wine tasting, board games, television and VCR, square grand piano

NAPA INN

1137 Warren Street
Napa, California 94559
707/257-1444 or 800/435-1144
Proprietors: Ann and Denny Mahoney

This stately Queen Anne house was built in 1899 for Harry and Madaline Johnston. It was a wedding gift from Harry's parents. The house sits on one of Napa's quiet tree-lined streets in the historic district, within walking distance of restaurants and downtown. All of the individually appointed guest rooms offer private baths and sitting areas. Most also have fireplaces. The Courtyard Room has a private entrance and courtyard. The Oak Room has a charming window seat overlooking the garden. Dormers and a peaked ceiling provide architectural interest in the Grand Suite, where a unique bathroom occupies the turret, and the sitting area is dominated by a floor-to-ceiling oak mantelpiece. Guests are welcomed with afternoon refreshments.

Open: year round **Accommodations:** 6 guest rooms with private baths; 2 are suites **Meals:** full breakfast included; complimentary refreshments; restaurants nearby **Rates:** $120 to $170; 10% discount to National Trust members and National Trust Visa cardholders **Payment:** AmEx, Visa, MC, Discover, personal and traveler's checks **Restrictions:** not suitable for children; no smoking; no pets **Activities:** board games, puzzles, library, piano

OLD WORLD INN
1301 Jefferson Street
Napa, California 94559
707/257-0112
Proprietor: Diane M. Dumaine

The Old World Inn was built in 1906 by local contractor E. W. Doughty as his private town residence. The home is an eclectic combination of architectural styles detailed with wood shingles, wide shady porches, clinker brick, and leaded and beveled glass. Inside are painted Victorian and other antique furnishings. Each of the eight guest rooms has been decorated with coordinating linens and fabrics, and each has a private bathroom, most with claw-foot tubs. Bright, fresh Scandinavian colors inspired by the works of Swedish artist Carl Larsson dominate the bedrooms as well as the parlor. The latter, with its fireplace and soft classical music, provides a soothing retreat. Complimentary tea and cookies, wines, appetizers, and desserts are offered daily.

Open: year round **Accommodations:** 8 guest rooms with private baths **Meals:** continental-plus breakfast included; complimentary refreshments; restaurants nearby **Rates:** $110 to $145 **Payment:** AmEx, Visa, MC, Discover, personal and traveler's checks **Restrictions:** no smoking; no pets **Activities:** outdoor spa, puzzles

PACIFIC GROVE

Nearby attractions: historic Pacific Grove, Cannery Row, Monterey Bay Aquarium, Monterey Maritime Museum, Pebble Beach Golf Course, 17-Mile Drive, Carmel-by-the-Sea, Carmel Mission, Big Sur, Point Lobos State Park, tennis, boating, fishing, kayaking, sailing, scuba diving, gift shops, galleries, hiking, biking, butterfly-watching, beaches

GRAND VIEW INN
557 Ocean View Boulevard
Pacific Grove, California 93950
408/372-4341
Proprietors: Susan, Ed, and John Flatley

After half a century as a Methodist summer camp, the town of Pacific Grove was becoming established as a year-round community by 1910, the same year that Dr. Julia Platt, a noted marine biologist, built her four-story home at the edge of Monterey Bay overlooking Lover's Point. Pacific Grove's first woman mayor, she was instrumental in preserving the Lover's Point beach and park for future generations. Her home has been completely restored by the Flatley family and opened as the Grand View Inn. Along with unsurpassed views of the bay from each room, guests enjoy the elegance of marble-tiled private baths, patterned hardwood floors, antique furnishings, and inviting grounds. The parlor is appointed with oak columns, a marble fireplace, and comfortable seating areas affording wraparound ocean views. A full breakfast and afternoon tea are served overlooking the Pacific Grove coastline.

Open: year round **Accommodations:** 10 guest rooms with private baths **Meals:** full breakfast included; complimentary refreshments; restaurants nearby **Wheelchair access:** 1 room **Rates:** $125 to $185 **Payment:** Visa, MC, personal and traveler's checks **Restrictions:** children over 12 welcome; no smoking; no pets **Activities:** oceanfront walks, touring, relaxing, gardens, viewing ocean

MARTINE INN
255 Ocean View Boulevard
Pacific Grove, California 93950
408/373-3388 or 800/852-5588
Proprietors: Marion and Don Martine

This elegant inn, perched high on the cliffs overlooking the rocky coastline of Monterey Bay, dates from 1899, when it was built as a Victorian house. Later, Laura and James Parke of Parke Davis Pharmaceuticals transformed it into a Mediterranean-style house with a stuccoed exterior. Fond of exotic woods, Parke installed gates of Siamese teak, a Spanish cedar staircase, and inlaid oak and mahogany floors. Guest rooms, many with working fireplaces, are furnished with museum-quality American antique bedroom suites. Guests receive fruit in a Victorian silver basket, a fresh rose, and chocolate mints on pillows at evening turn-down. Breakfast is served on antique silver, crystal, and lace in the dining room, which provides views of the bay. In 1993 Martine Inn was selected by *Bon Appétit* as one of eight best bed and breakfasts in historic homes.

Open: year round **Accommodations:** 19 guest rooms with private baths; 2 are suites **Meals:** full breakfast included; complimentary refreshments; restaurants nearby **Wheelchair access:** guest rooms, bathrooms, dining facilities **Rates:** $125 to $230 **Payment:** Amex, Visa, MC, personal and traveler's checks **Restrictions:** smoking limited; no pets **Activities:** billiards, spa, vintage car collection

SEVEN GABLES INN
555 Ocean View Boulevard
Pacific Grove, California 93950
408/372-4341
Proprietors: Susan, Ed, and John Flatley

Built in 1886, the Seven Gables Inn is one of a parade of large, showy Victorian homes found throughout Pacific Grove, a coastal town that began as a Methodist summer retreat in the 1850s. Bought in 1906 by Henry and Lucie Chase, this house was christened "The House of Seven Gables" to honor the Chase's Salem, Massachusetts, origins. The inn is perched on a rocky promontory overlooking Monterey Bay, a location that affords each guest room views of the Pacific coastline and encircling mountains. Ornate stained-glass windows and delicate plaster ceiling medallions are backdrops to the fine European antiques found throughout the inn. The Flatley family has owned this home for 25 years and attends to guests' needs with meticulous care and attention, resulting in a Mobil four-star rating and the honor of being named one of 1994's top 12 inns in the nation by *Country Inns* magazine.

Open: year round **Accommodations:** 14 guest rooms with private baths **Meals:** full breakfast included; complimentary afternoon tea; restaurants nearby **Wheelchair access:** 2 rooms accessible with assistance **Rates:** $105 to $205 **Payment:** Visa, MC, personal and traveler's checks **Restrictions:** children over 12 welcome; no smoking; no pets **Activities:** relaxing, porch sitting, gardens, viewing ocean

PALM SPRINGS

Nearby attractions: Desert Museum, historic village green, theaters, tennis, golfing, horseback riding, hiking, cross-country skiing, art galleries, shopping, botanical gardens, Aerial Tramway, Cahuilla Reservation

ORCHID TREE INN
261 South Belardo Road
Palm Springs, California 92262
619/325-2791 or 800/733-3435
619/325-3855 Fax
Proprietors: Robert and Karen Weithorn

Built mostly in the 1930s, the Orchid Tree offers accommodations ranging from intimate studios and suites to garden cottages, cabins, and bungalows. In the sheltered area between the famed Palm Springs village and the soaring San Jacinto Mountains, the Spanish-tiled roofs of the inn's various buildings nestle amid flowering gardens, fruit trees, towering palms, and two large swimming pools. Many accommodations offer private balconies, porches, patios, or gardens. Most rooms offer full kitchens, and all have color cable television. A desert garden retreat, the Orchid Tree offers the appeal of the 1920s and 1930s with contemporary comfort and convenience.

Open: year round **Accommodations:** 40 guest rooms with private baths; 15 are suites **Meals:** continental-plus breakfast included November 1 through May 31; restaurants nearby **Rates:** $55 to $270; 10% discount offered to National Trust members and National Trust Visa cardholders excluding holidays and high season **Payment:** AmEx, Visa, MC, Discover, travelers check **Restrictions:** inquire about children; smoking limited; no pets **Activities:** 3 swimming pools, 2 spas, shuffleboard, library, board games, seminars, retreats, tennis at neighboring private club

SACRAMENTO

Nearby attractions: state capitol, governor's mansion, convention center, railroad museum, Sacramento and American rivers, Old Sacramento Historic State Park, Sutter's Fort, Crocker Art Museum, Gold Country, dining, shopping

ABIGAIL'S BED AND BREAKFAST
2120 G Street
Sacramento, California 95816
916/441-5007 or 800/858-1568
916/441-0621 Fax
Proprietors: Susanne and Ken Ventura

This stately Colonial Revival house ws built in 1912 by Henry Bernard Drescher, a leader in the wholesale grocery business. After years as a boarding house, the building was renovated in the early 1980s and opened as Abigail's Bed and Breakfast. Just inside the ornate entry, with sidelights and fanlight, are the living room and parlor with fireplace. A piano is in the sitting room. Antiques-furnished guest rooms with sitting areas have private bathrooms of marble and granite with perhaps a claw-foot tub or hand-painted basin. Beds range from four-poster or canopy to brass. Terrycloth robes, magazines, and radios are provided. Breakfast is served in the dining room. In warm weather guests enjoy the hot tub in a secluded garden setting and the patio surrounded by flowerbeds. Abigail's is conveniently located just minutes from the capitol and the convention center.

Open: year round **Accommodations:** 5 guest rooms with private baths **Meals:** full breakfast included; complimentary refreshments; restaurants nearby **Rates:** $95 to $165; 10% discount to National Trust members and National Trust Visa cardholders **Payment:** AmEx, Visa, MC, CB, DC, Discover, personal and traveler's checks **Restrictions:** inquire about children; no smoking; no pets (resident cats) **Activities:** hot tub, gardens, patio

AMBER HOUSE BED AND BREAKFAST INN
1315 22nd Street
Sacramento, California 95816
916/444-8085 or 800/755-6526
Proprietors: Michael and Jane Richardson

Amber House consists of two neighboring early twentieth-century homes—one a Craftsman and the other a Mediterranean style. Just eight blocks from the state capitol, on a quiet street of old homes, the houses have been fully restored and offer a blend of elegance, comfort, and friendly hospitality. Each guest room is individually decorated and furnished with a full-service telephone, clock–radio–cassette player, and cable television. Some offer VCRs and whirlpool tubs for two. Morning brings gourmet breakfasts with special house-blend coffee, which may be enjoyed in the dining room, on the veranda, or in the privacy of guest rooms. Amber House is ideal for romantic getaways, executive retreats, and weddings and receptions. It has been praised by many, including California's Governor Pete Wilson and *Travel and Leisure*.

Open: year round **Accommodations:** 9 guest rooms with private baths; 1 is a suite **Meals:** full breakfast included; complimentary refreshments; restaurants nearby **Rates:** $89 to $199; 10% discount offered to National Trust members and National Trust Visa cardholders **Payment:** AmEx, Visa, MC, CB, DC, Discover, personal and traveler's checks **Restrictions:** no smoking; no pets **Activities:** library, bicycles (including a tandem)

HARTLEY HOUSE BED AND BREAKFAST INN
700 22nd Street
Sacramento, California 95816-4012
916/447-7829 or 800/831-5806
916/447-1820 Fax
Proprietor: Randy Hartley

Hartley House is a turn-of-the-century mansion surrounded by majestic elm trees and the grand old homes of historic Boulevard Park in midtown Sacramento. The stately character of the house is preserved in original inlaid hardwood floors, stained woodwork, leaded- and stained-glass windows, and original brass light fixtures converted from gas. Authentic antique furnishings and collectibles decorate the parlor, dining room, and guest rooms. Guest rooms, named for British cities, are appointed with private baths, cable television, clock radios, private telephones, and air conditioning. Fine soaps, shampoos, and bathrobes are provided. Breakfast is served in the dining room or courtyard. Close to downtown, Hartley House is equally suited to business and leisure travelers.

Open: year round **Accommodations:** 5 guest rooms with private baths **Meals:** full breakfast included; complimentary refreshments; restaurants nearby **Rates:** $95 to $155; 10% discount to National Trust members and National Trust Visa cardholders **Payment:** AmEx, Visa, MC, CB, DC, Discover, personal and traveler's checks **Restrictions:** children over 10 welcome; no smoking; no pets **Activities:** reading, porch swings, games, puzzles

ST. HELENA

Nearby attractions: Napa Valley wineries, Robert Louis Stevenson Museum, river, lake, hot-air ballooning, bicycling, hiking, tennis, golfing, antiques hunting, shopping

CHESTELSON HOUSE
1417 Kearney Street
St. Helena, California 94574
707/963-2238
Proprietor: Jackie Sweet

In the heart of the Napa Valley is Chestelson House, a 1904 Queen Anne cottage with inviting wrap-around porches. This comfortable bed and breakfast is in a quiet residential neighborhood, only a short walk from charming shops and nationally renowned restaurants. The light, spacious guest rooms, with names taken from Robert Louis Stevenson's *A Child's Garden of Verses*, have queen-size beds and touches of romantic lace and polished brass. All rooms have private baths, and one offers a double whirlpool tub. Complimentary beverages are served in the early evening in front of the fireplace or on the wide veranda. The innkeeper draws from her experience as a caterer and cooking teacher to prepare a mouth-watering, family-style breakfast.

Open: year round **Accommodations:** 3 guest rooms with private baths **Meals:** full breakfast included; complimentary refreshments; restaurants nearby **Rates:** $98 to $145; 10% discount to National Trust members and National Trust Visa cardholders **Payment:** Visa, MC, Discover, personal and traveler's checks **Restrictions:** no smoking; no pets **Activities:** porch rocking, fireside reading, walking

SAN FRANCISCO

Nearby attractions: San Francisco Bay region, Golden Gate Bridge, Fisherman's Wharf, Embarcadero, North Beach, Mission Dolores, historic districts, Japan Center, financial district, Chinatown, dining, theaters, shopping, opera, symphony, ballet, zoo, cable cars, museums, Golden Gate Park, bicycling, jogging paths, tennis, golfing

ANNA'S THREE BEARS
114 Divisadero
San Francisco, California 94117
415/255-3167 or 800/428-8559
415/552-2959 Fax
Proprietors: Frank and Anna Pope **Innkeeper:** Michael Hofman

World travelers of the Edwardian age maintained a pied-à-terre, or temporary home, in their favorite cities. Anna's Three Bears is a refined alternative for present-day travelers, tired of hotels, who long for the comfort and privacy of their own flat in San Francisco. Located on a quiet residential street in historic Buena Vista Heights, Anna's Three Bears offers two- and three-bedroom flats in a 1906 townhouse. Opulently and elegantly furnished with antiques in the Edwardian style, each has a view of the city, full kitchen, dining and living rooms, and working fireplaces. Guests rent an entire flat, yet the resident manager is available to help with restaurant selections, directions, and tips on how to enjoy the city. Ideal for both business and leisure travelers, the house is 10 minutes from the financial district and within walking distance of Golden Gate Park.

Open: year round **Accommodations:** 3 complete flats **Meals:** continental-plus breakfast included; each flat has a fully equipped kitchen and dining room; restaurants nearby **Rates:** $200 to $250 daily; $1000 to $1400 weekly; 10% discount offered to National Trust members and National Trust Visa cardholders **Payment:** AmEx, Visa, MC, personal and traveler's checks **Restrictions:** children over 12 welcome; no smoking; no pets

THE ARCHBISHOP'S MANSION
1000 Fulton Street
San Francisco, California 94117
415/563-7872 or 800/543-5820
415/885-3193 Fax
Proprietors: Jeffrey Ross and Jonathan Shannon

In 1904, after overseeing work on the Cathedral of St. Mary's, Archbishop Patrick Riordan had a new home built for himself, choosing fashionable Alamo Square for his stuccoed mansion with mansard roof. After Riordan's death in 1909 the house was occupied by succeeding archbishops until 1945. After 35 years of decline, the house was bought by the innkeepers, who undertook an extensive restoration that resulted in today's opulent inn, decorated with lavish fabrics, hand-painted ceilings, and French antiques. Guest rooms, most with fireplaces, contain elaborately carved beds dressed in embroidered linens. Private baths offer French-milled soaps. Breakfast is delivered to bedrooms and afternoon wine is offered in the parlor, with piano selections on the 1904 Bechstein grand. Attention to detail and service has garnered the inn three stars from Mobil, three diamonds from AAA, and kudos from *USA Today*.

Open: year round **Accommodations:** 15 guest rooms with private baths; 5 ares suites **Meals:** continental-plus breakfast included; complimentary refreshments; restaurants nearby **Rates:** $129 to $385; 10% discount to National Trust members and National Trust Visa cardholders, Sunday through Thursday **Payment:** AmEx, Visa, MC, travelers check, personal check for prepayment only **Restrictions:** smoking limited; no pets

CHATEAU TIVOLI
1057 Steiner Street
San Francisco, California 94115
415/776-5462 or 800/228-1647
Proprietors: Rodney Karr and Willard Gersbach

This opulent Queen Anne townhouse was built in 1892 for Daniel B. Jackson, an Oregon lumber baron, and his wife, Maria, who occupied the 22-room mansion until 1898. Ernestine Kreling, operator of the famous Tivoli Opera House, purchased and lived in the house from 1905 to 1917. Today, after years of decline, the building has been restored to its original splendor with 22 exterior colors plus gold-leaf trim. The unique roof has three colors of slate that form striped and diamond patterns. Inside, the hardwood floors, grand oak staircase, Wedgwood frieze and tiling, and elaborate woodwork all have been restored. Guests are surrounded by art and antiques from the Vanderbilt and Getty estates. Rooms and suites feature canopy beds, marble baths, balconies, fireplaces, stained-glass windows, and turrets. The entire chateau is available for special events.

Open: year round **Accommodations:** 8 guest rooms (6 have private baths); 3 are suites **Meals:** continental-plus breakfast included; complimentary refreshments; restaurants nearby **Rates:** $80 to $200; 10% discount offered to National Trust members and National Trust Visa cardholders **Payment:** AmEx, Visa, MC, personal and traveler's checks **Restrictions:** no smoking; no pets **Activities:** reading, piano, relaxing with wine by the fireplace

EAST BROTHER LIGHT STATION
c/o 117 Park Place
Point Richmond, California 94801
415/233-2385
Proprietors: John Barnett and Lore Hogan
Location: in San Francisco Bay, 1 mile west of Point San Pablo

Two rocky islands known as "The Sisters" and two known as "The Brothers" mark the straits separating San Francisco and San Pablo bays. The one-acre East Brother Island holds this 1873 light station, the oldest of 17 still in operation in the bay. Listed in the National Register of Historic Places, the station was manned continuously until 1969, when the Coast Guard automated the light and fog signals and closed the buildings. A nonprofit group was formed in 1979 to restore and preserve the structure and operate it as a living museum and inn. Guests are picked up by boat at 4 p.m. at Point San Pablo Yacht Harbor and given a tour of the island. Dinner at the inn is an innovative five-course California-French meal, replete with wines and champagne. Guest rooms sport Victorian furnishings, including brass beds. After breakfast guests are treated to a demonstration of the restored diaphone foghorn and are returned to the harbor at 11 a.m.

Open: year round Thursday through Sunday nights only **Accommodations:** 4 guest rooms (2 have private baths) **Meals:** full breakfast and dinner included; complimentary refreshments **Rates:** $295 double; $235 single **Payment:** AmEx, Visa, MC, personal and traveler's checks **Restrictions:** children welcome if one group rents all four rooms; no smoking; no pets; water supplied by cistern so showers available only by special arrangement **Activities:** fishing (bring your own gear and bait), pitching horseshoes, basketball, watching birds and seals

GOLDEN GATE HOTEL
775 Bush Street
San Francisco, California 94108
415/392-3702 or 800/835-1118
415/392-6202 Fax
Proprietors: John and Renate Kenaston

The Golden Gate Hotel is a bed-and-breakfast hotel located in the Lower Nob Hill Historic District. Built in 1913, the four-story hotel has a double-bay facade, providing many guest rooms with bay-window views and letting in plenty of light and air. The rear of the building faces an open, tree-filled garden. An antique birdcage elevator is a favorite attraction of hotel guests. Furnished with antiques, art, and imagination, the hotel maintains the mood of turn-of-the-century San Francisco, especially in its antique claw-foot tubs. The multilingual hosts of this small, family-owned-and-operated inn take pride in offering individual attention: They brighten each guest room with fresh flowers, provide concierge services, and arrange sightseeing tours.

Open: year round **Accommodations:** 23 guest rooms (14 have private baths); 1 is a suite **Meals:** continental breakfast included; complimentary afternoon tea; restaurants nearby **Rates:** $55 to $144; 10% discount offered to National Trust members and National Trust Visa cardholders November through April **Payment:** AmEx, Visa, MC, CB, DC, personal and traveler's checks **Restrictions:** smoking limited; with notice, arrangements can be made for pets **Activities:** relaxation, classical music in the parlor, conversation

RED VICTORIAN PEACE CENTER
BED AND BREAKFAST
1665 Haight Street
San Francisco, California 94117
415/864-1978
Proprietor: Sami Sunchild

The "Red Vic," built in 1904 as the Jefferson Hotel, was a country retreat for families on outings to the new Golden Gate Park. A few years later, a Victorian residential community grew up around the hotel and, in 1967, when the Summer of Love came to Haight-Ashbury, the hotel was its cornerstone. Sami Sunchild, owner and artist-in-residence since 1977, has created a living museum of San Francisco's famous neighborhood with her 18 guest rooms and Gallery of Meditative Art that commemorate the ideals of the 1960s. Peace, ecology, and community are the themes found throughout the Red Vic in rooms with names like Flower Child, Sunshine, Peace, and Rainbow. Most rooms share baths, also named: Aquarium (live goldfish in the toilet tank!), Starlight, Infinity, and Love, of course. Breakfast is served in the Global Village Center on the first floor, where guests from around the world converse over a simple, yet nutritious meal.

Open: year round **Accommodations:** 18 guest rooms (4 have private baths); 1 is a suite **Meals:** continental-plus breakfast included; restaurants nearby **Rates:** $86 to $200; 10% discount to National Trust members and National Trust Visa cardholders for stays of 3 days or more **Payment:** AmEx, Visa, MC, personal and traveler's checks **Restrictions:** well-supervised children welcome; no smoking; no pets **Activities:** 15-minute morning meditation, massage, life counseling by appointment, Gallery of Meditative Art

SHERMAN HOUSE

2160 Green Street
San Francisco, California 94123
415/563-3600 or 800/424-5777
Proprietors: Manou and Vesta
Mobedshahi

In 1876, Leander Sherman, an influential patron of the arts, created this elegant Second Empire home, which flourished for decades at the center of San Francisco's musical and artistic life. The focus of the house was a soaring, three-story music recital hall. In 1981 the structure's restoration and conversion into a world-class hotel took 11 months of meticulous work, with an average of 60 craftspeople on the job daily. Sherman House is now filled with antiques and international furnishings. Each unique guest room is designed in either a French Second Empire, Biedermeier, or English Jacobean motif. Canopied feather beds are draped in rich tapestry fabrics. Modern amenities include wet bars, wall safes, and whirlpool baths in the black granite bathrooms. A city and county landmark, Sherman House is a member of Historic Hotels of America.

Open: year round **Accommodations:** 14 guest rooms with private baths; 6 are suites **Meals:** restaurant on premises serving breakfast, afternoon tea, and dinner; 24-hour room service; restaurants nearby **Wheelchair access:** 1 suite **Rates:** $235 to $750; 10% discount offered to National Trust members and National Trust Visa cardholders **Payment:** AmEx, Visa, MC, DC, personal and traveler's checks **Restrictions:** smoking limited; no pets **Activities:** reading and board games in the gallery, relaxing in the garden

VICTORIAN INN ON THE PARK

301 Lyon Street
San Francisco, California 94117
415/931-1830 or 800/435-1967
415/931-1830 Fax
Proprietors: Lisa and William Benau and Shirley and Paul Weber

The Victorian Inn on the Park, also known as the Clunie House, was built in 1897 in the Queen Anne style. Overlooking Golden Gate Park, the house sports decorative gable vergeboards and finials and an octagonal, covered, third-story porch. Each guest room is uniquely designed to reflect Victorian San Francisco and provides comfort with fluffy comforters, down pillows, and private bathrooms. A newspaper and a breakfast of seasonal fruit, cheese, juice, croissants, and freshly brewed coffee greet guests each morning in the oak-paneled dining room. The innkeepers are always available to help guests plan local tours, make dining reservations, or obtain anything from a chauffeured limousine to theater tickets.

Open: year round **Accommodations:** 12 guest rooms with private baths; 2 are suites **Meals:** continental-plus breakfast included; complimentary refreshments; restaurants nearby **Rates:** $99 to $159; 10% discount to National Trust members and National Trust Visa cardholders **Payment:** AmEx, Visa, MC, CB, DC, Discover, personal and traveler's checks **Restrictions:** no smoking; no pets

---

SAN LUIS OBISPO

Nearby attractions: Hearst Castle, Mission San Luis Obispo, winery tours, walking and house tours, Pismo Beach, Morro Bay, Cambria, mountains, natural hot springs, horseback riding, hiking, picnicking, shopping, golfing, tennis, bicycling, antiques hunting

GARDEN STREET INN
1212 Garden Street
San Luis Obispo, California 93401
805/545-9802
Proprietors: Dan and Kathy Smith

Behind a wrought-iron fence, one block from an eighteenth-century mission, is this graceful 1887 Italianate building, home of the Garden Street Inn. Its guest rooms are appointed with antiques, fireplaces, whirlpool tubs, armoires, and rich wall coverings and fabrics. Historical, cultural, and personal memorabilia provide each room with its theme, such as Emerald Isle (shamrocks and Lilies of the Valley), Amadeus (eighteenth-century elegance), Edelweiss (Victorian Austria), and The Lovers (a print of Picasso's famed picture and a private deck). A full breakfast is served in the McCaffrey morning room with original stained-glass windows. Spacious outside decks and the well-stocked Goldtree library are open to guests.

Open: year round **Accommodations:** 13 guest rooms with private baths; 4 are suites **Meals:** full breakfast included; complimentary refreshments; restaurants nearby **Wheelchair access:** 1 room **Rates:** $95 to $165; 10% discount to National Trust members and National Trust Visa cardholders (requires two-night stay on weekends) **Payment:** AmEx, Visa, MC, personal and traveler's checks **Restrictions:** not suitable for young children; no smoking **Activities:** reading, relaxing, touring historic house

SANTA BARBARA

Nearby attractions: historic sites, mission, beach, ocean swimming, sailing, fishing, hiking, biking, riding, windsurfing, tennis, golfing, botanical gardens, wine-country tours, museums, theaters, shopping

OLD YACHT CLUB INN
431 Corona Del Mar Drive
Santa Barbara, California 93103
805/962-1277 or 800/676-1676 (reservations)
805/962-3989 Fax
Proprietors: Nancy Donaldson and Sandy Hunt

Built as a private home in 1912, this Craftsman house was used during the 1920s as temporary headquarters for the Santa Barbara Yacht Club. The house was restored in 1980 and opened as the city's first bed and breakfast. The Old Yacht Club Inn is furnished with classic European and Early American antiques. Oriental rugs cover the hardwood floors. Four sunny guest rooms are available upstairs and the Captain's Corner downstairs offers a private "aft" deck. The adjacent Hitchcock House features four guest rooms, each with a private entry. All rooms have private baths and telephones, fresh flowers, and a decanter of sherry. Guests may relax in front of the fireplace, on the covered front porch, or on the back deck. Gourmet breakfasts are prepared daily by Chef Nancy, who also offers five-course Saturday-night meals, which *Bon Appetit* has said "rival the finest the city has to offer."

Open: year round **Accommodations:** 9 guest rooms with private baths **Meals:** full breakfast included; complimentary refreshments; dinner available on Saturdays; restaurants nearby **Rates:** $90 to $155; 10% discount to National Trust members and National Trust Visa cardholders midweek only **Payment:** AmEx, Visa, MC, DC, Discover, personal and traveler's checks **Restrictions:** no smoking; no pets **Activities:** bicycles and beach equipment provided

OLIVE HOUSE INN
1604 Olive Street
Santa Barbara, California 93101
805/962-4902 or 800/786-6422
805/899-2754 Fax
Proprietor: Lois Gregg

The Olive House is a quiet bed and breakfast in Santa Barbara's beautiful Riviera section, offering mountain, city, and ocean views. This 1904 two-story home with hipped roof and center chimney contains six guest rooms, each individually decorated and offering different amenities, such as a private deck, a fireplace, or a hot tub. For business travelers there are in-room telephones and an available fax machine. Guests are welcomed in the living room with its wood wainscoting, beamed ceiling, window seats, fireplace, and studio grand piano. Breakfast can be enjoyed in the dining room, on the sundeck, or in the garden. The Olive House has been awarded three diamonds by AAA.

Open: year round **Accommodations:** 6 guest rooms with private baths **Meals:** full breakfast included; complimentary refreshments; restaurants nearby **Rates:** $105 to $175; 10% discount to National Trust members and National Trust Visa cardholders **Payment:** AmEx, Visa, MC, Discover, personal and traveler's checks (must have credit card to guarantee reservation) **Restrictions:** no smoking; no pets **Activities:** piano, board games, reading, garden, conversation

PARSONAGE BED AND BREAKFAST INN
1600 Olive Street
Santa Barbara, California 93101
805/962-9336
Proprietor: Hilde Michelmore

Built in 1892 as a parsonage for the Trinity Episcopal Church, one of Santa Barbara's most notable Queen Anne Victorians is now a bed-and-breakfast inn. The Parsonage has been furnished with antiques and reproductions to create an atmosphere of comfort and grace. Each guest room has its individual character: the Versailles Room, for example, faithfully reproduces the decor of Louis XIV with period furnishings and distinctive wallpaper; the Honeymoon Suite features a king-size canopy bed and an old-fashioned solarium. A full breakfast is served in the dining room by the fireplace or on the sundeck with its cozy gazebo. The living room with fireplace and garden with arbor are comfortable places to unwind. The Parsonage is located in a quiet residential neighborhood between downtown Santa Barbara and the foothills.

Open: year round **Accommodations:** 6 guest rooms with private baths; 1 is a suite **Meals:** full breakfast included; restaurants nearby **Rates:** $95 to $185; 10% discount offered to National Trust members and National Trust Visa cardholders **Payment:** AmEx, Visa, MC, personal and traveler's checks **Restrictions:** smoking limited; no pets

SECRET GARDEN INN AND COTTAGES (formerly Blue Quail Inn)
1908 Bath Street
Santa Barbara, California 93101
805/687-2300 or 800/676-1622
805/687-4576 Fax
Proprietor: Jack C. Greenwald

The Secret Garden Inn begins with a 1915 California bungalow and moves on to encompass four cottages built slightly later. Each guest room and cottage is decorated in a combination of English and American country styles, with antiques, white iron beds, wicker furnishings, down comforters, and claw-foot tubs. Guest rooms are named for prevalent birds—Hummingbird, Meadowlark, Wood Thrush, and so on—and each has some special treat such as a fireplace, a private patio, a view of the garden, or a bay window. Tree-shaded patios, gardens, and a sunny lawn with lounge chairs afford ample space for relaxing. The inn provides bicycles to take guests to nearby downtown shops, galleries, sights, and beaches.

Open: year round, except December 24 and 25 **Accommodations:** 9 guest rooms with private baths; 4 are suites **Meals:** full breakfast included; complimentary refreshments; restaurants nearby **Rates:** $95 to $165; 10% discount to National Trust members Monday through Thursday, except holidays **Payment:** AmEx, Visa, MC, DC, personal and traveler's checks **Restrictions:** no smoking; no pets **Activities:** bicycling, relaxing, sunning in the garden

SIMPSON HOUSE INN
1221 East Arrellaga
Santa Barbara, California 93101
805/963-7067 or 800/676-1280
Proprietors: Glyn and Linda Davies **Manager:** Gillean Wilson

Scotsman Robert Simpson built this Eastlake-style home in 1874 to remind himself of his native land. Today, the Simpson House Inn is considered one of the most distinguished Victorian homes of southern California and is a Santa Barbara Landmark. Sandstone walls and tall hedges screen the house from the street. Guests pass through wrought-iron gates and landscaped grounds into the house. Here the spacious sitting room adjoins the formal dining room, and French doors open onto garden verandas with teak floors and white wicker furniture. Guest rooms are elegantly appointed with antiques, English lace, oriental rugs, goose-down comforters, and fresh flowers. Four suites in the restored barn and three cottages in the gardens offer understated elegance, privacy, and fireplaces. Simpson House is surrounded by an acre of English gardens, mature oaks, magnolias, fountains, and arbors.

Open: year round **Accommodations:** 14 guest rooms with private baths; 4 are suites; 3 are cottages **Meals:** full breakfast included; complimentary refreshments; restaurants nearby **Wheelchair access:** 1 barn suite **Rates:** $105 to $245 **Payment:** AmEx, Visa, MC, Discover, personal and traveler's checks **Restrictions:** no smoking; no pets **Activities:** English croquet, bicycles, beach chairs and towels available, acre of gardens for sitting and strolling

UPHAM VICTORIAN HOTEL AND GARDEN COTTAGES
1404 De La Vina Street
Santa Barbara, California 93101
805/962-0058 or 800/727-0876
Proprietor: Jan Martin Winn

In 1871, Boston banker Amasa Lincoln sailed to Santa Barbara and built one of the city's first boarding houses to accommodate guests attracted to the area by reports of health-giving hot springs. Lincoln had the building designed in the Italianate style, complete with a wraparound porch and cupola to remind him of his New England origins. Situated on an acre of gardens in the heart of downtown, the Upham is now the oldest continuously operating hostelry in southern California. Antiques and period furnishings highlight the guest rooms, which are located in the main building, five garden cottages, and a carriage house.

A breakfast buffet, daily newspaper, and many guest services are provided by the helpful and friendly staff. Louie's Restaurant, adjoining the lobby, offers innovative California cuisine for lunch and dinner, featuring fresh seafood and pasta.

Open: year round **Accommodations:** 49 guest rooms with private baths; 2 are suites **Meals:** continental-plus breakfast included; complimentary wine and cheese; restaurant on premises **Wheelchair access:** dining room only **Rates:** $120 to $350 **Payment:** AmEx, Visa, MC, CB, DC, Discover, travelers check **Restrictions:** no pets **Activities:** relaxing in the garden

SANTA CRUZ

Nearby attractions: beaches; boardwalk and amusement park; swimming; surfing; sailing; seal-watching; tennis; golfing; shopping; wineries; villages of Aptos, Soquel, and Capitola

APPLE LANE INN
6265 Soquel Drive
Aptos, California 95003
408/475-6868
Proprietors: Doug and Diana Groom
Location: 10 miles south of Santa Cruz

Apple Lane Inn is a Victorian farmhouse with wraparound porch, patterned wood shingles, and decorative vergeboards. The house and barn were built in the 1870s on three acres, which included apple orchards. Today, the inn still enjoys its quiet country setting amid trim lawns and flowering gardens. Guest accommodations are handsomely furnished in the Victorian tradition. One elaborate room features redwood wainscoting, a pressed-tin ceiling, and a seventeenth-century Spanish four-poster bed. Others offer antique pine or walnut furnishings, lace canopies, claw-foot tubs, or antique quilts. A full country breakfast is served, always centering on a hearty main course. The brick patio offers both afternoon sun and cooling shade under wisteria and roses.

Open: year round **Accommodations:** 5 rooms with private baths; 1 is a suite **Meals:** full breakfast included; restaurant on premises **Rates:** $70 to $175; 10% discount offered to National Trust members or National Trust Visa cardholders **Payment:** Visa, MC, Discover, personal check **Restrictions:** children welcome Sunday through Thursday; no smoking; no pets **Activities:** barn and farm animals, pitching horseshoes, croquet, badminton, historic library

CHATEAU VICTORIAN
118 First Street
Santa Cruz, California 95060
408/458-9458
Proprietor: Alice June

This Queen Anne–style structure was built around the turn of the century as a single-family residence. In the 1950s the house was converted to apartments, but 30 years later it was restored to its original appearance and opened as a comfortable inn. Fireplaces adorn all of the guest rooms, and each room offers a touch of individuality. Ocean View Room—offering a peek at Monterey Bay—has a marble fireplace and a claw-foot tub. Garden View Room, on the main level, contains an original bay window and a canopy bed. Patio Room has a private entrance and an old-fashioned armoire. Two guest rooms are in the cottage on the other side of the brick patio. Guests may choose to enjoy breakfast in the lounge, on the secluded deck, or on the terrace.

Open: year round **Accommodations:** 7 rooms with private baths **Meals:** continental-plus breakfast included; complimentary refreshments; restaurants nearby **Rates:** $110 to $140 **Payment:** AmEx, Visa, MC, personal and traveler's checks **Restrictions:** children over 18 welcome; no smoking; no pets **Activities:** restful relaxation

---

SANTA ROSA

Nearby attractions: Railroad Square, Sonoma wineries, redwood forests, Pacific coast, San Francisco, museums, Luther Burbank Center for the Arts, art galleries, golfing, hot-air ballooning

HOTEL LA ROSE
308 Wilson Street
Santa Rosa, California 95401
707/579-3200 or 800/527-6738
707/579-3200 Fax
Proprietors: Debbie and Claus Neumann

First settled in the 1850s, Santa Rosa became a center of commerce and transportation when the railroad came to town in 1870. Hotel La Rose was built in 1907—during Santa Rosa's period of continued economic growth—of locally quarried stone. After an extensive renovation in 1984 that garnered top honors from the Sonoma County Historical Society, Hotel La Rose reopened with 29 guest rooms in the original building and 20 new guest rooms in the adjacent carriage house, each with a private balcony or patio. Each guest room is decorated in its own distinctive turn-of-the-century style. Original wainscoting has been preserved in the corridors, which are lit with simulated-gas light fixtures. The hotel's grand staircase was taken from the San Francisco cable car barn. Josef's Restaurant, in the hotel, serves continental cuisine. Hotel La Rose is a member of Historic Hotels of America.

Open: year round **Accommodations:** 49 guest rooms with private baths **Meals:** continental breakfast included; restaurant on premises; restaurants nearby **Wheelchair access:** yes **Rates:** $70 to $115; 10% discount to National Trust members and National Trust Visa cardholders **Payment:** AmEx, Visa, MC, travelers check **Restrictions:** smoking limited; no pets **Activities:** courtyard garden, specialty packages (hot-air ballooning, golfing, romance)

SEAL BEACH

Nearby attractions: Disneyland, the *Queen Mary*, beach, golfing, tennis, sailing, surfing, theater, antiques hunting, Catalina Island, Hollywood

SEAL BEACH INN AND GARDENS
212 Fifth Street
Seal Beach, California 90740
310/493-2416
310/799-0483 Fax
Proprietor: Marjorie Bettenhausen

Built in 1918 and 1923, Seal Beach Inn and Gardens has served as a seaside resort since its inception, making it the area's oldest continuously operating business. Architectural details—filigreed iron fences and newel posts, a brick courtyard, curved window arches, window boxes, tile murals, and iron fountains—reflect the area's early European and Mediterranean influences. The inn also features picturesque gardens, an elegant dining room with a fireplace and brass chandeliers, and bedrooms containing original hardwood floors and light fixtures, and many period furnishings. The innkeepers proudly cater special occasions, and will serve lunches, teas, and dinners by request. Picnic baskets are also available. The inn has been designated a historic landmark by the Seal Beach Historical Society. In 1995, the Seal Beach Inn was chosen as one of the top 12 inns of the year by *Country Inns* magazine.

Open: year round **Accommodations:** 23 guest rooms with private baths; 14 are suites **Meals:** full breakfast included; gourmet picnics on request; wine and cheese social in evening; restaurants nearby **Rates:** $118 to $185; 10% discount to National Trust members **Payment:** AmEx, Visa, MC, DC, travelers check, personal check for advance reservations only **Restrictions:** children discouraged; no smoking; no pets **Activities:** swimming pool, library, board games

SONOMA

Nearby attractions: National Register historic district, Jack London State Park, St. Franci de Solano Mission, wineries, art galleries, historic home tours, golfing, horseback riding, hiking, hot-air ballooning

HIDDEN OAK
214 East Napa Street
Sonoma, California 95476
707/996-9863
Proprietor: Catherine Cotchett

Hidden Oak, a restored California Craftsman bungalow, was built in 1913 as a refectory, or dining hall, for the small church located next door. A large two-story house, it has a brown-shingled exterior and a low-pitched gabled roof over the wide front porch. Guests are invited to feel at home at the Hidden Oak and browse in the library, sit by the tile-faced fireplace in the reading room, or relax in the parlor. Guest bedrooms—three located upstairs, some under the shed dormers—are large, airy, and welcoming with plush pillows, comfortable beds, antiques, and wicker. This country-style home is located in a historic neighborhood, less than two blocks from the downtown plaza, which is listed as a state and national landmark.

Open: year round **Accommodations:** 4 guest rooms with private baths; 1 is a suite **Meals:** full breakfast included; restaurants nearby **Rates:** $90 to $160 **Payment:** AmEx, Discover, personal check **Restrictions:** no smoking; no pets **Activities:** bicycles, puzzles, games

SONOMA HOTEL

110 West Spain Street
Sonoma, California 95476
707/996-2996 or 800/468-6016
707/996-7014 Fax
Proprietors: John and Dorene Musilli

Located on Sonoma's tree-lined plaza (a National Register historic district), this vintage hotel has offered accommodations and dining to the discriminating guest since the 1920s. It was first built in 1879 as a two-story adobe structure that housed a grocery shop and entertainment hall across a dirt road from the Sonoma State Depot. In 1922 the building was sold to Samual Sebastiani, who added a third floor and six dormers, and admitted guests to the rechristened Plaza Hotel. In today's Sonoma Hotel, each antique-filled guest room evokes California's early history, while the emphasis on comfort is decidedly European. From the wine offered on arrival to the morning's fresh-baked pastries, guests sample the wine country's hospitality. This romantic inn is a short walk to wineries, historic landmarks, art galleries, and unique shops.

Open: year round **Accommodations:** 17 guest rooms (5 have private baths); 1 is a suite **Meals:** continental breakfast included; complimentary refreshments; full bar and restaurant on premises **Rates:** $75 to $120; 10% discount offered to National Trust members and National Trust Visa cardholders November 1 through May 30 **Payment:** AmEx, Visa, MC, personal and traveler's checks

---

SOQUEL

Nearby attractions: museums, antiques hunting, wineries, Monterey Bay region, redwood forests, Carmel, Big Sur

BLUE SPRUCE INN

2815 Main Street
Soquel, California 95073-2412
408/464-1137 or 800/559-1137
Proprietors: Pat and Tom O'Brien
Location: 4 miles south of Santa Cruz

The Blue Spruce inn was built in 1875 as a home for one of the logging families who cut the redwoods in the Santa Cruz Mountains for shipment to San Francisco. In 1893 a barn was built adjacent to the house. Both the simple Victorian farmhouse and barn have been renovated to provide modern luxury in a lush garden setting. The innkeepers' interest in local art permeates the inn. Each guest room is named for the work of art that hangs in the room. The rooms are

further individualized by country antiques and Amish quilts that complement the colors in the pictures. Some rooms offer gas fireplaces, others whirlpool tubs. The Carriage House contains a stained-glass mural in the shower. Guests often unwind in the garden hot tub or before the fireplace in the living room.

Open: year round **Accommodations:** 6 guest rooms with private baths **Meals:** full breakfast included; complimentary refreshments; restaurants nearby **Rates:** $85 to $135; 10% discount offered to National Trust members and National Trust Visa cardholders Sunday through Thursday **Payment:** AmEx, Visa, MC, personal and traveler's checks **Restrictions**: children over 12 welcome; no smoking; no pets **Activities:** garden hot tub, board games

---

UKIAH

Nearby attractions: Mendocino coast, redwood forests, museums, water sports

VICHY HOT SPRINGS RESORT AND INN
2605 Vichy Springs Road
Ukiah, California 95482
707/462-9515
Proprietors: Gilbert and Marjorie Ashoff

The only warm and naturally carbonated mineral baths in North America, Ukiah's springs were first used thousands of years ago by Native Americans. The Vichy resort, named after the famous springs in France, opened in 1854 and is now a state historic landmark. It was a favorite of writers Mark Twain and Jack London, presidents Grant, Harrison, and Teddy Roosevelt, and pugilists John L. Sullivan and "Gentleman" Jim Corbett. The resort has been renovated to combine its natural and historic charm with modern comfort. Twelve guest rooms are in a redwood building dating from the 1860s; two cottages with fully equipped kitchens date from 1854 and are the oldest structures in Mendocino County. Just steps away are the renovated indoor and outdoor mineral bathing tubs, therapeutic massage building, hot pool, and Olympic-size swimming pool.

Open: year round **Accommodations:** 12 guest rooms with private baths; 2 cottages **Meals:** full breakfast included; restaurants nearby **Wheelchair access:** limited in dining facilities and bathrooms **Rates:** $89 to $165; 10% discount to National Trust members and National Trust Visa cardholders **Payment:** AmEx, Visa, MC, CB, DC, personal and traveler's checks **Restrictions:** no smoking; no pets **Activities:** swimming, massage, hot pool, carbonated mineral baths, hiking on 700-acre ranch with waterall, mountain biking, picnicking

WESTPORT

Nearby attractions: Skunk Train, Mendocino, deep-sea fishing from Noyo Harbor, wilderness, redwoods, tide pools

HOWARD CREEK RANCH
40501 North Highway One
P.O. Box 121
Westport, California 95488
707/964-6725
Proprietors: Charles (Sunny) and Sally Grigg
Location: 3 miles north of Westport, 180 miles north of San Francisco

Once part of a huge sheep and cattle ranch first settled in 1867, Howard Creek Ranch occupies a 40-acre valley on the Mendocino coast. Designated a Mendocino County historic site, the 1871 farmhouse sits on an expanse of green lawns and award-winning flower gardens. A 75-foot-long swinging footbridge spans Howard Creek as the waterway flows past barns and outbuildings to the beach 200 yards away. The ranch buildings are constructed of virgin redwood from the ranch's forest. The inn is furnished with antiques, collectibles, and memorabilia; the original fireplace still warms the parlor. A hot tub and sauna are set into the mountainside, forming a unique health spa with privacy and dramatic views. The magnificent area affords sweeping views of the ocean, sandy beaches, and rolling mountains.

Open: year round **Accommodations:** 10 guest rooms (8 have private baths); 3 are cabins **Meals:** breakfast included; barbecue grills available for beach picnics; some rooms with microwaves and refrigerators; restaurants nearby **Rates:** $55 to $145; 10% discount offered off-season **Payment:** AmEx, Visa, MC, personal and traveler's checks **Restrictions:** children by prior arrangement; smoking limited; arrangements can be made for pets **Activities:** horseback riding, games, books, musical instruments, beachcombing, watching birds and whales, tide pools

COLORADO

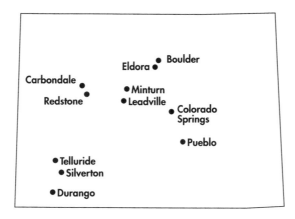

BOULDER

Nearby attractions: University of Colorado, Pearl Street pedestrian mall, Shakespeare festival, Chautauqua festival

BRIAR ROSE BED AND BREAKFAST
2151 Arapahoe Avenue
Boulder, Colorado 80302
303/442-3007
Proprietors: Bob and Margaret Weisenbach

In 1904, the McConnel family built a brick bungalow on this site. Over the next 77 years they expanded and improved their home until it was purchased in 1981 and converted to a bed and breakfast. The house is charmingly styled much like an English country cottage with arched windows, stone lintels and sills, and a shake roof. Period antiques, original art, and fresh flowers fill the nine guest rooms, giving each a distinctive character. All rooms have private baths, telephones, fine linens, and feather comforters on queen-size beds. The Honeymoon and Anniversary rooms have wood-burning fireplaces. Carefully groomed gardens offer a private retreat for guests, as well as the perfect

site for small meetings and receptions. The innkeepers provide a generous breakfast and afternoon tea, featuring the inn's own shortbread cookies.

Open: year round **Accommodations**: 9 guest rooms with private baths; 1 is a suite **Meals**: continental-plus breakfast included; complimentary refreshments; restaurants nearby **Rates**: $84 to $135; 10% discount offered to National Trust members and National Trust Visa cardholders **Payment**: check **Restrictions**: no smoking; no pets **Activities**: garden strolling, conversation

---

CARBONDALE

Nearby attractions: river rafting, hot-air ballooning, tennis, bungee jumping, skydiving, hayrides, horseback riding, art galleries, marble sculpture studios, iron works forge, hot springs, vapor caves, hiking, golfing, fishing, mountain biking, mountaineering, llama trekking, concerts, Aspen Music Festival, Glenwood Canyon, Physics and Biology Institute, fine dining

MT. SOPRIS INN
0165 Mt. Sopris Ranch Road
Box 126
Carbondale, Colorado 81623
Proprietor: Barbara Fasching
Location: 30 miles north of Aspen, 3 miles southwest of highways 82 and 133

This wooden mountain lodge was built in 1945. Its two-story lobby contains a unique log-and-rail staircase. The great room features a 15-foot-wide floor-to-ceiling river rock fireplace. On 14 acres, the inn provides a magnificent panorama of the Crystal Valley to Mount Sopris, McClure Pass, and Chair Mountain. Llamas graze in the inn's pasture and a hiking path leads to the Crystal River for stream fishing. Guest accommodations are in the Main House, the Guest House, and the newly completed Chalet East. All rooms have a private bath, television, telephone, and writing table. Some rooms have fireplaces and some have balconies, all offer grand views. Mt. Sopris Inn can accommodate wedding parties and business conferences as well as leisure travelers.

Open: year round **Accommodations:** 15 guest rooms with private baths; 1 is a suite **Meals:** full breakfast included; complimentary refreshments; restaurants nearby **Wheelchair access:** yes **Rates:** $85 to $250; 10% discount to National Trust members and National Trust Visa cardholders **Payment:** Visa, MC, personal and traveler's checks **Restrictions:** children over 12 welcome; no smoking; no pets **Activities:** swimming pool, hot tubs, fishing, hiking

COLORADO SPRINGS

Nearby attractions: Pikes Peak, Garden of the Gods, Cheyenne Cañon, U.S. Olympic Training Center, U.S. Air Force Academy, Old Colorado City, Manitou Springs, historic district, shopping, hiking, bicycling, fishing, ice skating, horseback riding

HOLDEN HOUSE – 1902 BED AND BREAKFAST INN

1102 West Pikes Peak Avenue
Colorado Springs, Colorado 80904
719/471-3980
Proprietors: Sallie and Welling Clark

This 1902 turreted Colonial Revival Victorian house, 1906 carriage house, and adjacent 1898 Victorian house were built by Isabel Holden, widow of prosperous Colorado Springs businessman Daniel M. Holden. The six guest rooms have been named after mining towns in which the Holdens owned interests: the Aspen, Cripple Creek, Leadville, Silverton, Goldfield, and Independence. All boast private baths, period furnishings, and queen beds. The three houses are filled with family treasures, antiques, heirloom quilts, and personal touches. A full gourmet breakfast is served in the formal dining room, and complimentary refreshments are provided. The four suites offer fireplaces and tubs for two. The inn's common areas include the living room with a tiled fireplace, the parlor with television, and the veranda with wicker furniture and mountain views.

Open: year round **Accommodations:** 6 guest rooms with private baths; 4 are suites **Wheelchair access:** 1 suite **Meals:** full breakfast included; complimentary refreshments; restaurants nearby **Rates:** $75 to $110 **Payment:** AmEx, Visa, MC, CB, DC, Discover, personal and traveler's checks **Restrictions:** not suitable for children; no smoking; no pets (resident cats)

ROOM AT THE INN BED AND BREAKFAST

618 North Nevada Avenue
Colorado Springs, Colorado 80903
719/442-1896
719/442-6802 Fax
Proprietors: Chick and Jan McCormick

A wealthy mine investor and his wife built this Queen Anne home in 1896. They incorporated many elements typical of the style including fish-scale siding, a wraparound porch, and a three-story turret. Inside, original hand-painted murals, Italian tiled fireplaces, and pocket doors remain. Today, as an inn, the house offers five guest rooms with private baths, queen-size beds, period antiques, and oriental rugs. Several rooms have whirlpool tubs and turret sitting areas, while the others have gas fireplaces. The adjacent cottage offers two guest accommodations; one is fully wheelchair accessible, the other has a kitchenette. Designer linens, cotton robes, and evening turn-down service are provided in all rooms. Guests may relax in the hot tub on the sundeck or play games and read in the third-floor upper parlor.

Open: year round **Accommodations:** 7 guest rooms with private baths; 2 are suites **Meals:** full breakfast included; complimentary refreshments; restaurants nearby **Wheelchair access:** 1 guest room **Rates:** $90 to $115 **Payment:** AmEx, Visa, MC, CB, DC, Discover, personal and traveler's checks **Restrictions:** children over 12 welcome; no smoking; no pets **Activities:** hot tub, library, board games, bicycles

DURANGO

Nearby attractions: Durango–Silverton Narrow Gauge Railroad, Mesa Verde National Park, historic districts, downhill and cross-country skiing, hiking, mountain biking, rafting, kayaking, fishing, rodeo, shopping, galleries, fine dining

ROCHESTER HOTEL
721 East Second Avenue
Durango, Colorado 81301
303/385-1920
303/385-1967 Fax
Proprietors: Diane and Kirk Komick

This two-story brick building, built in 1891, was originally known as the Peeples Hotel. Mary Francis Finn, who owned and operated the hotel from 1905 to 1920, renamed it the Rochester. By the 1950s it had sunk into disrepair and continued to decay until purchased in 1993 by Diane Komick and her son Kirk. Together they completed an extensive restoration, converting the derelict building into a spacious hotel furnished in a "cowboy-Victoriana" style. Original interior features that have been restored include the woodwork, staircase, hardware, doors, windows, and skylight in the upstairs ceiling. The Rochester Hotel offers 15 high-ceilinged rooms, each decorated in an Old West motif inspired by the many movies filmed in and around Durango. Among the rooms available are those named *Viva Zapata, Ticket to Tomahawk*, and *How the West Was Won*.

Open: year round **Accommodations:** 15 guest rooms with private baths; 2 are suites **Meals:** full breakfast included; complimentary refreshments; restaurant on premises; restaurants nearby **Wheelchair access:** yes **Rates:** $85 to $165; 10% discount to National Trust members and National Trust Visa cardholders **Payment:** AmEx, Visa, MC, Discover, personal and traveler's checks **Restrictions:** no smoking; no pets **Activities:** courtyard garden

ELDORA
Nearby attractions: Eldora Mountain Resort, downhill and cross-country skiing, ski school, Nederland, Indian Peaks Wilderness Area, Rocky Mountain National Park, hiking, bicycling, fishing, camping, horseback riding, antiques hunting, crafts shops, gambling towns of Central City and Black Hawk

GOLDMINER HOTEL
601 Klondyke Avenue
Eldora, Colorado 80466
800/422-4629
303/258-3850 Fax
Proprietor: Scott Bruntjen

The Goldminer Hotel is an 1897 two-story, hipped-roof, log-and-frame structure in the heart of the Eldora National Historic District. Guest rooms are decorated with period pieces to bring back the rustic and exciting gold-mining days of the area. Some rooms have fireplaces and a hot tub is available to all guests. Adjacent to Eldora Mountain Resort, the hotel offers free daily shuttle transportation to the resort, as well as nightly transporation to the close-by gambling towns of Central City and Black Hawk. The hotel also operates unique horseback, Jeep, cross-country ski, and snowcat tours of the area.

Open: year round **Accommodations:** 5 guest rooms (2 have private baths); 1 is a suite **Meals:** full breakfast included; restaurants nearby **Rates:** $49 to $115; 10% discount to National Trust members and National Trust Visa cardholders **Payment:** Visa, MC, traveler's check **Restrictions:** no smoking **Activities:** hot tub, hiking

LEADVILLE

Nearby attractions: National Mining Hall of Fame, Colorado and Southern Scenic Railroad, Heritage Museum, Tabor Opera House, Leadville Music Festival, Mts. Elbert and Massive, historic Ski Cooper, carriage rides, golfing, hiking, white-water rafting, fishing, hunting, bicycling, snowmobiling, downhill and cross-country skiing, antiques hunting, gold panning, swimming, tennis

DELAWARE HOTEL
700 Harrison Avenue
Leadville, Colorado 80461
719/486-1418 or 800/748-2004
719/486-2214 Fax
Proprietors: Susan and Scott Brackett

Leadville's gold- and silver-mining days brought desperados such as Billy the Kid, Doc Holiday, and Butch Cassiday to the Delaware Hotel. Built in 1886 by three brothers named Callaway from Delaware, and often referred to as the "crown jewel of Leadville," the hotel is notable for its Italianate and Second Empire elements. A recent renovation has resulted in a Victorian-style lobby that contains period antiques, crystal chandeliers, brass fixtures, and oak paneling. Thirty-six guest rooms and suites are appointed with brass and iron bed frames, heirloom quilts, lace curtains, and period antiques. Each room has a private bath and color cable television. In the hotel's restaurant, Callaway's, the breakfast and lunch menu offers local and traditional dishes, while the dinner menu offers continental cuisine.

Open: year round **Accommodations:** 36 guest rooms with private baths; 4 are suites **Meals:** full breakfast included; restaurant on premises; restaurants nearby **Rates:** $65 to $100; 10% discount to National Trust members and National Trust Visa cardholders **Payment:** AmEx, Visa, MC, DC, Discover, personal and traveler's checks **Restrictions:** no smoking in restaurant; no pets **Activities:** afternoon tea, hot tub; specialty weekend packages (murder mystery, medieval, Octoberfest, ski, golf)

ICE PALACE INN AND ANTIQUES
813 Spruce Street
Leadville, Colorado 80461
719/486-8272
Proprietors: Giles and Kami Kolakowski

In the winter of 1896 the citizens of Leadville erected a lumber frame around which they built a palace of ice carved from a nearby lake. The Leadville Ice Palace was the largest ice structure ever built. March that year was unexpectedly warm and the ice palace quickly melted away, leaving a wooden skeleton. An architect named Dimmick used the Ice Palace's wood to build five houses on Spruce Street, including this one, constructed in 1904 as a wedding gift to John Harvey and his wife. Today, the Harvey's home is the Ice Palace Inn, where romantic guest rooms—each with a private bath—are decorated with antiques and quilts. Photos of the Ice Palace are found throughout the house, including guest rooms, which are named after the rooms at the original Ice Palace: the grand ballroom, riding gallery, and king's tower. The inn also houses an antiques shop. This house was featured in Leadville's 1994 Victorian Homes Tour.

Open: year round **Accommodations:** 3 guest rooms with private baths; 1 is a suite **Meals:** full breakfast included; complimentary refreshments; restaurants nearby **Rates:** $79 to $119; 10% discount to National Trust members and National Trust Visa cardholders **Payment:** personal and traveler's checks **Restrictions:** no smoking; no pets **Activities:** games, croquet, television and VCR, stereo system

LEADVILLE COUNTRY INN
127 East Eighth Street
Leadville, Colorado 80461
719/486-2354 or 800/748-2354
719/486-0300 Fax
Proprietors: Sid and Judy Clemmer

Located in one of the nation's largest National Register historic districts, the Leadville Country Inn is a shining example of historic preservation and restoration. The 1892 Queen Anne home combines a mix of period antiques and decorating touches, even in the bathrooms. Some baths have fully functioning antique fixtures, including an 1870 copper-lined wooden tub and an 1880s wooden-rimmed, metal claw-foot tub. Guests are invited to relax in the courtyard complete with gazebo and hot tub or in the parlor filled with books.

Open: year round **Accommodations:** 9 guest rooms with private baths; 2 are suites **Meals:** full breakfast included; complimentary refreshments; candlelight dinners by reservation; restaurants nearby **Rates:** $69 to $149; 10% discount to National Trust members and National Trust Visa cardholders **Payment:** AmEx, Visa, MC, CB, DC, Discover, personal and traveler's checks **Restrictions:** children over 10 welcome; no smoking; no pets **Activities:** reading, hot tub, gift shop with handmade items, bicycles available

MINTURN

Nearby attractions: Vail and Beaver Creek ski areas, hiking, fishing, snowshoeing, hot-air ballooning, white-water rafting, mountain biking, snowmobiling, historic town

EAGLE RIVER INN

145 North Main Street
P.O. Box 100
Minturn, Colorado 81645
303/827-5761
303/827-4020 Fax
Proprietor: Richard Galloway

The Eagle River Inn dates to 1894 when the little town of Minturn was brought to life by the Rio Grande Railroad. Today, Minturn is the home of popular retaurants, shops, and galleries, just around the bend from the resorts of Vail and Beaver Creek. The 1986 renovation of the inn resulted in a Southwestern style captured in earth-red adobe walls, rambling riverside decks, and a gardenside hot tub. Inside, the lobby features Santa Fe–style furniture, a beehive fireplace, and a ceiling of traditional latillas and vegas. Baskets, rugs, and weavings add warmth. Twelve guest rooms welcome guests with fresh flowers and views of the river or mountains. Colorful tiles, thick towels, and fine toiletries are in the private baths. A hearty breakfast is served in the sala, where evening wine-and-cheese gatherings also take place.

Open: year round **Accommodations:** 12 guest rooms with private baths **Meals:** full breakfast included; complimentary wine and cheese; restaurants nearby **Rates:** $95 to $200 **Payment:** AmEx, Visa, MC, personal and traveler's checks **Restrictions:** children over 12 welcome; no smoking; no pets **Activities:** hot tub

PUEBLO

Nearby attractions: historic district, specialty shops, antiques hunting, art galleries, museums, mountain activities and sports, fishing, boating, swimming

ABRIENDO INN
300 West Abriendo Avenue
Pueblo, Colorado 80114
719/544-2703
719/542-6544 Fax
Proprietor: Kerrelyn M. Trent

Abriendo Inn, an estate home built in 1907, exhibits many classic qualities of the Colonial Revival style. Its two stories are topped by a hipped roof with gabled dormers. Its full-width front porch extends beyond and wraps around the sides of the house, supported by classical columns. Modillions and dentils decorate the cornice line. Inside, the guest rooms are individually decorated and richly appointed with antiques and period reproductions, oriental rugs, and fine linens. All beds are king or queen size; all rooms have private baths, writing desks, and telephones. A full breakfast is served in the window–filled dining room with hardwood floors. Afternoon refreshments and off-street parking are offered.

Open: year round **Accommodations:** 7 guest rooms with private baths; 1 is a suite **Meals:** full breakfast included; complimentary refreshments; restaurants nearby **Rates:** $54 to $89 **Payment:** AmEx, Visa, MC, DC, personal and traveler's checks **Restrictions:** children over 7 welcome; no smoking; no pets **Activities:** books, magazines, table games

REDSTONE

Nearby attractions: West Elk Loop Scenic and Historic Byway, world's largest hot springs pool in Glenwood Springs, horseback riding, river rafting, hiking, cross-country skiing

CLEVEHOLM MANOR, THE HISTORIC REDSTONE CASTLE
0058 Redstone Boulevard
Redstone, Colorado 81623
970/963-3463 or 800/643-4837
970/963-3463 Fax
Proprietors: Ken and Rose Marie Johnson
Location: 18 miles south of Carbondale on Highway 133

Cleveholm Manor was built in 1900 as a retreat for industrialist John Cleveland Osgood and his family. With 42 rooms and 27,000 squre feet of living area, the castle cost $2.5 million to build. Osgood employed the finest artisans from Austria and Italy to carve stone from nearby red sandstone cliffs for the exterior and to install marble fireplaces throughout the house. Louis Tiffany brasswork, from chandeliers to sconces, was used exclusively. Guests may reserve the entire castle or just one room, but all guests have full use of its library, music room, game room, armory, board room, sun parlor, and grand room with its huge fireplace. The professionally appointed kitchen is available along with the mahogany- and velvet-walled dining room with gold-leaf ceiling.

Open: year round **Accommodations:** 16 guest rooms (8 have private baths); 3 are suites **Meals:** continental-plus breakfast included; restaurant on premises serves on weekends; restaurants nearby **Rates:** $95 to $180 **Payment:** AmEx, Visa, MC, personal and traveler's checks **Restrictions:** no smoking **Activities:** hiking, fishing, cross-country skiing, sledding, snowshoeing, lawn games, game room, billiards

---

SILVERTON

Nearby attractions: Durango–Silverton Narrow Gauge Railroad, San Juan Mountains

TELLER HOUSE HOTEL
1250 Green Street
P.O. Box 2
Silverton, Colorado 81433
970/387-5423 or 800/342-4338
970/387-5423 Fax
Proprietors: Fritz Klinke and Loren Lew

Teller House Hotel is on the second floor of a two-story brick commercial building constructed in 1896 by Silverton Brewery owner Charles Fischer. The upstairs has always been a hotel and today's guests stay in the same comfortable rooms with original woodwork and high ceilings. Four of the nine guest rooms have private baths. Many rooms offer queen-size beds and all are filled with quaint furnishings and Victorian antiques. Along the hotel's hallway are comfortable rocking chairs, a piano, and bookcases containing old hotel registration books and collectibles. The downstairs retail space houses the French Bakery, where Teller House guests register and eat breakfast.

Open: year round **Accommodations:** 9 guest rooms (4 have private baths) **Meals:** full breakfast included; restaurant on premises; restaurants nearby **Rates:** $33 to $49; 10% discount to National Trust members and National Trust Visa cardholders **Payment:** AmEx, Visa, MC, CB, DC, Discover, personal and traveler's checks **Restrictions:** no pets

---

TELLURIDE

Nearby attractions: Telluride Historical Museum, historical walking tour, fly fishing, hiking, bicycling, rafting, horseback riding, mountain biking, downhill and cross-country skiing, summer festivals: film, bluegrass, jazz, chamber music, balloon, wine

ALPINE INN BED AND BREAKFAST
440 West Colorado Avenue
Telluride, Colorado 51435
970/728-6282
970/728-3424 Fax
Proprietors: Denise and John Weaver

Built in 1903, the Alpine Hotel was originally a 12-room lodge in this booming mining town. Fires destroyed the third story of the hotel in the 1940s and again in the 1950s, after which the owner remained satisfied with two stories. Over the years, the building has also been a brothel, real estate office, and private home. A renovation in 1988 resulted in today's Alpine Inn with eight Victorian-era guest rooms filled with handmade quilts, antique armoires, and, purportedly, a resident ghost. Breakfast is served in the sunroom with a view of Imogene Falls. Located in Telluride's National Register historic district, Alpine Inn is steps away from art galleries, gift shops, and fine dining.

Open: year round **Accommodations:** 8 guest rooms (6 have private baths); 1 is a suite **Meals:** full breakfast included; restaurants nearby **Rates:** $60 to $220; 10% discount to National Trust members and National Trust Visa cardholders **Payment:** Visa, MC, personal and traveler's checks **Restrictions:** children over 10 welcome; no smoking; no pets **Activities:** hot tub, après ski in winter

CONNECTICUT

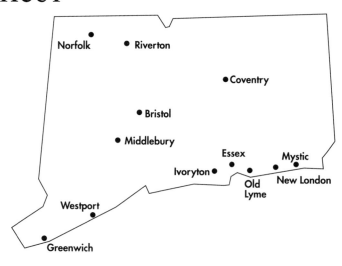

BRISTOL

Nearby attractions: New England Carousel Museum, clock and watch museum, nature center with hiking trails, amusement park

CHIMNEY CREST MANOR BED AND BREAKFAST
5 Founders Drive
Bristol, Connecticut 06010
203/582-4219
Proprietors: Dante and Cynthia Cimadamore
Location: 16 miles west of Hartford, 12 miles south of Litchfield

A 32-room, Tudor-style mansion overlooking Connecticut's Farmington Hills, Chimney Crest was built in 1930 of English brick with dark, exposed timbers and rough stucco. Multiflued chimneys tower above slab-tiled roofs. The manor is endowed with ornate plasterwork, beamed ceilings, and stately fireplaces. A 40-foot-long arcade leads to the cherry-paneled library, the Spanish-tiled sunroom, or the salon, welcoming visitors with its pair of Tudor fireplaces, deep oak paneling, and sculptured plaster ceiling. Five guest suites—two with fireplaces, four with kitchens—provide queen-size beds, private baths, air conditioning, and private entrances. Extra touches include turned-down beds, pillow chocolates, and fresh fruits and flowers.

Open: year round, except December 24 and 25 **Accommodations:** 5 suites with private baths **Meals:** full breakfast included; restaurants nearby **Rates:** $80 to $135; 10% discount offered to National Trust members and National Trust Visa cardholders **Payment:** AmEx, Visa, MC, personal and traveler's checks **Restrictions:** no smoking **Activities:** volleyball, croquet

COVENTRY

Nearby attractions: University of Connecticut, Nathan Hale Homestead, homes of Mark Twain and Harriet Beecher Stowe, Caprilands Herb Farm, Strong House Museum, antiques hunting, golfing

MAPLE HILL FARM BED AND BREAKFAST

365 Goose Lane
Coventry, Connecticut 06238-1215
203/742-0635 or 800/742-0635
Proprietors: Tony Felice and Marybeth Gorke-Felice

Nathaniel Woodward built this Cape Cod–style farmhouse in 1731 using stone, oak, and chestnut. Solid and comfortable, the house stands today at the center of Maple Hill Farm as a bed-and-breakfast inn, the first in Coventry. Four guest rooms are furnished with antiques—many, family heirlooms. Breakfast by candlelight is served on Limoges china brought from Austria by the innkeeper's great-grandmother. The meal includes fresh eggs from the inn's own free-range chickens. The library has a fireplace for winter comfort, and a screened porch, a solarium, and a swimming pool are available in the summer. Guests are encouraged to walk the inn's seven acres, enjoy the horses, or relax in a hammock suspended from large maple trees.

Open: year round **Accommodations:** 5 guest rooms share a bathroom **Meals:** full breakfast included; restaurants nearby **Rates:** $60 to $70 **Payment:** Visa, MC, personal check **Restrictions:** no smoking **Activities:** swimming pool, hot tub, picnic areas, hammocks, reading

---

ESSEX

Nearby attractions: Connecticut River Museum, Hammonaset Beach, Goodspeed Opera House, Ivoryton Playhouse, steam train, riverboat rides, golfing, Yale University, Connecticut College, U.S. Coast Guard Academy

GRISWOLD INN

36 Main Street
Essex, Connecticut 06426
203/767-1776
Proprietor: William G. Winterer

Not many businesses can match this claim: The Griswold Inn has been open for business every day since June 7, 1776. The main building was the first three-story

frame structure built in Connecticut. Three adjacent houses date from 1793 to 1801. Today's inn also includes a 1738 taproom (originally a schoolhouse moved to this site around 1800) and several dining rooms: one constructed from an abandoned covered bridge; one in the library, which includes a fireplace; one in the Steamboat Room, featuring a collection of Currier and Ives steamboat prints; and one in the Gun Room, with its collection of firearms dating to the fifteenth century. The floors of the guest rooms in the inn and neighboring houses list slightly after centuries of use. The rooms are charming with period furnishings and piped-in classical music. The inn has been praised by many, including *New York* magazine, *Town and Country*, and *House Beautiful*.

Open: year round **Accommodations:** 26 guest rooms with private baths; 12 are suites **Meals:** continental breakfast included; restaurants on premises **Wheelchair access:** dining room with public bathroom **Rates:** $90 to $175 **Payment:** AmEx, Visa, MC, personal and traveler's checks **Activities:** nightly musical entertainment, collections of firearms and marine art

GREENWICH

Nearby attractions: Bruce Museum, Audubon Society, hiking, nature preserves, antiques hunting, shopping

HOMESTEAD INN
420 Field Point Road
Greenwich, Connecticut 06830
203/869-7500
Proprietors: Lessie Davison and Nancy Smith
Location: 45 minutes north of New York City

Homestead Inn began as a New England farmhouse, home of Augustus Mead, the
judge and gentleman farmer who built it in 1799. In 1859 the property was sold
to innkeepers, who converted the colonial-style dwelling to the distinctive
Italianate Victorian it remains today, adding a square cupola, ornate eaves
brackets, and a wraparound porch. In the twentieth century the structure fell into
total disrepair before the innkeepers conducted a complete restoration in 1979.
Today, guest rooms are decorated with flair and whimsy—no two rooms are
alike—and antiques coexist with amenities such as electric blankets, reading
lights, makeup mirrors, and color television. The inn's renowned restaurant has
earned three stars from the *New York Times*, and *Country Inns* has called the
Homestead one of the nation's 12 best inns. *Interior Design* and *Colonial Homes*
magazines have touted the inn's style and design.

Open: year round **Accommodations:** 23 guest rooms with private baths; 5 are suites
Meals: continental breakfast included; restaurant and bar on premises **Wheelchair
access:** 1 guest room **Rates:** $92 to $185; 10% discount offered to National Trust
members and National Trust Visa cardholders **Payment:** AmEx, Visa, MC, DC,
Discover, traveler's check

IVORYTON

Nearby attractions: Goodspeed Opera House, Ivoryton Playhouse, Connecticut River Musuem, Essex Steam Train, Mystic Seaport and Aquarium, Gillette Castle State Park, sailing, antiques hunting

COPPER BEECH INN
46 Main Street
Ivoryton, Connecticut 06442
203/767-0330
Proprietors: Sally and Eldon Senner

The handsome Copper Beech Inn, once the private home of an ivory importer, stands behind a magnificent copper beech tree, one of the oldest and largest of its type in Connecticut. Lovely turn-of-the-century gardens and native woodlands complete the inn's setting in this quiet village. The house was built in the 1880s as an elegant Victorian country cottage, complete with carriage barn, root cellar, and terraced gardens. It was rescued from disrepair and vacancy in the 1970s, refurbished, and opened as the Copper Beech Inn. Guest rooms in the main house are decorated with country and antique furnishings; the old-fashioned baths are intact. Guest rooms in the renovated carriage house have four-poster or canopy beds, whirlpool baths, and French doors leading to decks. French country-style dining is available in the restaurant.

Open: year round, except first week of January **Accommodations:** 13 guest rooms with private baths **Meals:** continental-plus breakfast included; complimentary refreshments; restaurant on premises serving dinner Tuesday through Sunday (Wednesday through Sunday in January, February, and March) **Wheelchair access:** some guest rooms, dining room **Rates:** $105 to $165 **Payment:** AmEx, Visa, MC, CB, DC, personal and traveler's checks **Restrictions:** children over 7 welcome; smoking limited; no pets **Activities:** country gardens, gallery of antique Chinese porcelain

MIDDLEBURY

Nearby attractions: state parks, museums, theaters, concerts, historic sites, antiques hunting, Quassy Amusement Park, water sports, hiking, fishing, golfing, tennis, skiing

TUCKER HILL INN
96 Tucker Hill Road
Middlebury, Connecticut 06762
203/758-8334
Proprietors: Susan and Richard Cebelenski
Location: 1/2 hour east of Danbury

Tucker Hill Inn is a typical New England–style Colonial Revival home—large and spacious inside and out, and lightly shaded by ancient oaks and maples. Located one mile from the village green in Middlebury, Tucker Hill opened for business in 1923 as a tearoom, becoming a busy trolley stop on the line from Waterbury. Over time the tearoom evolved into an inn with a restaurant and catering facilities; hundreds of brides have descended the home's center-hall staircase. Today's inn is also host to weary travelers who want to relax and unwind. Guests stay in bright, sunny rooms and are invited to share the downstairs living room. A full breakfast is served either in the formal dining room or on the patio.

Open: year round **Accommodations:** 4 guest rooms, 2 with private baths **Meals:** full breakfast included; restaurants nearby **Rates:** $66 to $95; 10% discount to National Trust members and National Trust Visa cardholders **Payment:** AmEx, Visa, MC, personal and traveler's checks **Restrictions:** no smoking; no pets **Activities:** library, videotapes, compact discs

MYSTIC

Nearby attractions: Mystic Seaport Museum, Mystic Marinelife Aquarium, Old Mistick Village, Groton Submarine Base, U.S. Coast Guard Academy, tennis, golfing, sailing, deep-sea fishing, antiques hunting, classical music concerts, wildlife sanctuaries, historic houses, shopping

PALMER INN
25 Church Street
Noank, Connecticut 06340
203/572-9000
Proprietor: Patricia Ann White
Location: 2 miles south of Mystic

One block from Long Island Sound and two miles from Mystic Seaport, shipyard craftsmen built a grand seaside mansion for shipbuilder Robert Palmer in 1906. The house, described by the architects as a "Classic Colonial Suburban Villa," features a hip roof with dormers, a balustrade, dentil cornices, pilasters, Palladian windows, and a huge portico with two-story Ionic columns. Today, as the Palmer Inn, these architectural details remain, while inside the elegant inn 13-foot ceilings, a mahogany staircase and beams, brass fixtures, intricate woodwork, stained-glass windows, and original wall coverings have been restored. Guest rooms, filled with family heirlooms and antiques, also offer modern luxuries such as hair dryers, makeup mirrors, toiletries, and designer sheets. Balconies offer views of Long Island Sound, and fireplaces warm cold winter evenings.

Open: year round **Accommodations:** 6 rooms with private baths **Meals:** continental-plus breakfast included; restaurants nearby **Rates:** $125 to $185; 10% discount to National Trust members and National Trust Visa cardholders Sunday through Thursday, excluding holidays **Payment:** AmEx, Visa, MC, personal and traveler's checks **Restrictions:** children over 14 welcome; no smoking; no pets **Activities:** sailing lessons, tennis, art school in June

PEQUOT HOTEL BED AND BREAKFAST
Burnett's Corners
711 Cow Hill Road
Mystic, Connecticut 06355
203/572-0390
203/536-3380 Fax
Proprietors: Nancy and Jim Mitchell

The Pequot Hotel is an authentically restored 1840 stagecoach stop. The stately Greek Revival landmark is located in the center of the Burnett's Corners historic district, surrounded by many other historic buildings. Inside, original hardware, moldings, and fireplaces enhance the building's historic character. Two guest rooms with 12-foot-high coved ceilings have Rumford fireplaces. A two-room suite offers accommodations for up to four people. Guests will find a rare book collection in the library and wicker furniture on the screened porch. Two parlors are also open to guests. The hotel is surrounded by more than 20 acres of trailed woods, open fields, ponds, spacious lawns, and gardens.

Open: year round **Accommodations:** 3 guest rooms with private baths; 1 is a suite **Meals:** full breakfast included; complimentary refreshments; restaurants nearby **Rates:** $95 to $130; 10% discount to National Trust members **Payment:** Visa, MC, personal and traveler's checks **Restrictions:** well-supervised children welcome; no smoking; no pets **Activities:** horseshoe pitching, badminton, 22 acres of woods, fields, pond, and stream

RED BROOK INN
2750 Gold Star Highway, Route 184
P.O. Box 237
Mystic, Connecticut 06372
203/572-0349
Proprietor: Ruth Keyes
Location: 1 1/2 miles north of Mystic Seaport Museum

Red Brook Inn offers guest lodgings in two handsome historic buildings: the Haley Tavern (1740) and the Crary Homestead (1770). The Crary house was built on this site; the Haley Tavern (a National Register property) was moved here by owner Ruth Keyes to prevent its destruction by a proposed highway. For her outstanding preservation efforts, Keyes received an award in 1986 from the U.S. Department of Transportation and President Reagan's Advisory Council on Historic Preservation. Guest rooms in both buildings are appointed with period antiques and original early lighting fixtures. Extensive collections of early American glass, pewter, and lighting devices are on display in the downstairs common rooms. Fireplaces abound throughout the inn. The Red Brook Inn has been featured in *National Geographic Traveler.*

Open: year round **Accommodations:** 6 guest rooms with private baths **Meals:** full breakfast included; restaurants nearby **Rates:** $105 to $179; 10% discount to National Trust members and National Trust Visa cardholders **Payment:** Visa, MC, traveler's check **Restrictions:** no smoking; no pets **Activities:** picnic area, terrace, woodlands walking

NEW LONDON

Nearby attractions: Garde Arts Center, Foxwoods Casino, U.S. Naval Submarine Base, Mystic Seaport Museum and Marinelife Aquarium, Gillette's Castle, Eugene O'Neill Theater Center, U.S. Coast Guard Academy, marinas, beaches, sailing, sport fishing, outlet shops

LIGHTHOUSE INN

6 Guthrie Place
New London, Connecticut 06320
203/443-8411
203/437-7027 Fax
Proprietors: Jan and Jane Mavrak, Arthur Slaton

In 1902 steel magnate Charles S. Guthrie built his country home overlooking Long Island Sound and called it Meadow Court after the wildflowers that surrounded it. The formal grounds were designed by landscape architect Frederick Law Olmsted, who also designed Central Park. The Mediterranean-style mansion formed a half circle so that every room had a view of either the gardens or the water. Operated as an inn since 1927, the mansion and adjacent carriage house contain 50 guest rooms dressed in old and new furnishings, some of them original to the Guthrie family. Canopied beds and wing chairs blend easily with color television sets, whirlpool tubs, and bedside telephones. Two restaurants serve three meals daily. Lighthouse Inn, a member of Historic Hotels of America, provides a private beach for its guests just a block away.

Open: year round **Accommodations:** 50 guest rooms with private baths; 2 are suites **Meals:** 2 restaurants on premises **Rates:** $95 to $210; 10% discount to National Trust members and National Trust Visa cardholders **Payment:** AmEx, Visa, MC, DC, traveler's check **Restrictions:** no pets **Activities:** four acres of landscaped grounds, private beach

NORFOLK

Nearby attractions: skiing, water sports, horseback riding, Norfolk Music Festival, summer theater, antiques hunting, crafts shops, vineyards

GREENWOODS GATE BED AND BREAKFAST INN
105 Greenwoods Road East
Norfolk, Connecticut 06058
203/542-5439
Proprietor: George E. Schumaker

Greenwoods Gate exemplifies the tradition of Federal, or Adam, architecture in the northern states with its clapboard exterior, 12-over-12 double-hung windows, and paneled front door flanked by sidelights. Furnished throughout with an eclectic blend of fine antiques and collectibles, the handsome 1797 home is located less than a mile east of Norfolk's village green. Brass and iron beds, canopies suspended from walls, oriental rugs, and coordinating fabrics come together in four elegantly designed guest suites filled with such amenities as freshly cut flowers, monogrammed bathrobes, and crisp, ironed linens. All rooms retain original wide-board cherry floors. Afternoon tea is served in the library. Original fireplaces grace the grand parlor and breakfast room.

Open: year round **Accommodations:** 4 guest suites with private baths **Meals:** full breakfast included; complimentary refreshments; restaurants nearby **Rates:** $170 to $225; 10% discount to National Trust members and National Trust Visa cardholders **Payment:** personal and traveler's checks **Restrictions:** children over 12 welcome; no smoking; no pets

MANOR HOUSE
69 Maple Avenue
P.O. Box 447
Norfolk, Connecticut 06058
203/542-5690
Proprietors: Hank and Diane Tremblay

The original cherry paneling of the Manor House's foyer and grand staircase typifies the architectural elegance of this home. The Tudor-style house was built in 1898 for Charles Spofford, designer of London's underground system. As a housewarming present, Louis Comfort Tiffany installed 20 stained-glass windows. The baronial living room has a six-foot-wide raised hearth, and several of the bedrooms have fireplaces with ornate mantels. Guest rooms are furnished with four-poster, brass, sleigh, spindle, or lace-canopied beds, all covered with plush down comforters. The hearty breakfast menu changes daily but always includes

honey harvested from the Manor House's own hives. A grand piano is available for entertainment and a library offers solitude.

Open: year round **Accommodations:** 8 guest rooms with private baths **Meals:** full breakfast included; complimentary refreshments; restaurants nearby **Rates:** $95 to $190; 10% discount offered to National Trust members and National Trust Visa cardholders (some restrictions may apply) **Payment:** AmEx, Visa, MC, personal and traveler's checks **Restrictions:** children over 12 welcome; smoking limited; no pets **Activities:** croquet, hiking, bicycling, cross-country skiing

OLD LYME

Nearby attractions: Florence Griswold Museum, Lyme Art Academy, Connecticut River Museum, Mystic Seaport and Aquarium, Gillette Castle, Goodspeed Opera House, Essex Steam Train and Boat Ride, Mystic Seaport, boating, bicycling, swimming, hiking, antiques hunting

BEE AND THISTLE INN
100 Lyme Street
Old Lyme, Connecticut 06371
203/434-1667 or 800/622-4946
203/434-1667 Fax
Proprietors: Bob, Penny, Lori, and Jeff Nelson

The Bee and Thistle Inn, on more than five acres along the Lieutenant River, is located in the Old Lyme historic district. Built in 1756, the inn's early American tradition is recalled in its many fireplaces, antiques, comfortable parlors, formal garden, and bordering stone walls. A carved staircase leads from the center hall to tastefully decorated guest rooms. Most have private baths and each enjoys a distinctive style lent by canopied or four-poster beds, old quilts or afghans, and antiques. Breakfast is served on a tray to bedroom doors, on a porch, or before the fireplace in the dining room, which has been voted the "most romantic" place to dine in Connecticut for eight straight years by the *Connecticut Magazine* Readers' Choice Poll. The Bee and Thistle has also been selected as an Uncle Ben's "10 Best Inns in the County" award winner.

Open: year round **Accommodations:** 12 guest rooms with private baths; 1 is a cottage **Meals:** restaurant on premises serves breakfast, lunch, and dinner **Rates:** $70 to $205; 10% discount to National Trust members and National Trust Visa cardholders Monday through Thursday **Payment:** AmEx, Visa, MC, DC, presonal and traveler's checks **Restrictions:** children over 12 welcome; smoking limited; no pets **Activities:** flower and herb gardens, sitting by the river, reading, romance

OLD LYME INN
85 Lyme Street
Old Lyme, Connecticut 06371
203/434-2600 or 800/434-5352
Proprietor: Diana Field Atwood

The Champlain family built this house in the 1850s and worked its 300–acre farm until the turnpike came through town in the 1950s. The rambling farmhouse with its broad front porch was converted to an inn, which later fell into extreme disrepair following a fire. In 1976 the innkeeper purchased and restored the building, reopening it as the Old Lyme Inn. The inn, listed in the National Register of Historic Places, has a front hall adorned by hand–painted murals and stencils like those that were popular in the 19th century. Elsewhere in the inn are examples of the Old Lyme School of impressionist painting that flourished at the turn of the century. Guest rooms contain Empire and Victorian furnishings, and some rooms have canopied or four-poster beds. Awarded three stars by the *New York Times*, the inn's restaurant continues to be recognized in publications nationwide for its creativity and quality.

Open: year round **Accommodations:** 13 guest rooms with private baths; 8 are suites **Meals:** continental-plus breakfast included; restaurant on premises **Wheelchair access:** 4 guest rooms and restaurant **Rates:** $86 to $158; 10% discount offered to National Trust members and National Trust Visa cardholders **Payment:** AmEx, Visa, MC, CB, DC, Discover, personal and traveler's checks **Activities:** fine dining, relaxing, listening to classical guitar in the Grill Room

RIVERTON

Nearby attractions: historic house tours, Hitchcock Chair Company and Museum, Lake Compounce Festival Park, sleigh and carriage rides, state parks and forests, picnicking, fishing, hiking, hunting, cross-country and downhill skiing, camping, golfing, tennis, river tubing, canoeing, horseback riding, swimming, boating, bicycling

OLD RIVERTON INN

436 East River Road
Riverton, Connecticut 06065
203/379-8678
203/379-1006 Fax
Proprietors: Mark and Pauline Telford

This three-story Federal-style building was opened for business in 1796 by Jesse Ives and was known on the post route between Hartford and Albany as Ives Tavern or Ives Hotel. In the two intervening centuries, the inn has seen various architectural changes, but the National Register property remains true to its origins in style and hospitality. With white shutters gleaming against blue clapboards, the rechristened Old Riverton Inn offers quaint and cozy accommodations, some with canopy beds or fireplaces. All rooms have private baths and color cable television. For relaxing and dining, the inn offers the Hobby Horse Bar, Colonial Dining Room, and Grindstone Terrace.

Open: year round **Accommodations:** 12 guest rooms with private baths; 1 is a suite **Meals:** full breakfst included; restaurant on premises **Wheelchair access:** dining facilities **Rates:** $70 to $165; 10% discount offered to National Trust members and National Trust Visa cardholders off-peak only **Payment:** AmEx, Visa, MC, CB, DC, Discover, traveler's check **Restrictions**: pets accepted with prior approval

WESTPORT

Nearby attractions: Westport County Playhouse, historic waterfront district, Westport beaches, art galleries, antiques hunting, health club and indoor pool, shopping, dining

INN AT NATIONAL HALL
2 Post Road West
Westport, Connecticut 06880
203/221-1351 or 800/NAT-HALL
Proprietor: Nick Carter

Built in 1873 as Westport's First National Bank, this distinctive Italianate structure housed the town's meeting place—National Hall—on its third floor. Fashioned after Europe's elite manor houses, the inn displays a delightful mix of whimsy, privacy, and history. A recent rehabilitation produced elegant rooms with state-of-the-art amenities. Selected chambers feature loft bedrooms with soaring two-story ceilings, enhanced by expansive windows and sweeping river views. Guests should keep an eye out for fanciful trompe l'oeil paintings throughout the hotel. Embracing the understated elegance of the inn is its renowned Restaurant Zanghi, serving the latest French and Italian cuisine. Listed in the National Register of Historic Places, the Inn at National Hall is the cornerstone of Westport's restored historic waterfront district.

Open: year round **Accommodations:** 15 guest rooms with private baths; 7 are suites **Meals:** full breakfast included; complimentary refreshments; restaurant on premises; restaurants nearby **Wheelchair access:** restaurant **Rates:** $195 to $450; 10% discount offered to National Trust members and National Trust Visa cardholders **Payment:** AmEx, Visa, MC, DC, personal and traveler's checks **Restrictions:** no pipes or cigars; no pets **Activities:** billiards room, complimentary video library, cable television, complimentary use of local health facility

DELAWARE

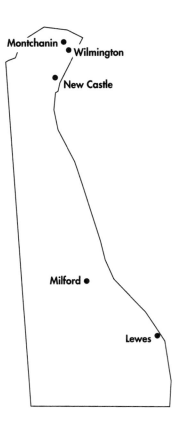

LEWES

Nearby attractions: Zwaanendael Museum, maritime museum, historic town with three centuries of architecture, ocean and bay beaches, watching whales and dolphins, sailing, harbor and Delaware Bay tours, Cape Henlopen State Park, Prime Hook Wildlife Refuge, charter boat fishing

WILD SWAN INN
525 Kings Highway
Lewes, Delaware 19958
302/645-8550
302/645-8550 Fax
Proprietors: Hope and Michael Tyler

Built just after the turn of the century, this classic example of a Queen Anne home is resplendent with ornate and delicate spindlework, wraparound porches, carved vergeboards, and fancy finials. Its pink-and-white exterior is accented by its surrounding flowering trees and shrubs. Guest rooms are decorated and furnished with an eclectic Victorian flair. All rooms are air conditioned and have private baths. The parlor, with its lavish wallpaper, antique furnishings, and player piano, provides a comfortable place to unwind. In summer months, the patio and pool offer a change of pace. A formal breakfast is served in the spacious dining room lighted by one of the inn's many antique brass chandeliers. Wild Swan is walking distance from downtown Lewes.

Open: year round **Accommodations:** 3 guest rooms with private baths **Meals:** full breakfast included; complimentary refreshments; restaurants nearby **Rates:** $85 to $120; 10% discount to National Trust members and National Trust Visa cardholders during off season, excluding holidays **Payment:** personal and traveler's checks **Restrictions:** not suitable for children; no smoking; no pets **Activities:** swimming pool, bicycles, music on antique player piano and Edison phonograph, porch sitting

MILFORD

Nearby attractions: Mispillion River; River Walk; Delaware Bay and Atlantic Ocean beaches; Bombay Hook National Wildlife Preserve; Dickerson Plantation; golfing; swimming; tennis; fishing; boating; antiques hunting; historic towns of Lewes, Rehoboth Beach, Odessa, Milton, and Milford

CAUSEY MANSION BED AND BREAKFAST

2 Causey Avenue
Milford, Delaware 19963
302/422-0979
Proprietors: Kenneth and Frances Novak

In 1763, Levin Crapper built this mansion in the Georgian style on 1000 acres of land, which he farmed with the help of many slaves. Today, two of the original slave quarters remain on the property. After ownership by Governor Daniel Rogers, the house was purchased by Governor Peter F. Causey in 1849. He enlarged the house by adding a third floor, changing the style from Georgian to the popular Greek Revival. Recently renovated, the Causey Mansion now offers accommodations that reflect the house's Early American heritage. Sitting on three acres in the heart of Milford, Causey Mansion is convenient to all the area's sites and activities.

Open: year round **Accommodations:** 5 guest rooms with private baths; 1 is a suite **Meals:** full breakfast included; complimentary refreshments; restaurants nearby **Wheelchair access:** 1 room **Rate:** $85 **Payment:** Visa, MC, personal and traveler's checks **Restrictions:** no smoking; no pets **Activities:** formal boxwood gardens

THE TOWERS BED AND BREAKFAST

101 Northwest Front Street
Milford, Delaware 19963
302/422-3814 or 800/366-3814
Proprietor: Dan Bond

Built in 1783, The Towers is one of the oldest buildings in Milford. Built in a typical Delawarean colonial style, the wooden structure was vastly remodeled in 1891, resulting in an engaging mix of Queen Anne and Steamboat Gothic styles. Craftsmen from the local shipyards enlarged the house, added whimsical embellishments, and created a stunning interior of stained glass and carved woodwork, including a sycamore coffered ceiling in the music room and an elaborate staircase crafted from walnut and mahogany. The carefully restored house sports an exterior paint scheme of six colors. It has been featured in the 1992 book, *America's Painted Ladies*. Inside, the furnishings are primarily French Victorian.

Guests often gather in the music room with its fireplace, 1899 grand piano, and working Victrola. In warm weather, guests are invited to enjoy the walled garden, swimming pool, or gazebo porch.

Open: Friday and Saturday nights only year round **Accommodations:** 6 guest rooms (4 have private baths); 2 are suites **Meals:** full breakfast included; restaurants nearby **Rates:** $95 to $125; 10% discount to National Trust members and National Trust Visa cardholders **Payment:** Visa, MC, personal and traveler's checks **Restrictions:** children over 13 welcome; no smoking; no pets **Activities:** swimming pool, bicycles

---

MONTCHANIN

Nearby attractions: Winterthur, Longwood Gardens, Brandywine River Museum, Hagley Museum and Library, Delaware Art Museum, Delaware Museum of Natural History

THE INN AT MONCHANIN VILLAGE
Route 100 and Kirk Road
Montchanin, Delaware 19710
302/888-2133 or 800/COW-BIRD (800/269-2473)
302/888-0389 Fax
Proprietors: Dan and Missy Lickle

Montchanin Village is a collection of 11 buildings constructed between 1799 and 1910, all of which have been restored and renovated to provide 37 elegant guest suites with private marble baths, fireplaces, individual garden and terrace settings, and state-of-the-art amenities. Each one- and two-bedroom suite has a different floor plan; some are two stories, and one is three stories high. The village was once the home of workers on the nearby DuPont estate, Winterthur, and accommodations and meeting rooms are in former residences, a barn, and a blacksmith shop. According to the National Register of Historic Places, Montchanin "remains today much as it did at the turn of the century. There are few other hamlets that have survived with so few intrusions in their environment and structural characteristics."

Open: year round **Accommodations:** 37 guest suites with private baths **Meals:** continental-plus breakfast included; complimentary refreshments; restaurant on premises **Rates:** $125 to $350 **Payment:** AmEx, Visa, MC, DC, Discover, personal and traveler's checks **Restrictions:** no smoking; no pets

NEW CASTLE

Nearby attractions: historic New Castle, Longwood Gardens, Winterthur, Brandywine River Museum, historic walking tour of eighteenth- and nineteenth-century buildings, tennis, golfing, biking, shopping, dining, Philadelphia

ARMITAGE INN
2 The Strand
New Castle, Delaware 19720
302/328-6618
Proprietors: Stephen and Rina Marks

Built in 1732, the Armitage Inn is situated on the bank of the Delaware River only a few feet from the spot where William Penn first set foot in the New World. The inn includes the main house, a wing, and a garden cottage. One of the rooms on the main floor is believed to have been built in the 1600s, being incorporated into the main house when built. Within this room is an original brick walk-in cooking fireplace. Guest rooms are individually decorated with attention to historic details. All furnishings, beds, linens, and towels have been carefully selected to pamper and comfort guests. Rooms feature king- and queen-size beds, private baths (some with whirlpool tubs), and central air conditioning. Guests are invited to enjoy the dining room, parlor, library, screened porch, and walled garden.

Open: year round **Accommodations:** 5 guest rooms with private baths **Meals:** breakfast buffet included; restaurants nearby **Rates:** $95 to $135 **Payment:** Visa, MC, personal check **Restrictions:** children over 12 welcome; no smoking; no pets

WILLIAM PENN GUEST HOUSE
206 Delaware Street
New Castle, Delaware 19720
302/328-7736
Proprietors: Irma and Richard Burwell

Pennsylvania's Quaker founder, William Penn, came upon the New World in 1682 at New Castle. In that same year this three-story brick house, where Penn later was an overnight guest, was built. Many of the house's original architectural features, including wide-planked floors, have been restored. Guests may choose from three cozy bedrooms overlooking the green in the center of town. Fine dining, walking tours, and Revolutionary War sites are within walking distance. Many visitors choose to stay in the quiet, historic, tree-filled town of New Castle when visiting nearby Philadelphia.

Open: year round **Accommodations:** 4 guest rooms with shared baths **Meals:** continental breakfast included; restaurants nearby **Rate:** $50 to $75 (for private bath) **Payment:** personal check **Restrictions:** children over 12 welcome; smoking limited; no pets

---

WILMINGTON

Nearby attractions: Winterthur, Longwood Gardens, Brandywine River Museum, Olde New Castle, Hagley Museum; Philadelphia, Pennsylvania

DARLEY MANOR INN BED AND BREAKFAST
3701 Philadelphia Pike
Wilmington, Delaware 19703
302/792-2127 or 800/824-4703
Proprietors: Ray and Judith Hester

Built in 1790 with four rooms plus attic, Darley Manor was expanded in 1810 and again in 1842. The house is named in honor of its most famous resident, Felix Darley, a popular book illustrator in the mid-nineteenth century. Darley's work was found in books by many notable authors, including Dickens, Poe, Longfellow, and Tennyson. Charles Dickens was guest here during his American tour in 1867. Darley lived in this home from 1859 until 1888. Today's guest rooms are decorated with colonial- and Victorian-style furnishings. All rooms are air conditioned and have refrigerators, coffeepots, pants pressers, and private baths with robes, hair dryers, and individual toiletries. Common rooms, dotted with fine antiques, include two parlors, meeting room, reading room, dining room, and foyer, where some of Darley's prints are on display.

Open: year round **Accommodations:** 6 guest rooms with private baths; 4 are suites **Meals:** full breakfast included; complimentary refreshments; 24-hour hospitality table; restaurants nearby **Rates:** $69 to $99
Payment: AmEx, Visa, MC, personal and traveler's checks **Restrictions:** children over 10 welcome; no smoking; no pets **Activities:** porch rockers, garden swing

DISTRICT OF COLUMBIA

ADAMS MORGAN

ADAMS INN
1744 Lanier Place, N.W.
Washington, D.C. 20009
202/745-3600 or 800/578-6807
202/332-5867 Fax
Proprietors: Gene and Nancy Thompson

The Adams Inn is in a three-story townhouse built in 1908 in what is now the city's most diverse neighborhood. The blocks surrounding the inn are filled with many of Washington's top-rated restaurants representing the cuisines of Europe, Asia, Africa, Latin America, and the Caribbean. Antiques shops and international boutiques fill in the gaps. Back at the Adams Inn, each guest room is unique in its home-style decor. All rooms are air conditioned. Guests from across the country and around the world gather in the breakfast room, parlor, television lounge, garden patio, or on the front porch. Refreshments are complimentary, as are an iron and ironing board. Coin-operated laundry and soda machines and pay telephones are available. Adams Inn is within walking distance of three major convention hotels and the city's Metro subway system.

Open: year round **Accommodations:** 25 guest rooms (12 have private baths) **Meals:** continental-plus breakfast; complimentary refreshments; restaurants nearby **Rates:** $45 to $90 **Payment:** AmEx, Visa, MC, CB, DC, Discover, personal and traveler's checks **Restrictions:** no smoking; no pets

---

DUPONT CIRCLE/ADAMS–MORGAN

1836 CALIFORNIA
1836 California Street, N.W.
Washington, D.C. 20009
202/462-6502
202/265-0342 Fax
Proprietors: Esen and Jimmy Cenkci

A large front gable punctuated by an arch-roofed, recessed balcony distinguishes this four-story brick row house. Built in 1899, the house was fully restored in 1988 to reflect its Victorian origin. Most notable is the maple and oak turned staircase in the center of the house. Spacious rooms with 12-foot-high ceilings are decorated with authentically styled wallcoverings and antique furnishings. Queen-size reproduction Victorian beds are dressed in fine linens. While six fireplaces warm the house, and south-facing bay windows capture the winter sun and bring in summer breezes, the updated guest rooms also contain central heat and air conditioning, telephones, and cable television. An extensive collection of books is available for guests' enjoyment. Breakfast, served in the formal dining room overlooking a deck and gardens, features home-baked breads.

Open: year round **Accommodations:** 5 guest rooms (2 have private baths); 2 are suites **Meals:** continental-plus breakfast included; restaurants nearby **Rates:** $60 to $70 **Payment:** AmEx, Visa, MC, personal and traveler's checks **Restrictions:** children over 10 welcome; no smoking; no pets **Activities:** reading, lounging on deck, walking neighbor's dog

KALORAMA/WOODLEY PARK

KALORAMA GUEST HOUSE AT WOODLEY PARK
2700 Cathedral Avenue, N.W.
Washington, D.C. 20008
202/328-0860
Proprietors: Roberta Pieczenik and Rick Fenstemaker

Built in 1910, The Kalorama Guest House at Woodley Park comprises two red-brick townhouses located on a tree-lined residential street close to downtown. This was a rural part of the city with scattered farmhouses until a streetcar line was laid at the turn of the century, spurring development. Today, the European-style bed and breakfast maintains a Victorian ambience, with polished hardwood floors, an oak staircase, and period oak and mahogany antiques. Guest rooms are furnished with brass beds, oriental carpets, and fresh flowers. A complimentary continental breakfast is served in the sunlit breakfast room, and each evening an aperitif is offered in both of the main parlors.

Open: year round **Accommodations:** 19 guest rooms (12 have private baths); 2 are suites **Meals:** continental breakfast included; complimentary refreshments; restaurants nearby **Rates:** $50 to $95; 10% discount offered to National Trust members or National Trust Visa cardholders **Payment:** AmEx, Visa, MC, DC, personal and traveler's checks **Restrictions:** no pets **Activities:** parlor games

MT. VERNON SQUARE/DOWNTOWN

HENLEY PARK HOTEL
926 Massachusetts Avenue, N.W.
Washington, D.C. 20001
202/638-5200
202/638-6740 Fax
General Manager: Ruedi Bertschinger

Making its debut in 1918 as the upscale Tudor Hall apartments, home to members of Congress and the Senate, this meticulously restored building was converted to a hotel in 1982. The lobby retains its original stained-glass windows and Mercer tile floor; traditional archways and moldings, carved walls, and leaded-glass windows are featured throughout. The facade of the building displays 118 gargoyles (including two depicting the faces of the architect and his wife), four others above the restaurant atrium were rescued from new York's Commodore

Hotel when razed. Guest rooms are furnished with Queen Anne or Chippendale reproductions; some rooms feature four-poster beds. Small to midsize business meetings are easily accommodated in the the Eton Room. The Henley Park, a member of Historic Hotels of America, is less than two blocks from the Convention Center and offers off-street parking.

Open: year round **Accommodations:** 96 guest rooms with private baths; 17 are suites **Meals:** continental breakfast included; restaurant on premises **Rates:** $165 to $235 **Payment:** AmEx, Visa, MC, DC, Discover, traveler's check, personal check with identification **Restrictions:** children under 16 free with parents; no pets **Activities:** fitness center, traditional tea daily, live entertainment nightly, dancing on weekends,

MORRISON–CLARK INN
1015 L Street, N.W.
Washington, D.C. 20001
202/898-1200 or 800/332-7898
Proprietor: Donard F. Schoen

The Morrison–Clark Inn, built in 1864, is the only inn in Washington, D.C., that is listed independently in the National Register of Historic Places. Originally two detached Victorian mansions built by David Morrison and Reuben Clark, one is festooned with an ornate Chinese Chippendale porch and topped by a mansard roof. In 1923, the houses became the Soldiers, Sailors, Marines, and Airmen's Club, offering lodging to servicemen for 75 cents per night. The 1980s restoration of the houses created the elegant small hotel that today is a charter member of Historic Hotels of America. Original interior ornaments include 12-foot-high mahogany-framed mirrors and elaborately carved marble fireplaces. Public and guest rooms are decorated with Victorian, neoclassical, and country furnishings. The inn's highly regarded restaurant has been featured in *Gourmet*.

Open: year round **Accommodations:** 54 guest rooms with private baths; 13 are suites **Meals:** continental breakfast included; restaurant on premises **Rates:** $115 to $185; 10% discount off regular room rates to National Trust members **Payment:** AmEx, Visa, MC, DC, Discover, En Route, personal and traveler's checks **Restrictions:** smoking limited; no pets **Activities:** fine dining, fitness center, conversation, relaxing in courtyard

WASHINGTON CIRCLE/WEST END

HOTEL LOMBARDY
2019 Pennsylvania Avenue, N.W.
Washington, D.C. 20006
202/828-2600
202/872-0503 Fax
Proprietors: The Classic Collection

Hotel Lombardy is a gracious, traditional establishment dating from 1929. Just blocks from the White House, the hotel is within easy walking distance of Georgetown and George Washington University and Hospital. Elegance is evident in the wood-paneled lobby with brass stair railings, crystal chandeliers, and decorative plaster ceiling. Each of the spacious 125 guest rooms and suites is designed with comfort in mind, from individual climate controls to coffeemakers and minibars. Most rooms offer fully equipped kitchens and dining areas. The multilingual staff offers attentive services that include valet, shoe shine, and nightly turn-down with imported chocolates. Cafe Lombardy, serving three meals daily, specializes in northern Italian cuisine. The hotel is ideally suited to small conferences and seminars.

Open: year round **Accommodations:** 125 rooms with private baths; 40 are suites **Meals:** restaurant on premises serves breakfast, lunch, and dinner **Rates:** $95 to $130; 10% discount to National Trust members and National Trust Visa cardholders **Payment:** AmEx, Visa, MC, CB, DC, Discover, traveler's check **Restrictions:** no pets

FLORIDA

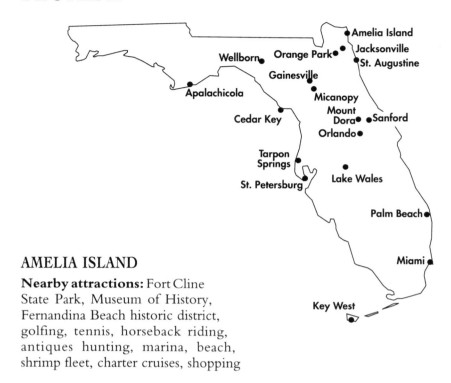

AMELIA ISLAND

Nearby attractions: Fort Cline
State Park, Museum of History,
Fernandina Beach historic district,
golfing, tennis, horseback riding,
antiques hunting, marina, beach,
shrimp fleet, charter cruises, shopping

BAILEY HOUSE
28 South Seventh Street
P.O. Box 805
Fernandina Beach, Florida 32034
904/261-5390 or 800/251-5390
Proprietors: Tom and Jenny Bishop
Location: on Amelia Island, 35 miles northeast of Jacksonville

Bailey House was designed by architect George W. Bailey of Knoxville,
Tennesee, in 1895. With its turrets, gables, bays, stained-glass windows, and fish-
scale shingles, the house took three years to build at the then-extravagant cost of
$10,000. The National Register home, an outstanding example of the Queen
Anne style, is in the heart of Fernandina Beach's historic district. Bailey House
guests enjoy ornately carved antique furniture. There are also brass beds, a pump
organ, fringed lamps, claw-foot bathtubs, and marble-topped dressers and tables.
The most spectacular of six fireplaces, located in the reception hall, bears the
inscription on its mantel: "Hearth Hall, Welcome All."

Open: year round **Accommodations:** 5 guest rooms with private baths; 1 is a suite **Meals:** deluxe continental breakfast included; restaurants nearby **Rates:** $75 to $115 **Payment:** AmEx, Visa, MC, personal check **Restrictions:** children over 8 welcome; no smoking; no pets **Activities:** bicycles, porch swings and rocking chairs, croquet

FAIRBANKS HOUSE
227 South Seventh Street
Fernandina Beach, Florida 32034
904/277-0500 or 800/261-4838
904/277-3103 Fax
Proprietors: Nelson and Mary Smelker
Location: on Amelia Island, 35 miles northeast of Jacksonville

Architect Robert Schuyler created this picturesque example of Italianate design in 1885. From the round-arched openings along the front piazza to the square tower with rows of round-topped windows, and decorative brackets, this house is an elegant showcase. Inside, nine carved fireplaces, polished hardwood floors, and intricately carved moldings grace spacious rooms, which are appointed with antiques and oriental rugs. Each guest room is furnished with a four-poster or canopied king, queen, or twin bed. Each private bathroom may contain a claw-foot or whirlpool tub. Most bedrooms have fireplaces. A private courtyard contains a swimming pool and gardens bursting with roses, palms, and magnolias. Guests may have breakfast in this outdoor setting or in the inn's formal dining room.

Open: year round **Accommodations:** 10 guest rooms with private baths; 2 are suites **Meals:** full breakfast included; complimentary refreshments; restaurants nearby **Rates:** $95 to $165 **Payment:** AmEx, Visa, MC, Discover, personal and traveler's checks **Restrictions:** no smoking; no pets **Activities:** swimming pool, bicycles

APALACHICOLA

Nearby attractions: historic district, Gorrie Museum, barrier islands, Apalachicola National Estuarine Research Reserve, local and state parks, sandy beaches, fishing, boating, hiking, Florida Seafood Festival, Carrabelle Waterfront Festival

COOMBS HOUSE INN
80 Sixth Street
Apalachicola, Florida 32320
904/653-9199
Proprietors: Lynn Wilson and William Spohrer **Innkeepers:** Charles and Marilyn Schubert

When timber baron James N. Coombs built this home in 1905, it was considered the most elegant residence in town. The mansion features 12-foot-high ceilings, nine fireplaces, a wood-paneled entrance hall, an ornate oak staircase, and leaded-glass windows. Today, the inn's clapboards and patterned shingles are dressed in bright yellow with white trim; shutters in dark green. Paintings and historical photographs complement the turn-of-the-century decor rendered by antique furniture: carved oak sideboards, armoires with mirrored doors, and Victorian sofas and chairs. Imported English chintz draperies frame large bay windows, and oriental carpets soften hardwood floors. Each distinctively decorated guest room has a full bath and cable television. Breakfast is served in the mansion's original dining room. Coombs House is in the heart of Apalachicola's historic district.

Open: year round **Accommodations:** 10 guest rooms with private baths; 1 is a suite **Meals:** continental-plus breakfast included; restaurants nearby **Wheelchair access:** 1 room **Rates:** $59 to $105 **Payment:** AmEx, Visa, MC, personal and traveler's checks **Restrictions:** no smoking; no pets **Activities:** bicycles, rocking chairs

---

CEDAR KEY

Nearby attractions: wildlife preserve, nature walks, boat tours, walking tours, swimming in freshwater springs, fresh and saltwater fishing, bird-watching

ISLAND HOTEL
Second and B Streets
P.O. Box 460
Cedar Key, Florida 32625
904/543-5111
Proprietors: Tom and Alison Sanders

Survivor of hurricanes, floods, economic depression, and arson, the 1859 Island

Hotel has truly stood the test of time and travail. One reason is its solid construction of 10-inch-thick tabby walls (a composite of oyster shells, sand, lime, and salt water) and 12-inch-thick oak beams. Recently restored by today's innkeepers and listed in the National Register of Historic Places, the hotel is a charming throwback to early life in Cedar Key. The two-story structure began life as a general store and was converted to a hotel in 1915. Its rooms are comfortably furnished in an old Florida style that includes feather beds, claw-foot tubs, mosquito netting and ceiling fans, although window screens and air conditioning have been added. But modern intrusions like telephones and television have been omitted. The hotel's restaurant continues a long tradition of serving gourmet island seafood, and the lounge bar, decorated with murals painted in 1948, has been refinished with genuine cedar from the key.

Open: year round **Accommodations:** 10 guest rooms (6 have private baths) **Meals:** full breakfast included; restaurant on premises **Wheelchair access:** dining room **Rates:** $85 to $95; 10% discount to National Trust members and National Trust Visa cardholders **Payment:** Visa, MC, traveler's check **Restrictions:** children by prior arrangement; smoking limited **Activities:** reading, conversing, dining, balcony sitting

---

GAINESVILLE

Nearby attractions: Hippodrome State Theater, cultural arts center, natural springs, canoeing, antiques hunting

MAGNOLIA PLANTATION BED AND BREAKFAST INN

309 S.E. Seventh Street
Gainesville, Florida 32601
904/375-6653
904/338-0303
Proprietors: Joe and Cindy Montalto

Magnolia Plantation derives its name from the many magnolias that surround the inn, formerly known as the Baird Mansion. The innkeepers and many of their family members have carefully restored this 1885 Italianate house and its gardens, resulting in awards from the city of Gainesville for historic preservation and beautification. The interior of the house boasts an eight-foot-wide central hallway with a mahogany staircase. The parlor and adjoining library, with two of the ten fireplaces at the inn, are favorite gathering spots for guests. Bedrooms feature white iron, sleigh, four-poster, or canopied queen-size beds. Nearly all rooms have gas-log fireplaces and ceiling fans. Each room also contains a music center and a selection of romantic tapes. A full breakfast, evening wine, and stocked guest refrigerator are complimentary.

Open: year round **Accommodations:** 5 guest rooms with private baths **Meals:** full breakfast included; complimentary refreshments; candlelight dinners offered; restaurants nearby **Rates:** $70 to $95; 10% discount to National Trust members and National Trust Visa cardholders **Payment:** AmEx, Visa, MC, personal and traveler's checks **Restrictions:** children over 6 welcome; no smoking; no pets **Activities:** candlelight dinners, carriage rides, massage therapist on call

JACKSONVILLE

Nearby attractions: Jacksonville Landing, historic districts, Cummer Art Museum and Gardens, Jacksonville Science Museum, antiques hunting, parks, tennis, swimming, beaches, Okefenokee Swamp, Gator Bowl, jazz festival

PLANTATION MANOR INN
1630 Copeland Street
Jacksonville, Florida 32204
904/384-4630
Proprietors: Kathy and Jerry Ray

Plantation Manor was built in 1905 on a high corner lot in the historic Riverside area of Jacksonville, only two blocks from the St. Johns River. First owned by a real estate mogul and then a bank president, this elegant Neoclassical house is distinguished by a full-height entry porch and first-floor wraparound porch supported by rows of massive Doric columns. Inside, crystal and brass chandeliers

glow above antique furnishings and oriental carpets. Guest rooms feature either fireplaces or sitting areas, as well as telephones and cable television. Guests are invited to enjoy the lap pool, spa, and garden. Plantation Manor Inn also hosts small business meetings, weddings, and receptions, and features a romantic honeymoon suite.

Open: year round **Accommodations:** 9 guest rooms with private baths; 3 are suites **Meals:** continental or full breakfast included; complimentary refreshments; restaurants nearby **Rates:** $95 to $150; 10% discount offered to National Trust members or National Trust Visa cardholders **Payment:** AmEx, Visa, MC, personal and traveler's checks **Restrictions:** smoking limited; no pets **Activities:** lap pool, spa

KEY WEST

Nearby attractions: Ernest Hemingway House, Audubon House, Duval Street, museums, live theater, tennis, beaches, fishing, snorkeling, scuba diving

ISLAND CITY HOUSE HOTEL
411 William Street
Key West, Florida 33040
305/294-5702 or 800/634-8230
305/294-1289 Fax
Proprietors: Stanley and Janet Corneal

Island City House Hotel comprises three unique guest houses that share private tropical gardens laced with red brick pathways. The Island City House, built as a private home in the 1880s, was enlarged and opened as a hotel in 1912 for the arrival of the railroad in Key West. The Cigar House is a recently built cypress house modeled after the cigar factory that once stood on the site. The Arch House, ca. 1880, the only remaining carriage house on the island, is a two-story, gingerbread-encrusted building. All three buildings offer parlor suites individually furnished with antiques or in contemporary or casual island decors. Hardwood floors, ceiling fans, color television, telephones, and private baths are standard. Most rooms offer balconies or porches.

Open: year round **Accommodations:** 24 guest suites with private baths **Meals:** continental-plus breakfast included; restaurants nearby **Rates:** $95 to $145; 10% discount to National Trust members and National Trust Visa cardholders **Payment:** Visa, MC, CB, DC, Discover, traveler's check, personal check for advance deposit only **Restrictions:** no pets **Activities:** swimming pool, sundecks, gardens

PALMS HOTEL

820 White Street
Key West, Florida 33040
305/294-3146 or 800/558-9374
305/294-8463 Fax
Proprietor: S. H. Stern

Built at the turn of the century, the Palms Hotel was meticulously restored in 1995. Its Victorian style is marked by double-decker, wraparound porches with gingerbread and a three-story corner tower. A sympathetic modern addition at the rear of the property surrounds a tropical garden and secluded swimming pool area where complimentary drinks are enjoyed at sunset. Handsomely appointed guest rooms feature ceiling fans, private baths, television, air conditioning, and French doors leading to the courtyard. The hotel is located away from Key West's busy main streets, yet just a short walk to the island's shops, restaurants, and bars. The beach is less than a 10-minute walk away. The Palms claims Ernest Hemingway, Key West's most famous inhabitant, as an early visitor; before the house was converted to a hotel, its first-floor apartment was rented to Hemingway's brother.

Open: year round **Accommodations:** 20 guest rooms with private baths; 5 are suites **Meals:** continental-plus breakfast included; restaurants nearby **Rates:** $95 to $175; 10% discount offered to National Trust members and National Trust Visa cardholders **Payment:** AmEx, Visa, MC, Discover, traveler's check **Activities:** swimming pool, bicycles, board games

WATSON HOUSE

525 Simonton Street
Key West, Florida 33040
305/294-6712 or 800/621-9405
305/294-7501 Fax
Proprietors: Joe Beres and Ed Czaplicki

The front double-decker veranda was one of the first areas that was restored in the 1980s to bring the Watson House back to its original Bahamian style. Built in 1860 by William and Susan Watson, the house was later sold and remodeled as a southern colonial mansion. After completing their restoration and expansion in 1987, the innkeepers received an award for preservation excellence from the Historical Florida Keys Preservation Board. Guest quarters blend tropical decor with Victorian romanticism using wooden paddle fans, wicker and rattan furnishings, floral patterns, and hardwood floors. A four-room apartment in the poolside cabana includes vaulted ceilings and a full kitchen. Guests relax in the swimming pool, heated spa, sundecks, and tropical gardens.

Open: year round **Accommodations:** 3 guest suites with private baths **Meals:** continental-plus breakfast included; restaurants nearby **Rates:** $105 to $380; 10% discount to National Trust members and National Trust Visa cardholders **Payment:** AmEx, Visa, MC, traveler's check **Restrictions:** not suitable for children; smoking limited; no pets **Activities:** heated swimming pool, spa, sunbathing

WHISPERS BED AND BREAKFAST INN
409 William Street
Key West, Florida 33040
305/294-5969 or 800/856-SHHH (800/856-7444)
Proprietor: John Marburg

This house, listed in the National Register of Historic Places, was built by Gideon Lowe, the youngest son of one of Key West's earliest Bahamian settlers. Located on a sleepy, shaded street within view of the Gulf harbor, the structure is surrounded by a 30-block historic district of distinctive nineteenth-century buildings. The oldest section of the house (ca. 1845) retains numerous significant architectural details. A later section, dating to 1866, reflects a typical Greek Revival floor plan, with Victorian embellishments. The house exhibits Bahamian influences in its scuttles, porches, shuttered windows, and numerous doors—all features well suited to the tropics. Guests can relax on cool porches, in the lush garden, or in rooms quietly cooled by ceiling fans. Whispers has appeared in many publications, including *National Geographic Traveler* and *Colonial Homes*.

Open: year round **Accommodations:** 7 guest rooms (5 have private baths) **Meals:** full breakfast included; restaurants nearby **Rates:** $69 to $150; 10% discount offered to National Trust members and National Trust Visa cardholders **Payment:** AmEx, Visa, MC, Discover, personal and traveler's checks **Restrictions:** smoking limited

LAKE WALES

Nearby attractions: Bok Tower Gardens, Cypress Gardens, Frank Lloyd Wright building at Florida Southern College, Black Hills Passion Play, tennis, golfing, beaches, central Florida attractions

CHALET SUZANNE COUNTRY INN AND RESTAURANT
U.S. Highway 27 and County Road 17A
3800 Chalet Suzanne Drive
Lake Wales, Florida 33853-7060
813/676-6011 or 800/433-6011
813/676-1814 Fax
Proprietors: Carl and Vita Hinshaw
Location: 4 miles north of Lake Wales

A winding road leads travelers to Chalet Suzanne's pastel-tinted cottages. Surrounded by cobblestone walkways and courtyards with fountains, the cottages are attached at odd angles and topped with a storybook assortment of steeples, gables, belfries, and cupolas. Built in various stages throughout the 1920s, 1930s, and 1940s, the cottages display a decor that is a little bit gingerbread, a little bit baroque, a touch medieval, and a touch Viking. Each guest room is uniquely proportioned and furnished; and fruits, candies, fresh flowers, complimentary sherry, and fine toiletries are standard. Chalet Suzanne is famous for its sprawling restaurant and delicious soups, which have been canned on the premises for more than 30 years. The inn has Mobil four-star and AAA three-diamond ratings and has been listed by *Women's Day* as one of the 10 most romantic spots for a honeymoon in Florida. Chalet Suzanne was voted one of the Top 10 Country Inns for 1991–1992 by Uncle Ben's.

Open: year round **Accommodations:** 30 guest rooms with private baths; 4 are suites **Meals:** full breakfast included; restaurants on premises **Wheelchair access:** 2 guest rooms **Rates:** $125 to $185 **Payment:** AmEx, Visa, MC, CB, DC, Discover, personal and traveler's checks **Restrictions:** additional charge for pets **Activities:** swimming, lawn games, fishing in private lake, jogging, rowboat, private airstrip, cannery, gift shop, antiques shop, ceramic studio

FORGET-ME-NOT BED AND BREAKFAST
301 East Sessoms Avenue
Lake Wales, Florida 33853
813/676-5499
Proprietor: Rebecca Hunter

This house, a grand, hip-roofed Colonial Revival home with wraparound porch, was built in 1914 for G. V. Tillman, a founder of Lake Wales. The house was listed in the National Register of Historic Places in 1990. Five guest rooms are decorated according to their names: Magnolia, Iris, Honeysuckle, Violet, and Rose. All rooms contain cable television and central air conditioning. Beds are turned down nightly. Breakfast is served in the Tillman Tearoom as is a traditional afternoon tea, which can also be enjoyed on the veranda overlooking Crystal Lake. The Forget-Me-Not is within walking distance of tennis courts, a city park, and Lake Wales.

Open: year round **Accommodations:** 5 guest rooms (3 have private baths); 2 are suites **Meals:** continental-plus breakfast included; restaurants nearby **Rates:** $85 to $100; 10% discount to National Trust members and National Trust Visa cardholders **Payment:** Visa, MC, personal and traveler's checks **Restrictions:** no smoking; no pets **Activities:** garden strolling

---

MIAMI
Nearby attractions: Center for Fine Arts, museums, Bayside Festival Marketplace, Knight Conference Center, Orange Bowl, Miami Arena, Vizcaya, Coconut Grove, Dadeland, beaches, swimming, shopping

MIAMI RIVER INN
118 S.W. South River Drive
Miami, Florida 33130
305/325-0045 or 800/HOTEL89 (800/468-3589)
305/325-9227 Fax
Proprietor: Sallye G. Jude

Old Miami lives at the Miami River Inn, a 1908 frame structure in much the same style it was when early visitors, arriving by train, were met by horse and carriage. It is the oldest continuously operating inn south of St. Augustine. Guests enjoy a turn-of-the-century environment overlooking Miami's vibrant riverfront and downtown. Each guest room is individually decorated and furnished with antiques, yet includes a telephone, television, and central air conditioning. Guests receive complimentary breakfast and a glass of welcoming wine. The lobby contains a library of historical publications about Miami and menus from restaurants in the river district. A swimming pool and hot tub are surrounded by tropical gardens.

Open: year round **Accommodations:** 40 guest rooms (38 have private baths) **Wheelchair access:** yes **Meals:** continental breakfast included; restaurants nearby **Rates:** $59 to $125; 10% discount to National Trust members, National Trust Visa cardholders, and members of other preservation organizations **Payment:** AmEx, Visa, MC, CB, DC, Discover, personal and traveler's checks **Restrictions:** no smoking; no pets **Activities:** swimming pool, hot tub

MICANOPY

Nearby attractions: Payne's Prairie State Park, University of Florida, Hippodrome Theater, Cross Creek, Marjorie Kinnan Rawlings Home, fresh watersprings, antiques hunting, canoeing, horseback riding

HERLONG MANSION
402 N.E. Cholokka Boulevard
P.O. Box 667
Micanopy, Florida 32667
800/HERLONG (800/437-5664)
904/466-3322 Fax
Proprietor: H. C. (Sonny) Howard, Jr.

The Herlong Mansion was originally a two-story Victorian house built in 1845. In 1910 it was encased in brick in a Colonial Revival design. Four two-story, carved-wood, Corinthian columns support the double porch that spans the front facade. Inside, the mansion boasts leaded-glass windows, 10 fireplaces, mahogany inlaid oak floors, 12-foot-high ceilings, walnut and tiger oak paneling, and floor-to-ceiling windows in the dining room. Each guest room offers different amenities, such as fireplaces, claw-foot tubs, private porches, antique brass beds, or leaded-glass windows. All provide private baths. A full breakfast features homemade pastries. Set back from the street, the mansion is surrounded by gardens and old oak and pecan trees.

Open: year round **Accommodations:** 11 guest rooms with private baths; 4 are suites **Meals:** full breakfast included; complimentary refreshments; catered meals available; restaurants nearby **Rates:** $50 to $150; 10% discount to National Trust members and National Trust Visa cardholders **Payment:** Visa, MC, personal and traveler's checks **Restrictions:** no smoking; no pets **Activities:** complimentary bicycles

MOUNT DORA

Nearby attractions: national forest, water sports, golfing, fishing, antiques hunting, historic Mount Dora, seasonal festivals, Disney World, Sea World, Universal Studios

FARNSWORTH HOUSE
1029 East Fifth Avenue
Mount Dora, Florida 32757
904/735-1894
Proprietors: Dick and Sandy Shelton

Leander Farnsworth, a shoe merchant from Michigan, built this large house with hipped dormers in 1886. In 1944 it was converted to an apartment house; broad screened porches were added upstairs and down for comfort. Today, Farnsworth House offers three suites in the main house and two in the adjacent carriage house. All guest rooms are decorated with designer fabrics, coordinating paint schemes, and antique furniture, ranging from mahogany to oak and wicker to wrought iron. All accommodations have private baths, kitchens, and air conditioning. Breakfast is served in guest rooms, while afternoon refreshments are served in the dining room. Guests may enjoy the spacious grounds, screened gazebo, and hot tub.

Open: year round **Accommodations:** 5 guest rooms with private baths; 3 are suites **Meals:** continental-plus breakfast included; complimentary refreshments; restaurants nearby **Rates:** $75 to $95; 10% discount to National Trust members and National Trust Visa cardholders **Payment:** Visa, MC, personal and traveler's checks **Restrictions:** no smoking; no pets **Activities:** hot tub, gazebo

ORANGE PARK

Nearby attractions: dog track, golfing, St. Johns River, boating, swimming, Jacksonville, museums, theater, St. Augustine

CLUB CONTINENTAL
2143 Astor Street
Orange Park, Florida 32073
904/264-6070 or 800/877-6070
904/263-4044 Fax
Proprietors: Karrie and Caleb Massee

For more than 70 years the Club Continental property has been preserved by the descendants of Caleb Johnson, founder of the Palmolive Soap Company. The

1923 Mediterranean-style mansion, originally known as Mira Rio, offers seven guest rooms individually decorated with an Old World ambience. A new building on the property offers 15 rooms with private riverfront balconies overlooking the broad St. Johns River. These rooms feature fireplaces, whirlpool tubs, and four-poster king-size beds. Club Continental's expansive grounds include Spanish moss-draped live oaks, magnolias, gardens, courtyards, seven tennis courts, three pools, and a pre-Civil War River House Pub with live entertainment. The inn is ideal for weddings, receptions, and corporate events.

Open: year round **Accommodations:** 22 guest rooms with private baths; 6 are suites **Wheelchair access:** yes **Meals:** continental breakfast included; restaurant on premises; restaurants nearby **Rates:** $60 to $140 **Payment:** AmEx, Visa, MC, personal and traveler's checks **Restrictions:** smoking limited **Activities:** 7 tennis courts, 3 swimming pools

ORLANDO

Nearby attractions: Disney World, Sea World, Church Street Station, downtown Orlando

COURTYARD AT LAKE LUCERNE
211 North Lucerne Circle, East
Orlando, Florida 32801
407/648-5188 or 800/444-5289
Proprietors: Charles, Sam, and Eleanor Meiner and Paula Bowers

Overlooking Lake Lucerne and encircling a lush garden, the Courtyard at Lake Lucerne is a cluster of three historic buildings: the Norment–Parry Inn, the Wellborn, and the I. W. Phillips House. The Norment–Parry Inn, built in 1883, is Orlando's oldest home. A clapboard Victorian with decorative vergeboards and a gingerbread porch, it is furnished with American and English antiques. Each of the guest rooms has been decorated by a different designer; the results range from flowered and airy to opulent and dramatic. The Wellborn is one of Orlando's finest examples of Art Deco design, with its pink stucco, corner and porthole windows, and wrought-iron screen doors. Elegant and streamlined guest suites bring back the 1930s in every detail from colors to furnishings. At the I. W. Phillips House, guests enjoy luxurious suites furnished in authentic Belle Epoque fittings. The house is a late nineteenth-century antebellum-style manor house complete with broad two-story verandas. Ceiling fans and a Tiffany window add to the setting.

Open: year round **Accommodations:** 22 guest rooms with private baths; 12 are suites, 2 are honeymoon suites with whirlpool baths **Meals:** continental-plus breakfast included; restaurants nearby **Rates:** $69 to $150; 10% discount offered to National Trust members and National Trust Visa cardholders **Payment:** AmEx, Visa, MC, CB, DC, personal and traveler's checks **Activities:** grand piano, tropical garden with fountain, walking, jogging, bicycling

PALM BEACH

Nearby attractions: Worth Avenue, Atlantic Ocean beaches, museums, tennis, golfing, swimming, fishing, sailing, boating, horseback riding, polo, jai alai, greyhound racing, ballet, opera, theater, antiques hunting, art galleries, boutiques, planetarium, botanical gardens, sculpture gardens, sightseeing cruises, scuba diving, snorkeling

PALM BEACH HISTORIC INN
365 South County Road
Palm Beach, Florida 334880
407/832-4009
407/832-6255 Fax
Proprietor: Melissa Laitman

This 1923 Palm Beach landmark building was designed by the architectural firm of Harvey and Clarke, which also designed the town hall. The stucco building with Mission-style parapet and red-tile roof, on a prominent corner lot, is most notable for its arcade of round arches with Tuscan columns that extends around its two street sides. Charming, intimate accommodations are individually appointed with coordinating paints, papers, and fabrics. Each room offers a private bath, refrigerator, color cable television, and telephone. A continental-plus breakfast is delivered to guest rooms, along with the morning newspaper. This historic inn is one block from the beach and two from the shops of world-famous Worth Avenue.

Open: year round **Accommodations:** 13 guest rooms with private baths; 4 are suites **Meals:** continental-plus breakfast included; complimentary refreshments; restaurants nearby **Rates:** $75 summer to $225 winter **Payment:** AmEx, Visa, MC, CB, DC, Discover, traveler's check **Restrictions:** smoking limited; no pets

ST. AUGUSTINE

Nearby attractions: Castillo de San Marcos, Lightner Museum, Ripley's Believe It or Not Museum, alligator farm, beaches, boating, swimming, Intracoastal Waterway

OLD CITY HOUSE INN AND RESTAURANT
115 Cordova Street
St. Augustine, Florida 32084
904/826-0113
904/829-3798 Fax
Proprietors: John and Darcy Compton

Old City House Inn, built in 1873, is a fine example of Colonial Revival architecture—St. Augustine style. The stone-and-stucco and tiled-roof building was first a stable, then a winter cottage rented to wealthy northerners. Later the building was used as a hat shop, antiques store, apartments, and an office building. In 1990, the building at 115 Cordova was returned to its original style and modernized with central heat and air conditioning. As a bed and breakfast, it offers individually decorated bedrooms with queen-size beds, cable television, and private entrances and bathrooms. All guests have access to the veranda and courtyard. Afternoon refreshments and a full breakfast are included in the rate. The inn, located in the historic district, provides bicycles for exploring the country's oldest city. Old City House Restaurant has been recommended by *Jacksonville Today*, *Florida Trend*, and *Food Arts*.

Open: year round **Accommodations:** 5 guest rooms with private baths; 1 is a suite **Meals:** full breakfast included; complimentary refreshments; restaurant on premises; restaurants nearby **Rates:** $65 to $110; 10% discount to National Trust members and National Trust Visa cardholders excluding weekends and holidays **Payment:** AmEx, Visa, MC, DC, Discover, personal and traveler's checks **Restrictions:** no smoking; no pets

ST. PETERSBURG

Nearby attractions: museums, Busch Gardens, Thunder Dome sports, beaches, golfing, sailing, fishing, tennis, antiques hunting

BAYBORO HOUSE
1719 Beach Drive, S.E.
St. Petersburg, Florida 33701
813/823-4955
Proprietors: Gordon and Antonia Powers

Built in 1905 by one of St. Petersburg's early entrepreneurs, C. A. Harvey, this Queen Anne house stayed in his family until the 1920s, when it became known as "the speakeasy." Today, the house has been restored and guests enjoy viewing the unspoiled waterfront from the old porch swing or rockers on the wraparound veranda. Inside, the innkeepers have amassed collections of gas and oil lamps, chiming clocks, marble-topped tables, dolls, trunks, and footstools. Each guest room is furnished with antiques and collectibles, provides a water view, and offers air conditioning, private bath, television and VCR, and a morning newspaper at the door. A continental-plus breakfast is served in the formal dining room; complimentary evening wine is served in the parlor. Bayboro House is across the street from Lassing Park on Old Tampa Bay, ideally situated for sunning, shelling, and relaxing.

Open: year round **Accommodations:** 4 guest rooms with private baths; 1 is a suite **Meals:** continental-plus breakfast included; complimentary refreshments; restaurants nearby **Rates:** $95 to $145; 10% discount to National Trust members and National Trust Visa cardholders **Payment:** Visa, MC, personal check **Restrictions:** not suitable for children; no smoking; no pets **Activities:** porch swings, player piano

---

SANFORD

Nearby attractions: historic Sanford, Centennial Park, St. Johns River, Wekiva River, Blue Spring State Park, Central Florida Zoo, Lake Monroe, Mt. Dora, Ocala National Forest, Cape Canaveral Wildlife Refuge, Walt Disney World, Sea World, Universal Studios

HIGGINS HOUSE VICTORIAN BED AND BREAKFAST
420 South Oak Avenue
Sanford, Florida 32771
407/324-9238 or 800/584-0014
Proprietors: Walter and Roberta Padgett

Higgins House was built in 1894 by James Cochran Higgins, Sanford's railroad superintendent. He chose to build in the Queen Anne style with cross gables, patterned wood shingles, bay windows, turned-post and spindle work, and a second-story round window. The Padgetts purchased the house, in a state of disrepair, in 1990 and performed most of the restoration and landscaping that has resulted in today's bed-and-breakfast inn. Three guest rooms with private baths are in the main house: The Queen Anne Room overlooks the garden, the Wicker Room has a bay window, and the Victorian Country Room has an antique brass bed and stenciled wood floor. Guests are invited to relax in the parlor, the pub, the front porch, the upstairs veranda, or in the hot tub. The adjacent Cochrans Cottage offers a two-bedroom, two-bath suite with full kitchen, living room, and porch. Also on premises is a gift and antiques shop.

Open: year round **Accommodations:** 4 guest rooms with private baths; 1 is a suite **Meals:** continental-plus breakfast included; complimentary refreshments; restaurants nearby **Rates:** $70 to $145; 10% discount to National Trust members and National Trust Visa cardholders **Payment:** AmEx, Visa, MC, Discover, personal and traveler's checks **Restrictions:** children welcome in cottage; no smoking; no pets **Activities:** hot tub, gardens, porch

---

TARPON SPRINGS

Nearby attractions: Greek Village and sponge docks, historic district with antiques shops, golfing, tennis, parks, beaches, fishing, bayou, Busch Gardens, Salvador Dali Museum

SPRING BAYOU INN
32 West Tarpon Avenue
Tarpon Springs, Florida
34689
813/938-9333
Proprietor: Sharon Birk

The artisanship of this turn-of-the-century Shingle Style home is reflected in such details as its wood-shingle exterior walls, a round corner tower, circular wrap-around porches, and a steep hip roof with boxed eaves. Guest rooms are laden with antiques and collectibles. Guests can also relax on the front porch or in the parlor with its baby grand piano and fireplace. Tarpon Springs, known as the sponge capital of the world, is an unusual mixture of new growth and quiet historic charm not easily found on the west coast of Florida. The Spring Bayou Inn is part of the town's National Register historic district. Stroll along the bayou or browse in local antiques shops. Nearby are the sponge docks and many excellent restaurants.

Open: year round **Accommodations:** 5 guest rooms (3 have private baths) **Meals:** continental-plus breakfast included; complimentary refreshments; restaurants nearby **Rates:** $80 to $110; 10% discount to National Trust members and National Trust Visa cardholders **Payment:** personal check **Restrictions:** children over 12 welcome; no smoking; no pets

WELLBORN

Nearby attractions: Stephen Foster Folk Culture Center, Suwannee River, Florida Sports Hall of Fame, state parks, freshwater springs, Osceola Forest National Park, carriage rides, bicycling, golfing, tennis, antiques hunting, Suwannee County Historical Museum, canoeing, hiking

1909 McLERAN HOUSE
12408 County Road 137
Wellborn, Florida 32094
904/963-4603
Proprietors: Robert and Mary Ryals

Banker E. B. McLeran built this two-story frame house in 1909. Although neglected for many years, it has been meticulously restored by the innkeepers. A huge porch spans the facade and wraps around the sides of the house. Inside are six fireplaces, each with a unique curly-pine mantel, elegant woodwork, and a grand stairwell. Paddle fans are in every room, recalling the ambience of north Florida a century ago. Furnishings are a tasteful blend of old and new, including a huge mirrored oak cabinet that graced a Wellborn store at the turn of the century. The downstairs guest room has a private entrance and refrigerator. Five manicured acres include a cedar gazebo and lush gardens with swing, fountain, arbor, walkways, goldfish pond, and the original open well.

Open: year round **Accommodations:** 2 guest rooms (1 has a privte bath) **Meals:** continental-plus breakfast included; complimentary refreshments; restaurants nearby **Rate:** $60; 10% discount to National Trust members and National Trust Visa cardholders **Payment:** personal and traveler's checks **Restrictions:** not suitable for children; no smoking; no pets **Activities:** collectibles shop, bird watching, walking, old books and records shop

GEORGIA

Clarkesville
Sautee ●
Athens ●
Atlanta ●
Thomson ●
● Senoia
● Hogansville
● Macon
Savannah ●
● Americus
St. Simons
Island
Thomasville
●

AMERICUS

Nearby attractions:
Plains/Jimmy Carter
National Historic Site,
Andersonville National
Historic Site, historical
walking tours, Habitat
for Humanity, tennis,
golfing, shopping

WINDSOR HOTEL
125 West Lamar Street
Americus, Georgia 31709
912/924-1555 or 800/678-8946
Proprietors: Max Wohlfarth, General Manager; Jo Childers, Sales and Marketing
Location: 9 miles east of Plains, 11 miles southwest of Andersonville National
Historic Site

The Windsor was a resort hotel and the site of elaborate parties, balls, and social
events for five decades, beginning in 1892. Years of neglect and decay followed
until a $6 million restoration reopened the Windsor in 1991 as a five-story wonder
of towers, balconies, grand arches, round-topped windows, and a three-story
atrium lobby, located in the city's National Register historic district. Each
uniquely configured guest room features period furnishings, 12-foot-high ceilings,
ceiling fans, and cable television. A member of Historic Hotels of America, the
Windsor offers all the amenities associated with a first-class, intimate hotel, including
valet and bell services, a full-service restaurant and bar, banquet and meeting
rooms, and complimentary coffee and daily newspaper. Palms, antique chandeliers, and wicker rockers typify the hotel's nostalgic blend of comfort and grace.

Open: year round **Accommodations:** 53 guest rooms with private baths; 4 are suites **Meals:** restaurant and bar on premises **Wheelchair access:** guest rooms, bathrooms, dining facilities **Rates:** $70 to $135; 10% discount offered to National Trust members and National Trust Visa cardholders **Payment:** AmEx, Visa, MC, CB, DC, Discover, personal and traveler's checks **Restrictions:** no pets **Activities:** Floyd's Pub, gift, clothing, art, and antiques shops

---

ATHENS

Nearby attractions: Cobbham Historic District, historic downtown, University of Georgia, parks, museums, botanical gardens

MAGNOLIA TERRACE GUEST HOUSE
277 Hill Street
Athens, Georgia 30601
706/891-1912 or 706/548-3860
706/369-3439 Fax
Proprietor: Shelia Hackney

This spacious Colonial Revival house, built in 1912, is located in the heart of downtown near the University of Georgia. Distinctive architectural features such as Corinthian columns, beveled-glass entrance, and original fireplace mantels showcase the area's talented craftsmen. Comfortably furnished with antiques, each of the seven unique guest rooms offers a large private bath with period clawfoot tub and modern shower or whirlpool. Beautifully appointed public areas are equally suited to intimate conversation and festive functions. Parking is available on premises, a porch is offered for smokers, and children and pets are welcome.

Open: year round **Accommodations:** 7 guest rooms with private baths **Meals:** continental-plus breakfast included; complimentary refreshments; restaurants nearby **Wheelchair access:** yes **Rates:** $90 to $150; 10% discount to National Trust members and National Trust Visa cardholders **Payment:** AmEx, Visa, MC, personal and traveler's checks **Restrictions:** smoking limited **Activities:** library with many National Trust publications, porch sitting

ATLANTA

Nearby attractions: Swan House, governor's mansion, state capitol, Museum of Science and Technology, Ansley Park, Inman Park, Buckhead, Woodruff Arts Center, Underground Atlanta, World of Coke, Zoo Atlanta, High Museum, Botanical Gardens, Piedmont Park, Stone Mountain, botanical gardens, symphony, shopping at Lenox Square and Phipps Plaza

BED AND BREAKFAST ATLANTA HILLTOP HOUSE IN ANSLEY PARK

1801 Piedmont Avenue, N.E.
Atlanta, Georgia 30324
404/875-0525
404/875-9672 Fax
Proprietor: Paula Gris

Located in the National Register neighborhood of Ansley Park, on a quiet, winding, tree-shaded street, Hilltop House was built ca. 1909. Its broad, low-pitched front dormer, wide overhanging eaves, side shed dormers, and front porch are evidence of Craftsman styling. The house is further distinguished by mock half-timbering that evokes a slightly Tudor feeling. Two large guest rooms share a bath. One bedroom offers a king-size bed, the other has twin beds. The decor of both is a mix of contemporary and traditional styles. A hearty continental breakfast is served in the glassed breakfast area, which affords views of the grounds. The innkeeper is knowledgeable about the city and also provides maps, brochures, and restaurant guides to help guests feel at home in Atlanta.

Open: year round **Accommodations:** 2 guest rooms share a bath **Meals:** continental-plus breakfast included; restaurants nearby **Rates:** $88 to $250 **Payment:** AmEx, Visa, MC, CB, DC, personal and traveler's checks **Restrictions:** no smoking; no pets **Activities:** bird-watching

BEVERLY HILLS INN

65 Sheridan Drive
Atlanta, Georgia 30305
404/233-8520 or 800/331-8520
Proprietor: Mit Amin

A European-style inn in the heart of Buckhead, Atlanta's premier business and residential district, the 1929 Beverly Hills Inn offers 18 unique suites for travelers who seek the unusual. Continental furnishings combine with leaded-glass French doors and wrought-iron balconies, creating a charming city retreat. Guests are invited to take breakfast in the garden room, relax in the parlor, play a tune on the piano, or enjoy a refreshing drink in the brick courtyard and garden. The inn

is just minutes from the governor's mansion, Atlanta Historical Society, state capitol, downtown Atlanta, and upscale shopping at the renowned Lenox Square and Phipps Plaza.

Open: year round **Accommodations:** 18 suites with private baths **Meals:** continental-plus breakfast included; restaurants nearby **Wheelchair access:** guest rooms, bathrooms, dining facilities **Rates:** $80 to $450; 10% discount to National Trust members and National Trust Visa cardholders **Payment:** AmEx, Visa, MC, CB, DC, Discover, personal and traveler's checks **Restrictions:** pets must be kept in carriers

OAKWOOD HOUSE BED AND BREAKFAST

951 Edgewood Avenue, N.E.
Atlanta, Georgia 30307
404/521-9320
404/688-6034 Fax
Proprietors: Robert and Judy Hotchkiss

In the early 1900s Joel Hurt developed Atlanta's first garden suburb, Inman Park, just two miles from downtown. Oakwood House, named for the huge tree in the backyard, was a "spec" house in the neighborhood—one of many similar houses built before being purchased. These houses, styled with Craftsman touches, had four bedrooms and one bath each and sat on 50-foot lots. Built in 1911, Oakwood House has seen use as a family home, boardinghouse, apartments, and offices. Renovations in the last decade spared the original heart pine woodwork. Today, Oakwood offers five guest accommodations decorated to complement the house's post-Victorian style. Some rooms have wall-size bookcases and exposed brick fireplaces. Others have lace curtains and shutters. All have private baths and telephones. Lighted off-street parking is provided.

Open: year round **Accommodations:** 5 guest rooms with private baths **Meals:** continental-plus breakfast included; complimentary refreshments; restaurants nearby **Wheelchair access:** 1 room **Rates:** $70 to $225; 10% discount to National Trust members and National Trust Visa cardholders **Payment:** AmEx, Visa, MC, personal and traveler's checks **Restrictions:** no smoking; no pets **Activities:** front-porch swing, books, back decks, television

SHELLMONT BED AND BREAKFAST LODGE

821 Piedmont Avenue, N.E.
Atlanta, Georgia 30308
404/872-9290
404/872-5379 Fax
Proprietors: Ed and Debbie McCord

A Colonial Revival house designed by renowned architect W. T. Downing in 1891, the Shellmont was owned by a single family until 1982, when it was acquired by the McCords. A thorough restoration has returned to the house original paint colors, period wallpapers, and fancy painted finishes. Stained, leaded, and beveled glass abound. The house is particularly noted for its hand-carved woodwork (both inside and out) depicting seashells, ribbons, garlands, flowers, fruits, and mythical creatures. Rare stenciling in geometric patterns graces the Turkish Corner—a room filled with oriental furnishings and memorabilia. This commendable restoration has gained a National Register listing and city landmark status for the Shellmont. Guests enjoy complimentary beverages, chocolates, and breakfast. Furnishings—beds, armoires, chairs—are Victorian, as are some of the plants in the front and back yards.

Open: year round **Accommodations:** 5 guest rooms with private baths; 1 is a suite **Meals:** full breakfast included; complimentary beverages; restaurants nearby **Rates:** $79 to $129 **Payment:** AmEx, Visa, MC, DC, personal and traveler's checks **Restrictions:** children over 12 welcome; no smoking; no pets **Activities:** games, three verandas with rockers, Victorian gardens with fish pond

CLARKESVILLE

Nearby attractions: Chattahoochee National Forest, Tallulah Falls, Helen, Dahlonega, lakes, hiking, white-water rafting, boating, mountain biking, horseback riding, tennis, golfing, gold panning, antiques hunting

GLEN–ELLA SPRINGS INN
Bear Gap Road
Route 3, Box 3304
Clarkesville, Georgia 30523
706/754-7295
706/754-1560 Fax
Proprietors: Barrie and Bobby Aycock

Originally home to Cherokee Indians, the site of Glen–Ella Springs Inn was part of a 600-acre tract awarded in the 1830s to Glen and Ella Davidson as part of the great Cherokee land give-away. Built in 1876 as the Davidson's home, the frame building was expanded in 1890 and again in 1905 to take in paying guests. After decades of decline, the inn was renovated by the innkeepers in 1986, leaving original heart-pine walls, floors, and ceilings and stacked-stone fireplaces intact. All guest rooms, featuring antiques and locally handcrafted pieces, open to porches with rocking chairs. Seventeen acres contain perennial and herb gardens, swimming pool and sundeck, and walking and hiking trails. National Register-listed Glen-Ella Springs has received awards from the state for outstanding preservation and kudos from the *Atlanta Constitution* for its cuisine.

Open: year round **Accommodations:** 16 guest rooms with private baths; 2 are suites **Meals:** full breakfast included; complimentary refreshments; restaurant on premises **Wheelchair access:** 5 rooms **Rates:** $95 to $175; 10% discount to National Trust members and National Trust Visa cardholders, December through April, weekdays only **Payment:** AmEx, Visa, MC, personal and traveler's checks **Restrictions:** children over 6 welcome; smoking limited; no pets **Activities:** swimming pool, hiking trails, gardens

HOGANSVILLE

Nearby attractions: Callaway Gardens, Warm Springs, Franklin D. Roosevelt's Little White House, Atlanta, bicycling, swimming, golfing, tennis

FAIR OAKS INN AT THE PLANTATION
703 East Main Street
Hogansville, Georgia 30230
706/637-8828
Proprietors: Ken Hammock and Wayne Jones
Location: 30 miles south of Atlanta Airport

Fair Oaks was a plantation founded in 1835. Fair Oaks Inn is a charming, yellow-and-white Colonial Revival home that was built in 1901 on the site of the plantation's original structure. The house's facade is dominated by a front gable that protrudes over a second-story porch and a pediment that crowns the entry. Paired columns on pedestals support the wraparound porch. The house's Victorian influences are noted inside where fretwork and stained-glass transoms accentuate doorways. Nine fireplaces with period mantels warm spacious rooms. The house offers five guest accommodations; the master suite has a whirlpool tub and steam room. The Carriage House contains a suite overlooking the formal gardens and pools. A full breakfast is served in the formal dining room, while complimentary wine and cheese are served on the veranda or poolside in warm weather. Horseback riding, lake fishing, and tennis are nearby for guests' use.

Open: year round **Accommodations:** 6 guest rooms with private baths; 2 are suites **Meals:** full breakfast included; complimentary refreshments; restaurants nearby **Rates:** $65 to $125; 10% discount to National Trust members and National Trust Visa cardholders **Payment:** AmEx, Visa, MC, CB, DC, Discover, personal and traveler's checks **Restrictions:** children over 14 welcome; no smoking; no pets **Activities:** swimming pool, hot tub, croquet, tennis, lake fishing, horseback riding

---

MACON

Nearby attractions: historic district walking tours, museum houses, antiques hunting, Grand Opera House

1842 INN
353 College Street
Macon, Georgia 31201
912/741-1842 or 800/336-1842
912/741-1842 Fax
Proprietors: Phillip Jenkins and Richard Meils

Listed in the National Register of Historic Places, the 1842 Inn is a classic example of southern Greek Revival architecture, with its full-colonnaded facade that continues around the sides of the house. Public and guest rooms are in this antebellum mansion and an adjoining Victorian house that share a courtyard and garden. The 21 guest rooms, parlors, and library are tastefully designed with fine English antiques, oriental carpets, tapestries, and paintings. Some bedrooms feature canopied beds, working fireplaces, and whirlpool tubs. An array of services include concierge, nightly turn-down, and complimentary in-room breakfast. Guests are offered access to an exclusive private dining and health club. Equally suited to corporate retreats and romantic getaways, the 1842 Inn is a member of Historic Hotels of America and is the recipient of Mobil's four-diamond award.

Open: year round **Accommodations:** 21 guest rooms with private baths **Meals:** continental-plus breakfast included; full breakfast optional; complimentary refreshments; restaurants nearby **Wheelchair access:** yes **Rates:** $95 to $145; 10% discount to National Trust members and National Trust Visa cardholders **Payment:** AmEx, Visa, MC, personal check **Restrictions:** children over 12 welcome; smoking limited; no pets **Activities:** gift shop, courtyard and garden, whirlpool tubs

ST. SIMONS ISLAND
Nearby attractions: historic St. Simons and Sea Island, golfing, tennis, shopping

LITTLE ST. SIMONS ISLAND
P.O. Box 1078
St. Simons, Georgia 31522
912/638-7472
912/634-1811 Fax
Proprietor: Debbie McIntyre

Little St. Simons Island is a secluded, unspoiled, 10,000-acre barrier island along the Georgia coast. Purchased for its lumber in the early 1900s by the owner of the Eagle Pencil Company, Little St. Simons Island proved better suited to a hunting and bird-watching retreat. Still privately owned by the same family, the island now accommodates guests in four separate buildings. Built in 1917, the Hunting Lodge remains the heart of the resort, serving as its dining and social centers; it also offers two guest rooms filled with rustic furniture and family memorabilia. In the lobby is a massive fireplace and vintage bar. The other houses provide a variety of guest lodgings with fireplaces, porches, and decks in natural woodland settings. *Forbes, House Beautiful, Gourmet,* and *Atlanta Magazine* have praised Little St. Simons Island. With never more than 24 visitors sharing the island, it becomes a guest's private retreat.

Open: year round **Accommodations:** 11 guest rooms with private baths; 1 is a suite **Meals:** all meals and refreshments provided on premises **Wheelchair access:** 1 room **Rates:** $375 to $500; 10% discount to National Trust members and National Trust Visa cardholders June through September **Payment:** Visa, MC, personal and traveler's checks **Restrictions:** children over 6 welcome October through May, children of all ages welcome June through September; no smoking; no pets **Activities:** expertly guided fly-fishing and angling excursions, bird-watching, horseback riding, hiking, bicycling, canoeing, boating, shelling, swimming, sunbathing, interpretive natural history tours, private boat docking

---

SAUTEE

Nearby attractions: state parks, arts and community center with museum and gallery, historic district

STOVALL HOUSE
1526 Highway 225 North
Sautee, Georgia 30571
706/878-3355
Proprietor: Hamilton Schwartz
Location: 5 miles southeast of Helen, 1 1/2 miles north of Highway 17

Constructed in 1837, the Stovall House was originally a one-story farmhouse with two rooms, each with a fireplace, on either side of a central passage known as a dogtrot hallway. The doors and mantels are made of black walnut taken from the property. William I. Stovall bought the house in 1893, making numerous changes that included the addition of three dormers to create a second floor and a wing to house the dining room and kitchen. Restored as an inn by the current owner in 1983, the Stovall House has been recognized by the Georgia Trust for Historic Preservation and by the Georgia Mountain Regional Planning Commission. Wall stenciling, handmade curtains, family antiques, and a serene mountain setting combine to put guests at their ease. The house, situated on a knoll surrounded by 26 acres of farmland, provides views of the valley and mountains in all directions.

Open: year round **Accommodations:** 5 guest rooms with private baths **Meals:** continental breakfast included; restaurant on premises serves dinner **Wheelchair access:** limited **Rates:** $45 single to $75 double; 10% discount offered to National Trust members and National Trust Visa cardholders **Payment:** Visa, MC, personal and traveler's checks **Restrictions:** smoking limited **Activities:** walking, bird-watching, boccie

SAVANNAH

Nearby attractions: historic district, River Street, City Market, museums, galleries, beach, riverfront, Fort Pulaski, Savannah Wildlife Refuge, tennis, golfing, deep-sea fishing, antiques hunting

BALLASTONE INN AND TOWNHOUSE
14 East Oglethorpe Avenue
Savannah, Georgia 31401
912/236-1484 or 800/822-4553
912/236-4626 Fax
Proprietors: Richard F. Carlson and Timothy C. Hargus

Built in 1835 for Major George Anderson, who would serve as commanding officer at Fort McAllister when it was attacked by General Sherman, this lovely townhouse was expanded in 1892. Preston Gibbons, prominent Boston architect, designed the addition for Captain Henry Blun, a former Confederate officer and blockade runner. Ballastone Inn is a showplace for the way Savannah once lived. Guest rooms are decorated in authentic colors with fabrics and wall coverings complementing original architectural motifs. Rice poster and canopy beds, marble-topped tables and dressers, comfortable love seats, and wing chairs provide a genteel elegance. Guests are pampered with plush robes, fresh fruit, chocolates, and turn-down and concierge services. Ballastone Inn, in the heart of the historic district, has been recommended by *Brides Magazine* and *Conde Nast Traveler.*

Open: year round **Accommodations:** 22 guest rooms with private baths; 7 are suites **Meals:** continental breakfast included; complimentary beverages; restaurants nearby **Wheelchair access:** guest rooms and public rooms **Rates:** $95 to $200; 10% discount offered to National Trust members and National Trust Visa cardholders **Payment:** AmEx, Visa, MC, personal check **Restrictions:** children over 12 welcome; small pets allowed on garden level **Activities:** landscaped courtyard, library, television with VCR, full service-bar, fireplaces, whirlpool tubs

FOLEY HOUSE INN
14 West Hull Street
Savannah, Georgia 31401
912/232-6622 or 800/647-3708
Proprietors: Mark A. Moore and Inge Svensson Moore

Two Savannah townhouses combine to create the Foley House Inn in the historic district of the city. Built in 1863 and 1896, the houses have been meticulously restored by master artisans. Each guest room is a seamless blend of traditional furnishings and contemporary pleasures. Antique furniture, silver, rugs, and engravings selected from around the world enhance rooms equipped with working fireplaces, whirlpool baths, and color televisions able to play the many selections in the inn's film library. Breakfast is served in the privacy of guest rooms, in the sunny courtyard, or in the newly expanded lounge. Wine, evening cordials, and tea are served daily in the parlor. Evening turn-down, shoeshine, and concierge services are standard at Foley House, which has been rated as one of the 10 most romantic inns by *Vacations* magazine.

Open: year round **Accommodations:** 19 guest rooms with private baths **Meals:** continental-plus breakfast included; complimentary refreshments; restaurants nearby **Rates:** $85 to $190; 10% discount to National Trust members and National Trust Visa cardholders **Payment:** AmEx, Visa, MC, personal and traveler's checks **Restrictions:** smoking limited; no pets **Activities:** golf or tennis by arrangement

THE GASTONIAN
220 East Gaston Street
Savannah, Georgia 31401
912/232-2869 or 800/322-6603
912/232-0710 Fax
Proprietors: Hugh and Roberta Lineberger

The Gastonian Inn combines two stately 1868 homes, one built for a prosperous insurance broker and the other for an affluent grocer. A costly restoration in 1985 helped the inn preserve its exemplary handcrafted design, evident in heart-of-pine floors, decorative moldings, brasses, and high ceilings. Each of the 13 guest rooms and suites has its own decorative theme, and all are furnished with English antiques, Persian rugs, whirlpool baths, and operating fireplaces. The Gastonian, in the middle of Savannah's internationally famous historic district, maintains an intimate atmosphere, treating guests with such amenities as concierge and turn-down service, nightly cordials and sweets, and a full southern breakfast. The hotel has earned Mobil four-star and AAA four-diamond ratings.

Open: year round **Accommodations:** 13 guest rooms with private baths; 2 are suites **Meals:** full breakfast included; complimentary refreshments; restaurants nearby **Wheelchair access:** 1 guest room **Rates:** $115 to $275 **Payment:** AmEx, Visa, MC, personal and traveler's checks **Restrictions:** children over 12 welcome; no smoking; no pets **Activities:** sundeck with hot tub

LION'S HEAD INN
120 East Gaston Street
Savannah, Georgia 31401
912/232-4580
Proprietor: Christy Dell'Orco

This three-story 9000-square-foot townhouse, built in 1883 for the William Wade family, is traditionally styled with dentils at roof and porch cornices and gently arched windows. A wraparound porch is supported by filigreed wrought-iron columns and railings. The fine materials used in the house's construction have been preserved: hand-carved marble mantels, detailed wood and plaster moldings, hardwood floors, a Waterford crystal chandelier in the dining room, and a French bronze chandelier in the parlor. Guest rooms are furnished with nineteenth-century American Federal antiques, king- and queen-size four-poster beds, fireplaces, cable television, and telephones. Guests are welcome in the parlor, library, dining room, and courtyard. The innkeeper serves a traditional English tea, plus wine and cheese each afternoon in the parlor or on the veranda. The elegant Lion's Head Inn has been featured in *Country Inns*.

Open: year round **Accommodations:** 6 guest rooms with private baths; 2 are suites **Meals:** continental-plus breakfast included; complimentary refreshments; restaurants nearby **Wheelchair access:** 1 room **Rates:** $85 to $150; 10% discount to National Trust members and National Trust Visa cardholders **Payment:** AmEx, Visa, MC, personal and traveler's checks **Restrictions:** no smoking; no pets **Activities:** house tours

SENOIA

Nearby attractions: Warm Springs, Callaway Gardens and Butterfly Center, driving tour of 113 places listed in the National Register, museums, tennis, golfing, antiques hunting, crafts shops, day trips to Atlanta

THE VERANDA
252 Seavy Street
Box 177
Senoia, Georgia 30276-0177
404/599-3905
404/599-0806 Fax
Proprietors: Jan and Bobby Boal
Location: 30 miles south of Atlanta airport

The Veranda, formerly known as the Hollberg Hotel, is a 1906 neoclassical building constructed of heart of pine, its wraparound porch supported by grand columns. The restored property is listed in the National Register of Historic Places. Among the hotel's many distinguished guests have been statesman William Jennings Bryan and *Gone With the Wind* author Margaret Mitchell, who interviewed Civil War veterans during their annual conventions here. The bookcases in the parlor once graced President McKinley's Ohio law offices. All nine guest rooms contain special touches, such as handmade quilts and antique armoires. Guests enjoy hearty complimentary breakfasts; delicious dinners are served by reservation. A collection of old and new kaleidoscopes, a 1930 Wurlitzer player piano, and an early twentieth-century pump organ provide entertainment. The picturesque town of Senoia was the setting for the films *Fried Green Tomatoes* and *The War.*

Open: year round **Accommodations:** 9 guest rooms with private baths **Meals:** full breakfast included; five-course candlelit dinner on premises by reservation; restaurants nearby **Wheelchair access:** 2 guest rooms and public rooms **Rates:** $90 to $110 **Payment:** AmEx, Visa, MC, personal and traveler's checks **Restrictions:** children must be supervised by parents **Activities:** bird-watching, nature walks, player piano and pump organ, gift shop, kaleidoscope collection

THOMASVILLE

Nearby attractions: plantation and house tours, historic district, Paradise Park, Rose Test Gardens, Birdsong Nature Center, Gulf coast, golfing, crafts shops, antiques hunting, greyhound racing

EVANS HOUSE BED AND BREAKFAST
725 South Hansell Street
Thomasville, Georgia 31792
912/226-1343 or 800/344-4717
912/226-0653 Fax
Proprietors: John and Lee Puskar

Located in the Parkfront Historic District, directly across from 27-acre Paradise Park, this late Victorian house is in a transitional style, combining the asymmetry of the Victorian era with the simpler formality of the emerging Neoclassical style. Robert R. Evans built the house for his family in 1898. The second story was added a few years later, then, after suffering the effects of a fire in 1908, the house was again remodeled. Four individually decorated guest rooms are now available, each with cozy seating area, private bath, and ceiling fan. The bedrooms, entrance hall, library, dining room, and parlor are furnished with antiques and contemporary pieces. Guests are served a full breakfast. Turn-down service and complimentary bicycles are available. Evans House is ideal for corporate retreats, offering all necessary amenities and corporate rates.

Open: year round **Accommodations:** 4 guest rooms with private baths; 1 is a suite **Meals:** full breakfast included; complimentary refreshments; restaurants nearby **Rates:** $70 to $115 **Payment:** personal and traveler's checks **Restrictions:** children over 12 welcome; no smoking; small pets acceptable, please inquire **Activities:** bicycling

SUSINA PLANTATION INN
1420 Meridian Road
Route 3, Box 1010
Thomasville, Georgia 31792
912/377-9644
Proprietor: Anne-Marie Walker

Susina Plantation Inn is located on 115 acres of lawns and woodlands in the heart of plantation country. Built in 1841 by the noted Greek Revival artichtect John Wind, the house is graced by four columns with Ionic capitals supporting its central pediment. The interior features a graceful flying staircase. Spacious, antiques-appointed dining and drawing rooms and screened verandas provide comfortable areas for relaxation. Eight elegant guest rooms offer four-poster beds and private baths with claw-foot tubs. This gracious residence stands among tremendous oaks and magnolias, atop the rolling Red Hills of Georgia, known as a center of quail, deer, turkey, and duck hunting.

Open: year round **Accommodations:** 8 guest rooms with private baths **Meals:** full breakfast and 5-course dinner included; restaurants nearby **Rates:** $175 **Payment:** personal and traveler's checks **Restrictions:** no smoking **Activities:** swimming pool, fishing pond, tennis court, walking and jogging trails

THOMSON
Nearby attractions: Clark Hill Lake; Augusta; Masters Golf Tournament; Belle Meade Fox Hunt; historic house tours; golfing; tennis; hunting; fishing; water sports; horseback riding; historic towns of Wrightsborough, Madison, Washington, and Sparta

1810 WEST INN
254 North Seymour Drive, N.W.
Thomson, Georgia 30824
706/595-3156
Proprietor: Virginia B. White
Location: 5 miles west of Thomson

Built in 1810, this house, first owned by Thomas Butler West, is locally referred to as a Piedmont Plains plantation style, its handsome façade symmetrical, windows five-ranked. It is constructed entirely of heart of pine. Attached to this building are four dependencies, which give the inn a comfortable rambling ambience, each room reflecting colonial touches. The inn contains five bed-rooms. A restored nineteenth-century country house on the property, known as Hobbs' House, contains four bedrooms and porches overlooking 11 acres dotted with magnolias, cedars, pecan trees, camellias, and a peacock. Guests are invited to enjoy the inn's informal country kitchen and the large breezy screened veranda, from which are visible a tobacco barn and several early tenant houses currently being renovated. Country club privileges are available for golf and tennis enthusiasts. The 1810 West Inn has been featured in *Country Inns* magazine.

Open: year round **Accommodations:** 10 guest rooms with private baths; 3 are suites **Meals:** continental-plus breakfast included; restaurants nearby **Rates:** $55 to $79; 10% discount to National Trust members and National Trust Visa cardholders **Payment:** AmEx, Visa, MC, Discover, personal and traveler's checks **Restrictions:** children over 12 welcome; no smoking; no pets **Activities:** hiking, horseshoe pitching, volleyball, croquet

HAWAII

Poipu, Kauai

Lahaina, Maui

POIPU BEACH, KAUAI

Nearby attractions: Spouting Horn,
Waimea Canyon, Na Pali Coast, Fern
Grotto, Old Koloa Town, beach, water
sports, free tennis and pool at neighboring
club, golfing, sightseeing tours by helicop-
ter and boat

POIPU BED AND BREAKFAST INN
2720 Hoonani Road
Poipu Beach, Kauai, Hawaii 96756-9635
808/742-1146 or 800/552-0095 or 800/22POIPU (800/227-6478)
808/742-6842 Fax
Proprietor: Dotti Cichon
Location: 13 miles south of Lihue Airport

This simple, yet elegant wooden house was built in 1933 for a former Kauai
County mayor and was moved to its present site in 1969. Its unique all-fir interior
and beautiful hand-hewn arch in the living room qualify it as an excellent example
of Hawaiian plantation-style architecture. The sympathetically added lanais
(porches) and 1987 restoration have won awards, including the Hawaii Visitors
Bureau's prestigious Kahili Award and a Great American Home Award from the

National Trust. Fur-
nished with white
wicker, pine antiques,
tropical prints, and an
authentic carousel
horse in each room,
Poipu Bed and Break-
fast Inn offers pamper-
ing amenities such as
robes, beach towels,
fine toiletries, cool

tropical drinks, free videos, concierge services, and an exotic garden where guests can often pick their breakfast fruit fresh from the trees. Guest rooms provide beautiful ocean or garden views.

Open: year round **Accommodations:** 9 rooms with private baths; 2 are suites **Meals:** continental-plus breakfast included; complimentary refreshments; restaurants nearby **Wheelchair access:** 1 suite, gathering room, and breakfast area **Rates:** $110 to $195; weekly discounts; 10% discount offered to National Trust members or National Trust Visa cardholders **Payment:** AmEx, Visa, MC, CB, DC, Discover, personal and traveler's checks **Restrictions:** no smoking; no pets; guests are expected to observe local custom of removing shoes before entering **Activities:** afternoon tea on lanai, free popcorn and videos on in-room VCR, library, croquet, Trivial Pursuit and Scrabble in the evening

LAHAINA, MAUI

Nearby attractions: Old Lahaina Town historical walks, dining, luaus, antiques hunting, shopping, art galleries, fine dining, sailing, snorkeling, whale watching

LAHAINA INN
127 Lahainaluna Road
Lahaina, Maui, Hawaii 96761-1502
808/661-0577 or 800/669-3444
808/667-9480 Fax
Proprietors: Rick and Tyler Ralston

The building now known as the Lahaina Inn was built by Tomezo Masuda in 1938 for his Maui Trading Company, a general merchandise store. It was a popular gathering place for servicemen stationed on Maui during World War II. Sold in 1949, the building subsequently changed hands several times and suffered subdivision and a disastrous fire in the 1960s. Rick Ralston bought the neglected building in 1986 and began transforming it into a small luxury inn that has been called "One of the Best Country Inns" by *Glamour*. Twelve individually appointed guest rooms present vignettes of historic Hawaii through rich fabrics and wall coverings, antique leaded-glass lamps, lace curtains, oriental carpets, and antique furnishings. The property is also home to the innkeeper's antiques shop, as well as David Paul's Lahaina Grill, voted "Best Maui Restaurant" by the readers of *Honolulu* magazine in 1994 and 1995.

Open: year round **Accommodations:** 12 guest rooms with private baths; 3 are suites **Meals:** continental breakfast included; restaurant on premises; restaurants nearby **Rates:** $89 to $129; 10% discount to National Trust members and National Trust Visa cardholders **Payment:** AmEx, Visa, MC, Discover, personal and traveler's checks **Restrictions:** children over 15 welcome; no smoking; no pets **Activities:** fine dining, antiques shopping, whale-watching from porches

IDAHO

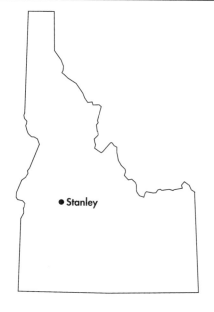

STANLEY

Nearby attractions: Centennial State Park, Sawtooth National Recreation Area, Salmon River, Sun Valley, hiking, camping, fishing, mountain lakes with endangered salmon, fish hatchery, ghost towns, white-water rafting and canoeing, mountain biking, shopping

IDAHO ROCKY MOUNTAIN RANCH
H.C. 64, Box 9934
Stanley, Idaho 83278
208/774-3544
Proprietors: Bill and Jeana Leavell

In 1930, carpenters handcrafted the lodge and surrounding cabins of the Idaho Rocky Mountain Ranch from native lodgepole pines. At that time it was an invitation-only guest ranch. Now open to the public, cozy lodge rooms and authentic duplex log cabins are handsomely decorated with log furniture fashioned by early craftsmen. Massive rock fireplaces warm the public rooms in the lodge as well as each log cabin. All accommodations provide private baths. The ranch is nestled in the heart of the Sawtooth National Recreation Area, surrounded by the Sawtooth and White Cloud mountain ranges of central Idaho. Encircling the ranch are hundreds of miles of trails through meadows and up mountains to trout-filled lakes. Full breakfasts and dinners can be provided. The dining room specializes in country cuisine featuring fresh Idaho trout, lamb, steaks, and vegetarian entrees.

Open: June 1 to September 21 **Accommodations:** 21 guest rooms with private baths; 17 are in log cabins **Meals:** full breakfast and dinner included on modified American Plan (MAP); picnic baskets available; restaurants nearby **Rates:** $130 to $215 MAP **Payment:** Visa, MC, Discover, personal and traveler's check **Restrictions:** no smoking; no pets **Activities:** horseback riding, natural hot springs swimming pool, hiking, walking, fishing, wildlife watching, rock climbing, horseshoes, volleyball, mountain biking

ILLINOIS

EVANSTON

Nearby attractions: cultural and educational activities at Northwestern University, Chicago sightseeing, lakefront parks

THE HOMESTEAD
1625 Hinman Avenue
Evanston, Illinois 60201
708/475-3300
Proprietor: David Reynolds

Evanston architect Philip Danielson designed and built The Homestead in 1927 as a colonial-style residence and hotel. The Depression and subsequent war years necessitated that he and his wife, Ruby, a noted interior decorator, run the hotel themselves. Under their 30-year direction, the Homestead reigned as one of Evanston's premier residences and hotels. Mrs. Herbert Hoover and Sinclair Lewis were among its guests. Lewis included reflections of his Homestead experiences in *Work of Art*, published two years after his visit. The Homestead lies close to Lake Michigan, Northwestern University, and downtown Evanston, and borders Evanston's historic lakeshore district. Its hotel rooms and furnished monthly apartments afford a quiet retreat in a busy metropolitan area.

Open: year round **Accommodations:** 35 guest rooms, 55 apartments, all with private baths **Meals:** complimentary morning coffee; restaurant on premises for dinner; restaurants nearby **Rates:** $65 to $80 **Payment:** personal and traveler's checks **Restrictions:** smoking limited; no pets

JERSEYVILLE

Nearby attractions: Center for American Archaeology, antiques hunting, golfing, tennis

THE HOMERIDGE BED AND BREAKFAST
1470 North State Street
Jerseyville, Illinois 62052
618/498-3442
Proprietors: Sue and Howard Landon
Location: 1 mile north of Jerseyville on Route 267

The Homeridge is a 14-room Italianate structure with deep eaves, decorative brackets, and a third-story, square cupola. It was built in 1867 by Cornelius B. Fisher. Senator Theodore S. Chapman purchased the home in 1891 and it remained in the Chapman family until 1960. Today, as a bed and breakfast, The Homeridge retains its original woodwork, 12-foot-high ceilings, crown molding, and elegant, hand-carved, curved stairway. The inn offers a choice of king-size, twin, or antique double beds. Each room, with its expansive view of the countryside, has a private bath. Favorite places to relax include the pillared front porch and private swimming pool.

Open: year round **Accommodations:** 4 guest rooms with private baths **Meals:** full breakfast included; complimentary refreshments; restaurants nearby **Rates:** $65 to $75; 10% discount to National Trust members and National Trust Visa cardholders **Payment:** Visa, MC, personal and traveler's checks **Restrictions:** children over 14 welcome; no smoking; no pets **Activities:** swimming pool, 20 acres for hiking, walking, jogging, and cross-country skiing

---

PEKIN

Nearby attractions: Illinois River, Dirksen Congressional Center, University of Illinois Medical School, Par-a-dice Riverboat Gambling, golfing, fishing

HERGET HOUSE BED AND BREAKFAST
420 Washington Street
Pekin, Illinois 61554
309/353-4025
Proprietor: Richard T. Walsh

Listed in the National Register of Historic Places, this Neoclassical home was built in 1912, in an era known in England as Edwardian. Accordingly, the house is furnished in an elegant English country style. Bedrooms—named for King Edward himself and some of his contemporaries—feature antiques, four-poster or sleigh beds, fine linens, down comforters and pillows, and writing desks. Guests are invited to have breakfast on the sunporch, take tea in the music room, relax in the living room, or browse through an eclectic selection of books. Herget House, with its four grand columns supporting a large trianular pediment, commands its setting on an acre of grounds. An outdoor swimming pool and off-street parking are available.

Open: year round **Accommodations:** 5 guest rooms (4 have private baths); 1 is a suite **Meals:** full breakfast included; restaurants nearby **Rates:** $85 to $100; 10% discount to National Trust members **Payment:** personal check **Restrictions:** no smoking; no pets (resident cats, dog, and rabbit) **Activities:** swimming pool, reading

---

WATERLOO

Nearby attractions: historic district, St. Louis, Mississippi River, Cahokia Mounds World Heritage Site, Waterloo Winery, Illinois Caverns, Fort de Chartres site, Prairie du Rocher Historic Village, seasonal festivals

SENATOR RICKERT RESIDENCE BED AND BREAKFAST
216 East Third Street
Waterloo, Illinois 62298
618/939-8242
Proprietors: Ed and Kathi Weilbacher

Located in Waterloo's historic district, this bed and breakfast was constructed in 1866 as a one-story brick house. Senator Joseph Rickert enlarged the house in 1897 to its present size. Fascinated with the French Second Empire style of architecture, he added a mansard roof, tower, widow's walk, and gingerbread detailing. The house is currently undergoing restoration and offers one guest suite. The spacious bedroom boasts antiques once owned by the senator's wife's family. Through pocket doors, the bedroom opens to a bright sitting room featuring a three-piece parlor set. The large bath includes a footed tub with oak rail. The country kitchen, formal dining room, and brick patio are available for enjoying full breakfasts that feature house specialties such as spinach and sausage strata.

Open: year round **Accommodations:** 1 guest suite with private bath **Meals:** full breakfast included; restaurants nearby **Rate:** $75; 10% discount offered to National Trust members and National Trust Visa cardholders **Payment:** Visa, MC **Restrictions:** no smoking; no pets

INDIANA

CENTERVILLE

Nearby attractions: historic district, museums, walking tours, antiques hunting at world's largest antiques mall, hiking, golfing, canoeing, fishing, farm activities

HISTORIC LANTZ HOUSE INN
214 National Road West
Centerville, Indiana 47330
317/855-2936 or 800/495-2689
317/855-2864 Fax
Proprietor: Marcia Hoyt

The original portion of Lantz House was built in 1823 by Israel Abrahams along the bustling National Road. In 1835, a man named Lantz added a large Federal-

style brick house to the front of the smaller house and a commercial space for his wagon shop next door. The two buildings are connected by one of Centerville's famous archways—a one-story, arched passage separating two buildings, with a room above connecting the two. As an intimate inn today, the house boasts original hardwood floors and fireplaces with mantels. Antiques add to the period decor. Each of the four comforable guest rooms has a private bath. Art, music, and books are found throughout the inn for guests' enjoyment. Surrounded by serene grounds and gardens, the inn is listed in the National Register of Historic Places.

Open: year round **Accommodations:** 4 guest rooms with private baths **Meals:** full breakfast included; complimentary refreshments; restaurants nearby **Rates:** $68.50 to $90; 10% discount to National Trust members and National Trust Visa cardholders **Payment:** Visa, MC, personal and traveler's checks **Restrictions:** children welcome by prior arrangement; no smoking; no pets **Activities:** garden and yard, television and VCR, games, cards, music

COLUMBUS

Nearby attractions: historical and contemporary architecture tours, outlet shops, golfing, hiking, walking and bicycling trails

COLUMBUS INN BED AND BREAKFAST
445 Fifth Street
Columbus, Indiana 47201
812/378-4289
812/378-4289 Fax
Innkeeper: Paul A. Staublin

The Columbus Inn was built in 1895 as the Columbus City Hall, the hub of this scenic small town for many years. The building housed public offices, a town library, a market house, and an auditorium for everything from dances to basketball and poultry shows. After standing empty for several years, this National Register building has been transformed into the Columbus Inn, the only historic lodging in downtown Columbus. Guest rooms are furnished with reproduction furnishings and are decorated with bright, bold wall coverings and paint schemes. Public rooms include the elegant lobby, lounges, and a library. In the heart of downtown, the Columbus Inn has meeting rooms fully equipped for business functions.

Open: year round **Accommodations:** 34 guest rooms with private baths; 5 are suites **Meals:** full breakfast included; complimentary refreshments; lunch and dinner for groups by reservation; restaurants nearby **Wheelchair access:** yes **Rates:** $89 to $225; 10% discount to National Trust members and National Trust Visa cardholders **Payment:** AmEx, Visa, MC, CB, DC, Discover, personal and traveler's checks **Restrictions:** smoking limited; no pets **Activities:** library

CORYDON

Nearby attractions: Indiana's first state capitol, historic downtown, scenic railroad tour, buffalo farm, Hayswood Nature Reserve, Civil War battleground, Squire Boone Caverns, Wyandotte Caves, Marengo Cave, golfing, swimming, tennis

KINTNER HOUSE INN

101 South Capitol Avenue
Corydon, Indiana 47112
812/738-2020
812/738-7430 Fax
Proprietor: Blaine H. Wiseman   **Innkeeper:** Mary Jane Bridgewater

In July 1873, Jacob Kintner opened the doors of the Kintner House as Corydon's finest hotel. Kintner's daughter operated the hotel until 1922, after which it fell into disrepair. The current owners restored the three-story brick Italianate building according to the Secretary's Standards for Rehabiliation, replacing the front porch and refinishing original floors where possible. In the hallways carpenters removed carpeting, two layers of vinyl, two layers of plywood, and several coats of paint to discover the original floors, which were patterned with alternating boards of light chestnut and dark walnut woods. The balusters in the sweeping staircase reveal the same pattern of carved light and dark woods. The inn now offers 15 individually decorated guest rooms. All rooms provide private baths, telephones, cable television, and antique furnishings. Five rooms have fireplaces.

Open: year round **Accommodations:** 15 guest rooms with private baths **Meals:** full breakfast included; complimentary refreshments; restaurants nearby **Wheelchair access:** yes **Rates:** $39 to $89 **Payment:** AmEx, Visa, MC, DC, Discover, personal and traveler's checks **Restrictions:** no smoking; no pets **Activities:** front porch swings, organ, piano, board games

EVANSVILLE

Nearby attractions: historic district, Evansville Museum, University of Evansville, University of Southern Indiana, riverside walking and jogging paths, riverboat casino, horse racing, convention center, tennis

RIVER'S INN BED AND BREAKFAST
414 S.E. Riverside Drive
Evansville, Indiana 47713
812/428-7777 or 800/797-7990
812/421-2902 Fax
Proprietors: Marsha and Allan Trockman

Built in 1866, this three-story Italianate house contains the innkeeper's large collection of antiques and collectibles. The furnishings are enhanced by stained glass, Battenburg lace, fine linens, crystal, art, and oriental rugs. Each guest room offers an antique Victorian bed with a new, comfortable mattress. Easy chairs, a luggage rack, good reading lights, extra pillows, cable television, and a private-line telephone are found in each room. Both third-floor rooms have access to balconies overlooking the Ohio river and the garden, as well as a private exterior staircase. An ample breakfast may feature house specialties such as Johnny Walker potato pie, cornbread and apple casserole, or fresh asparagus quiche. Private, off-street parking is available.

Open: year round **Accommodations:** 5 guest rooms with private baths **Meals:** full breakfast included; complimentary refreshments; restaurants nearby **Rates:** $85 to $135; 10% discount to National Trust members and National Trust Visa cardholders **Payment:** AmEx, Visa, MC, personal and traveler's checks **Restrictions:** children over 15 welcome; no smoking; no pets

HUNTINGTON

Nearby attractions: Forks of the Wabash Historic Park, Dan Quayle Center and Museum, walking tours, chief Richardville House, Sunken Gardens, Merillat Center for the Arts, Huntington College, nature trails, lake, swimming, boating, cross-country skiing, hiking, golfing, tennis, antiques hunting

PURVIANCE HOUSE BED AND BREAKFAST

326 South Jefferson Street
Huntington, Indiana 46750
219/356-4218 or 219/356-9215
Proprietors: Robert and Jean Gernand

Listed in the National Register of Historic Places, this Italianate house was built in 1859 by Samuel Purviance, a prominent early resident of Huntington who was noted for his kind deeds. Special architectural features remain and have been restored, including a winding cherry staircase, interior window shutters, ornate ceiling designs, unique parquet floors, and four tiled fireplaces. The house is decorated with period furnishings. Guests can choose from five bedrooms and are welcome in the gold parlor with television and well-stocked bookshelves. A full breakfast is served in the dining room. Special dinners and luncheons can be arranged for groups or small parties. The parlors are also available for weddings, meetings, retreats, or workshops.

Open: year round **Accommodations:** 5 guest rooms (2 have private baths) **Meals:** full breakfast included; complimentary refreshments; restaurants nearby **Wheelchair access:** yes **Rates:** $35 to $75; 10% discount to National Trust members and National Trust Visa cardholders **Payment:** Visa, MC, Discover, personal check **Restrictions:** no smoking; no pets **Activities:** television, card and board games, neighborhood strolls and roller-blading

---

MADISON

Nearby attractions: historic district, house tours, Ohio River walk, Clifty Falls State Park, antiques hunting

SCHUSSLER HOUSE BED AND BREAKFAST

514 Jefferson Street
Madison, Indiana 47250
812/273-2068 or 800/392-1931
Proprietors: Judy and Bill Gilbert

In 1849 physician Charles Schussler had this combination home and office built in a blend of the popular Federal and Greek Revival architectural styles. Three spacious, elegantly appointed guest rooms feature antique and reproduction furniture, coordinating fabrics and wall coverings, reading areas, and private baths. Guests may also relax in the front parlor with soft music and an abundance of reading materials. A full breakfast is served in the sun-filled dining room and may feature such treats as apple flan or caramel-glazed French toast. Additional amenities include afternoon refreshments and evening turn-down service. The Ohio River is within walking distance of Schussler House.

Open: year round **Accommodations:** 3 guest rooms with private baths **Meals:** full breakfast included; complimentary refreshments; restaurants nearby **Rates:** $75 to $120; 10% discount to National Trust members and National Trust Visa cardholders **Payment:** Visa, MC, personal and traveler's checks **Restrictions:** children over 12 welcome; no smoking; no pets

---

PERU

Nearby attractions: Miami County Museum; International Circus Hall of Fame; Cole Porter home and burial site; antiques hunting; golfing; tennis; Mississinewa Reservoir for boating, fishing, hiking, picnicking, and water skiing

ROSEWOOD MANSION INN
54 North Hood Street
Peru, Indiana 46970
317/472-7151
317/472-5575 Fax
Proprietors: Dave and Lynn Hausner

Rosewood Mansion Inn, built in 1872 by Elbert Shirk, combines elements of style from the Federal period—sidelights, fanlight, pedimented dormers—and those of the Victorian era—tower, porte cochere, asymmetry, stained glass. Inside is a three-story staircase, oak-paneled library, and a Victorian parlor. The mansion has 19 rooms, including 8 bedrooms, each with private bath. A full breakfast is

served in the unique oval dining room. Located near Peru's downtown area, Rosewood Mansion Inn is perfectly suited to romantic and corporate retreats alike.

Open: year round **Accommodations:** 8 guest rooms with private baths; 4 are suites **Meals:** full breakfast included; complimentary refreshments; restaurants nearby **Rates:** $70 to $85; 10% discount to National Trust members and National Trust Visa cardholders **Payment:** AmEx, Visa, MC, Discover, personal and traveler's checks **Restrictions:** smoking restricted; no pets **Activities:** gardens

SOUTH BEND

Nearby attractions: Oliver House Museum (Copshaholm), University of Notre Dame, St. Mary's College, Studebaker Museum, Tippecanoe Place, carriage rides in historic district

QUEEN ANNE INN
420 West Washington Street
South Bend, Indiana 46601
219/234-5959 or 800/582-2379
Proprietors: Robert and Pauline Medhurst

Samuel Good, a South Bend native who made his fortune in the gold rush, built this home in 1893, mixing elements of the Queen Anne and neoclassical styles. Good's contractor also built the nearby Frank Lloyd Wright house, the influence of which is particularly evident in the inn library's leaded-glass bookcase. Listed in the National Register of Historic Places, the 17-room home reflects Good's prominence in the community, attested to by oak and maple paneling, hand-painted silk wallcovering, crystal chandeliers, and crown moldings. Guest rooms feature antique furnishings and reproduction beds in sleigh, Jenny Lind, and brass styles. One room hides Samuel Good's wall safe behind a mirror, and another has a cozy window seat. Guests are invited to relax in front of the fireplace in the parlor, in the library, or on the wraparound porch.

Open: year round **Accommodations:** 6 guest rooms with private baths; 2 are suites **Meals:** full breakfast included; complimentary refreshments; restaurants nearby **Rates:** $70 to $105 **Payment:** AmEx, Visa, MC, personal and traveler's checks **Restrictions:** no smoking; no pets **Activities:** front porch sitting, library, in-room television, VCR and videotapes, games

IOWA

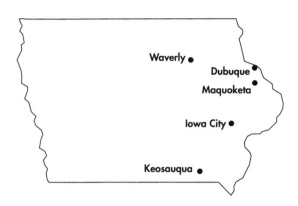

DUBUQUE

Nearby attractions: five historic districts, Mississippi River paddlewheel cruises, Cable Car Square, Woodward Riverboat Museum, National Rivers Hall of Fame, gambling, dog track, parks, walking trails, golfing, downhill and cross-country skiing

RICHARDS HOUSE
1492 Locust Street
Dubuque, Iowa 52001
319/557-1492
Proprietor: David C. Stuart

Constructed in 1883 by manu-facturer and financier B. B. Richards, this four-story Stick Style house with Eastlake effects is one of the finest and most original homes in Dubuque. Occupied by the same family until 1989, Richards House fea-tures nearly ninety stained-glass windows, eight ornate fireplaces, seven types of woodwork, ten patterns of embossed wallcoverings, original chandeliers, hand-painted tiles, and elaborate built-in cupboards. Guest rooms are furnished with period antiques. Most have concealed television sets and telephones, and working fireplaces. Bathrooms feature original fixtures. Queen-size beds and air condi-tioning are standard. Guests are served a full breakfast by the fireplace in the dining room, surrounded by pocket doors with stained-glass inserts, a bay window, and ornate fretwork. A music room with grand piano is open to guests at this National Register–listed inn.

Open: year round **Accommodations:** 6 guest rooms (4 have private baths); 1 is a suite **Meals:** full breakfast included; complimentary refreshments; restaurants nearby **Rates:** $40 to $95; 10% discount to National Trust members and National Trust Visa cardholders **Payment:** AmEx, Visa, MC, CB, DC, Discover, personal and traveler's checks **Restrictions:** smoking limited

IOWA CITY

Nearby attractions: University of Iowa, Kinnick Stadium, MacBride Museum, University of Iowa Art Museum, Amana Colonies German village, Amish community of Kalona, city park, Herbert Hoover birthplace and library

HAVERKAMPS LINN STREET HOMESTAY BED AND BREAKFAST
619 North Linn Street
Iowa City, Iowa 52245
319/337-4363
Proprietors: Clarence and Dorothy Haverkamp

John Koza emigrated from Czechoslovakia in 1868 when he was 19. His future wife, Barbara, had emigrated in 1857 at the age of 4. After they were married, they built this handsome house on North Linn Street in 1907. The house's design owes much to the Prairie style, evident in its hipped roof with widely overhanging eaves and massive square porch supports. Original floor plans and building contracts and old photographs indicate that little has been changed inside or out during the house's nearly 90 years and six family changes. Today's bed and breakfast welcomes children and, in fact, offers a crib for small visitors. Wake-up coffee is offered along with a full breakfast. Off-street parking is available.

Open: year round **Accommodations:** 3 guest rooms share a bath **Meals:** full breakfast included; restaurants nearby **Rates:** $30 to $45; 10% discount to National Trust members

and National Trust Visa cardholders **Payment:** personal and traveler's checks **Restrictions:** no smoking; no pets **Activities:** television, reading, card games

KEOSAUQUA

Nearby attractions: Villages of Van Buren, antiques hunting, crafts shops, National Register historic districts, Lacey State Park, hiking, Des Moines River, canoeing, fishing, Mormon Trail, Amish and Mennonite communities

HOTEL MANNING

100 Van Buren Street
Keosauqua, Iowa 52565
319/293-3232 or 800/728-2718
Proprietors: Ron and Connie Davenport

Named for a founder of Keosauqua, the Hotel Manning was built in 1839 to house a bank and general store. In the 1890s the second and third floors were added and the whole took on a style pegged "Steamboat Gothic," with verandas spanning the width of the first two stories. The hotel opened on April 27, 1899, and has been in continuous use as a hotel since then. The spacious lobby has 16-foot ceilings, original pine woodwork, and antique fixtures. The room features a rare Vose rosewood grand piano, a specially commissioned grandfather clock, and outstanding examples of early pine and oak furniture. Guest rooms are handsomely appointed with antiques. The hotel restaurant offers fresh meat and produce from the heartland. On weekends diners enjoy piano entertainment.

Open: year round **Accommodations:** 18 guest rooms (10 have private baths); 2 are suites **Meals:** restaurant on premises **Rates:** $35 to $65; 10% discount offered to National Trust members and National Trust Visa cardholders **Payment:** Visa, MC, Discover, personal and traveler's checks **Restrictions:** smoking limited; no pets

---

MAQUOKETA

Nearby attractions: Maquoketa State Caves Park, Lime Kilns, art galleries, Banowetz Antiques

SQUIERS MANOR BED AND BREAKFAST

418 West Pleasant
Maquoketa, Iowa 52060
319/652-6961
Proprietors: Kathy and Virl Banowetz

Squiers Manor, built in 1882, was the first house in Maquoketa to have running water and electric power. It was home to members of the Squiers family for more than 60 years. The Queen Anne brick mansion is notable for its massive brick chimneys, corbeling, and rectangular bays. The original cast-iron fence surrounds the property. Through the front door, with its stained-glass window, guests will note walnut, cherry, butternut, and pine woodwork as well as original light fixture, louvered shutters, and fireplace mantels. The innkeepers, who also run an antiques business known as Banowetz Antiques, have filled the inn with outstanding American Victorian furnishings, including a seven-foot-high brass bed and a mahogany bed carved with birds and flowers that is original to the house. Guest rooms also feature all modern comforts, including whirlpool baths and color television.

Open: year round **Accommodations:** 8 guest rooms with private baths; 3 are suites **Meals:** full breakfast and candlelight evening dessert included; complimentary refreshments; restaurants nearby **Rates:** $75 to $195; 10% discount to National Trust members and National Trust Visa cardholders midweek only **Payment:** AmEx, Visa, MC, personal check **Restrictions:** smoking limited; no pets **Activities:** Victorian garden, grape arbor, front porch swing

---

WAVERLY

Nearby attractions: Wartburg College, Little Brown Church, Iowa's Star Clipper Dinner Train, museums, theaters

VILLA FAIRFIELD
401 Second Avenue, S.W.
Waverly, Iowa 50677
319/352-0739
Proprietor: Inez B. Christensen

Wide eaves supported by decorative brackets and tall, narrow windows identify this striking home as Italiante. It was built in 1876 by A. C. Fairfield, owner of the local power company. The fully restored house is testament to the quality of materials used in its construction: locally made red brick, maple and oak flooring, brass hardware, and marble fireplaces. Hand-hewn limestone sidewalks and thresholds are still in excellent condition today. The inn is furnished with family antiques as well as items collected during the innkeeper's years living in Brazil. Four guest rooms range in decor from Victorian elegant to tropical retreat. Guest rooms have ceiling fans and are air conditioned. Guests are invited to relax in the parlor or help themselves to always-fresh coffee and the bottomless cookie jar.

Open: year round **Accommodations:** 4 guest rooms with private baths **Meals:** full breakfast included; complimentary refreshments; restaurants nearby **Rates:** $55 to $75; 10% discount to National Trust members and National Trust Visa cardholders **Payment:** Visa, MC, personal and traveler's checks **Restrictions:** smoking limited

KANSAS

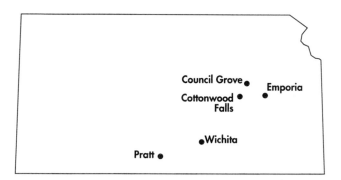

COTTONWOOD FALLS

Nearby attractions: historic sites, proposed Tall Grass Prairie National Park, antiques hunting, crafts shops, bicycling

1874 STONEHOUSE ON MULBERRY HILL
R.R. 1, Box 67A
Cottonwood Falls, Kansas 66845
316/273-8481
Proprietors: Carrie and Dan Riggs

Mulberry Hill contains 10 acres of river valley woods, a half-mile of old stone fencing, a stretch of Cottonwood River for wading and fishing, an old stone barn and corral ruins, an abandoned railway right-of-way, and the 1874 farmhouse, built of locally quarried stone. On the first floor is the fireplace room for reading and conversation and where breakfast is served, and the parlor, where guests can enjoy music and television. Three upstairs guest rooms have private baths. The Rose Room has a sleigh bed; the Blue Room overlooks the quarry pond; and the Yellow Room has a vista of the flint hills. With its rural setting and historic buildings, the 1874 Stonehouse appeals to naturalists, hikers, hunters, fishermen, and historians alike.

Open: year round **Accommodations:** 3 guest rooms with private baths **Meals:** full breakfast included; complimentary refreshments; restaurants nearby **Rate:** $75; 10% discount to National Trust members and National Trust Visa cardholders **Payment:** Visa, MC, personal and traveler's checks **Restrictions:** children over 12 welcome; no smoking; pets welcome in kennel facilities on property **Activities:** hiking, bird-watching, fishing, hunting

COUNCIL GROVE

Nearby attractions: Old Santa Fe Trail, "Old West" historic sites, lakes, boating, fishing, water skiing, golfing, shopping

COTTAGE HOUSE HOTEL
25 North Neosho
Council Grove, Kansas 66846
316/767-6828 or 800/727/7903
Proprietor: Connie Essington

This unusually styled brick hotel began as a three-room cottage in 1867, but was encapsulated in an 1871 two-story brick building. Then in 1879 the building gained a 5000-square-foot addition that encompassed a two-story turret with stained-glass windows to the east, a bank of bay windows on the northeast side, a corbelled brick parapet, and gazebo-style porches. Many of the interior's Victorian features have been restored, including pressed-tin ceilings in the hallways. Selected antique furnishings and lace curtains are featured throughout the building. Each guest room, from Aunt Minnie's Room to the Anniversary Suite, is individually decorated and contains a special accent, such as a stained-glass window, claw-foot tub, or brass bed. Private baths and all modern amenities complete each room.

Open: year round **Accommodations:** 26 guest rooms with private baths; 2 are suites **Meals:** continental-plus breakfast included; famous Hays House restaurant nearby **Wheelchair access:** limited **Rates:** $50 to $90; 10% discount offered to National Trust members and National Trust Visa cardholders **Payment:** AmEx, Visa, MC, CB, DC, Discover, personal and traveler's checks **Restrictions:** smoking limited; pets accepted at manager's discretion with an $8 charge **Activities:** porch sitting, whirlpool and sauna room

EMPORIA

Nearby attractions: William Allen White Memorial Drive, Charles Squires Tours, Flint Hills Adventure Tour of historic sites, lakes, reservoirs, fishing, antiques hunting, downtown shops, zoo

PLUMB HOUSE BED AND BREAKFAST
628 Exchange Street
Emporia, Kansas 66801
316/342-6881
Proprietor: Barbara Stoecklein

This 1910 Prairie-style house was once home to George and Ellen Plumb. Today it is the Plumb House Bed and Breakfast, its original beveled glass windows and pocket doors intact. The house is furnished with Victorian-era antiques. Guest rooms offer a variety of settings, such as the Garden Suite with a balcony, Horseless Carriage with garden views, or Grannie's Attic and The Loft, each with a private sitting room, television, refrigerator, and microwave oven. A full breakfast is served and guests are invited to end the day with complimentary tea or coffee.

Open: year round **Accommodations:** 5 guest rooms (4 have private baths); 2 are suites **Meals:** full breakfast included; complimentary refreshments; restaurants nearby **Rates:** $35 to $75; 10% discount to National Trust members and National Trust Visa cardholders **Payment:** AmEx, Visa, MC, personal check **Restrictions:** no smoking; nearby kennel for pets **Activities:** garden walk with pond, board games, horseshoe pitching

PRATT

Nearby attractions: Pratt County Historical Museum, Kansas Wildlife and Parks Museum and Ponds, Cheyenne Bottoms/Quivira National Wildlife Refuge, antiques hunting, auction houses, Santa Fe Trail

PRATT GUEST HOUSE BED AND BREAKFAST INN
105 North Iuka Street
P.O. Box 326
Pratt, Kansas 67124
316/672-1200
Proprietor: Marguerite Flanagan

A classic example of Colonial Revival architecture, Pratt Guest House was built in 1910 by Samuel P. "Geb" Gebhart, founder of the *Pratt Union* newspaper, and one-time mayor and councilman. Gebhart resided in this home until his death in

1935. Now listed in the National Register of Historic Places and the Register of Historic Kansas Places, the house recently was rehabilitated; an elegant oak staircase with hand-carved newel posts, leaded-glass windows and doors, and quarter-sawn oak cabinetry have been beautifully restored. Period antiques and family heirlooms complete the decor. A large third-floor suite has a king-size bed; all other guest rooms have queen-size beds. Whirlpool tubs are available in some bathrooms. Guests are welcome to relax in the parlor or gardens. Breakfast is served in the dining room or on the patio.

Open: year round **Accommodations:** 5 guest rooms with private baths **Meals:** full breakfast included; complimentary refreshments; restaurants nearby **Rates:** $45 to $90 **Payment:** Visa, MC, personal and traveler's checks **Restrictions:** inquire about children; no smoking; no pets **Activities:** backyard bird-watching, reading, porch swings and rockers

---

WICHITA

Nearby attractions: Old Town Wichita, Arkansas River, boathouse, tennis, Indian Center, Botanical Gardens, Cow Town, museums, convention center

CASTLE INN RIVERSIDE
1155 North River Boulevard
Wichita, Kansas 67203
316/263-9300
Proprietors: Dr. and Mrs.
Terry Lowry

This castle of Richardsonian Romanesque architecture was built in 1888 by cattle baron Colonel Burton Campbell, who modeled it after a castle in Scotland. The rough-faced stonework mansion, with round-arched porches and porte cochere, is notable for its four-story castellated tower. Completely restored and listed in the National Register of Historic Places, the house boasts original stained-glass windows, intricately carved woodwork in oak, mahogany, cherry, and walnut, and nine European fireplace mantels. Common areas include the foyer, parlor, library, and dining and billiard rooms. Guest rooms—most with working fireplaces—are furnished with antiques and reproduction pieces. Beds, dressed in luxurious linens, are brass and cast iron. Guests are served a full, seasonally changing breakfast, afternoon tea and aperitifs, and evening desserts, coffee, and cordials.

Open: year round **Accommodations:** 14 guest rooms with private baths; 2 are suites **Meals:** full breakfast included; complimentary refreshments; restaurants nearby **Wheelchair access:** 1 room **Rates:** $125 to $195; 10% discount to National Trust members and National Trust Visa cardholders **Payment:** AmEx, Visa, MC, Discover, personal and traveler's checks **Restrictions:** children over 12 welcome; no smoking; no pets **Activities:** exercise and meeting facilities, croquet, board games, book and videotape libraries, two acres of grounds with gardens and strolling paths

VERMILION ROSE — A BED AND BREAKFAST PLACE
1204 North Topeka
Wichita, Kansas 67214
316/267-7636
316/267-7642 Fax
Proprietors: Ken Kern and Marietta Anderson

This 1887 Queen Anne home, framed by decorative wrought-iron fencing, occupies a corner lot in historic midtown Wichita. The house is a compilation of decorated gables, bay windows, and wraparound porches. Inside, the living room offers a fireplace and a piano, while the library contains overstuffed chairs and a variety of reading materials. Four guest rooms are available; one has a brick fireplace, all have private baths. Antiques—an iron or Jenny Lind bed, wardrobes, desks, rockers—combine with contemporary pieces to create comfortable retreats. Breakfast is served in the dining room or, in warm weather, on the porch. Guests are invited to stroll through the antique rose gardens on brick walkways or sit on the patio or porches.

Open: year round **Accommodations:** 4 guest rooms with private baths **Meals:** continental-plus breakfast included; complimentary refreshments; restaurants nearby **Rates:** $60 to $90; 10% discount to National Trust members and National Trust Visa cardholders **Payment:** AmEx, Visa, MC, personal and traveler's checks **Restrictions:** no smoking; no pets **Activities:** croquet, badminton

KENTUCKY

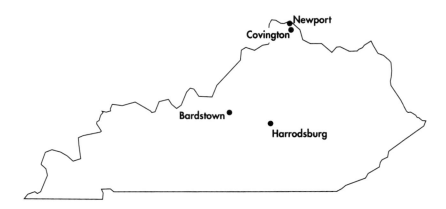

BARDSTOWN

Nearby attractions: Lincoln's birthplace, Federal Hill, Stephen Foster outdoor drama, Civil War battlefield, My Old Kentucky Home State Park, My Old Kentucky Dinner Train, Kentucky bourbon distilleries

JAILER'S INN
111 West Stephen Foster Avenue
Bardstown, Kentucky 40004
502/348-5551 or 800/948-5551
Proprietor: Fran McCoy

Built as a jail in 1819, the building originally housed prisoners upstairs while the jailer lived below. In 1874 prisoners were moved to a new jail built behind the old one, which remained the jailer's residence. Both facilities were used until 1987, at which time the complex was the oldest operating jail in the state of Kentucky. Listed in the National Register of Historic Places, the 1819 building has been completely rehabilitated to offer six individually decorated guest rooms filled with antiques, original rugs, and heirlooms. Accommodations range from the Victorian Room and the Garden Room to the former women's cell, which is adorned in prison black and white and features two of the original bunk beds and a more modern waterbed. Another room contains a double whirlpool bathtub. Guests are treated to refreshments and a hearty continental-plus breakfast.

Open: March to January **Accommodations:** 6 guest rooms with private baths **Meals:**

continental-plus breakfast included; complimentary refreshments; restaurants nearby **Wheelchair access:** limited **Rates:** $65 to $95 **Payment:** AmEx, Visa, MC, Discover, personal and traveler's checks **Restrictions:** smoking limited; no pets **Activities:** touring old jails, playing cards, board games, tandem bicycle

COVINGTON

Nearby attractions: Riverfront Stadium, Kings Island, horse racing at Turfway River Downs, boating, opera, ballet, symphony, walk to downtown Cincinnati

AMOS SHINKLE TOWNHOUSE BED AND BREAKFAST
215 Garrard Street
Covington, Kentucky 41011
606/431-2118
Proprietors: Bernie Moorman and Don Nash
Location: less than 1 mile south of downtown Cincinnati, Ohio

A fine example of upper-class lifestyle in antebellum northern Kentucky, this 1854 brick house was built for entrepreneur Amos Shinkle, one of the area's leading business figures in the mid-nineteenth century. The restored home, winner of several preservation awards, features an Italianate facade with a cast-iron filigreed porch. Superior local craftsmanship is evident in the plaster chandelier medallions—preserved intact—and interior cornices, elaborate crown moldings, and Italianate mantels. Guest rooms have four-poster or Victorian-style beds and period furnishings. Behind the house is the Carriage House, where original horse stalls have been redesigned as delightful sleeping accommodations for children.

Open: year round **Accommodations:** 7 guest rooms with private baths; 1 is a suite **Meals:** full breakfast included; restaurants nearby **Wheelchair access:** 2 guest rooms and baths **Rates:** $73 to $125; 10% discount to National Trust members and National Trust Visa cardholders **Payment:** AmEx, Visa, MC, CB, DC, Discover, personal and traveler's checks **Restrictions:** no pets

HARRODSBURG

Nearby attractions: Ft. Harrod State Park, Constitution Square Park, Kentucky Horse Park, Bright Leaf Golf Resort, fishing, boating

SHAKER VILLAGE OF PLEASANT HILL
3500 Lexington Road
Harrodsburg, Kentucky 40330
606/734-5411
Proprietor: James C. Thomas
Location: 7 miles east of Harrodsburg

Shaker Village of Pleasant Hill preserves 33 original nineteenth-century buildings (built between 1809 and 1844) that have been accurately restored to provide visitors with an insight into the Shaker way of life. To make a stay at Shaker Village even more interesting, visitors are invited to lodge in one of 80 guest rooms scattered throughout 15 of these buildings. Guest rooms are furnished with reproduction Shaker furniture and handwoven rugs and curtains. Despite their nineteenth-century decor, all rooms are air conditioned and have private baths. Pleasant Hill, a National Historic Landmark, provides a relaxing, yet educational look at one of America's most successful communal religious societies.

Open: year round **Accommodations:** 80 guest rooms with private baths; 7 are suites **Meals:** restaurant on premises **Wheelchair access:** Trustee's Office dining room **Rates:** $48 to $100 **Payment:** Visa, MC, personal check **Restrictions:** no pets **Activities:** touring historic village, hiking, riverboat excursions, nature programs, shopping for handmade crafts and reproductions

NEWPORT

Nearby attractions: historic district walking tour, Museum of Natural History, River Boat Row, Cincinnati Zoo, Riverfront Stadium

GATEWAY BED AND BREAKFAST

326 East Sixth Street
Newport, Kentucky 41071
606/581-6447
Proprietors: Ken and Sandy Clift

The architectural details on this 1878 Italianate townhouse are intact and preserved, from the round window hood moldings to the decorative eave brackets. Accordingly, the house was a recent winner of the Great American Homes Award for bed-and-breakfast restoration from the National Trust for Historic Preservation. Three guest rooms are offered. The Oak Room includes an antique oak high-back double bed and an unusual oak library table that unfolds into a single bed. The Victorian Room features Victorian-era furnishings. The Country Room is accentuated with rustic baskets, grapevine wreaths, and quilts. All rooms have fireplaces. Guests are invited to play the 1910 pump organ, 1904 Edison phonograph, or 1928 player piano in the common rooms. Breakfast is served in the formal dining room and city views are found from the rooftop deck. This National Register property is only five minutes from downtown Cincinnati.

Open: year round **Accommodations:** 3 guest rooms, 1 has a private bath **Meals:** full breakfast included; restaurants nearby **Rates:** $60 to $70; 10% discount to National Trust members and National Trust Visa cardholders **Payment:** AmEx, Visa, MC **Restrictions:** no smoking; no pets **Activities:** rooftop deck, antique musical instruments

LOUISIANA

St. Francisville ●

Ramsay/● Covington

Lafayette ●

Abbeville ● St. Martinville New Orleans

ABBEVILLE

Nearby attractions: shrimping fleet, Live Oak Gardens, Jungle Gardens, Avery Island, National Trust's Shadows-on-the-Teche, fresh and saltwater fishing, horse racing, Creole and Cajun cuisine

A LA BONNE VEILLÉE GUEST HOUSE—CIRCA 1860
Route 2, Box 2270
Highway 339
Abbeville, Louisiana 70510
318/937-5495
Proprietors: Ron and Carolyn Doerle Ray

A Louisiana French–style cottage resting beside a duck pond under century-old live oak trees and surrounded by 30 acres of farmland, this cottage has been owned by several prominent French Creole and Acadian families. Sturdily built of hand-cut cypress timbers, it features a steeply pitched shingled roof, front gallery, and brick piers to raise it above flooding bayou waters. Listed in the National Register of Historic Places, the cottage is available for rental and consists of two bedrooms, a full bath, kitchen, dining area, living room, and two working fireplaces. The temperature is controlled by central air and heat. Color television and telephone are also provided. The house is furnished with period antiques.

Open: year round **Accommodations:** cottage with 2 bedrooms and 1 bath **Meals:** continental breakfast included; restaurants nearby **Rates:** $85 single; $100 for 1 couple; $140 for 2 couples; 10% discount offered to National Trust members and National Trust Visa cardholders **Payment:** personal and traveler's checks **Restrictions:** no smoking; no pets **Activities:** jogging, bicycling, pond fishing

LAFAYETTE

Nearby attractions: bayou country and tourist attractions, shopping, dancing, golfing, tennis, hiking

T'FRERE'S HOUSE BED AND BREAKFAST
1905 Verot School Road
Lafayette, Louisiana 70508
318/984-9347 or 800/984-9347
Proprietors: Pat and Maugie Pastor

Built in 1880 of Louisiana red cypress hauled from the nearby Vermilion Bayou, the steeply pitched roof and wide galleries across the front and sides of the house are reminiscent of earlier Acadian colonial architecture. The inn's Cajun hosts welcome guests with complimentary T'Juleps and Cajun canapes served on a glass-enclosed gallery. This Lafayette landmark offers four elegant guest rooms furnished with period antiques, including canopied beds. Bedrooms also feature ceiling fans, fireplaces, and Victorian-style wallpapers. Wake-up coffee is served in guest rooms while the innkeepers prepare a full Cajun breakfast, served in the dining room. Guests at T'Frere's House cannot but help catch the contagious *joie de vivre* of Louisiana's bayou country from the Pastors.

Open: year round **Accommodations:** 4 guest rooms with private baths **Meals:** full breakfast included; complimentary refreshments; restaurants nearby **Rates:** $75 to $85; 10% discount to National Trust members and National Trust Visa cardholders **Payment:** Visa, MC, Discover, personal and traveler's checks **Restrictions:** no smoking; no pets

NEW ORLEANS

Nearby attractions: Audubon Park and Zoological Gardens, French Quarter, St. Louis Cathedral, Tulane University, Woldenberg Park, Riverwalk Mall, central business district, Superdome, U.S. Mint, Cajun food and dancing, Natchez paddlewheeler on Mississippi River, streetcar rides, antiques hunting, tennis, swimming, nature trips through swamps

COLUMNS HOTEL
3811 Saint Charles Avenue
New Orleans, Louisiana 70115
504/899-9308 or 800/445-9308
504/899-8170 Fax
Proprietors: Claire and Jacques Creppél

Designed by architect Thomas Sully and built by wealthy tobacco merchant Simon Hernsheim in 1883, the Columns is the only remaining example of a large group of Italianate houses Sully designed between 1883 and 1885. The surviving interior features are considered to be among the grandest known in any late nineteenth-century Louisiana residence. One of the most dramatic is a mahogany stairwell that rises to meet an extraordinary square-domed skylight made of stained glass in a stylized sunburst motif. The house is listed in the National Register and was the location for Louis Malle's film, *Pretty Baby*, which won an award at Cannes. Guest rooms, furnished with antiques, each feature some small delight—a unique fireplace, an armoire, or a claw-foot bathtub. The Columns serves New Orleans–style food, which combines the best of Creole, Cajun, and European cuisines.

Open: year round **Accommodations:** 19 guest rooms (12 have private baths); 3 are suites **Meals:** continental breakfast included; complimentary refreshments; restaurants and lounge on premises; catered parties available **Wheelchair access:** yes **Rates:** $65 to $150; 10% discount offered to National Trust members and National Trust Visa cardholders **Payment:** AmEx, Visa, MC, personal and traveler's check **Activities:** jazz nights, international nights

DUSTY MANSION
2231 General Pershing Street
New Orleans, Louisiana 70115
504/895-4576
Proprietor: Cynthia Riggs

This homey, casual inn is on a quiet residential street on the edge of the Garden District in the historic Bouligny Plantation District. The turn-of-the-century, two-story frame house sports a wide front porch where guests often relax on the wicker swing. Inside, the house is trimmed in original hardwood floors and cypress woodwork and doors. Guest rooms are air conditioned, have ceiling fans and televisions, and are furnished with antiques and reproduction pieces. Queen-size beds may be brass, canopied, sleigh, or white enameled iron. Guests are invited to linger over breakfast in the dining room, play pool in the game room, or relax on the sundeck or shaded patio. Just six blocks from the St. Charles Avenue streetcar, Dusty Mansion offers off-street parking.

Open: year round **Accommodations:** 4 guest rooms (2 have private baths) **Meals:** continental-plus breakfast included; champagne brunch on Sundays; complimentary refreshments; restaurants nearby **Rates:** $50 to $75; 10% discount to National Trust members and National Trust Visa cardholders **Payment:** personal and traveler's checks **Restrictions:** no smoking; no pets **Activities:** gazebo with hot tub, pool table, table tennis

FRENCH QUARTER COURTYARD HOTEL
1101 North Rampart Street
New Orleans, Louisiana 70116
504/522-7333 or 800/290-4BED (800/290-4233)
504/522-3908 Fax
Proprietors: April Casey, Layne Amacher, and Patrice Banks

Built in 1879 by renowned architect G. A. D'Hemecourt, this Italianate house exudes New Orleans elegance with its lacy wrought-iron balconies that face the streets and overlook historic Storyville, where jazz was born. Wooden balconies surround an inner courtyard with swimming pool and fountains. Inside, guests will discover antique hardwood and brick flooring, 13-foot ceilings, and many original architectural elements. Guest rooms are appointed with carved, four-poster beds, ceiling fans, oriental rugs, and private baths. Conveniently located across the street from the famed French Quarter, the Courtyard Hotel offers valet parking, nightly turn-down service, and a 24-hour bar.

Open: year round **Accommodations:** 33 guest rooms with private baths; 1 is a suite **Meals:** continental-plus breakfast included; restaurants nearby **Wheelchair access:** 2 rooms **Rates:** $59 to $159; 10% discount to National Trust members and National Trust Visa cardholders **Payment:** AmEx, Visa, MC, DC, Discover, personal and traveler's checks **Restrictions:** smoking limited **Activities:** swimming pool, garden, lounge

FRENCH QUARTER LANAUX HOUSE
Esplanade Avenue at Chartres Street
Box 52257
New Orleans, Louisiana 70152-2257
504/488-4640 or 800/729-4640
504/488-4639 Fax
Proprietors: Ruth Bodenheimer and Hazell Boyce

Charles Andrew Johnson built this Italianate town house in 1879. Although he died unmarried in 1896, he willed his 11,000-square-foot mansion to Marie Andry Lanaux, the daughter of his business partner, and object of his affections. The Lanaux family owned this home for generations. Ms. Bodenheimer has meticulously restored the house. The original ceiling medallions and moldings are in nearly perfect condition. The seven fireplaces wear their original mantels. A number of furnishings owned by Johnson remain in the house today. A private entrance leads to each guest suite, which includes a private sitting room, queen bed, bathroom, and country kitchenette. A self-served continental breakfast is provided for guests to enjoy at their leisure.

Open: year round **Accommodations:** 4 guest suites with private baths **Meals:** continental breakfast included; restaurants nearby **Rates:** $96 to $251; 10% discount to National Trust members **Payment:** personal and traveler's checks **Restrictions:** no smoking; no pets **Activities:** historic house tour

LAFITTE GUEST HOUSE
1003 Bourbon Street
New Orleans, Louisiana 70116
800-331-7971 or 504-581-2678
Proprietor: Robert D. Guyton

According to *Dixie Magazine*, Lafitte Guest House is "as New Orleans as streetcars, jazz musicians, and voodoo queens." Located in the heart of the French Quarter, the Lafitte offers easy access to the district's antiques shops, museums, world-famous restaurants, Bourbon Street nightclubs, and rows of colorful Creole and Spanish cottages. The inn, built in 1849 by P. J. Gelieses, is a three-story, New Orleans–style French Colonial, complete with lacy wrought-iron balconies. Each guest room is individually decorated with antiques and reproduction furnishings. A continental breakfast is served on the balconies or in the intimate courtyard. The tranquil and gracious atmosphere has been hailed by *Glamour*, *McCall's*, *Antique Monthly*, and *Country Living*.

Open: year round **Accommodations:** 14 guest rooms with private baths; 1 is a suite **Meals:** continental breakfast included; complimentary refreshments; restaurants nearby **Rates:** $85 to $165 **Payment:** AmEx, Visa, MC, Discover, traveler's check **Restrictions:** no pets

NICOLAS M. BENACHI HOUSE
2257 Bayou Road
New Orleans, Louisiana 70119
504/525-7040 or 800/308/7040
504/525-9760 Fax
Proprietors: James G. Derbes and Cecilia J. Rau

This Greek Revival house was constructed in 1858 for Nicolas M. Benachi, cotton broker, Consul of Greece, and a founder of the city's Greek Orthodox church. The home is located in the Esplanade Ridge National Register historic district; eighteenth- and nineteenth-century artifacts have been found in the inn's yard. An award-winning restoration by the innkeepers is evident in 14-foot ceilings with banded cornices and medallions, carved black marble mantels, Rococo Revival chandelieres, Greek key doorways, and heart-of-pine floors. The entire house is furnished with nineteenth-century American antiques. Guests are welcome in the parlor, library, and dining room, and are invited to stroll the tree-shaded grounds with gazebo and fountain. The inn has been featured in such publications as *American Home* and the *Times-Picayune* and two feature films have been filmed here.

Open: year round **Accommodations:** 4 guest rooms (3 with private baths); 1 is a suite **Meals:** full breakfast included; complimentary refreshments; restaurants nearby **Rates:** $85 to $130; 10% discount to National Trust members and National Trust Visa cardholders **Payment:** AmEx, Visa, MC, Discover, personal and traveler's checks **Restrictions:** no smoking; no pets

PRYTANIA PARK HOTEL
1525 Prytania Street
New Orleans, Louisiana 70130
504/524-0427 or 800/682-1984
504/522-2977 Fax
Proprietor: Edward Halpern

Located in the historic Garden District, the Prytania Park Hotel is only a half block from St. Charles Avenue, where the world's oldest continuously operating streetcar provides 24-hour access to the French Quarter. The original portion of this hotel is in a beautifully restored 1856 Victorian townhouse, complete with high ceilings, shiny hardwood floors, exposed brick walls, and old English furniture. Wrought-iron second-floor balconies lend the building an authentic New Orleans air. Many of the hotel's guest rooms are located in the recently constructed addition and are furnished with teak wall systems, microwave ovens,

refrigerators, and cable television. The courtyard provides a comfortable setting for a New Orleans continental breakfast.

Open: year round **Accommodations:** 62 guest rooms with private baths; 6 are suites **Meals:** continental breakfast included; restaurants nearby **Rates:** $79 to $200; 10% discount offered to National Trust members and National Trust Visa cardholders **Payment:** AmEx, Visa, MC, CB, DC, traveler's check; personal check in advance only **Restrictions:** no pets

RATHBONE INN

1227 Esplanade Avenue
New Orleans, Louisiana 70116
504/947-2100 or 800/947-2101
504/947-7454 Fax
Proprietors: Richard Mole and Robert Feldman

The Rathbone Inn was built in 1850 as a single-family residence. The Greek Revival building is adorned with a two-story front porch supported by Ionic columns on the first floor and Corinthian on the second. The wrought-iron front fence with filigreed gate is one of the finest in New Orleans. The house was restored in 1985 so that most rooms sport their original high ceilings and interesting architectural details. Accommodations range from small rooms with a king- or queen-size bed to large two- and three-room suites. All guest rooms have private baths and kitchenettes. The Rathbone Inn is located less than two blocks from the French Quarter.

Open: year round **Accommodations:** 9 guest rooms with private baths and kitchenettes **Meals:** continental breakfast included; restaurants nearby **Rates:** $70 to $125; 10% discount to National Trust members and National Trust Visa cardholders **Payment:** AmEx, Visa, MC, CB, DC, Discover, traveler's check **Restrictions:** no pets **Activities:** patio with hot tub

SULLY MANSION

2631 Prytania Street
New Orleans, Louisiana 70130
504/891-0457
Proprietor: Maralee Prigmore

Sully Mansion, designed by renowned architect Thomas Sully in 1890, is the most intact of the few remaining "Sullys" in New Orleans. Original stained-glass windows, ornate ceiling medallions, heart-of-pine floors, a grand stairway, 10-foot-high cypress doors, and 12-foot-high coved ceilings are just a few of the features of this rare Queen Anne–style home. A tasteful blend of antiques and today's comfortable furnishings creates an intimate atmosphere. Sully Mansion is located in the heart of New Orleans's historic Garden District. Nearby, the historic St. Charles streetcar takes visitors to all the city's attractions.

Open: year round **Accommodations:** 5 guest rooms with private baths; 2 suites **Meals:** continental breakfast included; restaurants nearby **Rates:** $89 to $175 **Payment:** Visa, MC, personal and traveler's checks **Restrictions:** not suitable for children

RAMSAY/COVINGTON

Nearby attractions: St. Joseph's Abby liberal arts college, Dom Gregory DeWitt painted frescoes, antiques hunting

MILL BANK FARMS
75654 River Road
Ramsay/Covington, Louisiana 70435
504/892-1606
Proprietor: "Miss Katie" Planche Friedrichs
Location: 4 miles outside Covington

Mill Bank Farms bed and breakfast was originally built in 1832 as the office of a lumber company and mill. The mill operated until 1915 when it was purchased by M. P. Planche, Sr., for farming. Guests have the use of the large living room and dining room with open fireplaces. Each of the bedrooms are enhanced by antique furnishings and private baths. Wake-up calls are made with coffee or tea served in bed. Then a full plantation breakfast is served indoors or on the front porch overlooking the pecan orchard and grazing horses. Mill Bank Farms sits back off River Road, one of the oldest and most scenic roads in the state, in the middle of 70 acres on the bluffs of the Bogue Falaya River, a registered Lousisana scenic river.

Open: year round **Accommodations:** 2 guest rooms with private baths **Meals:** full breakfast included; complimentary refreshments; restaurants nearby **Rates:** $85 first night; $80 second night; $75 third night; 10% discount to National Trust members and National Trust Visa cardholders **Payment:** AmEx, Visa, MC, Discover, personal check **Restrictions:** no smoking; no pets **Activities:** fishing, bicycling, river swimming, hiking

---

ST. FRANCISVILLE

Nearby attractions: golfing, historic sightseeing, plantations

BUTLER GREENWOOD PLANTATION
8345 U.S. Highway 61
St. Francisville, Louisiana 70775
504/635-6312
Proprietor: Anne Butler
Location: 2 1/2 miles north of St. Francisville on U.S. Highway 61

This plantation was established in 1796; the main house was built around 1810. Guest accommodations are in five dependencies located on the extensive grounds

filled with moss-draped live oaks and antebellum gardens of mature azaleas and camellias. The Old Kitchen, built in 1796, features exposed beams and bricks made on the plantation by its slaves. The nineteenth-century Cook's Cottage has a working fireplace, claw-foot tub, and porch swing. The Gazebo is notable for its three nine-foot-tall antique stained-glass church windows. The Pond House sleeps six and has a shaded gingerbread-trimmed porch overlooking the pond. The Treehouse is at the edge of a steep wooded ravine. It has a three-level deck, a king-size cypress four-poster bed, and a fireplace. All accommodations have kitchens and private baths.

Open: year round **Accommodations:** 5 guest cottages with private baths and kitchens **Meals:** continental-plus breakfast included; restaurants nearby **Wheelchair access:** limited **Rates:** $80 to $90 **Payment:** AmEx, Visa, MC, personal and traveler's checks **Restrictions:** no smoking in main plantation house **Activities:** gardens, swimming pool, pond with ducks and geese, guided nature walks and bird-watching, historic home tour

COTTAGE PLANTATION
10528 Cottage Lane
St. Francisville, Louisiana 70775
504/635-3674
Proprietors: Harvey and Mary T. Brown
Location: 5 miles north of St. Francisville

Cottage Plantation, built between 1795 and 1850, is one of the few complete antebellum plantations remaining in the South. The mansion—an English cottage with broad galleries and a steeply pitched roof with dormers—and its outbuildings stand as tributes to the skill and imagination of the designers and artisans of the early nineteenth century. In its time the cottage entertained such eminences as Andrew Jackson, who stopped on his way to Natchez as a guest of the original owner, shortly after the Battle of New Orleans. Today, the house and guest rooms are furnished with antiques, many original to the home. Located on nearly 400 rolling acres with moss-draped oaks and old gardens, this National Register property conveys the charm and hospitality of the Old South.

Open: year round **Accommodations:** 6 guest rooms with private baths **Meals:** full breakfast included; restaurant on premises **Rate:** $90 **Payment:** Visa, MC, personal and traveler's checks **Restrictions:** children over 12 welcome; smoking limited; no pets **Activities:** horseshoes, croquet, swimming pool, antiques shop

---

ST. MARTINVILLE

Nearby attractions: Bayou Teche, National Register historic district, St. Martin Square, St. Martin Catholic Church, Presbytère, Petit Paris Museum

OLD CASTILLO BED AND BREAKFAST
220 Evangeline Boulevard
P.O. Box 172
St. Martinville, Louisiana 70582
318/394-4010 or 800/621-3017
318/394-7983 Fax
Proprietor: Peggy Hulin

Pierre Vasseur built this stately Greek Revival structure in 1829 as a combination inn and residence. Later, under the management of Mrs. Edmond Castillo, widow of a well-known steamboat captain, the hotel became renowned as a center of superb hospitality, gala balls, and fine operas. Between 1899 and 1986 the building was owned by the Sisters of Mercy, who operated it as a high school for girls. Today, the building has been restored to its original use, now housing five antiques-filled guest rooms and La Place d'Evangeline restaurant featuring Acadian cuisine. The building's careful restoration has earned it a listing in the National Register of Historic Places.

Open: year round **Accommodations:** 5 guest rooms with private baths; 3 are suites **Meals:** full breakfast included; restaurants nearby **Wheelchair access:** limited **Rates:** $50 to $80; 10% discount to National Trust members and National Trust Visa cardholders **Payment:** AmEx, Visa, MC, traveler's check **Restrictions:** well-behaved children are welcome; smoking limited; no pets **Activities:** relaxing on balcony or along bayou

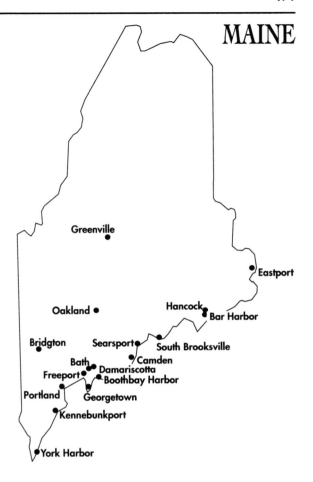

MAINE

BAR HARBOR

Nearby attractions: Acadia National Park, summer theater, golfing, tennis, boating, swimming, hiking, biking, walking, whale-watching, fine shops and restaurants

BREAKWATER 1904
45 Hancock Street
Bar Harbor, Maine 04609
207/288-2313 or 800/238-6309
207/288-2377
Proprietor: Bonnie P. Sawyer

In 1904, John Innes Kane, great-grandson of John Jacob Astor, built this oceanfront Tudor-style estate, replete with gables and half-timbering. An extensive restoration by the innkeeper in 1992 resulted in an inn that has been lauded by *Country Inns* and chosen by the American Bed and Breakfast Association as one of the top sixteen inns in the country. Columns, gothic arches, a winding, three-story staircase with a minstrel's gallery, and leaded-glass French doors leading to a piazza looking out to sea—all found in the great hall alone—have been restored to their original elegance. The entire house has been furnished as a showcase for Drexel Heritage Furniture's reproduction pieces and lush fabrics. Luxury and comfort combine in guest rooms, some with fireplaces, most with oceanfront views. Breakfast is served in the vast dining room with its custom-made oak table.

Open: mid-April to mid-November **Accommodations:** 6 guest rooms with private baths; 5 are suites **Meals:** full breakfast included; complimentary refreshments and evening social hour; restaurants nearby **Rates:** $155 to $325 (seasonal) **Payment:** AmEx, Visa, MC, personal and traveler's checks **Restrictions:** children over 12 welcome; no smoking; no pets **Activities:** billiards room, games, cards

MIRA MONTE INN
69 Mount Desert Street
Bar Harbor, Maine 04609
207/288-4263 or 800/553-5109
207/288-3115 Fax
Proprietor: Marian Burns

This elegant summer retreat was built in 1864 and was named Mira Monte ("behold the mountains") in 1892 by its wealthy Philadelphia owners. The rambling clapboard building is graced by porches, balconies, and bay windows, as well as several fireplaces. The wraparound porch, paved terraces, gardens, and sweeping lawns are a testament to style and beauty. Guests may relax in the living room or library and are encouraged to use the piano for their enjoyment. Each guest room is furnished in the Victorian style and offers a special feature: a balcony or porch, a bay window, an alcove, or a fireplace. Fresh flowers, freshly baked breads, and a friendly staff are relaxing additions. Ask about fly–drive packages.

Open: early May to late October **Accommodations:** 15 guest rooms with private baths **Meals:** full breakfast included; complimentary refreshments; restaurants nearby **Wheelchair access:** yes **Rates:** $115 to $180; 10% discount offered to National Trust members and National Trust Visa cardholders **Payment:** AmEx, Visa, MC, Discover, personal and traveler's checks **Restrictions:** smoking limited; no pets **Activities:** badminton, croquet, horseshoe tossing, library, piano, chess and board games

THE TIDES
119 West Street
Bar Harbor, Maine 04609
207/288-4968
Proprietors: Tom and Bonnie Sawyer

Built in 1887, this 16-room oceanfront Neoclassical estate is located in the historic district, on more than an acre of landscaped grounds accented by gardens and shade trees. The spacious living and dining rooms each boast working fireplaces and full ocean views. A casual elegance pervades the second-floor sitting room with cozy fireplace. Guest suites offer four-poster or Victorian furnishings and thoughtful amenities. Tastefully restored and decorated, the two-room suites all have oceanfront bed chamber, queen-size bed, private bath, and personal parlor with cable television. Two suites offer fireplaces. On summer mornings breakfast is served on the veranda overlooking the shore. In spring and fall breakfast is served by candlelight before a cheery fire.

Open: May 1 to December 31 **Accommodations:** 3 guest suites with private baths **Meals:** full breakfast included; complimentary refreshments; restaurants nearby **Rates:** $125 to $255 **Payment:** Visa, MC, personal and traveler's checks **Restrictions:** children over 14 welcome; no smoking; no pets **Activities:** watching the ocean from the veranda

BATH

Nearby attractions: historic Bath, Kennebec River, Maritime Museum, Chocolate Church Cultural Center, Bowdoin College, antiques hunting, art gallery, outlet shopping, beaches, state parks

GALEN C. MOSES HOUSE
1009 Washington Street
Bath, Maine 04530
207/442-8771
Proprietors: James M. Haught and Larry E. Kieft

Built in 1874 for Galen Clapp Moses, this Italianate house stands out in its National Register historic district thanks not only to its outstanding architecture but also to its current paint scheme of plum, pink, and teal. The interior of the house is just as commanding: fireplaces with elaborately carved and mirrored overmantels, built-in bookcases, leather upholstered seats, paneled walls, bay windows, plaster friezes. Guest rooms are individually appointed and dressed with antiques ranging from Victorian to vintage 1950s. Porches and elegant gardens are also open to guests. Surprises are found throughout the house, from the full theater located on the third floor that was once used to entertain officers from the nearby naval air station during World War II to the reputed friendly ghosts who often make their presence felt.

Open: year round **Accommodations:** 3 guest rooms with private baths **Meals:** full breakfast included; complimentary refreshments; restaurants nearby **Rates:** $65 to $95; 10% discount to National Trust members and National Trust Visa cardholders weekdays only **Payment:** personal and traveler's checks **Restrictions:** no smoking; no pets **Activities:** porch sitting, garden strolling, reading

BOOTHBAY HARBOR

Nearby attractions: boating, fishing, sightseeing, tennis, golfing, theaters, museums, specialty shops, restaurants

HARBOUR TOWNE INN ON THE WATERFRONT
71 Townsend Avenue
Boothbay Harbor, Maine 04538
207/633-4300 or 800/722-4240
Proprietor: George Thomas

This rambling Queen Anne inn sits among colorful gardens and giant shade trees on the shore of beautiful Boothbay Harbor. Built at the turn of the century, this fully refurbished structure offers scenic views of the quaint village and harbor that, together, are known as the "Boating Capital of New England." Waterfront accommodations in the inn and attached carriage house have outside decks, good for catching fresh breezes. A modern, spacious penthouse accommodates six people and affords a panoramic view not only of the harbor but also of outlying islands and the ocean. A continental breakfast is served in the sunroom. In cold weather, the parlor fireplace is kept burning. With charming accommodations and special off-season packages, the inn's proprietors have deemed it "The Finest B&B on the Waterfront."

Open: year round **Accommodations:** 6 guest rooms with private baths; 1 is a penthouse suite **Meals:** continental breakfast included; restaurants nearby **Rates:** $59 to $225 (seasonal); 10% discount off rack rate to National Trust members and National Trust Visa cardholders **Payment:** AmEx, Visa, MC, Discover, traveler's check, personal check with credit card and driver's license **Restrictions:** well-behaved children welcome; no smoking; no pets

BRIDGTON

Nearby attractions: Shaker Village, restored nineteenth-century village of Willowbrook, antiques hunting, crafts shops, Jones Gallery of glass and ceramics

THE NOBLE HOUSE

37 Highland Road
P.O. Box 180
Bridgton, Maine 04009
207/647-3733
Proprietors: Dick and Jane Starets
Location: 38 miles west of Portland, 1/2 mile from Bridgton

In the heart of the Lakes Region of Maine in the quaint town of Bridgton, this 1903 Queen Anne home overlooks peaceful Highland Lake. Built for State Senator Winfred Staples, the house is most notable for a second-story balcony topped by an unusual round arch tucked under a steep gable and for its wraparound porches. Inside, the inn is understated yet elegant. A front parlor contains the library, a grand piano, a pump organ, and a fireplace. The lounge in the rear of the house provides a comfortable setting for meeting other guests over complimentary refreshments or for watching television and videotapes. Some guest rooms have private porches; others provide whirlpool tubs. A full breakfast is served on the porch, by the fireside, or family-style in the dining room.

Open: year round **Accommodations:** 7 guest rooms (5 have private baths); 3 are suites **Meals:** full breakfast included; restaurants nearby **Rates:** $74 to $115 **Payment:** AmEx, Visa, MC, personal and traveler's checks **Restrictions:** no infants on weekends in season; no smoking; no pets **Activities:** swimming, canoeing, fishing, croquet, lakeside hammock

CAMDEN

Nearby attractions: Camden Harbor, Camden Opera House, shopping, museums, boating, cruises, lake swimming, windjammers, lighthouses, island day trips, golfing, tennis, hiking, horseback riding, downhill and cross-country skiing and all winter sports

BLACKBERRY INN

82 Elm Street
Camden, Maine 04843
207/236-6060 or 800/833-6674
Proprietors: Edward and Vicki Doudera

A stay at Blackberry Inn is made special by its spacious guest rooms decorated in Victorian style with brass beds, curved love seats, and antique dressers, and extra touches such as blackberry candies and large fluffy towels. Each morning brings a gourmet breakfast with entrees like brie souffle and blintzes with blackberry sauce. Two new deluxe rooms contain king-size beds, whirlpool tubs, and wood-burning fireplaces. Guests also enjoy the 1849 Victorian home for its airy parlors (one furnished with Bar Harbor wicker), polished parquet floors, original tin ceilings, working fireplaces, and ornate plaster moldings. The inn has been fitted with sprinklers for the safety of its guests and has been described as "just delightful" by the *Miami Herald*. This is a unique home, the only one from Maine featured in *Daughters of Painted Ladies: America's Resplendent Victorians*.

Open: year round **Accommodations:** 10 guest rooms with private baths, **Meals:** full breakfast included; dinner available by special arrangement; restaurants nearby **Wheelchair access:** 3 guest rooms, dining room, parlors **Rates:** $55 to $135 (seasonal); 10% discount offered to National Trust members and National Trust Visa cardholders **Payment:** Visa, MC, personal and traveler's checks **Restrictions:** children over 6 preferred; no smoking; no pets (resident dog)

CAMDEN HARBOUR INN

83 Bayview Street
Camden, Maine 04843
207/236-4200 or 800/236-4266
Proprietors: Sal Vella and Patti Babij

Camden Harbour Inn was built in 1874 when Camden was a working seaport village bustling with cargo and fishing schooners. The inn provided lodging for summer travelers whose steamships laid over on their way from Boston to Bangor. Then, as now, guests were delighted by the spectacular panorama the inn offered of the village, mountains, harbor, and open waters of Penobscot Bay. With its vast wraparound porch, balconies, and mansard roof, the inn itself is an impressive sight. Every guest room is individually decorated with Victorian antiques, wallpapers, and four-poster or canopy beds. Some rooms have working fireplaces, and some also offer private patios, decks, or balconies. The inn offers several specialty packages throughout the year.

Open: year round **Accommodations:** 22 guest rooms with private baths **Meals:** full breakfast included from May through November; continental-plus breakfast included from December through April; restaurant on premises; restaurants nearby **Wheelchair access:** yes **Rates:** $95 to $195 (seasonal); 10% discount offered to National Trust members and National Trust Visa cardholders **Payment:** Visa, MC, traveler's check **Restrictions:** children over 12 welcome; smoking limited; no pets **Activities:** lounge, television, porch sitting, harbor watching, charters on the inn's 52-foot motor yacht

DAMARISCOTTA

Nearby attractions: Fort William Henry, lighthouses, Audubon Center, museums, beaches, fresh and saltwater fishing, boating, hiking, bicycling, golfing, tennis, seal watching

BRANNON–BUNKER INN
H.C.R. 64, Box 045 Q
Route 129
Damariscotta, Maine 04543
207/563-5941
Proprietors: Jeanne and Joe Hovance
Location: 4 miles south of Damariscotta

In the 1920s the owners of this Cape-style house, which had been built one hundred years earlier, turned the barn behind the house into a dance hall known as La Hacienda. In the 1950s the owners converted the old barn and adjacent carriage house to comfortably furnished sleeping rooms and opened the inn, then known as the Homeport. It was the area's first bed and brakfast. Today, eight sleeping rooms are furnished in colonial, Victorian, and Empire themes. Stenciled walls and floors, quaint wallpapers, homemade quilts, dried flowers, and country crafts meld with each room's antique furnishings. Antiques also fill the breakfast nook and public room with fieldstone fireplace. The upstairs sitting area showcases the innkeeper's World War I memorabilia.

Open: April to December **Accommodations:** 8 guest rooms (6 have private baths) 1 is a suite **Meals:** continental-plus breakfast; restaurants nearby **Wheelchair access:** 3 rooms **Rates:** $55 to $110; 10% discount to National Trust members and National Trust Visa cardholders **Payment:** AmEx, Visa, MC, personal check **Restrictions:** no smokiing; no pets **Activities:** badminton, board games, television, reading, stream and pond

EASTPORT

Nearby attractions: Campobello Island and the Roosevelt summer cottage, whale-watching, Reversing Falls, hiking, fishing trips, tennis, beachcombing, museums, historic district walking tours, art galleries

MILLIKEN HOUSE
29 Washington Street
Eastport, Maine 04631
207/853-2955
Proprietors: Joyce and Paul Weber

In the mid-nineteenth century Eastport vied with New York City as the busiest port on the east coast. This Italianate house was built in 1846 by Benjamin F. Milliken, owner of a nearby wharf that serviced the tall trading ships using Eastport as their port of entry to the United States. Milliken filled his house with Victorian Renaissance furnishings, such as marble-topped tables and ornately carved high-backed beds. Many of these pieces remain in the house today, including in the guest rooms. Guests are welcome to explore the library and double living room with two marble fireplaces. Breakfasts are as elegant as the heavy carved dining room table on which they are served. Visiting artists are invited to share the innkeeper's skylit third-floor studio.

Open: year round **Accommodations:** 5 guest rooms share 2 baths **Meals:** full breakfast included; complimentary refreshments; restaurants nearby **Rates:** $50 to $60; 10% discount to National Trust members and National Trust Visa cardholders **Payment:** Visa, MC, personal and traveler's checks **Restrictions:** no smoking; no pets **Activities:** television, games, herb and perennial gardens, artist's studio

TODD HOUSE
1 Capen Avenue
Todd's Head
Eastport, Maine 04631
207/853-2328
Proprietor: Ruth M. McInnis

Built in 1775, Todd House is a classic New England Cape Cod house with a massive center chimney and a unique "good morning" staircase that rises toward the chimney, then divides left and right to lead toward two opposing bedroom doors. (When occupants of each room awake in the morning and open their doors, they are facing each other, hence the nickname.) One of these bedrooms has a working fireplace. In 1801, Eastern Lodge No. 7 of the Masonic Order was chartered here; a cornerstone marks the event. During the Civil War, the Todd House served as barracks for soldiers. The house, currently owned by a historian and listed in the National Register, has many volumes of local history in its library. Breakfast is served in the common room before a fireplace and bake oven in surroundings reminiscent of the Revolutionary era. The yard affords a view of Passamaquoddy Bay and its islands.

Open: year round **Accommodations:** 6 guest rooms (2 have private baths); 2 are suites **Meals:** continental-plus breakfast included; two rooms have kitchenettes; complimentary refreshments; restaurants nearby **Wheelchair access:** some guest rooms, common rooms **Rates:** $45 to $80 **Payment:** personal and traveler's checks **Restrictions:** no smoking **Activities:** deck and barbecue with water view, library of local history

WESTON HOUSE
26 Boynton Street
Eastport, Maine 04631
207/853-2907
Proprietors: Jett and John Peterson

Jonathan Weston built this Federal house in 1810 on a hill overlooking Passamaquoddy Bay. John James Audubon stayed here while awaiting passage to Labrador in 1833. At today's inn, listed in the National Register of Historic Places, afternoon sherry and tea are offered to guests in surroundings elegantly furnished with collections of antiques and oriental rugs. Some of the large and comfortable guest rooms overlook the bay while others afford views of the expansive lawn and garden. Sumptuous breakfasts are served in the dining room amid family treasures, to the relaxing strains of classical music.

Open: year round **Accommodations:** 5 guest rooms with shared baths **Meals:** full breakfast included; complimentary refreshments; dinners and picnic lunches by reservation; restaurants nearby
Rates: $45 to $65; 10% discount offered to National Trust members **Payment:** personal and traveler's checks **Restrictions:** smoking limited; no pets **Activities:** croquet, badminton, porch sitting to view the bay, gardens

FREEPORT

Nearby attractions: Maine Maritime Museum, famous Freeport factory outlets, including L. L. Bean; Bowdoin and Bates colleges; boat cruises; fishing; beaches; four state parks with nature trails; Marine Museum; golfing; bicycling; hiking; cross-country skiing

BAGLEY HOUSE BED AND BREAKFAST
1290 Royalsborough Road
Durham, Maine 04222
207/865-6566
Proprietor: Suzanne O'Connor and Susan Backhouse
Location: 6 miles north of Freeport on Route 136 in Durham

In 1772, Captain O. Israel Bagley built the first public inn in Durham, then known as Royalsborough. His home served as the site of the town's first worship services and school lessons. Today, the Bagley House contains five guest rooms, each furnished with antiques or beautifully crafted custom pieces, and featuring handmade quilts. The library has an extensive collection of books and games, and the country kitchen boasts a huge brick fireplace, pine floors, hand-hewn beams, and a beehive oven. This is where guests gather each morning for a hearty breakfast around the antique baker's table. Located on six acres of fields and woods, this country home is a bird watcher's and flower lover's dream in the summer and fall.

Open: year round **Accommodations:** 5 guest rooms with private baths **Meals:** full breakfast included; restaurants nearby **Rates:** $80 to $107 **Payment:** AmEx, Visa, MC, Discover, personal and traveler's checks **Restrictions:** no smoking; no pets (resident dog) **Activities:** games, books, magazines, hiking, bird-watching, studying wildflowers, berry picking, cross-country skiing, quilting weekends

BREWSTER HOUSE BED AND BREAKFAST
180 Main Street
Freeport, Maine 04032
207/865-4121 or 800/865-0822
Proprietors: Matthew and Amy Cartmell

Jarvis A. Brewster built this Queen Anne house in 1888. A local businessman, he owned J. A. Brewster, General Merchandise. His store was located on the block were L. L. Bean stands today, just two blocks south of Brewster House. The innkeepers have newly restored Brewster's home, incorporating antique furnishings and a traditional decor that compliment the house's nineteenth-century fixtures such as tin ceilings and carved moldings. Each large guest room is quiet and comfortable and has a private bath. Guests may also enjoy the sitting room. Breakfast, prepared by an experienced chef, is served in the dining room. Guests of Brewster House may park their cars in the inn's lot and walk the short distance to Freeport's many outlets, shops, and restaurants.

Open: year round **Accommodations:** 5 guest rooms with private baths **Meals:** full breakfast included; complimentary refreshments; restaurants nearby **Rates:** $70 to $95 **Payment:** Visa, MC, Discover, personal and traveler's checks **Restrictions:** children over 8 welcome; no smoking; no pets

HARRASEEKET INN
162 Main Street
Freeport, Maine 04032
207/865-9377
Proprietor: Nancy D. Gray

The last dairy farmhouse in town, built in 1798, was connected by a 1989 addition to an 1850 Greek Revival house to create this small luxury inn in the village of Freeport, the town where Maine was declared a state. Located on five acres of tree-shaded grounds, the Harraseeket Inn features 20 fireplaces, antique furnishings, three dining rooms, a library, a ballroom, and a tavern. Guest rooms with private baths (some with whirlpool tubs) offer canopied beds. A strong emphasis is placed on Maine-grown organic foods in the inn's restaurants. Complimentary afternoon tea is served in the mahogany-paneled drawing room. The innkeepers are Maine natives with a family history of innkeeping that dates to 1895. They offer amenities and services for discriminating travelers.

Open: year round **Accommodations:** 54 guest rooms with private baths; 6 are suites **Meals:** full breakfast included; complimentary afternoon tea; restarants on premises **Wheelchair access:** meets Americans with Disabilities Act regulations **Rates:** $145 to $225; 10% discount offered to National Trust members and National Trust Visa cardholders **Payment:** AmEx, Visa, MC, DC, Discover, traveler's check **Restrictions:** smoking limited **Activities:** croquet

GEORGETOWN

Nearby attractions: Reid State Park, beach, Maine Maritime Museum, Boothbay Harbor, antiques hunting, Freeport outlet shops, Bowdoin College, lobster boat charters, fishing

GREY HAVENS INN
Seguinland Road
P.O. Box 308
Georgetown, Maine 04548
207/371-2616
Proprietors: Bill and Haley Eberhart
Location: 12 miles east of Bath

Opened as the Seguinland in June 1904, this inn was built by Walter Reid, who later gave another parcel of his estate to become Reid State Park. The inn is believed to be the last Shingle-style hotel still in operation on the Maine coast. The National Register property has been altered only enough to bow to modern comforts, with baseboard heat and private guest baths. Nearly all guest rooms look on the water; four are turret rooms, offering 180-degree vistas. The porch wraps around three sides of the inn, providing a perfect setting from which to watch the sun rise, eat breakfast, or just mark the tides. For relaxing inside, there is the lounge with its enormous rock fireplace and original 12-foot-wide picture window. An honor bar is open to inn guests in the evening. The restaurant, featuring local seafood, serves dinner Tuesday through Saturday.

Open: year round **Accommodations:** 10 guest rooms with private baths; 1 is a suite **Meals:** continental-plus breakfast included; restaurant on premises; restaurants nearby **Rates:** $100 to $185; 10% discount to National Trust members and National Trust Visa cardholders November through April **Payment:** AmEx, Visa, MC, personal and traveler's checks **Restrictions:** children over 7 welcome; no smoking; no pets **Activities:** rowboats (to get to an island nature preserve), watching tides rise and fall

GREENVILLE

Nearby attractions: Steamboat Katahdin lake cruises, Moosehead Lake for water activities, skiing on Squaw Mountain, golfing, tennis, sightseeing plane rides, snowmobile trails

GREENVILLE INN
Norris Street
P.O. Box 1194
Greenville, Maine 04441
207/695-2206
Proprietors: Michael, Elfi, and Susie Schnetzer

The Greenville Inn, an 1895 lumber baron's mansion, is located on a hill overlooking Moosehead Lake—the largest lake completely contained in any one state—and the Squaw Mountains. It took 10 years for ships' carpenters from the coast to complete the house's cherry, mahogany, and oak paneling and other embellishments. A spruce tree painted on a leaded-glass window is the focal point of the stairway landing. Six fireplaces ornamented with mosaics and carved mantels, embossed wallpapers, and gaslights grace the inn. The intimate and elegant dining rooms offer fresh Maine seafood, glazed roast duckling, and grilled chops or steaks. Boating and water sports are available on the lake, whose surface in autumn reflects the brilliantly colored foliage on the mountainsides.

Open: year round **Accommodations:** 13 guest rooms (11 have private baths); 6 are cottages **Meals:** continental-plus breakfast included; restaurant on premises **Wheelchair access:** limited **Rates:** $75 to $115; 10% discount offered to National Trust members and National Trust Visa cardholders **Payment:** Visa, MC, Discover, personal and traveler's checks **Restrictions:** children over 10 welcome; no pets

HANCOCK

Nearby attractions: Acadia National Park, mountain climbing, boating, whale-watching, antiques hunting, golfing, tennis

CROCKER HOUSE COUNTRY INN
H.C. 77, Box 171
Hancock, Maine 04640
207/422-6806
207/422-3105 Fax
Proprietors: Richard and Elizabeth Malaby

Crocker House Country Inn, tucked away on the peninsula of Hancock Point, was built in 1884 and carefully restored in 1986. Crocker House has been operating since the days in which Hancock was a thriving shipbuilding community. In addition to having been the terminus of the Washington, D.C. to Bar Harbor Express, Hancock was the port from which the famed Sullivan quarries shipped their cobblestones to pave the streets of Boston and New York. Built as an adjunct to the great hotels of Hancock's past, the Crocker House is the lone survivor. Eleven guest rooms are uniquely decorated. All rooms have private baths and telephones. In addition to the full complimentary breakfast served to overnight guests, the dining room is open to the public for dinner. Breads and desserts are made daily on the premises. The inn is available for weddings and large parties.

Open: April to January **Accommodations:** 11 guest rooms with private baths; 1 is a suite **Meals:** full breakfast included; restaurant on premises; restaurants nearby **Wheelchair access:** limited **Rates:** $75 to $120 **Payment:** AmEx, Visa, MC, Discover, personal and traveler's checks **Restrictions:** smoking limited **Activities:** spa, croquet, bicycles available

KENNEBUNKPORT

Nearby attractions: Dock Square shops, walking tours, tennis, golfing, boating, deep-sea fishing, watching birds and whales, bicycling, hiking, beaches, museums, outlet shops, theaters, concerts, art galleries, antiques hunting

CAPTAIN LORD MANSION
Corner of Pleasant and Green Streets
P.O. Box 800
Kennebunkport, Maine 04046
207/967-3141
207/967-3172 Fax
Proprietors: Bev Davis and Rick Litchfield

This 20,000-square-foot Federal mansion was built during the War of 1812 by shipbuilder Nathaniel Lord, whose family continued to occupy the home until 1972. It is located at the head of a sweeping lawn known as the River Green, overlooking the Kennebunk River. Listed in the National Register of Historic Places, the mansion is graced with many fine architectural details, such as an octagonal cupola, a four-story spiral staircase, an 18-foot-wide bay window with curved sashes, 14 fireplaces, and a hand-pulled elevator. Guest rooms are furnished with antiques, reproduction wall coverings, plush linens, fine toiletries, and many other amenities. With a conference room that can accommodate up to 14 people and full meal service available, the inn is also perfect for executive retreats. Elegant yet intimate, the inn has enjoyed a four-diamond rating from AAA for 15 consecutive years.

Open: year round **Accommodations:** 16 guest rooms with private baths **Meals:** full breakfast included; complimentary refreshments; restaurants nearby **Rates:** $149 to $199; 10% discount to National Trust members and National Trust Visa cardholders **Payment:** Visa, MC, Discover, personal and traveler's checks **Restrictions:** children over 6 welcome; no smoking; no pets **Activities:** large gathering room with comfortable chairs for reading, game tables, puzzles, antique music box, and working fireplace

KENNEBUNKPORT INN
One Dock Square
P.O. Box 111
Kennebunkport, Maine 04046
207/967-2621 or 800/248-2621
207/967-3705 Fax
Proprietors: Rick and Martha Griffin

The Kennebunkport Inn began in 1890 as a private residence for wealthy tea and coffee merchant Burleigh S. Thompson. The Colonial Revival mansion boasted

400 feet of river frontage and was furnished without regard to expense. Today, guest rooms in the mansion and in the attached 1930s River House are individually decorated with period antiques. All accommodations include private baths and color television. The inn's dining room is renowned for its fresh native seafood and regional cuisine. The turn-of-the-century pub includes a piano bar. The inn boasts a swimming pool, deck, and white sand beach. Just steps from the inn are numerous shops and galleries.

Open: year round **Accommodations:** 34 guest rooms with private baths **Meals:** continental breakfast include in winter months; restaurant on premises serves breakfast and dinner; restaurants nearby **Wheelchair access:** yes **Rates:** $69.50 to $189 (seasonal) **Payment:** AmEx, Visa, MC, traveler's check **Restrictions:** smoking limited; no pets **Activities:** swimming pool, piano bar and lounge

KYLEMERE HOUSE, 1818
South Street
P.O. Box 1333
Kennebunkport, Maine 04046-1333
207/967-2780
Proprietors: Ruth and Helen Toohey

Kylemere House, historically known as "Crosstrees," is a Federal-style home built in 1818 by Daniel Walker, a member of one of the first four families in the port. In 1895, well-known Maine artist and architect Abbot Graves purchased the house and used the barn as his studio. Today, the barn is a charming innkeepers' apartment with the 1818 post-and-beam construction still visible. The house has been restored and each guest room individually decorated in period style. Creative breakfast cuisine is served in the formal dining room or on the porch overlooking the gardens. Kylemere House has been featured in *Glamour* magazine and on CBS television's "Regis and Kathie Lee Show."

Open: mid-May to mid-December **Accommodations:** 4 guest rooms with private baths **Meals:** full breakfast included; complimentary refreshments; restaurants nearby **Rates:** $80 to $135; 10% discount offered to National Trust members and National Trust Visa cardholders **Payment:** Visa, MC, Discover, personal and traveler's checks **Restrictions:** children over 12 welcome; no smoking; no pets **Activities:** reading, music, gardens with pond and sitting areas

MAINE STAY INN
34 Maine Street
P.O. Box 500A-NT
Kennebunkport, Maine 04046-1800
207/967-2117 or 800/950-2117
207/967-8757 Fax
Proprietors: Carol and Lindsay Copeland

Built as a home in 1860 in a square-block, Italianate style with a contoured, low-hipped roof, the Maine Stay Inn underwent numerous alterations around the turn of the century. The house's fine craftsmanship is still evident in a suspended flying staircase, sunburst-crystal glass windows, ornately carved mantels and moldings, a spacious wicker-bedecked wraparound porch, and a cupola that was once used to spot rum-runners offshore and now offers lovely views of the town. The delightful guest rooms, some with fireplaces, offer comfort and solitude. Both the house and surrounding district are listed in the National Register of Historic Places. The innkeepers join with Maine Stay guests each afternoon for tea and conversation, sharing the latest happenings in the "Port."

Open: year round **Accommodations:** 6 guest rooms with private baths; 2 are suites **Meals:** full breakfast included; complimentary afternoon refreshments; restaurants nearby **Rates:** $85 to $210 **Payment:** AmEx, Visa, MC, personal and traveler's checks **Restrictions:** smoking limited; no pets **Activities:** lawn games, porch for reading and relaxing

TIDES INN BY-THE-SEA
R.R. 2, 737 Goose Rocks Beach
Kennebunkport, Maine 04046
207/967-3757
Proprietor: Marie B.
Henriksen

Exceptionally clean, homey New England lodging is what guests encounter at the Tides Inn, a three-story Victorian clapboard-and-shingle hotel, designed by John Calvin Stevens and built in 1899. In its infancy, the inn was called the New Belvidere, and hosted such luminaries as Theodore Roosevelt and Sir Arthur Conan Doyle, whose signatures are in the guest register. The lobby boasts its original beachstone fireplace and an antique cabinet displaying items found in the hotel walls during its most recent renovation: snuff boxes, love letters, photographs, a large hat pin, and black hosiery! The front rooms, dining rooms, and open porches afford sunny, unobstructed views of the Atlantic Ocean. Guests enjoy a cozy pub, terrific Maine cooking, and a relaxed atmosphere.

Open: mid-May to mid-October **Accommodations:** 22 guest rooms (19 have private baths); 2 are suites **Meals:** restaurants on premises; restaurants nearby **Rates:** $85 to $210 **Payment:** AmEx, Visa, MC, personal and traveler's check **Restrictions:** smoking limited; no pets **Activities:** three miles of sandy beach for jogging, swimming, collecting shells, and building sand castles

OAKLAND

Nearby attractions: Belgrade Lakes Chain, swimming, boating, water skiing, fishing, ice skating, cross-country skiing, snowmobiling, ice fishing

PRESSEY HOUSE
85 Summer Street
Oakland, Maine 04963
207/465-3500
Proprietors: Terry and JoAnne Badger

Pressey House is a fine example of an architectural rarity: an octagon house. Built in the 1850s by H. T. Pressey, this local landmark (one of 14 known octagonal structures in the state of Maine) incorporates elements of the Greek Revival style in its simple ornamentation. Located in the quaint village of Oakland on Messalonskee Lake, Pressey House has an attached ell and barn in the typical New England rural style. The house boasts 22 rooms and five original fireplaces in 8000 square feet of living space. The rambling structure also includes five guest suites, many with excellent lake views. Listed in the National Register of Historic Places, Pressey House is decorated with traditional and Victorian furnishings.

Open: year round **Accommodations:** 5 guest suites with private baths **Meals:** full breakfast included; complimentary refreshments; restaurants nearby **Rates:** $75 to $100; 10% discount to National Trust members and National Trust Visa cardholders **Payment:** personal and traveler's checks **Activities:** lake beach, swimming, fishing, boating, gardens

PORTLAND

Nearby attractions: historic district walking tours, fine art museum, symphony, theater, beaches, Casco Bay, Calendar Islands, harbor cruises, whale-watching, ice skating, cross-country skiing, outlet shops, international ferry to Nova Scotia

POMEGRANATE INN

49 Neal Street
Portland, Maine 04102
207/772-1006 or 800/356-0408
207/773-4426 Fax
Proprietors: Isabel and Alan Smiles

In 1884, E. Russell Barbour built a Victorian house on this corner lot. In 1919 the house was sold to Frank E. Milliken, who remodeled it to its current Colonial Revival style, which features a two-story bow window, cornice modillions, and a classical portico. Today, the house is the Pomegranate Inn, an imaginative small inn dressed in eclecticism and offering personalized service. The walls of each bedroom have been painted by artist Heidi Gerquest in unique floral abstractions and geometric patterns that blend seamlessly with the elegant furnishings, which include four-poster beds in some rooms. All rooms are appointed with antiques, fine linens, telephone, television, and private bath. The inn's individuality extends to breakfast, with entrees such as currant pancakes. Pomegranate Inn has been featured in *Travel and Leisure.*

Open: year round **Accommodations:** 8 guest rooms with private baths; 1 is a suite **Meals:** full breakfast included; restaurants nearby **Wheelchair access:** 1 room **Rates:** $95 to $155; 10% discount to National Trust members and National Trust Visa cardholders **Payment:** AmEx, Visa, MC, DC, Discover, personal and traveler's checks **Restrictions:** children over 16 welcome; no smoking; no pets

SEARSPORT

Nearby attractions: Acadia National Park and other seacoast parks, coastal towns, museums, sailing, tennis, golfing, bay cruises, hiking, antiques hunting, fall foliage, downhill and cross-country skiing, snowmobiling

HOMEPORT INN
East Main Street
Route 1, Box 647H
Searsport, Maine 04974
207/548-2259 or 800/742-5814
Proprietors: Edith and George Johnson

Homeport, listed in the National Register of Historic Places, is a fine example of Italianate architecture, complete with decorative eaves brackets, arched windows, twin chimneys, and square cupola. Built in 1863 as a sea captain's mansion, the inn has been fully restored and now offers comfortable accommodations in elegant surroundings of family heirlooms and period antiques. The house sits neatly behind a white picket fence, its grounds extending beyond gardens and recreational areas to the seashore. Breakfast is served in the formal family dining room or in the sunporch overlooking Penobscot Bay. The family room on the lower level features an English pub, *The Mermaid*.

Open: year round **Accommodations:** 10 guest rooms (6 have private baths) **Meals:** full breakfast included in rate; pub on premises; restaurants nearby **Wheelchair access:** limited **Rates:** $55 to $85; 10% discount offered to National Trust members and National Trust Visa cardholders **Payment:** AmEx, Visa, MC, Discover, personal and traveler's checks **Restrictions:** smoking limited; no pets **Activities:** croquet, badminton, flower garden, seashore

---

SOUTH BROOKSVILLE

Nearby attractions: Acadia National Park, Bar Harbor, Camden, Castine, Blue Hill, Stonington, antiques hunting, crafts shops, hiking, swimming, rowing, sailing, golfing, tennis

BUCK'S HARBOR INN
Steamboat Wharf Road
South Brooksville, Maine 04617
207/326-8660
207/326-0730 Fax
Proprietors: Peter and Ann Ebeling
Location: 10 miles south of Blue Hill

This large clapboard building with dramatic mansard roof was built in 1901 as an annex to the Bay View Hotel, a large resort hotel that catered to summer vacationers from urban New England. The hotel, dependent on steamship passengers, closed in the 1930s and was dismantled; the annex became the private residence of Morris and Minnie Lou Chatto. The innkeepers purchased the annex and land in 1976, embarking on extensive renovations that resulted in the Buck's Harbor Inn, which opened in 1982. Six roomy and comfortable guest rooms are available. The inn exudes the quiet charm of an old resort hotel, yet pampers guests with modern comforts. The adjoining Landing Restaurant affords spectacular views of Buck's Harbor and Penobscot Bay.

Open: year round **Accommodations:** 6 guest rooms share 2¹/2 baths **Meals:** full breakfast included; seasonal restaurant next door **Rates:** $50 to $75 **Payment:** Visa, MC, personal check **Restrictions:** no smoking; no pets **Activities:** porch sitting, nature walks

YORK HARBOR

Nearby attractions: historic buildings, museums, outlet shops in Kittery, theater, boating, fishing, tennis, beach, water sports, art galleries, antiques hunting, cross-country skiing

TANGLEWOOD HALL
611 York Street
P.O. Box 12
York Harbor, Maine 03911
207/363-7577
Proprietor: Michael L. Stotts

Tanglewood, a Shingle Style Victorian house, was built in 1889 for Edward H. Banks. The house was once the summer home of Jimmy and Tommy Dorsey, and Winslow Homer also is said to have been a visitor. Tanglewood was the 1994 York Historical Society's Decorator Show House, welcoming more than 7000 people through its rooms. These expertly decorated rooms include a large foyer, parlor, morning room, and dining room, all with fireplaces. A T-shaped or "good morning" staircase leads to bedrooms on the second floor and mezzanine. The York Harbor Suite with four-poster bed has a fireplace and conservatory. The Winslow Homer Room is located on the mezzanine level in the former library. The Tommy Dorsey Room overlooks the gardens and woods. A large wrap-around veranda and the sounds of the ocean sooth guests.

Open: June 1 to October 31 **Accommodations:** 3 guest rooms; 1 is a suite **Meals:** full breakfast included; restaurants nearby **Rates:** $90 to $120; 10% discount to National Trust members and National Trust Visa cardholders **Payment:** Visa, MC, personal and traveler's checks **Restrictions:** children over 12 welcome; no smoking; no pets **Activities:** veranda, gardens

YORK HARBOR INN
Route 1A
P.O. Box 573
York Harbor, Maine 03911
207/363-5119 or 800/343-3869
207/363-3545, ext. 295 Fax
Proprietor: Garry Dominguez

The York Harbor Inn has been hosting visitors to this oceanside town for more than a century. Various owners have expanded the building over the years, but at its core is a 1637 fisherman's cabin that was moved here from the Isle of Shoals. This rustic structure, with its massive fieldstone fireplace, exposed wood beams, oriental rugs, and comfortable seating arrangements serves as a common room for guests. All guest rooms and public areas are furnished with colonial-era antiques and artifacts. Four-poster and iron beds are featured in guest rooms, which include such amenities as working fireplaces, clock-radios, and guest toiletries. The inn is a short walk away from the beach and a charming National Register historic district.

Open: year round **Accommodations:** 35 guest rooms (31 have private baths); 2 are suites **Meals:** continental-plus breakfast included; complimentary refreshments; restaurant on premises **Wheelchair access:** some guest and common rooms **Rates:** $79 to $139; 10% discount to National Trust members and National Trust Visa cardholders **Payment:** AmEx, Visa, MC, CB, DC, personal and traveler's checks **Restrictions:** smoking limited; no pets **Activities:** pub with live music, bicycles available

MARYLAND

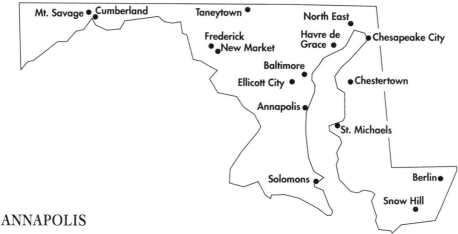

ANNAPOLIS

Nearby attractions: Maryland State Capitol, William Paca House, walking tours of historic district, City Dock, Chesapeake Bay, boating, U.S. Naval Adacemy, antiques hunting, shopping, dining

GIBSON'S LODGINGS

110 Prince George Street
Annapolis, Maryland 21401
410/268-5555
Proprietors: Claude and Jeanne Schrift

Three distinctive buildings in the heart of the Annapolis Historic District—in the area once known as infamous Hell's Point—make up Gibson's Lodgings. The oldest home is the Patterson House, built over the period 1760 to 1786 by businessman Richard MacDubbin. It combines Georgian and Federal styling with a few later Victorian elements. It contains six guest rooms sharing three baths, two parlors, and a formal dining room. The Berman House, a nineteenth-century two-story stucco home with double-decker front porches contains nine guest rooms with shared baths, a parlor, and dining room. The recently built brick Lauer House offers two suites and four rooms with private baths and conference facilities. Antiques are used to furnish all three homes.

Open: year round **Accommodations:** 21 guest rooms (7 have private baths); 2 are suites **Meals:** continental-plus breakfast included; restaurants nearby **Wheelchair access:** 1 room **Rates:** $68 to $125 **Payment:** AmEx, Visa, MC, personal and traveler's checks **Restrictions:** no smoking; no pets

BALTIMORE

Nearby attractions: National Aquarium, Inner Harbor, Oriole Park at Camden Yard, Maryland Science Center, Johns Hopkins University, historic Fell's Point, Little Italy, Pimlico Race Course (home of the Preakness), Baltimore Zoo, Babe Ruth Baseball Museum, H. L. Mencken House, Edgar Allan Poe House, Baltimore Symphony, Mechanic Theatre, historic neighborhoods, antiques hunting, tennis, bicycling, boating, swimming

ADMIRAL FELL
888 South Broadway
Baltimore, Maryland 21231
410/522-7377 or 800/292-INNS (800/292-4667)
410/522-0707 Fax
Proprietors: Matthias Eckenstein and Jim Widman

In the historic Fell's Point section of Baltimore is the mischievously named Admiral Fell Inn, seven adjoining buildings of Victorian design dating from 1850 to 1910. Originally a boardinghouse for sailors, later a YMCA, and then a vinegar bottling plant, this delightful facility was completely renovated in 1985, then expanded and renovated in 1995. The public areas include an antique-filled lobby and library, an English-style pub for light fare, and a full-service restaurant specializing in fresh seafood dishes. The 80 individually decorated guest rooms, many with four-poster beds, are named after figures in Maryland history. Ultimate convenience is provided by modern bathrooms (some with whirlpool tubs) containing color cable television sets and telephones. In addition to free continental breakfasts and daily newspapers, the inn provides complimentary transportation to the Inner Harbor, downtown, and Johns Hopkins Medical Institutions. The Admiral Fell inn is a charter member of Historic Hotels of America.

Open: year round **Accommodations:** 80 guest rooms with private baths; 4 are suites **Meals:** continental breakfast included; restaurants on premises; restaurants nearby **Wheelchair access:** guest rooms, bathrooms, dining rooms **Rates:** $98 to 195; 10% discount to National Trust members and National Trust Visa cardholders **Payment:** AmEx, Visa, MC, Discover, personal and traveler's checks **Restrictions:** no smoking; call for guidelines for pets **Activities:** pub and restaurant, courtyard for relaxing, books and games

BAUERNSCHMIDT MANOR BED AND BREAKFAST
2316 Bauernschmidt Drive
Baltimore, Maryland 21221-1713
410/687-ABED (410/687-2233) or 800/735-6360
Proprietors: Will and Sue Gerard

This house was once the summer residence of Frederick and Agnes Bauernschmidt, a family noted in Baltimore history for its beer-brewing fortune and philanthropy. The manor house was built ca. 1910 and its foundation is said to contain bricks salvaged from the Baltimore fire of 1904. The frame house with wraparound porch and balcony has wide eaves with decorative brackets and a central cupola that come from the Italianate style of architecture. The house was renovated in 1991 and now offers three spacious, air-conditioned guest rooms with cable, color television, and private bath. One guest room features a fireplace, whirlpool tub, and king-size bed. A pool table and an in-ground swimming pool are offered for relaxation.

Open: year round **Accommodations:** 3 guest rooms with private baths **Meals:** full breakfast included; restaurants nearby **Rates:** $75 to $125; 10% discount to National Trust members and National Trust Visa cardholders **Payment:** personal and traveler's checks **Restrictions:** no smoking; no pets **Activities:** swimming pool, pool table, bicycling, hiking

BETSY'S BED AND BREAKFAST
1428 Park Avenue
Baltimore, Maryland 21217
410/383-1274 or 800/899-7533
Proprietor: Betsy Grater

Betsy's Bed and Breakfast is in an 1870 four-story townhouse with center staircase that rises to a skylight. The interior features six carved marble fireplace mantels and 12-foot ceilings with medallions. A hallway is inlaid with strips of oak and walnut. The walls are decorated with handsome brass rubbings and family heirloom quilts and coverlets. Spacious guest rooms with marble mantelpieces contain queen- or king-size beds. The living room, in the back of the house, opens through French doors onto a garden, deck, and hot tub. Bolton Hill is a historic neighborhood, primarily residential, with tree-lined streets and brick sidewalks. Once it was home to F. Scott Fitzgerald and Gertrude Stein. Betsy's is within walking distance of Baltimore's cultural center and just seven minutes' driving time to the inner harbor and Harbor Place or a quick ride on the light rail to Camden Yard.

Open: year round **Accommodations:** 3 guest rooms with private baths **Meals:** continental breakfast included; restaurants nearby **Rates:** $65 to $85; 10% discount offered to National Trust members **Payment:** AmEx, Visa, MC, Discover, personal and traveler's checks **Restrictions:** no smoking; no pets **Activities:** hot tub in season

THE INN AT HENDERSON'S WHARF
1000 Fell Street
Baltimore, Maryland 21231
410/522-7777
410/522-7087 Fax
Proprietor: Tom Holohan

Henderson's Wharf, at the historic Fell's Point neighborhood, is home to the former Baltimore and Ohio Railroad tobacco warehouse. Built in 1894, now listed in the National Register of Historic Places, the warehouse has been artfully renovated to maintain its historical integrity while being converted to a bed-and-breakfast inn. The lobby and guest rooms use the structure's original brick walls as a backdrop to luxurious and spacious rooms offering every modern amenity. Guest rooms face the harbor, the marina, or the garden in the interior courtyard. Room service, next-day valet service, and an exercise studio are available. A leisurely stroll from the inn will take guests to fine dining, pubs, musical entertainment, antiques shops, and historic buildings.

Open: year round **Accommodations:** 38 guest rooms with private baths **Meals:** continental breakfast included; room service available; restaurants nearby **Wheelchair access:** yes **Rates:** $95 to $145; 10% discount to National Trust members and National Trust Visa cardholders **Payment:** AmEx, Visa, MC, CB, DC, traveler's check **Restrictions:** no smoking; no pets **Activities:** small health club, specialty packages

MR. MOLE BED AND BREAKFAST
1601 Bolton Street
Baltimore, Maryland 21217
410/728-1179
410/728-3379 Fax
Proprietors: Collin Clarke and Paul Bragaw

Mr. Mole Bed and Breakfast is located in historic Bolton Hill, a neighborhood of quiet, tree-lined streets and spacious brick row houses. The neighborhood was built by wealthy merchants of mid-nineteenth-century Baltimore. This house, built in 1870, is decorated in a comfortable English style with many eighteenth- and nineteenth-century antiques. On the first floor, the living, breakfast, and drawing rooms are made elegant by 14-foot-high ceilings, bay windows, and marble fireplaces. Each guest room is individually decorated to create a distinctive mood like that in the Explorer Suite, a soothing blue-and-white room appointed with prints and artifacts collected from around the world. The Garden Suite, with its third-floor sunroom and sitting area, is bright in floral prints and plaid. Garage parking (with an automatic garage door opener) is available. Mr. Mole Bed and Breakfast has a Mobil four-star rating.

Open: year round **Accommodations:** 5 guest rooms with private baths; 2 are suites **Meals:** continental breakfast included; restaurants nearby **Rates:** $82 single to $155 triple **Payment:** AmEx, Visa, MC, Discover, personal and traveler's checks **Restrictions:** children over 10 welcome; no smoking; no pets

---

BERLIN

Nearby attractions: Assateague Island National Seashore, Ocean City, antiques hunting, museums, horseback riding, golfing, tennis, fishing, crabbing, boating, swimming, beachcombing

MERRY SHERWOOD PLANTATION
8909 Worcester Highway
Berlin, Maryland 21811
410/641-2112 or 800/660-0358
Proprietor: Kirk Byrbage
Location: 6 miles west of Ocean City, Maryland

On 18 acres of Maryland's scenic Eastern Shore, Merry Sherwood is an Italianate plantation home built in 1859. Outside, the stately structure is heavily orna-mented with decorative cresting along the roofs of the main three-story house, the two-story wing, the wraparound arcaded porch, and the central tower. Inside, marble fireplaces, hardwood floors, fine antiques, and period light fixtures are complemented by deep, rich wall paints and Victorian-style papers. Each large guest room has been decorated with differently styled Victorian antiques. Bathrooms are luxurious with marble tile floors, marble showers, antique fixtures, and period wallcoverings. Guests are invited into the ballroom, parlor, dining room, library, and sunporch. Landscaped grounds include rare varieties of trees and shrubs. The plantation is listed in the National Register of Historic Places.

Open: year round **Accommodations:** 8 guest rooms (6 have private baths); 1 is a suite **Meals:** full breakfast included; complimentary refreshments; restaurants nearby **Rates:** $125 to $175; 10% discount to National Trust members and National Trust Visa cardholders **Payment:** Visa, MC, personal and traveler's checks **Restrictions:** no smoking; no pets **Activities:** lawn games, swings

CHESAPEAKE CITY

Nearby attractions: Canal Museum, Longwood Gardens, Winterthur, nature preserves, bicycling, shopping, antiques hunting

INN AT THE CANAL
104 Bohemia Avenue
Chesapeake City, Maryland 21915-0187
410/885-5995
410/885-3585 Fax
Proprietors: Mary and Al Ioppolo

Henry Brady had this house built for his family upon the birth of his first son in 1868. With a steeply pitched cross gable and tall, thin windows, the house is a charming example of the Gothic Revival style. Many of the fine architectural and decorative details that Brady incorporated are still intact. Today, as the Inn at the Canal, the house offers six distinct guest rooms with private baths and individual climate controls. The inn is filled with antique quilts and furnishings, and a large collection of old baking and cooking implements is displayed on the fireplace wall of the kitchen. Guests relax in the parlor or sit on the waterside porch to watch boats pass by on the canal. Located in the heart of historic Chesapeake City, Inn at the Canal owes much of its unique atmosphere to the thriving village at the banks of the Chesapeake and Delaware Canal.

Open: year round **Accommodations:** 6 guest rooms with private baths **Meals:** full breakfast included; complimentary refreshments; restaurants nearby **Rates:** $75 to $130; 10% discount to National Trust members and National Trust Visa cardholders **Payment:** AmEx, Visa, MC, CB, DC, Discover, personal and traveler's checks **Restrictions:** children over 10 welcome; no smoking; no pets **Activities:** croquet, waterside porches and rockers, antiques shop on premises

CHESTERTOWN

Nearby attractions: Chester River, Washington College, Eastern Neck Wildlife Reserve, Kent County Historical Society, sailing, boating, hunting, fishing, crabbing, antiques hunting, historic sightseeing

BRAMPTON
25227 Chestertown Road
Chestertown, Maryland 21620
301/778-1860
Proprietors: Michael and Danielle Hanscom
Location: 1 mile south of Chestertown on Route 20

Brampton, a three-story red brick Italianate house constructed in 1860, is situated on 35 quiet, rural acres with century-old trees and boxwoods on Maryland's Eastern Shore. This National Register property is located between the Chester River and the Chesapeake Bay in the heart of the Atlantic Flyway, the favorite spring and fall route of migrating Canada geese, ducks, and swans. Resting birds crowd Kent County's fields and sanctuary ponds in season. Guest rooms are decorated with antiques or custom reproductions and have either fireplaces or Franklin stoves. The house also features a guest parlor and a large dining room where guests receive a full country breakfast, complete with homemade cakes, breads, and jams.

Open: year round **Accommodations:** 8 guest rooms with private baths; 2 are suites **Meals:** full breakfast included; restaurants nearby **Wheelchair access:** 1 guest room **Rates:** $95 to $155 **Payment:** Visa, MC, personal and traveler's checks **Restrictions:** smoking limited; no pets **Activities:** bicycling, reading, relaxing, horseshoes

IMPERIAL HOTEL
208 High Street
Chestertown, Maryland 21620
301/778-5000
Proprietors: Robert and Barbara Lavelle

Built in 1903 by Wilbur W. Hubbard (whose 95-year-old son still lives in town), the Imperial Hotel offers views of quaint High Street from its lofty porches. Listed in the National Register of Historic Places, the hotel has undergone an elaborate restoration, winning an award from the Maryland Trust for Historic Preservation. The hotel's bedrooms, dining rooms, and parlors are furnished in lavish Victorian decor and feature such unique touches as original prints and lithographs. The elegant hotel provides every guest convenience, from towel warmers and designer toiletries to antique writing desks, telephones, and color cable television

tucked into antique armoires. The Imperial's restaurant, serving outstanding contemporary American food with emphasis on regional and seasonal specialties, has been acclaimed by *New York* magazine, the *Philadelphia Inquirer*, and the *Zagat Survey*, as well as by *Wine Spectator* for its wine list.

Open: year round **Accommodations:** 13 guest rooms with private baths; 2 are suites **Meals:** continental breakfast included; restaurant on premises **Wheelchair access:** guest rooms, bathrooms, dining rooms **Rates:** $125 to $250; midweek discounts available **Payment:** Visa, MC, Discover, personal and traveler's checks **Restrictions:** smoking limited; no pets

CUMBERLAND

Nearby attractions: historic districts, History House Museum, Western Maryland Station and Museum, Western Maryland Scenic Railroad, C&O Canal towpath, Cumberland Theater, Rocky Gap and New Germany state parks, Frostburg State University, Savage River and Greenridge recreation areas, bicycling, Frank Lloyd Wright's Fallingwater

INN AT WALNUT BOTTOM
120 Greene Street
Cumberland, Maryland 21502
301/777-0003 or 800/286-9718
Proprietor: Sharon Ennis Kazary

The Inn at Walnut Bottom comprises the 1820 Federal-style Cowden House, the adjoining 1890 Dent House, the Oxford House Restaurant, and from May through October, the Haystack Mountain Art Workshops. All guest rooms are uniquely decorated with antique and period reproduction furniture. All rooms have television and private telephones. The inn is air conditioned and bathrooms are modern. Two parlors and a gift shop are available to overnight guests. In addition to the art workshops hosted by the inn from spring to fall, the inn offers a variety of packages based on such activities as canoeing the Potomac River, bicycling along the C&O Canal, and Mountain Club golfing. The restaurant serves traditional country-inn fare.

Open: year round **Accommodations:** 12 guest rooms (8 have private baths); 2 are suites **Meals:** full breakfast included; complimentary refreshments; restaurant on premises; restaurants nearby **Wheelchair access:** 2 rooms **Rates:** $65 to $130; 10% discount to National Trust members and National Trust Visa cardholders Sunday through Thursday **Payment:** AmEx, Visa, MC, Discover, traveler's check **Restrictions:** no smoking; no pets **Activities:** parlor games, library, in-room cable television

ELLICOTT CITY

Nearby attractions: Railroad Station Museum, Baltimore's Inner Harbor, Savage Mill, antique hunting, specialty shops

WAYSIDE INN
4344 Columbia Road
Ellicott City, Maryland 21042-5910
410/461-4636
Proprietors: Margo and John Osantowski

The Wayside Inn is a stately Federal-style stone farmhouse situated on two acres with a pond, near the historic mill town of Ellicott City. The inn, built between 1800 and 1850, continues the tradition of setting a lighted candle in the window of each room available to guests. As guests enter the central hall, they glimpse the parlor on the left and the adjoining music room, both inviting them to read and relax. Individually decorated guest rooms or suites feature pencil-post, iron and brass, canopy, or spool beds. Two guest rooms offer working fireplaces.

Open: year round **Accommodations:** 2 guest rooms with shared baths; 2 suites with private baths **Meals:** continental breakfast included; restaurants nearby **Rates:** $70 to $90; 10% discount offered to National Trust members and National Trust Visa cardholders **Payment:** AmEx, Visa, MC, personal and traveler's checks **Restrictions:** not suitable for small children; no smoking; no pets **Activities:** games, music room, walking

FREDERICK

Nearby attractions: historic district, carriage rides, Civil War battlefields and tours, antiques hunting, golfing, tennis, bicycling, swimming

TYLER SPITE HOUSE
112 West Church Street
Frederick, Maryland 21701
301/831-4455
Proprietors: William and Andrea Myer

Tyler Spite House derives its name from the fact that Dr. John Tyler built the 1814 Federal mansion expressly to prevent the city from extending Record Street through to West Patrick Street. The foundation was constructed literally overnight and the home became known as the Spite House. Today, the National Register house is located in prestigious courthouse square in the heart of the historic district. The house's interior features 14-foot-high ceilings, elaborate woodwork with raised paneling, intricate moldings, eight working fireplaces, and a winding staircase. Guest rooms are appointed with comfortable antiques, oriental carpets, fresh flowers, down comforters, spring water, and toiletries. A multicourse breakfast is served in the dining room or on adjacent patios in the walled garden. High tea is in the library, music room, or garden.

Open: year round **Accommodations:** 6 guest rooms with private baths; 2 are suites **Meals:** full breakfast included; complimentary refreshments and high tea; restaurants nearby **Rates:** $175 to $230; 10% discount to National Trust members and National Trust Visa cardholders **Payment:** AmEx, Visa, MC, Discover, personal and traveler's checks **Restrictions:** not suitable for children; no smoking; no pets **Activities:** swimming pool

---

HAVRE DE GRACE

Nearby attractions: Concord Point Lighthouse, boat rentals, decoy museum, swimming, antiques hunting, walking tour of historic district, state park

SPENCER SILVER MANSION
200 South Union Avenue
Havre de Grace, Maryland 21078
410/939-1097 or 800/780-1485
Proprietors: Jim and Carol Nemeth

Located in the heart of Havre de Grace's National Register historic district, the Spencer Silver Mansion is just two blocks from the water. The inn is a stone mansion in the Queen Anne style, its design embellished by a two-story bay window, a tower, four gables, a dormer, and a variety of window shapes and placements. The house was constructed in 1896 for John Spencer, a merchant and foundry owner. Later the house was purchased by Charles Silver, a local canner. Restored to reflect late Victorian styles, the house features intricate oak wood-work, impressive fireplace mantels, 10-foot-high quarter-sawn oak doors, and parquet floors with fancy inlaid borders. Guest rooms are decorated with Victorian antiques. A reading nook invites guests to curl up with a good book and relax. The recently restored carriage house (ca. 1919) has become a luxurious suite with whirlpool bath.

Open: year round **Accommodations:** 4 guest rooms (2 have private baths); 1 is a suite **Meals:** full breakfast included; restaurants nearby **Rates:** $70 to $125; 10% discount offered to National Trust members **Payment:** personal check **Restrictions:** smoking limited; no pets **Activities:** croquet, badminton

MT. SAVAGE

Nearby attractions: New Germany State Park, Frank Lloyd Wright's Fallingwater, Allegheny scenic train rides, lakes, streams, water sports, bicycling, hiking, fishing, cross-country skiing

THE CASTLE
Route 36
Mt. Savage, Maryland 21545
301/759-5946
Proprietors: William and Andrea Myer

Scotland's Craig Castle is replicated in Mt. Savage at The Castle. Built in the mid-nineteenth century, the building exudes a distint Old World feeling in its Gothic styling with a steeply pitched roof punctured by peaked gables, arched windows, and massive round-arched entryway. The masonry building is further detailed with quoins and a balustraded railing. The Castle's guest rooms—Thompson, Highland, Ramsay, St. Andrews, Robert Burns, and Thistle—are furnished with four-poster, canopy, sleigh, and brass beds. The house's authentic antique decor is complemented by English gardens and vistas of western Maryland's mountains.

Open: year round **Accommodations:** 6 guest rooms (4 have private baths); 1 is a suite **Meals:** full breakfast included; complimentary high tea; restaurants nearby **Rates:** $100 to $140; 10% discount to National Trust members and National Trust Visa cardholders **Payment:** AmEx, Visa, MC, Discover, personal and traveler's checks **Restrictions:** not suitable for children; no smoking; no pets

NEW MARKET

Nearby attractions: historic New Market; antiques hunting, historic Frederick; Cunningham Falls National Park; Washington, D.C.; Gettysburg, Pa.; Baltimore; Harpers Ferry

STRAWBERRY INN
17 West Main Street
New Market, Maryland 21774
301/865-3318
Proprietors: Jane and Ed Rossig

This 1837 wood-siding farmhouse shows a Gothic influence in its steeply pitched center gable with arched window. Across the symmetrical facade are slightly arched windows. The house is located in the heart of New Market, founded in 1793, and now a National Register historic district. New Market is also known as the antiques capital of Maryland, thus all rooms at the Strawberry Inn are furnished with antiques, including the five guest rooms with private baths. The first-floor guest room is wheelchair accessible and has a private porch. A large grape arbor covers the cafe-style back porch, where breakfast is served on warm mornings, allowing guests to appreciate the landscaped yard. Afternoon tea is served in the Victorian gazebo. A restored log building on the grounds is suitable for small conferences and workshops.

Open: year round **Accommodations:** 5 guest rooms with private baths **Meals:** full breakfast included; complimentary refreshments; restaurants nearby **Wheelchair access:** 1 room **Rates:** $85 to $95; 10% discount to National Trust members and National Trust Visa cardholders **Payment:** personal check, cash **Restrictions:** children over 7 welcome; no smoking; no pets **Activities:** garden, gazebo

NORTH EAST

Nearby attractions: waterfront community, antiques hunting, craft shops, Town Park, North East River, canoeing, Upper Bay Museum, golfing, outlet shops, Baltimore, Pennsylvania Dutch country, Winterthur, Brandywine River Museum, Longwood Gardens

MILL HOUSE BED AND BREAKFAST
102 Mill Lane
North East, Maryland 21901
410/287-3532
Proprietors: Lucia and Nick Demond

The Mill House was built ca. 1710 as two houses, one for the mill owner and the other as kitchen and servants' quarters. Guests are invited to stay in the more formal mill owner's side. In the large Thomas Moffitt Room, furnished with a canopied bed, is a copy of an 1807 document in which Thomas Moffitt reserved this room for his own use when he deeded the property to his son. In the Victorian Room, the furnishings include a four-poster bed with a three-paneled headboard and a pair of slipper chairs. An eighteenth-century case clock and warming fireplace in the parlor create a colonial atmosphere. A full breakfast includes homemade breads. The inn sits along the North East River, which was used in early days to bring grain to the mill, now in ruins at the rear of the property.

Open: March 1 to December 1 **Accommodations:** 2 guest rooms share a bath **Meals:** full breakfast included; restaurants nearby **Rates:** $60 to $75; 10% discount to National Trust members and National Trust Visa cardholders **Payment:** Visa, MC, personal and traveler's checks **Restrictions:** children over 12 welcome; no smoking; no pets **Activities:** river canoeing

---

ST. MICHAELS

Nearby attractions: Chesapeake Bay Maritime Museum, St. Mary's Square Museum, St. Michael's historic district, antiques hunting, golfing, tennis, hunting, boating, bicycling, fishing, crabbing

INN AT PERRY CABIN
308 Watkins Lane
St. Michaels, Maryland 21663
410/745-2200 or 800/722-2949
410/745-3348 Fax
Proprietor: Sir Bernard Ashley

Named for Commodore Oliver Hazzard Perry, veteran of the War of 1812, this waterside inn was built in the 1820s by Samuel Hambleton, who served under Perry and much admired him. The original building was a Federal farmhouse, but many expansions over the years have left a Colonial Revival estate. The inn is decorated in the warm style of a classic country house, with fine antiques, prints, and Laura Ashley fabrics and furnishings throughout. Guests are welcome to browse in the library, stroll in the rose and herb gardens, or dine in the restaurant, featuring fresh produce and local flavor. Superbly appointed bedrooms are furnished with fresh flowers, seasonal fruit, and mineral water. Evening turn-down and concierge services complete the personal assistance that is the hallmark of the Inn at Perry Cabin.

Open: year round **Accommodations:** 41 guest rooms with private baths **Meals:** full breakfast included; restaurant on premises; restaurants nearby **Wheelchair access:** yes **Rates:** $175 to $525 **Payment:** AmEx, Visa, MC, personal and traveler's checks **Restrictions:** children over 10 welcome; no smoking; no pets **Activities:** indoor pool, exercise equipment, sauna, steam room, river and bay cruises, croquet

PARSONAGE INN
210 North Talbot Street
St. Michaels, Maryland 21663
410/745-5519 or 800/394-5519
Proprietors: Anthony and Jodie Deyesu

Henry Clay Dodson, a prominent businessman and politician, built this house as his private residence in 1883, using bricks from his St. Michaels brickyard. This Victorian house, with its steeple-topped entry tower flanked by paneled chimneys and its porches adorned with gingerbread, is one of the major architectural gems in the town's historic district. Dodson's daughter donated this building to the Union Methodist Church in 1924, and it served as the parsonage until 1985, when it was purchased by the current owners and meticulously restored. The Parsonage Inn is furnished in late Victorian garb, right down to its lighting fixtures, yet modern amenities assure guest comfort. Guest rooms are decorated with English country-style fabrics, bed linens, and wallpapers. Three guest rooms have working fireplaces, as does the parlor.

Open: year round **Accommodations:** 7 guest rooms with private baths; 1 is a suite **Meals:** full breakfast included; catering available for lunch and business meetings; restaurants nearby **Wheelchair access:** 1 guest room and bath **Rates:** $80 to $130; 10% discount offered to National Trust members weeknights **Payment:** Visa, MC, personal and traveler's checks **Restrictions:** no smoking; no pets **Activities:** bicycles, patio and charcoal grill, library

SNOW HILL

Nearby attractions: historic Snow Hill (founded 1642), Pocomoke River, canoeing, ocean beaches, museums, Chincotegue and Assateague National Wildlife Refuge, parks, Crisfield, Chesapeake Bay, bicycling, swimming

CHANCEFORD HALL BED AND BREAKFAST INN
209 West Federal Street
Snow Hill, Maryland 21863
410/632-2231
Proprietors: Michael and Thelma Driscoll

It is said that Chanceford Hall was built by Robert Morris, financier of the Revolutionary War. The house, 32 feet wide and 100 feet long, was built in three sections: the original house; a ballroom built shortly after as a separate building, which now contains the kitchen; and a middle section built in the late eighteenth century to join the other two. This part is now the dining room. Original hand-carved mantels and woodwork, ten working fireplaces (four in bedrooms), original hardwood floors, and two staircases are all intact. Canopied beds with down comforters and oriental rugs are found in all guest rooms. Formal common rooms with fireplaces and an informal solarium are available for guest use, as are the lap pool and brick patio outside.

Open: year round **Accommodations:** 5 guest rooms with private baths; 1 is a suite **Meals:** full breakfast included; complimentary refreshments; restaurants nearby **Rates:** $110 to $130 **Payment:** personal and traveler's checks **Restrictions:** children over 12 welcome; no pets **Activities:** lap pool, complimentary bicycles, lawn games

RIVER HOUSE INN
201 East Market Street
Snow Hill, Maryland 21863
410/632-2722
410/632-2866 Fax
Proprietors: Susanne and Larry Knudsen

River House Inn comprises three historic buildings situated on more than two acres of lawn that lead to the Pocomoke River. The Little House is an 1835 Tidewater cottage with wide floorboards and a picket fence. The River Cottage was built in 1890 as a carriage barn and now offers private accommodations with a porch overlooking the river. The Main House is a stunning 1860 Gothic Revival home. It was built by a Mr. Smith, and shortly thereafter sold to a Mr. Payne. In 1877 it was purchased by George Washington Purnell, an attorney. The house stayed in Purnell's family, being owned by his youngest daughter, Frances

Thebaud, until 1975. Today, the inn combines modern amenities with the charm of fireplaces in spacious rooms and old-fashioned porches. All guest rooms have private baths. Guests may tie up their boats along the inn's waterfront at no charge.

Open: year round **Accommodations:** 9 guest rooms with private baths; 2 are suites **Meals:** full breakfast included; complimentary refreshments; dinner available by arrangement; restaurants nearby **Wheelchair access:** River Cottage **Rates:** $89 to $135; 10% discount to National Trust members and National Trust Visa cardholders **Payment:** AmEx, Visa, MC, personal and traveler's checks **Restrictions:** no smoking; no pets **Activities:** fishing, river tours, bicycling, canoe rentals

---

SOLOMONS

Nearby attractions: fishing, boating, tennis, golfing, swimming, harbor tours, surfboard and bicycle rentals, marine and paleontological museum

SOLOMONS VICTORIAN INN AT THE DAVIS HOUSE
125 Charles Street
P.O. Box 759
Solomons, Maryland 20688
301/326-4811
Proprietors: Helen and Richard Bauer

The Davis House was built at the turn of the century by Clarence Davis, son of M. M. Davis, renowned builder of wooden workboats and sailing yachts. It is a charming Victorian house, commanding a striking view of the harbor and overlooking the mouth of the Patuxent River and entrance to the Chesapeake Bay. The house and its guest rooms have been carefully restored and comfortably and stylishly furnished to celebrate the great shipbuilding tradition of Solomons.

The living and breakfast rooms are pleasant and restful, opening onto a large, sunny veranda. The hosts at Solomons Victorian Inn are happy to help guests plan recreational and leisure activities in the area.

Open: year round **Accommodations:** 6 guest rooms with private baths; 1 is a suite **Meals:** full breakfast included; complimentary refreshments; restaurants nearby **Rates:** $85 to $140; 10% discount offered to National Trust members and National Trust Visa cardholders **Payment:** Visa, MC, personal and traveler's checks **Restrictions:** children over 15 welcome; no smoking; no pets **Activities:** relaxing, reading, games

TANEYTOWN

Nearby attractions: Carroll County Farm Museum, Homestead Museum, antiques hunting, golfing, bicycling, hiking; Gettysburg, Pennsylvania

GLENBURN
3515 Runnymede Road
Taneytown, Maryland 21787
410/751-1187
Proprietor: Robert Neal
Location: 3 miles east of Taneytown

The first structure to occupy this 600-acre Carroll County farm was a log cabin. In 1840 a large, brick Federal home was built here and became a boys' boarding school called Glenburn until 1880. In 1905 Joseph Goulden, a U.S. congressman bought the house and added a Victorian-style wing, replacing the original log home. Glenburn, furnished with American and European antiques, offers guests a sitting room with fireplace, a dining room with a display of heirloom china, and a wraparound porch with rocking chairs overlooking Bear Branch. Each air-conditioned bedroom has a view of lawns, pastures, creek, or woods. Just across the shaded lawn is a guest house with two large bedrooms, a living room, and a kitchenette.

Open: year round **Accommodations:** 5 guest rooms with private baths; 2 are suites **Meals:** full breakfast included; complimentary refreshments; restaurants nearby **Rates:** $75 to $125; 10% discount to National Trust members and National Trust Visa cardholders **Payment:** personal check **Restrictions:** smoking limited; no pets **Activities:** swimming pool, walking, bird-watching, croquet

MASSACHUSETTS

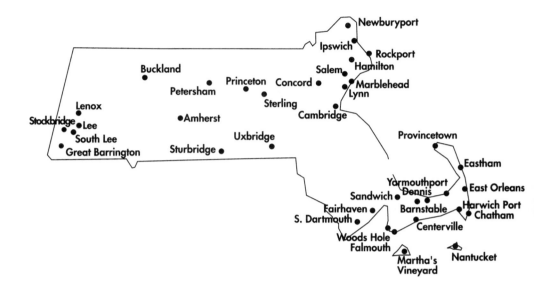

Newburyport
Ipswich
Rockport
Buckland
Salem Hamilton
Princeton Concord
Marblehead
Petersham
Lynn
Sterling
Lenox
Cambridge
Stockbridge Lee
Amherst
South Lee
Uxbridge
Great Barrington
Sturbridge
Provincetown
Eastham
Yarmouthport
Dennis
East Orleans
Sandwich
Fairhaven
Barnstable
Harwich Port
S. Dartmouth
Chatham
Centerville
Woods Hole
Falmouth
Martha's
Nantucket
Vineyard

AMHERST

Nearby attractions: Emily Dickinson Homestead, historic Deerfield, Old Sturbridge Village, galleries, museums, theaters, shopping, five-college area: Amherst College, University of Massachusetts, Hampshire College, Smith College, Mount Holyoke College

ALLEN HOUSE
599 Main Street
Amherst, Massachusetts
01002
413/253-5000
Proprietors: Alan and Ann Zieminski

Allen House was built in the Stick Style—steeply pitched gables contain decorative trusses and patterned stickwork accentuates the clapboard walls. On three scenic acres, just across

Millikan

the road from Emily Dickinson's home, Allen House was built in 1886 by Lysander H. Allen, a local wire goods manufacturer. A detailed restoration has earned a Historic Preservation Award from the Amherst Historical Commission. Guest accommodations are spacious and comfortable with private baths and air conditioning. Eastlake style furnishings are enhanced by reproduction wallcoverings from the Aestheic period of Victorian design. The innkeepers provide a full breakfast, afternoon tea, free pickup service from the nearby train and bus stations, and a complimentary collection of selected poems by Emily Dickinson.

Open: year round **Accommodations:** 5 guest rooms with private baths **Meals:** full breakfast included; complimentary refreshments; restaurants nearby **Rates:** $45 to $115; 10% discount to National Trust members and National Trust Visa cardholders **Payment:** AmEx, Visa, MC, CB, DC, Discover, personal and traveler's checks **Restrictions:** children over 10 welcome; no smoking; no pets **Activities:** chamber music concerts, baby grand piano, flower gardens, cross-country skiing

BARNSTABLE (CAPE COD)

Nearby attractions: Barnstable Harbor for fishing and whale watching, Sturgis Library, historic courthouse, Old King's Highway, Sandy Neck beach, Sandwich Glass Museum and Heritage Plantation, antiques hunting, gift shops, arts-and-crafts galleries, museums, auctions, tennis, golfing, biking, island ferries

ASHLEY MANOR
3660 Old King's Highway (Route 6A)
P.O. Box 856
Barnstable, Massachusetts 02630
508/362-8044
Proprietors: Donald and Fay Bain
Location: 1/2 mile east of Barnstable Village

Intimate and romantic, Ashley Manor occupies a two-acre estate in the heart of one of Cape Cod's historic districts. Built in 1699, the inn has seen many additions. Evidence of its age and history is in the wide-board flooring (made of wood usually reserved for the king during colonial times), huge open-hearth fireplaces, and a secret passageway connecting the upstairs and downstairs suites; the passageway is thought to have been a hiding place for Tories during the Revolutionary War. Elegant public rooms and spacious guest rooms are furnished with antiques, oriental rugs, and graceful country furniture. All but one guest room contain working fireplaces. A full gourmet breakfast is served fireside in the formal dining room or on the charming brick terrace. The beach, village, and harbor are within walking distance.

Open: year round **Accommodations:** 6 guest rooms with private baths; 4 are suites **Meals:** full breakfast included; complimentary refreshments; restaurants nearby **Rates:** $115 to $175 **Payment:** AmEx, Visa, MC, personal and traveler's checks **Restrictions:** children over 14 welcome; smoking limited; no pets **Activities:** tennis, croquet, bicycles, board games

BEECHWOOD
2839 Main Street
Barnstable, Massachusetts 02630
508/362-6618 or 800/609-6618
Proprietors: Debbie and Ken Traugot

Beechwood is a carefully restored example of the Queen Anne style, and takes its name from the old beech trees that shade the spacious wraparound porch. Centrally located on Cape Cod along the Old King's Highway in Barnstable Village, the inn offers six large guest rooms. The Rose Room features a carved, antique four-poster bed, tall shuttered windows overlooking the bay, and a fireplace. The Marble Room offers a brass bed, and a marble fireplace, and a view of the garden through lace-curtained windows. In the Cottage Room, guests enjoy rare hand-painted furniture in the Cottage style made popular in the 1860s. The Eastlake, Garret, and Lilac rooms are equally unique. Breakast is served in the paneled dining room, afternoon tea on the porch. The inn is rated with three diamonds by AAA.

Open: year round **Accommodations:** 6 guest rooms with private baths; 1 is a suite **Meals:** full breakfast included; complimentary refreshments; restaurants nearby **Rates:** $110 to $150; 10% discount to National Trust members and National Trust Visa cardholders **Payment:** AmEx, Visa, MC, personal and traveler's checks **Restrictions:** inquire about children under 12; smoking limited; no pets **Activities:** croquet, badminton

BUCKLAND

Nearby attractions: historic Deerfield, Tanglewood, Sturbridge Village, Shaker Village, tennis, hiking, white-water rafting, downhill and cross-country skiing, swimming

1797 HOUSE
Charlemont Road
Buckland, Massachusetts 01338
413/625-2975
Proprietor: Janet Turley
Location: 5 miles west of Shelburne Falls, 15 miles northwest of Deerfield

Zenas Graham built this Georgian house in 1797 for his bride on a rural eighteenth-century crossroad. It retains its 12-over-12 double-hung windows, four fireplaces, mantels, chair rails, and random-width hardwood floors. The house served as an inn in the early nineteenth century, before Mary Lyon taught her Winter School for Young Ladies here in 1830 and 1831. She went on to found Mt. Holyoke College in 1837. In the late 1920s the house once again took in overnight guests as the Wayside Inn. Guests in today's 1797 House may choose from three guest rooms offering either a four-poster, brass, or iron bed. Guests are invited to share the living room, dining room, and screened porch, all handsomely decorated with nineteenth-century antiques. A full breakfast and afternoon refreshments are served.

Open: January 15 to October 31 **Accommodations:** 3 guest rooms with private baths **Meals:** full breakfast included; complimentary refreshments; restaurants nearby **Rates:** $60 to $75; 10% discount offered to National Trust members and National Trust Visa cardholders **Payment:** personal and traveler's checks **Restrictions:** no smoking; no pets **Activities:** hiking, reading

CAMBRIDGE

Nearby attractions: Harvard University, Harvard Square, downtown Boston, Faneuil Hall Market Place, Freedom Trail, Boston Common, Museum of Fine Arts, Beacon Hill, shopping, theaters, symphony, beaches, harbor cruises, whale watching

A CAMBRIDGE HOUSE, BED AND BREAKFAST INN

2218 Massachusetts Avneue
Cambridge, Massachusetts 02140
617/491-6300 or 800/232-9989
617/868-2848 Fax
Proprietors: Ellen Riley and Anthony Femmino

Built in 1892 and listed in the National Register of Historic Places, A Cambridge House is a stately Colonial Revival home, turned bed-and-breakfast inn. It offers elegant guest rooms filled with antiques and reproduction pieces and private baths. Most rooms feature canopied beds and some rooms have fireplaces. All rooms are dressed in designer fabrics and linens, creating a plush atmosphere. A full breakfast, "not to be missed," according to *Glamour*, is served on small tables set among estate sale finds in the Victorian parlor or in the richly appointed den, with its herringbone-pattern wood flooring. A few minutes from downtown Boston, A Cambridge House is considered by *Country Inns* to be "Boston's finest gem." The inn also has received kudos from the *Los Angeles Times*, the BBC, and the *Oprah Winfrey Show*, where it was deemed a "dream vacation."

Open: year round **Accommodations:** 16 guest rooms with private baths **Meals:** full breakfast included; complimentary refreshments; restaurants nearby **Rates:** $89 to $225 **Payment:** AmEx, Visa, MC, Discover, personal and traveler's checks **Restrictions:** children over 6 welcome; no smoking; no pets

CENTERVILLE (CAPE COD)

Nearby attractions: Craigville Beach, Hyannis, ferry to Nantucket and Martha's Vineyard, tennis, golfing, bicycling, shops, theaters

COPPER BEECH INN ON CAPE COD
497 Main Street
Centerville, Massachusetts 02632
508/771-5488
Proprietor: Joyce Diehl

Hospitality begins at the sight of the largest beech tree on Cape Cod. Located in the heart of Centerville's historic district amid private estates and venerable homes, the Copper Beech Inn offers a charming glimpse of life from the clippership days. Now listed in the National Register of Historic Places, this Cape Cod–style house was built by Captain Hillman Crosby in 1830. Today's inn has been updated with private baths and air conditioning, and its guest rooms are tastefully furnished with traditional decor. The family-sized kitchen, with a wood-burning stove that dates from 1898, is a friendly gathering place for full country breakfasts. The parlors also are popular spots for reading, relaxing, or conversation. The Copper Beech Inn has been featured in *Innsider* and *Country* magazines.

Open: year round **Accommodations:** 3 guest rooms with private baths **Meals:** full breakfast included; restaurants nearby **Rates:** $80 to $90 **Payment:** AmEx, Visa, MC, personal and traveler's checks **Restrictions:** children over 12 welcome; smoking limited; no pets **Activities:** porch sitting, yard, walk to beach

---

CHATHAM (CAPE COD)

Nearby attractions: village of Chatham, National Seashore, whale-watching, antiques hunting, golfing, tennis, bicycling, fishing, harbor and boat tours, horseback riding, swimming, nature walks, bird-watching

CHATHAM BARS INN
Shore Road
Chatham, Massachusetts 02633
508/945-0096 or 800/527-4884
508/945-5491 or 508/945-4978 Fax
Director of Sales: Tony Guthrie

On June 9, 1914, Boston stockbroker Charles Ashley Hardy officially opened Chatham Bars Inn, an elegant oceanfront resort offering "surf and still water bathing, sailing and motor boating in land-locked waters, the best of deep-sea fishing, harbor fishing and shore bird shooting." The sprawling seaside inn, surrounded by verandas and terraces, soon became a favorite of the wealthy and sporting, including Henry Ford, William Rockefeller, and the Dutch royal family, who spent part of their World War II exile here. Today's Chatham Bars offers 152 guest accommodations in the main inn and 26 cottages, combining historic elegance, modern conveniences, and ocean views. An endless assortment of activities and personal service are hallmarks of the Chatham Bars Inn, a member of the National Trust's Historic Hotels of America.

Open: year round **Accommodations:** 152 guest rooms with private baths; 8 are suites **Meals:** complimentary refreshments November through April; restaurant on premises; restaurants nearby **Wheelchair access:** yes **Rates:** $160 to $1000 **Payment:** AmEx, Visa, MC, CB, DC, personal and traveler's checks **Restrictions:** smoking limited; no pets **Activities:** tennis, heated pool, fitness room, children's program, putting green, volleyball, badminton

CYRUS KENT HOUSE INN
63 Cross Street
Chatham, Massachusetts 02633
508/945-9104
508/945-9104 Fax
Proprietor: Sharon Mitchell-Swan

Cyrus Kent was the sea captain who built this two-story home in 1877. Decorative eave brackets under its steeply pitched roof and tall windows give this home an Italianate feel. A bay window in the living room fills it with sunlight, accentuating the original marble fireplace, plaster moldings, and ceiling rosette. Guest room floors are made of wide pine boards on which rest four-poster beds. Private baths, telephones, and television are standard. The adjoining carriage house contains two additional guest accommodations. Breakfast is served in the main house dining room on individual tables, before a marble fireplace. Guests will find historic Chatham village a short stroll away from the inn, which has been featured in *Country Inns*.

Open: year round **Accommodations:** 9 guest rooms with private baths; 2 are suites **Meals:** continental-plus breakfast included; complimentary refreshments; restaurants nearby **Rates:** $75 to $165; 10% discount to National Trust members and National Trust Visa cardholders **Payment:** AmEx, Visa, MC **Restrictions:** children over 10 welcome; no smoking; no pets

CONCORD

Nearby attractions: Walden Pond; Old North Bridge; wildlife sanctuary; canoeing; picnicking; walking; homes of Emerson, Alcott, and Hawthorne

HAWTHORNE INN
462 Lexington Road
Concord, Massachusetts 01742
508/369-5610
508/287-4949 Fax
Proprietor: Marilyn Mudry

Located in Concord's historic district, the Hawthorne Inn was built in 1870 on the famed Battle Road once traveled by revolutionists. The site has an impressive literary pedigree: at various times the land was owned by Ralph Waldo Emerson, Louisa May Alcott, and Nathaniel Hawthorne. The inn itself sits across the road from Hawthorne's house, Wayside; the Alcott's Orchard House; and Grapevine Cottage, where the Concord grape was developed. The Hawthorne Inn's rooms are appointed with antique furnishings, handmade quilts, and oriental and rag rugs on the hardwood floors. Original art, displayed throughout the inn, includes antique Japanese ukiyoe prints and sculptures by the innkeeper. Guest rooms feature canopy beds, fresh flowers or fruit, and a selection of poetry books. When the weather turns cold, the common room's fireplace is kept burning.

Open: year round **Accommodations:** 7 guest rooms with private baths **Meals:** continental-plus breakfast included; complimentary refreshments; restaurants nearby **Rates:** $95 to $160 **Payment:** AmEx, Visa, MC, Discover, personal and traveler's checks **Restrictions:** no smoking; no pets (resident dogs and cats) **Activities:** playground for children, gardens and paths, lily pool, many works of art, poetry books

DENNIS (CAPE COD)

Nearby attractions: beach, swimming, theater, antiques hunting, crafts shops, museums, sightseeing, golfing, tennis, bicycling

ISAIAH HALL BED AND BREAKFAST INN

152 Whig Street
P.O. Box 1007
Dennis, Massachusetts 02638
508/385-9928 or 800/736-0160
Proprietor: Marie Brophy

Tucked away on a quiet historic street, this 1857 Greek Revival farmhouse was the home of Isaiah B. Hall, a builder and cooper. A short distance behind the house, his brother Henry cultivated the first cranberry bogs in America. The house has been kept as an inn since 1948, with cheerful guest rooms in both the main house and carriage house featuring iron and brass beds and homemade quilts. Nearly all guest rooms enjoy private baths and air conditioning. Guests enjoy relaxing on porch rockers, in front of a Victorian parlor stove surrounded by antiques and oriental rugs, or in the converted carriage house, decorated in white wicker and knotty pine. Centrally located on the Cape, the inn is within walking distance of the beach or village.

Open: April through mid-October **Accommodations:** 11 guest rooms (10 have private baths); 1 is a suite **Meals:** continental-plus breakfast included; complimentary refreshments; restaurants nearby **Wheelchair access:** limited **Rates:** $59 to $112 **Payment:** AmEx, Visa, MC, personal and traveler's checks **Restrictions:** children over 7 welcome; smoking limited; no pets **Activities:** board games, badminton, croquet, library, television

EASTHAM (CAPE COD)

Nearby attractions: Cape Cod National Seashore, bicycle trail, Audubon Wildlife Sanctuary, Nauset Lighthouse, hiking, swimming, windsurfing, museums, historic homes, antiques hunting, art galleries

OVER LOOK INN, CAPE COD

3085 County Road (Route 6)
Eastham, Massachusetts 02642
508/255-1886 or 800/356-1121
508/240-0345 Fax
Proprietors: Aitchison family

This Victorian house, built in 1869 by Captain Barnabus Chipman as a wedding gift to his wife Sarah, sits on a hill across from the saltpond and marshes of Coast Guard Beach and the first visitors center of the Cape Cod National Seashore. Carefully restored, the Over Look is furnished in comfortable antiques and period reproductions of the Victorian era, including queen-size brass beds, cozy wicker, down comforters, and lace. A Scottish breakfast is served in the Edward Hopper Dining Room. Afternoon tea is served in the Sarah Chipman Parlor. Guests will also enjoy the Windston Churchill Library and the Ernest Hemingway Billiard Room. The inn has played host to such notables as Henry Beston, the author and naturalist, and the mayor and mayoress of Eastham, England.

Open: year round **Accommodations:** 10 guest rooms with private baths; 3 are suites **Meals:** full breakfast included; complimentary afternoon tea; restaurants nearby **Rates:** $75 to $125; 10% discount to National Trust members and National Trust Visa cardholders **Payment:** AmEx, Visa, MC, CB, DC, Discover, personal and traveler's checks **Restrictions:** smoking limited; no pets **Activities:** billiards, library, porches

EAST ORLEANS

Nearby attractions: Nauset Beach swimming and sunbathing, bicycle trails, fishing, sailing, boating, whale watching, golfing, horseback riding, antiques hunting, shopping

NAUSET HOUSE INN
143 Beach Road
P.O. Box 774
East Orleans, Massachusetts 02643
508/255-2195
Proprietors: Diane and Al Johnson and Cindy and John Vessella

At the Nauset House Inn, sea and shore, orchard and field create a refreshing, tranquil setting. Built in 1810 in the Cape Cod style, the Nauset House Inn has undergone numerous changes over the years, including the addition of dormers and a turn-of-the century conservatory filled with flowering plants and wicker furniture. The brown clapboard inn with a cherry red front door also offers a large common room with fireplace and 14 cozy guest rooms. An old-fashioned country breakfast is served. A warm and intimate atmosphere permeates the inn, and the hosts are happy to share their love for the Cape with their guests. Nauset House, only a half mile to the beach, has been recommended by *Country Living*, *Travel and Leisure*, and *Glamour*.

Open: April 1 to October 31 **Accommodations:** 14 guest rooms (8 have private baths) **Meals:** full or continental breakfast for an additional fee ($3.00 to $5.00); complimentary refreshments; restaurants nearby **Rates:** $65 to $105 **Payment:** Visa, MC, personal and traveler's checks **Restrictions:** children over 12 welcome; no smoking; no pets **Activities:** relaxing in conservatory, in front of fireplaces, on brick patio, or under 100-year-old apple trees

SHIP'S KNEES INN
186 Beach Road
P.O. Box 756
East Orleans, Massachusetts 02643
508/255-1312
508/240-1351 Fax
Proprietors: Donna Anderson and Peter Butcher

Built more than 170 years ago, with a section added in 1970, this rehabilitated sea captain's home offers an intimate setting just a short walk from the sand dunes of beautiful Nauset Beach. Inside the lantern-lighted doorways are 19 guest rooms, each distinctively decorated in a nautical style and furnished with such antiques as hand-painted trunks, braided rugs, four-poster beds, and authentic ship's knees (the wooden braces used in shipbuilding). Some rooms have an ocean view, and the master suite has a working fireplace. The inn has a swimming pool and tennis court. Three miles away overlooking Town Cove, the proprietors also offer accommodations in three quaint buildings: a turn-of-the-century Cape Cod–shuttered house with three guest rooms (with private baths) and an efficiency apartment, and two cedar-shingled cottages (a one-bedroom unit and a two-bedroom unit) that predate World War II. This cluster of buildings is nestled on a small hillside leading to the water's edge.

Open: year round **Accommodations:** 19 guest rooms (5 have private baths) **Meals:** continental breakfast included; restaurants nearby **Rates:** $45 to $100; 10% discount offered to National Trust members and National Trust Visa cardholders **Payment:** Visa, MC, personal and traveler's checks **Restrictions:** no smoking, no pets **Activities:** swimming pool, tennis

---

FAIRHAVEN

Nearby attractions: New Bedford; Plymouth; Cape Cod; ferries to Cuttyhunk and Martha's Vineyard; factory outlet shops; antiques hunting; Tabor Academy; University of Massachusetts at Dartmouth; beaches; tennis; golfing; Newport, R.I.

EDGEWATER BED AND BREAKFAST
2 Oxford Street
Fairhaven, Massachusetts 02719
508/997-5512
Proprietor: Kathleen Reed

Built in 1760 by Elnathan Eldridge as his home and store, which serviced the local shipbuilding industry, this historic waterfront structure was greatly expanded in the 1880s by later owner Clara Anthony. Today, the well-kept, tastefully decorated home offers beautiful views of the New Bedford and Fairhaven shorelines along with a feeling of comfort. Each guest accommodation is unique, such as the Captain's Suite with water view and working fireplace in the cozy sitting room, or the Clara Anthony room with a romantic cherry canopy bed. Another suite offers a working fireplace, kitchenette, and private entrance for guests who plan a lengthy stay. Edgewater is conveniently located to many popular attractions, including the old whaling city of New Bedford, historic Plymouth, the mansions of Newport, Rhode Island, Cape Cod, and the islands of Cuttyhunk and Martha's Vineyard.

Open: year round **Accommodations:** 5 guest rooms with private baths; 2 are suites **Meals:** continental breakfast included; restaurants nearby **Rates:** $65 to $85 **Payment:** AmEx, Visa, MC, personal and traveler's checks **Restrictions:** children over 4 welcome; no smoking; no pets **Activities:** reading, croquet, sunbathing, bird-watching

FALMOUTH (CAPE COD)

Nearby Attractions: Shining Sea Bikeway, Woods Hole Oceanographic Institute, Plymouth, ferry to Martha's Vineyard and Nantucket, historic district, museums, shopping, beach, swimming, boating, golfing, fishing, tennis

CAPTAIN TOM LAWRENCE HOUSE, BED AND BREAKFAST
75 Locust Street
Falmouth, Massachusetts 02540
508/540-1445 or 800/266-8139
508/457-1790 Fax
Proprietor: Barbara Sabo-Feller
Location: southwestern corner of Cape Cod, 68 miles south of Boston

Tom Lawrence first sailed on a Nantucket whaler in 1838. As he met with success, he built a fine residence on Locust Street, sparing no expense. His Italianate home, built in 1861, is today an intimate bed-and-breakfast inn. With its circular staircase, hardwood floors, and high ceilings, the house remains much as it was when Captain Lawrence lived here. Guests may play the Steinway piano or read by a cozy fire in the sitting room, with its antique furnishings and old paintings. Six corner guest rooms are available, all with private baths and some with canopy beds. The complimentary full breakfast includes specialties like Belgian waffles with strawberry sauce and whipped cream. The innkeeper speaks German.

Open: year round **Accommodations:** 6 guest rooms with private baths **Meals:** full breakfast included; restaurants nearby **Rates:** $80 to $110; 10% discount to National Trust members and National Trust Visa cardholders **Payment:** Visa, MC, personal and traveler's checks **Restrictions:** children over 12 welcome; smoking limited; no pets **Activities:** relaxing, playing piano

MOSTLY HALL BED AND BREAKFAST INN
27 Main Street
Falmouth, Massachusetts 02540
508/548-3786 or 800/682-0565
Proprietors: Caroline and Jim Lloyd
Location: southwestern corner of Cape Cod

In 1849 Albert Nye built this striking home for his New Orleans bride. The house, Falmouth's first summer residence, features a wide porch completely surrounding the house, a front-to-back central hallway, and 13-foot-high ceilings. Its name derives, legend has it, from a young child who, upon entering, exclaimed, "Why, it's mostly hall!" Majestically set back from the road, Mostly Hall provides comfortable seclusion in more than an acre of gardens, yet is close to shops, beaches, and island ferries. The spacious corner guest rooms are furnished with antiques and canopied, queen-size beds. All rooms are air conditioned and have comfortable reading areas with large windows, ensuring plenty of light and fresh air. Breakfast is served either fireside in the dining room or on the porch overlooking the gazebo; the menu is highlighted by recipes that have been featured in *Bon Appetit*, the *Boston Globe*, and in the cookbook *Mostly Hall Breakfast at 9*.

Open: February 15 through December 31 **Accommodations:** 6 guest rooms with private baths **Meals:** full breakfast included; complimentary refreshments; restaurants nearby **Rates:** $85 to $125; 10% discount to National Trust members and National Trust Visa cardholders **Payment:** AmEx, Visa, MC, Discover, traveler's check **Restrictions:** children over 16 welcome; no smoking; no pets **Activities:** piano, library, croquet, veranda, widow's walk and garden gazebo for relaxing and reading, bicycles to use on the Shining Sea Bikeway to Woods Hole

PALMER HOUSE INN
81 Palmer Avenue
Falmouth, Massachusetts 02540-2857
508/548-1230 or 800/472-2632
508/540-1878 Fax
Proprietors: Ken and Joanne Baker

The Palmer House Inn, located in the historic district of Falmouth, offers the ambience of a turn-of-the-century Victorian home. The romance of its Queen Anne styling is displayed in the stained-glass windows, wraparound porch, and tower. Rich woodwork and hardwood floors run throughout the inn. Guest rooms are individually appointed with antiques, and some feature a sleigh, brass, or canopy bed. Quilts, lace doilies, silk flowers, and old photographs add the finishing touches. Gourmet breakfasts often include cheese blintzes with blue-

berry compote, Finnish pancakes and strawberry soup, and pain perdu (French toast) with orange cream. The elegance and old-fashioned hospitality of the Palmer House have been featured in *Country Inns* magazine.

Open: year round **Accommodations:** 13 guest rooms with private baths; 1 is a suite **Meals:** full breakfast included; complimentary refreshments; restaurants nearby **Wheelchair access:** 1 guest room **Rates:** $54 to $160 **Payment:** AmEx, Visa, MC, CB, DC, Discover, personal check (for deposit only), and traveler's check **Restrictions:** children over 10 welcome; no smoking; no pets **Activities:** relaxing in front of parlor fireplace or in rockers on front porch; bicycles, cable television, whirlpool tubs

VILLAGE GREEN INN
40 West Main Street
Falmouth, Massachusetts 02540
508/548-5621
Proprietors: Diane and Don Crosby

Built in 1804 in the Federal style, Village Green Inn stands today as it has since being remodeled in 1875 and 1894, making it Victorian in appearance with a wraparound porch, decorative shingles, bay windows, and a turretlike dormer. Today, the house contains tastefully appointed guest rooms decorated in soft colors. Each room has a private bath and uniquely designed fireplace. Two large porches furnished in white wicker and hanging pots of red geraniums overlook the flower gardens and lawns that surround the inn and adjacent carriage house. A formal parlor is well stocked with a varied choice of books, magazines, and games. Breakfast may include such specialties as apple-plum crumble or tangy ambrosia.

Open: April to December **Accommodations:** 5 guest rooms with private baths; 1 is a suite **Meals:** full breakfast included; complimentary refreshments; restaurants nearby **Rates:** $85 to $140; 10% discount to National Trust members and National Trust Visa cardholders **Payment:** AmEx, Visa, MC, personal and traveler's checks **Restrictions:** children over 12 welcome; no smoking; no pets

---

GREAT BARRINGTON

Nearby attractions: National Trust's Chesterwood, skiing, concerts, theater, hiking, antiques hunting, golfing

SEEKONK PINES INN
142 Seekonk Cross Road, corner of Route 23
Great Barrington, Massachusetts 01230
413/528-4192 or 800/292-4192
Proprietors: Linda and Christian Best
Location: 1 mile east of South Egremont; 2 miles west of Route 7 in Great Barrington

Seekonk Pines is conveniently located along one of the main routes into the Berkshires, but the feeling is definitely rural. The inn dates to 1832, when Horace Church purchased a 200-acre parcel of land and built a typical New England frame farmhouse. Later owners added a Dutch Colonial wing and other alterations, but by the 1970s the house had fallen into severe neglect. Now beautifully restored, Seekonk Pines Inn invites guests to share the comforts of its library and large living room with piano. Antiques, quilts, stenciling, and original watercolors adorn the guest rooms, while lovely gardens and a swimming pool are outside. A country breakfast served daily features the inn's home-grown fruit and garden produce and heart-healthy inn specialties.

Open: year round **Accommodations:** 6 guest rooms with private baths **Meals:** full breakfast included; complimentary guest pantry and beverage-stocked refrigerator; restaurants nearby **Rates:** $70 to $110; 10% discount to National Trust members and National Trust Visa cardholders, with some restrictions **Payment:** AmEx, Visa, MC, personal and traveler's checks **Restrictions:** no smoking, no pets **Activities:** swimming pool, bicycles, piano, picnics, naps in the hammock under the pines

HAMILTON

Nearby attractions: world-class horse events, colonial villages, antiques hunting, Cape Ann and Crane's beaches, hiking, bicycling, bird watching, sailing, cross-country skiing, whale-watching, Parker River Wildlife Refuge

MILES RIVER COUNTRY INN
823 Bay Road
Hamilton, Massachusetts 01936
508/468-7206
508/468-3999 Fax
Proprietor: Gretel T. Clark

Set among Boston's fabled North Shore estates, this New England farmhouse was built in the late eighteenth century. In 1919 the president of Harvard gave the house to his daughter and son-in-law as a wedding gift, moving it to its present site from his estate a half mile away. A ballroom and glassed-in porch were added at that time. Today the 24-room house with 12 fireplaces (four in guest rooms) is filled with the family's antique furniture. The grounds—more than 30 acres— are landscaped in the grand estate style of the early 1900s with sweeping lawns, a grass allée (passage between two rows of trees), ponds, streams, and a giant arborvitae "secret garden" to explore. The estate contains a flock of chickens that provide fresh eggs, gardens that produce fresh fruit, and an apiary that offers honey for country breakfasts. The Miles River flows through the property. Surrounding meadows and woodlands invite countless varieties of ducks, geese, birds, and other wildlife.

Open: year round **Accommodations:** 7 guest rooms (3 have private baths) **Meals**: full breakfast included; complimentary refreshments and afternoon tea; restaurants nearby **Rates:** $65 to $90; 10% discount to National Trust members and National Trust Visa cardholders **Payment:** personal check **Restrictions:** no smoking; no pets **Activities:** walking, hiking, jogging, bird-watching, croquet, badminton, cross-country skiing, ice skating

HARWICH PORT (CAPE COD)

Nearby attractions: harbor, historic town, Nantucket Sound, beaches, Nantucket ferry, golfing tennis, bicycling, fishing, swimming

HARBOR WALK
6 Freeman Street
Harwich Port, Massachusetts 02646
508/432-1675
Proprietors: Marilyn and Preston Barry

Located in the scenic Wychmere Harbor area of Harwich Port, this Victorian summer guest house was built in 1880 by Ensign Rogers, on his return from sea. Today, as a guest house, Harbor Walk offers six comfortable rooms, with twin or king-size beds, for rent daily or weekly. A completely furnished and heated summer house that sleeps six is available by the week from April until October. Homemade quilts, antiques, and freshly baked kuchen enhance the Cape Cod spirit of the inn. An attractive garden and porch invite guests to sit and read or just lounge and enjoy the constant sea breeze.

Open: April to November **Accommodations:** 6 guest rooms (4 have private baths) **Meals:** continental-plus breakfast included; restaurants nearby **Rates:** $45 to $60 **Payment:** personal and traveler's checks **Restrictions:** children over 3 welcome; no smoking; inquire about pets **Activities:** rest and relaxation, television

IPSWICH

Nearby attractions: Crane Beach, Ipswich River, canoeing, bird sanctuary, historical walking tours, hiking, horseback riding, antiques hunting, golfing, shopping

TOWN HILL BED AND BREAKFAST
16 North Main Street
Ipswich, Massachusetts 01938
508/356-8000 or 800/457-7799
Proprietors: Robert and Cheryl Statho

Formerly known as the Coburn House, Town Hill Bed and Breakfast is an 1850 house showing Greek Revival influences in the bands of trim at the cornice line, the entry porch supported by classical columns, and the front door flanked by sidelights. The house is located in Ipswich's National Register historic district, where more than 40 homes built before 1725 are still in use today. Eleven comfortable, individually decorated guest rooms contain queen-size brass beds. Five rooms have fireplaces. Guests receive a buffet breakfast to start their day. The inn is centrally located among the historic communities of Salem, Gloucester, Rowley, and Newburyport.

Open: year round **Accommodations:** 11 guest rooms (4 have private baths); 2 are suites **Meals:** continental-plus breakfast included; restaurants nearby **Rates:** $75 to $150; 10% discount to National Trust members and National Trust Visa cardholders **Payment:** AmEx, Visa, MC **Restrictions:** children over 12 welcome; smoking limited; no pets **Activities:** television, sunporch, reading

LEE

Nearby attractions: Tanglewood, Berkshire Theater Festival, Jacob's Pillow, Berkshire Ballet, National Trust's Chesterwood, antiques hunting, galleries, museums, historic sites, hiking, fishing, downhill and cross-country skiing, golfing

HAUS ANDREAS
85 Stockbridge Road
Lee, Massachusetts 01238
413/243-3298 or 800/664-0880
Proprietors: Sally and Ben Schenck

Overlooking a pastoral setting that includes birch trees and 40 acres of rolling lawn and fields, rests Haus Andreas. Built by a Revolutionary War soldier, the house was modernized and landscaped in the early 1900s for George Westinghouse, Jr., son of the noted manufacturer. During the summer of 1942, the estate was the residence of Queen Wilhelmina of the Netherlands. Today as Haus Andreas, the country house offers 10 spacious and traditionally styled guest rooms, some of which contain canopied beds and fireplaces. Antique furnishings are found throughout the house. The large living room contains a stereo system, library, and fireplace, making it restful and friendly. Guests have use of a heated swimming pool and tennis court. A nine-hole public golf course is across the road.

Open: year round **Accommodations:** 10 guest rooms with private baths; 4 are suites **Meals:** full breakfast included; restaurants nearby **Rates:** $60 to $250 **Payment:** AmEx, Visa, MC, personal and traveler's checks **Restrictions:** children over 10 welcome; smoking limited; no pets **Activities:** swimming pool, tennis, lawn sports, bicycles, television

LENOX

Nearby attractions: Tanglewood, Jacob's Pillow, Berkshire Theater Festival, Shakespeare and Company, Wharton and Melville houses, National Trust's Chesterwood, Hancock Shaker Village, Norman Rockwell Museum, Williams College, Clark Art Institute, Bashbish Falls, Appalachian Trail, Mount Greylock, Berkshires, downhill and cross-country skiing, tennis, golfing, swimming, horseback riding, fishing, hiking

BIRCHWOOD INN
7 Hubbard Street
P.O. Box 2020
Lenox, Massachusetts 01240
413/637-2600 or 800/524-1646
Proprietors: Joan, Dick, and Dan Toner

The Birchwood Inn, located at the top of a hill overlooking the historic village of Lenox, is the town's only inn listed in the National Register of Historic Places. The inn's tradition of hospitality dates to 1767 when the first town meeting was held in this building, replete with dormers and chimneys. Guests enjoy the large library and common rooms with fireplaces, antiques, and colonial-era decor. A spacious, covered porch and gardens enclosed by authentic New England stone fences offer outdoor places to relax. A multicourse, country breakfast is served daily, complemented by homemade breads and muffins. The inn is adjacent to Kennedy Park, a popular place for hiking, bicycling, and cross-country skiing.

Open: year round **Accommodations:** 12 guest rooms (10 have private baths); 2 are suites **Meals:** full breakfast included; restaurants nearby **Rates:** $60 to $199 **Payment:** AmEx, Visa, MC, CB, DC, Discover, personal and traveler's checks **Restrictions:** children over 12 welcome; no smoking; no pets **Activities:** library, videotapes, croquet, therapeutic massage

BLANTYRE
16 Blantyre Road
P.O. Box 995
Lenox, Massachusetts 01240
413/637-3556 (summer) or 413/298-3806 (winter)
413/637-4282 Fax
Proprietor: Ann Fitzpatrick

Robert W. Paterson, a native of Scotland, built this mansion in 1902, modeling it after his wife's ancestral home in Lanarkshire, Scotland. He intended, he wrote, to build a "castle of feudal architectural features, ressembling the medieval castle of Scotland and modern as to convenience and interior arrangements." He called the resulting Tudor-style manor home, complete with arches, towers, and turrets, Blantyre. Today, the fully restored home offers eight exquisite bedrooms and suites, many with fireplaces. Twelve rooms in the nearby carriage house echo the plush fabrics, antiques, and opulent style of the main house. Courteous and discreet service accompany Blantyre's elegant style, evident in its crystal chandeliers, carved mantels, rich wood paneling, and tapestries. In the dining rooms, candlelit tables are laid with damask, sterling silver, antique crystal, and bone china.

Open: May 17 to November 1 **Accommodations:** 23 guest rooms with private baths; 5 are suites **Meals:** continental breakfast included; restaurant on premises; restaurants nearby **Wheelchair access**: limited **Rates:** $175 to $550 **Payment:** AmEx, Visa, MC, CB, DC, personal and traveler's checks **Restrictions:** children over 12 welcome; no pets **Activities**: Har-Tru tennis courts, heated pool, professional croquet lawns, hiking trails, hot tub and sauna

GABLES INN
81 Walker Street
Lenox, Massachusetts 01240
413/637–3416 or 800/382–9401
Proprietors: Mary and Frank Newton

The Gilded Age is embodied in this 1885 Queen Anne Berkshire "cottage" and one-time home of novelist Edith Wharton. Built when Lenox was at its peak as a fashionable summer resort, competing with Newport and Bar Harbor, Pine Acre (as the house was called then) exemplified grand living. Today, after extensive reconstruction, the house is a showcase of authentic period antiques— even down to the lamps—and classic furnishings, most notably Wharton's bedroom with its four-poster bed. The famous octagonal library where Edith Wharton once wrote her memorable short stories has been recreated, enhanced by the owner's fine art and rare document and book collection. This elegant inn also offers a heated swimming pool, a private tennis court, and a peaceful garden.

Open: year round **Accommodations:** 18 guest rooms with private baths; 3 are suites **Meals:** full breakfast included; complimentary refreshments; restaurants nearby **Rates:** $75 to $195 **Payment:** Visa, MC, Discover, personal and traveler's checks **Restrictions:** children over 12 welcome; smoking limited; no pets **Activities:** swimming pool, tennis, garden, television, library, 2 pianos

SUMMER WHITE HOUSE
17 Main Street
Lenox, Massachusetts 01240
413/637–4489
Proprietors: Mary and Frank Newton

In 1885, Edith Wharton's cousin J. E. Schermerhorn built his "cottage" on then-rural Main Street in Lenox. He named it "Lanai" for its many porches. In the early 1900s, Schermerhorn sold the house to a druggist who opened it as a shop on then-busy Main Street. During the 1920s, the house belonged to the Curtis Hotel, hence its many bathrooms. Purchased in 1992 by the Newtons, the Summer White House is fully renovated to show off gleaming hardwood floors, ornate ceiling medallions, and classical mantelpieces. Elegant accommodations— some with fireplaces or canopy beds—with private baths are offered. Antique furnishings throughout the house are the result of shopping excursions up and down the east coast. Guests are welcome in the formal dining room, the parlor, and the library–music room, with a Yamaha concert grand piano.

Open: June through October **Accommodations:** 6 guest rooms with private baths **Meals:** continental-plus breakfast included; restaurants nearby **Rate:** $160 **Payment:**

Visa, MC, Discover, personal and traveler's checks **Restrictions:** children over 12 welcome; no smoking; no pets **Activities:** library, concert grand piano, swimming pool and tennis courts at nearby Gables Inn

UNDERLEDGE INN
106 Cliffwood Street
Lenox, Massachusetts 01240
413/637-0236
Proprietors: Marcie and Cheryl Lanoue

The Underledge estate, built ca. 1890, was at one time the summer home of two wealthy sisters, Olivia and Caroline Stokes. Their home was built in the Colonial Revival style with a pedimented front porch, a corner turret, and a spacious solarium. Today, the inn offers eight individually appointed guest rooms with parlors and fireplaces. The richly paneled foyer offers a common resting area, complete with fireplace, while the front porch and sunny terrace provide fresh-air settings. The house sits on four acres adjacent to Kennedy Park with 26 miles of trails for hiking and cross-country skiing.

Open: year round **Accommodations:** 8 guest rooms with private baths **Meals:** continental-plus breakfast included; restaurants nearby **Rates:** $60 to $195 seasonal; 10% discount to National Trust members and National Trust Visa cardholders **Payment:** AmEx, Visa, traveler's check **Restrictions:** children over 10 welcome; no smoking; no pets

VILLAGE INN
16 Church Street
P.O. Box 1810
Lenox, Massachusetts
01240
413/637-0020 or 800/
253-0917
413/637-9756 Fax
Proprietors: Clifford
Rudisill and Ray Wilson

In 1771 the Whitlock family built a large residence and two nearby barns on their property. In 1775 they connected the barns to the main house by building an adjoining dining room. Then the barns were adapted to provide guest accommodations. That was the beginning of the Village Inn, which has operated continuously ever since. Except for two bay windows added in the Victorian era, the building has retained its eighteenth-century architectural styling. In recent years the interior has been renovated and decorated with antiques, oriental carpets, and period wallpapers. Some guest rooms have working fireplaces and four-poster canopied beds. To promote its pre-Revolutionary heritage, the inn serves authentic English high tea in the afternoon and British beers and ales in the cellar pub.

Open: year round **Accommodations:** 32 guest rooms with private baths; 1 is a suite **Meals:** restaurant on premises serves breakfast, English tea, and dinner **Wheelchair access:** guest rooms, bathrooms, dining facilities **Rates:** $50 to $195 (seasonal); 10% discount to National Trust members and National Trust Visa cardholders midweek only **Payment:** AmEx, Visa, MC, CB, DC, personal and traveler's checks **Restrictions:** children over 6 welcome; smoking limited; no pets **Activities:** tavern; television room; common room with games, piano, and reading; weekend packages

WALKER HOUSE
64 Walker Street
Lenox, Massachusetts
01240
413/637-1271 or
800/235-3098
413/637-2387 Fax
Proprietors: Richard
and Peggy Houdek

Built in 1804 in historic
Lenox Village, Walker
House is one of the town's
last remaining examples of
Federal architecture. Among its residents have been two judges and a state senator. Guest rooms in the restored building, situated on three acres of woods and gardens, bear the names of composers—Mozart, Chopin, Beethoven, and others—and are decorated with art and antiques that recall the lives and times of their namesakes. Some rooms have warming fireplaces. The parlor contains a grand piano, lots of books, and a fireplace with hearth. Guests can relax on the open and screened porches in warm weather. A video theater shows classic films, operas, plays, and notable events nightly on a seven-foot screen. Breakfast and afternoon tea are served in the dining room.

Open: year round **Accommodations:** 8 guest rooms with private baths **Meals:** continental-plus breakfast included; complimentary refreshments; restaurants nearby **Wheelchair access:** 1 guest room **Rates:** $60 to $180; 10% discount offered to National Trust members and National Trust Visa cardholders from November 1 to April 30, excluding holidays **Payment:** personal check **Restrictions:** children over 12 welcome; no smoking; pets accepted with prior approval **Activities:** croquet, tennis

LYNN

Nearby attractions: Lynn Historical Society, Mary Baker Eddy home, beach, walking and jogging paths, Salem, Marblehead

DIAMOND DISTRICT BED AND BREAKFAST
142 Ocean Street
Lynn, Massachusetts 01902-2007
617/599-5122
617/599-4470 Fax
Proprietors: Sandra and Jerry Caron

This 17-room architect-designed clapboard mansion was built in 1911 by a Lynn shoe manufacturer. Its Colonial Revival design is defined by its hipped roof, pedimented dormers, modillions, quoins, and Palladian-style window above the front door. The 44-page architect specifications permitted only the best of materials, evident, for example, in the Mexican mahogany used in the living room. This room features a large fireplace and French doors leading to a veranda that overlooks the gardens and ocean. A winding staircase ascends three floors. Like the remainder of the house, guest rooms are furnished with antiques and oriental rugs. A piece of note is the 1895 rosewood Knabe concert grand piano. In the dining room are a custom-made Chippendale-style table and chairs signed by Joseph Gerty, a 1940s Boston furniture maker.

Open: year round **Accommodations:** 8 guest rooms (4 have private baths) **Meals:** full breakfast included; complimentary refreshments; restaurants nearby **Rates:** $58 to $105 **Payment:** AmEx, Visa, MC, CB, DC, Discover, personal and traveler's checks **Restrictions:** not suitable for young children; no smoking; inquire about pets **Activities:** ocean watching

MARBLEHEAD

Nearby attractions: Audubon bird sanctuary, historic homes and sites, Abbott Hall Spirit of '76 painting, museums, antiques hunting, art galleries, swimming, sailing, tennis, windsurfing, harbor cruises, whale watching, seasonal festivals, Boston, Salem

HARBOR LIGHT INN
58 Washington Street
Marblehead, Massachusetts 01945
617/631–2186 or 617/631–7407
Proprietors: Peter and Suzanne Conway

Located in this sailing capital's National Register historic district, the Harbor Light Inn was first constructed in 1712. An 1820 remodeling transformed the building into a Federal mansion. Completely renovated in 1986, it is today an elegant, modern inn that preserves its rich past. The feeling of a previous era is conveyed by the brass chandeliers, finely tooled eighteenth-century mahogany furniture, bedside fireplaces, local period art, and authentic oriental rugs— treasures frequently brought home from exotic ports. Many guest rooms offer fireplaces, and some have whirlpool tubs. The inn has a conference room and easily accommodates business meetings. A swimming pool offers exercise and a rooftop walk provides a clear view of the famous Marblehead Light.

Open: year round **Accommodations**: 20 guest rooms with private baths **Meals**: continental breakfast included; restaurants nearby **Rates**: $80 to $185; 10% discount offered to National Trust members and National Trust Visa cardholders **Payment**: AmEx, Visa, MC, personal and traveler's checks **Restrictions**: children over 5 welcome; smoking limited; no pets

HARBORSIDE HOUSE
23 Gregory Street
Marblehead, Massachusetts 01945
617/631-1032
Proprietor: Susan Livingston
Location: 1/2 hour to Boston/Logan Airport

This handsome 1850 home, built by a ship's carpenter, overlooks the picturesque harbor in the historic district of Marblehead. Guests enjoy water views from the wood-paneled and beamed living room with fireplace, the period dining room, the sunny breakfast porch, and the third-story deck. Antique furnishings and reproduction wallpapers enhance the charm of this comfortable, quiet home. One large guest room with twin beds overlooks the harbor. Another, a romantic room with a double bed and an antique mirrored dressing table, looks out on flower gardens and the deck. The spacious third guest room enjoys a private deck and views of the harbor. A generous breakfast features homemade breads and muffins. Guests are just a short stroll from historic sites, quaint shops, and fine restaurants.

Open: year round **Accommodations:** 3 guest rooms, 1 has a private bath **Meals:** continental-plus breakfast included; afternoon tea available; restaurants nearby **Rates:** $65 to $90; 10% discount to National Trust members and National Trust Visa cardholders **Payment:** personal and traveler's checks **Restrictions:** children over 10 welcome; no smoking; no pets **Activities:** television, sundeck, secluded garden, quiet relaxation

SPRAY CLIFF
25 Spray Avenue
Marblehead, Massachusetts 01945
617/631-6789 or 800/626-1530
Proprietors: Roger and Sally Plauche

The sea is the most enticing amenity offered at Spray Cliff. It is viewed through picture windows from nearly every room in this 1910 Tudor-style mansion. Built as a summer home, Spray Cliff offers seven spacious bedrooms, elegantly appointed with antiques, wicker, and fresh-cut flowers. In addition to the panoramic vistas, each room contains a sitting area, refreshments, reading materials, and toiletries. Living and dining areas for guests are cozy and relaxed. But it is the brick terrace, nestled in lush flower gardens, that is most memorable with its sights and sounds of the ocean. Three guest rooms and the hospitality room offer working fireplaces.

Open: year round **Accommodations:** 7 guest rooms with private baths **Meals:** continental-plus breakfast included; restaurants nearby **Rates:** $150 to $200; 10% discount offered to National Trust members and National Trust Visa cardholders **Payment:** AmEx, Visa, MC, personal and traveler's checks **Restrictions:** not suitable for children, no smoking

MARTHA'S VINEYARD (CAPE COD)

Nearby attractions: villages of Edgartown, Oak Bluffs, and Vineyard Haven; beaches; bicycle rentals; tour buses; fishing; sailing; movie house; health club; tennis; golfing; summer theater; shopping; antiques hunting; island ferries; yacht club

THE ARBOR
222 Upper Main Street
P.O. Box 1228
Edgartown, Massachusetts 02539
508/627-8137
Proprietor: Peggy Hall

Some people say this 1890 farmhouse was brought to Martha's Vineyard on a barge from the neighboring island of Chappaquidick. Others say it was pulled by oxen on a sled across the icy narrows of Katama Bay. Now firmly set on Martha's Vineyard, the Arbor beckons to guests from along the bicycle path in historic Edgartown, inviting island visitors to sample its comforts and charms, like the front-porch rockers and flower-filled window boxes. The rooms are delightfully New England; the atmosphere is warm and friendly. Guests enjoy the dining-room fireplace, the English tea garden, and the fragrance of fresh flowers in their rooms.

Open: May 1 through October 31 **Accommodations:** 10 guest rooms (8 have private baths) **Meals:** continental breakfast included; restaurants nearby **Rates:** $90 to $135 June through September; $65 to $95 off season **Payment:** Visa, MC, personal and traveler's checks **Restrictions:** children over 12 welcome; smoking limited; no pets **Activities:** walking trails

CAPTAIN DEXTER HOUSE
100 Main Street
P.O. Box 2457
Vineyard Haven, Massachusetts 02568
508/693-6564
301/319-1262 Fax
Proprietors: Roberta Pieczenik and Rick Fenstemaker

This elegant house was built in 1843 as the home of sea captain Rodolphus Dexter. Its original wide floorboards, graceful moldings, Rumford fireplaces, and hand-stenciled walls have been meticulously restored, and the house is now furnished with eighteenth-century antiques, early American oil paintings, and oriental rugs. Each guest room is unique in style and distinctive in decor. Several rooms have working fireplaces and four-poster beds with white lace canopies. In-room amenities include hand-sewn quilts, color-coordinated linens, period reproduction wallpapers, velvet wing chairs, fresh-cut flowers, and complimentary sherry. Breakfast is served in the formal dining room or in the garden. The inn is located in the heart of town on a street of fine historic homes, only a short stroll to the beach, shops, and restaurants.

Open: April to December **Accommodations:** 8 guest rooms with private baths; 1 is a suite **Meals:** continental-plus breakfast included; restaurants nearby **Rates:** $55 to $170; 10% discount to National Trust members and National Trust Visa cardholders **Payment:** AmEx, Visa, MC, DC, personal and traveler's checks **Restrictions:** no smoking; no pets **Activities:** garden lounge chairs

CAPTAIN DEXTER HOUSE OF EDGARTOWN
35 Pease's Point Way
P.O. Box 2798
Edgartown, Massachusetts 02539
508/627-7289
Proprietor: Rick Fenstemaker

Built in 1840 by a seafaring merchant, this country colonial inn on the island of Martha's Vineyard is traditionally New England—from its white clapboard siding and black shutters to its original double-width floorboards. The home is located on a quiet residential street, just a short stroll to the harbor, shops, and restaurants. Guest rooms retain their colonial character with canopied beds, period antiques, and working fireplaces, yet offer all of today's conveniences. The cutting garden provides fresh flowers for the inn, while the landscaped garden is a haven for relaxation. Guests start their days with a home-baked continental breakfast served in the elegant dining room. Afternoons bring complimentary aperitifs or lemonade.

Open: May through October **Accommodations** 11 guest rooms with private baths **Meals:** continental-plus breakfast included; complimentary refreshments; restaurants nearby **Rates:** $65 to $180; 10% discount offered to National Trust members and National Trust Visa cardholders **Payment:** AmEx, Visa, MC, DC, personal and traveler's checks **Restrictions:** smoking limited; no pets **Activities:** sunbathing, garden lounge chairs

EDGARTOWN INN
56 North Water Street
Edgartown, Massachusetts 02539
508/627-4794
Proprietors: Liliane and Earle Radford

Whaling captain Thomas Worth built this Federal home in 1798. His son, William Jenkins Worth, later became a hero of the Mexican War and the namesake of Fort Worth, Texas. The house was first used for lodging in 1820. During its long career, the house has been host to many notable guests, including Daniel Webster, Nathaniel Hawthorn, Senator Charles Sumner, and later, Senator John F. Kennedy. The inside of Captain Worth's house is much unchanged, except for the addition of spotless tiled baths and a paneled dining room at the rear of the building. Here are served full country breakfasts, featuring homemade breads and muffins. Beyond the patio is the Garden House with two spacious rooms with private balconies. Many period antiques are found throughout the property.

Open: April to November **Accommodations:** 20 guest rooms (16 have private baths) **Meals:** full and continental breakfast served; restaurants nearby **Rates:** $75 to $165 **Payment:** personal and traveler's checks **Restrictions:** children over 6 welcome; no pets **Activities:** television, sunbathing, porch sitting

LOTHROP MERRY HOUSE
P.O. Box 1939
Vineyard Haven, Massachusetts 02568
508/693-1646
Proprietors: John and Mary Clarke

The Lothrop Merry House is an eighteenth-century guest house overlooking Vineyard Haven harbor and the ocean beyond. Built in the late 1790s, the house retains its original latch-lock doors, wide pine floors, and wainscotting. Most guest rooms offer a harbor view; some have their own fireplaces. All are charmingly furnished with antiques. The lawn slopes gently down to the inn's private beach. Continental breakfasts, featuring homemade breads, are served

---

outside on the sunny, flower-bordered terrace in warm weather. For those who enjoy sailing, the inn owns and operates a 54-foot Alden ketch, which can be chartered for daily, evening, or overnight cruises among the many coves and harbors of the Vineyard and the Elizabeth Islands. In addition, the inn offers free use of a canoe and sunfish.

Open: year round **Accommodations:** 7 guest rooms (4 have private baths) **Meals:** continental breakfast included; restaurants nearby **Wheelchair access:** 1 guest room **Rates:** $68 to $180 **Payment:** Visa, MC, personal check **Restrictions:** no pets **Activities:** private beach, swimming, canoeing, sunfish sailing

NANTUCKET (CAPE COD)

Nearby attractions: Steamship Wharf, swimming, beaches, boating, wind surfing, tennis, golfing, bicycling, historic sites, museums, shopping, antiques hunting, theaters, nature walks

CENTERBOARD GUEST HOUSE
8 Chester Street
Box 456
Nantucket, Massachusetts 02554
508/228-9696
508/228-1957 Fax
Proprietor: Marcia Wasserman   **Manager:** Reggie Reid

One of a very few examples of Victorian architecture in the historic whaling town of Nantucket, the Centerboard is a restored 1885 home built the fashionable Second Empire style. It is located on the edge of the historic district, just a few blocks from cobblestone streets, shops, and white sand beaches. The pastel guest rooms are luxuriously appointed with private baths, telephones, refrigerators, and color television. A gentle romantic atmosphere is achieved through such details as Battenburg lace and fresh and dried flower arrangements. A living room window seat is a great place for curling up on a summer day and a cozy fireplace provides warmth on a snowy winter afternoon.

Open: year round **Accommodations:** 6 guest rooms with private baths; 1 is a suite; 1 is a studio with kitchen **Meals:** continental-plus breakfast included; complimentary refreshments; restaurants nearby **Rates:** $110 to $265 (seasonal) **Payment:** AmEx, Visa, MC, personal and traveler's checks **Restrictions:** children over 12 welcome; no smoking; no pets

COBBLESTONE INN
5 Ash Street
Nantucket, Massachusetts 02554
508/228-1987
Proprietors: Robin Hammer-Yankow and Keith Yankow

Built in 1725 as a simple, two-story dwelling by Tristram Coffin, a member of one of Nantucket's founding families, this house was later expanded to a six-bedroom guest house offering charm and privacy (no two guest rooms have adjoining walls). The weathered-shingle building managed to survive the great fire of 1846 and now proudly displays it plaque from the Nantucket Historical Association. Retained are such original features as four fireplaces, wide floorboards, and curved corner support posts from a ship's frame. Guest rooms are spacious and contain period furnishings; some have fireplaces and canopy beds. A sunporch, fenced yard, brick patio, and garden are delightful places to relax. Guests like to gather around the living-room fireplace in cold weather.

Open: year round **Accommodations:** 5 guest rooms with private baths **Meals:** continental-plus breakfast included; restaurants nearby **Rates:** $50 to $150 (seasonal); 10% discount to National Trust members and National Trust Visa cardholders **Payment:** Visa, MC, personal and traveler's checks **Restrictions:** no smoking; no pets **Activities:** books about Nantucket, games, croquet, television–VCR and film library

1739 HOUSE
43 Centre Street
P.O. Box 997
Nantucket, Massachusetts 02554
508/228-0120 or 305/781-4895
Proprietor: Robert (Bob) Martin

In the early eighteenth century Solomon Gardner gave this parcel of Centre Street land to his daughter Sarah and her husband, David Joy. They built their clapboard, Georgian-style home here in 1739, and it stands just as elegantly today. Its five fireplaces and center chimney still provide warmth and comfort, and the wide floorboards have been carefully preserved. The 1739 House is furnished with antiques, oriental rugs, and canopy beds. Guests are invited to enjoy two living rooms, the garden patio, and a rose garden. Located in the heart of Nantucket's historic district, the house is a short walk to shops, restaurants, museums, wharves, and beaches.

Open: June 15 to October 15 **Accommodations:** 6 guest rooms (3 have private baths); 2 are suites **Meals:** continental breakfast included; restaurants nearby **Rates:** $55 to $85 **Payment:** personal and traveler's checks **Restrictions:** no pets **Activities:** television–VCR and movie library, patio parties

WOODBOX INN
29 Fair Street
Nantucket, Massachusetts 02554
508/228-0587
Proprietor: Dexter Tutein

The Woodbox is Nantucket's oldest inn. Built in 1709 by a whaling captain named Bunker, it was joined to its neighboring 1711 house in the early 1900s to create a guest establishment. The low-beamed, pine-paneled dining room serves breakfast (some say the best on the island) and gourmet dinners by the light of tall candles in brass candlesticks. Furnishings throughout the Woodbox feature fine American antiques from the colonial period. Six of the nine guest rooms are suites with fireplaces, and some contain canopy beds. Less than two blocks from Main Street, the Woodbox Inn is located in a quiet part of town, promising peaceful nights.

Open: June through mid-October **Accommodations:** 9 guest rooms with private baths; 6 are suites with fireplaces **Meals:** restaurant on premises serving breakfast and gourmet dinners **Wheelchair access:** limited **Rates:** $120 to $200 **Payment:** personal and traveler's checks

---

NEWBURYPORT

Nearby attractions: Custom House Maritime Museum, Plum Island National Wildlife Refuge, Cushing House; Maudslay State Park for cross-country skiing, hiking, picnicking, and bird-watching; concerts and plays, Firehouse Center for Performing and Visual Arts, antiques hunting, speciality shops, golfing, swimming, tennis, fishing, boating, Lowell's Boat Shop, Sturbridge Village, Hancock Shaker Village, New Hampshire's White Mountains

CLARK CURRIER INN
45 Green Street
Newburyport, Massachusetts 01950
508/465-8363
Proprietors: Mary, Bob, and Melissa Nolan

The Clark Currier Inn is a classic Federal home built in 1803 by Thomas March Clark, a prominent citizen, entrepreneur, and shipbuilder. Lovely architectural details such as a wide center hall, decorative dentil moldings, window seats, Indian shutters, and an elegant "good morning" staircase, lend grace to the dwelling. The name of the inn honors memories of its builder and a longtime owner, and each guest room bears the name of a former owner or resident. All rooms are furnished with antiques and have private baths and air conditioning. There is a sunny garden room, comfortable parlor, library, and garden for guests to enjoy. The inn is located just one block from an award-winning restored historic downtown and three blocks from the waterfront.

Open: year round **Accommodations:** 8 guest rooms with private baths **Meals:** buffet breakfast included; complimentary afternoon tea; restaurants nearby **Wheelchair access:** 3 guest rooms, common areas **Rates:** $75 to $125; 10% discount offered to National Trust members and National Trust Visa cardholders **Payment:** AmEx, Visa, MC, personal and traveler's checks **Restrictions:** children over 12 welcome; smoking limited; no pets **Activities:** reading

WINDSOR HOUSE
38 Federal Street
Newburyport, Massachusetts 01950
508/462-3778
508/465-3443 Fax
Proprietors: Judith and John Harris

This three-story Federal-style brick building was built in 1786 to serve as both a ships' chandlery and residence. It was Aaron Pardee's wedding gift to Jane Perkins. Each spacious room in today's Windsor House has been refurbished to hold a memory of its original use. The Merchant Suite contains the hand-hewn beamed ceiling that was part of the ships' chandlery. The Bridal Suite was first the bedroom shared by Jane and Aaron Pardee. The Nursery and Nanny's Room saw the birth of 21 Pardee children through the years. The Library was Aaron's study; today it houses 500 books on one wall. The Rose Room was, for many years, Aaron and Jane's youngest daughter's room; today it recalls a typical English cottage bedroom. Traditional Cornish and English regional cooking is featured for breakfast and tea.

Open: year round **Accommodations:** 5 guest rooms (3 have private baths) **Meals:** full breakfast included; complimentary afternoon tea; restaurants nearby **Rates:** $75 to $125; 10% discount offered to National Trust members and National Trust Visa cardholders **Payment:** AmEx, Visa, MC, Discover, personal and traveler's checks **Restrictions:** no smoking **Activities:** Cornish crafts center

PETERSHAM

Nearby attractions: Harvard University forestry division, golfing, hiking, skiing, summer band concerts, museums, Old Sturbridge Village

WINTERWOOD AT PETERSHAM
North Main Street
Petersham, Massachusetts 01366
508/724-8885
Proprietors: Jean and Robert Day

Winterwood is an elegant 16-room country inn just off the common in the historic district of Petersham. The inn was built in 1842 in the Greek Revival style as a private summer home. Recently restored, the house has undergone few changes over the years and is listed in the National Register of Historic Places. Guest rooms are professionally decorated to reflect the grace and history of the house; most rooms have working fireplaces. Guests may enjoy tea or linger over cocktails in front of the living room fireplace or on one of the inn's several porches. Across from a 32-acre wildlife meadow preserve, Winterwood offers views of Mount Wachusett and the countryside.

Open: year round **Accommodations:** 6 guest rooms with private baths **Meals:** continental breakfast included; restaurant on premises for private parties; restaurants nearby **Rates:** $65 to $85; 10% discount offered to National Trust members and National Trust Visa cardholders **Payment:** AmEx, Visa, MC, personal and traveler's checks **Restrictions:** no smoking in guest rooms; no pets

---

PROVINCETOWN (CAPE COD)

Nearby attractions: Pilgrim's Monument and Museum, art galleries, beaches, swimming, whale watching, shopping, fine dining

ASHETON HOUSE
3 Cook Street
Provincetown, Massachusetts 02657
508/487-9966
Proprietor: Jim Bayard

Asheton House is a fully restored 1840 whaling captain's house. Its gracious atmosphere is retained outside by a surrounding Nantucket fence and flowing two-sided staircase, and inside by the many American, French, English, and Oriental antiques from the innkeeper's private collection. Three distinctively decorated guest rooms are available—one with African and Asian decor, one with American antiques, and one a suite with French furnishings and fireplace. Bordered by gardens and brick walks, Asheton House is located in the quiet east end of town. The *New England Guest House Book* says, "Of all the guest houses in Provincetown, this is perhaps the most elegant and beautifully furnished, down to the last perfect detail."

Open: year round **Accommodations:** 3 guest rooms (1 has a private bath); 1 is a suite **Meals:** continental breakfast included; restaurants nearby **Rates:** $55 to $105 **Payment:** personal check **Restrictions:** children over 8 welcome; no pets **Activities:** informal English garden with sitting area

---

ROCKPORT

Nearby attractions: Cape Ann, art colony and galleries, ocean beaches, swimming, sailing, park, whale-watching, boating, shopping, antiques hunting, golfing, tennis, trolley tours, schooner trips, June chamber music festival, fine dining

INN ON COVE HILL
37 Mount Pleasant Street
Rockport, Massachusetts
01966
508/546-2701
Proprietors: John and
Marjorie Pratt

Behind a white picket fence just a block from the harbor is this gracious Federal home built in 1791, many of its decorative and architectural features carefully preserved or restored. On arrival, guests are welcomed into the entrance hall, with its artfully crafted spiral staircase. The living room is an inviting blend of comfortable and antique furnishings. Wide pine floorboards and dentil molding remind visitors of the inn's 200-year heritage. Guest rooms feature canopy beds and period antiques. Carefully selected wallcoverings and fabrics create a cozy yet lavish atmosphere, while personal touches and amenities add comfort.

Open: April through October **Accommodations:** 11 guest rooms (9 have private baths)

Meals: continental breakfast included; restaurants nearby **Rates:** $49 to $103 **Payment:** personal and traveler's checks **Restrictions:** appropriate for children over 16; no smoking; no pets **Activities:** reading, relaxation

SEACREST MANOR

131 Marmion Way
Rockport, Massachusetts 01966
508/546-2211
Proprietors: Leighton T. Saville and Dwight B. MacCormack, Jr.

Seacrest Manor is decidedly small, intentionally quiet. Situated on the rugged heights of Cape Ann, surrounded by acres of garden and woodland, it offers a panoramic view of the sea. Built in 1911 as a luxurious Colonial Revival home, it has operated as an inn for more than 40 years, garnering countless accolades from guests and travel critics. Guest rooms are large and sunny, tastefully furnished with antiques and traditional pieces. Turn-down service, evening mints, shoe-shine service, floral bouquets, and morning newspapers are some of the amenities that have earned Seacrest Manor its Mobil three-star rating. A hearty breakfast is served in the dining room overlooking the gardens. The inn's natural setting is furthered by a nine-acre nature preserve across the street.

Open: April through November **Accommodations:** 8 rooms (6 have private baths) **Meals:** full breakfast included; complimentary afternoon tea; restaurants nearby **Rates:** $90 to $128 **Payment:** personal and traveler's checks **Restrictions:** not recommended for children; no smoking; no pets **Activities:** gardens, woods, bird-watching, sundeck, library, bicycles

SALEM

Nearby attractions: Witch Museum, Essex Institute, Peabody Museum, Salem Maritime National Historic Site, House of the Seven Gables, Pickering Wharf, historic homes, harbor cruises, whale-watching, boat rentals, swimming, movie theaters

AMELIA PAYSON HOUSE

16 Winter Street
Salem, Massachusetts 01970
508/744-8304
Proprietors: Ada May and Donald C. Roberts

Built in 1845 for Amelia and Edward Payson, 16 Winter Street is one of Salem's finest examples of Greek Revival architecture, its front-gabled facade distinguised by four two-story pilasters. Carefully restored, the elegant inn offers individually decorated guest rooms featuring period antiques, charming wallpapers, and hardwood floors. A generous continental breakfast is served family style, providing guests with an opportunity to learn about historic Salem and its witchcraft mystique from the innkeepers. Guests appreciate the inn's convenient location within the town's historic district.

Open: March through December **Accommodations:** 4 guest rooms with private baths; 1 is a suite **Meals:** continental-plus breakfast; restaurants nearby **Rates:** $75 to $95 **Payment:** AmEx, Visa, MC, traveler's check **Restrictions:** children over 12 welcome; no smoking; no pets

STEPHEN DANIELS HOUSE
1 Daniels Street (corner of Essex)
Salem, Massachusetts 01970
508/744-5709
Proprietor: Catherine B. Gill

The Stephen Daniels House was built in 1667 by a sea captain and remained a family home until it was converted to an inn in 1945. Originally a four-room gambrel-roofed building, the house was greatly enlarged in 1756. Since then there have been no major changes except for the installation of modern plumbing and electricity; all the eighteenth-century architectural details—and some from the seventeenth century—are intact. The house is of such significance that its plans are in the Library of Congress. Of ten working fireplaces, three are in guest rooms. Another is in the dining room and breakfast is served before it. The rooms are large, colorful, and furnished with antiques, including canopy beds. At the inn, listed in the National Register, great care has been taken to ensure that nothing intrudes on the eighteenth-century New England atmosphere.

Open: year round **Accommodations:** 6 guest rooms (3 have private baths); 1 is a suite **Meals:** continental breakfast included; complimentary refreshments; restaurants nearby **Rates:** $50 to $90; 10% discount to National Trust members and National Trust Visa cardholders **Payment:** AmEx, personal and traveler's checks **Activities:** checkers, board games, private English garden, conversing

SANDWICH (CAPE COD)

Nearby attractions: Sandwich Glass Museum, Heritage Plantation, Thornton Burgess Museum, Hoxie House, Yesteryear's Doll Museum, Cape Cod Bay Beach, antiques hunting, whale-watching, golfing, tennis

SUMMER HOUSE

158 Main Street
Sandwich, Massachusetts 02563
508/888-4991
Proprietors: David and Kay Merrell

Summer House is a beautiful example of Cape Cod Greek Revival architecture set among other equally grand historic homes and public buildings. Built around 1835 by Dr. Jonathan Leonard, Jr., Summer House is located in the heart of the historic district of Sandwich Village, the oldest town on Cape Cod (settled in 1637). Guest rooms are decorated to evoke the spirit of previous centuries. Antiques, hand-stitched quilts, heirloom linens, working fireplaces, painted hardwood floors, and original woodwork and hardware set the mood of a gracious nineteenth-century home. Breakfast is served in the vibrant breakfast room, where Chinese red walls contrast with white window molding and paneling, a black-and-white checkerboard floor, and a black marble fireplace. Afternoon tea is served on the wicker-furnished porch or in the flower garden.

Open: year round **Accommodations:** 5 rooms (1 has a private bath) **Meals:** full breakfast included; complimentary afternoon tea; restaurants nearby **Rates:** $55 to $75; 10% discount offered to National Trust members and National Trust Visa cardholders **Payment:** AmEx, Visa, MC, Discover, personal and traveler's checks **Restrictions:** children over 6 welcome; no smoking; no pets **Activities:** flower gardens and lawns, library

SOUTH DARTMOUTH

Nearby attractions: New Bedford Historic District; whaling museum; walking tours; beaches; hiking; biking; day trips to Plymouth, Cape Cod, Boston, Martha's Vineyard, Mystic Seaport, and Newport, R.I.

SALT MARSH FARM
322 Smith Neck Road
South Dartmouth, Massachusetts 02748
508/992-0980
Proprietors: Larry and Sally Brownell
Location: 7 miles southwest of New Bedford

In 1665 when John Smith found the town of Plymouth too crowded, he exchanged his house there for land in Dartmouth, which became known as Smith's Neck. The portion of that land which is now Salt Marsh Farm was known in 1727 as the Homestead Farm of Isaac Howland, ancestor of Hetty Green, the "Witch of Wall Street." Owned today by one of John Smith's descendants, Howland's post-and-beam, hip-roofed Georgian farmhouse retains many original features. The uneven floors give a little, and the wide boards creak. Narrow stairs and low doorways lead into cozy guest rooms furnished with family antiques. Original fireplaces provide warmth and comfort. Dotted with old stone walls, Salt Marsh Farm is a 90-acre nature preserve with trails that lead through fields and woods to salt meadows and tidal marshes.

Open: year round **Accommodations:** 2 guest rooms with private baths **Meals:** full breakfast included; complimentary refreshments; restaurants nearby **Rates:** $65 to $85 **Payment:** Visa, MC, personal and traveler's checks **Restrictions:** children over 5 welcome; no smoking; no pets; two-night minimum at holidays and on weekends May into October **Activities:** walking trails, nature hikes, bicycling, library–living room, organic flower and vegetable gardens, bicycles available

STERLING

Nearby attractions: Wachusett Mountain skiing, Worcester Art Museum, Sterling Millworks, historic Lexington and Concord

STERLING INN
240 Worcester Road
Route 12
Sterling, Massachusetts 01564
508/422-6592 or 800/370-0239
Proprietors: Mark and Patricia Roy
Location: 15 miles north of Worcester

The Sterling Inn has served central Massachusetts since 1890. The current building was designed in 1907 by G. Henri Desmond, a Boston architect. The inn is an excellent example of the Craftsman style of architecture that swept the country at the turn of the century, and its half-timbering and flower-filled window boxes give it a Swiss chalet feel. The dining rooms and tap room, where working fireplaces generate warmth on chilly evenings, have always been popular with both travelers and local patrons. For generations local families have considered the inn a second home where they entertain at holidays, hold intimate wedding receptions, or simply sit together on the front porch. The second floor has six comfortable guest rooms decorated in a homespun, country style.

Open: year round **Accommodations:** 6 guest rooms with private baths **Meals:** continental-plus breakfast included (full breakfast on Sunday); complimentary refreshments; restaurant on premises **Wheelchair access:** dining rooms and public bathrooms **Rates:** $51 to $55; 10% discount offered to National Trust members and National Trust Visa cardholders **Payment:** AmEx, Visa, MC, personal and traveler's checks **Restrictions:** children over 8 welcome; no pets

STOCKBRIDGE–SOUTH LEE

Nearby attractions: Tanglewood Music Festival; Jacob's Pillow Dance Festival; Berkshire Festival Theater; skiing; fall foliage tours; Norman Rockwell Museum; National Trust's Chesterwood, Wharton, and Melville houses; Hancock Shaker Village; Mission House; Naumkeag

HISTORIC MERRELL INN

1565 Pleasant Street
South Lee, Massachusetts
01260
413/243-1794
Proprietors: Charles and
Faith Reynolds
Location: 1 mile east of
Stockbridge

An eighteenth-century brick stagecoach inn, the Historic Merrell Inn commemorated its bicentennial in 1994. One of the most authentic buildings in New England, the inn retains most of its original architectural features, including a circular bird cage bar with original faux-grain painting, one of the few remaining in America. Original woodwork and eight Rumford fireplaces are also intact. A full breakfast is served in the tavern room, while afternoon tea is served in the keeping room from an eighteenth-century breakfront. Guest rooms are furnished with canopy beds and antiques collected by the innkeepers. Visitors like to roam the inn's two acres of grounds with their eighteenth-century stone walls and foundations or stroll down to the shore of the Housatonic River, which borders the inn's property. The tavern is listed in the National Register and the Historic American Buildings Survey.

Open: year round **Accommodations:** 9 guest rooms with private baths **Meals:** full breakfast included; complimentary afternoon tea; restaurants nearby **Rates:** $85 to $155; 10% discount offered to National Trust members and National Trust Visa cardholders **Payment:** Visa, MC, personal checks **Restrictions:** no smoking; no pets **Activities:** gardens and grounds for strolling, riverside gazebo, television room

INN AT STOCKBRIDGE
30 East Street (Route 7 North)
P.O. Box 618
Stockbridge, Massachusetts 01262
413/298-3337   Fax: 413/298-3406
Proprietors: Alice and Len Schiller

In 1906, Boston attorney Philip Blagdon built an elegant vacation home in Stockbridge. He had it designed in the Colonial Revival style, complete with Georgian detailing and classical columns. The house, now the Inn at Stockbridge, remains structurally unchanged; its interior still boasts finely detailed molding throughout the first floor and on the staircase. The inn, on 12 secluded acres, offers an atmosphere of warmth and friendliness attested to by numerous publications, including *Country Inns, New York Magazine* and the *Boston Globe*. Individually decorated guest rooms are traditional and cozy. A full breakfast is served on a grand mahogany table set with china, silver, crystal, linen, and lighted candles. Guests also gather for wine and cheese each afternoon, often after a dip in the pool.

Open: year round **Accommodations:** 8 guest rooms with private baths; 2 are suites **Meals:** full breakfast included; complimentary refreshments; restaurants nearby **Rates:** $75 to $225; 10% discount offered to National Trust members and National Trust Visa cardholders **Payment:** AmEx, Visa, MC, personal and traveler's checks **Restrictions:** children over 12 welcome; no smoking; no pets **Activities:** swimming, exploring 12 acres, extensive library

RED LION INN
Main Street
Stockbridge, Massachusetts 01262
412/298-5545
413/298-5130 Fax
Proprietors: Fitzpatrick family

Established as a stagecoach stop in 1773 by Silas Pepoon and rebuilt in 1897 following a devastating fire, the Red Lion is one of the few remaining American inns in continuous use since the eighteenth century. Immortalized in Norman Rockwell's painting *Main Street, Stockbridge*, the inn epitomizes New England hospitality. It is filled with a fine collection of Staffordshire china, colonial pewter, and eighteenth-century furnishings, many of which have belonged to the inn for more than a century. Every guest room is uniquely decorated in keeping with the inn's history. Meals are prepared from the freshest ingredients and are served in the main dining room, the tavern room, or the lounge. Host to five presidents as well as Nathaniel Hawthorne, William Cullen Bryant, and Henry Wadsworth Longfellow, the Red Lion Inn is central to Stockbridge's and the Berkshires' historic and cultural attractions.

Open: year round **Accommodations:** 110 guest rooms (85 have private baths); 19 are suites **Meals:** restaurants on premises **Rates:** $60 to $235 **Payment:** AmEx, Visa, MC, CB, DC, Discover, personal and traveler's checks **Restrictions:** no pets **Activities:** massage therapist, outdoor swimming pool, exercise room, pub with nightly entertainment

---

STURBRIDGE
Nearby attractions: Old Sturbridge Village, museums, galleries, tennis, golfing, hiking trails, antiques hunting, shopping

EBENEZER CRAFTS INN
Fiske Hill
Sturbridge, Massachusetts 01566
800/PUBLICK (800/782-5425)
508/347-5073 Fax
Proprietors: Publick House Historic Inn

This classic New England Federal farmhouse was built in 1786 by David Fiske. The house is owned and operated today by the nearby Publick House, first opened in 1771 by Colonel Ebenezer Crafts. Except for the addition of modern conveniences, Fiske's house is as it was when built. Large, airy guest rooms are individually furnished with colonial antiques and period reproductions. Each has its own bath. All offer sweeping views of unspoiled rolling hills. On arrival, guests are given a tour of the historic house. Before retiring at night, beds are turned down, terrycloth robes are laid out, and chocolates are left on bedside tables. A fresh bakery breakfast and afternoon tea are offered daily. The entire inn may be reserved for special occasions.

Open: year round **Accommodations:** 8 guest rooms with private baths; 1 is a suite **Meals:** continental breakfast included; complimentary refreshments; restaurants nearby **Wheelchair access:** yes **Rates:** $65 to $155; 10% discount to National Trust members and National Trust Visa cardholders **Payment:** AmEx, Visa, MC, CB, DC, personal and traveler's checks **Restrictions:** smoking limited; no pets **Activities:** swimming pool, specialty packages

UXBRIDGE

Nearby attractions: Sturbridge Village; Blackstone Canal Heritage Corridor; Worcester; Providence, R.I.; factory outlets; walking tours of historic district

CHARLES CAPRON HOUSE
2 Capron Street
Uxbridge, Massachusetts 01569
508/278-2214
Proprietors: Ken and Mary Taft

Listed in the National Register of Historic Places, Capron House is considered Uxbridge's best example of Victorian Gothic architecture. It was built in 1874 by Charles Capron, a wealthy woolen mill owner, whose mill in the center of town was powered by the river that runs behind the inn. Capron is also credited with introducing electricity and telephones to Uxbridge. Three guest rooms are charmingly furnished in antiques, lace, handmade quilts, and relaxing upholstered chairs. One room features a four-poster bed, and another contains an antique sleigh bed. Guests are invited to use the living room and the sunporch filled with wicker rockers, gliders, and greenery. Breakfast is served in one of two dining rooms or on the porch, and may feature cranberry pancakes or apple crêpes with crème fraîche.

Open: April to December **Accommodations:** 3 guest rooms (2 have private baths) **Meals:** full breakfast included; complimentary refreshments; restaurants nearby **Rates:** $55 to $70; 10% discount offered to National Trust members and National Trust Visa cardholders **Payment:** personal and traveler's checks **Restrictions:** children over 12 welcome; smoking limited; no pets **Activities:** canoeing, biking, croquet, house tours

WOODS HOLE (CAPE COD)

Nearby attractions: lighthouse, aquarium, beaches, whale watching, National Seashore, bicycling, Falmouth, antiques hunting, ferries to Martha's Vineyard and Nantucket

THE MARLBOROUGH

320 Woods Hole Road
Woods Hole, Massachusetts 02543
508/548-6218 or 800/320-2322 (reservations only)
508/457-7519 Fax
Proprietor: Diana Smith
Location: 1 1/2 miles from Woods Hole Village; 2 1/2 miles from Falmouth

A 1940s Cape Cod cottage, the Marlborough exhibits architectural and decorative details copied from its centuries-old predecessors: slanted second-story ceilings, dormers, a steep staircase, a picket fence, and a rambling rose climbing a trellis next to the doorway. Unlike its antecedents, the Marlborough provides modern plumbing and air conditioning. Professionally decorated guest rooms are furnished with quilts, needlework, and collectibles. Beds are dressed in lavender-scented linens, and freshly cut flowers cheer each room. A complimentary breakfast is served poolside or before a fire according to the season. Afternoon tea and homemade sweets are available in the parlor during the summer and on Sunday and Wednesday afternoons from fall through spring.

Open: year round **Accommodations:** 6 guest rooms with private baths and 1 poolside cottage **Meals:** full breakfast included; complimentary refreshments; restaurants nearby **Rates:** $65 to $125 (seasonal) **Payment:** AmEx, Visa, MC, personal and traveler's checks **Restrictions:** well-traveled children over 2 welcome; no smoking **Activities:** swimming pool, English paddle tennis, croquet, hammocks

YARMOUTHPORT (CAPE COD)

Nearby attractions: historic houses, museums, art galleries, antiques hunting, beaches and water sports, whale-watching, golfing, tennis, theater

WEDGEWOOD INN
83 Main Street
Yarmouthport, Massachusetts 02675
508/362-5157 or 508/362-9178
Proprietors: Milt and Gerrie Graham

Built in 1812 for an attorney, the Wedgewood Inn was the first structure in the village of Yarmouthport to have been designed by an architect. A stately Federal-style home located in the town's historic district, it has been handsomely restored and updated to include air conditioning. In each guest room, attention to detail is evident in the handcrafted, cherry pencil-post beds with antique quilts, wood-burning fireplaces, period wallpapers, distinctive paintings, and daily arrangements of fresh flowers. The Wedgewood Inn, listed in the National Register of Historic Places, has been acclaimed by the *New York Times* and *Colonial Homes* magazine, among others.

Open: year round **Accommodations:** 6 guest rooms with private baths; 2 are suites **Meals:** full breakfast included; tea trays and fresh fruit in rooms; restaurants nearby **Wheelchair access:** 2 guest rooms; dining room **Rates:** $110 to $160; off-season rates available; 10% discount to National Trust members and National Trust Visa cardholders **Payment:** AmEx, Visa, MC, DC, personal and traveler's checks **Restrictions:** children over 10 welcome; smoking limited; no pets **Activities:** lawn, gardens, patio

MICHIGAN

BIG BAY

Nearby attractions: maritime museum, harbor cruises, walking tours, antiques hunting, hiking, waterfall tours, fishing, rock climbing, canoeing, downhill and cross-country skiing, art and music festivals

BIG BAY POINT LIGHTHOUSE BED AND BREAKFAST
3 Lighthouse Road
Big Bay, Michigan 49808
906/345-9957
Proprietors: Linda and Jeff Gamble
Location: 30 miles north of Marquette

Beginning in 1896, the Big Bay Point Lighthouse guided mariners on Lake Superior from its vantage point high atop a cliff jutting into the water. Although automated signals replaced the original lamp in 1941, the 1500-pound Third Order Fresnel Lens, the second largest ever used on the Great Lakes, is still intact and available for inspection by guests. In 1986 the two-story brick building and its adjoining 60-foot-high square tower were adapted to a bed-and-breakfast facility. The 18-room inn has seven guest rooms and a common living room with fireplace, a dining room, a library, and a sauna located in the tower. A visit to the lantern, 125 feet above the lake surface, reveals vistas of Lake Superior, the Huron Mountains, fields of windflowers, dense forests, and the drama of offshore lightning bolts and the Aurora Borealis in the night sky.

Open: year round **Accommodations:** 7 guest rooms (5 have private baths); 2 are suites **Meals:** full breakfast included; restaurants nearby **Rates:** $85 to $150; 10% discount to National Trust members **Payment:** traveler's check **Restrictions:** not suitable for children; no smoking; no pets **Activities:** sauna, nature trail, 1/2 mile of lakefront, cross-country skiing

COLDWATER

Nearby attractions: Tibbits Opera House, Shipshewana Amish Country, Allen (antiques capital of Michigan), Colon Magic Festival, Michigan International Speedway, Kalamazoo, winery, museums, Pokagon State Park, golfing, boating, fishing, ice fishing, swimming, cross-country skiing, hiking, Binder Park Zoo

CHICAGO PIKE INN
215 East Chicago Street
Coldwater, Michigan 49036
517/279-8744
Proprietors: Harold and Jane Schultz

Built for Morris G. Clarke, a wealthy Coldwater merchant, this 1903 mansion exhibits elegant neoclassical styling in its full-height porch supported by massive columns with Ionic capitals. After more than 50 years as a rooming house, it was sold in 1988 and transformed into the luxurious bed and breakfast of today. A careful restoration preserved the sweeping cherry staircase, stained-glass windows, parquet and marble floors, and gas and electric chandeliers. Richly designed wallpapers and fabrics from Schumacher and Waverly are accentuated by oriental rugs and Victorian-era antiques. Guest rooms, recalling former house occupants with names like Miss Sophia's Suite, the Hired Girls' Suite, and the Grandchildrens' Room, all assure comfort, with individual climate controls and comfortable chairs and reading lamps. Chicago Pike Inn has been featured in an *Innsider* cover story.

Open: year round **Accommodations:** 8 guest rooms with private baths; 1 is a suite **Meals:** full breakfast included; complimentary refreshments; restaurants nearby **Rates:** $80 to $165 **Payment:** AmEx, Visa, MC, personal check **Restrictions:** children over 12 welcome; smoking limited; no pets **Activities:** bicycling, reading, relaxing in gazebo, gift shop

GRAND RAPIDS

Nearby attractions: Meyer May House (designed by Frank Lloyd Wright), museums, concert halls, theater, historic district walking tours, Grand River, skiing, Lake Michigan

FOUNTAIN HILL BED AND BREAKFAST
222 Fountain, N.E.
Grand Rapids, Michigan 49503
616/458-6621
Proprietors: Sally Coburn and Chuck Carter

This classic Italianate home was built by John and Sarah Wenham in 1874. Overlooking downtown Grand Rapids, it is in the historic Heritage Hill district and cultural center. Elegant architectural details such as the high ceilings, elaborate plasterwork, and a circular staircase set off the fine wall coverings, lighting fixtures, and period furnishings found throughout the home. Guest accommodations are spacious and distinctive, and filled with modern comforts, including private baths with whirlpool tubs, television, and air conditioning. Guests may eat breakfast in the dining room or in the privacy of their bedroom. Surrounded by delightful gardens, Fountain Hill is within walking distance of fine restaurants, theaters, and museums.

Open: year round **Accommodations:** 4 guest rooms with private baths **Meals:** full breakfast included; complimentary refreshments; restaurants nearby **Rates:** $55 to $85 **Payment:** AmEx, Visa, MC, personal and traveler's checks **Restrictions:** no smoking; no pets **Activities:** television

HOLLAND

Nearby attractions: Windmill Island, DeWitt Cultural Center, Manufacturers' Marketplace, Lake Michigan beaches, bicycle paths

DUTCH COLONIAL INN
560 Central Avenue
Holland, Michigan 49423
616/396-3664
616/396-0461 Fax
Proprietors: Bob and Pat Elenbaas

This 1928 Dutch Colonial Revival home was built as a wedding gift. Today, it is a bed-and-breakfast inn offering Dutch hospitality and five comfortable, air-conditioned guest rooms, one a cozy hideaway suite tucked under the eaves. Several rooms feature whirlpool tubs for two. The decor spans several generations, from Victorian country to 1930s chic. Guests are invited to relax in the common room with fireplace, television and VCR, in the bright solarium, or on the open porch in white wooden rockers. Located in a lovely residential neighborhood, the Dutch Colonial Inn is ideally suited to business as well as leisure travelers.

Open: year round **Accommodations:** 5 guest rooms with private baths; 2 are suites **Meals:** full breakfast included; complimentary refreshments; restaurants nearby **Rates:** $60 to $150 **Payment:** AmEx, Visa, MC, Discover, personal and traveler's checks **Restrictions:** no smoking; no pets

LAKESIDE

Nearby attractions: Lake Michigan beaches, swimming, state parks, art galleries, summer theater, antiques hunting, winery tours, cross-country skiing

PEBBLE HOUSE
15093 Lakeshore Road
Lakeside, Michigan 49116
616/469-1416
Proprietors: Jean and Ed Lawrence

The Pebble House, consisting of three guest buildings, a screened summer house, and a tennis court, was built in 1912 as a vacation retreat. Buildings are connected by wooden walkways and pergolas covered with wisteria and grapevines. The main house and fence posts are built of decorative stones that inspired the inn's name. The house decor celebrates the American Arts and Crafts Movement, which flourished between 1900 and 1916 as a rebellion against the excesses of Victorian design. The inn's emphasis on handcraftsmanship and simple, solid construction typifies Arts and Crafts design. Guest rooms are furnished in either Mission or Victorian styles. The glassed-in porch is a welcoming retreat, with rockers surrounding the stone fireplace.

Open: year round **Accommodations:** 7 guest rooms with private baths; 4 are suites **Meals:** full breakfast included; complimentary refreshments; restaurants nearby **Wheelchair access:** 1 guest room and bath; dining room with assistance **Rates:** $100 to $140 **Payment:** Visa, MC, personal and traveler's checks **Restrictions:** smoking limited; no pets (resident cats) **Activities:** tennis, parlor games, library, screenhouse for hammocks, games, picnicking

---

LUDINGTON

Nearby attractions: Lake Michigan beaches, Ludington State Park, Stearns Park, White Pine Village, Michigan–Wisconsin car ferry

THE INN AT LUDINGTON
701 East Ludington Avenue
Ludington, Michigan 49431
616/845-7055
Proprietor: Diane Shields

The Inn at Ludington occupies an antique-laden Queen Anne house that was built in 1889 by Dr. F. R. Latimer. The corner tower is the focal point of this house, which retains its original leaded- and stained-glass windows, four working fireplaces and their oak mantels, oak floors, and a grand staircase. Guest bedrooms, including two with fireplaces, have queen-size poster or brass beds. Handmade quilts, fresh flowers, and turn-down service are evidence of the friendly, attentive atmosphere. Early morning coffee and homemade muffins are served in the parlor, followed by a complete breakfast in the dining room. The inn also offers special-occasion packages, picnic baskets, and fall and winter weekend events.

Open: year round **Accommodations:** 6 guest rooms with private baths; 1 is a suite **Meals:** full breakfast included; complimentary refreshments; restaurants nearby **Wheelchair access:** 1 guest room, dining room, parlor **Rates:** $65 to $85; 10% discount offered to National Trust members and National Trust Visa cardholders **Payment:** AmEx, Visa, MC, personal and traveler's checks **Restrictions:** smoking limited; no pets (resident dog) **Activities:** library, relaxing before fire or on patio

MACKINAC ISLAND

Nearby attractions: Fort Mackinac, horse-carriage tours, bicycling, historic town, park trails, golfing, tennis, horseback riding, fine dining, museums, shopping

HAAN'S 1830 INN
Huron Street
P.O. Box 123
Mackinac Island, Michigan 49757
906/847-6244
Winter address:
3418 Oakwood Avenue
Island Lake, Illinois 60042
708/526-2662
Proprietors: Joyce and Vernon Haan and Nicholas and Nancy Haan

A survey conducted under provisions of the National Historic Preservation Act of 1966 identified Haan's 1830 Inn as the oldest example of Greek Revival architecture in the Northwest Territory. It is the oldest building used as an inn in the state of Michigan. Haan's was once the home of Colonel William Preston, the first mayor of Mackinac Island City. Each of the inn's guest rooms is furnished with antiques from the mid-nineteenth century and artifacts from the island's fur-trading period. A hearty continental breakfast is served on the 12-foot-long, Civil War–era dining table. The inn, featured in the *Chicago Tribune* and *Innsider*, among others, is a short distance from the island's quaint downtown, old Fort Mackinac, and the ferry docks. Automobile traffic is not allowed on the island, and visitors have their choice of bicycling, walking, or renting a horse and carriage.

Open: mid-May to mid-November **Accommodations:** 7 guest rooms (5 have private baths); 1 is a suite with kitchen **Meals:** continental-plus breakfast included; restaurants nearby **Rates:** $80 to $120 **Payment:** personal and traveler's checks **Restrictions:** no smoking; no pets **Activities:** open and screened porches with views of water and gardens; reading; games; benches throughout yard and gardens

---

PETOSKEY

Nearby attractions: historic Gaslight District, skiing, golfing, art galleries, shopping, boating, antiques hunting, nature preserves, museums, beaches, Traverse City, Mackinac Island, Tahquamenon Falls

STAFFORD'S PERRY HOTEL
Bay and Lewis Streets
Petoskey, Michigan 49770
616/347-4000 or 800/456-1917
616/347-0636 Fax
Proprietors: Stafford Smith and Dudley Marvin

The city's first brick hotel, the Perry Hotel was built in 1899 by Dr. Norman J. Perry, a dentist who quit his practice and took up the hospitality business when one of his patients died following a multiple tooth extraction. Listed in the

National Register of Historic Places, the hotel offers panoramic views of Little Traverse Bay from the porches, dining room, and a number of guest rooms. Public rooms and guest rooms alike are decorated with the color and lavish wallpaper patterns popular at the turn of the century. Bedrooms are individually decorated for charm and comfort, each with a private bath, telephone, and color cable television. Some rooms have balconies. A full-service restaurant serves three meals daily. Live musical entertainment is offered nightly in the Noggin Room Pub.

Open: year round **Accommodations:** 80 guest rooms with private baths; 1 is a suite **Meals:** complimentary refreshments; restaurant and pub on premises **Wheelchair access:** yes **Rates:** $69 to $165; 10% discount to National Trust members and National Trust Visa cardholders **Payment:** AmEx, Visa, MC, personal and traveler's checks **Restrictions:** no pets **Activities:** exercise bike, hot tub

---

ST. JOSEPH

Nearby attractions: wineries, museums, beaches, sailing, charter fishing, cross-country skiing, antiques hunting, golfing, shopping

SOUTH CLIFF INN BED AND BREAKFAST
1900 Lakeshore Drive
St. Joseph, Michigan 49085
616/983-4881
616/983-7391 Fax
Proprietor: Bill Swisher

This 1920 brick cottage, influenced by Tudor styling in its peaked front entry gable, sits on a cliff overlooking Lake Michigan. One of the inn's most attractive amenities is the spectacular view of the lake, seen from many guest rooms as well as from the sunroom, where breakfast is served. Guest rooms have been designed by combining imported fabrics with antique and traditional furnishings. Some rooms offer whirlpool tubs, others may contain a sitting area with reading chairs, each has its own character. Guests enjoy the living room fireplace in cool weather and the two decks overlooking the lake in summer. Color cable television is available in the den. Downtown St. Joseph is an easy walk away.

Open: year round, except December 23–25 **Accommodations:** 7 guest rooms with private baths; 2 are suites **Meals:** continental-plus breakfast included; restaurants nearby **Rates:** $60 to $125 **Payment:** AmEx, Visa, MC, Discover, traveler's check **Restrictions:** smoking limited; no pets **Activities:** lake swimming, sundecks

---

SALINE

Nearby attractions: Greenfield Village, Henry Ford Museum, Ford Heritage Trails, Ann Arbor Antiques Market, Irish Hills, golfing, tennis, theaters

THE HOMESTEAD BED AND BREAKFAST
9279 Macon Road
Saline, Michigan 48176-9305
313/429-9625
Proprietor: Shirley H. Grossman

Saline is named for the local salt wells where Native Americans once salted their fish for preservation. Their arrowheads and stone axes are still found among the woods and fields of the Homestead's 50-acre organic farm. The country and Victorian antiques throughout the farmhouse have been here for more than 100 years. (The Grossman family purchased the large, two-story brick farmhouse completely furnished more than 30 years ago.) Bedrooms also contain antiques, and each room has a sitting area. Bathrooms are in the hall, so robes and towels are provided in each bedroom. The living room, library, and parlor are open to guests at all times, as is the upright grand piano. Complimentary refreshments are served in the living room each evening. The Homestead is convenient to Saline, Ann Arbor, and Ypsilanti.

Open: year round **Accommodations:** 5 guest rooms (1 has a private bath) **Meals:** full breakfast included; complimentary refreshments; restaurants nearby **Rates:** $35 single to $70 double; 10% discount to National Trust members and National Trust Visa cardholders **Payment:** AmEx, Visa, MC, Discover, personal and traveler's checks **Restrictions:** smoking limited; no pets **Activities:** walking, cross-country skiing, reading, piano

SAUGATUCK

Nearby attractions: Holland Tulip Festival, Lake Michigan beaches and charter fishing, Dune State Park for hiking and cross-country skiing, farmers' markets, museums, golfing, shopping

KEMAH GUEST HOUSE
633 Pleasant Street
Saugatuck, Michigan 49453
616/857-2919
Proprietors: Cindi and Terry Tatsch

Kemah Guest House is a turn-of-the-century mansion evocative of an English cottage with false thatched roof and a porte cochere. The interior sports a combination of Old World charm in its antiques and Bavarian rathskeller, Art Deco grace from a 1920s remodeling, and Southwestern airiness in a solarium designed by a local artist, Carl Hoerman. Six quaint guest rooms combine antique furnishings and hardwood floors with original tile bathrooms for a charming historic atmosphere. Chantilly Corner is accented with lace. The Captain's Quarters features an oak gentleman's suite with six-foot headboard. The Deco Dormer's unique mahogany bedroom suite was featured in a 1926 issue of *Architectural Digest.* Needlepoint Nook is cozy, country Victorian. The study provides a warming fireplace; the parlor contains a baby grand piano. In the rathskeller, a game room offers billiards and television.

Open: year round **Accommodations:** 6 guest rooms (4 have private baths) **Meals:** continental-plus breakfast included; complimentary refreshments, restaurants nearby **Rates:** $85 to $140; 10% discount offered to National Trust members and National Trust Visa cardholders **Payment:** AmEx, Visa, MC, Discover, personal and traveler's checks **Restrictions:** not suitable for children; no smoking; no pets **Activities:** game room, bird watching, strolling the grounds

MINNESOTA

Stillwater •

Dundas •

DUNDAS

Nearby attractions: Cannon Valley Wilderness for hiking and cross-country skiing, Dundas Dukes baseball, St. Olaf and Carleton colleges, canoeing, antiques hunting, golfing, state parks, Mall of America

MARTIN OAKS BED AND BREAKFAST
(Historic Archibald–Martin House)
107 First Street
P.O. Box 207
Dundas, Minnesota 55019
507/645-4644
Proprietors: Marie and
Frank Gery

Built in 1869 by the treasurer of
the thriving Archibald Mills, this
Italianate house is now in the
National Register of Historic
Places. It is one of several large
homes built at the same time in
the Cannon River community
of Dundas, then a thriving mill

town. Guest rooms at Martin Oaks are decorated with antique furnishings. Martin Suite features a spoon-carved high bed and a Baltimore Album quilt. Sarah Etta's Room was stenciled in 1811 and looks out on spring and summer gardens. The tiny Hideaway offers a quiet retreat. An elegant candlelight breakfast is served in the Victorian dining room. Afternoon tea is available on request.

Open: year round **Accommodations:** 3 guest rooms with shared baths **Meals:** full breakfast included; complimentary refreshments; restaurants nearby **Rates:** $55 to $69; 10% discount to National Trust members and National Trust Visa cardholders **Payment:** Visa, MC, personal and traveler's checks **Restrictions:** not suitable for children; no smoking; no pets (resident cat)

STILLWATER

Nearby attractions: St. Croix River, art galleries, antiques hunting, skiing, hot-air ballooning, trolley tours, golfing, water and jet skiing, paddlewheeler rides

WILLIAM SAUNTRY MANSION
626 North Fourth Street
Stillwater, Minnesota 55082
612/430-2653 or 800/828-2653
612/430-9315 Fax
Proprietors: Martha and Duane Hubbs

Listed in the National Register of Historic Places, this 25-room Queen Anne mansion with Eastlake detailing was built in 1890 by lumber baron William Sauntry. The house reflecs Sauntry's love of the opulent, with 10 fireplaces, parquet floors, painted canvas ceilings, cherry and oak woodwork, and many stained-glass windows. The house is furnished in the late Victorian style. Each guest room is a tribute to an original family member with colors and decor selected to reflect their personalities. Most rooms have fireplaces and two have double whirlpool tubs. A full breakfast is served in the dining room and guests are invited to explore the parlors, music room, and library.

Open: year round **Accommodations:** 6 guest rooms with private baths; 2 are suites **Meals:** full breakfast included; restaurant on premises; restaurants nearby **Rates:** $89 to $149 **Payment:** AmEx, Visa, MC, CB, DC, Discover, personal and traveler's checks **Restrictions:** children over 12 welcome; no smoking; no pets

MISSISSIPPI

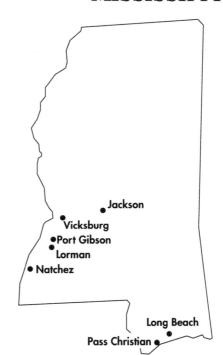

Jackson
Vicksburg
Port Gibson
Lorman
Natchez

Long Beach
Pass Christian

JACKSON

Nearby attractions: Old Capitol Museum, Mississippi Museum of Art, New Stage Theater, Dizzy Dean Baseball Museum, Jackson Zoological Park, Petrified Forest, Natchez, Vicksburg, golfing, tennis

FAIRVIEW INN
734 Fairview Street
Jackson, Mississippi 39202-1624
601/948-3429
601/948-1203 Fax
Proprietors: William J. and Carol N. Simmons

This elegant Colonial Revival mansion was built by lumber tycoon Cyrus G. Warren in 1908. In 1930 it was purchased by banker D. C. Simmons, in whose family the house remains today. Designed by the Chicago architectural firm of Spencer and Powers, the house is one of a small number of architecturally designed homes remaining in Jackson. The Simmonses have gathered a rich array of antiques from the surrounding area as well as from their travels in New England and Europe. Seven bedrooms, located in the main building and in the carriage house, are appointed with fine antiques and heirlooms. Hardwood floors gleam throughout the house. Rich tapestries, fine oil paintings, marble mantels, and crystal chandeliers add to the warm opulence of the home. Fairview offers catering services and chef-prepared dinners and is a favorite setting for weddings. The inn has been featured on the cover of *Country Inns*.

Open: year round **Accommodations:** 7 guest rooms with private baths; 4 are suites **Meals:** full breakfast included; complimentary refreshments; dinners available with advance notice; restaurants nearby **Wheelchair access:** some rooms **Rates:** $80 to $150; 10% discount to National Trust members and National Trust Visa cardholders **Payment:** AmEx, Visa, MC, Discover, personal and traveler's checks **Restrictions:** no smoking; no pets **Activities:** walking and jogging track, library, exercise equipment

---

LONG BEACH

Nearby attractions: Jefferson Davis home, 14 golf courses, 26 miles of gulf beaches, casinos, historic sites

RED CREEK COLONIAL INN
7416 Red Creek Road
Long Beach, Mississippi 39560
601/452-3080
Proprietors: Dr. and Mrs. Karl Mertz
Innkeepers: Ed and Chantell Rhoton

In 1899 an Italian sea captain built this house to entice his young bride to move here from her parents' home in New Orleans. He copied that home's raised French Colonial style with its high brick foundation, 64-foot-wide front porch, 10-foot-high ceilings, six fireplaces, and roof dormers. Six ceiling fans help cool the house. A variety of antiques from different periods help define the Victorian, French, and English rooms. The most elaborate room features an 8 1/2-foot-high headboard and a pink marble-topped dresser and chest of drawers. The inn's 11 acres are punctuated by huge magnolias and ancient live oak trees (two of which are registered with the Live Oak Society). An electrified Victorian organ and a wooden tabletop radio with an overseas band provide entertainment.

Open: year round **Accommodations:** 5 guest rooms (3 have private baths); 1 is a suite **Meals:** continental-plus breakfast included; restaurants nearby **Rates:** $59 to $79; 10% discount offered to National Trust members and National Trust Visa cardholders **Payment:** personal check **Restrictions:** no smoking; no pets **Activities:** porch swings, organ, Victrola, radio

LORMAN

Nearby attractions: historic homes, antiques hunting; battlefields in Natchez, Vicksburg, and Port Gibson

ROSSWOOD PLANTATION
Route 552 East
Route 1, Box 6
Lorman, Mississippi 39096
601/437-4215 or 800/533-5889
601/437-6888 Fax
Proprietors: Jean and Walt Hylander
Location: 2 1/2 miles east of U.S. 61

Rosswood Plantation, completed in 1857, is a Greek Revival mansion of 14 rooms and 10 fireplaces that Dr. Walter Wade built for his bride Mabella Chamberlain. The journal he kept of their life on a cotton plantation before and during the Civil War makes fascinating reading for overnight guests. The National Register house has 14-foot-high ceilings, a winding staircase, columned galleries, and slave quarters. It is completely restored and furnished with antiques, such as the Jacobean dining table, where breakfast is served. Four-poster beds and fireplaces grace each guest room. Rosswood occupies 100 acres of rolling fields where deer and other wildlife abound, and Christmas trees stand where cotton once grew.

Open: March through December **Accommodations:** 4 guest rooms with private baths **Meals:** full breakfast included; complimentary refreshments; restaurants nearby **Wheelchair access:** bathrooms, dining facilities **Rates:** $99 to $125 **Payment:** Visa, MC, personal and traveler's checks **Restrictions:** no pets **Activities:** walking, fishing, movies on videotape, antiques, Civil War history, swimming pool and heated spa

NATCHEZ

Nearby attractions: Mississippi River, riverboat gambling, Native American sites, Natchez Trace, historic house tours, golfing, fishing, tennis, antiques hunting

DUNLEITH
84 Homochitto Street
Natchez, Mississippi 39120
601/446-8500 or 800/433-2445
601/446-6094 Fax
Proprietor: William F. Heins

Surrounded by 40 acres of pastures and bayous, Dunleith stands as a monument to the southern Greek Revival tradition of architecture. Somtimes called the most-photographed house in America, the white-colonnaded Dunleith has been the backdrop for numerous feature films and has appeared in the Southern Accents book *Historic Houses of the South*. Having undergone extensive restoration since the 1970s, the mansion now offers 11 guest rooms in the main house and the courtyard wing. Each room has a unique decor and contains a fireplace, television, and telephone. The walls in the dining room are covered with rare turn-of-the-century French Zuber wallpaper printed from wood blocks carved in 1855. The mural-like paper reflects the climatic zones of the world: arctic, temperate, and tropical. A southern breakfast is served in the renovated poultry house. Dunleith is a National Historic Landmark.

Open: year round except Sundays, Thanksgiving, and Christmas **Accommodations:** 11 guest rooms with private baths **Meals:** full breakfast included; complimentary refreshments; restaurants nearby **Rates:** $85 to $130 **Payment:** AmEx, Visa, MC, Discover, traveler's check **Restrictions:** not suitable for children; smoking limited; no pets **Activities:** daily house tours, strolling through gardens and grounds, porch sitting

PASS CHRISTIAN

Nearby attractions: beaches, antiques hunting, casinos, parks, historic homes, art galleries, golfing, swimming, fishing, boating

INN AT THE PASS

125 East Scenic Drive
Pass Christian, Mississippi 39571
601/452-0333 or 800/217-2588
601/452-0449 Fax
Proprietors: Brenda and Vernon Harrison
Location: 8 miles west of Gulfport

The Inn at the Pass is an Eastlake-influenced planter's cottage built in 1879 on the Gulf coast at Pass Christian, one of three intact examples of nineteenth-century coastal resorts (the other two being Newport, Rhode Island, and Cape May, New Jersey). Victorian period furnishings and accessories are found throughout the inn. Accommodations are in the main house and adjacent cottage. The inn is one block from a fine sand beach, part of the 26 miles of coastline from Bay Saint Louis to Biloxi, where visitors will find fine restaurants, southern mansions, parks, beaches, boating, shopping, and a world of family entertainment.

Open: year round **Accommodations:** 4 guest rooms (2 have private baths); 1 is a cottage **Meals:** continental-plus breakfast included; complimentary refreshments; restaurants nearby **Rates:** $65 to $125; 10% discount to National Trust members and National Trust Visa cardholders **Payment:** Visa, MC, Discover, personal check **Restrictions:** children over 10 welcome in main house, all ages welcome in cottage; smoking limited; small pets welcome in on-site indoor kennels **Activities:** cable television, relaxing

PORT GIBSON

Nearby attractions: Grand Gulf Military State Park, driving and walking tours of historic town, hiking, bicycling; Civil War battlefields, museums, and forts

OAK SQUARE
1207 Church Street
Port Gibson, Mississippi 39150
601/437-4350 or 800/729-0240
601/437-5768 Fax
Proprietors: Mr. and Mrs. William D. Lum

Oak Square, named for the massive trees on its grounds, was once the home of a cotton planter. Built in 1850, the house is Greek Revival in design with six 22-foot-tall fluted Corinthian columns supporting the front gallery. Inside, the house's grandeur endures in ornate millwork, a grand staircase, and spacious, high-ceilinged rooms. Fine rare antiques fill the house's public rooms. Guest rooms in the mansion and the guest house are furnished with family heirlooms and have canopied beds. Guests receive a full southern breakfast and a tour of the mansion. National Register–listed Oak Square is the largest antebellum mansion in Port Gibson, the town Ulysses S. Grant said was "too beautiful to burn." Rated with four diamonds by AAA, Oak Square is home to the annual 1800s Spring Festival, a "top 20 event" in the southeast.

Open: year round **Accommodations:** 11 guest rooms with private baths **Meals:** full breakfast included; complimentary refreshments; restaurants nearby **Rates:** $85 to $105 **Payment:** AmEx, Visa, MC, Discover, personal check **Restrictions:** not suitable for young children; no smoking; no pets **Activities:** house tours, nineteenth-century Spring Festival last weekend of March each year with 200 costumed participants creating a living history weekend

VICKSBURG

Nearby attractions: Vicksburg National Military Park, Center for Southern Culture, Old Court House Museum, historic house tours, casinos, boat rides, golfing

BALFOUR HOUSE
1002 Crawford Street
P.O. Box 781
Vicksburg, Mississippi 39181
601/638-7113 or 800/294-7113
Proprietors: Bob and Sharon Humble

Balfour House is considered to be one of the finest Greek Revival structures in the state by the Mississippi Department of Archives and History. The house was a center of activity during the Siege of Vicksburg and became the business headquarters for the Union Army after the fall of the city. In 1982, when the house was restored according to the Secretary of the Interior's Standards for Rehabilitation, a cannonball and other Civil War artifacts were discovered hidden in the walls. The restoration, which included work on the three-story elliptical staircase and patterned, inlaid, hardwood floors, received the 1984 Award of Merit from the state historical society. Balfour House, a National Register property and designated Mississippi landmark, offers overnight guests authentically decorated bedrooms, house tours, and a full southern-style breakfast.

Open: year round **Accommodations:** 4 guest rooms with private baths **Meals:** full breakfast included; complimentary refreshments; restaurants nearby **Rates:** $85 to $150; 10% discount to National Trust members and National Trust Visa cardholders **Payment:** AmEx, Visa, MC, personal and traveler's checks **Restrictions:** no smoking; no pets **Activities:** house tours

THE CORNERS MANSION
601 Klein Street
Vicksburg, Mississippi 39180
800/444-7421
Proprietors: Clifford and Bettye Whitney

A wedding gift for Susan Klein of Cedar Grove upon her marriage to Issaac Bonham in 1872, The Corners is an artful combination of Greek Revival and Victorian styles. The home's most outstanding features are the front-porch columns, which are pierced with heart, diamond, and club patterns. These were the first and most ornate of an architectural feature that is thought to be unique to this area of Mississippi. Inside, the house has been fully restored, and antiques fill the rooms. Guests may wander through original parterre gardens, or relax in rocking chairs on the 68-foot-long gallery overlooking the Mississippi River. Breakfasts are served on heirloom porcelain and silver in the formal dining room. The Corners, listed in the National Register of Historic Places, has been given four diamonds by AAA.

Open: year round **Accommodations:** 9 guest rooms with private baths; 2 are suites **Meals:** full breakfast included; complimentary refreshments; restaurants nearby **Wheelchair access:** some rooms **Rates:** $75 single to $105 double; suites sleeping 4 are $150; 10% discount to National Trust members and National Trust Visa cardholders **Payment:** AmEx, Visa, MC, CB, DC, Discover, personal and traveler's checks **Restrictions:** no smoking **Activities:** library, piano, porch rockers, house tours

DUFF GREEN MANSION
1114 First East Street
Vicksburg, Mississippi 39180
800/992-0037 or 601/638-6662 or 601/636-6968
Proprietors: Harry Carter Sharp and Alicia Shrader

Listed in the National Register of Historic Places, the Duff Green Mansion is located in Vicksburg's historic district. The home is noted for the lacy wrought-iron double porches that span its front facade. Built in 1856 by Duff Green, a prosperous merchant, the 12,000-square-foot mansion was the site of many parties in the antebellum days, but was hastily converted to a hospital for both Confederate and Union soldiers during the siege of Vicksburg and the remainder of the war. Recently restored, the mansion offers six elegant guest rooms furnished with antiques and private baths, room service, a swimming pool, and a southern breakfast served in the formal dining room under a grand crystal chandelier.

Open: year round **Accommodations:** 6 guest rooms with private baths **Meals:** full breakfast included; complimentary refreshments; dinner available by request; restaurants nearby **Wheelchair access:** yes **Rates:** $85 to $160 **Payment:** AmEx, Visa, MC, personal and traveler's checks **Restrictions:** smoking limited **Activities:** swimming pool

MISSOURI

KANSAS CITY

Nearby attractions: Nelson Atkins Museum of Art, Kemper Museum of Contemporary Art and Design, Country Club Plaza, Royals and Arrowhead Stadium, toy and miniature museum, theater

SOUTHMORELAND ON THE PLAZA—AN URBAN INN
116 East 46th Street
Kansas City, Missouri 64112
816/531-7979
816/531-2407 Fax
Proprietors: Susan Moehland Penni Johnson

Centuries-old shade trees, native-rock walls, sweeping lawns, and formal gardens create a feeling of country in the city at Southmoreland on the Plaza. The Colonial Revival styling of the 1913 mansion inspires quaint touches such as a croquet lawn, white wicker solarium, and traditional decor enhanced by antiques. The Plaza locale calls for sophisticated conveniences like in-room telephones, parking, fax service, and airport shuttle for business travelers. Guest rooms are named after notable Kansas City residents, with each room reflecting the era and personality of its namesake. The rooms all boast some special feature, such as a private deck, wood-burning fireplace, or double whirlpool bath. Guests are invited to use the tennis and swimming facilities at nearby Rockhill Tennis Club, listed in the National Register of Historic Places. Southmoreland on the Plaza holds a four-

star rating from the *Mobil Travel Guide* and is a four-crown winner from the American Bed and Breakfast Association.

Open: year round **Accommodations:** 12 guest rooms with private baths **Meals:** full breakfast included; complimentary wine and cheese; restaurants nearby **Wheelchair access:** 1 guest room and bath, dining room, common rooms **Rates:** $90 to $145 **Payment:** AmEx, Visa, MC, personal and traveler's checks **Restrictions:** children over 13 welcome; smoking limited; no pets **Activities:** croquet, badminton, conference facilities

NEW FRANKLIN

Nearby attractions: Katy Trail State Park, Old Cooper County Jail and Hanging Barn, start of the Santa Fe Trail, Boone's Lick State Park, Kemper Military Academy and Junior College, Missouri River Festival of the Arts, antiques hunting, hiking, bicycling

RIVERCENE BED AND BREAKFAST
127 County Road 463
New Franklin, Missouri 65274
816/848-2497 or 800/531-0862
816/848-2142 Fax
Proprietors: Jody and Ron Lenz
Location: 4 miles north of Boonville, just over the Missouri River

Rivercene was built in 1869 by riverboat captain Joseph Kinney. After selecting this site directly on the Missouri River, Captain Kinney was warned by the locals that the river would claim his home, and thus it was dubbed Kinney's Folly. But Kinney persevered, building a Second Empire mansion containing nine Italian marble fireplaces, black walnut front doors, and a hand-carved mahogany grand staircase. So spectacular was the house that the state of Missouri duplicated its architectural plan for the present governor's mansion. Today's ongoing restoration has resulted in 9 spacious guest rooms filled with period antiques. Nearly all rooms have private baths, one has a whirlpool tub. Guests are served a full breakfast in the dining room or cozy breakfast room.

Open: year round **Accommodations:** 9 guest rooms (8 have private baths); 1 is a suite **Meals:** full breakfast included; restaurants nearby **Rates:** $70 to $120 **Payment:** AmEx, Visa, MC, Discover, personal and traveler's checks **Restrictions:** children over 10 welcome; no smoking; no pets **Activities:** horseshoe pitching, softball, volleyball, badminton, porch sitting

ST. CHARLES

Nearby attractions: Katy Trail State Park, Goldenrod Showboat, Casino St. Charles, Lewis and Clark Museum, Lindenwood College, Missouri's first state capitol, French Town, Shrine of Ste. Phillipine Duchesne, antiques hunting, crafts shops

BOONE'S LICK TRAIL INN
1000 South Main Street
St. Charles, Missouri 63301
314/947-7000 or 800/366-2427
Proprietors: V'Anne and Paul Mydler

The Carter–Rice building has stood along the historic Boone's Lick Trail since 1840. The Federal-style building, now known as Boone's Lick Trail Inn, has had various owners, ranging from doctor and mayor to "Madame" Duquette and a unisex hair salon. In 1981 the Mydler family restored the brick building, opening it as an inn. Five guest rooms contain nineteenth-century American and European antiques, lace curtains, warm comforters, fresh and dried flower arrangements, ceiling fans, and gleaming pine floors. A suite is under the sloping ceiling and dormers of the third floor; it offers a panoramic view of the Missouri River. The National Register–listed inn has been featured in *Midwest Living*, *Missouri Magazine*, and the Walt Disney film *Back to Hannibal*.

Open: year round **Accommodations:** 5 guest rooms with private baths; 1 is a suite **Meals:** full breakfast included; complimentary refreshments; restaurants nearby **Rates:** $85 to $125 **Payment:** Visa, MC, CB, DC, Discover, personal and traveler's checks **Restrictions:** no smoking; no pets **Activities:** rose and herb gardens, antique duck decoy collection, located in the state's largest historic district

ST. LOUIS

Nearby attractions: Gateway Arch, Museum of Westward Expansion, Busch Stadium, Union Station, Anheuser–Busch Brewery, Missouri Botanical Gardens, Laclede's Landing, St. Louis Zoo, art and history museums, Muny Opera, Fox Theater, Science Center, shopping, dining

LEHMANN HOUSE BED AND BREAKFAST
10 Benton Place
St. Louis, Missouri 63104
314/231-6724
Proprietors: Marie and Michael Davies

This 20-room Richardsonian Romanesque mansion, just off Lafayette Square, was built in 1893 for Edward S. Rowse, a wealthy financier. But the house's second owners, Frederick and Nora Lehmann, who lived there for 31 years, are best remembered and today's inn bears their name. The current owners are carefully restoring the oak, maple, and cherry woodwork throughout the house. For their lodging, guests may choose from the Sun Room, the Maids' Room, or the President's Room, so named because Lehmann, a lawyer and statesman, is reputed to have entertained three presidents in this home. Breakfast is served in the formal dining room with oak-paneled walls and ceiling. Children are welcome at Lehmann House, and cribs and highchairs are available.

Open: year round **Accommodations:** 3 guest rooms (1 has a private bath) **Meals:** full breakfast included; complimentary refreshments; restaurants nearby **Rates:** $60 to $75; 10% discount offered to National Trust members and National Trust Visa cardholders **Payment:** AmEx, Visa, MC, DC, Discover, personal and traveler's checks **Restrictions:** no smoking; no pets

SPRINGFIELD

Nearby attractions: Southwest Missouri State University, Hammons Sports Center, Wilson's Creek National Battlefield, Springfield Nature Center, Walnut Street National Register historic district, Bass Pro Shop

WALNUT STREET INN
900 East Walnut Street
Springfield, Missouri 65806
417/864-6346 or 800/593-6346
417/864-6184 Fax
Proprietors: Karol and Nancy Brown

Deemed one of the "Top Twelve Inns in the Country" by *Country Inns*, Walnut Street Inn is an 1894 Queen Anne house, bay windows on first and second floors and Corinthian columns supporting the broad front porch. Located in a National Register historic district, convenient to Southwest Missouri State University, the inn offers antique four-poster beds, whirlpool or claw-foot tubs, cable television, and fireplaces. Guests can choose to have breakfast served in the dining room, on the deck, or on trays in bed. Business travelers are invited to "relax and fax"—private in-room phones, fax service, honor bar and beverages, and writing desks make it easy. Two doors away, the inn offers a cozy Cottage Inn with three additional suites with kitchenettes.

Open: year round **Accommodations:** 10 guest rooms with private baths; 6 are suites **Meals:** full breakfast included; complimentary refreshments; restaurants nearby **Wheelchair access:** limited **Rates:** $65 to $150; 10% discount to National Trust members **Payment:** AmEx, Visa, MC, CB, DC, Discover, personal and traveler's checks **Restrictions:** children over 12 welcome; no smoking; no pets **Activities:** flower gardens, porch swings

WARRENSBURG

Nearby attractions: Central Missouri State University, Whiteman Air Force Base, Windsor Amish community, state fair in Sedalia, Civil War battlefields, Old Courthouse Museum, horseback riding, cross-country skiing, antiques hunting

CEDARCROFT FARM BED AND BREAKFAST

431 S.E. Y Highway
Warrensburg, Missouri 64093
816/747-5728 or 800/368-4944
Proprietors: Sandra and Bill Wayne
Location: 8 miles southeast of Warrensburg

Cedarcroft Farm Bed and Breakfast is unique in Missouri as the only privately owned farm recognized as a National Register historic district. The farmhouse was built in 1867 by Sandra Wayne's great-grandfather, John A. Adams, a pioneer soil conservationist. The network of field drainage tiles and dams that Adams devised remains on the farm today. The antiques-filled farmhouse has been modernized for comfort, but otherwise looks essentially as it did when Adams lived there. A guest suite consists of two bedrooms, a parlor, gathering room, and dining area. The suite is rented to one party at a time and can sleep up to eight people. Plentiful breakfasts feature Amish-made breads and country specialties. An evening snack offers everything from fruit to fudge. Guests are invited to explore the farm's 80 acres of woods, creeks, and meadows.

Open: year round **Accommodations:** 1 guest suite with private bath **Meals:** full breakfast included; complimentary refreshments; restaurants nearby **Rates:** $65 to $75; 10% discount to National Trust members and National Trust Visa cardholders **Payment:** AmEx, Visa, MC, Discover, personal and traveler's checks **Restrictions:** no smoking; no pets **Activities:** hiking, horseshoe pitching, bird-watching, farm activities

MONTANA

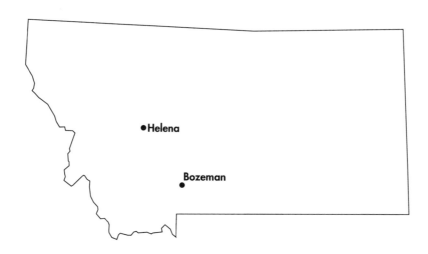

BOZEMAN

Nearby attractions: Montana State University, Museum of the Rockies, Yellowstone National Park, state parks, ice skating, skiing at Bridger Bowl and Big Sky, trout fishing

TORCH AND TOES BED AND BREAKFAST
309 South Third Avenue
Bozeman, Montana 59715
406/586-7285 or 800/446-2138
Proprietors: Ronald and Judy Hess

Set back from the street, Torch and Toes looks much as it did when it was built in 1906—a tall, trim brick-and-frame house in the Colonial Revival style. Located in the Bon Ton historic district, the house was built for Wilbur F. Williams, vice-president of the Bozeman Milling Company. Today, the house retains its high ceilings, oak wainscoting, and leaded-glass windows. These elements are complemented by turn-of-the-century furnishings and

whimsical collections of gargoyles, mousetraps, and old postcards. There are four guest accommodations, each offering a unique setting. A full breakfast is served before the fireplace in the dining room in winter, or on the redwood deck in summer.

Open: year round **Accommodations:** 4 guest rooms with private baths; 1 is a suite **Meals:** full breakfast included; complimentary refreshments; restaurants nearby **Rates:** $65 to $85; 10% discount to National Trust members and National Trust Visa cardholders **Payment:** Visa, MC, personal and traveler's checks **Restrictions:** no smoking; no pets

---

HELENA

Nearby attractions: St. Helena's Cathedral, the original Governor's Mansion, State Capitol, Montana Historical Museum, Holter Museum, Grand Street Theater, fishing on the Missouri River

THE SANDERS – HELENA'S BED AND BREAKFAST
328 North Ewing
Helena, Montana 59601
406/442-3309
Proprietors: Bobbi Uecker and Rock Ringling

Wilbur Sanders, Montana's first U.S. senator, built this three-story Victorian home in 1875. His family, and only one other, owned the house until it was purchased by the innkeepers in 1986. After a thorough restoration, the house was opened as a bed and breakfast, incorporating Sanders' original furnishings in the elegant and comfortable bedrooms and public areas. Each richly detailed guest rooms has a private bath, telephone, color television, alarm clock, hair dryer, and easy chair, and provides views of the mountains and downtown Helena. Gourmet Montana breakfasts, featuring such specialties as orange souffle and Grand Marnier French toast, are served in the wainscoted dining room. The Sanders has welcomed guests from around the world, most notably Archbishop Desmond Tutu. The inn has been featured in the *Washington Post*, the *New York Times*, and the *Boston Sunday Globe*.

Open: year round **Accommodations:** 7 guest rooms with private baths **Meals:** full breakfast included; catering available; restaurants nearby **Rates:** $75 single to $98 double **Payment:** Visa, MC, Discover, personal and traveler's checks **Restrictions:** no smoking; no pets **Activities:** reading, listening to music, porch sitting

NEVADA

EAST ELY

Nearby attractions: Nevada Northern Railway Museum and steam train excursions, Great Basin National Park, Cave Lake State Park, garnet hunting, back country trails, ghost towns, golfing, tennis

STEPTOE VALLEY INN
220 East 11th Street
P.O. Box 151110
East Ely, Nevada 89315-1110
702/289-8687 (June–September)
702/435-1196 (October–May)
Proprietors: Jane and Norman Lindley

East Ely ●

When the Nevada Northern Railway reached the copper mines of Eastern Nevada, promoters laid out a new community called Ely City to attract miners and their families. Steptoe Valley Inn was built in 1907 as the Ely City Grocery and Meat Market and had rooms upstairs for railroad workers. In 1990 the structure was remodeled into Steptoe Valley Inn, with a Victorian cottage decor accentuated by hand-painted accents, decorative wood trim, brass hardware, high embossed ceilings, etched and stained glass, and an old-fashioned rose garden with gazebo. Guest rooms contain white iron, canopy, pine, or wicker beds, lace curtains, and ceiling fans. Some rooms have private balconies overlooking mountains, valley, or rose garden. A library, television room, living room, and upstairs veranda are open to guests.

Open: June through September **Accommodations:** 5 guest rooms with private baths **Meals:** full breakfast included; complimentary refreshments; restaurants nearby **Rates:** $68 single to $90 triple **Payment:** AmEx, Visa, MC **Restrictions:** supervised, well-behaved children welcome; no smoking; no pets **Activities:** croquet, parlor games, television and VCR, chess, library, rose garden and gazebo

NEW HAMPSHIRE

ASHLAND

Nearby attractions: White Mountains, Squam and Winnepesaukee lakes, Plymouth State College, Science Center of New Hampshire, Wellington State Park, Franconia Notch State Park, downhill and cross-country skiing, antiques hunting, swimming, boating, hiking, bicycling, fishing, golfing, tennis, covered bridges

GLYNN HOUSE VICTORIAN INN
43 Highland Street
P.O. Box 710
Ashland, New Hampshire 03217
603/968-3775 or 800/637-9599
Proprietors: Betsy and Karol Paterman

From its round tower and patterned shingles to its irregular roof line and gingerbreaded wraparound porch, Glynn House is a fine example of Queen Anne architecture. Built in 1895, the house contains carved oak woodwork and pocket doors in the foyer, ornate oriental wallpaper in the living room, and period furniture and amenities in the individually designed guest rooms. Each guest room features a private bath, two with whirlpool tubs. Fireplaces throughout the house, including one in the Honeymoon Suite, create a cozy ambience. Nestled in the Lakes Region and the White Mountains, Glynn House is in the quaint village of Ashland.

Open: year round **Accommodations:** 8 guest rooms with private baths; 2 are suites **Meals:** full breakfast included; restaurants nearby **Rates:** $75 to $150; 10% discount to National Trust members and National Trust Visa cardholders **Payment:** Visa, MC, personal and traveler's checks **Restrictions:** children over 12 welcome; no smoking; no pets

BETHLEHEM

Nearby attractions: Mount Washington, White Mountain National Forest, downhill and cross-country skiing, Littleton Historical Museum, Robert Frost Museum, New England Ski Museum, antiques hunting, Franconia Notch State Park, outlet shopping, North Country Chamber Players, golfing

ADAIR

Old Littleton Road
Bethlehem, New Hampshire 03574
603/444-2600 or 800/441-2606
Proprietors: Hardy, Pat, and Nancy Banfield

Frank Hogan built the hilltop mansion called Adair in 1927 as a gift to his daughter Dorothy on the occasion of her marriage to John William (Duke) Guider. Dorothy Hogan Guider lived in the elegant gambrel-roofed Colonial Revival house until her death in 1991. Situated on 200 acres and surrounded by gardens designed by the Olmsted Brothers (of Central Park and Boston Common fame), Adair offers eight guest rooms furnished with period antiques and reproductions. Each room, with private bath, offers a view of the White Mountains or the landscaped grounds. Some rooms have fireplaces. A full breakfast, afternoon tea, and bar setups are complimentary. Adair's restaurant, Tim-Bir Alley, offers fine dining. The Granite Tap room contains a pool table and a television set with VCR and film library. Adair is rated by AAA with four diamonds.

Open: year round **Accommodations:** 8 guest rooms with private baths; 1 is a suite **Meals:** full breakfast included; complimentary refreshments; restaurant on premises; restaurants nearby **Rates:** $105 to $175 **Payment:** AmEx, Visa, MC, personal and traveler's checks **Restrictions:** no smoking; no pets **Activities:** tennis, shuffleboard, swimming pool, billiards, hiking

CENTER HARBOR

Nearby attractions: Squam Lake, Lake Winnipesaukee, White Mountains, Shaker Village at Canterbury, cross-country and downhill skiing, swimming, boating, hiking

RED HILL INN
R.F.D. 1, Box 99M
Center Harbor, New Hampshire 03226
603/279-7001 or 800/5-REDHIL (800/573-3445)
603/279-7003 Fax
Proprietors: Rick Miller and Don Leavitt

On 60 wooded acres high on Overlook Hill is this meticulously restored Colonial Revival brick mansion, built in 1903 by Leonard Tufts, whose father invented the ice cream soda fountain. Many other distinguished families have owned the property through the decades, as well as royalty escaping wartorn Europe. On the first floor, a wide central hallway draws guests into the spacious living room with fireplace. Each guest room on the second and third floors varies in size and differs in elegant appointments. Most have fireplaces; some have private balconies. Guests are also welcome in cottages adjacent to the inn or in the 1850 farmhouse just down the hill. Many of these rooms have fireplaces and whirlpool baths. The restaurant features fresh fare seasoned with herbs from the inn's extensive garden.

Open: year round **Accommodations:** 21 guest rooms with private baths; 5 are suites **Meals:** full breakfast included; restaurant on premises; restaurants nearby **Wheelchair access:** limited **Rates:** $85 to $165 **Payment:** AmEx, Visa, MC, CB, DC, Discover, personal and traveler's checks **Restrictions:** no pets **Activities:** horseshoe pitching, badminton, walking trails, herb garden

---

CHARLESTOWN

Nearby attractions: French and Indian War Fort at No. 4, St. Gauden's National Historic Site, covered bridges, Simon Pearce Glass Blowers, Connecticut River Valley, water sports, golfing, hiking, skiing, antiques hunting

MAPLE HEDGE BED AND BREAKFAST INN
Main Street
Charlestown, New Hampshire 03603
603/826-5237
Proprietors: Joan and Dick DeBrine

Maple Hedge has stood beside the Great Road (Route 12) for almost 250 years.

Built in 1755 with an addition in 1830, this large colonial home is listed in the National Register of Historic Places. Each of the five bedrooms has been decorated with distinctive antiques and memorabilia to create unique settings: the Victorian Beale Room, the elegant Ellcee's Boudoir, the pine-wainscoted Lt. R.A.D.'s Quarters, the mahogany-furnished Cobalt Room, and the wicker-filled Butterfly Suite. The innkeepers host a a predinner social time and provide a full breakfast. This historic home has been updated to include all modern amenities, including central air conditioning and alarm system, smoke detectors, and sprinklers.

Open: year round **Accommodations:** 5 guest rooms (4 have private baths); 1 is a suite **Meals:** full breakfast included; complimentary refreshments; restaurants nearby **Rates:** $75 to $90; 10% discount to National Trust members and National Trust Visa cardholders excluding September 20 through October 20 and some weekends **Payment:** Visa, MC, personal and traveler's checks **Restrictions:** children over 12 welcome; no smoking; no pets **Activities:** horseshoe pitching, croquet, badminton, games, books, puzzles

---

CORNISH

Nearby attractions: Saint-Gaudens National Historic Site, Connecticut River Valley, Dartmouth College, downhill and cross-country skiing, ice skating, bicycling, hiking, fishing, canoeing, antiques hunting, museums, crafts and specialty shops, seasonal theater and concerts

THE CHASE HOUSE – BED AND BREAKFAST INN
Route 12A
R.R. 2, Box 909
Cornish, New Hampshire 03745
603/675-5391 or 800/401-9455
603/675-5010 Fax
Proprietors: Bill and Barbara Lewis

The Chase House, situated on 160 acres on the New Hampshire bank of the Connecticut River, offers outstanding views of Vermont's Mount Ascutney and the scenic Upper Valley. The original portion of the house was built in 1766. In

1795 it was joined to a Federal-style building. The house's most famous resident was Salmon Portland Chase, born there in 1808. He is remembered as a founder of the Republican Party, namesake of the Chase Manhattan Bank, and as the man on the first $1 bill in 1862 and on the recently retired $10,000 bill. Today, the Chase House is honored as one of 22 National Historic Landmarks in New Hampshire. Furnishings and decor, including canopied beds, antiques, and period pieces, reflect the house's historic and elegant past. A function room, previously the second story of an 1810 house moved from West Topsham, Vermont, accommodates up to 70 people.

Open: year round **Accommodations:** 7 guest rooms with private baths; 2 are suites **Meals:** full breakfast included; complimentary refreshments; restaurants nearby **Rates:** $75 to 115 **Payment:** AmEx, Visa, MC, personal check **Restrictions:** children over 12 welcome; no smoking; no pets **Activities:** Alpine and Nordic skiing, hiking, canoeing, bicycling

---

EATON CENTER

Nearby attractions: White Mountain National Forest, Mount Washington Valley, Crystal Lake, Ossipee Lake, canoeing, boating, ice skating, cross-country and downhill skiing, sleigh rides, snowmobiling, shopping

INN AT CRYSTAL LAKE
Route 153
P.O. Box 12
Eaton Center, New Hampshire 03832
603/447-2120 or 800/343-7336
603/447-3599 Fax
Proprietors: Richard and Janice Octeau

In 1884, Nathaniel G. Palmer built a home with spacious rooms and airy balconies around a small home previously built by his father. Making enterprising use of a steep hillside site, Palmer built a Victorian-influenced Greek Revival split-level home—a highly unusual architectural style. By the turn of the century, Palmer was taking in overnight guests who came to enjoy the mountains during the summer, and the establishment became known as Palmer House. After stints as a day camp and a school, the house was converted back to an inn in the 1970s. Now known as the Inn at Crystal Lake, the house has been renovated to include private baths for all guest rooms and to remove 1960s paneling and restore original plaster walls. Victorian lighting and antiques are found throughout. A full country breakfast is served in the sun-filled dining room.

Open: year round **Accommodations:** 10 guest rooms with private baths; 2 are suites sleeping up to 7 people **Meals:** full breakfast included; complimentary refreshments; restaurants nearby **Rates:** $60 to $130; 10% discount to National Trust members and National Trust Visa cardholders during off-season **Payment:** AmEx, Visa, MC, DC, Discover, personal and traveler's checks **Restrictions:** smoking limited; no pets **Activities:** across the street is Crystal Lake for swimming, fishing, hiking, and cross-country skiing

FRANCONIA

Nearby attractions: White Mountains National Forest, skiing, hiking, Lost River, Echo Lake, Cannon Mountain Tramway, Robert Frost Museum, golfing, antiques hunting

BUNGAY JAR
Easton Valley Road
P.O. Box 15
Franconia, New Hamp-
shire 03580
603/823-7775
603/444-0100 Fax
Proprietors: Kate
Kerivan and Lee
Strimbeck
Innkeeper: Janet Engle

Named for a wind that roars out of the southern Easton Valley, shaking and jarring in a rhythmic fashion, Bungay Jar is of post-and-beam construction, with beams taken from an eighteenth-century barn. The inn has six guest rooms and a two-story living room reminiscent of a hayloft. Informal dining areas overlook the White Mountains. A small library, sauna, large fireplace, and private balconies invite guests to relax. Guest rooms feature such architectural details as leaded-glass windows, original beams and wide-planked pine floors, French doors, skylights, and private balconies. Handmade quilts, ornate beds, and comfortable reading chairs add to the enjoyment of stunning woodland and mountain views from each room. The Bungay Jar has been featured on the cover of *Country Accents*.

Open: year round **Accommodations:** 6 guest rooms (4 have private baths); 3 are suites **Meals:** full breakfast included; restaurants nearby **Rates:** $60 to $120; 10% discount offered to National Trust members and National Trust Visa cardholders **Payment:** AmEx, Visa, MC, Discover, **Restrictions:** children over 6 welcome; no smoking; no pets **Activities:** hiking, skating, cross-country and alpine skiing

HAVERHILL

Nearby attractions: tennis, hiking, canoeing, bicycling, antiques hunting, auctions, antique auto show

HAVERHILL INN
Route 10
R.R. 1, Box 320
Haverhill, New Hampshire 03765
603/989-5961
Proprietors: Stephen Campbell and Anne Baird

One of the many Federal homes that grace Haverhill's National Register historic district, the 1810 Haverhill Inn commands sweeping views of the Upper Connecticut Valley and the Vermont hills. Originally the home of Dr. Edmund Carleton, the property remained in the Carleton family until 1882. Clapboard construction, a fanlight and sidelights, and pilasters mark the outside of the home. Inside are antiques, Indian shutters, and fireplaces in every room. The old kitchen hearth and bake oven add to the country setting. The town attracts antiques collectors, and the countryside offers many outdoor sports.

Open: June through February **Accommodations:** 4 guest rooms with private baths **Meals:** full breakfast included; restaurants nearby **Wheelchair access:** guest rooms, bathrooms, dining facilities **Rate:** $85 **Payment:** personal and traveler's checks **Restrictions:** children over 8 welcome; no smoking; no pets **Activities:** reading, conversation, cross-country skiing, river canoeing

---

JACKSON

Nearby attractions: village of Jackson, Mount Washington, four downhill ski areas, North Conway outlet shops, golfing, tennis

EAGLE MOUNTAIN HOUSE, EST. 1879
Carter Notch Road
Jackson, New Hampshire 03846
603/383-9111 or 800/966-5779
603/383-0854 Fax
Proprietor: Paul W. Mayer

Up the hill from the village of Jackson, past the falls of the Wildcat River, stands the Eagle Mountain House, a resort inn built in 1915 to replace the inn that was originally built here in 1879. The vast white structure with black-shuttered

windows, cross gables, and dentils has been restored to offer cozy guest rooms and suites, all with private baths, decorated with a country flair. The hotel dining room serves breakfast, brunch, and dinner featuring New England specialties. Lunch and cocktails are available in the Eagle Landing Tavern. Each season at Eagle Mountain House presents an array of activities, from golf, tennis, and swimming in the heated pool to viewing fall foliage and cross-country and downhill skiing. A health club with whirlpool is available year round. Eagle Mountain House is a member of Historic Hotels of America.

Open: year round **Accommodations:** 94 guest rooms with private baths; 30 are suites **Meals:** complimentary refreshments; restaurants on premises **Wheelchair access:** yes **Rates:** $105 to $210; 10% discount to National Trust members and National Trust Visa cardholders **Payment:** AmEx, Visa, MC, CB, DC, Discover, personal and traveler's checks **Activities:** golfing, tennis, trout fishing, cross-country skiing, swimming pool

NORTH CONWAY

Nearby attractions: downhill and cross-country skiing, ice skating, hiking and walking trails, bicycling, climbing, mountaineering, golfing, fishing, canoeing, white-water rafting, river and lake swimming, tennis, outlet shops, summer theater

CENTER CHIMNEY – 1787
River Road
P.O. Box 1220
North Conway, New Hampshire 03860-1220
603/356-6788
Proprietor: Farley Ames Whitley

Built in 1787, the Center Chimney is one of North Conway's oldest buildings, and with its quaint New England farmhouse style one of its most photographed, having been featured on postcards and calendars throughout the country. While there are modern conveniences—even a whirlpool bath—much of the original charm of the building has been carefully preserved. The tremendous center chimney is surrounded by three fireplaces. Guests are always invited to gather in front of the fire in the common room for a friendly game of cribbage or backgammon and hot spiced cider. Wide-board floors throughout the house have been beautifully maintained for two centuries. One guest bed is as old as the house, although it is outfitted with a new box spring and mattress. One guest room has a sitting area and sundeck.

Open: year round **Accommodations:** 4 guest rooms share baths **Meals:** continental breakfast included; restaurants nearby **Rates:** $40 to $55; 10% discount to National Trust members and National Trust Visa cardholders **Payment:** personal check **Restrictions:** no pets but kennels nearby

STONEHURST MANOR
Route 16
P.O. Box 1937
North Conway, New Hampshire 03860
603/356-3113 or 800/525-9100
Proprietor: Peter Rattay
Location: 1 mile north of North Conway Village

In 1876, Erastus and Eliza Bigelow, owners of Bigelow Carpet Mills, built a summer home on this piece of pine-forested hillside. Their daughter Helen embarked on a massive remodeling job in 1894 that transformed the simple structure into her vision of a grand English country manor. The two-story clapboard house became a three-story, multigabled, dormered mansion. Rooms were added, existing ones enlarged. A library was created, featuring a massive hand-carved oak mantelpiece imported from England. Windows were replaced with stained and cut glass, and a stone porte cochere was added. This grandeur remains for the pleasure of overnight guests. Wicker abounds in the bedrooms and dining rooms, and seven guest rooms contain fireplaces or porches.

Open: year round **Accommodations:** 24 guest rooms (22 have private baths); 2 are suites **Meals:** breakfast and dinner included; restaurant and lounge on premises **Rates:** $48 to $78 per person **Payment:** Visa, MC, traveler's check **Restrictions:** no pets **Activities:** hot tub, swimming pool, tennis, guided or unguided walking and hiking tours beginning at the inn, free cross-country skiing on 65 miles of groomed trails

NORTHWOOD

Nearby attractions: Shaker village tours, antiques hunting, hiking, skiing, Concord, capitol

MEADOW FARM BED AND BREAKFAST
Jenness Pond Road
Northwood, New Hampshire 03261
603/942–8619
603/942–5731 Fax
Proprietors: Douglas and Janet Briggs
Location: 18 miles east of Concord

Meadow Farm Bed and Breakfast is in an eighteenth-century colonial home, a classic Georgian clapboard structure with central chimney. The interior boasts original ceiling beams, fireplaces, paneling, and wide floorboards, and is furnished accordingly with period pieces. A full breakfast is served in the keeping room in front of the huge brick fireplace. Fields and woods surround the property and horses graze in the pastures. A short walk down a country lane brings guests to the inn's private beach on Jenness Pond, where they are welcome to swim. The quiet country setting is ideal for enjoying long wallks, or in the winter, cross-country skiing on trails.

Open: year round **Accommodations:** 3 guest rooms share a bath **Meals:** full breakfast included; restaurants nearby **Rates:** $45 to $65; 10% discount to National Trust members **Payment:** AmEx, MC **Restrictions:** no smoking **Activities:** swimming, canoeing, cross-country skiing, carriage drives, rose gardens

---

PORTSMOUTH

Nearby attractions: Strawberry Banke, Portsmouth Trail, Prescott Park, arts festival, Seacoast Repertory Company

MARTIN HILL INN
404 Islington Street
Portsmouth, New Hampshire 03801
603/436–2287
Proprietors: Jane and Paul Harnden

The land on which the Martin Hill Inn stands was sold in 1710 by New Hampshire Lieutenant Governor George Vaughan to the Martin family for 50 British pounds. Today's inn comprises the Main House, built in 1815, and to the rear, the Guest House, built ca. 1850. The houses are linked by a flower-lined brick walk and patio. Three guest rooms in the Main House are furnished with period furniture including canopy or four-poster beds. The Guest House's four bedrooms have queen-size canopy, spindle, or iron and brass beds. All rooms have

writing tables and sofas or separate sitting areas. Each room enjoys a private bath and air conditioning. A full breakfast is served in the formal dining room.

Open: year round **Accommodations:** 7 guest rooms with private baths; 3 are suites **Meals:** full breakfast included; restaurants nearby **Rates:** $83 to $105; 10% discount to National Trust members and National Trust Visa cardholders **Payment:** Visa, MC, personal and traveler's checks **Restrictions:** children over 12 welcome; no smoking; no pets

SHELBURNE

Nearby attractions: White Mountains, Appalachian Trail, Mt. Washington Auto Road, downhill skiing, hunting, fishing, hiking, Storyland (summer), antiques hunting, outlet shops

PHILBROOK FARM INN
881 North Road
Shelburne, New Hampshire 03581
603/466-3831
Proprietors: Constance Leger and Nancy Philbrook
Location: 6 miles east of Gorham, N.H.; 20 miles west of Bethel, Maine

This property was purchased by Susannah and Harvey Philbrook in 1853. They added on to the 1834 farmhouse (now the living room and office) in 1861 and welcomed their first guests. Their son added a wing in 1905 and his son built an addition in 1934. In all, five generations of Philbrooks have welcomed guests to the now liberally gabled and dormered farmhouse, painted white with green shutters. Cozy, comfortable guest rooms are furnished with the family's treasures. Cottages that were built in the 1890s offer accommodations for groups during the summer. Wholesome meals featuring fresh farm ingredients are served in the inn's dining room daily. Listed in the National Register of Historic Places, Philbrook Farm Inn is a refreshing country retreat offering myriad activities for families.

Open: May 1 through October 31 and December 26 through March 31 **Accommodations:** 18 guest rooms (10 have private baths); 6 summer cottages **Meals:** full breakfast and dinner included (MAP) **Rates:** $109 to $139 [Modified American Plan (MAP)]; rates for single guests and B&B rates (including breakfast only) available **Payment:** personal and traveler's checks **Restrictions:** no smoking in dining room; pets allowed in summer cottages only **Activities:** swimming pool, table tennis, pool table, board games, antique wooden puzzles, badminton, horseshoes, shuffleboard, library, hiking, cross-country skiing, porch rocking

TILTON

Nearby attractions: Mt. Washington, Lake Winnipesaukee, Lake Winnisquam, Tilton Prep School, Shaker village, golfing, tennis, boating, downhill and cross-country skiing

TILTON MANOR
28 Chestnut Street
Tilton, New Hampshire 03276
603/286-3457
Proprietors: Chip and Diane

Tilton Manor, once known as the Pillsbury Estate, was the first private home in the Lakes Region of New Hampshire to have electricity. Built in 1882, the 16-room house is dominated by a large front gable and many shuttered windows. The roof of the wing terminates in a jerkinhead, or clipped gable, lending interest to the roofline. Guest rooms are furnished with antiques and handmade afgans. The sitting room offers books, games, and television, while the living room is a comfortable setting with its fireplace. A hearty breakfast includes freshly baked muffins. The innkeepers can provide dinner with advance notice. The inn sits amid more than three tranquil acres.

Open: year round **Accommodations:** 4 guest rooms (3 have private baths); 1 is a suite **Meals:** full breakfast included; dinner available with advance notice; restaurants nearby **Rates:** $60 to $70 **Payment:** AmEx, Visa, MC, Discover, personal and traveler's checks **Restrictions:** well-supervised children welcome; smoking limited; small pets can be accommodated **Activities:** walking, reading

WENTWORTH

Nearby attractions: Appalachian Trail, mountain biking, scenic drives, skiing, snowmobiling, swimming, boating, fishing, antiques hunting, New Hampshire Music Festival, Polar Caves

HILLTOP ACRES

East Side and Buffalo Road
P.O. Box 32
Wentworth, New Hampshire 03282
603/764-5896
Proprietor: Marie A. Kauk

Built in 1806, this house was one of the first built in Wentworth, a small town in the White Mountains. Located on 20 acres of field and pine forest, the inn offers a peaceful country retreat with spectacular views of the surrounding landscape available from each guest accommodation. The large pine-paneled recreation room is equipped with an antique piano, board games, a fireplace, an extensive library, and cable television. Two housekeeping cottages are also paneled in pine. Each contains a kitchen, bedroom, bathroom, and screened porch. Guests are welcome to wander through the grounds and explore the woods and winding brook.

Open: May 1 to November 1 **Accommodations:** 4 guest rooms with private baths; 2 are cottages **Meals:** continental-plus breakfast included; complimentary refreshments; restaurants nearby **Rates:** $65 to $80; 10% discount to National Trust members and National Trust Visa cardholders **Payment:** AmEx, Visa, MC, Discover, personal and traveler's checks **Restrictions:** no smoking; no pets **Activities:** library, board games, lawn games, cable television

WILTON CENTER

Nearby attractions: three summer theaters (including one for children), antiques hunting, flea markets, arts center, summer chamber-music concerts, hiking, nature center, golfing, canoeing

STEPPING STONES BED AND BREAKFAST
R.F.D. 1, Box 208
Bennington Battle Trail
Wilton Center, New Hampshire 03086
603/654-9048
Proprietor: Ann Carlsmith
Location: 5 miles west of Wilton (town); 3/4 mile north of Wilton Center (village)

The house that is Stepping Stones Bed and Breakfast was originally a settler's cabin built in the early nineteenth century. In the late 1800s the original structure was incorporated into a country-style Greek Revival house with gable front and wing. This quaint structure sits along the route taken by the militia from nearby towns as they joined to fight the Revolutionary Battle of Bennington. Visitors will enjoy the artistry of the innkeeper, a garden designer, in the extensively landscaped terraces, paths, and gardens that surround the house. Inside, handwoven throws, pillows, and rugs display her talent as a weaver. Fresh flowers, quilts, down comforters, and an art collection contribute to the comfortable atmosphere. Home-baked breakfast specialties are served in a solar-heated garden room.

Open: year round **Accommodations:** 3 guest rooms (1 has a private bath) **Meals:** full breakfast included; complimentary refreshments; restaurants nearby **Rates:** $35 single to $50 double; 10% discount offered to National Trust members and National Trust Visa cardholders **Payment:** personal and traveler's checks **Restrictions:** no smoking; well-behaved and controlled pets allowed **Activities:** gardens, weaving studio, television, library, bird-watching (birdhouses, baths, and feeders)

NEW JERSEY

CAPE MAY

Nearby attractions: National Historic Landmark district, Victorian house tours, antiques hunting, horse and buggy rides, trolley and walking tours, bicycling, beach and swimming, Cape May Lighthouse, boating, fishing, bird sanctuary, nature walks, hiking, golfing, tennis, festivals (music, seafood, and kite), theater, shopping

THE ABBEY

34 Gurney Street at Columbia Avenue
Cape May, New Jersey 08204
609/884-4506
Proprietors: Jay and Marianne Schatz

In 1987 two houses were joined to form The Abbey: a Gothic Revival structure (now the main house), dating to 1869, and a Second Empire cottage, dating to 1873. The main house is dominated by a 60-foot-high tower and accented by ruby-glass arched windows, spacious rooms, and shaded verandas. The cottage boasts an unusual convex mansard roof. Both houses are furnished with Victorian antiques, including 12-foot-wide mirrors, ornate glass fixtures, tall walnut beds,

and marble-topped dressers. The Abbey is listed in the National Register of Historic Places, and measured drawings of it are recorded in the Library of Congress. Fine accommodations and merriment are The Abbey's trademarks; an evening hat fashion show often takes place with hats from the innkeepers' extensive—and exotic—collection. This establishment has been heralded by many, including the *New York Times* and *Conde Nast Traveler.*

Open: April to January **Accommodations:** 14 air-conditioned guest rooms with private baths and mini-refrigerators; 2 are suites **Meals:** full breakfast included; complimentary afternoon tea and refreshments; restaurants nearby **Rates:** $95 to $200 **Payment:** Visa, MC, Discover, traveler's check; personal check for room deposit only **Restrictions:** young adults over 12 welcome; no smoking **Activities:** house tours, croquet, rocking and people-watching on veranda

BARNARD–GOOD HOUSE
238 Perry Street
Cape May, New Jersey 08204
609/884-5381
Proprietors: Nan and Tom Hawkins

In the center of Cape May's historic district is the colorful Barnard–Good House. Sitting neatly behind a white picket fence, the 1865 Second Empire house sports a lively color combination of lavender, blue, purple, and tan. Inside, the decor is decidedly Victorian, from the antiques to the lace curtains and fringed lamp shades. But the most outstanding feature of the Barnard–Good House is its four-course breakfast. The constantly changing menu has been acclaimed by *New Jersey Monthly* as the best in New Jersey. The *New York Times* has said that the "table groans at the Barnard–Good House." *McCall's* and the *Philadelphia Enquirer* have published the inn's gourmet recipes. Guests can take a short walk to the beach to work off one of these repasts. The inn provides air-conditioned guest rooms and on-site parking for all guests.

Open: April to November **Accommodations:** 5 guest rooms with private baths; 2 are suites **Meals:** full breakfast included; restaurants nearby **Rates:** $89 to $128; 10% discount to National Trust members and National Trust Visa cardholders **Payment:** Visa, MC, personal and traveler's checks **Restrictions:** children over 14 welcome; no smoking; no pets **Activities:** rocking on veranda, relaxing, reading

BRASS BED INN
719 Columbia Avenue
Cape May, New Jersey 08204
609/884-8075
Proprietors: John and Donna Dunwoody

A Gothic Revival cottage built in 1872, the inn takes its name from the fine collection of nineteenth-century brass beds in the individually decorated bedrooms. Many furnishings, now antiques, have remained in the house throughout its history. Lace curtains, dramatic period wallcoverings, and patterned oriental carpets help produce the cozy ambience. The house retains many historic architectural features: outside, it boasts a turn-of-the-century veranda, original vergeboard detailing, and finial; inside, most of the architectural details, such as plaster crown moldings, and medallions are original to the house. Christmas at the Brass Bed is an especially festive season with extravagant decorations, including antique Christmas tree ornaments. The Brass Bed Inn has been featured in *Innsider, National Geographic Traveler, Country,* and *New Jersey Monthly,* among others.

Open: year round **Accommodations:** 8 air-conditioned guest rooms (6 have private baths) **Meals:** full breakfast included; restaurants nearby **Rates:** $65 to $165; 10% discount offered to National Trust members and National Trust Visa cardholders **Payment:** Visa, MC, personal and traveler's checks **Restrictions:** no smoking; no pets **Activities:** front-porch swing and rockers

GINGERBREAD HOUSE
28 Gurney Street
Cape May, New Jersey 08204
609/884-0211
Proprietors: Fred and Joan Echevarria

Built in 1869, the Gingerbread House is one of the original Stockton Row Cottages designed by Stephen Decatur Button and intended as a summer retreat for wealthy families, their servants, and nannies. This charming Victorian house, loaded with gingerbread woodwork, has been skillfully restored, incorporating the innkeeper's craftsmanship as a cabinetmaker: he recreated the double front doors of teak and beveled glass that provide an inviting entrance. His handmade furniture complements the Victorian furnishings, lace curtains, and period wallpapers that decorate the house. Original watercolors by the innkeeper's mother, award-winning photographs, and fresh bouquets from the garden add to the lovely atmosphere. In the heart of the historic district, Gingerbread House is less than a block from the beach.

Open: year round **Accommodations:** 6 guest rooms (3 have private baths); 1 is a suite with private porch **Meals:** full breakfast included; complimentary afternoon tea; restaurants nearby **Rates:** $98 to $185 **Payment:** Visa, MC, personal and traveler's checks **Restrictions:** children over 7 welcome; smoking limited; no pets

INN OF CAPE MAY
601 Beach Drive
Cape May, New Jersey 08204
609/884-3500
609/884-0669 Fax
Proprietor: D. B. Eastman

Upon completion in 1894, the Inn of Cape May was the tallest building on the coast. The structure is characterized by "witch-hat" turrets, mansard roofs, fish-scale shingles, and a long wraparound porch from which guests can enjoy a view of the beach. All of the guest rooms are furnished with antiques, many in white

wicker. Etched-glass doors add to the Victorian ambience. Over the years celebrity guests have included Diamond Jim Brady, Henry Ford, and Wallis Warfield (later the Duchess of Windsor), who had her coming-out ball at the hotel. John Philip Sousa's band gave nightly concerts here in 1912. Following an attentive restoration, the building has been listed in the National Register of Historic Places.

Open: May to October **Accommodations:** 77 guest rooms (55 have private baths); 50 are suites **Meals:** full breakfast included; restaurant on premises; restaurants nearby **Rates:** $48 to $228 **Payment:** AmEx, Visa, MC, DC, Discover, traveler's check **Restrictions:** no pets **Activities:** swimming pool

LEITH HALL HISTORIC SEASHORE INN
22 Ocean Street
Cape May, New Jersey 08204
609/884-1934
Proprietors: Elan
and Susan
Zingman-Leith

A deep mansard roof, bay windows, a wrap-around porch, and ocean views from every room define Leith Hall, an 1885 seaside struc-ture. Inside, Leith Hall has been decorated with rich wall coverings and paint to faithfully reproduce the Victorian era in which it was built. Bedrooms are furnished with Victorian antiques, including walnut or brass beds, hand-carved mahogany tables, laces and linens, fringes and tassels. Each room offers a private bath, and several rooms include refrigerators. Downstairs are a parlor and library for guests' use; stained-glass French doors open onto the chair-lined veranda. Breakfast is served from antique silver, crystal, and Royal Worcester china. An English tea is offered in the afternoon.

Open: year round **Accommodations:** 7 guest rooms with private baths; 2 are suites **Meals:** full breakfast included; complimentary refreshments; restaurants nearby **Rates:** $85 to $160 **Payment:** Visa, MC, personal and traveler's checks **Restrictions:** children over 12 welcome; no smoking; no pets **Activities:** library, cabinet grand piano, parlor games

MAINSTAY INN AND COTTAGE

635 Columbia Avenue
Cape May, New Jersey 08204
609/884–8690
Proprietors: Tom and Sue Carroll

A pair of wealthy gamblers pooled their resources in 1872 to build an exclusive gambling club. They hired an architect to design a grand Italianate villa with 14-foot-high ceilings, ornate plaster moldings, a sweeping veranda, and a cupola to top it off. For the interior, they selected the finest, richly ornamented furnishings: 12-foot-wide mirrors, glittering chandeliers, marble-topped sideboards, and graceful love seats. Yesterday's gambling palace has become today's Mainstay Inn, an elegant Victorian inn in the heart of historic Cape May. All rooms are furnished in antiques, most in a somewhat ornate manner suited to the period. This applies even to rooms in the Cottage, an 1870s summer cottage adjacent to the inn. The Mainstay is listed in the National Register and has been lauded by the *New York Times, Town and Country, Good Housekeeping,* and *Smithsonian.*

Open: year round **Accommodations:** 12 guest rooms with private baths; 3 are suites **Meals:** full breakfast included; restaurants nearby **Wheelchair access:** 1 guest room; dining room **Rates:** $95 to $185; 10% discount offered to National Trust members and National Trust Visa cardholders during off-season **Payment:** personal and traveler's checks **Restrictions:** children over 12 welcome; no smoking; no pets **Activities:** croquet, porch rocking, conversation, tour of historic inn

THE MASON COTTAGE

625 Columbia Avenue
Cape May, New Jersey 08204
609/884–3358 or 800/716–2766 (reservations)
Proprietors: Dave
and Joan Mason

This summer residence was built in 1871 for Edward A. Warne, a wealthy Philadelphia entrepreneur. The Second Empire cottage, with its telltale wood-shingled mansard roof, is endowed with lofty ceilings, full-length windows, and a sweeping veranda, all characteristic of Victorian

homes of the period. When the Masons bought the house from a Warne cousin in 1945, they became only the second family to own it. Today, the restored cottage, which survived the great fire of 1878 and several major hurricanes, proudly displays its original color scheme, tin gutters, and roof shingles. The interior, including original Warne family furniture, also has been carefully restored. Situated just one block from the beach, the Mason Cottage is cooled by summer breezes.

Open: March through December **Accommodations:** 9 guest rooms with private baths; 4 are suites **Meals:** full breakfast included; afternoon refreshments; restaurants nearby **Rates:** $95 to $255; 10% discount offered to National Trust members and National Trust Visa cardholders **Payment:** AmEx, Visa, MC, personal and traveler's checks **Restrictions:** children over 12 welcome; no smoking; no pets **Activities:** house tour, rocking on veranda, reading, conversation

SEVENTH SISTER GUESTHOUSE
10 Jackson Street
Cape May, New Jersey 08204
609/884-2280
Proprietors: Bob and Jo-Anne Echevarria-Myers

One of seven identical houses built in 1888, the Seventh Sister was designed by prominent nineteenth-century architect Stephen Decatur Button. Three floors are joined by a central circular staircase. The inn features 80 percent of its original furniture, which was specified by the architect, and a collection of more than 50 wicker pieces. Most of the six individually designed guest rooms have ocean views. A guest living room has the original coal fireplace, and a sunporch faces the ocean. The Seventh Sister, a contributing structure to Cape May's National Historic Landmark district, also earned an individual listing in the National Register of Historic Places on the basis of it own historic merit. The house is decorated to reflect the skills of its owners, an artist and a designer.

Open: year round **Accommodations:** 6 guest rooms with shared baths **Meals:** no meals on premises; guest refrigerator available; restaurants nearby **Rates:** $70 to $85; 10% discount offered to National Trust members and National Trust Visa cardholders **Payment:** Visa, MC, personal and traveler's checks **Restrictions:** children over 7 welcome; smoking limited; no pets **Activities:** croquet

SUMMER COTTAGE INN
613 Columbia Avenue
Cape May, New Jersey 08204
609/884-4948
Proprietors: Skip and Linda Loughlin

The renowned architect Stephen Decatur Button designed this Italianate summer cottage in 1867 for the S. A. Harriman family. The three-story structure is complete with wide eaves supported by decorative brackets and a square rooftop cupola. In the early part of the twentieth century the house was converted to a guest house and restaurant. Each of the inn's guest rooms is individually decorated with country Victorian furnishings. Guests are invited to relax, play games at the antique game table, read, or visit in the parlor or sitting room. During warm weather, the veranda—with wicker rockers, a porch swing, and ferns—is a favorite spot to catch sea breezes. The inn provides its guests with beach passes, hot and cold outside showers with dressing rooms, and bicycles.

Open: year round **Accommodations:** 8 guest rooms with private baths **Meals:** full breakfast included; complimentary refreshments; restaurants nearby **Rates:** $85 to $160; 10% discount to National Trust members and National Trust Visa cardholders **Payment:** Visa, MC, personal check

WHITE DOVE COTTAGE
619 Hughes Street
Cape May, New Jersey 08204
609/884-0613 or 800/321-DOVE
Proprietors: Frank and Sue Smith

Built in 1866, this Second Empire–style house boasts a mansard roof faced with original octagonal slate tiles. The three floors were built with spacious rooms and large windows to take advantage of ocean breezes. The inn, furnished with American and European antiques, is decorated with period wallpapers, soft carpeting, paintings, prints, and hand-made quilts. Blending seamlessly with the old are the new: modern private baths, air conditioning, up-to-date systems. Guests enjoy a multicourse breakfast at a banquet table set with lace, fine china, and heirloom crystal. The wicker-furnished front veranda looks out on a quiet, gaslit residential street in the historic district.

Open: year round **Accommodations:** 6 guest rooms with private baths; 2 are suites

Meals: full breakfast included; complimentary afternoon tea; restaurants nearby **Rates:** $85 to $195; 10% discount to National Trust members and National Trust Visa cardholders **Payment:** personal and traveler's checks **Restrictions:** children over 10 welcome; no smoking; no pets **Activities:** total relaxation, mystery and romance packages

FLEMINGTON

Nearby attractions: Flemington outlet shops, New Hope and Bucks County, Pa.; antiques hunting; summer theater; Princeton University; hiking; bicycling; Delaware River tubing and rafting

JERICA HILL – A BED AND BREAKFAST INN
96 Broad Street
Flemington, New Jersey 08822
908/782-8234
908/782-8234 Fax
Proprietor: Judith S. Studer

Built at the turn of the century, Jerica Hill is located in the historic district of Flemington. The focal point of the house is a graceful center-hall staircase that leads to airy, spacious guest rooms with canopy, brass, and four-poster beds. Bay windows keep the rooms bright; reading chairs and old-fashioned ceiling fans provide comfort; a full complement of toiletries are offered for convenience; and fresh flowers and greenery soften the corners. Guests also enjoy the living room with its wood-burning fireplace, deep wing chairs, and well-stocked bookcases. In warm weather, guests relax on the screen porch filled with white wicker and green plants. The inn offers two specialty packages that feature hot-air ballooning or a country winery tour. Jerrica Hill has been praised in many publications, including the *New York Times*.

Open: year round **Accommodations:** 5 guest rooms with private baths **Meals:** continental-plus breakfast included; complimentary refreshments from 24-hour guest pantry; restaurants nearby **Rates:** $70 to $105; 10% discount offered to National Trust members and National Trust Visa cardholders **Payment:** AmEx, Visa, MC, personal and traveler's checks **Restrictions:** no smoking; no pets (resident cats) **Activities:** color televisions in rooms; specialty packages arranged; hot-air balloon rides from the inn; country picnic and winery tour

HOPE

Nearby attractions: Delaware Water Gap National Recreation Area, Pocono Mountains, skiing, golfing, bicycling, antiques hunting, historic Moravian village tours

INN AT MILLRACE POND
Box 359
Hope, New Jersey 07844
908/459-4884
908/459-5276 Fax
Proprietors: Charles and Cordie Puttkammer

The Inn at Millrace Pond sits on a hillside on 23 acres in historic Hope. The town was founded in 1769 by Moravian pioneers and is now listed in the National Register of Historic Places. The inn comprises three historic buildings: the grist mill, a landmark limestone building constructed in 1770; the miller's house; and the wheelwright's cottage. For 150 years the mill was the heart of Hope's economy. Now it offers colonial-styled overnight accommodations furnished with period reproductions and handcrafted oriental rugs. Original wide-board pumpkin-pine floors gleam throughout the inn. A massive stone wall and exposed beams accent the formal dining room, where award-winning meals are served. From the dining room a staircase descends to the Tavern, which is highlighted by a walk-in fireplace, grain chute, and 180 years of mill memorabilia.

Open: year round **Accommodations:** 17 guest rooms with private baths **Meals:** continental breakfast included; restaurant on premises **Wheelchair access:** 2 guest rooms **Rates:** $85 to $165; 10% discount to National Trust members and National Trust Visa cardholders **Payment:** AmEx, Visa, MC, CB, DC, personal and traveler's checks **Restrictions:** smoking limited; no pets **Activities:** tennis, hiking

PRINCETON

Nearby attractions: Princeton University, McCarter Theater, governor's mansion, antiques hunting in Bucks County, Pa.

PEACOCK INN
20 Bayard Lane
Princeton, New Jersey 08540
609/924-1707
609/924-0788 Fax
Proprietor: Michael Walker

The gambrel-roofed building that houses the Peacock Inn was built in 1775 on the campus of Princeton University. It was moved to its present location, one block from the campus, 100 years later. Originally the home of John Deare, the Peacock Inn has been a Princeton landmark and gathering place since opening its doors to the public in 1912 and has hosted many illustrious guests, such as Bertrand Russell, Albert Einstein, and F. Scott Fitzgerald. Guest rooms are decorated with individually chosen antiques in a number of styles, including French, Early American, and English. Each room is decorated with a cheerful mixture of prints, plants, and authentic country crafts. Guests are served a continental-plus breakfast and the inn's elegant restaurant, Le Plumet Royal, serves fresh, seasonal French cuisine for dinner and lunch.

Open: year round **Accommodations:** 15 guest rooms **Meals:** continental-plus breakfast included; restaurant on premises; restaurants nearby **Rates:** $80 to $125; 10% discount to National Trust members and National Trust Visa cardholders **Payment:** AmEx, Visa, MC, personal and traveler's checks **Restrictions:** smoking limited

SPRING LAKE

Nearby attractions: ocean beach, tennis, golfing, antiques hunting, state park, horseback riding, surf and deep-sea fishing, thoroughbred racing

NORMANDY INN
21 Tuttle Avenue
Spring Lake, New Jersey 07762
908/449-7172
Proprietors: Michael and Susan Ingino

This National Register house stands as a prime example of a Victorian seaside inn. Built as a summer home in 1888, the Normandy is an Italianate villa (square towers and tall, round-arched windows) with Queen Anne modifications (wraparound porches and lacey brackets). Formerly known as the Audenried House, the original structure was moved to its present location—only five houses from the beach—in the early 1900s and became known as one of the Johnson cottages. The Johnson family began the Normandy's heritage of innkeeping nearly 90 years ago. The prized furnishings of all common rooms and each guest room are original American Victorian antiques that are accented with reproduction wallpaper. A full country breakfast is served, after which guests often explore this picturesque oceanfront village on bicycles provided by the inn.

Open: year round **Accommodations:** 17 guest rooms with private baths **Meals:** full breakfast included; complimentary refreshments; restaurants nearby **Rates:** $92 to $171 **Payment:** AmEx, Visa, MC, DC, Discover, personal and traveler's checks **Restrictions:** smoking limited; no pets **Activities:** bicycles, beach chairs, and towels provided free of charge

NEW MEXICO

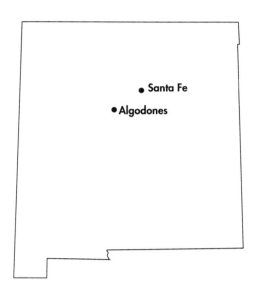

ALGODONES

Nearby attractions: museums, Santa Fe Opera House, Albuquerque, casinos, horseback riding, golfing, water sports, downhill skiing, Rio Grande River, horse racing, International Balloon Fiesta

HACIENDA VARGAS BED AND BREAKFAST INN
1431 El Camino Real
P.O. Box 307
Algodones, New Mexico 87001
505/867-9115 or 800/261-0006
505/867-1902 Fax
Proprietors: Paul and Jule De Vargas

This nineteenth-century adobe structure has been a stagecoach stop and an Indian trading post. Complete with a chapel, Hacienda Vargas captures the spirit of the Old West, the influence of the original Spanish settlers, and the presence of the Pueblo culture. The inn is decorated with antique furniture, all of which was purchased in New Mexico. Each bedroom has a private entrance, its own handmade kiva fireplace, and a private bath; some offer whirlpool tubs. In some guest rooms the original adobe walls are visible. A courtyard and gardens are open to guests. Hacienda Vargas also offers a picturesque setting for private parties and garden weddings. AAA has given the inn three diamonds.

Open: year round **Accommodations:** 6 guest rooms with private baths; 3 are suites **Meals:** full breakfast included; restaurants nearby **Wheelchair access:** 1 room **Rates:** $69 to $129; 10% discount to National Trust members and National Trust Visa cardholders **Payment:** Visa, MC **Restrictions:** children over 12 welcome; no smoking; no pets **Activities:** romance packages, hot tub, barbeque area

---

SANTA FE

Nearby attractions: Indian pueblos, museums, art galleries, shopping, mountains, desert, skiing

CANYON ROAD CASITAS
652 Canyon Road
Santa Fe, New Mexico 87501
505/988-5888
Proprietor: Trisha Ambrose

This 80-year-old Territorial adobe structure offers two luxury guest accommodations. Both provide comfort with handmade quilts, feather beds, down pillows, fireplaces, kitchenettes, and separate entrances wtih private walled gardens. The suite is outfitted with southwestern designer furnishings and contains a separate dining room and a kiva fireplace. The innkeeper offers a complimentary continental breakfast and a bottle of wine to greet guests on their arrival. The inn is located on Santa Fe's famous Canyon Road within walking distance of art galleries, museums, historic landmarks, and unique shops.

Open: year round **Accommodations:** 2 guest rooms with private baths; 1 is a suite **Meals:** continental breakfast included; complimentary refreshments; restaurants nearby **Rates:** $85 to $175; 10% discount to National Trust members and National Trust Visa cardholders **Payment:** AmEx, Visa, MC, CB, DC, Discover, personal and traveler's checks **Restrictions:** no smoking; no pets **Activities:** relaxation

DON GASPAR COMPOUND

623 Don Gaspar
Santa Fe, New Mexico 87501
505/986-8664
505/986-0696 Fax
Proprietors: David and Shirley Alford

Built in 1912 in Santa Fe's Don Gaspar historic district, the compound is a classic example of Mission and adobe architecture. Six private suites enjoy a secluded adobe-walled garden courtyard with fountain and heirloom flowers. The Main House, in the Mission style, is rented to one party at a time. It has two wood-burning fireplaces, three bedrooms, two baths, and a fully equipped kitchen. There are two casitas in the courtyard, both with saltillo-tiled floors and gas-burning fireplaces; one has a kitchen, the other has a whirlpool tub for two. The Southwest Suite has a wood-burning fireplace and Mexican-tiled bath. The Aspen Suite with king-size bed has a kitchenette. The western-style Colorado Room opens onto a patio through French doors. The compound is a short walk from Santa Fe's famed Plaza.

Open: year round **Accommodations:** 6 guest rooms with private baths; 5 are suites **Meals:** continental-plus breakfast included; restaurants nearby **Wheelchair access:** 2 rooms **Rates:** $95 to $220 May through October; $85 to $195 November through April **Payment:** AmEx, Visa, MC, personal and traveler's checks **Restrictions:** no smoking; no pets **Activities:** gardens with fountain

DOS CASAS VIEJAS

610 Agua Fria Street
Santa Fe, New Mexico 87501
505/983-1636
Proprietors: Jois and Irving Belfield

In the Guadelope historic district of Santa Fe, Dos Casas Viejas (Two Old Houses) sits tucked into a half-acre walled compound. The two buildings, built in 1860 with 18-inch-thick adobe walls, represent the blending of Santa Fe's three cultures: Anglo, Indian, and Hispanic. In the guest house, rooms are entered through private brick patios surrounded by six-foot-high adobe walls. French doors open into rooms containing original roof beams known as vigas, Mexican-tiled floors, and wood-burning kiva fireplaces. Furnished with authentic south-western antiques and original art, all rooms have telephone, television, and private baths. Some rooms have canopy beds. The main building houses the lobby–library with fireplace and dining area. Breakfast is served in the dining area or outside by the lap pool, or may be taken back to guest rooms in baskets.

Open: year round **Accommodations:** 5 guest rooms with private baths; 1 is a suite **Meals:** continental breakfast included; restaurants nearby **Rates:** $145 to $195 **Payment:** Visa, MC, personal and traveler's checks **Restrictions:** no smoking; no pets **Activities:** lap pool, library

HOTEL ST. FRANCIS
210 Don Gaspar Avenue
Santa Fe, New Mexico 87501
505/983-5700 or 800/529-5700
505/989-7690 Fax
Proprietors: Patricia and Goodwin Taylor

Built in 1923, joining two structures—a two-story building that dates to 1888 and the current three-story building—the southwestern adobe-style hotel is listed in the National Register of Historic Places. The hotel's unique charm is created by a combination of 1920s style and distinctly southwestern elements, such as clay tile floors and wrought-iron chandeliers. Public rooms feature high ceilings, decorative moldings, and an ornate fireplace. Antique furnishings have been blended with reproduction pieces. Guest rooms with casement windows, many offering mountain views, are furnished with brass or iron beds and period pieces in cherry and oak, and also offer in-room refrigerators and personal safes. Baths feature original hexagonal tiles and porcelain pedestal sinks. The St. Francis, a member of the National Trust's Historic Hotels of America, is located one block from the plaza in Santa Fe.

Open: year round **Accommodations:** 82 guest rooms with private baths; 2 are suites **Meals:** restaurants on premises; afternoon tea **Rates:** $75 to $185; 10% discount to National Trust members and National Trust Visa cardholders **Payment:** AmEx, Visa, MC, Discover, personal and traveler's checks **Restrictions:** no pets **Activities:** veranda sitting, pub

NEW YORK

Lake Placid

Thendara

Hague

Bolton Landing
Lake Luzerne • Warrensburg

Saratoga
Schenectady • Springs

Leonardsville

Berlin

Clarence
• Bushnell Basin Cooperstown

Canandaigua • Geneva

Cincinnatus

Ithaca •

Lew Beach

• Candor

Rhinebeck

Kingston •

Stone Ridge •
High Falls •

• Dover Plains
• Cornwall
• Garrison

Croton-on-Hudson •

Westhampton Beach

BERLIN

Nearby attractions: Tanglewood, Shaker Village, Williamstown, museums, National Trust's Chesterwood, state parks, swimming, hiking, cross–country and downhill skiing

SEDGWICK INN
Route 22
Berlin, New York 12022
518/658-2334 or 800/845-4886
Proprietor: Edith Evans

Located on the New York side of the Berkshire Mountains, the Sedgwick Inn sits on 12 acres in the scenic Taconic Valley. The original deed to the property, dated 1791 and signed by Stephen Van Rensselaer, hangs in library of the house, which was built in that same year. The elegant Federal-style house is filled with antiques and has a large parlor with fireplace and a well-stocked library. In summer, the wraparound porch with wicker furniture provides a cool place to relax. For many years the building was known as the Ranch Tavern. Now, as the Sedgwick Inn, it offers distinctive period accommodations and a choice of dining areas—the original tavern room or the airy dining porches overlooking the garden. The inn's restaurant has an outstanding reputation in the area. Behind the mansion, a converted carriage house has been turned into a gift shop, and an unusual one-room, tin-lined building dating from 1834 now serves as an antiques shop.

Open: year round **Accommodations:** 5 guest rooms with private baths; 1 is a suite **Meals:** full breakfast included; restaurant on premises **Wheelchair access:** restaurant **Rates:** $70 to $115; 10% discount offered to National Trust members and National Trust

Visa cardholders **Payment:** AmEx, Visa, MC, DC, Discover, personal and traveler's checks **Restrictions:** children over 12 welcome; smoking limited; no pets (a motel annex accepts children of all ages and pets) **Activities:** gift and antiques shops

BOLTON LANDING

Nearby attractions: Sembrich Opera Museum, Lake George Opera, Bolton Historical Museum, Ft. Ticonderoga, Lake George village, lake cruise ships, antiques hunting, outlet shops, public beaches, tennis, ice fishing, cross-country and downhill skiing, swimming, water skiing, boating, Adirondack Mountains, hiking

HILLTOP COTTAGE BED AND BREAKFAST
6883 Lakeshore Drive
P.O. Box 186
Bolton Landing, New York 12814
518/644-2492
Proprietor: Anita Richards

Upon retiring in 1921, Metropolitan Opera diva Marcella Sembrich owned a summer estate on Millionaire's Row along the Lake George-to-Bolton Road. Here, in 1926, she built a teaching studio—now the Sembrich Opera Museum—and a combined caretaker cottage and student dormitory—now Hilltop Cottage. The recently renovated cottage contains three homey guest rooms with ceiling fans that look toward the old estate homes. Guests can choose from twin, queen-size, or king-size beds. A full breakfast, served in summer on the vine-shaded screen porch, includes German apple pancakes or quiche with homemade breads and jams. Hilltop Cottage is a comfortable walk to beaches, restaurants, tennis courts, and marinas.

Open: year round **Accommodations:** 3 guest rooms (1 has a private bath) **Meals:** full breakfast included; restaurants nearby **Rates:** $50 to $70; 10% discount to National Trust members and National Trust Visa cardholders **Payment:** Visa, MC, personal and traveler's checks **Restrictions:** no smoking; no pets (resident dog and cats)

BUSHNELL BASIN

Nearby attractions: Finger Lakes, Strong Museum, George Eastman House, International Museum of Photography, Letchworth Park, Niagara Falls

OLIVER LOUD'S INN
Mailing address:
1474 Marsh Road
Pittsford, New York 14534
716/248-5200 or 716/248-5000—restaurant only
Proprietor: Vivienne Tellier
Location: 12 miles southeast of Rochester in Bushnell Basin; 4 miles from New York State Thruway exit 45

Oliver Loud built this simple Federal-style tavern around 1812 in the hamlet of Egypt on a busy stagecoach route to Syracuse. In 1825 the opening of the Erie Canal a few miles away cost the tavern much of its trade. By the 1980s the building was abandoned and slated for demolition. Fortunately, it was rescued by Vivienne Tellier. Moved in 1985 to its present location on the canal, it was reopened as an inn after a painstaking restoration in which wood moldings and wallpapers were reproduced from remnants. Today, high-quality reproduction furniture and artifacts grace the building's interior. Faux-grained doors follow Loud's "recipe for making any wood look like mahogany," spelled out in his almanac. Guest rooms are elegantly appointed in period furnishings, yet contain modern amenities. The innkeeper speaks French and Spanish.

Open: year round **Accommodations:** 8 guest rooms with private baths **Meals:** continental breakfast included; complimentary refreshments; restaurant on premises **Wheelchair access:** yes **Rates:** $135 to $155; corporate rates available; 10% discount offered to National Trust members and National Trust Visa cardholders **Payment:** AmEx, Visa, MC, DC, CB, personal and traveler's checks **Restrictions:** children over 12 welcome; smoking limited; no pets (kennels nearby) **Activities:** Erie Canal towpath, walking, jogging, cross-country skiing, croquet, restaurant

CANANDAIGUA

Nearby attractions: Bristol Mountain ski resort, Sonnenberg Gardens and Mansion, winery tours, Granger Homestead and Carriage Museum, Finger Lakes Performing Arts Center, Cumming Nature Center, Canandaigua Lake, boating, fishing, swimming, golfing, hiking

ACORN INN
4508 Route 64 South
Bristol Center
Canandaigua, New York 14424
716/229-2834
716/229-5046 Fax
Proprietors: Joan and Louis Clark
Location: 8 miles west of Canandaigua; 30 miles south of Rochester

This dark-brown-shingled Federal stagecoach inn was built by Ephraim Wilder in 1795. Today it is operated as an antiques shop and bed and breakfast. On the first floor there are five rooms of eighteenth- and early nineteenth-century English and American antiques. More period pieces are found in the four air-conditioned, sound-proofed guest rooms upstairs. Each room has a canopy bed, sitting area, reading lamps, and private bath. Two rooms have fireplaces and two have whirlpool tubs. Books (many on antiques, and architecture) fill the house— in guest rooms, the living room, and the common room. The dining room and garden terrace are where the Clarks serve a full breakfast. Beds are turned down (and warmed in cold weather) nightly. Guests are invited to stroll the grounds filled with perennial gardens, brick walks, nature trails, and a creek.

Open: year round **Accommodations:** 4 guest rooms with private baths **Meals:** full breakfast included; complimentary afternoon tea and sherry; restaurants nearby **Rates:** $95 to $175; 10% discount to National Trust members and National Trust Visa cardholders **Payment:** Visa, MC, Discover, personal and traveler's checks **Restrictions:** children over 10 welcome; no smoking; no pets **Activities:** extensive library, gardens, tennis club available

CANDOR

Nearby attractions: Cornell University, Ithaca College, Watkins Glen, wineries, state parks, Mark Twain country, Tioga Train Ride

EDGE OF THYME
6 Main Street
P.O. Box 48
Candor, New York 13743
607/659-5155 or 800/722-7365 (outside New York state)
Proprietors: Frank and Eva Mae Musgrave

At the turn of the century, Rosa Murphy, the private secretary of John D. Rockefeller, met Dr. Amos Canfield in New York City. They married and decided to spend their summers in Candor, New York. Their Colonial Revival home was built in the center of the village, and Rosa's elegant style of entertaining became widely known. The well-maintained formal home retains its marble fireplaces, parquet floors, porch with leaded-glass windows, sweeping stairway, gardens, pergola, and gracious atmosphere. The decor is in keeping with the Canfield's era, as are the recipes used for the full breakfasts. The Edge of Thyme is located in the center of the Finger Lakes region, a short drive to Cornell University and Ithaca College.

Open: year round **Accommodations:** 4 guest rooms (2 have private baths); 1 is a suite **Meals:** full breakfast included; complimentary refreshments; high tea by appointment; restaurants nearby **Rates:** $55 to $75; 10% discount offered to National Trust members **Payment:** Visa, MC, personal and traveler's checks **Restrictions:** no smoking; no pets (kennels nearby) **Activities:** parlor games, croquet, gift shop

CINCINNATUS

Nearby attractions: Ithaca College, Cornell University, Colgate University, SUNY–College at Cortland, Otselic Valley, Finger Lakes, golfing, skiing, fishing, antiques hunting

ALICE'S DOWRY BED AND BREAKFAST
2789 Route 26
Box 306
Cincinnatus, New York 13040
607/863-3934
Proprietors: Lois and Rich Kearney

Alice's Dowry, an 1876 Italianate home, is named for the bride for whom it was built. Listed in the State and National Registers of Historic Places, the inn offers guests a formal parlor, a comfortable common room with television, an enclosed sunporch, and a wicker rocker–filled veranda. Two guest rooms, decorated with antiques like the rest of the house, have private baths. Before coming downstairs for a full breakfast, guests are awakened by the aroma of coffee, tea, and muffins just outside bedroom doors. Situated in the center of a small farming community, the inn is convenient to area colleges, yet sits nestled in the Otselic Valley between the Finger Lakes and Leather Stocking regions.

Open: year round **Accommodations:** 2 guest rooms with private baths **Meals:** full breakfast included; complimentary refreshments; dinner, tea, and private parties by reservation; restaurants nearby **Rates:** $55 to $65; 10% discount to National Trust members and National Trust Visa cardholders **Payment:** personal and traveler's checks **Restrictions:** children over 12 welcome; no smoking; no pets **Activities:** parlor games, television, antique slot machine, Adirondack chairs under shade trees

CLARENCE

Nearby attractions: Niagara Falls, Amherst Old Colony Museum, Lancaster Opera House, Buffalo, antiques hunting, Town Park, tennis, golfing, swimming, skiing, Fort Niagara, Genesee County Village, winery tours

ASA RANSOM HOUSE

10529 Main Street (Route 5)
Clarence, New York 14031
716/759-2315
76/759-2791 Fax
Proprietors: Robert and Judy Lenz
Location: 16 miles northeast of Buffalo

In 1799 the Holland Land Company offered a lot to anyone who would build and operate a tavern on it. Asa Ransom was first to accept this offer, building a combination tavern and log cabin home. He also built a sawmill (1801) and a gristmill (1803), the ruins of which are at the rear of the property. Another building, incorporating the original tavern, was constructed in 1853. Today, it offers guest accommodations plus a library, gift shop, and tap room. Guest rooms are furnished with antiques and period reproductions. Some rooms have fireplaces, some have canopied beds, all have private baths. Guests are invited to work puzzles, play board games, read, or listen to old radio program tapes in the antiques-appointed library. The inn offers two fine restaurants featuring fresh New York farmland fare.

Open: February 1 to December 31 **Accommodations:** 9 guest rooms with private baths; 2 are suites **Meals:** full breakfast included; complimentary refreshments; restaurants nearby **Wheelchair access:** yes **Rates:** $85 to $145; 10% discount to National Trust members and National Trust Visa cardholders Monday through Thursday **Payment:** Visa, MC, Discover, personal and traveler's checks **Restrictions:** no smoking; no pets **Activities:** library, chess, board games, more than 200 old-time radio program tapes, gift shop

COOPERSTOWN

Nearby attractions: National Baseball Hall of Fame, Farmers' Museum/ Fenimore House, Glimmerglass Opera, art galleries, Lake Otsego, Glimmerglass State Park, golfing, boating, fishing, swimming, hiking, bicycling, antiques hunting, museums

ÄNGELHOLM BED AND BREAKFAST

14 Elm Street
Cooperstown, New York 13326
607/547-2483
607/547-2309 Fax
Proprietors: Fred and Janet Reynolds

Ängelholm is a Federal-style home built in 1805 on historic Phinney's Farm, now in the heart of Cooperstown. Phinney's Farm was the site of the first baseball game, invented by Abner Doubleday. Today, Ängelholm's backyard and Doubleday Field have common boundaries. Charming guest rooms are decorated individually: the Doubleday room with white iron bed has a view of historic Doubleday Field and Stadium; the Elihu Phinney and Roby Mae rooms each boast original board-and-batten walls; the Glimmerglass room is early American in style; Ann's Cabbage Rose room is Victorian. A living room and library are offered to guests, along with the veranda overlooking the formal flower gardens. Guests are provided with off-street parking.

Open: year round **Accommodations:** 5 guest rooms with private baths **Meals:** full breakfast included; complimentary refreshments; restaurants nearby **Rates:** $85 to $95 Memorial Day through October; $65 to $75 off season **Payment:** Visa, MC, personal check **Restrictions:** children over 6 welcome; no smoking; no pets

INN AT COOPERSTOWN
16 Chestnut Street–NT
Cooperstown, New York 13326
607/547-5756
Proprietor: Michael Jerome

The Inn at Cooperstown, built in 1874 as an annex to the Hotel Fenimore, was designed by Henry J. Hardenbergh, architect of the Dakota Apartments and the Plaza Hotel in New York City. Originally known as the Fenimore Cottages, the inn is an excellent example of Second Empire style. The impressive three-story structure has a sweeping veranda, bracketed cornices, and large dormered windows gracing the mansard roof. The innkeeper's restoration of the building earned him the New York State Certificate of Achievement for Historic Preservation in 1986 and the tourism award from the Preservation League of New York in 1992. The 17 guest rooms are comfortably furnished with period reproductions. The sitting rooms, furnished with antiques, are inviting places to watch television or enjoy a book by a warming fire. Or guests may choose to rock idly on the porch. AAA gives the Inn at Cooperstown three diamonds.

Open: year round **Accommodations:** 17 guest rooms with private baths **Meals:** continental breakfast included; restaurants nearby **Wheelchair access:** 1 room **Rates:** $80 to $98 **Payment:** AmEx, Visa, MC, Discover, DC, personal and traveler's checks **Restrictions:** smoking limited; no pets **Activities:** reading, porch rocking, television

CORNWALL

Nearby attractions: West Point, Roosevelt's Hyde Park, Vanderbilt Mansion, Boscobel, New York Renaissance Festival, Brotherhood Winery (America's oldest), Goshen Historic Race Track, Black Rock Forest, Harriman State Park, antiques hunting, outlet shops, hiking, swimming, ice skating, skiing

CROMWELL MANOR INN
Angola Road
Cornwall, New York 12518
914/534-7136
Proprietors: Dale and Barbara O'Hara
Location: 5 miles north of West Point

This country estate, on seven acres of woodlands and gardens, was built in 1820 by David Cromwell, a descendant of Oliver Cromwell. It was constructed on the site of an earlier dwelling, incorporating that building's chimnies, which date from 1764. Guest rooms are decorated with period antiques and fine furnishings. Many rooms have working fireplaces, whirlpool tubs, or steamrooms. The inn is fully air-conditioned for guest comfort. A full breakfast is served in the country dining room or on the veranda. Guests are invited to relax in front of the common room's fireplace in winter and to stroll through the formal gardens, play croquet on the lawn, or sit by the goldfish pond in warm weather.

Open: year round **Accommodations:** 13 guest rooms with private baths; 2 are suites **Meals:** full breakfast included; restaurants nearby **Wheelchair access:** 1 room **Rates:** $120 to $250; 10% discount to National Trust members and National Trust Visa cardholders **Payment:** Visa, MC, personal and traveler's checks **Restrictions:** children over 5 welcome; no smoking; no pets

CROTON-ON-HUDSON

Nearby attractions: historic house tours, including National Trust's Lyndhurst, Kykuit, Sunnyside, and Pocantico Historic Area; West Point; hiking trails; Harriman State Park; antiques hunting; sailing; one hour from New York City

ALEXANDER HAMILTON HOUSE
49 Van Wyck Street
Croton-on-Hudson, New York 10520
914/271-6737
Proprietor: Barbara Notarius

Westchester County's first bed and breakfast, the Alexander Hamilton House was built in 1889 as a home for Croton-on-Hudson's village doctor. The Queen Anne house, loaded with bay and bow windows, sits on a cliff above the historic Hudson River. It is a short walk to the picturesque village of Croton-on-Hudson, gateway to the Hudson River Valley. The house is furnished with an eclectic blend of Victorian antiques, handicrafts (including hair art), and Hudson River paintings. Guests enjoy comfortable bedrooms and are invited to share the living room, with its stone fireplace, and a 35-foot-long sunporch with windows that offer a view of the river in winter and of the apple orchard in summer. A bridal chamber on the newly renovated third floor comes with a whirlpool tub, fireplace, window seat, king-size bed, and private bath. Four other guest rooms have fireplaces.

Open: year round **Accommodations:** 7 guest rooms with private baths; 3 are suites **Meals:** full breakfast included; restaurants nearby **Rates:** $75 to $250; 10% discount to National Trust members and National Trust Visa cardholders **Payment:** AmEx, Visa, MC, Discover, personal and traveler's checks **Restrictions:** no smoking; no pets **Activities:** swimming pool, television and VCR

DOVER PLAINS

Nearby attractions: Hyde Park, Roosevelt, and Vanderbilt estates; Culinary Institute of America; Hudson riverboat tours; Mary Flagler Cary Arboretum; wineries; Tanglewood; antiques hunting; canoeing; horseback riding; golfing

OLD DROVER INN
Old Route 22
Dover Plains, New York 12522
914/832-9311
Proprietors: Alice Pitcher and Kemper Peacock

Nestled in the Berkshire foothills, the Old Drovers Inn is a traditional colonial inn

that has survived almost 250 years of continuous service. Guests enter the original Tap Room, with its crackling fire, heavy wood-smoked beams, and stone walls, that greeted cattle drovers in 1750. These New England "cowboys" purchased herds of cattle and swine and drove them down the post roads to New York City markets. The drovers disappeared in the mid-nineteenth century, but their stopping place remains. Today's guests may choose from four antique-furnished bedrooms: the largest has a unique barrel-shaped ceiling; three have working fireplaces; all have private baths. The inn is famed for its blend of traditional and innovative fare at breakfast, lunch, and dinner. As only the third owners of Old Drovers, the proprietors continue the inn's heritage of hospitality and comfort.

Open: year round **Accommodations:** 4 guest rooms with private baths **Meals:** continental breakfast included weekdays; full breakfast and dinner included weekends; restaurant on premises **Wheelchair access:** dining room and bathrooms **Rates:** $150 to $395 (includes tax and service); 10% discount offered to National Trust members and National Trust Visa cardholders on Mondays and Thursdays **Payment:** Visa, MC, CB, DC, personal and traveler's checks **Restrictions:** pets allowed with a $20 per night charge **Activities:** biking, croquet, badminton, cross-country skiing

GARRISON

Nearby attractions: West Point, Boscobel restoration, Hudson River, Franklin Roosevelt home, Vanderbilt mansion

BIRD AND BOTTLE INN
Old Albany Post Road
Route 9
Garrison, New York 10524
914/424-3000 or 914/424-4035
Proprietor: Ira Boyar
Location: 8 miles north of Peekskill, 8 miles south of Fishkill and Route 84

Since opening in 1761, Warren's Tavern—now the Bird and Bottle Inn—has been closely identified with the history of the Hudson River Valley. It was a stagecoach stop on the New York–Albany Post Road (a National Historic Landmark) and quartered defense troops during the Revolutionary War. The Bird and Bottle Inn is a three-story, wood-frame structure, decorated in authentic American colonial style. Low-timbered ceilings and long, narrow hallways look today as they did when the building was constructed more than 200 years ago. Well known since 1940 for its extraordinary cuisine, the inn recently reopened for overnight accommodations. Wood-burning fireplaces warm the guest rooms, each of which is meticulously furnished with period furniture and a four-poster or canopied bed.

Open: year round **Accommodations:** 4 guest rooms with private baths **Meals:** full breakfast and dinner included; restaurant on premises **Wheelchair access:** guest rooms, bathrooms, dining facilities **Rates:** $210 to $240; 10% discount offered to National Trust members and National Trust Visa cardholders **Payment:** AmEx, Visa, MC, DC **Restrictions:** no pets

---

GENEVA

Nearby attractions: Finger Lakes wineries, Watkins Glen, Corning Glass Center, Sonnenberg Gardens

BELHURST CASTLE
Route 14 South
Geneva, New York 14456
315/781-0201
Proprietor: Duane R. Reeder

Belhurst Castle was constructed over a four-year period beginning in 1885. The turreted, red medina-stone structure was built mostly of materials imported from Europe in a style known as Richardsonian Romanesque, which emphasizes round-topped arches over windows. In the century since the structure was completed, Belhurst Castle has been at various times a home, speakeasy, casino, and restaurant. Today the 100-year-old mansion contains 11 romantic bedrooms; two guest houses offering unique accommodations are also located on the grounds. The castle features atmospheric dining in the library, parlor, center room, conservatory, or on the veranda overlooking Seneca Lake. Belhurst Castle is rated with four diamonds by AAA.

Open: year round **Accommodations:** 13 guest rooms with private baths; 2 are suites **Meals:** restaurant on premises **Rates:** $65 to $295 **Payment:** Visa, MC **Restrictions:** no pets **Activities:** fishing and sailing 100 yards from castle

HAGUE

Nearby attractions: Lake George, boating, town beach, swimming, lake cruises, water skiing, fly fishing, golfing, tennis, Saratoga Springs, horse racing, Saratoga Performing Arts Center

LOCUST INN
Route 9N
Hague, New York 12836
518/543-6035
Proprietor: James Coates

Built in 1865, this frame Victorian house with tall windows and decorative front porch was rennovated in 1992, opening as a bed and breakfast. Furnished in period antiques from the early 1900s, the inn features an extensive collection of regional art. Five guest suites have private baths, sitting areas, and views of northern Lake George and the surrounding Adirondack Mountains. Guests are served a home-cooked country breakfast each morning. In season, Saturday nights feature a casual gathering for a barbecue or lobster bake dinner. Next door to the inn is Hague Brook, a salmon and smelt spawning ground well known as a fly-fisherman's paradise. The inn is also adjacent to the town beach and a boat ramp.

Open: year round **Accommodations:** 5 guest suites with private baths **Meals:** continental-plus breakfast included; restaurants nearby **Rates:** $55 to $95 **Payment:** Visa, MC, Discover, personal and traveler's checks **Restrictions:** smoking limited

HIGH FALLS

Nearby attractions: New Paltz; Woodstock; historic Kingston; Hyde Park, Vanderbilt, and Roosevelt estates; state parks; hiking

CAPTAIN SCHOONMAKER'S BED AND BREAKFAST
R.D. 2, Box 37
High Falls, New York 12440
914/687-7946
Proprietors: Sam and Julia Krieg

The inn's namesake was a Hudson Valley Revolutionary War hero who built this stone cottage in 1760 and lived here with his 13 sons before they were summoned to serve in the regiment protecting New York's then-capital, Kingston. Original fireplaces, beams, and flooring in this early Dutch Colonial home have all been preserved and restored to their original beauty. Early American country antiques and fine oil portraits of family members and other notables add to the house's warmth and hospitality. The post-and-beam barn, once part of the working farm, has been renovated to house guests. The 1810 structure, situated along a creek and waterfall, provides private porches overlooking woodlands. Canopy beds and puffy feather beds are part of the early American decor. A six-course breakfast features home-baked breads and sweet cakes.

Open: year round **Accommodations:** 6 guest rooms (2 have private baths) **Meals:** six-course breakfast included; complimentary refreshments; restaurants nearby **Rates:** $80 to $90; 10% discount offered to National Trust members and National Trust Visa cardholders **Payment:** personal check **Restrictions:** not suitable for children under 6 on weekends; no pets **Activities:** trout fishing in stocked stream, library

ITHACA

Nearby attractions: Salmon Creek and Falls, Finger Lakes region, Cornell Univeristy, Ithaca College, wineries, state parks, Lake Cayuga, swimming, fishing, boating, picnicking, bicycling

FEDERAL HOUSE BED AND BREAKFAST
P.O. Box 4914
Ithaca, New York 14852-4914
607/533-7362 or 800/533-7362
Proprietor: Diane Carroll

Federal House was built ca. 1815 by Abijah Miller, whose daughter, Frances, wed

William Henry Seward, secretary of state under Abraham Lincoln. The house features spacious rooms furnished with antiques, original woodwork, and hand-carved fireplace mantels reputedly made by Brigham Young, who worked as an apprentice carpenter in the area in the early nineteenth century. Four individually appointed guest rooms are offered: one has a white iron bed, one has hand-painted furniture, one has a canopy bed and fireplace. The English Ivy Room is a guest sitting room with television, a refrigerator, and a hot pot. Here guests will find fresh fruit, beverages, and snacks, as well as books, magazines, and games. Sitting on an acre of landscaped grounds, Federal House is less than two miles from a public beach on Lake Cayuga.

Open: year round **Accommodations:** 4 guest rooms (3 have private baths); 1 is a suite **Meals:** full breakfast included; complimentary refreshments; restaurants nearby **Rates:** $55 to $150; 10% discount to National Trust members and National Trust Visa cardholders with restrictions **Payment:** AmEx, Visa, MC, Discover, personal and traveler's checks **Restrictions:** children over 14 welcome; no smoking; no pets **Activities:** gardens, gazebo, bicycles

---

KINGSTON

Nearby attractions: Hudson River cruises, lighthouses, Urban Cultural Park, Trolley Museum of New York, Firemen's Museum, Old Dutch Church and Museum, Maritime Museum, Senate House and Museum, historic Stockade area of New York's first capital, art galleries, theaters, antiques hunting, specialty shops

RONDOUT BED AND BREAKFAST
88 West Chester Street
Kingston, New York 12401
914/331-2369
Proprietors: Adele and Ralph Calcavecchio

It is said that J. Graham Rose, the wealthy industrialist who built this Colonial Revival home in 1906, had piles of dirt dumped at the building site at $1 per truckload in order to make his home the highest in Kingston. Then he had built this 4000-square-foot, 12-room house with lofty ceilings, numerous windows (some with leaded and beveled glass), and chestnut paneling. Nearly all of the house's original architectural details remain intact, including brass wall sconces, having been converted from gas to electricity. Both the living and dining rooms contain pianos, and the entire house is filled with antiques and paintings, prints, and ceramics by local artists. The glassed-in porch sports rattan and wicker furniture that belonged to Adele Calcavecchio's grandmother. Hearty breakfasts feature Belgian waffles and homemade maple syrup.

Open: year round **Accommodations:** 4 guest rooms (2 have private baths) **Meals:** full breakfast included; complimentary refreshments; restaurants nearby **Rates:** $65 to $80; 10% discount offered to National Trust members and National Trust Visa cardholders **Payment:** AmEx, Visa, MC, personal check **Restrictions:** no smoking; no pets **Activities:** croquet, boccie, bicycles, player piano, television, reading

---

LAKE LUZERNE

Nearby attractions: Lake George, Saratoga Springs, historic sites, horseback riding, downhill and cross-country skiing, white-water rafting, antiques hunting, outlet shops, ballet and symphony in summer

LAMPLIGHT INN BED AND BREAKFAST
2129 Lake Avenue
P.O. Box 70
Lake Luzerne, New York 12846-0070
518/696-5294 or 800/262-4668
Proprietors: Gene and Linda Merlino
Location: 10 miles south of Lake George; 18 miles north of Saratoga Springs

In 1890, Howard Conkling, a wealthy lumberman and summer resident of Lake Luzerne, built a Victorian estate here, designed for entertaining. Sparing no expense, he hired English craftsmen to make the first floor's 12-foot-high beamed ceilings, chestnut wainscoting and moldings, and a chestnut keyhole staircase. Now as the Lamplight Inn, the house continues to entertain guests. Five doors lead from the parlor to the spacious wraparound porch and lawns. The inn contains comfortable Victorian furnishings and working fireplaces. Guest rooms are individually decorated with romantic quilts, flowered wallpaper, and lace curtains. Gas-burning fireplaces and canopy beds are featured in some rooms. Guests also enjoy relaxing on the porches with wicker rockers and porch swings.

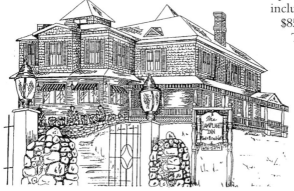

Open: year round **Accommodations:** 10 guest rooms with private baths **Meals:** full breakfast included; restaurants nearby **Rates:** $85 to $150; 10% discount to National Trust members and National Trust Visa cardholders **Payment:** AmEx, Visa, MC, personal and traveler's checks **Restrictions:** children over 12 welcome; smoking limited; no pets (resident dog) **Activities:** board games, books, garden, porch swings, nature walk/cross-country trail, gift shop

LAKE PLACID

Nearby attractions: U.S. Olympic Training Center, John Brown's grave and homestead, Adirondack Park, Lake Center for the Arts, Whiteface Mountain Ski Center, golfing, tennis, canoeing

STAGECOACH INN
370 Old Military Road
Lake Placid, New York 12946
518/523-9474
Proprietor: Peter Moreau

The Stagecoach Inn has been serving travelers—many in stagecoaches—since 1833. The two-story clapboard building with gabled dormers is distinguished outside by its balustraded porch and balcony and inside by its unique yellow birch staircase. Nine guest rooms are individually furnished with brass or white iron beds, handmade quilts, wicker pieces, and antiques. Memorable breakfasts may feature cheese souffles, French toast, or homemade breads. The inn was host to the CBS Sports broadcast team during the 1980 Winter Olympics and has been praised by *Gourmet* and *Vogue*.

Open: year round **Accommodations:** 9 guest rooms (5 have private baths); 2 are suites **Meals:** full breakfast included; restaurants nearby **Rates:** $60 to $85; 10% discount to National Trust members and National Trust Visa cardholders **Payment:** Visa, MC **Restrictions:** no pets

LEONARDSVILLE

Nearby attractions: Cooperstown, Baseball Hall of Fame, Farmers Museum, antiques hunting, lake activities, cross-country skiing, hiking

HORNED DORSET INN
Route 8
P.O. Box 142
Leonardsville, New York 13364
315/855-7898
315/855-7820 Fax
Proprietors: Bruce Wratten and Donald Lentz

Constructed in 1830, the house that is now the Horned Dorset Inn was remodeled in 1889 by its owner John Wheeler, president of the Leonardsville National Bank. Incorporating the bank into his house, Wheeler gave the building a distinctive Italianate appearance with elaborately bracketed cornices at the roof and porches.

At the same time, Wheeler had a commercial building constructed next door, which now houses the Horned Dorset's AAA-rated, four-diamond French restaurant, a destination in its own right. Guest accommodations are in two rooms, one with fireplace, and two suites, each with king-size bed and a sitting room (one with fireplace). The inn is decorated throughout with antique furnishings and architectural antiques.

Open: year round **Accommodations:** 4 guest rooms with private baths; 2 are suites **Meals:** continental breakfast included; restaurant on premises **Rates:** $90 to $110 **Payment:** AmEx, Visa, MC, personal and traveler's checks **Restrictions:** children over 12 welcome; no pets

LEW BEACH

Nearby attractions: Beaverkill Valley, Catskill Mountains, downhill skiing, fly-fishing museum, Wulff Fishing School, boating, horseback riding

BEAVERKILL VALLEY INN
Beaverkill Road
Box 136
Lew Beach, New York 12753
914/439-4844
Proprietor: Laurance Rockefeller

Since 1893 this inn in the Beaverkill Valley has hosted sportsmen and nature enthusiasts. First opened as the Bonnie View Inn, it was in a state of decline when purchased in 1981 by Larry Rockefeller, an environmental lawyer, who restored the white clapboard, red-shingled building and set about claiming surrounding acreage for conservation and protection. Now listed in the National Register of Historic Places, the inn contains 21 guest rooms individually outfitted with brass-and-iron beds, quilts, oak furniture, and Laura Ashley wallpapers. The inn also contains game rooms, a Victorian bar, a sundeck, and a dining room featuring seasonal foods and home-baked breads and pastries. An old barn has been renovated to include a 60-foot heated indoor swimming pool and a self-serve ice cream parlor. Sixty acres of pristine wilderness surround the inn.

Open: year round **Accommodations:** 21 guest rooms (13 have private baths) **Meals:** breakfast, lunch, and dinner included on full American Plan (FAP) **Rates:** $160 to $195 single FAP; $260 to $330 double FAP **Payment:** AmEx, Visa, MC, personal and traveler's checks **Restrictions:** no smoking; no pets **Activities:** fly fishing, cross-country skiing, indoor swimming pool, tennis, ice cream parlor

RHINEBECK

Nearby attractions: FDR library and home, Old Rhinebeck Aerodrome, state historic sites of Clermont and Olana, mansion tours, Culinary Institute of America, golfing, tennis, skiing

BEEKMAN ARMS
4 Mill Street
Rhinebeck, New York 12752
914/876-7077
Proprietor: Chuck LaForge

Since this inn first opened its doors in 1776 as the Traphagen Inn on Kings Highway (now Route 9), the Beekman Arms has been a strategic meeting place for Revolutionary War generals and the center of business and government for the town of Rhinebeck and the Hudson Valley. Wide-planked floors, ceiling beams, and a huge stone hearth greet visitors as the enter the lobby. Authentic furnishings are found throughout, including the Colonial Tap Room—the center of the original inn—and guest rooms—many with fireplaces. The hotel's restaurant, serving fine country fare, has been awarded a rating of excellent by the *New York Times*. This distinctive inn has hosted both the famous and the infamous, from George Washington and Franklin Delano Roosevelt to Benedict Arnold. Directly behind the main building is the Beekman Arms Antique Barn, with more than 30 dealers.

Open: year round **Accommodations:** 59 guest rooms with private baths; 3 are suites **Meals:** restaurant and taproom on premises **Wheelchair access:** yes **Rates:** $85 to $150 **Payment:** AmEx, Visa, MC, personal and traveler's checks **Restrictions:** children, smoking, and pets are limited to certain rooms **Activities:** antiques center

DELAMATER HOUSE
44 Montgomery Street (Route 9)
Rhinebeck, New York 12572
914/876-7080
Proprietors: Doris Masten and
Chuck LaForge

Delamater House is one of the architectural jewels of the Hudson Valley. Built in 1844, it was designed by noted architect Alexander Jackson Davis for Henry Delamater, founder of

the First National Bank of Rhinebeck. Davis designed many state capitol buildings as well as mansions, the most famous of which is the National Trust's Lyndhurst in Tarrytown. Delamater House has been excellently preserved (it is listed in the National Register of Historic Places) and is one of few early examples of an American Gothic residence still in existence. It is elaborately decorated with fancy vergeboards, pointed-arched windows, and diamond-paned sashes. Accommodations at Delamater House are reminiscent of those at a country manor. A living room, enclosed porch, and pantry also are available for guests.

Open: year round **Accommodations:** 7 guest rooms with private baths **Meals:** continental breakfast included; complimentary refreshments; restaurants nearby **Wheelchair access:** limited **Rates:** $85 to $99; 10% discount offered to National Trust members and National Trust Visa cardholders **Payment:** AmEx, Visa, MC, personal and traveler's checks **Restrictions:** children over 12 welcome; no pets **Activities:** spacious lawns for strolling, lounging, and croquet

SARATOGA SPRINGS

Nearby attractions: National Museum of Dance, National Museum of Racing, Saratoga Raceway, Saratoga Performing Arts Center, New York City Ballet in July, New York City Opera in June, state park, Lake George, mineral baths, antiques hunting, Saratoga National Battlefield, tennis, golfing, swimming, downhill and cross-country skiing, outlet shops

INN ON BACON HILL
P.O. Box 1462
Saratoga Springs, New York 12866
518/695-3693
Proprietor: Andrea Collins-Breslin
Location: 7 miles east of city of Saratoga Springs

The Inn on Bacon Hill was built by New York State legislator Alexander B. Baucus in 1862. Although an engineer and surveyor by profession, Baucus engaged extensively in business, farming, and produce distribution before serving in the state senate in the 1880s. The recently restored 16-room Italianate home is still nestled in a peaceful rural setting, close to historic Saratoga Springs. Its interior boasts original marble fireplaces, an antique kerosene chandelier, high ceilings, and finely crafted plaster moldings and woodwork. Restful places can be found in the living room, on the wicker-filled porch, in the flower garden, and in the screened-in gazebo.

Open: year round **Accommodations:** 4 guest rooms (2 have private baths); 1 is a suite **Meals:** full breakfast included; complimentary refreshments; restaurants nearby **Rates:** $65 to $85; $115 to $135 during August racing season; 10% discount to National Trust members and National Trust Visa cardholders **Payment:** Visa, MC, personal and traveler's checks **Restrictions:** children over 13 welcome; no smoking; no pets (resident dog) **Activities:** relaxation, walking down country lanes

SARATOGA BED AND BREAKFAST
434 Church Street
Saratoga Springs, New York 12866
518/584-0920 or 800/584-0920
518/584-4500 Fax
Proprietors: Noel and Kathleen Smith

Saratoga Bed and Breakfast consists of two historic homes: an 1860 Victorian frame farmhouse and an 1850 brick home in the Greek Revival style. The rambling farmhouse was used as lodging for summer visitors after World War II and converted to a bed and breakfast in 1984. It is furnished with maple and oak antiques and colorful handmade quilts. Each guest room is named for old hotels or estates in Saratoga. The 1850 House, next door, was originally known as the Oscar Granger Farm, and was constructed with the profits of the Mount Pleasant Glass Works, manufacturers of the glass bottles used to bottle Saratoga waters. The house retains its hardwood floors, tall ceilings, and fireplaces. Four suites in this house are distinctively decorated with walnut and mahogany antiques. A full country breakfast is served.

Open: year round **Accommodations:** 8 guest rooms with private baths; 2 are suites **Meals:** full breakfast included; restaurants nearby **Rates:** $65 to $135 (higher during thoroughbred racing season); 10% discount to National Trust members and National Trust Visa cardholders **Payment:** AmEx, Visa, MC, Discover, personal and traveler's checks **Restrictions:** children over 12 welcome; no smoking; no pets **Activities:** gardens, stream, specialty packages

WESTCHESTER HOUSE
102 Lincoln Avenue
P.O. Box 944
Saratoga Springs, New York 12866
518/587-7613
Proprietors: Bob and Stephanie Melvin

This 1885 Queen Anne Victorian was built by master carpenter Almeron King as his family home. Examples of King's skill and imagination abound. A main

staircase and two elaborate hand-carved fireplace mantels reflect a strong Eastlake influence. The whimsical roofline includes a cupola and balcony. Decorative exterior shingles, a wraparound porch, and a seven-color paint scheme tie the whole together. The proprietors have combined antique furnishings with contemporary art and collectibles and up-to-date comforts. Guest rooms contain luxury linens, queen- and king-size beds, ceiling fans, fresh flowers, and chocolates. Guests may enjoy the library, baby grand piano, and gardens. The dining room, where breakfast is served on crystal and china, is brightened by large arched windows. The innkeepers have earned several local and state awards for their extensive restoration work on the house.

Open: February through December **Accommodations:** 7 guest rooms with private baths **Meals:** continental-plus breakfast included; complimentary refreshments; restaurants nearby **Rates:** $75 to $150 (higher in August racing season); 10% discount to National Trust members and National Trust Visa cardholders **Payment:** AmEx, Visa, MC, personal and traveler's checks **Restrictions:** well-behaved children welcome; smoking limited; no pets (resident dog) **Activities:** library, games, piano, gardens, walking distance to all Saratoga attractions

SCHENECTADY

Nearby attractions: Riverside Park, historic neighborhood, bicycling, ice skating, antiques hunting, theaters, colleges, General Electric, Mohawk River, downhill skiing

WIDOW KENDALL HOUSE
10 North Ferry Street
Schenectady, New York 12305
518/370-5972 or 518/370-5511
Proprietors: Richard H. Brown and Matthew G. Moross

A classic saltbox built before 1788, the Widow Kendall House is a two-story brick and wood frame structure in the heart of Schenectady's Stockade Historic District. Each guest room is unique: a fireplace, original 14-inch-wide floorboards, and a private entrance are some distinguishing features. The 1830s brought elegant Greek Revival changes to the house; an ongoing 10-year restoration has painstakingly retained these, along with original architectural features. Listed in the National Register of Historic Places, the home is attractively furnished with antiques. Guests are served a four-course breakfast overlooking the gardens.

Open: year round **Accommodations:** 3 guest rooms with shared baths **Meals:** full breakfast included; guests have kitchen privileges; restaurants nearby **Rate:** $95; 10% discount offered to National Trust members and National Trust Visa cardholders except in August **Payment:** AmEx, Visa, MC, personal and traveler's checks **Restrictions:** smoking limited **Activities:** sun bathing, sitting in the herb garden

STONE RIDGE

Nearby attractions: Catskill Mountains, lakes, Woodstock art colony, Kingston, Hyde Park, hiking, bicycling, cross-country skiing, ice skating, fishing, tennis, golfing, Hudson River cruises, bird-watching, wine region, antiques hunting, crafts shops

INN AT STONE RIDGE – HASBROUCK HOUSE
Route 209
Stone Ridge, New York 12484
914/687-0736
Proprietors: Dan and Suzanne Hauspurg

This eighteenth-century Dutch colonial mansion, with a full-facade double-decker porch, is set on 40 acres of lawns, gardens, and woods with a lake. The guest parlor area includes a full-size antique billiard table, a sitting room with library, and a television room. Guest rooms are furnished in colonial and Victorian antiques. Located on the first floor of the mansion, Milliways Restaurant features regional cuisine and specials representing America's different heritages. A craft and gift shop, located in the original carriage house of the estate, features the works of local artisans. Hasbrouck House, only 95 miles from midtown Manhattan, is listed in the National Register of Historic Places.

Open: year round **Accommodations:** 11 guest rooms (2 have private baths); 1 is a suite **Meals:** full breakfast included; restaurant on premises; restaurants nearby **Rates:** $60 to $145; 10% discount to National Trust members and National Trust Visa cardholders **Payment:** AmEx, Visa, MC, Discover, personal and traveler's checks **Activities:** gardens, hiking, swimming, billiards

---

THENDARA

Nearby attractions: Adirondack Museum, Fulton Chain of Lakes, arts center, Old Forge, Blue Mountain Museum, Enchanted Forest, Water Safari, golfing, horseback riding, hiking, downhill and cross-country skiing

MOOSE RIVER HOUSE BED AND BREAKFAST
12 Birch Street
Thendara, New York 13472
315/369-3104
Proprietors: Kate and Bill Labbate

Built in 1884 as a small hotel, Moose River House was then accessible only by boat. The double-decked *Fawn*, a tiny sidewheeler, steamed upstream from

Minnehaha, where the only wooden train rails ended. Four delightful guest rooms overlook the river, which offers miles of canoeing and fishing. Guests are also welcome in the fireplaced living room for conversation, reading, games, or television. A full breakfast is served in the dining room or on the outside deck, both of which overlook Moose River. A canoe trip originates at the inn that goes through the eight lakes of the Fulton Chain as well as Raquette, Forked, Long, and Saranac lakes.

Open: year round **Accommodations:** 4 guest rooms (2 have private baths) **Meals:** full breakfast included; restaurants nearby **Rates:** $65 to $85 **Payment:** Visa, MC, personal and traveler's checks **Restrictions:** children over 12 welcome; no smoking; no pets **Activities:** gardens, hiking, canoeing, mountain biking

WARRENSBURG

Nearby attractions: Lake George, museums, Saratoga Performing Arts Center, swimming, fishing, boating, skiing

HOUSE ON THE HILL BED AND BREAKFAST
Route 28, Box 248
Warrensburg, New York 12885
518/623-9390 or 800/221-9390
518/623-9390 Fax
Proprietors: Joe and Lynn Rubino

The House on the Hill, dating to the eighteenth century, is a Federal-style building with a twist. When a major addition was built in 1890, decorative vergeboards—decidedly Victorian—were added under the gables of the colonial-era house. In 1989 a huge sunroom, where guests enjoy breakfast, was added. The kitchen, part of the original house, has slanted floors and a hand-operated water pump to go along with all the modern appliances. The innkeepers, collectors of antiques, original paintings, and musical memorabilia, have filled the house with these items. There are five distinctive bedrooms with air conditioning, telephones, and television. While baths are shared, sinks are provided in each bedroom. House on the Hill is located in the six-million-acre Adirondack Park. The Rubinos speak Italian, French, and German.

Open: year round **Accommodations:** 5 guest rooms (1 has a private bath) **Meals:** full breakfast included; complimentary in-room refreshments; restaurants nearby **Wheelchair access:** limited **Rates:** $89 to $109; 10% discount to National Trust members and National Trust Visa cardholders **Payment:** Visa, MC, DC, Discover, personal and traveler's checks **Restrictions:** children over 12 welcome; younger children by special arrangement; no smoking; no pets **Activities:** cross-country ski trails, hiking, mountain biking, hunting, bird-watching

WESTHAMPTON BEACH

Nearby attractions: Quogue Wildlife Refuge, Montauk Point, ocean and beach, golfing, fishing, shopping

1880 SEAFIELD HOUSE
2 Seafield Lane
P.O. Box 648
Westhampton Beach, New York 11978
516/288-1559 or 800/346-3290
Proprietor: Elsie Pardee Collins

Seafield House is a rural retreat just 90 minutes from Manhattan but 100 years from the present in style, decor, and atmosphere. The estate, including a swimming pool and tennis court, is only a short, brisk walk to the ocean beach. The home is filled with family heirlooms, antiques, and personal touches, especially in the guest suites, with their flower arrangements, fruit and candies, and English toiletries. The eclectic furnishings harmonize to create a casual, country-inn feeling. When the weather turns cool, the parlor fire and 1907 potbelly stove continually blaze to keep Seafield House warm and comforting. Guests are treated to a full breakfast, and all leave Seafield House carrying one of Mrs. Collins's complimentary home-baked goodies.

Open: year round **Accommodations:** 3 guest suites with private baths **Meals:** full breakfast included; complimentary refreshments; restaurants nearby **Rates:** $100 to $200; 10% discount to National Trust members **Payment:** AmEx, Visa, MC, personal and traveler's checks **Restrictions:** no smoking **Activities:** swimming pool, tennis

NORTH CAROLINA

ABERDEEN
Nearby attractions: Pinehurst, championship-quality golf; PGA Hall of Fame; antiques hunting; historic sites; nature preserves; horse shows; horseback riding; polo; hunting; swimming; tennis; auto racing

INN AT THE BRYANT HOUSE
214 North Poplar Street
Aberdeen, North Carolina 28315
919/944-3300 or 800/453-4019
Proprietors: Bill and Abbie Gregory
Location: 5 miles southeast of Pinehurst

Built in 1913 by Julia Thaggard Bryant as a guest house, the Inn at the Bryant House is located in Aberdeen's downtown historic district. The symmetrical brick Colonial Revival house is decorated throughout in tranquil pastels. The spacious sitting, dining, and living rooms open to one another for easy access and a relaxed, friendly environment. A large wraparound porch is also inviting. A generous continental breakfast is served to guests buffet style in the dining or garden room. The inn's quiet setting also suits small business meetings, wedding parties, family gatherings, and weekend retreats.

Open: year round **Accommodations:** 8 guest rooms with private baths **Meals:** continental-plus breakfast included; restaurants nearby **Rates:** $45 to $70; 10% discount offered to National Trust members and National Trust Visa cardholders **Payment:** AmEx, Visa, MC, Discover, personal and traveler's checks **Restrictions:** no smoking **Activities:** picnic area

ASHEVILLE

Nearby attractions: Biltmore Estate, Thomas Wolfe home, Carl Sandburg home, Great Smoky Mountains National Park, Blue Ridge Parkway, arts and science center, crafts shops, tennis, golfing, hiking, white-water rafting, horseback riding

BEAUFORT HOUSE

61 North Liberty Street
Asheville, North Carolina 28801
704/254-8334
Proprietors: Jacqueline and Robert Glasgow

Having celebrated its centennial in 1994, Beaufort House stands out as a local landmark among many elegant homes in historic Asheville. The house, an elegant Queen Anne, was designed by noted architect A. L. Melton, who designed some of the area's finest turn-of-the-century buildings. The home was owned by Asheville Mayor Theodore Fulton Davidson, who also served as a state senator and state attorney general. Carved wood paneling and moldings are accented by fine Victorian antiques. An expansive wraparound porch, incorporating a corner gazebo, is filled with wicker and hanging and potted plants. On landscaped grounds, under giant shade trees, Beaufort House offers spacious guest rooms and suites. Listed in the National Register of Historic Places, the house is an easy walk to Asheville's downtown attractions.

Open: year round **Accommodations:** 7 guest rooms with private baths; 1 is a suite **Meals:** full breakfast included; complimentary refreshments; restaurants nearby **Rates:** $95 to $195; 10% discount offered to National Trust members and National Trust Visa cardholders **Payment:** Visa, MC, personal and traveler's checks **Restrictions:** smoking limited **Activities:** tea garden, free bicycles, in-room television and VCR, fitness facility

CEDAR CREST VICTORIAN INN

674 Biltmore Avenue
Asheville, North Carolina 28803
704/252-1389
704/252-5522 Fax
Proprietors: Jack and Barbara McEwan

Perched on a hill just north of Biltmore Village, this opulent Queen Anne mansion is prominently situated on its four-acre site. Built in 1891 for Confederate veteran and businessman William E. Breese, Cedar Crest is known for its captain's walk, turrets, and expansive verandas. Ornate woodwork, said to be that of the same artisans employed by Vanderbilt at his nearby Biltmore estate, is featured prominently inside, perhaps most ornately in the parlor's carved oak corner mantel and crown molding. Spacious bedrooms are furnished with period antiques and may have canopied or brass beds, Victorian laces, fireplaces, or claw-foot tubs. The Guest Cottage, just above the garden, is a 1915 bungalow ideal for families and those seeking additional privacy. Cedar Crest is listed in the National Register of Historic Places.

Open: year round **Accommodations:** 11 guest rooms with private baths; 3 are suites **Meals:** continental-plus breakfast included; complimentary refreshments; restaurants nearby **Rates:** $120 to $175; winter discounts; 10% discount offered to National Trust members and National Trust Visa cardholders **Payment:** AmEx, Visa, MC, DC, Discover, personal and traveler's checks **Restrictions:** children over 10 welcome; no smoking; no pets **Activities:** croquet, badminton, gardens, music room

INN ON MONTFORD
296 Montford Avenue
Asheville, North Carolina 28801
704/254-9569
Proprietor: Alexa Royden

The Inn on Montford sits behind a boxwood-lined walkway, under enormous shade trees, on a street traveled by Scott and Zelda Fitzgerald and memorialized by Thomas Wolfe. Architect Richard Sharp Smith, supervising architect of nearby Biltmore house, designed this house in an English cottage style with its two front gables, eaves flared, and an expansive wraparound porch. Today, the inn is furnished with English and American antiques, fine paintings, oriental rugs, and porcelains. Guest rooms feature canopied beds and fireplaces. Three bathrooms have whirlpool tubs and one has an old-fashioned claw-foot tub. All are stocked with scented soaps and plush towels. The innkeeper serves a full breakfast that features daily specialties and an afternoon tea.

Open: year round **Accommodations:** 4 guest rooms with private baths **Meals:** full breakfast included; complimentary refreshments; restaurants nearby **Rates:** $100 to $130 **Payment:** AmEx, Visa, MC, Discover, personal and traveler's checks **Restrictions:** no smoking; no pets (resident dogs) **Activities:** porch sitting, hammock

OLD REYNOLDS MANSION
100 Reynolds Heights
Asheville, North Carolina 28804
704/254-0496
Proprietors: Helen and Fred Faber

One of the few brick houses in Asheville that predates the Civil War, the Old Reynolds Mansion maintains its solitary perch on Reynolds Mountain surrounded by acres of trees. This large home was built in 1855 by Daniel and Susan Reynolds. Their son Nathaniel renovated it, adding a third story with a mansard roof, a kitchen, and two verandas, and transformed the house to a Second Empire style. Restored by the innkeepers, the Old Reynolds Mansion is listed in the National Register of Historic Places. All guest rooms are adorned with antiques, and most have private baths and fireplaces. Guests can enjoy breakfasts and sunsets on the verandas, stroll through the pines surrounding the house, or tour historic Asheville.

Open: year round, weekends only January and February **Accommodations:** 10 guest rooms (8 have private baths) **Meals:** continental-plus breakfast included; complimentary refreshments; restaurants nearby **Rates:** $55 to $100 **Payment:** personal and traveler's checks **Restrictions:** children over 12 welcome; no pets **Activities:** swimming pool, porch sitting, walking

REED HOUSE BED AND BREAKFAST
119 Dodge Street
Asheville, North Carolina 28803
704/274-1604
Proprietor: Marge Turcot

In 1892 Samuel Harrison Reed built this imposing Queen Anne frame house on a hill above Biltmore Village. A porch with swings and rockers surrounds half the house, and an octagonal turret, capped by a bell-shaped roof, looks out over the village. The house is encased in weatherboard and has interior chimneys. High-quality millwork includes a variety of mantels, molded door and window surrounds, and a spindled Chinese Chippendale balustrade on the stairway. Comfortable, homey guest rooms feature rocking chairs for relaxing. A complimentary breakfast features homemade muffins and jams. The Reed House is listed in the National Register of Historic Places and has been declared a Local Historic Property by the Historic Resources Commission of Asheville.

Open: May 1 to November 1 **Accommodations:** 3 guest rooms (1 has a private bath); separate two-bedroom cottage **Meals:** continental breakfast included; restaurants nearby **Rates:** $45 to $95 **Payment:** Visa, MC, personal and traveler's checks **Restrictions:** no pets **Activities:** porch rockers and swing, games and puzzles, pool table, television

RICHMOND HILL INN
87 Richmond Hill Drive
Asheville, North Carolina 28806
704/252-7313 or 800/545-9238
Proprietors: Dr. Albert J. and Margaret Michel

An impressive Queen Anne Victorian, this mansion was built in 1889 as the private residence of Richmond Pearson, a former congressman and ambassador. Designed by James. G. Hill, supervising architect for the U.S. Treasury buildings, the home was one of the most elegant and innovative residential structures of its era, with running water, its own communication system, and a pulley-operated elevator for luggage. The Richmond Hill Inn, as the house is known today, boasts a grand entrance hall paneled in rich native oak and 10 fireplaces with neoclassical mantels. The cottages and garden rooms at Richmond Hill reflect the Victorian style of the mansion. The house, listed in the National Register of Historic Places, the cottages, and the garden complex offer guests individually decorated, antique-filled bedrooms with such extras as turn-down service, fresh flowers, and down pillows.

Open: year round **Accommodations:** 12 rooms with private baths in the mansion, 1 is a suite; 15 rooms with private baths in garden complex, 1 is a suite; 9 rooms with private baths in the cottages, 1 is a suite **Meals:** full breakfast included; complimentary refreshments; 2 restaurants on premises **Wheelchair access:** limited **Rates:** $130 to $350 **Payment:** AmEx, Visa, MC, personal and traveler's checks **Restrictions:** no smoking; no pets **Activities:** croquet, rare book collection

WRIGHT INN AND CARRIAGE

235 Pearson Drive
Asheville, North Carolina 28801
704/251-0789 or 800/552-5724
Proprietors: Carol and Art Wenczel

Asheville's historic Montford District contains the grand homes of turn-of-the-century industrialists and real estate developers. The fully restored Wright Inn is one of the finest examples of Queen Anne architecture found in the district and in all of western North Carolina. Built in 1899 for Osella B. and Leva Wright, the house, heavily ornamented with gingerbread trim and known fondly by local residents as "Faded Glory," features original hand-fashioned oak trim inside and numerous gables outside. Each guest rooms is decorated in early twentieth-century style; two rooms have fireplaces. A Victorian parlor and drawing room, each with a fireplace, provide restful places for afternoon tea. In warm weather, tea is served in the gazebo. The Carriage House contains a living room, dining room, kitchen, three bedrooms, and two baths for group vacationers, especially those with children. The former owners of the Wright Inn received two preservation awards for their work on the historic home.

Open: year round **Accommodations:** 9 guest rooms with private baths; 1 carriage-house unit with 3 bedrooms and 2 baths **Meals:** full breakfast included in the inn rates; complimentary refreshments; restaurants nearby **Rates:** $85 to $115; carriage house $190 **Payment:** Visa, MC, personal and traveler's checks **Restrictions:** children over 12 welcome in the inn **Activities:** reading, porch sitting, bicycling (bicycles provided free of charge)

BALSAM

Nearby attractions: Blue Ridge Parkway, Great Smoky Mountain National Park, Smoky Mountain Scenic Railroad, Shining Rock National Wilderness Area, Biltmore Estate, fishing, hiking, white-water rafting

BALSAM MOUNTAIN INN

Balsam Mountain Inn Road (S.R. 1700)
P.O. Box 40
Balsam, North Carolina 28707
704/456-9498
Proprietor: Merrily Teasley

Built in 1908, the year the railroad came to Balsam, Balsam Mountain Inn is situated just above the highest depot east of the Rockies. A symmetrical Colonial Revival structure, it is dominated by broad double-decker porches across the main facade, bounded on each end by three-story towers capped with hipped roofs. At an elevation of 3500 feet, Balsam Mountain Inn provides guests with crisp, cool air and a dramatic view of the surrounding mountains. Many original furnishings remain, including pretty iron beds, wicker chairs, oak rockers, and dressers, but modern comforts have been added along with firm mattresses and springs. Delightful areas to relax and make friends include the wicker- and chintz-filled lobby, game room, library, porches, and dining room, where plentiful meals are served.

Open: year round **Accommodations:** 34 guest rooms with private baths; 3 are suites **Meals:** full breakfast included; restaurant on premises **Wheelchair access:** some guest rooms, dining room, public bathrooms, lobby, library **Rates:** $90 to $150; 10% discount to National Trust members and National Trust Visa cardholders **Payment:** Visa, MC, personal and traveler's checks **Restrictions:** smoking limited; no pets **Activities:** hiking on 26 acres with trails, library, croquet, game room with cards and puzzles

---

BRYSON CITY

Nearby attractions: Great Smoky Mountains National Park, hiking, Nantahala River Gorge, whitewater rafting, Blue Ridge Parkway, Fontana Dam and Reservoir, fishing, boating, Biltmore House, Cherokee Indian Reservation, Great Smoky Mountain Railway, Joyce Kilmer Memorial Forest

FRYEMONT INN
Fryemont Road
P.O. Box 459
Bryson City, North
Carolina 28713
704/488-2159 or 800/
845-4879
Proprietors: Suzette and
George Brown

Opened in 1923, the
Fryemont Inn sits on a
mountain shelf overlooking
the village of Bryson City
and the Great Smoky
Mountains National Park. The inn owes its rustic beauty to Amos Frye, who established a timber empire in the late nineteenth century and built the inn out of chestnut, oak, and maple. The exterior was covered with bark from huge poplar trees. The lodge contains 37 chestnut-paneled guest rooms. No two rooms

are alike in decor, but all have private baths and pocket windows that slide back to let in crisp mountain air. Each suite in the adjacent stone cottage has a loft-bedroom, a living area with fireplace, a television, and a wet bar. Full breakfast and dinner, often featuring mountain trout, are included in the rates. A National Register property, the Fryemont Inn has been praised by the *Atlanta Journal-Constitution*, the *Los Angeles Times*, and the *Miami Herald*.

Open: mid-April to November 1 **Accommodations:** 44 guest rooms with private baths; 7 are suites **Meals:** full breakfast and dinner included **Rates:** $90 to $166 **Payment:** Visa, MC, Discover, personal and traveler's checks **Restrictions:** smoking limited; no pets **Activities:** swimming pool, basketball

---

CASHIERS

Nearby attractions: Chimney Top Mountain, Highlands, shopping, horseback riding, white-water rafting

HIGH HAMPTON INN AND COUNTRY CLUB
N.C. Highway 107 South
P.O. Box 338
Cashiers, North Carolina 28717-0338
Proprietors: William D. McKee, Sr., president, and Will McKee, Jr., vice-president

High Hampton was the summer home of Civil War General Wade Hampton, later governor of South Carolina and U.S. Senator. On 1400 acres in the Cashiers Valley of the Blue Ridge Mountains, at 3600 feet, High Hampton offers today what it did then—mountain breezes, clear lakes, pine forests, picnics, fishing, and solitude. The current inn, a rambling building swathed in shaggy chestnut bark, was built in 1933 by the McKee family. Still family owned and operated, this National Register property offers 130 guest rooms in the inn and adjacent cottages. Rustic simplicity defines the decor. The large lobby has a four-sided stone fireplace; a porch wraps around three sides of the inn, affording mountain views. Three buffet-style meals are served daily. A complete resort, High Hampton offers activities for the whole family, including tennis, golfing, and children's programs, and has been praised by the *New York Times*, *Golf Magazine*, and *Better Homes and Gardens*.

Open: April to December **Accommodations:** 130 guest rooms with private baths, plus 35 2-, 3-, or 4-bedroom Vacation Homes **Meals:** buffet breakfast, lunch, and dinner included on full American Plan (FAP); restaurants nearby **Wheelchair access:** yes **Rates:** $75 to $90 per person FAP **Payment:** AmEx, Visa, MC, personal and traveler's checks **Restrictions:** smoking limited; no pets **Activities:** golfing, tennis, golf and tennis clinics, hiking, bicycling, fitness/exercise trails, 35-acre lake, swimming, boating, fishing, children's programs

CHAPEL HILL

Nearby attractions: University of North Carolina, historic Hillsborough, Raleigh/Durham, Research Triangle Park, Burlington outlet shops, fishing

INN AT BINGHAM SCHOOL
P.O. Box 267
Chapel Hill, North Carolina 27514
919/563-5583 or 800/566-5583
919/563-9826
Proprietors: François and Christina Deprez
Location: 11 miles west of Chapel Hill

Bingham School was a preparatory school that operated from 1845 to 1865. The school is no longer standing, but the headmaster's house, listed in the National Register of Historic Places, has received an award for its meticulous restoration. A combination of Greek Revival and Federal styles, the early nineteenth-century house contains five spacious guest rooms with private baths. Guests will find thick bathrobes, designer soaps, and homemade cookies in their rooms. One guest room offers a pencil-post canopy bed, another has a whirlpool tub. Elaborate breakfasts include such entrees as pear-almond waffles or baked German pancakes. Guests are invited to relax on a porch, roam the surrounding woodlands, swing in a hammock, or play a game of croquet. Books, games, and old movies are provided for indoor entertainment.

Open: year round **Accommodations:** 5 guest rooms with private baths; 1 is a suite **Meals:** full breakfast included; complimentary wine and cheese; dinner available with 3-day advance notice; restaurants nearby **Rates:** $75 to $110; 10% discount to National Trust members and National Trust Visa cardholders **Payment:** AmEx, Visa, MC, personal and traveler's checks **Restrictions:** no smoking; no pets **Activities:** croquet, hammocks, books, games, porch rockers

ELLERBE

Nearby attractions: Seagrove Pottery Village, Town Creek Indian Mount, North Carolina Zoological Park, Pinehurst golfing, Morrow Mountain State Park, Rankin Museum of American Heritage, North Carolina Motor Speedway, antiques hunting

ELLERBE SPRINGS INN

2537 North Highway 220
Ellerbe, North Carolina 28338
910/652-5600 or 800/248-6467
Proprietor: Beth Cadieu-Diaz
Location: 70 miles south of Greensboro, 75 miles southeast of Charlotte

In 1820, Captain William F. Ellerbe, South Carolina plantation owner, purchased 300 acres of land surrounding the natural mineral springs here and built a summer home. After the Civil War the property was sold to a group of investors, who built a boarding house and a dozen summer cottages, thus creating the Ellerbe Springs resort. The present Colonial Revival inn was built in 1906. Victorian antiques accent the lobby, restaurant, and guest rooms, each with private bath. Two guest suites with fireplaces are in the Guest Cottage, formerly known as the Murdock McAskill House. The grounds of this National Register property also contain a picnic pavilion, the 90-year-old springhouse (used for meetings and dances), the gazebo-covered natural spring, tennis courts, a five-acre lake, and a jogging trail. Breakfast, lunch, and dinner are available in the spacious dining room.

Open: year round **Accommodations:** 15 guest rooms with private baths; 3 are suites **Meals:** restaurant on premises **Wheelchair access:** limited **Rates:** $48 to $94 **Payment:** AmEx, Visa, MC, Discover, personal and traveler's checks **Restrictions:** no smoking; no pets **Activities:** tennis, lake fishing, jogging/walking trail, murder-mystery weekends

---

HERTFORD

Nearby attractions: historic Edenton, Hope Plantation, Somerset Plantation, Newbold–White house, golfing, canoeing

BEECHTREE INN

Route 1, Box 517 (Pender Road)
Hertford, North Carolina 27944
919/426-7815
Proprietors: Ben and Jackie Hobbs

Beechtree Inn consists of the rear wing of the Richard Pratt House, built in 1760 by brick mason Richard Pratt; the Bear Swamp House, ca. 1800, with plaster walls, original woodwork, and fireplace; and the Bennetts Creek House, a ca. 1790 frame house with fireplace and loft bedroom. The three buildings are furnished with period reproduction furniture made by the Hobbses in their on-site shop, where furniture-making classes are offered each month. A full breakfast, served in the dining room of the Pratt House, may include country sausage, corn fritters, or pecan waffles. The inn is in a secluded wooded setting, sharing its grounds with 14 pre–Civil War buildings that have been moved here for protection and restoration.

Open: year round **Accommodations:** 3 guest houses with private baths **Meals:** full breakfast included; complimentary refreshments; restaurants nearby **Rates:** $45 to $75; 10% discount to National Trust members and National Trust Visa cardholders **Payment:** personal and traveler's checks **Restrictions:** no smoking **Activities:** bicycles, table tennis, furniture-making classes, studying pre–Civil War buildings

KILL DEVIL HILLS

Nearby attractions: Wright Brothers Memorial, Cape Hatteras National Seashore, Jockey's Ridge State Park, Oregon Inlet Fishing Center, Pea Island Wildlife Refuge, Roanoke Island, North Carolina Aquarium, Fort Raleigh, Elizabethan Gardens, *Queen Elizabeth II*, charter fishing, lighthouses, shipwrecks, bird-watching, beachcombing, sand dunes, wild ponies, golfing, tennis, swimming, sailing, hang gliding, surfing, jet skiing, shopping, art galleries

CHEROKEE INN BED AND BREAKFAST
500 North Virginia Dare Trail
Kill Devil Hills, North Carolina 27948
919/441-6127 or 800/554-2764
Proprietors: Bob and Kaye Combs

This spacious house, 500 feet from the Atlantic Ocean, was built in the 1940s as a hunting and fishing lodge. The interior is notable for its tongue-and-groove paneled cypress walls and ceilings throughout. Guest rooms are made comfortable and cheery with ruffled curtains, ceiling fans, air conditioning, and private baths. The common room provides a restful location for reading, card playing, puzzle solving, and visiting. Fresh-brewed coffee and a continental breakfast are enjoyed in guest rooms or on the wraparound porch. Cherokee Inn is located in the heart of the Outer Banks, affording visitors the chance to sun and swim, fish and sightsee, study nature and history, or just sit back and relax.

Open: April to November **Accommodations:** 6 guest rooms with private baths **Meals:** continental breakfast included; restaurants nearby **Rates:** $60 to $95 **Payment:** AmEx, Visa, MC, personal and traveler's checks **Restrictions:** not suitable for children; no smoking; no pets **Activities:** beach and water sports, reading, games, puzzles, cards, television

NAGS HEAD

Nearby attractions: Jockey's Ridge State Park, Wright Brothers Memorial, Cape Hatteras National Seashore, Oregon Inlet Fishing Center, Pea Island Wildlife Refuge, Roanoke Island, North Carolina Aquarium, Fort Raleigh, Elizabethan Gardens, *Queen Elizabeth II*, charter fishing, lighthouses, shipwrecks, bird-watching, beachcombing, sand dunes, wild ponies, golfing, tennis, swimming, sailing, hang gliding, surfing, jet skiing, shopping, art galleries

FIRST COLONY INN
6720 South Virginia Dare Trail
Nags Head, North Carolina 27959
919/441-2343 or 800/368-9390
Proprietor: Alan Lawrence

Built in 1932 as LeRoy's Seaside Inn, and renamed in 1937, the First Colony Inn is the only remaining beach hotel from Nags Head's early glory days. Slated for demolition in the 1980s, the Shingle-style hotel was saved only by moving it in three pieces nearly four miles down the road. A three-year historic rehabilitation returned the multidormered roof and encircling double veranda to their original appearances, and earned the building a place in the National Register and a preservation award from the Preservation Foundation of North Carolina. A reconfigured interior transformed 60 tiny bedrooms into 26 deluxe rooms plus a breakfast room and elegant library with exposed beams and fireplace. Wet bars or kitchenettes with dishwashers, remote-controlled television and VCR, individual climate control, heated towel bars, and imported toiletries complement antique-filled rooms. The inn has been rated with four diamonds by AAA.

Open: year round **Accommodations:** 26 guest rooms with private baths; 6 are suites **Meals:** continental-plus breakfast included; afternoon tea; restaurants nearby **Wheelchair access:** limited **Rates:** $125 to $220 in season; $75 to $150 off season **Payment:** Visa, MC, Discover, personal and traveler's checks **Restrictions:** no smoking; no pets **Activities:** boardwalk to beach, pool and ocean swimming, croquet, board games, reading, fishing, hot tub

OLD FORT

Nearby attractions: Blue Ridge Parkway, Chimney Rock, Biltmore House, Mt. Mitchell, Lake Lure, Pisgah National Forest, museums, antiques hunting, crafts shops, golfing, hiking, white-water rafting, horseback riding

INN AT OLD FORT
116 West Main Street
P.O. Box 1116
Old Fort, North Carolina 28762
704/668-9384 or 800/471-0637
Proprietors: Debbie and Chuck Aldridge

The Inn at Old Fort was built in 1871 as a summer retreat. Twin, steeply pitched, front gables and pointed-arched windows announce this two-story, frame house's style as Gothic Revival. It is one of the best remaining examples of the style in McDowell County. Located on more than three acres, the house is surrounded by terraced lawns and gardens that were created when the house was built. Furnished with antiques, the house has been extensively renovated and now welcomes overnight guests to its comfortable accommodations. Rooms may be rented individually with private baths or may be combined to create a two-bedroom suite with den and private bath. Guests are invited to relax in the library, parlor, garden, and on the rocker-filled front porch.

Open: year round **Accommodations:** 4 guest rooms with private baths; 1 is a suite **Meals:** continental-plus breakfast included; complimentary refreshments; restaurants nearby **Rates:** $45 to $90; 10% discount to National Trust members and National Trust Visa cardholders **Payment:** personal and traveler's checks **Restrictions:** no smoking **Activities:** porch rocking, garden walks and sitting areas, croquet, library, parlor games

---

SALISBURY

Nearby attractions: historic districts, Civil War sites, historic railroad yard

ROWAN OAK HOUSE
208 South Fulton Street
Salisbury, North Carolina 28144
704/633-2086 or 800/786-0437
Proprietors: Barbara and Les Coombs

Milton S. Brown, a wealthy merchant, built this Queen Anne home for his bride in 1901. Attention to detail is evident in the carved oak door surrounded by stained glass. There are seven tiled fireplaces, each with a uniquely carved mantel;

one is bird's-eye maple and another features the ribbon-and-leaf motif found on the front of the house and in the stained-glass Palladian window in the library. Guest rooms are furnished with antiques, historically patterned wallpaper, down comforters, reading lights, fruit, and fresh flowers. Rowan Oak House, with its octagonal cupola, is located in Salisbury's 13-block historic district.

Open: year round **Accommodations:** 4 guest rooms (2 have private baths) **Meals:** full breakfast included; complimentary refreshments; restaurants nearby **Rates:** $75 to $110; 10% discount offered to National Trust members and National Trust Visa cardholders **Payment:** Visa, MC, personal check **Restrictions:** not suitable for children; smoking limited; no pets **Activities:** television, reading, puzzles, garden strolling, porch sitting

---

VALLE CRUCIS

Nearby attractions: USS *North Carolina*, golfing, swimming, tennis, boating, historic house tours, fishing, canoeing, downhill skiing, craft fairs, hiking

MAST FARM INN
Camp Broadstone Road
P.O. Box 704
Valle Crucis, North Carolina 28691
704/963-5857
704/963-6404 Fax
Proprietors: Sibyl and Francis Pressly

The Mast Farm has been operated as an inn since the early 1900s by descendants of the Mast family, who built this mountain home in 1885. Placed in the National Register of Historic Places as one of the best examples of a self-contained mountain homestead in North Carolina, the 18-room farmhouse has been restored by the current innkeepers, along with a two-room log cabin, and a variety of outbuildings. Originally a 13-bedroom, 1-bath house, it now has 9 guest rooms, 7 with private baths. Guest accommodations are also available in the Loom House, Blacksmith Shop, and Woodwork Shop. Rooms are furnished with plain, turn-of-the-century antiques and are tastefully decorated with mountain crafts and fresh flowers. Mast Farm Inn has been featured in *Country* magazine, the *New York Times*, and on the PBS television series "Inn County USA."

Open: May through February **Accommodations:** 12 guest rooms (10 have private baths); 3 are suites **Meals:** continental-plus breakfast and dinner included on modified American Plan (MAP); restaurant on premises **Wheelchair access:** 1 room **Rates:** $95 to $175 MAP **Payment:** Visa, MC, Discover, personal check **Restrictions:** children over 12 welcome; no smoking; no pets **Activities:** fishing, walking, vegetable and flower gardens

WILMINGTON

Nearby attractions: Cape Fear Museum, USS *North Carolina*, beaches, riverfront shops, antiques hunting, Old Cotton Exchange, Chandler's Wharf

TAYLOR HOUSE INN
14 North Seventh Street
Wilmington, North Carolina 28401
910/763-7581 or 800/382-9982 (reservations)
Proprietor: Glenda Moreadith

Located in the Wilmington Historic District, Taylor House Inn is the 1908 home of John Allen Taylor, a local merchant. The house's quaint Victorian style is accentuated by golden oak fireplace mantels and inlaid parquet and heart-of-pine floors. Four guest rooms offer a variety of accommodations, ranging from the Jacobean Room with king-size bed to the Garden Room with its brass bed and fireplace. All rooms contain private baths and sitting areas. The innkeeper serves a candlelit breakfast on bone china and crystal. Guests are welcomed in the public rooms and on the front porch with swings and high-backed rocking chairs. Taylor House Inn was the setting for the movie *Against Her Will*.

Open: year round **Accommodations:** 4 guest rooms with private baths; 1 is a suite **Meals:** full breakfast included; complimentary refreshments; restaurants nearby **Rates:** $65 to $85; 10% discount to National Trust members and National Trust Visa cardholders **Payment:** AmEx, Visa, MC, personal check **Restrictions:** children over 12 welcome; no smoking; no pets **Activities:** reading, card playing, puzzles, porch rocking and swinging, music on compact discs

WILSON

Nearby attractions: antiques hunting, Arts Council, Imagination Station (children's science museum), Tobacco Farm Life Museum, Doctor's Museum, tennis, golfing, swimming

MISS BETTY'S BED AND BREAKFAST INN
600 West Nash Street
Wilson, North Carolina 27893-3045
919/243-4447 or 800/258-2058
Proprietors: Betty and Fred Spitz

Wilson, known as the "antique capital of North Carolina," is a fitting site for Miss Betty's Bed and Breakfast Inn, an 1858 Italianate home listed in the National Register of Historic Places with carved eave brackets and detailed window surrounds. A multicolored paint scheme highlights the house's decorative trim, especially on the porch, which spans the front facade. Selected as one of the "best places to stay in the South," in the guidebook by the same name, the inn also includes the adjacent Riley House (circa 1900) and the 1943 house known as Rosebud. Located in Wilson's downtown historic district, Miss Betty's offers 10 Victorian-styled guest rooms and three spacious parlors. One parlor is also available for small weddings. Six covered porches provide ample space to relax and enjoy the mature trees and shrubs of the landscaped grounds.

Open: year round **Accommodations:** 10 guest rooms with private baths; 3 are suites with king-size beds **Meals:** full breakfast included; restaurants nearby **Rates:** $50 single to $75 double **Payment:** AmEx, Visa, MC, CB, DC, Discover, personal and traveler's checks **Restrictions:** not suitable for children; smoking limited; no pets **Activities:** cable television with remote control in each room, VCR available, classic film library, reading, board games, American Victorian antiques for sale

WINSTON-SALEM

Nearby attractions: Old Salem National Register historic district, Museum of Early Southern Decorative Arts, Revolutionary War military park, Reynolda Village, Tanglewood Park, tennis, swimming, hiking, golfing

AUGUSTUS T. ZEVELY INN
803 South Main Street
Old Salem
Winston-Salem, North Carolina 27101
910/748-9299 or 800/928-9299
Proprietor: John Seitz

Augustus Theophilus Zevely purchased this house in 1845, a year after its construction. The symmetrical brick house is a contributing structure in the National Register village known as Old Salem, founded by the Moravian religious sect in 1766. Zevely began using his house as an inn in 1848; that use continued until around 1900. After nearly a century as a tenement and apartment house, Zevely's house received a museum-quality restoration in 1993. The Zevely Inn is furnished today with Old Salem licensee's furniture, fixtures, accessories, textiles, and floor coverings. Each individually decorated guest room has a private bath, television, radio-alarm clock, and built-in hairdryer. Some rooms have fireplaces, whirlpool tubs, steam baths, refrigerators, and microwaves. The parlor and dining room each contain a corner fireplace, a characteristic of Moravian architecture. A two-story porch at the rear of the building is comfortable even on cool days, due to its radiant-heated floors.

Open: year round **Accommodations:** 12 guest rooms with private baths; 1 is a suite **Meals:** full breakfast included on weekends; continental-plus breakfast included weekdays; complimentary refreshments; restaurants nearby **Wheelchair access:** yes **Rates:** $80 to $185; 10% discount to National Trust members and National Trust Visa cardholders **Payment:** AmEx, Visa, MC, personal and traveler's checks

COLONEL LUDLOW INN
434 Summit at West Fifth Street
Winston-Salem, North Carolina 27101
910/777-1887 or 800/301/1887
910/777-1890 Fax
Proprietor: Ken Land

The Colonel Ludlow Inn comprises two neighboring Victorian homes: the 1887 Queen Anne–styled Jacob Lott Ludlow House and the 1895 Benjamin Joseph Sheppard House. Located in the West End historic district, both homes are listed in the National Register of Historic Places. Guest rooms are furnished with Victorian antiques accented by works of art, books, fresh flowers, and plants. Nearly all rooms have king-size beds and whirlpool tubs, and all feature a stereo system with a wide selection of tapes, television and VCR, telephone, coffeemaker, iron, hair dryer, microwave, and mini-refrigerator. Some rooms have working fireplaces. Bathrobes have been thoughtfully provided by the innkeeper, as are a full breakfast, a morning newspaper, and in-room movies. Guests can walk to restaurants, shops, and parks.

Open: year round **Accommodations:** 9 guest rooms with private baths; 3 are suites **Meals:** full breakfast included; restaurants nearby **Rates:** $89 to $189 **Payment:** AmEx, Visa, MC, Discover, personal and traveler's checks **Restrictions:** children over 12 welcome; no pets **Activities:** exercise room, recreation room with bar and pool table

OHIO

CINCINNATI

Nearby attractions: King's Island, downtown Cincinnati, picturesque Mariemont village for strolling and shopping, pond, parks, convention center

BEST WESTERN MARIEMONT INN
6880 Wooster Pike
Cincinnati, Ohio 45227
513/271-2100 or 800/528-1234
Proprietor: Bonnie Malone, General Manager

The Cincinnati suburb of Mariemont was designed and constructed in the 1920s as a planned community modeled after English country villages. It was envisioned as a rural alternative to nearby Cincinnati. Now a Cincinnati suburb listed in the National Register of Historic Places, Mariemont is still a quaint village of English Tudor-style commercial buildings and quiet, tree-lined residential neighborhoods. At the Tudor-style Mariemont Inn, guest rooms contain four-poster or canopy beds and Queen Anne chairs, along with antiques and portraits of British royalty. Massive beams stretch across the ceilings, and polished dark wood accents

each room. Modern amenities include television and hair dryers. Hearty meals and grog are served up in the National Exemplar restaurant and Southerby's Pub.

Open: year round **Accommodations:** 60 guest rooms with private baths; 2 are suites **Meals:** restaurant and pub on premises **Rates:** $49 to $84; 10% discount offered to National Trust members and National Trust Visa cardholders **Payment:** AmEx, Visa, MC, Discover, CB, DC, personal and traveler's checks **Restrictions:** no pets

POLAND

Nearby attractions: historic Poland Village, boyhood home of President William McKinley; Village Woods with hiking, jogging, and cross-country skiing trails; Mill Creek Park with golfing, tennis, walking trails, and gardens; Butler Institute of American Art; Amish country; antiques hunting

INN AT THE GREEN
500 South Main Street
Poland, Ohio 44514
216/757-4688
Proprietors: Ginny and Steve Meloy
Location: 7 miles southeast of Youngstown

The Inn at the Green, an 1876 Second Empire home notable for its steeply pitched mansard roof and decorative eave brackets, sits on a slight rise at the southern end of the Poland Village green in a National Register historic district. Its interior architecture is dignified by 12-foot-high ceilings, wood moldings, five fireplaces, interior window shutters, and original poplar floors. Three of the four guest rooms have working fireplaces, and all are furnished with four-poster beds and antiques. The inn's various public rooms are furnished with original American art, antiques, and oriental rugs. The greeting room and parlor contain working fireplaces. A pantry with sink, refrigerator, and microwave is available for guests. An enclosed porch and an English perennial garden with deck and patio offer outdoor relaxation.

Open: year round **Accommodations:** 4 guest rooms with private baths **Meals:** continental breakfast included; complimentary refreshments; restaurants nearby **Rate:** $60; 10% discount offered to National Trust members and National Trust Visa cardholders **Payment:** Visa, MC, personal and travlers checks **Restrictions:** no pets **Activities:** library, piano, classical music on compact disc, audiotape library with players in rooms, room televisions, video collection, lawn games, garden

WILLIAMSBURG

Nearby attractions: East Fork State Park, Rocky Fork State Park, Riverbend Amphitheater, Cincinnati Nature Center, downtown Cincinnati, boating, fishing, swimming, horseback riding, hunting

LEWIS McKEVER FARMHOUSE BED AND BREAKFAST
4475 McKeever Pike
Williamsburg, Ohio 45176
513/724-7044
Proprietors: John and Carol Sandberg
Location: 30 miles east of Cincinnati

This elegant example of rural Italianate architecture was built in 1841 by Lewis McKever, a prominent businessman, farmer, and horse breeder. The two-story farmhouse was part of the Underground Railroad during the Civil War and was forced to host some of Morgan's raiders when they passed through Williamsburg. Listed in the National Register of Historic Places, the bed and breakfast is located on 10 acres of rolling fields and woods. Three spacious guest rooms have private baths and queen beds, air conditioning, and ceiling fans. The library has an inviting fireplace and a second-floor porch is a comfortable alternative to the spacious dining room for breakfast.

Open: year round **Accommodations:** 3 guest rooms with private baths **Meals:** continental-plus breakfast included; complimentary refreshments; restaurants nearby **Rate:** $65 **Payment:** Visa, MC, personal and traveler's checks **Restrictions:** inquire about children; no smoking; no pets **Activities:** walking paths, country tranquility

WORTHINGTON

Nearby attractions: Ohio State University, Ohio State Fair, Columbus Museum of Art, Center of Science and Industry, Worthington Historical Society, Columbus Zoo, Olentangy Indian Caverns, skiing, hiking, jogging, shopping, swimming

WORTHINGTON INN
649 High Street
Worthington, Ohio 43085
614/885-2600
Proprietors: Steve and Susan Hanson

The Worthington Inn was built as a residence in 1834 by Rensselaer W. Cowles. After Cowles's death, the house was enlarged by the new owner and became a stagecoach stop on the toll road, and later a hotel. Originally a Federal structure, it was altered numerous times, and after a fire in 1901, the third floor and mansard roof were added. This National Register property has recently been renovated and provides guest rooms handsomely appointed with vintage furnishings and antiques, personally collected by the owners in a five-state search. Reproductions of rich textiles and period wallpapers complete the turn-of-the-century effect. A full-service restaurant specializes in regional American cuisine. The Worthington inn has been featured in *Country Inns* magazine and has received Mobil's four-star award.

Open: year round **Accommodations:** 26 guest rooms with private baths; 5 are suites **Meals:** full breakfast included; complimentary refreshments; restaurant on premises; restaurants nearby **Wheelchair access:** yes **Rates:** $140 to $215; 10% discount to National Trust members and National Trust Visa cardholders **Payment:** AmEx, Visa, MC, DC, Discover, personal and traveler's checks **Restrictions:** smoking limited; no pets

OKLAHOMA

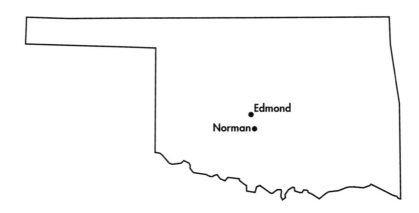

EDMOND

Nearby attractions: University of Central Oklahoma, antiques hunting, theaters, tearooms, golfing, tennis, swimming, Oklahoma City, Guthrie

ARCADIAN INN
328 East First
Edmond, Oklahoma 73034
405/348-6347 or 800/299-6347
Proprietors: Gary and Martha Hall

This Queen Anne home of A. M. Ruhl was built in 1908. In 1928 Dr. Ruhl had the home raised 12 feet and built another story beneath it, resulting in the three-story house that is now the Arcadian Inn. Six guest rooms are decorated in sumptuous Victorian style with yards of lace, velvet, and satin, brass, and canopy beds, claw-foot and whirlpool tubs, bubble bath, and candles. Some rooms have fireplaces. All guests are invited to relax in the parlor, on the wraparound porch, or in the garden spa. Breakfast can be served privately in guest rooms or in the dining room beneath a ceiling painting of angels by a local artist. Arcadian Inn is the 1991 winner of the Edmond Historic Preservation Award.

Open: year round **Accommodations:** 6 guest rooms with private baths; 4 are suites **Meals:** full breakfast included; restaurants nearby **Rates:** $85 to $195; 10% discount to National Trust members and National Trust Visa cardholders **Payment:** AmEx, Visa, MC, Discover, personal check **Restrictions:** not suitable for young children; no smoking; no pets **Activities:** whirlpool tubs, garden spa

NORMAN

Nearby attractions: DeBarr Historic District, University of Oklahoma, Campus Corner, Oklahoma Museum of Natural History, Cowboy Hall of Fame, Thunderbird Lake

HOLMBERG HOUSE BED AND BREAKFAST

766 DeBarr
Norman, Oklahoma 73069
405/321-6221
Proprietors: Jo Meacham and Richard Divelbiss

Located in Norman's National Register historic district across the street from the University of Oklahoma campus, this handsome 1914 Craftsman house was built by Professor Fredrik Holmberg and his wife, Signy. The current innkeepers bought the house in 1993 and it now provides overnight accommodations for many of the university's visiting scholars and students' parents. Each of the four guest rooms is individually decorated with antiques and has a private bath with claw-foot tub, and color cable television. A parlor with fireplace, porches with rockers, and gardens are available for guest use. A full breakfast is served in the formal dining room.

Open: year round **Accommodations:** 4 guest rooms with private baths **Meals:** full breakfast included; restaurants nearby, 15 within walking distance **Rates:** $55 to $85; 10% discount to National Trust members and National Trust Visa cardholders **Payment:** AmEx, Visa, MC, Discover, personal and traveler's checks **Restrictions:** no smoking; no pets **Activities:** parlor games, edible gardens, rest and relaxation

OREGON

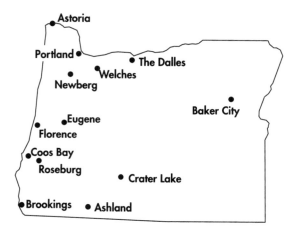

ASHLAND

Nearby attractions: historic district, Oregon Shakespeare Festival, Britt Music Festival, Natural History Museum, Crater Lake National Park, fishing, downhill and cross-country skiing, Rogue and Klamath Rivers, rafting, wineries, historic Jacksonville, golfing, tennis, horseback riding

HERSEY HOUSE
451 North Main Street
Ashland, Oregon 97520
503/482-4563 or 800/482-4563
Proprietors: Gail E. Orell and K. Lynn Savage

Hersey House was built in 1904 for William and Ella Breeden. In 1916, James and Carrie Hersey purchased the house, where several generations of their family lived for the next 60 years. The house blends elements of two architectural styles: patterned shingles on the gables and porch reflect the late Queen Anne period, and the porch's substantial, grouped, boxed columns are reminiscent of Craftsman houses. All original interior woodwork remains, including baseboards with distinctive quarter-turned finial detailing in the corners. Today, as a bed and breakfast, Hersey House is filled with family treasures, such as an early twentieth-century Victrola and record collection, a player piano, and many books about Oregon and its history. Antique furnishings distinguish each of the comfortable guest rooms.

Open: May 1 to November 1 **Accommodations:** 4 guest rooms with private baths **Meals:** full breakfast included; restaurants nearby **Rates:** $85 to $125; 10% discount offered to National Trust members and National Trust Visa cardholders **Payment:** Visa, MC, personal and traveler's checks **Restrictions:** children over 12 welcome; no smoking; no pets (kennel nearby) **Activities:** parlor games, player piano, sundeck, croquet

IRIS INN

59 Manzanita Street
Ashland, Oregon 97520
503/488-2286 or
800/460-7650
Proprietor: Vicki Lamb

A beautiful iris design in the front door's stained-glass window gives this 1905 Victorian frame house its name. Five guest rooms are delicately decorated with antique iron beds, flower-printed fabrics and wallpapers, and antique oak, maple, and wicker furniture. Private bathrooms contain thoughtful touches of hospitality, including terry robes. Elegant and creative breakfasts start the day. Specialties include peaches-and-cream French toast and apple pancakes. The inn is situated in a quiet neighborhood with views of the Rogue Valley and the Grizzly and Siskiyou Mountains. Guests often spend time relaxing on the deck overlooking these sights and the inn's own rose garden.

Open: year round **Accommodations:** 5 guest rooms with private baths **Meals:** full breakfast included; complimentary refreshments; restaurants nearby **Rates:** $60 to $98; 10% discount offered to National Trust members and National Trust Visa cardholders **Payment:** Visa, MC, personal and traveler's checks **Restrictions:** children over 7 welcome; no smoking; no pets

MORICAL HOUSE
668 North Main Street
Ashland, Oregon 97520
503/482-2254 or 800/208-0960
503/482-1775 Fax
Proprietors: Gary and Sandye Moore

This 1882 frame farmhouse is dressed up by patterned shingles in the front gable, leaded- and stained-glass windows, original red fir floors, and finely crafted woodwork. With the Cascade Mountains providing the backdrop, the dining room and enclosed sunporch overlook an acre of grounds filled with flowers and trees. In the afternoon refreshments are served in the parlor or on the sun porch. Five guest rooms are uniquely decorated with period furniture, comforters, quilts, and family heirlooms. All rooms have mountains views and private baths with brass fixtures. Two additional bedrooms are in the garden carriage house. Each of these offers a king-size bed, fireplace, wet bar, microwave, and refrigerator. Morical House is one mile from the downtown plaza in historic Ashland.

Open: year round **Accommodations:** 7 guest rooms with private baths **Meals:** full breakfast included; complimentary refreshments; restaurants nearby **Wheelchair access:** 2 rooms **Rates:** $76 to $150; 10% discount to National Trust members and National Trust Visa cardholders **Payment:** Visa, MC, Discover, personal and traveler's checks **Restrictions:** children over 12 welcome; no smoking; no pets **Activities:** bird-watching, sundeck

---

ASTORIA
Nearby attractions: Fort Clatsop, museums, walking tour of historic homes, Pacific Ocean beaches, Astoria Column

MARTIN AND LILLI FOARD HOUSE
690 17th Street
Astoria, Oregon 97103
503/325-1892
Proprietor: Melissa A. Yowell

Martin and Lilli Foard built this Queen Anne house in 1892. Its exterior is replete with an array of patterned shingles and wood siding, its asymmetrical shape determined by a dual-arched front porch, bay windows, gables, and second-story porches. The interior is authentically Victorian with original fixtures, wainscoting, woodwork, and antiques, all overseen by the Foard's great-granddaughter, Melissa Yowell. Two charming guest rooms share a bath. Accommodations are available only on Friday and Saturday nights and nights preceding holidays. The Foard House is in a neighborhood of historic homes on a hill overlooking the Columbia River and is included in Astoria's walking tour. Listed in the National Register of Historic Places, Foard House appears in the book *America's Painted Ladies: The Ultimate Celebration of Our Victorians.*

Open: February to November, Friday and Saturday nights only **Accommodations:** 2 guest rooms share a bath **Meals:** continental-plus breakfast included; restaurants nearby **Rate:** $48 **Payment:** personal and traveler's checks **Restrictions:** children over 10 welcome; no smoking; no pets **Activities:** garden, reading, music

BAKER CITY

Nearby attractions: downtown historic district, Oregon Trail Interpretive Center, Hells Canyon National Recreation Area, Sumpter Dredge State Park, Sumpter Valley Railroad, Oregon Trail Regional Museum, Phillips Lake, downhill skiing, hiking, bicycling, swimming, boating

GRANT HOUSE BED AND BREAKFAST
2525 Third Street
Baker City, Oregon 97814
503/523-6685
Proprietor: Diane Pearson

The oldest part of the Grant House was built in 1881 as the Catholic parish hall, located next to the cathedral on First Street. Tom E. Grant, builder of the cathedral, bought the building and moved it to its present location and converted it to a home for his family, who lived there for more than 50 years. The 12-room Tudor house is dominated by steep front and side gables decoratively finished with half-timbering. The Arts-and-Crafts-style interior is furnished with antiques. Three individual bedrooms are named after area mines: Blue Bucket, Rosebud, and Maiden's Dream. Guests are welcome in the upstairs sitting room, downstairs living room, and hot tub in the rock garden. Full breakfasts include fresh-baked goods.

Open: year round **Accommodations:** 3 guest rooms share a bath **Meals:** full breakfast included; restaurants nearby **Rates:** $65 to $70; 10% discount to National Trust members and National Trust Visa cardholders **Payment:** Visa, MC, personal and traveler's checks **Restrictions:** no smoking; no pets **Activities:** hot tub, musical performances on piano, guitar, violin, and percussion instruments—guests are invited to join in

BROOKINGS

Nearby attractions: Pacific Ocean, beaches, Chetco River, Azalea Park, redwood forests, mountains, Oregon Caves, swimming, fishing, hiking, camping, boating, golfing, museums, performing arts center, festivals, antiques hunting, crafts shops

SOUTH COAST INN BED AND BREAKFAST
516 Redwood Street
Brookings, Oregon 97415
514/469-5557 or 800/525-9273
514/469-6615 Fax
Proprietors: Ken Raith and Keith Pepper

Located on Oregon's rugged, unspoiled southern coast, the South Coast Inn was built in 1917 by William Ward, president of the Brookings Lumber Mill. San Francisco architect Bernard Maybeck designed the house in the Craftsman style, expressed by its low-pitched, multiple gabled roofs, overhanging eaves, and exposed roof beams. The 4000-square-foot inn offers a reading parlor with stone fireplace and vintage grand piano, indoor hot tub and sauna, protected sundecks, and four antiques-filled bedrooms, two with ocean views. All bedrooms contain queen-size beds, ceiling fans, and television. The innkeepers serve a full breakfast in the dining room. The style of the South Coast Inn is tailored, the atmosphere is relaxed.

Open: year round **Accommodations:** 4 guest rooms with private baths **Meals:** full breakfast included; restaurants nearby **Rates:** $74 to $94; 10% discount to National Trust members and National Trust Visa cardholders **Payment:** AmEx, Visa, MC, Discover, personal and traveler's checks **Restrictions:** children over 12 welcome; no smoking; no pets **Activities:** hot tub, sauna, television

---

COOS BAY

Nearby attractions: Coos Bay, boardwalk, beaches, tide pools, Oregon Dunes Recreational Area, botanical gardens, antiques hunting, art museum, whale watching, seal rookery, hunting, lighthouses, festivals

COOS BAY MANOR BED AND BREAKFAST (NERDRUM HOUSE)
955 South Fifth Street
Coos Bay Oregon 97420
503/269-1224 or 800/269-1224
Proprietor: M. Patricia Williams

This National Register–listed Colonial Revival house was built in 1912 by two Finnish brothers, the Nerdrums, who worked for the C. A. Smith Lumber

Company. The house has a unique open-air bannister that surrounds the second floor, detailed woodwork throughout, high ceilings, and spacious rooms. Five individually styled guest rooms are offered: the Victorian Room with lace, ruffles, and a canopied bed; the Cattle Baron's Room with authentic bear and coyote rugs; the Country Room, with brass bed and handmade quilts; the Garden Room, with white rattan furnishings; and the Colonial Room, with two twin four-poster beds. The grounds include giant redwood trees and a rhododendron garden. The innkeeper serves a generous specialty breakfast.

Open: year round **Accommodations:** 5 guest rooms (3 have private baths) **Meals:** continental-plus breakfast included; restaurants nearby **Rates:** $65 to $75; 10% discount to National Trust members and National Trust Visa cardholders **Payment:** personal and traveler's checks **Restrictions:** children over 4 welcome; no smoking; mannerly pets welcome

CRATER LAKE

Nearby attractions: Crater Lake, boat tours, back country camping, hiking, wildlife viewing, Diamond Lake, downhill and cross-country skiing, Lost Creek Reservoir

CRATER LAKE LODGE
565 Rim Village Drive
P.O. Box 128
Crater Lake, Oregon 97604
503/594-2255 (summer) or 503/830-8700 (winter)
503/594-2622 (summer) Fax or 503/830-8514 (winter) Fax
Director of Sales: Michael Romick

At 1932 feet deep, Crater Lake is the deepest lake in the United States and the seventh deepest in the world. Its depth and clarity account for the blue brilliance of its waters. Along the south side of the lake is the lodge, built between 1909 and 1924. The mammoth stone-and-shingle lodge served the public until 1989, when it was closed due to years of snow damage. The National Park Service restored the lodge and reopened it in 1995. Seventy-one guest rooms are available, each with its own character and style. Many offer spectacular views of the lake. All guest rooms have private baths—some with claw-foot tubs. Rustic stone walls and fireplaces, hardwood floors, and beamed ceilings define the public rooms. The terrace affords vistas of the sun setting on the crater—or caldera—rim. The lodge restaurant serves elegant Northwest cuisine and there are other dining options in the adjacent Rim Village.

Open: May to October **Accommodations:** 71 guest rooms with private baths; 4 are suites **Meals:** restaurant on premises; restaurants nearby **Wheelchair access:** yes **Rates:** $99 to $119 **Payment:** Visa, MC, personal and traveler's checks **Restrictions:** no smoking; no pets **Activities:** boat tours, hiking, cross-country skiing, showshoeing, gift shop

EUGENE

Nearby attractions: Hult Center for the Performing Arts, 5th Street Public Market, Autzen Stadium, University of Oregon, bicycling, Pre's Trail jogging path, white-water rafting, fishing, golfing, wineries

THE CAMPBELL HOUSE, A CITY INN

252 Pearl Street
Eugene, Oregon 97401
503/343-1119 or 800/264-2519
503/343-2258 Fax
Proprietor: Myra Plant

The Campbell House was built in 1892 by gold miner and timber baron John Cogswell for his daughter Idaho and her husband, Ira Campbell. One of Eugene's most lavish homes, Campbell House is located on the east side of Skinner's Butte, overlooking downtown Eugene. The house features original hardwood floors, bay windows, high ceilings, and a unique curved corner window. Each of the elegantly styled guest rooms has a private bath, hidden television with VCR, and telephone. Selected rooms also feature a gas fireplace, four-poster bed, and claw-foot or whirlpool tub. Campbell House offers specialty packages such as birthday tea parties for little girls, Victorian high teas, murder-mystery parties, and a holiday package that includes a limousine tour of Christmas lights and dinner on the town.

Open: year round **Accommodations:** 14 guest rooms with private baths; 2 are suites **Meals:** full breakfast included; complimentary refreshments and coffee room service; restaurants nearby **Wheelchair access:** 1 guest room **Rates:** $75 to $225; 10% discount to National Trust members and National Trust Visa cardholders **Payment:** AmEx, Visa, MC, traveler's check **Restrictions:** no smoking; no pets

FLORENCE

Nearby attractions: Old Town Florence, Siuslaw River, ocean beaches, lakes, fishing, swimming, crabbing, clamming, mushrooming, bicycling, bird-watching, horseback riding, whale-watching, golfing

JOHNSON HOUSE
216 Maple Street
Florence, Oregon 97439
503/997-8000 or 800/768-9488
Proprietors: Jayne and Ronale Fraese

Johnson House, the oldest house in Florence, was built in 1892 for Dr. O. F. Kennedy, who lived here until 1907. It served as a private residence for several owners, the last of whom were Milo and Cora Johnson, who made it their home for 60 years. The clapboard house, with its minimal decorative detailing, reflects the warm, plain living style of the Oregon coast of a century ago. Antique furnishings in every room are complemented by original prints and photographs. Beds are dressed in top-quality linens and down comforters and pillows. Guests are provided with a daily newspaper and diverse current periodicals. A gourmet breakfast may include a soufflé, salmon crepes, a frittata, or an omelette aux fines herbes. The Johnson House garden provides, in season, flowers for all rooms, as well as herbs, strawberries, cherries, blueberries, and apples served with breakfast.

Open: year round **Accommodations:** 6 guest rooms (3 have private baths) **Meals:** full breakfast included; complimentary refreshments; restaurants nearby **Wheelchair access:** guest rooms, bathrooms, dining facilities **Rates:** $75 to $105; 10% discount offered to National Trust members and National Trust Visa cardholders **Payment:** Visa, MC, personal and traveler's checks **Restrictions:** young children discouraged; no smoking; no pets **Activities:** croquet, boccie

NEWBERG

Nearby attractions: wineries, hot-air ballooning, bicycling, antiques hunting, Portland

SPRINGBROOK HAZELNUT FARM

30295 North Highway 99W
Newberg, Oregon 97132
503/538-4606 or 800/793-8528
Proprietors: Chuck and Ellen McClure

Springbrook Hazelnut Farm, with its four matching Craftsman-style buildings dating from 1912, is listed in the National Register of Historic Places. The main residence has a spectacular entry hall extending from the covered front porch to the comfortably furnished back porch. A glassed-in sunporch is filled with plants and wicker furniture. Breakfast is served in the paneled dining room. Four guest rooms provide views of the pond or gardens. The carriage house has a master bedroom, adjoining bath with claw-foot tub, a living room, and a kitchen. The buildings are nestled among 10 acres of gardens and enormous old trees. The grounds are further enhanced by a pool, tennis court, and pond, complete with canoe and resident blue heron. Beyond the garden is a 60-acre hazelnut orchard, through which guests can walk to the adjoining winery.

Open: year round **Accommodations:** 5 guest rooms (3 have private baths); 1 is a suite **Meals:** full breakfast included; restaurants nearby **Rates:** $90 to $135; 10% discount to National Trust members and National Trust Visa cardholders **Payment:** personal and traveler's checks **Restrictions:** inquire about children; no smoking; no pets **Activities:** swimming pool, tennis court, pond with canoe, orchard walking

PORTLAND

Nearby attractions: Oregon Historical Society museum, Performing Arts Center, Riverplace, YMCA, historic conservation district, Oregon Health Science Center, Portland State University, parks, Mt. Hood, Mt. St. Helens, jogging tracks, shopping, convention center, ocean beaches, wineries

GENERAL HOOKER'S BED AND BREAKFAST

125 S.W. Hooker Street
P.O. Box 69292
Portland, Oregon 97201
503/222-4435 or 800/745-4135
503/295-6410 Fax
Proprietor: Lori Hall

Built in 1888 and condemned in 1975, General Hooker's house has been rehabilitated to accommodate travelers in style and comfort. A simple Victorian with just enough gingerbread to be interesting, General Hooker's is located on a quiet, residential street just a few minutes from downtown Portland. Rooms are eclectically furnished, blending antiques and rattan with custom-made batik quilts, modern art, neutral colors, and textured fabrics. The effect produced is an airy, contemporary feeling in a comfortable, old setting. The parlor fireplace provides warmth in winter; air conditioning and a roof deck accommodate the guest in summer. A guest refrigerator, a large videotape library, and a relaxed attitude complete the package. The innkeeper is a fourth-generation Portlander and an excellent source of local information. General Hooker's is recommended by AAA.

Open: year round **Accommodations:** 4 guest rooms (2 have private baths) **Meals:** continental-plus breakfast included; complimentary refreshments; restaurants nearby **Rates:** $65 to $105 single occupancy (add $10 for double); corporate rates available **Payment:** AmEx, Visa, MC, personal and traveler's checks **Restrictions:** children over 10 welcome; no smoking; no pets (resident cat) **Activities:** view from roof deck; telephones, cable television, and VCRs in rooms; videotape library; regional and local reference library

JOHN PALMER HOUSE BED AND BREAKFAST INN

4314 North Mississippi Avenue
Portland, Oregon 97217
503/284-5893
503/284-1239 Fax
Proprietors: Mary, Richard, and David Sauter

This elaborate Queen Anne residence was erected in 1890 by builder John Palmer. The house delights the eye with its fish-scale shingles, lacy wrought-iron roof cresting, decorative vergeboards, and porches and balconies dripping with gingerbread and spindles. Inside this National Register house, Victorian furnishings provide an elegant and relaxing atmosphere, which is carried through to the bedrooms, decorated with much attention to detail. Walls are covered with 1880-period wallpapers by Christopher Dresser and William Morris. The gas-electric light fixtures, with their ceiling medallions, reflect the colors in the original stained-glass windows. Leisurely breakfasts are served daily. Like the Victorians, guests may "take the waters," meaning today that a relaxing hot tub is in the gazebo.

Open: year round **Accommodations:** 5 guest suites with private baths **Meals:** full breakfast included; high tea and dinner available; restaurants nearby **Rates:** $45 to $125 **Payment:** AmEx, Visa, MC, Discover, personal and traveler's checks **Restrictions:** no smoking; no pets **Activities:** reading, piano, hot tub, high teas, seasonal carriage transport to city center and return

PORTLAND GUEST HOUSE
1720 N.E. 15th Avenue
Portland, Oregon 97212
503/282-1402
Proprietor: Susan Gisvold

Located in the historic Irvington neighborhood, just 10 minutes from downtown, the Portland Guest House is in an 1890 Queen Anne home, complete with patterned wall shingles and bay windows. The entire house is open to guests, who sleep on vintage linens in seven antiques-filled guest rooms. Summer guests can enjoy breakfast among the roses at garden tables. Omelets are flavored with fragrant herbs from the garden. Home-grown blueberries and strawberries are also served. Winter visitors sit before a crackling fireplace to enjoy such items as banana chocolate chip muffins or Grand Marnier French toast. The guest house offers off-street parking and is convenient to public transportation.

Open: year round **Accommodations:** 7 guest rooms (5 have private baths); 3 are suites **Meals:** full breakfast included; restaurants nearby **Rates:** $45 to $75 single; $55 to $85 double **Payment:** travelers and personal checks preferred; AmEx, Visa, MC require 5% extra charge **Restrictions:** no smoking; no pets **Activities:** herb, flower, and vegetable gardens, patio, deck

ROSEBURG

Nearby attractions: Umpqua River, Crater Lake, museums, fishing, rafting, art galleries, wineries, antiques hunting, Wildlife Safari

HOKANSON'S GUEST HOUSE
848 S.E. Jackson
Roseburg, Oregon 07470
503/672-2632
503/673-5253 Fax
Proprietors: John and Victoria Hokanson

The land on which this house stands was once owned by Roseburg's founding father, Aaron Rose. The house, built in 1882 in the Gothic Revival style, is Douglas county's only bed and breakfast listed in the National Register of Historic Places. The steep front gable and dormers are fitted with decorative vergeboards and topped with finials. The house has been fully restored by the innkeepers. Two upstairs guest rooms share a common sitting room. Each bedroom has a private bath with claw-foot tub. The Marietta Room contains original vertical-grained fir walls, a king-size and a double bed, and handmade quilts. The Frances Room features period oak furniture, including a high-backed bed. The Hokanson's children and Fritz the cat are in residence at the Guest House.

Open: year round **Accommodations:** 2 guest rooms with private baths **Meals:** full breakfast included; restaurants nearby **Rates:** $65 to $85; 10% discount to National Trust members and National Trust Visa cardholders **Payment:** Visa, MC, personal and traveler's checks **Restrictions:** children over 11 welcome; no smoking; no pets **Activities:** piano, porch with swing, pond, garden, parlor games and puzzles

---

THE DALLES

Nearby attractions: wind surfing, white-water rafting, golfing, hiking, skiing, fishing, swimming, tennis, historical walking tours

WILLIAMS HOUSE INN
608 West Sixth Street
The Dalles, Oregon 97058
503/296-2889
Proprietors: Don and Barbara Williams

Williams House was built in 1899 by Judge Alfred Bennet, who served on the Supreme Court of Oregon. He sold the house in 1926 to Mr. and Mrs. Edward M. Williams, descendants of an early pioneer family and parents of the current innkeeper. The inn is a large Queen Anne Victorian, occupying its own wooded hilltop in historic The Dalles, which is located in the Columbia River Gorge. Inside Williams House, a National Register property, the innkeepers display a collection of early Chinese objets d'art. One bedroom contains Victorian antiques; the other features a Georgian-period canopy bed and highboy; both rooms have private balconies. The three-room suite features an original marble-topped basin and claw-foot tub. Guests are invited to enjoy the comfortable parlor, with its games and tables and warm fire in winter.

Open: year round **Accommodations:** 3 guest rooms (2 have private baths); 1 is a suite **Meals:** full breakfast included; restaurants nearby **Rates:** $65 to $75 **Payment:** AmEx, Visa, MC, Discover, personal and traveler's checks **Restrictions:** no smoking; no pets **Activities:** parlor games, reading, musical instruments, photography, rest and relaxation

---

WELCHES

Nearby attractions: Mt. Hood, Hoodland Recreation Area, downhill and cross-country skiing, mountain climbing, fishing, hiking, golfing, museums

OLD WELCHES INN BED AND BREAKFAST
26401 East Welches Road
Welches, Oregon 07067
503/622-3754
Proprietors: Judith and Ted Mondun

Old Welches Inn was built in 1890 by Samuel Welch and his son Billy. They operated it as the first summer resort and hotel on Mt. Hood until the late 1930s, when the structure was converted to a single-family home. The Monduns have renovated the traditionally styled, Colonial Revival inn, offering comfortable lodging in three individually decorated guest rooms. Beds may be sleigh, cannonball, or iron. A two-bedroom, one-bath cottage with fully equipped kitchen and river-rock fireplace is adjacent to the inn. Dating to 1901, it was the first cottage built at the old summer resort. Breakfast in the dining room overlooks the Salmon River. Wildflower gardens fill the grounds surrounding Old Welches Inn.

Open: year round **Accommodations:** 3 guest rooms share 2 baths; 1 suite with private bath **Meals:** full breakfast included; complimentary refreshments; restaurants nearby **Rates:** $79.50 to $94.50; 10% discount to National Trust members and National Trust Visa cardholders **Payment:** AmEx, Visa, MC, Discover, personal and traveler's checks **Restrictions:** children over 12 welcome; no smoking; well-trained dogs allowed **Activities:** river fishing

PENNSYLVANIA

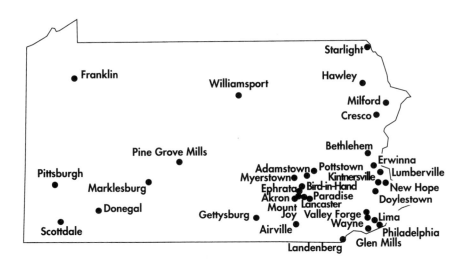

ADAMSTOWN

Nearby attractions: antiques hunting, Pennsylvania Dutch country, Amish farms, Reading outlet shops, hiking and bicycling trails, golfing, tennis, swimming

ADAMSTOWN INN
62 West Main Street
Adamstown, Pennsylvania 19501
717/484-0800 or 800/594-4808
Proprietors: Tom and Wanda Berman

Although this house was built in the early nineteenth century, it was remodeled in 1925, resulting in this handsome two-story, hipped roof house with broad wraparound porch supported by stout columns. Leaded-glass windows and doors were added, as well as elegant chestnut woodwork. The innkeepers renovated the house in 1988, refinishing the woodwork and hardwood floors, adding modern baths, and papering walls in Victorian motifs. Today's guest rooms are decorated with family heirlooms, handmade quilts, lace curtains, and fresh flowers. All rooms have private baths; two feature two-person whirlpool tubs. Each day begins with hot beverages waiting at guest room doors. A continental-plus breakfast that includes muffins, sweet breads, cheeses, or sausage balls, is served downstairs. Adamstown Inn is located in a small town brimming with antiques dealers and is only minutes from Reading and Lancaster.

Open: year round **Accommodations:** 4 guest rooms with private baths; 1 is a suite **Meals:** continental-plus breakfast included; complimentary refreshments; restaurants nearby **Rates:** $65 to $105; 10% discount to National Trust members and National Trust Visa cardholders **Payment:** Visa, MC, personal and traveler's checks **Restrictions:** children over 12 welcome; no smoking; no pets (resident dog) **Activities:** picnic area, lawn games

AIRVILLE

Nearby attractions: Amish country, horseback riding, fishing, swimming, canoeing, wineries, antiques hunting, golfing, scenic railroad rides, museums, auctions

SPRING HOUSE
1264 Muddy Creek Forks Road
Airville, Pennsylvania 17302
717/927-6906
Proprietor: Ray Constance Hearne
Location: in Muddy Creek Forks, 5 miles south of Brogue and Route 74

Built of local fieldstone in 1798 by Pennsylvania legislator Robert Turner, Spring House was for years the main residence of the village of Muddy Creek Forks, first settled in the 1730s. Now listed in the National Register of Historic Places, the house is situated over and protects an abundant spring, the village's main source of water. The house has massive, 26-inch-thick fieldstone walls that have been restored inside to their original whitewash and stenciling. Spring House offers local wine and Amish-made cheeses to travelers. Sunlit guest rooms, furnished with country antiques and handwoven rugs, are made cozy with feather beds in winter and freshened by fragrant breezes in summer. The porch swing is a relaxing place to take in the beautiful rural setting and scenic Muddy Creek.

Open: year round **Accommodations:** 5 guest rooms (3 have private baths) **Meals:** full breakfast included; complimentary refreshments; restaurants nearby **Rates:** $60 to $85; 10% discount offered to National Trust members and National Trust Visa cardholders **Payment:** personal and traveler's checks **Restrictions:** no smoking; pets can be accommodated outside or in nearby kennels (resident dog and cats) **Activities:** bird-watching, herb gardening, porch swing, rockers, games, library, music room

---

AKRON

Nearby attractions: Amish farms, Ephrata Cloister, antiques hunting, outlet shops, Hershey, tennis, swimming

SPRINGHOUSE INN BED AND BREAKFAST
806 New Street
Akron, Pennsylvania 17501
717/859-4202
Proprietors: Ray and Shirley Smith

Built in 1797, Springhouse Inn is a typical Lancaster County farmhouse. It boasts original hardware, bubble-glass windows, and random-width pine floors. Beams and joists are joined with wooden pegs. Attic floorboards are 16 inches wide. Stone walls, deep windows, and a walk-in firepalce are features of the cellar. Guest rooms include the Dickens Room, with vintage wardrobe and antique chandelier; Gatsby Room, with twin-size pineapple beds and fringed lampshades; or Poet's Corner, with queen-size spindle bed. Quiet, intimate breakfasts are served at small tables. Guests are invited to stroll through the acre of lawns, where the pure spring from which the inn takes its name flows. It is said that Springhouse Inn may be haunted by the ghosts of several young owners who died soon after occupying the residence.

Open: year round **Accommodations:** 3 guest rooms (2 have private baths) **Meals:** full breakfast included; complimentary refreshments; restaurants nearby **Rates:** $55 to $75 **Payment:** Visa, MC, personal check **Restrictions:** no smoking

BETHLEHEM

Nearby attractions: historic Bethlehem, Lehigh University, Moravian College, Binney and Smith Museum

WYDNOR HALL INN
3612 Old Philadelphia Pike
Bethlehem, Pennsylvania 18015
610/867-6851 or 800/839-0020
610/866-2062 Fax
Proprietors: Kristina and Charles Taylor

Wydnor Hall Inn, a late Georgian (ca. 1810) fieldstone manor, is located on the historic Old Philadelphia Pike, minutes from Lehigh University and Bethlehem's restored district. Wydnor Hall Inn is noted for its impeccable service, from coffee trays and morning newspapers outside bedroom doors to the varied and unusual breakfast menu and afternoon tea. Guests are pampered with down bedding, terrycloth robes, and freshly pressed linens. Each guest room is equipped with telephone, television, private baths, and central air conditioning. The atmosphere of an elegant private club is evident in everything from a breakfast table set with silver and Herend china to the homemade breads, cakes, and rich pastries served at tea time.

Open: year round **Accommodations:** 5 guest rooms with baths; 1 is a suite with private steam room **Meals:** continental-plus breakfast included; full breakfast menu on weekends; restaurants nearby **Rates:** $75 to $130 **Payment:** AmEx, Visa, MC, CB, DC, personal and traveler's checks **Restrictions:** children welcome with prior notice; smoking limited; small dogs allowed by prior arrangement

BIRD-IN-HAND

Nearby attractions: Lancaster County, Amish farms, farmers' market, quilt and crafts shops, outlet shops, antiques hunting, golfing, Gettysburg, Hershey

VILLAGE INN OF BIRD-IN-HAND
2695 Old Philadelphia Pike
P.O. Box 253
Bird-in-Hand, Pennsylvania 17505
717/293-8369
717/768-1511
Proprietors: John E. Smucker and George and Pat Desmond

The Old Philadelphia Pike was surveyed and built in 1734, the same year the Village Inn of Bird-in-Hand was built. The inn is a three-story brick building; its facade features an unusual second-story porch with fretwork railings, supported by turned Tuscan columns. A Quaker by the name of William McNabb was the inn's first proprietor. Today, the inn still welcomes guests traveling along the pike. Each guest room has a private bath and deluxe down-filled bedding. Four rooms are suites, three with king-size beds, two with whirlpool baths, one with a working wood stove, and one with a fireplace. The decor is in the Victorian tradition. Breakfast is served on the sunporch. Guests can enjoy free use of indoor and outdoor swimming pools and tennis courts located within walking distance of the inn. A complimentary tour of the surrounding Amish farmlands is offered daily.

Open: year round **Accommodations:** 11 guest rooms with private baths; 4 are suites **Meals:** continental breakfast included; complimentary refreshments; restaurants nearby **Rates:** $59 to $139 **Payment:** AmEx, Visa, MC, Discover, personal and traveler's checks **Restrictions:** smoking limited; no pets

CRESCO

Nearby attractions: Pocono Mountains, state parks, waterfalls, Lake Wallenpaupack, boating, hiking, golfing, swimming, tennis, downhill and cross-country skiing

LA ANNA GUEST HOUSE
R.R. 2, Box 1051
Cresco, Pennsylvania 18326
717/676-4225
Proprietor: Kathryn Gilpin Swingle
Location: 8 miles north of Cresco in village of LaAnna

In 1877, Kay Swingle's grandfather, Civil War veteran and owner of the Gilpin lumber mill, built this Victorian farmhouse of hemlock clapboards. He adorned the house with an elaborately trimmed wraparound porch, which stands intact today. Mrs. Swingle, who grew up in this house and raised her own family here, has maintained the house in much the same fashion as when her grandparents were living, furnishing rooms with their Victorian and Empire furniture, oriental rugs, and Victorian reproduction wallpapers. Both guest rooms look out on a pond, where guests are invited to paddle the inn's canoe. Strolling the grounds, guests will encounter breathtaking views of waterfalls and surrounding mountains.

Open: year round **Accommodations:** 2 guest rooms share a bath **Meals:** continental-plus breakfast included; restaurants nearby **Rates:** $30 to $40 **Payment:** personal and traveler's checks **Restrictions:** no smoking; no pets **Activities:** hiking, fishing, canoeing, cross-country skiing

---

DONEGAL

Nearby attractions: Frank Lloyd Wright's Fallingwater, Laurel Highlands, Fort Ligonier, Fort Necessity, skiing (Hidden Valley and Seven Springs), hiking, golfing, white-water rafting

MOUNTAIN VIEW BED AND BREAKFAST INN
Mountain View Road (Exit 9, Pennsylvania Turnpike)
Donegal, Pennsylvania 15628
412/593-6349 or 800/392-7773
Proprietors: Gerard and Lesley O'Leary

Mountain View, a classically styled farmhouse built in 1853, is located on 10 acres of the Pennsylvania land patent given to John Alexander in 1788 and witnessed by Benjamin Franklin. The property was then defined as "Alexandria." The house's windows still contain original hand-blown glass, and the interior retains original moldings, doors, and a carved walnut center-hall staircase. Guest rooms in the farmhouse as well as in the adjacent converted barn are furnished with eighteenth- and early nineteenth-century American antiques. Mountain View is in a quiet, pastoral setting with a magnificent view of the surrounding Laurel Mountains.

Open: year round **Accommodations:** 6 guest rooms (3 have private baths) **Meals:** full breakfast included; restaurants nearby **Wheelchair access:** some guest rooms, dining facilities **Rates:** $95 to $150 **Payment:** AmEx, Visa, MC, CB, DC, Discover, personal and traveler's checks **Restrictions:** children over 10 welcome; no smoking; no pets

DOYLESTOWN

Nearby attractions: Mercer Museum, Moravian Tileworks, Delaware River, New Hope, Peddler's Village, antiques hunting, crafts shops, hiking, river tubing, swimming, sailing, bicycling, horseback riding, tennis, golfing, skiing

INN AT FORDHOOK FARM
105 New Britain Road
Doylestown, Pennsylvania 18901
215/345-1766
Proprietors: Jonathan Burpee and Blanche Burpee Dohan

For more than 100 years Fordhook Farm has been the private home of W. Atlee Burpee, founder of the Burpee Seed Company, and his family. Nine major historic buildings constitute Fordhook Farm. Three of these are used for the inn: the main house, which began as a typical mid-eighteenth-century Pennsylvania fieldstone farmhouse; the two-story carriage house, built in 1868 and converted into a private library in 1915 (it features a Gothic-style great room with exposed beams and rafters and chestnut paneling); and the converted Bucks County–style barn. Guest rooms and common areas are filled with family antiques, furnishings, and mementos. There are 60 acres of meadows, woodlands, gardens, and seed-development trial grounds to explore.

Open: year round **Accommodations:** 7 guest rooms (5 have private baths); 2 have working fireplaces; 2 are suites **Meals:** full breakfast included; complimentary refreshments; restaurants nearby **Rates:** $100 to $300; 10% discount offered to National Trust members and National Trust Visa cardholders except in October **Payment:** AmEx, Visa, MC, personal and traveler's checks **Restrictions:** children over 12 welcome; no smoking; no pets **Activities:** gardens, paths through meadows and woods, badminton, croquet, cross-country skiing, tobogganing

PINE TREE FARM

2155 Lower State Road
Doylestown, Pennsylvania 18901
215/348-0632
Proprietors: Ron and Joy Feigles
Location: 1 mile west of Doylestown

Pine Tree Farm is a 1730 Bucks County fieldstone farmhouse on 16 acres that were part of William Penn's original grant. The house has had numerous additions throughout the years, resulting in a meandering floor plan. Fireplaces are found throughout the home; the one in the library is framed by Delft tiles, and the fireplace in an upstairs sitting room has Moravian tiles made in Doylestown. Each guest room is furnished with a queen-size bed, a convenient writing desk, and a telephone, if desired. Turn-down service in the evening is standard. Guests enjoy the inn's library, solarium, living room, and kitchen with its stocked pantry. The inn puts forth a fresh country look with coordinating colors and fabrics, shining brass, American antiques, and fresh flowers.

Open: year round **Accommodations:** 3 guest rooms with private baths **Meals:** full breakfast included; complimentary refreshments; restaurants nearby **Rates:** $135 to $160 **Payment:** personal check **Restrictions:** not suitable for children; no smoking; no pets **Activities:** swimming pool, 16 acres with pond and wildlife

SIGN OF THE SORREL HORSE

4424 Old Easton Road
Doylestown, Pennsylvania 18901
215/230-9999 or 800/BUCK-CTY (800/282-5289)
215/230-8053 Fax
Proprietors: Monique Gaumont and Jon Atkin
Location: 5 miles south of Quakertown

The Sign of the Sorrel Horse hangs on this 1714 gristmill, which supplied flour to Washington's troops and provided lodging for Lafayette and his officers during the Revolution. Today, the mill is an inn offering six guest rooms decorated in traditional American and French antiques, queen-size four-poster beds, and collectibles that reflect the inn's history. The rustic Sign of the Sorrel Horse is best known for its gourmet restaurant, which received *Food and Wine* magazine's 1992–1993 Distinguished Restaurant of the Year award and was named "Best Inn Dining of the Year" for 1993–1994 by *Country Inns Bed and Breakfast*. With innovative French-Continental cuisine prepared by master chef Jon Atkin and Monique Gaumont, a Cordon Bleu graduate, the restaurant has received accolades from the *New York Times*, *Philadelphia Inquirer*, *Gourmet*, and *Country Inns*.

Open: year round except March **Accommodations:** 5 guest rooms with private baths **Meals:** continental breakfast included; restaurant on premises **Rates:** $85 to $175; 10% discount offered to National Trust members and National Trust Visa cardholders **Payment:** AmEx, Visa, MC, CB, DC, personal and traveler's checks **Restrictions:** not suitable for children; smoking limited; no pets **Activities:** garden weddings are a specialty of the inn

EPHRATA

Nearby attractions: Ephrata Cloister; Pennsylvania Farm Museum; Pennsylvania Dutch country; historical sites; museums; farmers' market; art studios and galleries; shopping for antiques, collectibles, and fine fashions

HISTORIC SMITHTON INN
900 West Main Street
Ephrata, Pennsylvania 17522
717/733-6094
Proprietors: Dorothy Graybill and Allan Smith

The people of the religious Ephrata Cloister community built this inn in 1763; it has taken in guests ever since. Big square guest rooms are bright and airy and can be lighted by candles during evening hours. Each room has a working fireplace and a sitting area with comfortable leather-upholstered chairs, reading lamps, and a writing desk. Canopy or four-poster beds are made up with goose-down pillows and handmade Pennsylvania Dutch quilts. All rooms are provided with chamber music, books, and a refrigerator. Night shirts are available for guests to wear, and fresh flowers are in every room. Leisurely evenings can be enjoyed before the fire in the great room or in the adjacent library. Antiques and gleaming hardwood floors unite each room in the inn.

Open: year round **Accommodations:** 8 guest rooms with private baths; 1 is a suite **Meals:** full breakfast included; complimentary refreshments; restaurants nearby **Wheelchair access:** 1 room **Rates:** $65 to $170 **Payment:** AmEx, Visa, MC, personal and traveler's checks **Restrictions:** well-mannered, supervised children welcome; no smoking; well-trained, supervised pets allowed **Activities:** library, gardens, fountains and fish pond, parlor games

1777 HOUSE AT DONECKERS
301 West Main Street
Ephrata, Pennsylvania 17522
800/377-2217
Proprietor: H. William Donecker

Named after the year of its construction, the 1777 House at Doneckers is a stately, late-Georgian home built by Jacob Gorgas, a clockmaker in the religious Ephrata Cloister community located in scenic Lancaster County. Later the house was run as a tavern for travelers in Conestoga wagons en route from Philadelphia to Pittsburgh. A careful restoration has retained the structure's original stone masonry, handsome tile flooring, and many other authentic architectural details. Guest rooms (some with fireplaces) are named for brothers and sisters of the cloister, and are decorated with beautiful linens, fine antiques, and hand-cut stenciling. For the comfort of guests, the 1777 House has added queen-size beds and whirlpool baths in many rooms. The adjacent Carriage House offers two suites with lofts.

Open: year round **Accommodations:** 12 guest rooms with private baths; 6 are suites **Meals:** continental-plus breakfast included; restaurants nearby **Wheelchair access:** some guest rooms, dining room **Rates:** $69 to $175 **Payment:** AmEx, Visa, MC, CB, DC, Discover, personal and traveler's checks **Restrictions:** no pets

---

ERWINNA

Nearby attractions: antiques hunting, historic sites, galleries, museums, parks, canoeing, horseback riding, bicycling, rafting, shopping

EVERMAY ON-THE-DELAWARE
River Road
Erwinna, Pennsylvania 18920
610/294-9100
610/294-8249 Fax
Proprietors: Ronald L. Strouse and Frederick L. Cresson

Evermay, constructed in the 1700s, then remodeled and enlarged in 1871, is listed in the National Register of Historic Places. Its three stories are covered in clapboard, its facade evenly punctuated by rows of shuttered windows. A broad porch spans the first level. Evermay on-the-Delaware was a popular riverfront resort from 1871 until the 1930s, frequented by prominent families, including the theatrical Barrymores. The inn is located on 25 acres of pastures, woodlands, and gardens. Guest rooms with private baths are furnished with collectibles and antiques from the Victorian era as well as fresh flowers and fruit. Some guest rooms are contained in the restored carriage house. Afternoon tea is served in the parlor or on the patio.

Open: year round **Accommodations:** 16 guest rooms with private baths; 1 is a two-bedroom suite **Meals:** continental-plus breakfast included; complimentary refreshments and afternoon tea; restaurant on premises serving dinner **Wheelchair access:** carriage house guest rooms, dining rooms **Rates:** $85 to $170; 10% discount offered to National Trust members and National Trust Visa cardholders **Payment:** Visa, MC, personal and traveler's checks **Restrictions:** children over 12 welcome; smoking limited; no pets **Activities:** strolling grounds and gardens, hiking, bicycling, Delaware River swimming and fishing

---

FRANKLIN

Nearby attractions: walking tour of historic district, DeBence Antique Music World, Barrow Civic Theater, Oil Creek–Titusville Railroad, Allegheny River, bicycling, canoeing, fishing, hunting

QUO VADIS BED AND BREAKFAST

1501 Liberty Street
Franklin, Pennsylvania 16323
814/432-4208 or
800/360-6598
Proprietors: Allan and Janean Hoffman

Quo Vadis, listed individually and as a contributing structure to a historic district in the National Register of Historic Places, is an 1867 Queen Anne house built by lawyer Samuel Plumer. Detailed woodwork and friezes, parquet floors, and terra-cotta tile distinguish the house. Later owned by David Barcroft, the house contains heirloom furniture that has been owned now by his family for four generations. David and Anna Barcroft's daughters, Grace and Maude, made all the quilts, embroidery, and crocheting that are in Quo Vadis today. Also remaining is their hand-painted china. Spacious guest rooms with private baths are offered. The town of Franklin, celebrating its bicentennial in 1995, is noted for its Victorian architecture, and the historic area has recently been designated as the Oil Region Heritage Park by the state of Pennsylvania.

Open: year round **Accommodations:** 6 rooms with private baths **Meals:** full breakfast included; restaurants nearby **Rates:** $60 to $80 **Payment:** AmEx, Visa, MC, personal and traveler's checks **Restrictions:** no smoking; no pets **Activities:** piano, Victrola, games, books

GETTYSBURG

Nearby attractions: Gettysburg Battlefield; Lancaster Amish farms; skiing; golfing; antiques hunting; winery tours; Codorus State Park for swimming, boating, fishing, hiking, bicycling, golfing, and horseback riding

BEECHMONT INN
315 Broadway, Route 194
Hanover, Pennsylvania
17331
717/632-3013 or
800/553-7009
Proprietors: William and Susan Day
Location: 13 miles east of Gettysburg

Restored to its Federal-period elegance, Beechmont Inn offers traditional hospitality to visitors to historic Hanover and Gettysburg. The 1834 house has changed little except for a pantry and side porch added in 1900. The additions mirror the style of the main section with matching brick and woodwork. Guests at Beechmont can relax in the parlor, the library, or the quiet, formally landscaped courtyard. A winding staircase leads to guest rooms named in honor of the Civil War generals who fought at the Battle of Hanover; the rooms are appointed with period furnishings. Suites with working fireplaces may also feature whirlpool tubs or balconies. Breakfasts feature Beechmont's own granola (which took a prize at the York Fair) and gourmet entrees such as sausage crepes with corn soufflé or herb cheese tart with ambrosia cup.

Open: year round **Accommodations:** 7 guest rooms with private baths; 3 are suites **Meals:** full breakfast included; complimentary refreshments; restaurants nearby **Rates:** $80 to $135 **Payment:** AmEx, Visa, MC, Discover, personal and traveler's checks **Restrictions:** children over 12 welcome; no smoking; no pets **Activities:** honeymoon, anniversary, and golf packages available

BRAFFERTON INN
44 York Street
Gettysburg, Pennsylvania 17325
717/337-3423
Proprietors: Jane and Sam Back

In 1786 James Gettys bought 116 acres of farmland from his father. Soon after, he erected this fieldstone house and the village of Gettysburg was born. Today, this National Register stone structure and an adjoining nineteenth-century brick-and-clapboard building house the Brafferton Inn. A National Register home, it has been fully restored to show off its original woodwork, hardwood floors, wall stenciling, and fireplaces. During the Battle of Gettysburg in 1863 a bullet shattered the glass in an upstairs window of the house, lodging in the fireplace mantel, where it remains. Guest rooms, retaining the flavor of colonial times, are comfortably furnished with handmade quilts, pine antiques, samplers, and nineteenth-century wall hangings. Guests often gather in the atrium, garden, or patio. The Brafferton has been featured in *Country Living* and *Early American Life*.

Open: year round **Accommodations:** 10 guest rooms with private baths; 2 are suites **Meals:** full breakfast included; complimentary refreshments; restaurants nearby **Rates:** $85 to $125; 10% discount to National Trust members and National Trust Visa cardholders, Sunday through Thursday **Payment:** Visa, MC, personal and traveler's checks **Restrictions:** children over 8 welcome; smoking limited; no pets **Activities:** reading, relaxation

MULBERRY FARM
616 Flohrs Church Road
Biglerville, Pennsylvania 17307
717/334-5827
Proprietors: Mimi and James Agard
Location: 8 miles west of Gettysburg

In the summer of 1863, Robert E. Lee and his army passed directly in front of the house on Mulberry Farm on their march to and retreat from the Battle of Gettysburg. Now the 1817 Georgian farmhouse has been restored by the innkeepers, who received an award from the Adams County Historical Society for their work. Pine floors, protected by stenciled floor mats and braided and oriental rugs, are found throughout the house, which is decorated with early pine and cherry antiques. The large living room/library contains matching fireplaces. Guest rooms are decorated individually with antiques and collectibles. A decorative mantel over the fireplace is the focal point of the dining room, where breakfast is served on Wedgwood china. The inn sits on more than four acres in the orchard-lined foothills of the Appalachian Mountains, surrounded by perennial gardens, lawns, and mulberry trees.

Open: year round **Accommodations:** 4 guest rooms with private baths; 1 is a suite **Meals:** full breakfast included; restaurants nearby **Rates:** $90 to $125; 10% discount to National Trust members and National Trust Visa cardholders **Payment:** personal check **Restrictions:** no smoking; no pets **Activities:** garden, orchards, lawn

GLEN MILLS

Nearby attractions: Brandywine River Museum, Longwood Gardens, Winterthur, Franklin Mint

SWEEETWATER FARM
50 Sweetwater Road
Glen Mills, Pennsylvania 19342
610/459-4711
610/358-4945 Fax
Proprietors: Grace LeVine and Richard Hovsepian

Surrounded by 50 acres of fields and farmland, at the end of a winding country road lined by a canopy of trees, lies this stone Georgian mansion, built in 1734. The six guest rooms are appointed with country antiques, four-poster and canopied beds, wildflowers, and handmade quilts. The house's colonial country ambience is enhanced by working fireplaces throughout. A full breakfast features farm fresh-eggs and country sausage. Guests are encouraged to wander about the farm to enjoy its horses and sheep, herb and flower gardens, and in-ground pool.

Open: year round **Accommodations:** 6 guest rooms with private baths **Meals:** full breakfast included; restaurants nearby **Rates:** $145 to $250; 10% discount to National Trust members and National Trust Visa cardholders **Payment:** AmEx, Visa, MC **Restrictions:** no smoking

---

HAWLEY

Nearby attractions: Poconos, Lake Wallenpaupack, swimming, boating, golfing, picnicking, blueberry picking, antiques hunting, theater

ACADEMY STREET BED AND BREAKFAST
528 Academy Street
Hawley, Pennsylvania 18428
717/226-3430
Proprietor: Judith Lazan

Academy Street Bed and Breakfast is an outstanding Italianate Victorian built in 1863 by Civil War Captain, Joseph Atkinson, whose family was one of the earliest settlers in the Wayne County-Hawley area. Atkinson was discharged after being badly wounded at Gettysburg and became the first Sheriff of Wayne County. Conveniently located near beautiful recreational Lake Wallenpaupack and all its activities, the inn boasts antique-furnished rooms throughout. All guest rooms are large, bright, and air conditioned. The innkeeper, an avid cook, serves a full gourmet buffet breakfast and afternoon high tea.

Open: May to October **Accommodations:** 6 guest rooms (3 have private baths) **Meals:** full breakfast included; complimentary refreshments; restaurants nearby **Rates:** $65 to $80; 10% discount offered to National Trust members and National Trust Visa cardholders **Payment:** Visa, MC **Restrictions:** children over 12 welcome; smoking limited; no pets

KINTNERSVILLE

Nearby attractions: New Hope, Peddler's Village, Pearl Buck home, Mercer Museum, Michner Art Museum, Delaware Canal Museum, historic Bethlehem, antiques hunting, arts and crafts galleries, Nockamixon State Park for horseback riding, swimming, fishing, cross-country skiing, and sailing

LIGHTFARM
2042 Berger Road
Kintnersville, Pennsylvania 18930
610/847-3276 or 610/VIP-FARM (610/847-3276)
Proprietors: Max and Carol Sempowski

The stone farmhouse on this historic Bucks County plantation was built ca. 1815 on a quiet country road. A 1784 deed lists the property as "Lightfarm," which was owned by Solomon and Anna Maria Lightcap. Four period guest rooms are dedicated to this founding family. An archeological dig (featured in the October 1992 issue of *Early American Life*) is located at the stone foundation of the farm's early log cabin. Artifacts found there, and on display to guests, reveal the lifestyle of the Lightcap family. Guests are invited to relax by the open-hearth fire in the common room. The house is surrounded by a 92-acre working farm that includes sheep and flower gardens. Guests enjoy fresh, seasonal foods from the farm for breakfast, which features Pennsylvania Dutch fare.

Open: year round **Accommodations:** 4 guest rooms with private baths; 1 is a suite **Meals:** full breakfast included; complimentary refreshments; restaurants nearby **Rates:** $99 to $140; 10% discount to National Trust members and National Trust Visa cardholders **Payment:** AmEx, Visa, MC, personal and traveler's checks **Restrictions:** no smoking **Activities:** nature walks, farm chores, Lightfarm Artifact Museum, historic preservation and archeology lectures, open-hearth cooking (by reservation), cross-country skiing, relaxing in the garden porch spa

---

LANCASTER

Nearby attractions: Amish country tours, antiques and quilt auctions, villages of Bird-in-Hand and Intercourse, Valley Forge, Gettysburg, Winterthur, Longwood Gardens, Hershey, historic walking tours, museums, outlets shops, golfing

AUSTRALIAN WALKABOUT INN
837 Village Road
P.O. Box 294
Lancaster, Pennsylvania 17537
717/464-0707
Proprietors: Richard and Margaret Mason

Originally a Mennonite farmhouse, Walkabout Inn was built in 1925 by a local cabinetmaker. He used solid chestnut for the doors and trim throughout and for the floor-to-ceiling kitchen cabinets. Evidence of his skill is seen in the wood floors, which are laid in decorative patterns. The inn, now owned by an Australian family, is a British-style bed and breakfast located in the heart of Amish country. All guest rooms contain antique furnishings, Pennsylvania Dutch quilts, and hand-painted wall stenciling. Breakfast at the inn is served by candlelight on silver and crystal. Featured are the innkeeper's homemade Australian and British pastries, muffins, and jellies. Guests relax on the wraparound porch, sipping a cup of imported Australian tea while watching the Amish buggies go by and enjoying the grounds, which feature Australian and American wildflower gardens and a mermaid fountain.

Open: year round **Accommodations:** 6 guest rooms with private baths; 1 is a suite **Meals:** full breakfast included; restaurants nearby **Rates:** $79 to $189; 10% discount offered to National Trust members and National Trust Visa cardholders **Payment:** AmEx, Visa, MC, personal and traveler's checks **Restrictions:** children over 12 welcome; no smoking; no pets **Activities:** croquet, badminton, sunbathing in garden or park behind inn, outdoor whirlpool in cedar-lined spa house, picnics, barbecues, three-hour car-cassette tours of the Amish countryside

KING'S COTTAGE, A BED AND BREAKFAST INN
1049 East King Street
Lancaster, Pennsylvania 17602
717/397-1017 or 800/747-8717
717/397-3447 Fax
Proprietors: Karen and Jim Owens

Listed in the National Register of Historic Places, King's Cottage is a 1913 Spanish Mission-style mansion with its red-tiled roof, widely overhanging eaves, and parapeted entryway. Recipient of the C. Emlen Urban Award for Historic Preservation, King's Cottage features a sweeping staircase, Art Deco fireplaces, and crystal chandeliers. Guest rooms are furnished with antiques and reproduction pieces, dhurrie carpets over hardwood floors, and comfortable sitting areas. Queen- and king-size beds are brass, four-poster, canopied, Victorian, or Art Deco. Several rooms are favored by original stained-glass windows. Full breakfasts are served family style and afternoon tea is served in the library.

Open: year round **Accommodations:** 9 guest rooms with private baths **Meals:** full breakfast included; complimentary afternoon tea; restaurants nearby **Wheelchair access:** separate honeymoon cottage **Rates:** $80 to $160; 10% discount to National Trust members and National Trust Visa cardholders **Payment:** Visa, MC, Discover, personal and traveler's checks **Restrictions:** children over 12 welcome; no smoking; no pets **Activities:** reading, games, small gift shop, bicycling maps

WITMER'S TAVERN–HISTORIC 1725 INN
2014 Old Philadelphia Pike
Lancaster, Pennsylvania 17602
717/299-5305
Proprietors: Jeanne, Brant, Pamela, Keith, and Melissa Hartung

Witmer's Tavern is the sole survivor of 62 inns that once lined the nation's first turnpike joining Philadelphia and Lancaster. The four-story blue limestone inn with individual room fireplaces, original iron door hinges and latches, nine-over-six bubbly glass windows, and handcrafted woodwork was built in 1725 and underwent several expansions through 1773. Witmer's provisioned thousands of immigrants with Conestoga wagons, rifles, and other supplies and put together

the wagon trains heading into the wilderness. Listed in the National Register of Historic Places, Witmer's has been described by historians as "the most completely intact and authentic eighteenth-century inn in south-central Pennsylvania." Today's guests enjoy fresh flowers, antiques, quilts, and fireplaces in every romantic room.

Open: year round **Accommodations:** 7 guest rooms (2 have private baths) **Meals:** continental breakfast included; restaurants nearby **Rates:** $60 to $90 **Payment:** personal and traveler's checks **Restrictions:** no cigars, no pets **Activities:** five-room Pandora's Antique Shop, library, tavern, Amish farm behind inn

LANDENBERG

Nearby attractions: Brandywine River Museum, Winterthur, Longwood Gardens, Brandywine Battlefield, Hagley Museum, University of Delaware, Delaware and Lincoln Univerity, Equestrian Center, golfing, antiques hunting, outlet shops

DAYBREAK FARM BED AND BREAKFAST
R.R. 2, Box 173, Route 841
Landenberg, Pennsylvania 19350
610/255-0282
Proprietors: Ann C. and John C. Day
Location: 15 miles south of Kennett Square

Daybreak Farm Bed and Breakfast, a 1744 Quaker farmhouse, is situated on 20 wooded acres in historic southern Chester County, near the village of Kemblesville. The house is furnished with family heirlooms and simple country antiques. One guest room features old English pine antiques, complete with a four-poster bed. Another guest room's decor is devoted to a toy collection that features a child's carousel horse. A small third-floor suite contains antiques furnishings and a canopy bed. The farm's fresh garden vegetables, herbs, and fruit are prepared for a full, country breakfast. Guests are invited to relax before the living room fireplace in winter or enjoy with swimming pool and screened porch in warm weather.

Open: year round **Accommodations:** 3 guest rooms (2 have private baths); 1 is a suite **Meals:** full breakfast included; complimentary refreshments; restaurants nearby **Rates:** $65 to $85; 10% discount to National Trust members and National Trust Visa cardholders **Payment:** Visa, MC, personal and traveler's checks **Restrictions:** children over 12 welcome; no smoking; no pets (nearby kennels available) **Activities:** swimming pool, horsehoe pitching, croquet, bass pond (bring your fishing pole), 20 acres for walking and hiking

LIMA

Nearby attractions: Brandywine Valley, Longwood Gardens, Winterthur, Brandywine Museum (Wyeth), Brandywine Battlefield, canoeing, bicycling, Tyler Arboretum, hot-air ballooning, Chadds Fords, antiques hunting

**HAMANASSETT BED AND
BREAKFAST**
P.O. Box 129
Lima, Pennsylvania 19037
610/459-3000
610/459-3000 Fax
Proprietor: Evelene H.
Dohan
Location: 15 miles south-
west of Philadelphia; 15
miles northeast of
Wilmington, Del.

Hamanasset, named for a nearby river, was built in 1856 by Dr. Charles D. Meigs. The estate has been in the innkeeper's family since 1870. Built of dark gray fieldstone, the house is distinguished by a cross-grambrel roof and a massive Palladian window, which illuminates the staircase landing. Guest rooms feature canopied beds, private baths, television, fresh flowers and fruit, and comfortable seating arrangements. The living room contains more than 2000 contemporary and classical books. A full breakfast is served in the formal dining room before the corner fireplace and alcoved floor-to-ceiling French doors that overlook gardens, lawns, and ancient trees. Afternoon tea and refreshments may be enjoyed in the drawing room, in the solarium, or on the loggia in warm weather. Forty-eight acres of gardens, fields, and trails are available for guests to wander through.

Open: year round **Accommodations:** 6 guest rooms with private baths; 1 is a suite **Meals:** full breakfast included; complimentary refreshments; restaurants nearby **Wheel-chair access:** first-floor common rooms **Rates:** $90 to $125 **Payment:** personal and traveler's checks **Restrictions:** children over 14 welcome; no smoking; no pets **Activities:** trail walking, bird-watching, gardens, television

LUMBERVILLE

Nearby attractions: Washington's Crossing, New Hope, Peddler's Village, winery, state parks, antiques hunting, fishing, golfing, tennis, summer theater, barge rides, museums, shopping

BLACK BASS HOTEL
Route 32, River Road
Lumberville, Pennsylvania 18933
215/297-5770
215/297-0262 Fax
Proprietor: Herbert Ward
Location: 8 miles north of New Hope

The Black Bass Hotel was built in the 1740s as a fortified haven for river travelers anxious to steer clear of Native Americans who roamed the forest. It prospered as an inn for early traders. Since that time, the Black Bass has hosted thousands of guests. In 1949, when the current innkeeper took over, the structure underwent a thorough restoration. The guest rooms were filled with eighteenth- and nineteenth-century antiques, creating the mellow atmosphere of an English pub or colonial tavern. Hospitality—the inn's trademark—is readily conveyed in its several dining rooms as well as in the guest rooms, some of which have private balconies viewing the Delaware River. Dining is also available on the screened-in veranda, and the hotel boasts an unusual pewter bar from the famed Maxim's in Paris. The Black Bass is located next to the only footbridge across the Delaware River.

Open: year round **Accommodations:** 9 guest rooms (2 have private baths); 2 are suites **Meals:** continental breakfast included; restaurant on premises; restaurants nearby **Wheelchair access:** dining rooms **Rates:** $55 to $175 **Payment:** AmEx, Visa, MC, DC, Discover, personal and traveler's checks **Activities:** river boating, fishing, hiking

MARKLESBURG

Nearby attractions: Raystown Lake Recreational Area, boating, swimming, fishing, hunting, hiking, bird-watching, state parks, antiques hunting

A. ZEIGLER HOUSE
Route 26 and Aitch Road
Marklesburg, Pennsylvania
Mailing address:
Raystown Rentals
P.O. Box 435
James Creek, Pennsylvania 16657
814/658-3203 or 800/422-3203
Proprietors: Gwen and Chuck Keating

The A. Zeigler House is one of the original homes in the village of Marklesburg, a small rural community less than a half-mile from Raystown Lake. Adam Zeigler converted the original 1780 log structure into the Zeigler Hotel in 1845, sheathing it in clapboards and adding bay windows and a spindlework front porch. Zeigler's hotel also housed the local saloon; the orignal eight-foot cherry bar was found under the rear porch during the hotel's recent renovation and was reinstalled inside. Guest rooms and the parlor are furnished with antiques original to the house. All rooms have private baths; some have adjacent sitting areas. Raystown Lake is an easy walk from the inn.

Open: Memorial Day to mid-December **Accommodations:** 3 guest rooms with private baths; 2 are suites **Meals:** continental-plus breakfast included; restaurants nearby **Rates:** $50 to $65 **Payment:** Visa, MC, Discover **Restrictions:** children over 4 welcome; no smoking; no pets **Activities:** yard games, porch sitting, pump organ, reading

MILFORD

Nearby attractions: Delaware River for swimming, fishing, and canoeing; Grey Towers National Site, town of Milford, antiques hunting

CLIFF PARK INN AND GOLF COURSE
R.R. 4, Box 7200
Milford, Pennsylvania 18337-9707
717/296-6491 or 800/225-6535
717/296-3982 Fax
Proprietor: Harry W. Buchanan III

In 1820, George Buchanan built this family farmstead in a meadow bordered by woodlands and the stone cliffs of the Delaware River Valley. In 1900, Annie Buchanan turned the old farmhouse into Cliff Park House, a small summer hotel. A few years later the surrounding fields were converted into a nine-hole golf course. Since then the course has been enlarged to keep pace with the game and times. Some traditions have been maintained, however: today, as in the early part of the century, spectators may watch players from the inn's long front veranda. The inn's fireplaces, wide floorboards, front door with sidelights, and staircase maintain their original appearance. Guest parlors and bedrooms are filled with ancestral portraits and Victorian furnishings, including velvet settees and globe lamps hung with brilliant crystal pendants. Guests are invited to peruse the family's Civil War–era bible, which is on display.

Open: year round **Accommodations:** 18 guest rooms with private baths **Meals:** full breakfast included; restaurants nearby **Wheelchair access:** 6 rooms **Rates:** $93 to $155 **Payment:** AmEx, Visa, MC, CB, DC, Discover, personal and traveler's checks **Restrictions:** no pets **Activities:** golfing, hiking, cross-country skiing

MOUNT JOY

Nearby attractions: Amish country, Hersheypark, farmers' market, antiques hunting, outlet shops, Gettysburg, Baltimore's Inner Harbor

CEDAR HILL FARM BED AND BREAKFAST
305 Longenecker Road
Mount Joy, Pennsylvania 17552
717/653-4655
Proprietors: Russel and Gladys Swarr
Location: 12 miles west of Lancaster

Located midway between Lancaster's Amish country and Hershey, this 1817 limestone farmhouse overlooks a peaceful stream. The house, with its two-foot-thick walls, is fronted by a double veranda. Inside, original pine floors are found throughout and an open winding staircase leads to the second floor. Five comfortable guest rooms are furnished with many family heirlooms and antiques. Each room has a private bath and is centrally air conditioned. Breakfast is served before a walk-in fireplace, which originally was used for cooking meals. The sitting room contains books and a chess table. Another room contains a television set, VCR, stereo system, and computer. For outdoor relaxation there are the wicker rockers on the broad front porch.

Open: year round **Accommodations:** 5 guest rooms with private baths **Meals:** continental-plus breakfast included; restaurants nearby **Rates:** $65 to $75 **Payment:** AmEx, Visa, MC, Discover, personal and traveler's checks **Restrictions:** no smoking; no pets **Activities:** hiking, bicycling, croquet, chess

---

MYERSTOWN

Nearby attractions: swimming, golfing, bicycling; nearby towns of Lebanon, Hershey, Reading, and Lancaster

TULPEHOCKEN MANOR INN AND PLANTATION
650 West Lincoln Avenue
Myerstown, Pennsylvania 17067
717/866-4926 or 717/392-2311
Proprietors: Esther Nissly and James Henry
Location: on Route 422, 2 miles west of Myerstown, 3 miles east of Lebanon

This estate consists of four stone and two clapboard homes built between 1769 and 1885. Michael Ley's eight-room stone colonial house, which was later expanded into a 27-room Second Empire mansion with mansard roof, was once host to the the country's most famous overnight guest, George Washington. While others may make this claim, the innkeepers have letters proving that Washington slept here on at least three occasions. Today, the inn has antiques-filled parlors and guest rooms. Tours of the mansion point out its many outstanding architectural details, such as nailless walnut doors, painted slate mantels from Germany, walnut and pine woodwork, and etched glass from Belgium. Group accommodations are also available in the historic Cyrus Sherk House, which sleeps six guests, and the Christopher Ley Spring House, with room for 12. Guests enjoy viewing the estate's large barn and related outbuildings, grazing cattle, 18-acre quarry lake, and trout stream.

Open: year round; closed in extremely cold or icy weather **Accommodations:** 6 guest rooms share 2 baths **Meals:** no meals on premises; restaurants nearby **Rates:** $85 to $100 in manor house; $150 for Cyrus Sherk House; $300 for Christopher Ley Spring House **Payment:** personal check **Restrictions:** children over 12 welcome in mansion; strictly supervised children welcome in smaller houses; no smoking; no pets; no alcohol; no parties **Activities:** house tours; 150 acres for walking, picnicking, relaxing

---

NEW HOPE

Nearby attractions: New Hope historic district, Delaware River and canal, Bucks County Playhouse, Washington Crossing State Park, Mercer Museum, Fonthill, antiques hunting, arts and crafts shops, tileworks, galleries, scenic Bucks County, bicycling, skiing, ice skating, swimming pool, tennis

AARON BURR HOUSE
80 West Bridge Street
New Hope, Pennsylvania 18938
215/862-2520 or 215/862-2343
Proprietors: Nadine and Carl Glassman

In the heart of New Hope's historic district, the Aaron Burr House is named for the vice-president who sought a haven in Bucks County after his famous duel with Alexander Hamilton in 1804. Nestled under century-old shade trees, the 1873 inn is a two-story clapboard home, accented by the tall arched windows, single-story bay window, and decorative eave brackets characteristic of the Italianate style. High ceilings and beautifully restored black-walnut floors grace the interior, as does a fireplace that warms the parlor in cold months. Antique-filled guest rooms have four-poster canopy beds and private baths; some have fireplaces. Evening turn-down service includes chocolate mints and homemade almond liqueur at bedside. Guests have 24-hour access to a telephone, fax–copier machine, television, and kitchen.

Open: year round **Accommodations:** 6 guest rooms with private baths; 2 are suites with fireplaces **Meals:** continental-plus breakfast included; complimentary refreshments; restaurants nearby **Wheelchair access:** guest rooms, bathrooms, dining facilities **Rates:** $110 to $195; 10% discount offered to National Trust members and National Trust Visa cardholders **Payment:** Visa, MC, personal and traveler's checks **Restrictions:** no smoking; no pets **Activities:** croquet, badminton, swimming pool, tennis

HOLLIFEIF BED AND BREAKFAST
677 Durham Road
Wrightstown, Pennsylvania 18940
215/598-3100
Proprietors: Ellen and Richard Butkus
Location: 6 miles west of New Hope

The name Hollileif honors the 40-foot holly trees that grace the entrance to this pre-Revolutionary plaster-and-fieldstone farmhouse. Family artwork and antiques collected over many years adorn the establishment. Guest rooms are nostalgically appointed with lace, frills, and fresh flowers. Each room has a comfortable sitting area and one has a gas fireplace. All are centrally air conditioned and have private baths. A full breakfast is served in the intimate paneled-and-beamed breakfast room. Afternoon refreshments are enjoyed before the parlor fireplace or on the arbor-covered patio. Hollileif is in a natural setting of more than five rolling acres marked by trees, flowers, gardens, a stream, and occasional wildlife.

Open: year round **Accommodations:** 5 guest rooms with private baths **Meals:** full breakfast included; complimentary refreshments; restaurants nearby **Rates:** $85 to $135; 10% discount to National Trust members and National Trust Visa cardholders, Sunday through Thursday, excluding holidays **Payment:** AmEx, Visa, MC, Discover, personal and traveler's checks **Restrictions:** children over 12 welcome; no smoking; no pets **Activities:** badminton, croquet, hammocks, sledding, gardens

WEDGWOOD INN
111 West Bridge Street
New Hope, Pennsylvania 18938
215/862-2570
Proprietors: Nadine Silnutzer and Carl Glassman

Wedgwood Inn offers lodgings in two adjacent historic houses. The 1870 clapboard Victorian is distinguished by a wraparound porch, hipped gables, and a porte cochere. The stone and plaster house next door, built in 1833, boasts 26-inch-thick stone walls. Each of the inn's distinctive accommodations offers lofty windows, hardwood floors, and brass ceiling fans. The rooms are furnished with antiques, original art, scented English soaps, plush towels, and handmade quilts and comforters. Guests are served breakfast on the sunporch, in the gazebo, or in the privacy of their rooms. Evening turn-down service includes mints and liqueur at bedside. The inn, once featured on the cover of *National Geographic Traveler*, is just steps from New Hope's National Register historic district.

Open: year round **Accommodations:** 6 guest rooms with private baths; 2 are suites with fireplaces **Meals:** continental-plus breakfast included; complimentary refreshments; restaurants nearby **Wheelchair access:** limited **Rates:** $90 to $195; 10% discount to National Trust members and National Trust Visa cardholders **Payment:** Visa, MC, personal and traveler's checks **Restrictions:** no smoking; no pets **Activities:** badminton, croquet, porch swings, parlor fireplace, 2 acres of landscaped grounds, Victorian gazebo

PARADISE

Nearby attractions: Amish farms and shops, museums, antiques hunting, historic house tours, outlet shops, hot-air ballooning, bicycling

PEQUEA CREEKSIDE INN
44 Leacock Road
P.O. Box 435
Paradise, Pennsylvania 17562
717/687-0333
717/687-8200 Fax
Proprietors: Dennis and
Cathy Zimmerman

Pequea Creekside Inn is located in the heart of Lancaster County, surrounded by picturesque farms, on spacious grounds alongside Pequea Creek. The stone house, built in 1781, is adorned wth multipaned windows surmounted by triangular pediments. The inn contains six guest rooms, two with fireplaces. Some rooms have four-poster or tester beds, and all rooms are air conditioned. A full breakfast is served in the dining room, and a sitting room and porch also are available for guests. The inn is convenient to all of the Amish country sights.

Open: year round **Accommodations:** 6 guest rooms (4 have private baths) **Meals:** full breakfast included; complimentary refreshments; restaurants nearby **Rates:** $60 to $100 **Payment:** Visa, MC, personal check **Restrictions:** children over 12 welcome; no smoking; no pets **Activities:** swing overlooking creek, books, games

PHILADELPHIA

Nearby attractions: Independence National Historic Park, Independence Hall, downtown Philadelphia, Penn's Landing, National Trust's Cliveden, theaters, museums, shopping, Academy of Music and Philadelphia Orchestra

LA RESERVE CENTER CITY BED AND BREAKFAST

1804 Pine Street
Philadelphia, Pennsylvania 19103
215/735-1137 or 800/354-8401
Proprietor: Bill Buchanan

This four-story townhouse, built in 1868, sits conveniently in the center of Philadelphia, just minutes from Independence Hall, the Liberty Bell, U.S. Mint, and the Betsy Ross House. The inn offers an elegant historical setting adorned with decorative crown molding, original hardwood floors, and lovely fireplace mantels ranging in style from Federal to Rococo. Formal French antiques are found throughout the house, including bedrooms and suites. Guests are served a full breakfast in the chandeliered dining room and are invited to play the 1903 Steinway grand piano in the parlor or select a book from the library. A summer garden at the side of the house provides a quiet retreat in the heart of the city.

Open: year round **Accommodations:** 8 guest rooms (3 have private baths); 2 are suites **Meals:** full breakfast included; restaurants nearby **Wheelchair access:** 1 room **Rates:** $45 to $85; 10% discount to National Trust members and National Trust Visa cardholders **Payment:** Visa, MC **Restrictions:** no smoking **Activities:** piano, library, garden

SHIPPEN WAY INN

418 Bainbridge Street
Philadelphia, Pennsylvania 19147
215/627-7266 or 800/245-4873
Proprietors: Raymond Rhule and Ann Foringer

Two eighteenth-century houses—one brick, the other frame (which is unusual in Philadelphia)—constitute Shippen Way Inn. The houses are listed in the National Register and are located in the historic Queens Village district. Nine guest rooms are available ranging from spacious to cozy. One room has a fireplace, some rooms are reached via a spiral staircase, one is a third-floor dormer room, two have private garden entrances. Antiques, Laura Ashley wallpapers, and stenciling (on floors as well as walls) adorn the rooms. A courtyard with rose and herb gardens is shared by the two houses. The courtyard garden is where breakfast is served in warm weather. Afternoon wine and cheese may be enjoyed in the garden or before the living room fireplace. The innkeepers use fresh herbs from the garden in all the foods they prepare.

Open: year round **Accommodations:** 9 guest rooms with private baths **Meals:** continental-plus breakfast included; complimentary refreshments; restaurants nearby **Rates:** $70 to $105; 10% discount to National Trust members and National Trust Visa cardholders **Payment:** AmEx, Visa, MC, personal and traveler's checks **Restrictions:** limited space available for children; smoking limited; no pets

THOMAS BOND HOUSE BED AND BREAKFAST
129 South Second Street
Old City
Philadelphia, Pennsylvania 19106
215/923-8523 or 800/845-BOND (800/845-2663)
215/923-8504 Fax
Proprietor: George L. Phillips

Dr. Thomas Bond, together with Benjamin Franklin and Dr. Benjamin Rush, founded the the first public hospital in the United States in 1751. Bond built this house in 1769 in the Georgian style, the Ionic-modillioned cornice being its most elaborate feature. Additions were made in 1824 and 1840. The "borrowed-light" window on the garret floor, which allows light to get from an outside room to an inside room, is an interesting architectural detail. The house served as a residence until 1810 and then as several kinds of factories and businesses, until restored as a bed and breakfast in 1988. Thomas Bond House offers guest rooms furnished with canopy, four-poster, wrought-iron, or cannonball beds. Chippendale-style and period pine furnishings fill the rooms. Two suites contain fireplaces and whirlpool baths. The parlor, with Rumford fireplace, and dining room are designed in late eighteenth-century style.

Open: year round **Accommodations:** 12 guest rooms with private baths; 2 are suites **Meals:** full breakfast included on weekends; continental-plus breakfast included on weekdays; complimentary refreshments; restaurants nearby **Rates:** $85 to $150; 10% discount to National Trust members and National Trust Visa cardholders **Payment:** AmEx, Visa, MC, personal and traveler's checks **Restrictions:** no pets **Activities:** access to health club next door, parlor games

PINE GROVE MILLS

Nearby attractions: Pennsylvania State University, college football, outlet shops, caverns, boating, hiking, theaters, festivals, Amish market, dinner train, historic villages

THE CHATELAINE, A BED AND BREAKFAST AT SPLIT PINE FARMHOUSE
347 West Pine Grove Road
Box 326
Pine Grove Mills, Pennsylvania 16868
814/238-2028 or 800/251-2028
Proprietor: Mae McQuade

Split Pine Farmhouse was built in the Federal style in 1830 and expanded in 1860. Its spacious rooms are filled with elegant, yet unusual furnishings that have been collected by the innkeeper during 45 years of world travel. Guests may choose accommodations with either private or shared baths, each with a unique element like a lavender art-glass window or a split-pine mosaic-tiled shower for two. To complement their distinctive decor and antique pieces, bedrooms contain bits of whimsy, such as decorative swans, a multicolored bird cage with fantasy occupant, or old toys and games. The Chatelaine offers guests full breakfasts featuring entrees such as mushroom charlottes with currant sauce or Santa Fe strata. In summertime, guests may choose to take the picnic hamper filled with breakfast cookout fixings and the hibachi to Whipple's Dam or Shaver's Creek for a private meal al fresco.

Open: year round **Accommodations:** 4 guest rooms (2 have private baths) **Meals:** full breakfast included; complimentary refreshments; restaurants nearby **Rates:** $65 single to $135 double (seasonal) **Payment:** AmEx, Visa, MC, Discover, personal and traveler's checks **Restrictions:** children over 12 welcome; no smoking; no pets **Activities:** reading, television, strolling the grounds

PITTSBURGH

Nearby attractions: Three Rivers Stadium, Carnegie Science Center, Pittsburgh Aviary and Children's Museum, Andy Warhol Museum, historic house tours, symphony, opera, ballet, galleries, riverboat cruises

THE PRIORY

614 Pressley Street
Pittsburgh, Pennsylvania 15212
412/231-3338
412/231-4838 Fax
Proprietor: Mary Ann Graf

Carefully restored and updated, the Priory is a European-style hotel with the appointments of a large establishment and the personality of a small inn. The Priory was once a temporary haven for Benedictine priests traveling through Pittsburgh. Built in 1888, the red brick building, notable for its Romanesque-arched windows and parapeted gables, is adjacent to St. Mary's German Catholic Church, the oldest Catholic church in Pittsburgh. The Priory's maze of rooms and corridors is distinctly Old World. Each guest room is uniquely decorated with Victorian-style furnishings and has a private bath and cable television. Complimentary evening wine is enjoyed by guests in the sitting room, library, or courtyard.

Open: year round **Accommodations:** 24 guest rooms with private baths; 3 are suites **Meals:** continental-plus breakfast included; complimentary refreshments; restaurants nearby **Wheelchair access:** limited **Rates:** $92 to $160; 10% discount to National Trust members and National Trust Visa cardholders **Payment:** AmEx, Visa, MC, CB, DC, Discover, personal and traveler's checks **Restrictions:** no pets

POTTSTOWN

Nearby attractions: Valley Forge, Brandywine Valley Museum, Longwood Gardens, Philadelphia, Audubon Wildlife Sanctuary, Chadds Ford, Bryn Mawr College, Villanova University, Valley Forge Music Fair, Amish country, antiques hunting, tennis, golfing, state and local parks

COVENTRY FORGE INN
3360 Coventryville Road
Pottstown, Pennsylvania 19465
610/469-6222
Proprietors: June and Wallis Callahan
Location: 14 miles west of Valley Forge Park

Coventry Forge Inn comprises a guest house, built in 1806, and a restaurant, built in 1717. The guest house, resting among gardens and rolling pastures, offers comfortable and simple accommodations in a quiet rural setting. These spacious rooms, each with a private bath and air conditioning, are decorated in period antiques and reproductions. Breakfast is served on the porch of the restaurant next door. The inn is notable for its fine French cuisine. For more than 30 years, Coventry Forge Inn has offered the freshest, locally obtained ingredients, prepared according to classic French recipes, and served with the care and expertise that continue to gain national recognition, including a four-star rating from the *Mobil Travel Guide.*

Open: year round **Accommodations:** 5 guest rooms with private baths **Meals:** continental breakfast included; restaurant on premises **Rates:** $65 to $75 **Payment:** AmEx, Visa, MC, DC **Restrictions:** children over 12 welcome; no pets **Activities:** French dining, relaxation

---

SCOTTDALE

Nearby attractions: Frank Lloyd Wright's Fallingwater, West Overton Museum, Forts Necessity and Ligonier, Compass Inn Museum, Hannastown Museum, Seven Springs and Hidden Valley ski resorts, theater, bicycling, tennis, white-water rafting, hiking, nature walks, antiques hunting

ZEPHYR GLEN BED AND BREAKFAST
205 Dexter Road
Scottdale, Pennsylvania 15683
412/887-6577
Proprietors: Noreen and Gilbert McGurl

Abraham Stauffer, the son of a Mennonite minister, built this Federal brick home

in the 1820s. The house is nestled in a glen called Zephyr, which means gentle west wind. Three guest rooms are offered with private baths. All three have stenciled walls and ceiling fans. Anna's Room has two three-quarter rope beds, hooked rugs, and antique quilts. Elizabeth's Room has two Victorian antique beds—one single, one double. Katrina's Room has a working fireplace, and antique quilts on the 1850 Jenny Lind double bed. Guests are invited before the fireplace in the parlor or on the front porch, which spans the facade. The yard is filled with trees, wildflowers, and perennial and herb gardens. The innkeepers operate an antiques shop on the property.

Open: year round **Accommodations:** 3 guest rooms with private baths **Meals:** continental-plus breakfast included; complimentary refreshments; grill and picnic table provided; restaurants nearby **Rates:** $70 to $80 **Payment:** Visa, MC, Discover, personal and traveler's checks **Restrictions:** inquire about children; no smoking; no pets **Activities:** musical instruments, porch sitting, garden strolls, hands-on history weekends for children, antiques shop

---

STARLIGHT

Nearby attractions: Steamtown National Park; historic sites; museums, antiques hunting; golfing; Delaware River for fly fishing, canoeing, and rafting

INN AT STARLIGHT LAKE
P.O. Box 27
Starlight, Pennsylvania 18461
717/798-2519 or 800/248-2519
717/798-2672 Fax
Proprietors: Jack and Judy McMahon
Location: 5 miles south of Hancock, N.Y., off Route 370

Since 1909 the Inn at Starlight Lake has been providing comfortable accommodations to visitors seeking year-round activities and the region's famous natural beauty. The main house is a large three-story frame structure with hipped roof. It contains 14 guest rooms, a lakeside dining room, a library of recorded music, and the Stovepipe Bar. Additional accommodations are found in four cottages. One is a single-family house that sleeps up to 12 people. All facilities are furnished with a mix of antiques, collectibles, and contemporary furniture. Guests will find

a welcoming bowl of fruit in their rooms. Breakfast and dinner, included in the rate, feature home-baked bread and healthy fresh foods, including vegetarian dishes. Guests can explore the surrounding woods, use the lake for boating, swimming, or fishing, and cross-country ski on miles of groomed trails.

Open: year round **Accommodations:** 20 guest rooms with private baths; 1 is a suite with whirlpool tub **Meals:** full breakfast and dinner included on modified American Plan (MAP) **Rates:** $110 to $154 MAP; 10% discount, with restrictions, to National Trust members and National Trust Visa cardholders **Payment:** Visa, MC, personal and traveler's checks **Restrictions:** smoking limited; no pets **Activities:** lake swimming, boating, fishing, shuffleboard, tennis, hiking, cross-country skiing, bicycling, lawn sports

VALLEY FORGE

Nearby attractions: Valley Forge National Historical Park, Brandywine Valley Museum, Longwood Gardens, Philadelphia, Audubon Wildlife Sanctuary, Chadds Ford, Bryn Mawr College, Villanova University, Valley Forge Music Fair, antiques hunting, tennis, golfing

GREAT VALLEY HOUSE OF VALLEY FORGE
110 Swedesford Road
R.D. 3
Malvern, Pennsylvania 19355
215/644-6759
Proprietor: Pattye Benson
Location: 2 miles west of Valley Forge

A Welsh settler began building this fieldstone farmhouse in 1690. It was added to in 1740, and again in 1791. One of the oldest homes in the area, the Great Valley House, is complete with original fireplaces, random-width wood floors, and hand-hewn nails. Also notable are the hand-forged iron hinges used throughout and an old stone sink, said to be one of only two such pre-1700 sinks in the country. The old kitchen contains a walk-in fireplace with its original swing crane and 300-year-old mantel. Each of the three guest rooms are hand stenciled, decorated with antiques, and accented with handmade quilts. A refrigerator, coffeepot, and microwave oven are located in the center hall for guests' convenience. The surrounding three acres contain an old smokehouse, a cold storage keep, and ancient trees as well as a more modern diversion—a large swimming pool. The inn has been featured in the *Washington Post, New York Times*, and *Philadelphia Inquirer*.

Open: year round **Accommodations:** 3 guest rooms (2 have private baths) **Meals:** full breakfast included; complimentary refreshments; restaurants nearby **Rates:** $65 to $85; 10% discount offered to National Trust members and National Trust Visa cardholders **Payment:** personal and traveler's checks **Restrictions:** no smoking; no pets **Activities:** swimming pool, hiking, walking, fishing

WAYNE

Nearby attractions: Valley Forge National Park, Longwood Gardens, Amish country, historic center city Philadelphia, shopping

WAYNE HOTEL
139 East Lancaster Avenue
Wayne, Pennsylvania 19087
610/687-5000 or 800/962-5850
610/687-8387 Fax
Proprietor: Susan Prevost, General Manager

This Tudor-influenced hotel, originally called the Waynewood, was built in 1906, a time when the village of Wayne was changing from a summer resort to a permanent residential community. The restored Wayne Hotel retains a memory of that resort with its wide front porch that stretches across the facade, inviting guests to relax. An elegant environment is presented in the lobby with its floral carpet, Victorian furnishings, chandeliers, fireplace, and potted palms. Each guest room has a personality of its own that reflects the elegant impression created in the lobby. A few rooms have small kitchenettes. Guests are invited to relax in the

cozy library or in the hotel's bar. The restaurant offers predominantly French cuisine with an American bistro influence. This historic hotel is listed in the National Register of Historic Places.

Open: year round **Accommodations:** 35 guest rooms with private baths; 5 are suites **Meals:** continental breakfast included; restaurant on premises; restaurants nearby **Wheelchair access:** yes **Rates:** $94.50 to $135 **Payment:** AmEx, Visa, MC, CB, DC, personal and traveler's checks **Restrictions:** smoking limited; no pets **Activities:** porch sitting, bar, nearby outdoor pool and exercise facilities

WILLIAMSPORT

Nearby attractions: Lycoming College; Pennsylvania College of Technology; Little League Baseball Museum; mountain hiking; skiing; hunting; fishing; white-water canoeing; Penn State, Bucknell, Susquehanna, Mansfield, Bloomsburg, and Lock Haven universities

REIGHARD HOUSE
1323 East Third Street
Williamsport, Pennsylvania 17701
717/3326-3593 or 800/326-8335
717/323-4734 Fax
Proprietor: Susan L. Reighard

Reighard House is a 1905 stone-and-brick Victorian home. It is lent a Tudor air by mock half-timbering and a round two-story tower. The house once functioned as the county's first state police barracks, hence one of its six guest rooms is called the State Trooper Room. Two rooms offer canopied beds, while another contains a queen-size bed with trundle. All bedrooms are spacious and contain private baths, color television, telephones, and air conditioning. Guests are invited to relax in the formal parlor, music room with grand piano, or library. Breakfast is served in the formal oak-paneled dining room or in the cheery breakfast room with wood-burning stove. In mild weather the old-fashioned front porch is perfect for rocking and relaxing. The inn is within walking distance of restaurants and shopping. Inn guests receive complimentary membership in a nearby health club during their stay.

Open: year round **Accommodations:** 6 guest rooms with private baths **Meals:** full breakfast included; complimentary refreshments; restaurants nearby **Rates:** $48 to $78 **Payment:** AmEx, Visa, MC, CB, DC, personal and traveler's checks **Restrictions:** no smoking; no pets **Activities:** complimentary health club membership

RHODE ISLAND

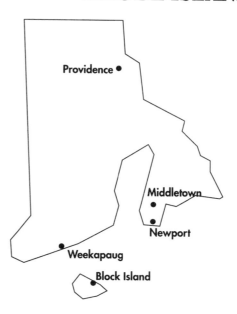

BLOCK ISLAND

Nearby attractions: art galleries, bicycling, swimming, beaches, sailing, bluffs, lighthouses, national landmarks, Nature Conservancy trails, bird-watching, shopping

HOTEL MANISSES
1 Spring Street
Block Island, Rhode Island 02807
401/466-2421 or 401/466-2063
Proprietors: Joan and Justin Abrams

When the Manisses was built in 1870, it was known as one of the best summer hotels in the east. With its mansard roof, clapboard siding, and lookout tower, it was a picturesque beach structure. The current innkeepers purchased this Block Island landmark in 1972 and began restoring it. Now listed in the National Register of Historic Places, the inn has 17 Victorian-style guest rooms featuring turn-of-the-century furniture and some fireplaces, as well as modern conveniences such as private baths (some with whirlpool tubs) and telephones. Brandy and candy are bedside treats. The hotel has a restaurant of note, serving meals in the garden terrace dining room or on the deck in summer. Many of the herbs, vegetables, and flowers used are grown in the hotel's own gardens.

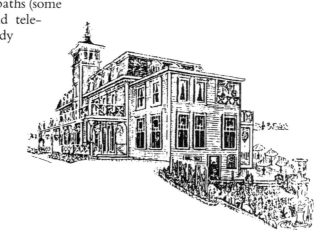

Open: year round **Accommodations:** 17 guest rooms with private baths; 4 are suites **Meals:** full breakfast included; complimentary refreshments; restaurant on premises serving dinner **Wheelchair access:** some guest rooms, bathrooms, dining room **Rates:** $90 to $250; 10% discount to National Trust members **Payment:** AmEx, Visa, MC, personal and traveler's checks **Restrictions:** children over 10 welcome; smoking limited; no pets **Activities:** lawn games, petting zoo, sailing, bicycling

SHEFFIELD HOUSE

High Street
P.O. Box C2
Block Island, Rhode Island 02807
401/466-2494
401/466-5067 Fax
Proprietors: Steve and Claire McQueeny

This Queen Anne house sports decorative wall shingles, a three-story tower, and a wraparound porch. Sitting on the gentle rise of High Street, overlooking the historic Old Harbor district, the house was built in 1888 for Dr. J. E. Bennett. The house passed through several families until purchased in 1911 by George G. Sheffield, whose name remains. The current owners have operated the house as an inn since 1984, offering seven custom-decorated guest rooms. Furnishings have been collected from around the country and in Europe, resulting in a comfortable and relaxing environment. Home-baked breakfasts are served in the day room or in the private flower and herb garden. A stroll through town or swim at the beach is a comfortable walk away.

Open: year round **Accommodations:** 7 guest rooms (5 have private baths) **Meals:** continental-plus breakfast included; complimentary refreshments; restaurants nearby **Wheelchair access:** yes **Rates:** $50 to $150; 10% discount to National Trust members and National Trust Visa cardholders **Payment:** AmEx, Visa, MC, personal and traveler's checks **Restrictions:** not suitable for childen; smoking restricted; no pets **Activities:** relaxation, porch rocking

MIDDLETOWN

Nearby attractions: mansion tours, Cliff Walk, Touro Synagogue, Newport Art Museum, Museum of Yachting, Tennis Hall of Fame, antiques hunting, Brick Market Place shops, Redwood Library, live theater, beaches, sailing, swimming, boating, fishing, golfing, hiking, bicycling, tennis

FINNEGAN'S INN AT SHADOW LAWN
120 Miantonomi Avenue
Middletown, Rhode Island 02842
401/849-1298 or 800/828-0000
401/849-1306 Fax
Proprietors: Selma and Randy Fabricant

Finnegan's Inn is an 1853 Italianate frame house. Its arcaded front porch is accented with green-and-white striped awnings, and its white clapboards are set off by green window shutters. Inside, the inn has been elegantly styled, from original French crystal chandeliers and stained-glass windows to tasteful wallcoverings and plush carpeting. Each color-coordinated guest room is individually decorated and provides an intimate sitting area, private tiled bath, color television, air conditioning, and refrigerator. Three bedrooms have working fireplaces. The inn's first floor contains a parlor, a paneled library, and a dining room. Complimentary shuttle service is offered to and from downtown Newport, only one mile away.

Open: year round **Accommodations:** 8 guest rooms with private baths **Meals:** continental plus breakfast included; restaurants nearby **Rates:** $65 to $129 **Payment:** Visa, MC, traveler's check **Restrictions:** no smoking; no pets **Activities:** television, newspapers, magazines, books

NEWPORT

Nearby attractions: mansion tours, Cliff Walk, Touro Synagogue, Newport Art Museum, Tennis Hall of Fame, more than 500 restored colonial homes, antiques hunting, Brick Market Place shops, oldest continuously used library in the country, live theater, beaches, sailing, swimming, boating, fishing, golfing, hiking, bicycling, tennis

ADMIRAL BENBOW INN

93 Pelham Street
Newport, Rhode Island 02840
401/848-8000 or 800/343-2863
401/848-8006 Fax
Proprietors: Jane and Bruce Berriman **Innkeeper:** Cathy Derigan

The Admiral Benbow was built in 1855 by a Block Island sea captain, Augustus Littlefield. He designed the house after those he had seen in Italy, incorporating an octagonal, two-story tower and tall, arched windows. The house was built as an inn and, for a few years, operated as a speakeasy. Accordingly, the inn has hosted many famous—and infamous—guests. Today's guest rooms are decorated with brass beds and fine antiques. A collection of eighteenth- and nineteenth-century barometers are on display and for sale in the hall and common room. The inn is a short walk from Bellevue Avenue shops, restaurants, art galleries, and all that Newport has to offer. Listed in the National Register and named after Mrs. Hawkins' inn in *Treasure Island*, the Admiral Benbow has been featured in *Country Inns, Bed and Breakfast* and *New York* magazines.

Open: year round **Accommodations:** 15 guest rooms with private baths; 1 is a suite **Meals:** continental-plus breakfast included; restaurants nearby **Rates:** $45 to $195; 10% discount to National Trust members and National Trust Visa cardholders **Payment:** AmEx, Visa, MC, DC, personal and traveler's checks **Restrictions:** children over 12 welcome; smoking limited; no pets

ADMIRAL FARRAGUT INN

31 Clarke Street
Newport, Rhode Island 02840
401/848-8000 or 800/343-2863
401/848-8006 Fax
Proprietors: Jane and Bruce Berriman **Innkeeper:** Maryann Brett

The original portion of this nearly 300-year-old home was built in 1702 by a man named Stevens. He expanded the two-story, two-room house to its present configuration in 1755. It was left untouched until 25 years ago, thus preserving all original features. Twelve-over-twelve double-hung windows and authentic colonial cove moldings outside give no hint of the modern conveniences inside. The current owners upgraded the interior in 1987 with new wiring and plumbing, salvaged beams, and wrought-iron hardware. Throughout the inn, guests will find a fresh interpretation of colonial themes. Each guest room is different with a combination of handmade and antique furnishings. There are Shaker-style four-poster beds, painted and stenciled armoires, and imported English antiques. Breakfast is served in the keeping room. This National Register property has been featured in *Country Living*.

Open: year round **Accommodations:** 9 guest rooms with private baths **Meals:** full breakfast included; restaurants nearby **Rates:** $55 to $185 **Payment:** AmEx, Visa, MC, DC, personal and traveler's checks **Restrictions:** children over 12 welcome; no smoking; no pets

ADMIRAL FITZROY INN

398 Thames Street
Newport, Rhode Island 02840
401/848-8000 or 800/343-2863
401/848-8006 Fax
Proprietors: Jane and Bruce Berriman **Innkeeper:** Holly Eastman

Built in 1854 to designs by architect Dudley Newton, the Admiral Fitzroy is a three-story weathered-shingle structure sitting above an English basement, which houses fashionable shops. The inn's guests rooms are decorated in a distinctive fashion with unique hand-painted details, and furnished with brass or sleigh beds, marble-topped tables, reading lamps, and comfortable sitting areas. A full breakfast is served in the breakfast room. The Admiral Fitzroy is named for the famous Englishman who commanded the *Beagle* on Charles Darwin's voyage while he was writing the *Origin of Species*. Careful attention to its restoration has earned the Admiral Fitzroy a listing in the National Register of Historic Places.

Open: year round **Accommodations:** 17 guest rooms with private baths **Meals:** full breakfast included; restaurants nearby **Wheelchair access:** 1 room **Rates:** $85 to $225 **Payment:** AmEx, Visa, MC, DC, personal and traveler's checks **Restrictions:** smoking limited; no pets

CLIFFSIDE INN
2 Seaview Avenue
Newport, Rhode Island 02840
401/847-1811 or 800/845-1811
Proprietor: Winthrop Baker **Innkeeper:** Stephan Nicolas

One of Newport's many imposing "cottages," Cliffside Inn was built in 1880 as a summer retreat for Governor Thomas Swann of Maryland. In 1897 the Second Empire cottage became the site of St. George's School, a prestigious preparatory school. Later the inn was the home of artist Beatrice Turner, who spent many reclusive years at Cliffside, painting more than 1000 self-portraits. Only 70 of her paintings survived a massive bonfire set by the estate's executors to destroy her work after her death in 1950; today, most are in private collections. Cliffside Inn's many bay and floor-to-ceiling windows wash it with light. The decor blends the richness of victorian furnishings with the freshness of Laura Ashley fabrics. Each unique guest room provides a variety of luxuries such as fireplaces, canopy beds, bay windows, window seats, skylights, or whirlpool tubs. The inn is situated on a quiet street one block from Cliff Walk, the city's seaside walking trail. Cliffside has received accolades from *Country Inns*, *New York*, and *Boston* magazines, as well as ABC-TV's "Good Morning, America."

Open: year round **Accommodations:** 13 guest rooms with private baths; 6 are suites **Meals:** full breakfast included; complimentary refreshments; restaurants nearby **Rates:** $145 to $325 **Payment:** AmEx, Visa, MC, Discover, DC, personal and traveler's checks **Restrictions:** children over 13 welcome; no smoking; no pets

COVELL GUEST HOUSE
43 Farewell Street
Newport, Rhode Island 02840
401/847-8872
Proprietor: Jeanne M. Desrosiers

John Williams built this colonial home in 1810, just three blocks from Newport's harbor. In 1885, the Covell family, who lived here for 110 years, added its mansard roof, front porch and side wing, resulting in this attractive architectural hybrid. Five guest rooms—some with four-poster beds—are found on the second and third floors, each decorated in its own style, comfortably mixing antiques and traditional furnishings. A guest sitting room on the second floor offers a warming fireplace and a television. Breakfast is served in the chandeliered breakfast room. Guests are invited to relax on the front porch to enjoy the professionally landscaped gardens. Covell Guest House is one block from the famous White Horse Tavern and Friends Meeting House. In the heart of the Point historic district, Covell House offers convenient off-street parking.

Open: year round **Accommodations:** 5 guest rooms with private baths **Meals:** continental-plus breakfast included; restaurants nearby **Rates:** $75 to $125; 10% discount to National Trust members and National Trust Visa cardholders **Payment:** Visa, MC, personal and traveler's checks **Restrictions:** children over 5 welcome; no pets **Activities:** porch sitting, gardens

MELVILLE HOUSE
39 Clarke Street
Newport, Rhode Island 02840
401/847-0640
Proprietors: Vince DeRico and David Horan

A country inn located in bustling Newport, Melville House is a 1750 shingled colonial structure built by Henry Potter, who once quartered officers of the French army here during the Revolutionary War. It was later owned by the Melville family (no relation to Herman) and is listed today in the National Register of Historic Places. Melville House is one of the few inns in Newport dedicated to the colonial style and decorated in the simple tastes of the early colonists. A full breakfast is served in the sunny breakfast room and features the inn's homemade granola, muffins, and home-baked breads. Afternoon tea is served daily and includes homemade biscotti and a hearty soup on cold days. The inn has earned a AAA three-diamond rating and has been featured in *Good Housekeeping* magazine.

Open: year round **Accommodations:** 7 guest rooms (5 have private baths); 1 is a winter fireplace suite **Meals:** full breakfast included; complimentary afternoon tea; restaurants nearby **Rates:** $60 to $125; 10% discount to National Trust members and National Trust Visa cardholders **Payment:** AmEx, Visa, MC, Discover, personal and traveler's checks **Restrictions:** children over 12 welcome; no smoking; no pets **Activities:** bicycles available

THE WILLOWS OF NEWPORT, ROMANTIC INN AND GARDEN
8 and 10 Willow Street, Historic Point
Newport, Rhode Island 02840
401/846-5486
Proprietor: Pattie Murphy

The Willows of Newport begins with the 1740 John Rogers House at number 10 Willow Street. Attached to its side is a Greek Revival house, which was built onto the Rogers House in 1840 so that family and friends could vacation in Newport, fast becoming the country's first summer resort. Listed as a National Landmark, the Willows is an inn that caters to the romantic traveler. Five guest rooms are uniquely designed, each with a private bath. Most rooms have canopied brass beds; one has an antique rosewood bedroom suite. Bone china and silver are used for breakfast, which is served to guests in bed by a black-tied host. Evening turn-down service with mints on pillows is standard. Guests are invited to use the wet bar and parlor with fireplace. The inn's award-winning flower gardens also contain a waterfall and heart-shaped fish pond. Private garage parking is provided at this Mobil three-star inn.

Open: April to November **Accommodations:** 5 guest rooms with private baths **Meals:** continental-plus breakfast in bed included; complimentary refreshments; restaurants nearby **Rates:** $88 to $185 **Payment:** personal and traveler's checks **Restrictions:** not suitable for children; no smoking; no pets **Activities:** garden

PROVIDENCE

Nearby attractions: historic architecture, Trinity Repertory Theater, Rhode Island School of Design, Brown University, shopping

OLD COURT BED AND BREAKFAST
144 Benefit Street
Providence, Rhode Island 02903
401/751-2002 or 401/351-0747
Proprietor: Jon Rosenblatt

Originally a rectory built in 1863 by Alpheus Morse, Old Court sits next to the historic Rhode Island Courthouse, which currently houses the Rhode Island Historical Preservation Commission. The Italianate inn reflects early Victorian taste in its ornate Italian mantelpieces, plaster moldings, and 12-foot ceilings. Antique furniture, chandeliers, and memorabilia display a range of nineteenth-century styles from the ornate Rococo Revival to the intricate and refined Eastlake. Yet contemporary standards of luxury and comfort are ever present. Breakfast, with espresso or cappuccino, is served in the dining room at the antique claw-foot table. Listed in the National Register of Historic Places, the inn is only a three-minute walk from downtown Providence or the campuses of Brown University and the Rhode Island School of Design.

Open: year round **Accommodations:** 11 guest rooms with private baths; 3 are suites **Meals:** continental-plus breakfast included; restaurants nearby **Rates:** $110 to $260; 10% discount offered to National Trust members and National Trust Visa cardholders **Payment:** Visa, MC, Discover, personal and traveler's checks

WEEKAPAUG

Nearby attractions: Watch Hill, Mystic Seaport and Aquarium, Babcock Smith House, Stonington Village, antiques hunting, golfing

WEEKAPAUG INN
25 Spring Avenue
Weekapaug, Rhode Island 02891
401/322-0301
803/722-2041 (October–April)
Proprietor: Darryl Forrester
Location: 7 miles east of Westerly Center, 5 miles east of Watch Hill

Frederick C. Buffum opened the Weekpaug Inn in 1899 as a summer retreat, beginning a tradition of providing his guests with the best in food and service in a spectacular natural setting. When a hurricane totally destroyed the inn in 1938, it was rebuilt and reopened in 1939, without missing a season. Today, the trademarks of the rambling, weathered gray clapboard inn remain the same: attentive service, clean and comfortable rooms, and hearty, healthy meals. The inn has a pristine beach for long walks and clear water for swimming and offers a variety of sports in an idyllic, relaxed environment. On its own peninsula with a pond on one side and the ocean on the other, the Weekapaug Inn has a scenic beauty that has attracted guests to this unique resort for 100 years.

Open: mid-June to Labor Day **Accommodations:** 62 guest rooms (52 have private baths); 6 are suites **Meals:** breakfast, lunch, and dinner included; restaurants nearby **Wheelchair access:** some guest rooms, bathrooms, dining facilities **Rates:** $140 to $155 per person **Payment:** personal and traveler's checks **Restrictions:** children over 3 welcome; no pets **Activities:** tennis, croquet, shuffleboard, lawn bowling, sailing, rowing, wind surfing

SOUTH CAROLINA

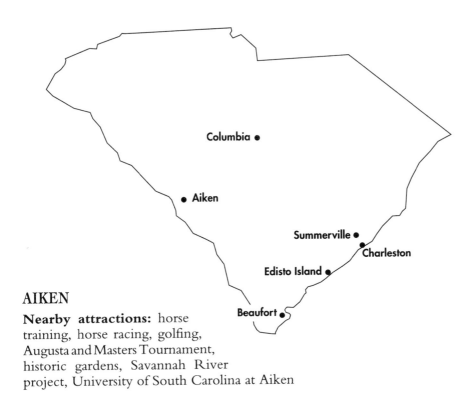

AIKEN

Nearby attractions: horse
training, horse racing, golfing,
Augusta and Masters Tournament,
historic gardens, Savannah River
project, University of South Carolina at Aiken

WILCOX INN

100 Colleton Avenue
Aiken, South Carolina 29801
803/649-1377 or 800/368-1047
803/643-0971 Fax
Proprietors: Management Counselors of Florida/Grand Heritage Hotels

Aiken is the home of world-famous thoroughbred horse trainers and the
renowned Aiken Triple Crown, and is just 15 miles from Augusta, home of the
Masters golf tournament. Located in Aiken's historic district, the National
Register Willcox Inn is an 1898 Neoclassical structure of white clapboard, its full-
facade porch supported by six enormous columns. Many of the inn's guest rooms
have four-poster beds and decorative fireplaces. Individually decorated suites
feature porches, ceiling fans, and window seats. Guest amenities include nightly
turn-down service and complimentary shoe shine, morning coffee, and newspapers. The lobby offers a wood-burning fireplace, while the Polo Pub has

handsome leather chairs and rich wood paneling. The Pheasant Room restaurant serves continental cuisine and traditional southern specialties.

Open: year round **Accommodations:** 30 guest rooms with private baths; 6 are suites **Meals:** restaurant on premises; restaurants nearby **Rates:** $60 to $150; 10% discount to National Trust members and National Trust Visa cardholders **Payment:** AmEx, Visa, MC, CB, DC, Discover, personal and traveler's checks **Activities:** honeymoon, golf, corporate, and other specialty packages available

BEAUFORT

Nearby attractions: Waterfront Park, Penn Center, Hunting Island State Park, antiques hunting, Beaufort National Register Historic District

TWOSUNS INN BED AND BREAKFAST
1705 Bay Street
Beaufort, South Carolina 29902
803/522-1122 or 800/532-4244
Proprietors: Carrol and Ron Kay

Designed by Savannah architect Morton Levy, this Neoclassical home, built for the Keyserling family in 1917, incorporated a host of modern conveniences: central baseboard vacuum system, a Roman heat distribution system, a brass full-body shower, an electric call-box system, and an open floor-plan ventilation system culminating in a classic hipped-roof skylight. Five guest rooms in today's inn are furnished with antiques and collectibles and decorated with Carrol Kay's custom window and bed ensembles. The parlor features Carrol's weaving looms, the living room is cozy with a fireplace, and the veranda rockers invite a lazy afternoon overlooking Beaufort Bay. Guest bicycles are available for touring Beaufort's National Landmark historic district.

Open: year round **Accommodations:** 5 guest rooms with private baths **Meals:** full breakfast included; complimentary afternoon "tea and toddy"; restaurants nearby **Wheelchair access:** yes **Rates:** $105 to $129; 10% discount to National Trust members and National Trust Visa cardholders **Payment:** AmEx, Visa, MC, personal and traveler's checks **Restrictions:** children over 12 welcome; no smoking; no pets **Activities:** lawn games, bicycles, reading, specialty weekends and B&B workshops available

CHARLESTON

Nearby attractions: Battery, Charleston Harbor, White Point Gardens, Fort Sumter, Gibbes Art Gallery, Charleston Museum, National Trust's Drayton Hall, plantations, waterfront park, beaches, golfing, hiking, swimming, tennis, fishing, concerts, theaters, shopping

BATTERY CARRIAGE HOUSE INN

20 South Battery
Charleston, South Carolina 29401
800/775-5575
803/727-3130 Fax
Proprietors: Katharine and Drayton Hastie

Built in 1843 and renovated in 1870, this antebellum mansion on the Battery was purchased in 1874 by the innkeeper's great-great grandfather, Andrew Simonds. Guests are invited to stay in the historic carriage house and kitchen of this landmark home in White Point Gardens, the most stately residential district of old Charleston. Elegant rooms overlooking a serene, private garden combine a romantic and historical ambience with many amenities, including private steam baths, whirlpool tubs, terrycloth robes, cable television, afternoon wine, turn-down service, free local phone calls, and ample free parking. Guests are served breakfast and a morning newspaper on silver trays in the privacy of their rooms or under the rose arbor in the garden.

Open: year round **Accommodations:** 11 guest rooms with private baths **Meals:** continental breakfast included; complimentary refreshments; restaurants nearby **Rates:** $99 to $199 **Payment:** AmEx, Visa, MC, Discover, personal and traveler's checks **Restrictions:** not suitable for young children; smoking limited; no pets **Activities:** relax in garden, house tour

BELVEDERE
40 Rutledge Avenue
Charleston, South Carolina 29401
803/722-0973 or 803/722-0750
Proprietor: David S. Spell **Manager:** Rick Zender

A handsome white house dominated by a two-story circular portico supported by massive columns with Ionic capitals, the Belvedere is an impressive example of the Neoclassical style so popular in 1900, when the house was built. A local physician, who bought the home in 1925, salvaged elegant Adam-style woodwork from nearby Belvedere Plantation (ca. 1800) and had the carved door surrounds and mantels installed in all the rooms and hallways of this house, where they remain today. Belvedere's guest suite surrounds a large common sitting area that opens to the spacious round porch overlooking Colonial Lake and the Ashley River beyond. Each bedroom features high ceilings, an ornamental fireplace, antique furnishings with oriental rugs, a private bath, and color television.

Open: mid-February to December 1 **Accommodations:** 3 guest rooms with private baths **Meals:** continental-plus breakfast included; complimentary refreshments; restaurants nearby **Rate:** $110; 10% discount offered to National Trust members **Payment:** personal and traveler's checks **Restrictions:** children over 8 welcome; no smoking; no pets

BRASINGTON HOUSE BED AND BREAKFAST
328 East Bay Street
Charleston, South Carolina 29401
803/722-1274 or
800/722-1274
803/722-6785 Fax
Proprietors: Dalton and Judy Brasington

Located in the heart of Charleston's historic district, Brasington House, a 200-year-old antebellum Charleston "single house," was meticulously restored in 1987 by its current owners. The antique furnishings blend with the Greek Revival features, marble mantels, and decorative plaster cornices in the formal living and dining rooms. The raised foundation and wide piazzas running the length of the facade are typical of this Charleston-style house. Four guest rooms appointed in period furnishings include telephones, cable television, and tea, coffee, and hot chocolate–making services. Late each afternoon, the proprietors serve wine and cheese in the living room. Elegant breakfasts are served on fine china, crystal, and silver in the dining room.

Open: year round **Accommodations:** 4 guest rooms with private baths; 1 is a suite **Meals:** full breakfast included; complimentary refreshments; restaurants nearby **Rates:** $75 to $115 **Payment:** Visa, MC, personal and traveler's checks **Restrictions:** not suitable for children; no smoking; no pets

FULTON LANE INN
202 King Street
Charleston, South Carolina 29401
803/720-2600 or 800/720-2688
803/720-2940 Fax
Proprietor: Randall Felkel

This 1902 brick inn is on a quiet pedestrian lane just off King Street, in the heart of the city's famous historic district. The inn is decorated in a classic blend of contemporary and traditional styling. Many of the spacious guest rooms feature large whirlpool baths and tall, canopied beds draped with hand-strung netting. Other rooms enjoy cathedral ceilings and several offer fireplaces. Each room is furnished with a private stocked refrigerator. Throughout, soaring windows frame vistas of the city's historic skyline, punctuated with the many trademark church spires. Complimentary breakfast is delivered to guest rooms on silver trays. Wine and sherry are offered in the lobby each eveing and nightly turn-down service is provided along with chocolates. Fulton Lane Inn has been awarded four diamonds by AAA.

Open: year round **Accommodations:** 27 guest rooms with private baths; 5 are suites **Meals:** continental-plus breakfast included; complimentary refreshments; restaurants nearby **Wheelchair access:** 2 rooms **Rates:** $100 to $240; 10% discount to National Trust members and National Trust Visa cardholders **Payment:** Visa, MC, traveler's check **Restrictions:** no smoking; no pets

JASMINE HOUSE
64 Hasell Street
Charleston, South Carolina 29401
803/577-5900
803/577-0378 Fax
Proprietors: Mr. and Mrs. H. B. Limehouse

Benjamin F. Smith was a well-to-do building supply merchant who built this Greek Revival mansion in 1843. His home is a stunning example of detailed ornamentation, perhaps because of his knowledge of materials, particularly wood and plaster. At every turn are foliate friezes, egg-and-dart cornices, carved door and window frames, and Corinthian pilasters. Wrought-iron and hammered foliate work is also found on the steps leading to the front piazza. Each of the named guest rooms and suites has been individually decorated; all contain hardwood floors, oriental rugs, 14-foot ceilings, and Italian marble bathrooms. A private brick and flagstone courtyard contains a whirlpool and tables and chairs for outdoor dining. A complimentary morning newspaper is served with breakfast. Jasmine House is located in Ansonborough, Charleston's eighteenth-century subdivision in the heart of the historic district.

Open: year round **Accommodations:** 10 guest rooms with private baths; 2 are suites **Meals:** continental breakfast included; complimentary refreshments; restaurants nearby **Rates:** $95 to $175; 10% discount to National Trust members and National Trust Visa cardholders with restrictions **Payment:** AmEx, Visa, MC, Discover, personal and traveler's checks **Restrictions:** not suitable for children; no pets **Activities:** outdoor whirlpool, private porches

JOHN RUTLEDGE HOUSE INN
116 Broad Street
Charleston, South Carolina 29401
803/723-7999 or 800/476-9741
Proprietor: Linda Bishop

John Rutledge, signer of the Constitution of the United States, built this home in 1763. The house is one of only 15 that once belonged to original signers of the Constitution and have survived the two intervening centuries. Designated a National Historic Landmark, the John Rutledge House Inn is located in the heart of Charleston's historic district. Careful restoration has renewed the house's beautiful eighteenth- and nineteenth-century craftsmanship, including carved Italian marble fireplaces, plaster moldings, inlaid floors, and graceful ironwork. Guest rooms are located in the main house or in its two carriage houses. Antiques and historical reproductions give each guest room its own character; each room also has a private bath and television. The inn is a charter member of Historic Hotels of America and has earned the four-diamond award from AAA and the four-star award from Mobil.

Open: year round **Accommodations:** 19 guest rooms with private baths; 3 are suites **Meals:** continental-plus breakfast included; complimentary wine and sherry; restaurants nearby **Wheelchair access:** 2 guest rooms and baths **Rates:** $125 to $195 single; $140 to $215 double; $235 to $295 suites **Payment:** AmEx, Visa, MC, traveler's checks **Restrictions:** smoking limited; no pets

KINGS COURTYARD INN
198 King Street
Charleston, South Carolina 29401
803/723-7000 or 800/845-6119
Proprietor: Laura Fox

Built in 1853, Kings Courtyard Inn is a three-story, Greek Revival structure with unusual Egyptian detailing. It is one of historic King Street's largest and oldest buildings and has had many uses in its 140 years: It has housed shops, residences, and at one time, an inn catering to plantation owners and shipping agents. Today's inn maintains the residential flavor of lower King Street. Guest rooms feature oversized beds, some with canopies, and fireplaces. Many have a view of one of the two inner courtyards, and other rooms overlook the rear garden. Guests receive wine or sherry on arrival. Daily extras include a morning newspaper and evening turn-down service with chocolates at bedside. The inn has a AAA four-diamond rating and is a member of Historic Hotels of America.

Open: year round **Accommodations:** 41 guest rooms with private baths; 4 are suites **Meals:** continental-plus breakfast included; full breakfast available; complimentary refreshments; restaurants nearby **Wheelchair access:** guest rooms, bathrooms, dining facilities **Rates:** $85 to $200; 10% discount offered to National Trust members and National Trust Visa cardholders **Payment:** AmEx, Visa, MC, traveler's check **Restrictions:** smoking limited; no pets **Activities:** outdoor hot tub

THE KITCHEN HOUSE
126 Tradd Street
Charleston, South
Carolina 29401
803/577-6362
Proprietor: Lois Evans

Dr. Peter Fayssoux, surgeon general in the Continental Army during the Revolutionary War, built the house at 126 Tradd Street. The Kitchen House is a completely renovated eighteenth-century kitchen/dwelling, attached to the Fayssoux house, but with a separate entrance. The Kitchen House is

centered around its four original fireplaces, and contains a living room and kitchen with dining area on the first floor and two spacious bedrooms and a bathroom on the second. The kitchen is fully equipped with every modern convenience; the refrigerator stocked with items for a complimentary full breakfast. The house is designed to accommodate up to four people. With its secluded patio overlooking a colonial herb garden and magnolia tree, it offers absolute privacy in the heart of the historic district.

Open: year round **Accommodations:** guest house with 2 bedrooms and 1 bath sleeps up to 4 **Meals:** full breakfast included; complimentary refreshments; restaurants nearby **Rates:** $99 to $195 **Payment:** Visa, MC, personal and traveler's checks **Restrictions:** inquire about children; no smoking; no pets **Activities:** fish pond, garden, library

MAISON DUPRÉ
317 East Bay Street
Charleston, South Carolina 29401
803/723-8691 or 800/844-INNS (800/844-4667)
Proprietors: Lucille, Robert, and Mark Mulholland

Three early nineteenth-century Charleston single houses and two carriage houses have been restored to create Maison DuPré. The main house was built in 1804 by Frenchman M. Benjamin DuPré. Stately columned piazzas overlook landscaped gardens and brick patios accented by flowering trees, shrubs, fountains, and a wishing well. Guest rooms are decorated with oriental carpets and antiques. Each room has a marble and tile bath with brass fittings. Throughout are paintings by innkeeper Lucille Mulholland. Morning newspaper, nightly turn-down service, and chocolates are among the special amenities at Maison DuPré. Located in the Ansonborough historic district, the inn has received a Carolopolis Award denoting houses of historic importance from the Preservation Society of Charleston, and has been featured in *Country Inns, Bed and Breakfast*.

Open: year round **Accommodations:** 15 guest rooms with private baths; 3 are suites **Meals:** continental-plus breakfast included; complimentary afternoon Low Country tea; restaurants nearby **Rates:** $98 to $200; 10% discount to National Trust members and National Trust Visa cardholders **Payment:** Visa, MC, personal and traveler's checks **Restrictions:** no smoking; no pets **Activities:** card room

PLANTERS INN
112 North Market Street
Charleston, South Carolina
29401
803/722-2345
803/577-2125 Fax
Proprietors: Larry Spelts and
Leigh Behling

Planters Inn, an 1844 commercial building at the corner of Market and Meeting streets, is a recipient of the Preservation Society of Charleston's award for renovation. The inn offers spacious guest rooms with traditional high ceilings and oversize baths of marble and hardwood. Furnishings are from Baker's museum-quality Historic Charleston Collection. Each room is distinct from the others in objets d'art, hues, and decor. Television and radio are concealed in an armoire. Many rooms have working fireplaces with adjacent seating areas. Turn-down service and pillow chocolates are standard. Breakfast, served on crystal and china, is brought to each bedroom door on a silver tray. A lobby, sitting room, courtyard, and rooftop deck are public places to relax. Planters Inn is also home to a critically acclaimed restaurant.

Open: year round **Accommodations:** 41 guest rooms with private baths; 5 are suites **Meals:** continental-plus breakfast included; complimentary wine and cheese; restaurant on premises; restaurants nearby **Wheelchair access:** yes **Rates:** $90 to $200; 10% discount to National Trust members and National Trust Visa cardholders **Payment:** AmEx, Visa, MC, DC, Discover, traveler's check **Restrictions:** no pets **Activities:** courtyard, carriage tours from inn

THOMAS LAMBOLL HOUSE

19 King Street
Charleston, South Carolina 29401
803/723-3212
803/724-6352 Fax
Proprietor: Marie W. Read

Located just off the Battery, this house is known as the Thomas Lamboll House, for its original owner. Built in 1735, the house is a fine example of the Charleston single-house style with raised basement and double-decker porch. Two large bedrooms, elegantly furnished with reproduction and antique furniture, are offered. Each room has a fireplace, cable television, a telephone, central air conditioning, a private bath, and French doors that lead to the third-floor balcony. A continental breakfast is served in the dining room on the first floor.

Open: year round **Accommodations:** 2 guest rooms with private baths **Meals:** continental breakfast included; restaurants nearby **Rates:** $85 to $115; 10% discount to National Trust members and National Trust Visa cardholders **Payment:** personal check **Restrictions:** smoking limited; no pets

TWENTY-SEVEN STATE STREET BED AND BREAKFAST

27 State Street
Charleston, South Carolina 29401
803/722-4243
Proprietors: Paul and Joye Craven

A significant structure in the city's historic district, the house at 27 State Street was built just after 1800 in the Adam, or Federal, style. Its outward appearance has been carefully preserved along with much of the interior, including elegant woodwork. The carriage house, behind wrought-iron gates and beyond the courtyard, contains two guest suites furnished in antiques and reproductions. Each suite has a private entrance and consists of a bedroom, living room, private bath, and kitchenette. Suites are made comfortable with fresh fruit and flowers, cable television, telephone, and central heat and air. Each evening the next day's breakfast is delivered to guest suites. Twenty-Seven State Street has been the location for several film productions, including the television minseries *Queen* and *Scarlett*.

Open: year round **Accommodations:** 2 guest suites with private baths **Meals:** continental-plus breakast included; complimentary refreshments; restaurants nearby **Rates:** $95 to $130 **Payment:** personal and traveler's checks **Restrictions:** no smoking; no pets **Activities:** courtyard and veranda sitting, bicycles available

VICTORIA HOUSE INN

208 King Street
Charleston, South Carolina 29401
803/720-2944 or 800/933-5464
Proprietor: Mary Kay Smith

Built in 1889 as the city's second YMCA, this three-story brick building was financed by prominent civic-minded Charlestonians who recognized the need to reestablish the association for young men. One of Charleston's few Victorian-era structures built in the Romanesque Revival style, the building, in the heart of the Market Area, has through the years housed retail shops as well as apartments. In 1991 it was meticulously refurbished to offer distinctive guest rooms and small suites, some with fireplaces and whirlpool baths. Today, the Victoria House is decorated in Victorian furnishings and fabrics. Period wallpapers and paint colors adorn the walls. Guests receive evening turn-down service, a continental-plus breakfast, and free on-site parking. Victoria House Inn is convenient to shopping, dining, and touring.

Open: year round **Accommodations:** 18 guest rooms with private baths; 4 are suites **Meals:** continental-plus breakfast included; complimentary refreshments; restaurants nearby **Wheelchair access:** some guest rooms, bathrooms, public spaces **Rates:** $105 to $200; 10% discount offered to National Trust members and National Trust Visa cardholders **Payment:** Visa, MC, traveler's check **Restrictions:** smoking limited; no pets

COLUMBIA

Nearby attractions: Riverbanks Zoo, Columbia Museum, State House, historic homes, University of South Carolina, Five Points shopping and restaurants, golfing, tennis

CLAUSSEN'S INN
2003 Greene Street
Columbia, South Carolina 29205
803/765-0440 or 800/622-3382
803/799-7924 Fax
Proprietor: Dan Vance

Since 1928 when it was built as Claussen's Bakery, this historic brick building has been a familiar sight in the Five Points area of Columbia. To save the landmark, the owners skillfully adapted it as an inn, carefully preserving the historic architectural features while modernizing the structure with a wide vaulted skylight and terra-cotta tiles. With four-poster or iron-and-brass beds, rich colors, and handsome traditional furnishings, every room has its own decor. Many have original hardwood floors; some are suites with loft bedrooms. All the expected amenities are here at this AAA four-diamond inn: private baths, color television, radios, air conditioning, and telephones. Nightly turn-down service includes chocolates and brandy.

Open: year round **Accommodations:** 29 guest rooms with private baths; 8 are suites **Meals:** continental breakfast included; restaurants nearby **Rates:** $100 to $125; 10% discount offered to National Trust members and National Trust Visa cardholders **Payment:** AmEx, Visa, MC, traveler's check **Restrictions:** no pets **Activities:** outdoor whirlpool

---

EDISTO ISLAND

Nearby attractions: Edisto Island, Edisto Beach, Charleston

CASSINA POINT PLANTATION
(off Clark Road)
P.O. Box 535
Edisto Island, South Carolina 29438
803/869-2535
Proprietors: Bruce and Tecla Earnshaw
Location: 45 miles south of Charleston

This sea-island cotton-plantation home was built in 1847 by Carolina Lafayette Seabrook and her husband, James Hopkinson. She was named for and by General

Lafayette and he was the grandson of Francis Hopkinson, signer of the Declaration of Independence. During the Civil War, Union troops occupied Edisto; their presence is still visible in the drawings they left behind on Cassina's ground-floor walls. The four-story Federal-style house rests on a raised foundation. Sitting 100 feet from a quiet creek and salt marsh, the house is surrounded by towering pine, palmetto, pecan, and live oak trees. Now listed in the National Register of Historic Places, Cassina Point has four guests rooms overlooking either the salt marsh or the landscaped grounds. Each antique-furnished bedroom has a fireplace and, for privacy, a half bath. Guests may choose the formal dining room or the screened piazza as a breakfast setting.

Open: year round **Accommodations:** 4 guest rooms with half baths share 2 full baths **Meals:** full breakfast included; complimentary afternoon refreshments **Rates:** $75 single to $105 double **Payment:** personal and traveler's checks **Restrictions:** no smoking; no pets **Activities:** bird and wildlife watching; catching fish, crab, and shrimp; lawn sports; rockers and hammocks; 145 acres of grounds; canoe and kayak rentals

SUMMERVILLE

Nearby attractions: Charleston; Francis Beidler Forest and Swamp; Cypress Gardens, historic homes of Middleton, Magnolia, and National Trust's Drayton Hall; bicycling

BED AND BREAKFAST OF SUMMERVILLE
304 South Hampton Street
Summerville, South Carolina 29483
803/871-5275
Proprietors: Dusty and Emmagene Rhodes

Accommodations at Bed and Breakfast of Summerville are in a restored slave cottage set behind the main house, which was built in 1862 when the land was worked as a plantation. The cottage, rustic with fireplace and beamed ceiling, is furnished with country reproduction furnishings, including a queen-size tester bed, and antiques. Modern comforts are seen to with central heat and air conditioning, full bath, telephone, color television, and fully equipped small kitchen. Guests enter the cottage through a small English garden with seating. A swimming pool is located on the grounds, replete with azalea, camillia, and gardenia bushes. Breakfast is served in the cottage, or in summer, may also be taken in the greenhouse, attached to the main dwelling.

Open: year round **Accommodations:** 1 guest cottage with private bath **Meals:** continental-plus breakfast included; complimentary refreshments; restaurants nearby **Rates:** $45 to $50 **Payment:** personal and traveler's checks **Restrictions:** infants and children over 11 welcome **Activities:** swimming pool, guest bicycles

TENNESSEE

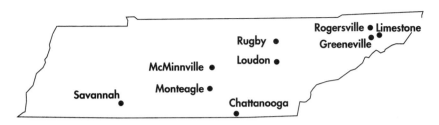

Rogersville ● Limestone
Greeneville ●

Rugby ●

Loudon ●

McMinnville ●

Monteagle ●

Savannah ●

Chattanooga ●

CHATTANOOGA

Nearby attractions: Tennessee Aquarium, Civil War battlefields, the Incline passenger railway, Chattanooga Choo-Choo, Hunter Museum of Art, Children's Discovery Museum, symphony, Tivoli Theater, Rock City, hiking

ADAMS HILBORNE
801 Vine Street
Chattanooga, Tennessee 37403
423/265-5000
423/265-5555
Proprietors: Wendy and Dave Adams

Located in the Fort Wood historic district, a neighborhood of architectural diversity, Adams Hilborne is a majestic Richardsonian Romanesque home. Built in 1889 of native mountain stone, the house's castlelike proportions are emphasized by a round-arched entryway, steeply pitched gables, balconies, balustrades, and a conically roofed round porch. The house, originally designed for former Chattanooga Mayor Edmond G. Watkins, has been renovated by the innkeepers

to show off its original hand-carved coffered ceilings, arched doorways, and leaded, beveled, and Tiffany glass windows. Guest rooms, with 16-foot ceilings and hand-carved moldings, are filled with fine antiques and original art. Many rooms offer fireplaces with original mantels. A continental breakfast is served in the banquet room with its views of historic Lookout Mountain.

Open: year round **Accommodations:** 9 guest rooms with private baths; 4 are suites **Meals:** continental breakfast included; restaurant on premises; restaurants nearby **Wheelchair access:** 1 room **Rates:** $75 to $295; 10% discount to National Trust members and National Trust Visa cardholders midweek only **Payment:** AmEx, Visa, MC, personal and traveler's checks **Restrictions:** children over 6 welcome; no smoking; no pets **Activities:** gift shop, music

MILTON HOUSE BED AND BREAKFAST
508 Fort Wood Place
Chattanooga, Tennessee 37403
615/265-2800
615/756-5191 Fax
Proprietor: Susan E. Mehlen

Located in Chattanooga's Fort Wood historic district, Milton House is a grand 1915 Neoclassical home originally built for the George Fort Milton, Sr. family. Milton was then president and owner of the *Chattanooga News*. The red-brick house is dominated by a full-height entry porch supported by fluted Ionic columns and pilasters. The foyer features a gilt Adam-style embossed garland just below the cove-ceiling cornice. Equally impressive are the well-preserved maple and heart pine floors and the three pillared fireplace mantels throughout the house. A gothic window illuminates the winding staircase. Each guest room is furnished with antiques and is decorated in its own style. Two rooms offer fireplaces; one has a balcony; one has a private bath hand-painted in a garden motif. Guests enjoy the billiard room, terrace, and gazebo.

Open: year round **Accommodations:** 4 guest rooms (3 have private baths); 1 is a suite **Meals:** full breakfast included; restaurants nearby **Rates:** $65 to $125; 10% discount to National Trust members and National Trust Visa cardholders **Payment:** AmEx, Visa, MC, Discover, personal and traveler's checks **Restrictions:** no smoking; no pets **Activities:** pool table, cable television, gazebo with swing, pond with fountain, terrace with view of historic Missionary Ridge

GREENEVILLE

Nearby attractions: historic sites, Smoky Mountain National Park, Cherokee National Forest, hiking, bicycling, golfing, white-water rafting, trout fishing, waterfalls, covered bridges, antiques hunting, Appalachian crafts shops

BIG SPRING INN, DOUGHTY–RICKER HOME

315 North Main Street
Greeneville, Tennessee 37745
615/638-2917
Proprietors: Marshall and Nancy Ricker
Location: 70 miles east of Knoxville

Big Spring Inn is a turn-of-the-century classically styled home with hipped roof and dormers, large covered porches, and porte cochere. Two guest parlors have fireplaces and provide diversions with a music collection, library, and games. A swimming pool, porches, and gardens with 100-year-old trees are offered in warm weather. Bedrooms are individually furnished with antiques and special amenities such as fresh flowers, fine soaps, and terrycloth robes. The inn's decor is elegant with its antiques, high quality reproductions, and original chandeliers throughout. A unique feature in the dining room is the early hand-painted wallpaper imported from France. Breakfast includes entrees such as cheese-stuffed French toast with apricot sauce. Located in Greeneville's historic district, the inn has been praised by the *Los Angeles Times* and *Knoxville News Sentinel*.

Open: year round **Accommodations:** 6 guest rooms with private baths; 1 is a suite **Meals:** full breakfast included; complimentary refreshments; dinners and picnics available; restaurants nearby **Rates:** $60 to $76; 10% discount to National Trust members and National Trust Visa cardholders **Payment:** AmEx, Visa, MC, personal and traveler's checks **Restrictions:** children over 4 welcome; no smoking; no pets (nearby kennels) **Activities:** swimming pool, lawn games, gardens, library, porch sitting

LIMESTONE

Nearby attractions: Davy Crockett State Park, golfing, white-water rafting, fishing, boating, swimming, hiking, bicycling, horseback riding, Andrew Johnson Home, historic Jonesborough

SNAPP INN BED AND BREAKFAST

1990 Davy Crockett Park Road
Limestone, Tennessee 37681
423/257-2482
Proprietors: Dan and Ruth Dorgan
Location: 10 miles west of Jonesborough; 12 miles east of Greeneville

Located in Upper East Tennessee's farm country, Snapp Inn affords expansive views of the Great Smoky Mountains. The Federal brick house, built in 1815 by John Snapp, shows elements of the Classical Revival in its full-height entry porch supported by massive fluted columns, and of the Gothic Revival in its Gothic-arched window in the gable, between two chimneys. Most of the house's original elements are intact, including detailed mantelpieces. The living room is furnished in the Empire style, an ornate reed organ its centerpiece. Both guest rooms, furnished with Victorian antiques, have private baths down the hall; guests are provided terrycloth robes. Guests are welcome to relax in the living room with television and VCR, books, and newspapers. Davy Crockett Birthplace State Park is within walking distance, with its large swimming pool and picnic areas.

Open: year round **Accommodations:** 2 guest rooms with private baths **Meals:** full breakfast included; restaurants nearby **Rates:** $40 to $50; 10% discount to National Trust members and National Trust Visa cardholders **Payment:** personal and traveler's checks **Restrictions:** no smoking; inquire about pets **Activities:** pool table, walk to park and swimming pool

LOUDON

Nearby attractions: museums, aquarium, Tennessee River, TVA waterways, The Lost Sea, Smoky Mountains, Cherokee National Forest, Gatlinburg, tennis, horseback riding

MASON PLACE BED AND BREAKFAST

600 Commerce Street
Loudon, Tennessee 37774
615/458-3921
Proprietors: Bob and Donna Siewert

Built in 1865, this Greek Revival house with two-tiered front porch sits among three acres of lawns, gardens, and towering shade trees. Troops from both sides camped on these grounds during the Civil War, and bullets and artifacts from those times are still found here today. Bob and Donna Siewert have spent six years restoring the 7000-square-foot home, receiving an award for outstanding restoration from the East Tennessee Development District. Guests at Mason Place find a grand entrance hall, 10 working fireplaces, and five antique-filled guest rooms, each complete with a gas-log fireplace, authentic feather bed, and private bath. Outdoors, guests are invited to enjoy the wisteria-covered arbor, gazebo, hammock, porch swings, and swimming pool at this National Register property.

Open: year round **Accommodations:** 5 guest rooms with private baths **Meals:** full breakfast included; restaurants nearby **Wheelchair access:** limited **Rates:** $96 to $120 **Payment:** personal and traveler's checks **Restrictions:** children over 12 welcome; no smoking; no pets **Activities:** swimming pool, horseshoe pitching, croquet, hammock, porch swings and rockers

MCMINNVILLE

Nearby attractions: "nursery capital of the world," Cumberland Caverns, Rock Island, Fall Creek Falls, Savage Gulf and Old Stone Fort state parks, Center Hill Lake, Nashville, Chattanooga

FALCON MANOR BED AND BREAKFAST
2645 Faulkner Springs Road
McMinnville, Tennessee 37110
615/668-4444
Proprietors: George and Charlien McGlothin

This National Register Victorian mansion was built in 1896 by manufacturer Clay Faulkner (who produced Gorilla jeans, "so strong, even a gorilla couldn't tear them apart"). The 6000-square-foot brick Queen Anne home is surrounded by gingerbreaded porches filled with rockers and shaded by century-old trees. Inside, 12-foot ceilings, a sweeping staircase, exquisite woodwork, rich colors, and museum-quality antiques create an elegant setting. All guest rooms are lavishly furnished with period antiques, including the double beds. The Honeymoon Suite, across the breezeway in the original kitchen, has a king-size brass bed. The house was used as a country hospital from the 1940s until 1968, after which it sat vacant until 1983. Recently, the innkeepers completed five years of restoration on the house and delight in sharing their experiences with guests.

Open: year round **Accommodations:** 5 guest rooms (1 has a private bath) **Meals:** full breakfast included; complimentary refreshments; restaurants nearby **Wheelchair access:** 2 rooms **Rates:** $75 to $85; 10% discount to National Trust members and National Trust Visa cardholders **Payment:** Visa, MC, personal and traveler's checks **Restrictions:** children over 11 welcome; no smoking; no pets **Activities:** porch rocking, library, complimentary house tours, picnics, creek across the street

MONTEAGLE

Nearby attractions: Monteagle Assembly Grounds, University of the South, Chattanooga Aquarium, South Cumberland State Park, mountain arts and crafts, Jack Daniel's and George Dickel distilleries, swimming, golfing, horseback riding, music festivals

ADAMS EDGEWORTH INN

Monteagle Assembly
Monteagle, Tennessee 37356
615/924-4000
615/924-3236 Fax
Proprietors: Wendy and David Adams

Situated amid the natural beauty of the Monteagle Assembly Grounds—96 acres of historic homes, giant trees, and rolling hills that are also known as the Chatauqua of the South—Adams Edgeworth Inn is an 1896 Victorian inn. Listed in the National Register of Historic Places, the inn features chintz fabrics, antique furniture, and wicker. A cast-iron wood-burning stove and four fireplaces warm guests on cold days. Outside, rockers line 200 feet of gingerbread-trimmed porches. Guests are invited to browse the museum-quality collection of Asian, European, and American art on display throughout the house. Guest rooms are decorated with antiques and family collectibles, and a colorful variety of bedcoverings from American quilts to hand-embroidered Pakistani cashmere blankets. Several rooms contain fireplaces. When weather permits, breakfast is served in the rose-scented courtyard.

Open: year round **Accommodations:** 12 guest rooms with private baths; 1 is a suite **Meals:** continental-plus breakfast included; 5-course dinner prepared by Culinary Institute of America–trained chef served nightly by candlelight; complimentary refreshments **Rates:** $65 to $150; 10% discount offered to National Trust members and National Trust Visa cardholders midweek only **Payment:** AmEx, Visa, MC, personal and traveler's checks **Restrictions:** children under 5 by special arrangement only; no smoking; no pets **Activities:** tennis; nature trails; strolling through historic village; music, art, and lectures during chatauqua season

ROGERSVILLE

Nearby attractions: Cherokee Lake, museum, walking tours of historic district with the oldest courthouse in Tennessee, swimming, tennis, golfing

HALE SPRINGS INN
110 West Main Street
Rogersville, Tennessee 37857
615/272-5171
Proprietors: Carl and Janet Netherland-Brown

Built in 1824, this three-story brick hostelry is the oldest continuously operating inn in the state. The Federal-style inn has hosted many famous people through the years, most notably presidents Andrew Jackson, Andrew Johnson, and James K. Polk. Originally called McKinney's Tavern after its founder, the inn became a Union headquarters during the Civil War. It was renamed the Hale Springs Inn in 1884, in honor of the mineral springs 15 miles to the north. Today, the fully restored inn retains its original wainscoting and heart-of-pine floors and is furnished with antiques and reproduction pieces. Eight of the nine guest rooms have working fireplaces.

Open: year round **Accommodations:** 9 guest rooms with private baths; 3 are suites **Meals:** continental breakfast included; restaurant on premises; restaurants nearby **Wheelchair access:** dining facilities **Rates:** $45 to $70 **Payment:** AmEx, Visa, MC, traveler's checks **Restrictions:** no pets **Activities:** tours of the inn, reading, in-room televisions, garden with gazebo and benches

RUGBY

Nearby attractions: Alvin York State Historic Site, Highland Manor Winery, Big South Fork National River and Recreation Area for swimming, hiking, white-water rafting, canoeing, and horseback riding

NEWBURY HOUSE AT HISTORIC RUGBY
Highway 52
P.O. Box 8
Rugby, Tennessee 37733
615/628-2441 or 615/628-2430
Proprietors: Historic Rugby, Inc.

In 1880, amid worldwide publicity, English author and social reformer Thomas Hughes launched a utopian colony in Tennessee. Calling Rugby a "lovely corner of God's earth," he urged English and American colonists to treat it lovingly while working cooperatively for individual freedoms. Newbury House was the colony's first boarding house, opening in 1880. It was prosperous during Rugby's early years yet fell into disrepair by 1950. Now the board-and-batten siding, front porch, mansard roof, and dormer windows are restored, and the house is furnished with Victorian antiques, some original to the colony. There are five guest rooms in Newbury House as well as a three-bedroom suite, with kitchen, parlor, and porch, in Pioneer Cottage. Guests may have tea in the parlor with its ceiling fans, fireplace, and Victorian library. A full-service restaurant specializes in British and Appalachian fare. The entire colony has been listed in the National Register of Historic Places.

Open: year round **Accommodations:** 5 guest rooms (3 have private baths); 1 suite **Meals:** full breakfast included; complimentary refreshments; restaurant on premises **Rates:** $50 to $70 **Payment:** Visa, MC, personal and traveler's checks **Restrictions:** children over 12 welcome in Newbury House; any age allowed in cottage; smoking limited **Activities:** tours of historic village with restored schoolhouse, church, and library; Rugby Commissary featuring handmade crafts and Victorian bookshop

SAVANNAH

Nearby attractions: historic district, Shiloh National Military Park, Pickwick Landing Dam and Lake, Tennessee River, Tennessee River Museum, Natchez Trace, bicycling

ROSS HOUSE BED AND BREAKFAST
504 Main Street
P.O. Box 398
Savannah, Tennessee 38372
901/925-3974 or 800/467-3174
901/925-4472 Fax
Proprietor: John J. Ross

This Neoclassical house was built in 1908 by Mr. and Mrs. E. W. Ross. It features a two-story portico with Ionic columns and a one-story wraparound porch with 24 columns. The exterior of the house, with original metal shingle roof, is unaltered except by an addition to the second floor made in the 1930s. The interior also remains in its original condition, having on the first floor an entry hall with oak staircase, library, music parlor, dining room, family room, children's room, and kitchen. The second floor has four original bedrooms and two sitting rooms and Art Deco–style bathrooms added in the 1930s. Today, these rooms compose two guest suites, each with two bedrooms, a bath, and a sitting room. The house recently has been redecorated in historical colors and is furnished with antiques. A library containing many early twentieth-century volumes and a Victrola with its record collection are original to the house.

Open: year round **Accommodations:** 2 guest suites with private baths **Meals:** continental-plus breakfast included; restaurants nearby **Rates:** $65 to $150 **Payment:** AmEx, Visa, MC, Discover, personal and traveler's checks **Restrictions:** children over 10 welcome; no smoking; no pets **Activities:** bocce, flower garden

TEXAS

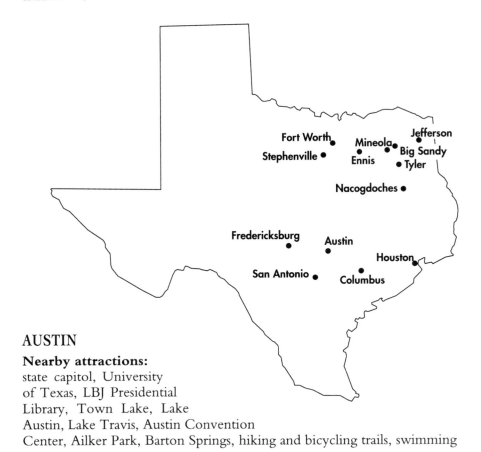

Fort Worth•
Stephenville •
Mineola•
Ennis•
Jefferson
•
Big Sandy
• Tyler
Nacogdoches •
Fredericksburg
•
Austin
•
Houston•
San Antonio •
Columbus
•

AUSTIN

Nearby attractions:
state capitol, University
of Texas, LBJ Presidential
Library, Town Lake, Lake
Austin, Lake Travis, Austin Convention
Center, Ailker Park, Barton Springs, hiking and bicycling trails, swimming

GOVERNORS' INN

611 West 22nd Street
Austin, Texas 78705
512/477-0711
Proprietors: Gwen and David Fullbrook

Just blocks from the Texas State Capitol and the University of Texas, Governors'
Inn is an 1897 Neoclassical yellow frame house. Restored in 1993, the inn offers
10 guest rooms, each named for a Texas governor. Furnished with tasteful
antiques and coordinating linens, each room has a private bath with claw-foot tub.
A parlor and wraparound porches provide quiet places to relax. Large trees shade
the porches, which are complete with Victorian rockers and porch swings. A full
breakfast is served in the dining room before the fireplace. The Fullbrooks

combine Texas hospitality (Gwen is a native) with British charm (David is English) to create a unique bed-and-breakfast experience. Governors' Inn has been featured in *USA Today*, *Dallas Morning News*, *Houston Chronicle*, and *Texas Monthly*.

Open: year round **Accommodations:** 10 guest rooms with private baths; 1 is a suite **Meals:** full breakfast included; complimentary refreshments; restaurants nearby **Wheelchair access:** yes **Rates:** $59 to $99 **Payment:** AmEx, Visa, MC, CB, DC, Discover, personal and traveler's checks **Restrictions:** children over 10 welcome; no smoking; no pets

---

BIG SANDY

Nearby attractions: historic house tours; antiques hunting; state and local parks; festivals; nearby towns of Longview, Tyler, and Gladewater

ANNIE'S BED AND BREAKFAST
106 North Tyler
Big Sandy, Texas 75755
903/636-4355
903/636-4744 Fax
Proprietors: Clifton and Kathy Shaw

Annie's Bed and Breakfast has a long history of ownership beginning with W. B. and Annie Mask, who built a one-story bungalow on this spot in 1901. Their small house is now the parlor and dining room of the larger house created by Wylie and Virgie Kay in 1916. The Kay's doubled the size of the house, adding two fireplaces. Further adornments and refinements were added by G. A. Tohill and his family, who lived here for 33 years, beginning in 1927. Today, bed and breakfast guests stay in rooms individually decorated with floral wallpaper, antique furnishings, afghans, and a small old-fashioned refrigerator. Bathrooms contain claw-foot tubs and some rooms have balconies. A full breakfast is served in Annie's Tea Room and Restaurant, a big blue-and-white 1905 house across the street.

Open: year round **Accommodations:** 12 guest rooms (11 have private baths); 5 area suites **Meals:** full breakfast included; restaurant on premises **Wheelchair access:** 1 room **Rates:** $70 to $115; 10% discount to National Trust members and National Trust Visa cardholders **Payment:** AmEx, Visa, MC, Discover, personal and traveler's checks **Restrictions:** children over 3 welcome; no smoking; no pets **Activities:** television; games; reading; Annie's Victorian Village, which includes Annie's Gift Shop, Annie's One Stop Craft Shoppe, and Annie's Needlecraft Gallery

COLUMBUS

Nearby attractions: walking tours of historic area, opera house, antiques hunting, tennis, golfing, arts and crafts cooperatives, spring wildflower tours

GANT GUEST HOUSE
936 Bowie Street
P.O. Box 86
Columbus, Texas 78934
409/732-5135 or 409/732-2190
Proprietor: Laura Ann Rau

This German-style cottage was built in the 1870s in Alleyton. From the early 1900s until 1978, it was owned and occupied by the Gant family. Then, in 1984, the current owners purchased it and moved it to nearby Columbus to save it from demolition. The house is an interesting example of the period, with original stenciling and paint colors. The lacy stenciling in the green and white room was copied for the walls of the Texas Room in the Daughters of the American Revolution Museum in Washington, D.C. The house is completely furnished in antiques. One of the oldest settlements in Texas, the site of Columbus was first occupied in 1823 by some of Stephen F. Austin's original colonists.

Open: year round **Accommodations:** 2 guest rooms share a bath **Meals:** continental breakfast included; restaurants nearby **Wheelchair access:** guest rooms, bathrooms, dining faciliites **Rates:** $65 to $85 **Payment:** personal check **Restrictions:** not suitable for small children; no smoking; no pets

RAUMONDA
1100 Bowie Street
P.O. Box 112
Columbus, Texas 78934
409/732-5135 or 409/732-2190
Proprietor: R. F. "Buddy" Rau

Built in 1887 by Henry Ilse, a farmer, rancher, and saloon owner, this symmetrical Victorian house with double-decker, gingerbread-encrusted verandas shows Italianate influences in its bracketed eaves and low-pitched hipped roof. The completely restored home has nine rooms, including a butler's pantry and glassed gallery. Two stairways and an elevator connect the two floors. Three fireplaces boast white marble mantels. Interior pine woodwork retains its faux-grain painting, a style popular during the Victorian period. One guest room leads to a gallery overlooking the formal garden and pool. Another contains a suite of turn-of-the-century mahogany furniture. The third room has a mahogany Second

Empire suite. In addition to continental breakfast, guests are offered a tour of this historic home.

Open: year round **Accommodations:** 3 guests rooms with private baths **Meals:** continental breakfast included; restaurants nearby **Rate:** $80 **Payment:** personal check **Restrictions:** not suitable for small children; no smoking; no pets **Activities:** swimming pool in landscaped garden, historic site tour

---

ENNIS

Nearby attractions: National Register historic district, Railroad Museum, Ellis County Museum, antiques hunting, driving tours, historic house tours, tennis, golfing, fishing

RAPHAEL HOUSE
500 West Ennis Avenue
Ennis, Texas 75119
214/875-1555
214/875-0308 Fax
Proprietors: Brian and Danna Cody Wolf

A French banker and community leader, Edmond Raphael, and his wife, Fannie Jolesch, built this grand Neoclassical home in 1906 for their family of five children, who continued to own the house for 82 years. The mansion commands attention with its massive Ionic columns that support the two-story front porch.

The house's 19 rooms boast 12-foot-high ceilings, pocket doors, transom windows, and heart-pine floors. This National Register house has been fully restored and is now a showcase of museum-quality antiques, rich wall coverings, and luxurious fabrics. Many furnishings belonged to the Raphael family, including three bedroom suites and an 1865 rosewood baby grand piano. Bedrooms, named and decorated for Raphael family members, have down comforters and pillows. Bathrooms offer claw-foot tubs, scented soaps, and toiletries. Breakfast brings an unusual Czech–Tex blend of cuisines.

Open: year round **Accommodations:** 6 guest rooms with private baths **Meals:** full breakfast included on weekends; continental-plus breakfast included weekdays; complimentary refreshments on weekends; restaurants nearby **Rates:** $60 to $105; 10% discount offered to National Trust members and National Trust Visa cardholders midweek only **Payment:** AmEx, Visa, MC, CB, DC, Discover, personal and traveler's checks **Restrictions:** children over 6 welcome; no smoking; no pets **Activities:** rocking chairs and porch swings, VCR and classic movies, piano, gardens, privileges at private tennis and health club

FORT WORTH

Nearby attractions: Stockyards National Historic District, Tarantula Railroad Station, Billy Bob's Texas, Cowtown Coliseum, Cowtown Rodeo, Livestock Exchange Building and Museum

MISS MOLLY'S HOTEL
109 1/2 West Exchange Avenue
Fort Worth, Texas 76106
817/626-1522 or 800/99MOLLY (800/996-6559)
817/624-2414
Proprietor: Mark Hancock

Miss Molly's Hotel is on the second floor of this 1910 building, above the Star Cafe, one of the district's oldest and best restaurants. The hotel originated as a legitimate business, but in the 1940s it became a popular bawdy house known as the Gayette Hotel. Operating legally again, Miss Molly's offers eight guest rooms dressed in turn-of-the-century Texas style with iron beds, carved oak furniture, and even a pot-bellied stove in one room. Each room contains memorabilia to honor a different sector of Texas society: cowboys, cattle barons, gunslingers, oilmen, railroad men, and even the establishment's previous madam, Miss Josie. Miss Josie's room features a draped fabric ceiling and a private bath. The remaining rooms share three bathrooms in the hallway—robes are provided for guests' use. Lace curtains and antique quilts are found in all rooms. Breakfast is served in the parlor beneath the stained-glass skylight.

Open: year round **Accommodations:** 8 guest rooms (1 has a private bath) **Meals:** continental-plus breakfast included; restaurants nearby **Rates:** $95 to $160; 10% discount to National Trust members and National Trust Visa cardholders **Payment:** AmEx, Visa, MC, DC, Discover, personal and traveler's checks **Restrictions:** children over 12 welcome; no smoking; no pets

---

FREDERICKSBURG

Nearby attractions: Admiral Nimitz Museum, LBJ State and National Park, Enchanted Rock, wineries and wine tastings, Guadalupe River, Austin, San Antonio

MAGNOLIA HOUSE
101 East Hackberry
Fredericksburg, Texas 78624
210/997-0306
Proprietors: Joyce and Patrick Kennard

This house was built in 1923 by architect Edward Stein for his family. Designer of the Gillespie County Courthouse in Fredericksburg, Stein personally selected each piece of lumber for his own home. The Craftsman-influenced house with clipped front gable and wide low-pitched roofline has been designated a Texas Historic Landmark by the Texas Historical Commission. Inside, the original kitchen has antique glass cabinets, a working cistern in the butler's pantry, and antique built-in iceboxes. Unique antique-decorated guest rooms offer terrycloth robes and Magnolia House soaps. Each room has color television with premium cable channels. Some rooms have fireplaces and private entrances. Southern-style breakfasts served on antique china and silver inclue biscuits and gravy. A stone patio with fish pond and waterfall invites guests outdoors. Wicker furniture graces the porches.

Open: year round **Accommodations:** 6 guest rooms (4 have private baths); 2 are suites **Wheelchair access:** limited **Meals:** full breakfast included; complimentary refreshments; restaurants nearby **Rates:** $75 to $105; 10% discount to National Trust members and National Trust Visa cardholders, weekdays only **Payment:** Visa, MC, personal and traveler's checks **Restrictions:** children over 12 welcome; no smoking **Activities:** patio and porch sitting

HOUSTON

Nearby attractions: museums, galleries, jogging trails, historical walking tours, theaters, downtown Houston attractions

DURHAM HOUSE BED AND BREAKFST INN
921 Heights Boulevard
Houston, Texas 77008
713/868-4654
713/868-7965 Fax
Proprietors: Marguerite Swanson

Listed in the National Register of Historic Places, Durham House was built in 1902 for newlyweds Mr. and Mrs. Jay L. Durham. Jay Durham later became the first fire chief of Houston Heights, this big-city community with a small-town feel. The Durham's is a Queen Anne house complete with turret and wraparound porch. Six elegantly styled guest rooms feature Victorian antiques. All bathrooms contain antique claw-foot tubs with overhead showers. A full breakfast is served in the formal dining room or in the wicker-furnished solarium. The inn's garden gazebo welcomes guests and is often used for romantic wedding ceremonies. The inn also hosts murder-mystery dinner parties using original mysteries written exclusively for Durham House.

Open: year round **Accommodations:** 6 guest rooms (5 have private baths) **Meals:** full breakfast included; complimentary refreshments; murder mystery dinner parties available; restaurants nearby **Rates:** $55 to $95; 10% discount to National Trust members and National Trust Visa cardholders **Payment:** AmEx, Visa, MC, Discover, personal and traveler's checks **Restrictions:** children over 12 welcome; no smoking; no pets **Activities:** in-room radio and television, tandem bicycles, parlor player piano

JEFFERSON

Nearby attractions: museums, riverboat tours, buggy tours of historic district, antebellum house tours, antiques hunting, steam-engine train ride, bayou excursions, Lake Caddo, Lake o' the Pines, golfing, boating, fishing

PRIDE HOUSE
409 Broadway
Jefferson, Texas 75657
903/665-2675 or 800/894-3526
Proprietor: Sandra J. Spalding

The Pride House is a two-story Stick Style structure built in 1888 for lumberman George Brown. Painted a rich caramel color with white gingerbread trim and sky-blue accents, Pride House recalls the past with a wraparound porch, original bronze hardware in heavy doors, and stained glass in every window. Rooms have high ceilings and tall windows, and exceptional millwork is evident in the beaded wainscoting and door and window moldings. The house is filled with Victorian furniture. Guest rooms, including those in the guest cottage, contain period decor and wallpaper, armoires, and private baths. (The crimson West Room has an enormous antique claw-foot bathtub that was voted best in the state by *Houston Style* magazine.) The Pride House, which opened to guests in 1980, is said to be Texas's first bed and breakfast.

Open: year round **Accommodations:** 10 guest rooms with private baths; 1 is a suite **Meals:** full breakfast included; restaurants nearby **Rates:** $55 to $100; 10% discount to National Trust members and National Trust Visa cardholders **Payment:** Visa, MC, personal and traveler's checks **Restrictions:** no smoking **Activities:** reading, porch rocking

MINEOLA

Nearby attractions: Lake Fork (bass capital), Little Theater, pottery factory, Canton First Monday Trade Days, state parks, golfing, hiking, peach and blueberry orchards, Christmas tree farms

MUNZESHEIMER MANOR
202 North Newson
Mineola, Texas 75773
903/569-6634
Proprietors: Bob and Sherry Murray

Gustav Munzesheimer, a German immigrant, built this Queen Anne home at the turn of the century, incorporating elements typical of the eclectic style: wrap-around porches, bay windows, and numerous gables. The house, built entirely of pine and cedar, was home to several prominent Mineola families over the years. Two parlors, a formal dining room, and four guest rooms are in the main house; three guest rooms are available in the adjacent cottage. Guest rooms are furnished with English and American antiques and each has its own bathroom with a period footed tub. All rooms are centrally heated and air conditioned and are equipped with ceiling fans. Three rooms have fireplaces. Victorian gowns and nightshirts are provided for each guest. A full family-style breakfast is served. Munzesheimer Manor is available for special occasions such as weddings, showers, and receptions.

Open: year round **Accommodations:** 7 guest rooms with private baths **Meals:** full breakfast included; complimentary refreshments; restaurants nearby **Wheelchair access:** limited **Rates:** $75 to $95; 10% discount to National Trust members and National Trust Visa cardholders **Payment:** Visa, MC, DC, Discover, personal and traveler's checks **Restrictions:** no smoking; no pets **Activities:** porch rocking

NACOGDOCHES

Nearby attractions: tours of historic Nacogdoches, golfing, fishing, hiking, rodeos, horse shows, county fairs, antiques hunting, museums, art galleries, lakes for swimming and water skiing

LLANO GRANDE PLANTATION BED AND BREAKFAST

Llano Grande Plantation
Press Road, Route 4
Box 9400
Nacogdoches, Texas 75961
409/569-1249
Proprietors: Ann and Charles Phillips
Location: 5 miles south of Nacogdoches, oldest town in Texas

Llano Grande Plantation contains three separate guest houses, none visible from the other. The Tol Barret House (1840) was the home of the man who drilled the first producing oil well in Texas in 1866. This National Register structure has been restored and furnished with antiques of the period. Its outbuildings include a large detached kitchen, with a second-story bedroom that is now a guest suite. The Sparks House (1851), a restored and antique-filled pioneer structure, is a Texas Historic Landmark offering a two-bedroom suite, complete with wood-burning fireplace and stove. The Gate House is a charming 1938 Texas farmhouse with a parlor fireplace and two sunny bedrooms. It is set among lofty oaks and surrounded by a well house, cattle barns, a corral, and pastures.

Open: year round **Accommodations:** 3 2-bedroom suites with private baths **Meals:** full or continental-plus breakfast included (varies with guest house); restaurants nearby **Rates:** from $65; 10% discount offered to National Trust members and National Trust Visa cardholders **Payment:** personal and traveler's checks **Restrictions:** inquire about children; smoking limited; inquire about pets **Activities:** 600 acres of forest with hiking trails, fishing in stocked pond, croquet, wildlife watching

SAN ANTONIO

Nearby attractions: Alamo, Riverwalk, Institute of Texan Cultures, Market Square, Spanish Governor's Palace, Fort Sam Houston, Brackenridge Park and Zoo, Sea World, Fiesta Texas, San Pedro Springs Park, jogging paths, tennis, botanical center, museums

BECKMANN INN AND
CARRIAGE HOUSE
222 East Guenther Street
San Antonio, Texas 78204
210/229-1449 or 800/945-1449
Proprietors: Betty Jo and Don Schwartz

This house was built in 1886 by Albert Beckmann for his bride, Marie Dorothea, daughter of the Guenther flour-mill family. Located on the mill grounds, the one-story house gained additions over the years, including a wraparound porch, which resulted in its current rambling floor plan. In the living room, ceilings are 14 feet high, tall windows have beveled glass, and the floor is an intricately designed wood mosaic imported from Paris. Arched pocket doors with opaque glass inserts open to the formal dining room. Guest rooms feature high ceilings with fans, tall, ornately carved Victorian beds, and colorful floral fabrics and wallpapers. Adjacent to the main house is the carriage house with two suites. This building's shuttered windows are adorned with flower-filled boxes. A full breakfast, including dessert, is served daily.

Open: year round **Accommodations:** 5 guest rooms with private baths; 2 are suites **Meals:** full breakfast included; restaurants nearby **Wheelchair access:** limited **Rates:** $80 to $130; 10% discount to National Trust members and National Trust Visa cardholders, midweek only **Payment:** AmEx, Visa, MC, DC, Discover, personal and traveler's checks **Restrictions:** children over 12 welcome; no smoking; no pets **Activities:** patio and gardens, wicker-filled sunporch, porch sitting

BULLIS HOUSE INN
621 Pierce Street
P.O. Box 8059
San Antonio, Texas 78208
210/223-9426
210/299-1479 Fax
Proprietors: Steven and Alma Cross

General John Lapham Bullis was famous for fighting Indians on the Texas frontier and was instrumental in the capture of the Apache chief Geronimo. Bullis's house, built between 1906 and 1909, is said to be haunted by Geronimo's spirit. The house is a white Neoclassical mansion, notable for the grouped Ionic columns that support the two-story portico. Stairways and paneling are of dark oak and mahogany. Marble fireplaces warm each parlor. The house is also graced with parquet floors and intricately designed ceilings with large plaster medallions framing crystal chandeliers. Several guest rooms have gas- and wood-burning fireplaces and French windows. All are individually decorated with antiques and contemporary furnishings. The Bullis House Inn is located in the Fort Sam Houston Historic District.

Open: year round **Accommodations:** 7 guest rooms (1 has a private bath) **Meals:** continental-plus breakfast included; lunch available with reservations; restaurants nearby **Rates:** $49 to $69; additional adult $10; additional child $6 **Payment:** AmEx, Visa, MC, Discover, traveler's check **Restrictions:** smoking limited; no pets **Activities:** badminton; swimming pool; volleyball; table tennis; summer barbecues; movie nights with complimentary popcorn, cookies, coffee, and tea

NORTON–BRACKENRIDGE HOUSE
230 Madison
San Antonio, Texas 78204
210/271-3442 or 800/221-1412
219/271-3442 Fax
Proprietors: Bennie and Sue Blansett

Located in the King William Historic District, the Norton–Brackenridge House is a 1901 Neoclassical house, its front gable supported by four Corinthian columns. Inside, the house boasts its original pine floors, double-hung windows, and high ceilings. Guest rooms contain king- and queen-size beds, telephones, private baths (three with footed tubs), and private entrances. Two rooms have kitchenettes; the other guest rooms have mini-refrigerators. A full breakfast is served and can be enjoyed on the veranda, weather permitting. Porch swings offer quiet relaxation in this quiet historic neighborhood just six blocks from downtown. The inn also offers a two-bedroom guest house with kitchen, living room, dining room, and bath.

Open: year round **Accommodations:** 5 guest rooms with private baths; 3 are suites **Meals:** full breakfast included; complimentary refreshments; restaurants nearby **Rates:** $89 to $125; 10% discount to National Trust members and National Trust Visa cardholders **Payment:** AmEx, Visa, MC, Discover, personal and traveler's checks **Restrictions:** children over 12 welcome (all ages welcome in guest house); no smoking; no pets, except in guest house **Activities:** hot tub, afternoon tea on veranda, King William district walking tour

RIVERWALK INN
329 Old Guilbeau
San Antonio, Texas 78204
210/212-8300 or 800/254-4440
210/229-9422
Proprietors: Tracy and Jan Hammer

Five two-story log homes built ca. 1842 have been moved from their original sites in Tennessee to this spot along the banks of the San Antonio River to form Riverwalk Inn. The homes were brought to this location log by log and reconstructed as originally built. Each guest room has been named in honor of Tennesseeans, such as Davy Crockett and James Bowie, who fought for Texas independence at the Battle of the Alamo. While guest rooms exude a rustic atmosphere, they come fully outfitted for comfort with private baths, telephones, television, fireplaces, and refrigerators. Period antiques, four-poster beds, and handmade quilts complete the setting. The inn is located within walking distance of most major San Antonio attractions, although there is an 80-foot-long porch filled with rocking chairs for those who choose to just relax.

Open: year round **Accommodations:** 11 guest suites with private baths **Meals:** full breakfast included on weekends; continental-plus breakfast included weekdays; restaurants nearby **Wheelchair access:** 1 room **Rates:** $89 to $135; 10% discount to National Trust members and National Trust Visa cardholders **Payment:** AmEx, Visa, MC, Discover, personal and traveler's checks **Restrictions:** no smoking; no pets **Activities:** walking and jogging along Riverwalk from inn door

STEPHENVILLE

Nearby attractions: Stephenville Country Opry, Granbury Opry House, Fossil Rim Wildlife Preserve and Dinosaur Park, Hoka Hey Foundry, golfing, swimming, horseback riding

OXFORD HOUSE
563 North Graham
Stephenville, Texas 76401
817/965-6885
Proprietors: Bill and Paula Oxford

Construction of this elaborate Queen Anne home of Judge W. J. Oxford

and his family was begun in 1889 but not completed until 1898. Widowed twice, the judge married a third time in 1911. This wife outlived him and remained in the home until her death in 1983. The judge's grandson and his wife have restored the house, opening it as a bed-and-breakfast establishment. Antique beds, marble-topped dressers, beveled-glass mirrors, and armoires enhance the Victorian atmosphere of the four upstairs bedrooms. Each has a private bath with antique claw-foot tub. Oxford House also contains a tearoom serving high tea, lunch, dinner, and dessert, and a gift shop offering vintage jewelry and dolls, imported toiletries, and tea accessories.

Open: year round **Accommodations:** 4 guest rooms with private baths **Meals:** full breakfast included; complimentary refreshments; restaurants nearby **Wheelchair access:** yes **Rates:** $65 to $85 **Payment:** AmEx, Visa, MC, personal check **Restrictions:** children over 6 welcome; no smoking; no pets **Activities:** tearoom, gift shop

---

TYLER

Nearby attractions: museums, zoo, antiques hunting, Tyler Municipal Rose Garden, Texas Rose Festival, house tours, golfing, lakes, parks, symphony, theaters, bicycle tours

CHARNWOOD HILL INN BED AND BREAKFAST
223 East Charnwood
Tyler, Texas 75701
903/597-3980
Proprietor: Andy Walker

Built in 1855, this residence underwent a series of owners and remodelings until it was purchased by H. L. Hunt in the early 1900s. Hunt remodeled the home extensively, resulting in the Neoclassical style evident today. On the third floor he built an Art Deco suite for his daughters, Margaret and Caroline. This 1500-square-foot suite with skylight, opaque glass walls, two bedrooms, and living room is a luxurious guest room today. The H. C. Miller family, who bought the house in 1938, converted some second-floor space into a wood-paneled and beamed trophy room with built-in gun cabinet and bar. This room is also offered to guests today. Other guest rooms range in style from rustic to sylvan in a room with a willow-canopied bed and garden statuary. Numerous common areas include the great hall, library, gathering hall, balconies, screened swing porch, and gardens. Located in the Azalea historic district, the inn offers off-street parking.

Open: year round **Accommodations:** 7 guest rooms with private baths; 1 is a suite **Meals:** full breakfast included; complimentary refreshments; restaurants nearby **Rates:** $95 to $275; 10% discount to National Trust members and National Trust Visa cardholders **Payment:** Visa, MC, Discover, personal and traveler's checks **Restrictions:** children over 13 welcome; no smoking; no pets **Activities:** library, television–VCR and video library, walking, gift shop, gardens with fountain

UTAH

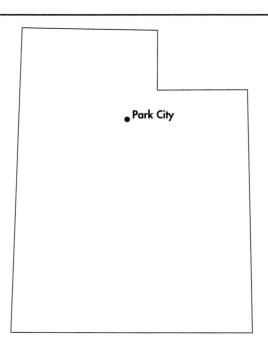

•Park City

PARK CITY

Nearby attractions: museum, historic Main Street, shops, galleries, Town Lift to Park City Ski Area for downhill skiing, cross-country skiing, golfing, tennis, mountain biking, hiking, fishing, hot-air ballooning, horseback riding, concerts, festivals

OLD MINERS' LODGE – A BED AND BREAKFAST INN

615 Woodside Avenue
P.O. Box 2639
Park City, Utah 84060-2639
801/645-8068 or 800/648-8068
801/645-7420 Fax
Proprietors: Hugh Daniels and Susan Wynne

Old Miners' Lodge is located in the National Register historic district of the colorful resort town of Park City. This two-story frame inn was established in 1889 as a boarding house for local miners seeking fortune in the surrounding ore-rich mountains. Named for historic Park City personalities, the lodge's 10 guest rooms are restored and furnished to their period with antique and country pieces, down pillows, and comforters. All guest baths contain terrycloth robes. Guests start the day with a full breakfast in the cozy dining room. A large fireplace in the living room draws guests in the evening. An outdoor hot tub is available year round and extra-large towels are provided in each room. The lodge is equipped to host groups for workshops, seminars, or family gatherings.

Open: year round **Accommodations:** 10 guest rooms with private baths; 3 are suites **Meals:** full breakfast included; complimentary refreshments; catering available for groups; restaurants nearby **Rates:** $50 to $190 seasonal **Payment:** AmEx, Visa, MC, Discover, personal and traveler's checks **Restrictions:** no smoking; no pets **Activities:** outdoor hot tub

VERMONT

ANDOVER

Nearby attractions: Okemo Mountain Ski Area, Weston Priory, Green Mountain National Forest, hiking, antiques hunting, Weston Playhouse (seasonal)

INN AT HIGHVIEW

East Hill Road
R.R. 1, Box 201A
Andover, Vermont 05142
802/875-2724
802/875-4021 Fax
Proprietor: Gregory T. Bohan
Location: 10 minutes from Weston, Chester, and Ludlow (Okemo Mountain)

A spacious, rambling farmhouse, the Inn at Highview sits high on East Hill, providing panoramic views of the surrounding Green Mountains. Built in 1800, the cozy, yet elegant inn retains much of its original farmhouse appeal, although it has been fully modernized. Guest rooms contain antiques, family heirlooms, and comfortable beds. But the real attention-getters here are the lands around the inn, specifically the trails that were developed for the Swedish Ski Club in the 1950s, and the magnificent gardens and views. After skiing on the inn's own scenic 72 acres and beyond, or cycling through quaint towns and past trout streams and waterfalls, guests return to the inn to relax by the warm fire, cool off in the rock garden pool, or unwind in the sauna.

Open: year round **Accommodations:** 8 guest rooms with private baths; 2 are suites **Meals:** full breakfast included; complimentary refreshments; dinner available on weekends; restaurants nearby **Rates:** $80 to $125; 10% discount offered to National Trust members and National Trust Visa cardholders **Payment:** Visa, MC, personal and traveler's checks **Restrictions:** in peak season, children over 12 welcome; no smoking; small pets accepted **Activities:** cross-country skiing and hiking trails, outdoor swimming pool, sauna, relaxing in gazebo

BRANDON–MIDDLEBURY

Nearby attractions: Middlebury College, Shelburne Museum, Fort Ticonderoga, Billings Farm Museum, Drowley Cheese Factory, New England Maple Museum, state parks, Lake Dunmore, swimming, boating, trout fishing, bicycling, hiking, downhill and cross-country skiing, UVM Morgan Horse Farm, antiques hunting, auctions, golfing

CHURCHILL HOUSE INN
R.R. 3, Box 3265
Brandon, Vermont 05733
802/247-3078
802/247-6851 Fax
Proprietors: Jackson Family

From the beginning, this century-old farmhouse has offered warm hospitality to weary travelers. Built by the Churchill family in 1871, the house was a stopover for farmers bringing their grain and lumber to the mills. That welcoming spirit remains today, as the Churchill House Inn offers an intimate setting with comfortable rooms that are a blend of original furnishings, antique pieces, and modern bedding. A full breakfast and dinner are included in overnight rates, and guests dine by candlelight around the old oak table. The inn's location at the edge of the Green Mountain National Forest provides numerous recreational opportunities, after which guests often retreat to the inn for a swim in the pool, a session in the sauna, or a drink by the fireplace.

Open: year round **Accommodations:** 8 guest rooms with private baths; 1 is a suite **Meals:** full breakfast and dinner included in modified American Plan (MAP) **Rates:** $150 to $220 MAP **Payment:** Visa, MC **Restrictions:** no smoking; no pets **Activities:** swimming pool, sauna, hiking, bicycle rentals, cross-country skiing and ski rentals

ROSEBELLE'S VICTORIAN INN
Route 7
P.O. Box 370
Brandon, Vermont 05733-0370
802/247-0098 or 800/556-7673
Proprietors: Ginette and Norm Milot

Rosebelle's Victorian Inn, an impressive three-story Second Empire house dating to 1860, is listed in the National Register of Historic Places. Its telltale mansard roof is punctuated by dormer windows. The innkeepers have collected authentic

Victorian furnishings to dress the public rooms and each of the six bedrooms. The front porch is inviting with wicker rockers, the common room offers a warming fireplace, and the gardens are overflowing with flowers in summer. Guests are served a hearty country breakfast and afternoon tea. Candlelight dinners can be arranged. French is spoken.

Open: year round **Accommodations:** 6 guest rooms (4 have private baths) **Meals:** full breakfast included; complimentary refreshments; restaurants nearby **Rates:** $65 to $85; 10% discount offered to National Trust members and National Trust Visa cardholders **Payment:** Visa, MC, personal and traveler's checks; gift certificates available **Restrictions:** children over 12 welcome; no smoking; no pets **Activities:** lawn games, bicycling, reading

---

CHELSEA

Nearby attractions: historic sites and house tours, museums, skiing, boating, hiking, bicycling, golfing, swimming, ice skating, tennis, antiques hunting, auctions

SHIRE INN
Main Street
Chelsea, Vermont 05038
802/685-3031 or 800/441-6908
Proprietors: Jay and Karen Keller

The elegant Shire Inn, solidly constructed of Vermont red brick and granite, has been skillfully restored and upgraded for modern conveniences. Inside the 1832 Federal-style structure are a spiral staircase, wide-planked pumpkin pine floors, and 10-foot-high ceilings. Fireplaces occupy four of the six guest rooms and a spacious, sunny parlor. The house is furnished with antiques throughout. The inn, listed as part of a National Register historic district, serves a full breakfast and a gourmet five-course dinner. Guests are invited to enjoy the parlor, porch, or yard at their leisure. The inn is located in the heart of what is frequently called "the quintessential New England village." The *New York Times* describes Chelsea as "one of the prettiest towns in Vermont."

Open: year round **Accommodations:** 6 guest rooms with private baths **Meals:** full breakfast included (B&B); dinner also included [modified American Plan (MAP)] **Wheelchair access:** guest rooms, bathrooms, dining facilities **Rates:** $80 (B&B) to $194 (MAP); 10% discount to National Trust members and National Trust Visa cardholders **Payment:** AmEx, Visa, MC, personal and traveler's checks **Restrictions:** children over 7 welcome; no smoking; no pets **Activities:** cross-country skiing, use of inn's bicycles, hiking, fishing, sledding

CHESTER

Nearby attractions: Vermont Historical Railroad, downhill and cross-country skiing, golfing, swimming, canoeing, picnicking, fishing, hiking, bicycling, tennis, antiques hunting

GREENLEAF INN
Depot Street
P.O. Box 188
Chester, Vermont 05143
802/875-3171
Proprietors: Jerry and Robin Szawerda

The abundant Italianate and Queen Anne decorations on this house reflect its construction in 1867 and ownership until 1880 by William H. H. Cram, one of Chester's foremost carpenters of that time. The inn is a two-and-a-half-story white clapboard house with gables, porches, bays, dormers, and a cupola. E. J. Davis owned the house during most of the first half of this century, causing it to be called the Cram–Davis House until its transformation in the 1980s to the Greenleaf Inn. Nearly all of the former owners' marks on the house have been carefully preserved, earning the house a National Register listing. Lovely antiques fill the ample guest rooms, which overlook the lawn and brook.

Open: year round **Accommodations:** 5 guest rooms with private baths **Meals:** full breakfast included; complimentary refreshments; restaurants nearby **Rates:** $75 to $115; 10% discount to National Trust members **Payment:** Amex, Visa, MC, Discover, personal and traveler's checks **Restrictions:** children over 12 welcome; no smoking **Activities:** board games, cards, volleyball, croquet, bicycles, swimming, hiking, golfing

HENRY FARM INN
Green Mountain Turpike
Chester, Vermont 05143
802/875-2674 or 800/723-8213
Proprietors: Robert and Barbara Bowman

Nestled between a sloping meadow and a pond, adjoining 50 acres of forested foothills near a sparkling river, is the Henry Farm and its inn, a mid-eighteenth-century classic New England colonial. With its white clapboards and black roof set off by dark green shutters on its many double-hung windows, the inn retains the ambience of its earlier days, when it served as a stagecoach stop and tavern. The rooms retain their original wide-planked pine floors, hand-hewn paneling, eight fireplaces, and a beehive oven. Spacious bedrooms with private baths look out on the picturesque landscape. Two cozy sitting rooms and a country dining room welcome guests.

Open: year round **Accommodations:** 7 guest rooms with private baths **Meals:** full breakfast included; complimentary refreshments; restaurants nearby **Rates:** $50 to $90; 10% discount offered to National Trust members and National Trust Visa cardholders **Payment:** AmEx, Visa, MC, personal and traveler's checks **Restrictions:** no smoking; no pets **Activities:** hiking in the hills, river fishing

HUGGING BEAR INN AND SHOPPE

Main Street
Chester, Vermont 05143
802/875-2412 or 800/325-0519
Proprietors: Georgette, Diane, and Paul Thomas

Set back from the street on landscaped grounds, the Hadley–Carpenter House—now known as the Hugging Bear Inn—was built in 1850 in the Italianate style. Later came Queen Anne and Colonial Revival additions. The inn's dominant feature is a three-story octagonal tower that rises to a pyramid-peaked roof. Indoors, teddy bears abound as symbols of warmth and family ties, emphasizing the inn's policy of welcoming children of all ages. Guests will find a teddy in each bed, along with sheets and towels decorated with teddy bear motifs. These are accompanied by comfortable, Victorian furnishings. Guests are invited to unwind in the cozy den or on the spacious front porch. The Hugging Bear Inn is located in one of Chester's two National Register historic districts.

Open: year round except Thanksgiving and Christmas **Accommodations:** 6 guest rooms with private baths **Meals:** full breakfast included; complimentary refreshments; restaurants nearby **Rates:** $55 to $65 single; $75 to $95 double; 10% discount offered to National Trust members and National Trust Visa cardholders November through June, excluding holidays **Payment:** AmEx, Visa, MC, Discover, personal and traveler's checks **Restrictions:** no smoking **Activities:** Teddy Bear Shoppe (with over 4000 bears), games, books

GRAFTON

Nearby attractions: historic village, Grafton Historical Society Museum, Grafton Museum of Natural History, antiques hunting, hiking, bicycling, walking trails, downhill and cross-country skiing, tennis, golfing, music festivals

THE OLD TAVERN AT GRAFTON
Main Street
Grafton, Vermont 05146
802/843-2231
802/843-2245 Fax
Proprietor: Tom List, Jr.

First opened just 12 years after the American colonies gained independence from England, the Old Tavern at Grafton was originally a stop along the Boston-to-Montreal stagecoach route. Restored with historical accuracy by the Windham Foundation in 1965, the Old Tavern retains its hand-hewn beams, wide pine flooring, and peace and quiet that were its hallmarks when it hosted such notables as Daniel Webster, Oliver Wendell Holmes, Ulysses S. Grant, Nathaniel Hawthorne, Rudyard Kipling, and Henry David Thoreau. Today's guest rooms—in the main tavern and adjacent cottages—are individually furnished with antiques and comfortable furnishings. A range of outdoor activities is offered year round, from pond swimming to cross-country skiing. A member of Historic Hotels of America, the Old Tavern at Grafton is an integral part of the historic community of Grafton.

Open: year round, except month of April **Accommodations:** 66 guest rooms with private baths **Meals:** continental breakfast included; complimentary afternoon tea; restaurant and bar on premises **Wheelchair access:** yes **Rates:** $95 to $200; guest houses sleeping up to 10 are $460 to $510; 10% discount to National Trust members and National Trust Visa cardholders **Payment:** Visa, MC, personal and traveler's checks **Restrictions:** children over 7 welcome (under 7 welcome in some guest houses); no pets **Activities:** pond swimming, bicycles, tennis courts, cross-country skiing on groomed trails, shuffleboard, billiards, table tennis, stables for guests' horses

GREENSBORO

Nearby attractions: Green Mountains, White Mountains, quaint villages, antiques hunting, golfing, fishing

HIGHLAND LODGE
Caspian Lake Road
R.R. 1, Box 1290
Greensboro, Vermont 05841
802/533-2647
802/533-7494 Fax
Proprietors: David and Wilhelmina Smith
Location: 2 miles north of Greensboro

Highland Lodge was built in 1865 as a Greek Revival farmhouse. Queen Anne–style porches were added in 1910 and 1926, the year it was converted to an inn. The lodge and its cottages are located deep in the Vermont countryside on the shores of Lake Caspian. Each of the eleven cottages has a living room, bath, porch and one, two, or three bedrooms. Guests enjoy imaginative meals served in the dining rooms of the lodge. At the lodge the playroom offers table tennis and other games, the playhouse is base for the supervised play program for youngsters, and the library and lounges are available for quieter activities. The beach house, with its fireplace and grills, is the center of lake activities. Highland Lodge has been in the Smith family since 1954.

Open: late May to mid-October and late December to mid-March **Accommodations:** 11 cottages with private baths **Meals:** full breakfast and dinner included on modified American Plan (MAP) **Wheelchair access:** 1 cottage **Rates:** $87.50 to $107.50 per person MAP **Payment:** Visa, MC, Discover, personal and traveler's checks **Restrictions:** smoking limited **Activities:** tennis, lawn games, lake swimming from sandy beaches, rowboats, paddleboats, canoes, sailboats, fishing

HYDE PARK

Nearby attractions: Stowe, downhill and cross-country skiing, hiking, walking, antiques hunting, swimming, golf, tennis, bicycling, opera house, summer theater

FITCH HILL INN
Fitch Hill Road
R.F.D. 1, Box 1879
Hyde Park, Vermont 05655
802/888-3834 or 800/639-2903
Proprietors: Richard A. Pugliese and Stanley E. Corklin
Location: 9 miles north of Stowe on Route 100

This gable-and-wing-style farmhouse was built in 1794 by Darius Fitch, son of a Hyde Park founder and Revolutionary War captain. First a farmhouse, then a school, the house has been used as an inn for more than a decade. The interior is filled with antiques, each guest room exhibiting an individual character. The Quebec Room has a Vermont-made quilt on a hardwood Victorian bed that sits on the original maple wide-board floor. The West is represented in the Wyoming Room with its nineteenth-century bed and quilt and huge Wyoming state flag on the wall. The suite has a country cottage decor. Full breakfasts—with such entrees as raspberry cream cheese–filled French toast—are served on Wedgewood and Lennox china. Sterling silver flatware and Waterford crystal complete the table settings. Guests may relax or read in the sitting room, den, or on one of three porches; outside, guests are welcome to explore the inn's five acres of lawns, fields, and maple and pine groves.

Open: year round **Accommodations:** 5 guest rooms (1 has a private bath); 1 is a suite **Meals:** full breakfast included; restaurant on premises (dinner available on modified American Plan); restaurants nearby **Rates:** $69 to $105; 10% discount to National Trust members and National Trust Visa cardholders **Payment:** AmEx, Visa, MC, personal and traveler's checks **Restrictions:** children over 3 welcome; no smoking; no pets **Activities:** video library, Civil War library, the complete works of Louis L'Amour, barbecue, hiking, walking

MANCHESTER

Nearby attractions: Hildene (Robert Todd Lincoln home), Southern Vermont Art Center, summer theater, factory-outlet shops, fishing, canoeing, downhill and cross-country skiing, tennis, golfing, hiking, bicycling

1811 HOUSE
Historic Route 7A, Box 39
Manchester Village, Vermont 05254-0039
802/362-1811 or 800/432-1811
802/362-2443 Fax
Proprietors: Marnie and Bruce Duff

This house has been operated as an inn since 1811, except for a period when it was the private residence of Mary Lincoln Isham, the granddaughter of Abraham Lincoln. The structure was built in 1775 and is true to its Federal styling today, Victorian porches and excessive molding having been removed. Old handmade glass has replaced modern windowpanes. The interior also reflects the house's heritage, with period antiques filling the rooms. Six of the 14 guest rooms have fireplaces; one has a private balcony. Canopied beds (mostly king- and queen-size), oriental rugs, air conditioning, and private baths are provided in all rooms. This National Register property sits on more than seven acres of lawn containing flower gardens and pond, and offers an exceptional view of the Equinox golf course and the Green Mountains beyond.

Open: year round **Accommodations:** 14 guest rooms with private baths **Meals:** full breakfast included; complimentary refreshments; restaurants nearby **Rates:** $110 to $200 **Payment:** AmEx, Visa, MC, Discover, personal and traveler's checks **Restrictions:** not suitable for children; no smoking; no pets **Activities:** English pub with pool table, table tennis and darts; library with games and puzzles

INN AT MANCHESTER
Historic Route 7A, Box 41
Manchester Village, Vermont 05254
802/362-1793
Proprietors: Stan and Harriet Rosenberg

The Inn at Manchester was built in 1880 as a two-story white clapboard home with gray shutters and multiple dormers. Today, the inn has been carefully restored, leaving original architectural details intact. The common rooms and guest rooms are furnished with antiques (most refinished by the owner) and an extensive art collection. The carriage house, recently rehabilitated according to the Secretary of the Interior's Standards for Rehabilitation, also contains antique-furnished guest rooms. Good places to unwind include the wraparound front porch, the parlor with its fireplace, the library, and a swimming pool, which hides in a secluded meadow. The congenial innkeepers like to assist their guests with reservations, travel plans, and directions as needed.

Open: year round **Accommodations:** 18 guest rooms with private baths; 4 are fireplaced suites **Meals:** full breakfast included; complimentary afternoon tea; restaurants nearby **Rates:** $95 to $130; 10% discount to National Trust members and National Trust Visa cardholders **Payment:** AmEx, Visa, MC, Discover, personal and traveler's checks **Restrictions:** children over 8 welcome; smoking limited; no pets **Activities:** swimming pool

VILLAGE COUNTRY INN
Historic Route 7A
P.O. Box 408
Manchester, Vermont 05254
802/362-1792 or 800/370-0300
Proprietors: Jay and Anne Degen

Listed in the National Register of Historic Places, the three-story clapboard-and-shuttered Village Country Inn was built in 1889. The wide porch that spans the first level is lined with cushioned rockers and seasonal flowers. The inn offers a variety of accommodations: luxury suites, large and midsize rooms, and cozy chambers. All guest rooms are dressed in lace, flowers, and ruffles to create romantic settings. Many rooms have canopied beds and luxury baths. All rooms have television and telephones. Lodging includes a full country breakfast and a four-course candlelight dinner in the Rose Room. Cocktails are available in the tavern, next to the terrace of fountains. Guests enjoy a swimming pool and tennis courts in warm weather and a skating rink in winter. Village Country Inn has been featured in *Country Inns, Country Living, Gourmet,* and *USA Today.*

Open: year round **Accommodations:** 32 guest rooms with private baths; 16 are suites **Meals:** full breakfast and dinner included on modified American Plan (MAP); restaurant on premises **Rates:** $150 to $225 MAP; extra person $65 **Payment:** AmEx, Visa, MC, Discover, personal and traveler's checks **Restrictions:** children over 12 welcome; smoking limited; no pets **Activities:** swimming pool, tennis, gift shop, gazebo, tandem bicycle, porch rockers

---

MIDDLEBURY

Nearby attractions: Shelburne Museum, Vermont State Craft Center, Morgan Horse Farm, Middlebury College, Sheldon Museum, boutique shops in historic district, golfing, skiing, ice skating, maple-sugaring tours, hiking, swimming, boating, antiques hunting

MIDDLEBURY INN
14 Courthouse Square
P.O. Box 798
Middlebury, Vermont 05753
802/388-4961 or 800/842-4666
Proprietors: Frank and Jane Emanuel

The Middlebury Inn has been welcoming guests since it was built in 1827 for Nathan Wood. A National Register property, it is an imposing three-story brick Georgian structure, which has seen a variety of changes over the years. Once it had a cupola, later a wraparound porch. The inn today is classic red brick, accented by white shutters and festive yellow and white awnings. Beautifully landscaped grounds complete the setting. Guest rooms reflect the traditions of the past with historical wall coverings, brass fixtures, and decorative moldings, while incorporating present-day amenities such as television and alarm clocks. The staff of the Middlebury Inn, a member of Historic Hotels of America, offers wake-up calls, complimentary early morning beverages, afternoon tea, and assistance with sightseeing plans.

Open: year round **Accommodations:** 75 guest rooms with private baths; 2 are suites **Meals:** complimentary morning coffee and afternoon tea; restaurants on premises; restaurants nearby **Wheelchair access:** some guest rooms, all public area **Rates:** $80 to $200; packages available to National Trust members and National Trust Visa cardholders **Payment:** AmEx, Visa, MC, personal and traveler's checks **Restrictions:** inquire about pets **Activities:** library, game and puzzle corner, gift shop

ORWELL

Nearby attractions: Sheldon Museum, Shelburne Museum, Vermont Folklife Museum, Fort Ticonderoga, Morgan Horse Farm, horseback riding, golfing, swimming, tennis

HISTORIC BROOKSIDE FARMS
Highway 22A
P.O. Box 36
Orwell, Vermont 05760
802/948-2727
Proprietors: Joan and Murray Korda

Tall white Ionic columns grace the front of this stately mansion. Known historically as the Wilcox–Cutts House, it was built in 1789 with the proceeds of a sale of two merino rams for $30,000. The original farmhouse was enlarged in 1843 to a design by architect James Lamb, reflecting the Greek Revival style. The building is also significant for having the only coffered ceiling in a private home in the state. A National Register building, the inn has been featured in numerous books about New England architecture. Bedrooms in the restored tenant farmer's house (1810) are furnished in early American style. The main house contains an enormous library and a major collection of pre-Columbian art. Still a working farm, the 300-acre estate produces maple syrup, feeds farm animals, and grows fresh vegetables and herbs.

Open: year round **Accommodations:** 7 guest rooms, 3 with private baths; 1 is a suite **Meals:** full breakfast included; complimentary refreshments; restaurants nearby **Wheelchair access:** 1 guest suite, all common areas **Rates:** $92 to $162; 10% discount to National Trust members and National Trust Visa cardholders **Payment:** personal and traveler's checks **Restrictions:** smoking limited; no pets **Activities:** hiking trails, cross-country skiing, canoeing on 26-acre lake, fishing, antiques hunting

---

PUTNEY

Nearby attractions: Yellow Barn Music Festival, numerous crafts shops, swimming, boating, skiing, antiques hunting

HICKORY RIDGE HOUSE
Hickory Ridge Road
RR 3, Box 1410
Putney, Vermont 05346
802/387-5709
Proprietors: Steve Anderson and Jacquie Walker

Theophilus and Annis Crawford, owners of a prosperous sheep farm and water mill, built this brick Federal-style country home in 1808, and their farmer descendants lived here for more than a century. An inn since 1984, Hickory Ridge House sits on 12 acres of rolling fields and woodlands, two miles from Putney Village, a noted crafts center. The house's original molding, flooring, hardware, and window lights have been preserved, and authentic colors and furnishings are used throughout. There are working fireplaces in the parlor, the dining room, and four of the seven guest rooms. A hearty breakfast features the inn's own jams and jellies, fresh eggs from its small flock of chickens, and local maple syrup. Guests may stroll through the perennial garden or let Crawford, the resident black lab, be their guide on the inn's network of hiking and cross-country trails.

Open: year round **Accommodations:** 7 guest rooms (3 have private baths) **Meals:** full breakfast included; restaurants nearby **Wheelchair access:** yes **Rates:** $50 to $90; 10% discount to National Trust members and National Trust Visa cardholders **Payment:** AmEx, Visa, MC, personal and traveler's checks **Restrictions:** no smoking; no pets **Activities:** woodland walks, cross-country skiing, swimming hole

QUECHEE

Nearby attractions: Quechee Gorge, Saint Gaudens National Historic Site, Quechee Club golfing, fly fishing, downhill and cross-country skiing, canoeing, bicycling, horseback riding, hiking, hot air ballooning, antiques hunting, covered bridges, Shaker village, Dartmouth College, Montshire Museum of Science

PARKER HOUSE INN
16 Main Street
Quechee, Vermont 05059
802/295-6077
Proprietors: Barbara and Walt Forrester

This three-story brick building is named for the man who built it in 1857. Joseph C. Parker was a woolen mill owner, farmer, lumber mill owner, and state senator. His Italianate home is replete with decorative cornices at the eaves, tall thin windows, and metal roof cresting. Recent renovations uncovered original wall stenciling in the entrance hall, which has been painstakingly restored. Elaborate moldings have been painted in rich hues. Seven comfortable guest rooms are furnished in period antiques, wall coverings, and fixtures. Parker House is also home to the widely acclaimed Isabelle's Restaurant, which features contemporary cuisine made with seasonal ingredients and fresh local products. Parker House guests enjoy easy access to the Ottauquechee River, which flows behind the inn, and Quechee Gorge, just two miles away.

Open: year round **Accommodations:** 7 guest rooms with private baths **Meals:** full breakfast included; restaurants nearby **Rates:** $105 to $130; 10% discount to National Trust members and National Trust Visa cardholders **Payment:** AmEx, Visa, MC, personal and traveler's checks **Restrictions:** smoking limited; no pets **Activities:** television and VCR in sitting room, river swimming

RIPTON

Nearby attractions: Middlebury sites, Shelburne Museum, Fort Ticonderoga, hiking the Long Trail and other trails, downhill and cross-country skiing

CHIPMAN INN
Route 125
P.O. Box 115
Ripton, Vermont 05766
802/388-2390 or 800/890-2390
Proprietors: Joyce Henderson and Bill Pierce

Built in 1828 by Daniel Chipman, a prominent legislator and founder of Middlebury College, Chipman Inn is situated eight miles from Middlebury in the midst of the Green Mountain National Forest. The inn is small, informal, and very comfortable. Guest rooms are individually furnished with attractive antiques and have private baths. Public rooms include a lounge where guests may relax before a large fireplace. The dining room is lighted by candles, warmed by a fireplace, and decorated with colonial stenciling. Here the innkeepers serve a full breakfast and, with notice, a five-course dinner. The Chipman Inn is located in the picturesque village of Ripton, home of Robert Frost.

Open: May 1 through October 31; December 26 through March 31 **Accommodations:** 9 guest rooms with private baths **Meals:** full breakfast included; restaurant on premises **Rates:** $80 to $115 **Payment:** AmEx, Visa, MC, personal and traveler's checks **Restrictions:** children over 12 welcome; smoking limited; no pets

SHELBURNE

Nearby attractions: Shelburne Museum, Vermont Mozart Concert Series, hiking, fishing, biking, sailing, golfing

INN AT SHELBURNE FARMS
Shelburne Farms
Bay and Harbor Roads
Shelburne, Vermont 05482
802/985-8498
Proprietors: Shelburne Farms

Shelburne Farms, originally the agricultural estate of William Seward Webb and Lila Vanderbilt Webb, is a 1000-acre historic site situated on the eastern shores of Lake Champlain. The Inn at Shelburne Farms, built in 1899, is the Webb's completely restored country manor house, evoking both Queen Anne and Tudor styles. Original furnishings and decor in its 24 bedrooms and spacious common rooms recall the grandeur of the Webb era. Guests may warm themselves before the library fireplace, stroll the formal perennial gardens, or explore the entire farm by walking trails. The grounds were designed at the turn of the century with help from Frederick Law Olmsted. Today, the estate is listed in the National Register of Historic Places. Shelburne Farms is a nonprofit organization that teaches and demonstrates the stewardship of natural and agricultural resources.

Open: mid-May to mid-October **Accommodations:** 24 guest rooms (17 have private baths) **Meals:** restaurant on premises serving breakfast, afternoon tea, and dinner daily **Rates:** $100 to $230 **Payment:** AmEx, Visa, MC, DC, personal and traveler's checks **Restrictions:** no smoking; no pets **Activities:** tennis, walking trails, rowing and canoeing, croquet, lake fishing, swimming, game room, tours of Shelburne Farms, concerts and special events

SHOREHAM

Nearby attractions: Fort Ticonderoga, Sheldon Museum, Shelburne Museum, downhill skiing, swimming, boating, horseback riding, covered bridges, country auctions

SHOREHAM INN AND COUNTRY STORE

Route 74 West (Main Street)
P.O. Box 182
Shoreham, Vermont 05770
802/897-5861 and 800/255-5081
Proprietors: Cleo and Fred Alter
Location: 12 miles southwest of Middlebury

Shoreham Inn, built around 1790 on the village green, is a traditional Federal-style New England clapboard and shuttered house. The balustrade on the original stairway is from an old church in town. The dining room, with its exposed beams and open fireplace, is a welcoming place where guests often make quick friendships over shared tables. Guest rooms, named for local personalities, are furnished simply with country-auction antiques. Restored nineteenth-century sitting rooms provide guests with areas for quiet reading, letter writing, or just relaxing. In the antique-laden Shoreham Room, visitors may try on turn-of-the-century clothing or browse through memorabilia. Adjacent to the inn is the Country Store, dating to 1828 and offering local crafts, beer, wine, and groceries.

Open: year round, except month of November **Accommodations:** 11 guest rooms (4 have private baths); 1 is a suite **Meals:** full breakfast included; dinner by special arrangement; restaurants nearby **Rates:** $50 single; $80 double **Payment:** personal and traveler's checks **Restrictions:** no smoking; no pets **Activities:** walking paths, cross-country skiing, snowshoeing, bird-watching

---

SHREWSBURY

Nearby attractions: maple and marble museums, Calvin Coolidge homestead, Appalachian trails for hiking, state parks, swimming, boating

BUCKMASTER INN

Lincoln Hill Road
R.R. 1, Box 118
Shrewsbury, Vermont 05738
802/492-3485
Proprietors: Sam and Grace Husselman
Location: 8 miles southeast of Rutland

This country inn, built as a stagecoach stop in 1801, stands on a knoll overlooking a picturesque valley in the Green Mountains. The colonial-styled building has a center hall, grand staircase, wide-planked pine floors, and many fireplaces. Family antiques gathered for more than 50 years fill the inn. The wood-burning stove in the kitchen, a library, huge porches, and the dining room

invite guests to linger. In winter a hearty breakfast is served in the country kitchen, in summer it is served on one of the spacious porches. Guests will find the inn within walking distance of a fishing and swimming pond, and only minutes from craft and gift shops in Shrewsbury Center.

Open: year round **Accommodations:** 3 guest rooms (2 have private baths) **Meals:** full breakfast included; complimentary refreshments; restaurants nearby **Wheelchair access:** 1 room **Rates:** $55 to $70; 10% discount to National Trust members and National Trust Visa cardholders **Payment:** personal and traveler's checks **Restrictions:** no smoking; no pets **Activities:** picnicking, cross-country skiing, porch sitting, badminton

---

STOWE

Nearby attractions: Stowe Mountain Resort, Mt. Mansfield, downhill and cross-country skiing, sleigh rides, gondola rides and alpine slide in summer, historic walking tours, covered bridges, Ben and Jerry's Ice Cream Factory, Cold Hollow Cider Mill, ice skating, hiking, bicycling, swimming, golfing, horseback riding, antiques hunting, music festivals, summer theater, concerts in Trapp Family Meadow

BRASS LANTERN INN
717 Maple Street
Stowe, Vermont 05672
802/253-2229 or 800/729-2980
802/253-7425 Fax
Proprietor: Andy Aldrich

At the edge of this 200-year-old village is the Brass Lantern Inn, a restored 1810 farmhouse and carriage barn. The inn offers nine guest rooms, each with its own identity and decor. Furnished with antiques and handmade quilts, all guest rooms have planked floors and private baths. Most offer spectacular views, and some have wood-burning fireplaces, canopy beds, or whirlpool tubs. A full country breakfast is served up along with views of Mt. Mansfield. A fireplace in the living room is kept burning in winter, and the patio, open in warm weather, is a fine place for viewing a sunset over the mountains. Brass Lantern Inn has earned three diamonds from AAA.

Open: year round **Accommodations:** 9 guest rooms with private baths **Meals:** full breakfast included; restaurants nearby **Rates:** $80 to $175 **Payment:** AmEx, Visa, MC, traveler's check **Restrictions:** not suitable for children; no smoking; no pets **Activities:** flower garden, putting green, enjoying views from patio

GREEN MOUNTAIN INN
Main Street
Stowe, Vermont 05672
802/253-7301 or 800/445-6629
802/253-5096 Fax
Proprietor: Marvin Gameroff

Built as the home of Peter Lovejoy in 1833, the Green Mountain Inn became one of Stowe's early resort hotels in the mid-1800s. In 1897, the Mt. Mansfield Electric Railroad Depot was built next door. The two buildings, now connected, are listed in the National Register of Historic Places. Fully restored for its 150th anniversary, the inn offers a blend of modern comforts and country charm with replica colonial wall coverings, stenciling, draperies, and eighteenth-century furnishings. Many guest rooms feature canopy beds, fireplaces, and whirlpool tubs. A member of Historic Hotels of America, Green Mountain Inn offers two acclaimed restaurants, a fully equipped health club, and specialty shops. Famous guests have included President Chester A. Arthur, CBS broadcaster Lowell Thomas, and a young Gerald Ford as a model for *Look* magazine.

Open: year round **Accommodations:** 68 guest rooms with private baths; 18 are suites **Meals:** 2 restaurants on premises; complimentary refreshments **Wheelchair access:** 3 rooms **Rates:** $89 to $229; 20% discount offered to National Trust members and National Trust Visa cardholders, some restrictions apply **Payment:** AmEx, Visa, MC, personal and traveler's checks **Activities:** outdoor heated pool; beauty salon; specialty shops; complimentary full-service health club, including aerobic and Nautilus equipment, free weights, sauna, and whirlpool

---

SUNDERLAND

Nearby attractions: Mount Equinox, Manchester Village, downhill and cross-country skiing, antiques hunting, art museums, golfing, hiking, bicycling, canoeing, fishing, Battenkill River, shopping

BATTENKILL INN
Historic Route 7A
R.R. 2, Box 2240
Sunderland, Vermont 05254
802/362-4213 or 800/441-1628
Proprietors: Mary Jo and Ramsay Gourd
Location: 4 miles south of Manchester

Nestled on the banks of the Battenkill River is the Battenkill Inn, an 1840 Victorian farmhouse showing distinctive Italianate touches in its low-pitched hipped roof with wide eaves, cornice brackets, tall windows, and entry porch. Inside, the ceilings are high and the fireplaces are marble. Ten distinctive guest rooms, each with a private bath, are decorated with fine antiques. Four have wood-burning fireplaces, and several open onto balconies looking out to the river and the Green Mountains. A full country breakfast is served in one of two dining rooms, and two fireplaced sitting rooms offer comfortable spots to relax. Just minutes from Manchester Village, Battenkill Inn offers dinner, ski, and picnic packages. The entire inn can be reserved for special occasions.

Open: year round **Accommodations:** 10 guest rooms with private baths **Meals:** full breakfast included; complimentary refreshments; restaurants nearby **Wheelchair access:** yes **Rates:** $75 to $165 **Payment:** AmEx, Visa, MC, traveler's check **Restrictions:** no smoking; no pets **Activities:** croquet, hiking, duck pond, ice skating

VERGENNES

Nearby attractions: Lake Champlain Maritime Museum, Fort Ticonderoga, Shelburne Museum, Vermont Artists Exhibit

BASIN HARBOR CLUB

Basin Harbor Road
Vergennes, Vermont 05491
802/475-2311 or 800/622-4000
Proprietors: Beach family
Location: in town of Ferrisburgh, 6 miles west of Vergennes

The Basin Harbor Club—including a main house, a lodge, and dozens of cottages—has been owned and operated by the Beach family since 1886, making it one of the oldest documented family-owned resorts in the United States. Basin Harbor was first settled in 1790 by General Platt Rogers, who started a shipyard and ferry landing here. The Harbor Homestead, built in 1790, is the oldest house in the settlement and was operated as an inn from its earliest days. The lodge was built in 1880 on 700 acres, which remain in the club's possession today. Over the years, cottages sprang up along the waterfront and golf course. A century's worth of experience is evident in the way the Beach family runs the resort—with beautifully decorated accommodations, fresh local food, and plenty of opportunities to enjoy Vermont's natural beauty.

Open: mid-May to mid-October **Accommodations:** 137 guest rooms with private baths; 77 are in cottages **Meals:** continental breakfast (B&B) included during May, June, September, and October; full breakfast, lunch, and dinner included on full American Plan (FAP) in July and August; restaurants nearby **Wheelchair access:** 8 rooms **Rates:** $130 to $200 B&B; $198 to $350 FAP **Payment:** Visa, MC, personal and traveler's checks **Restrictions:** smoking limited **Activities:** 18-hole golf course, tennis, all water sports, nature trails, children's programs, garden walks, bird-watching, pastel and watercolor workshops

WAITSFIELD

Nearby attractions: Vermont Historical Society, historic Waitsfield, Ben and Jerry's Ice Cream Factory, covered bridges, cultural arts center and theater, bicycling, boating, tennis, golfing, gift and crafts shops, fairs, auctions, Long Trail and other hiking trails

KNOLL FARM GUEST HOUSE
Bragg Hill Road
R.F.D. Box 179
Waitsfield, Vermont 05673
802/496-3939 or 3527
Proprietor: Ann Day
Location: 1/2 mile from junction of Routes 100 and 17

A century after the Knoll Farm was started in 1803 as a small family farm, a white clapboard Victorian farmhouse went up on the property; that structure is today's inn. Decor is simple, built around old-fashioned wallpaper, wainscoting, antique furniture, and a large kitchen with a wood-burning stove. Ample guest bedrooms have comfortable beds, chairs, roomy closets, and writing desks. Knoll Farm Inn maintains an unpretentious rural atmosphere, with farm animals outside, home-cooked food inside, and good fellowship all around. The 150-acre combination farm and country inn, with a significant early nineteenth-century barn at its core, has been preserved in a conservation land trust and nominated to the National Register of Historic Places.

Open: May 1 to October 31 **Accommodations:** 4 guest rooms with shared baths **Meals:** full breakfast and dinner included; complimentary refreshments **Rates:** $40 to $60 per person; 10% discount offered to National Trust members **Payment:** personal and traveler's checks **Restrictions:** children over 12 welcome; no smoking; no pets **Activities:** pond for swimming and boating, croquet, archery, volleyball, badminton, horseshoes, player piano, organ, farm activities, 150 acres for hiking and horseback riding, library, VCR and video collection

WARREN

Nearby attractions: Sugarbush and Mad River Glen ski areas, Vermont Mozart Festival, sailplanes, tennis, horseback riding, Shelburne Museum

BEAVER POND FARM INN
Golf Course Road
R.D. Box 306
Warren, Vermont 05674
802/583-2861
Proprietors: Betty and Bob Hansen

This classically styled farmhouse, built about 1840, has a wing and attached barn built at a later date. The whole has been beautifully restored, leaving Greek Revival and Italianate details intact. Beaver Pond Farm Inn is furnished with antiques; guest rooms have down comforters and candles in the windows. Gourmet breakfasts are served, thanks to Betty Hansen, the chef, who attended the Sorbonne in Paris. Prix fixe dinners are also offered three times weekly in winter. The inn derives its name from several beaver ponds in the rear of the property, which adjoins the Sugarbush Golf Course. Cross-country skiing is just outside the door in winter. Downhill skiing is less than one mile away.

Open: December to April; late May to Thanksgiving **Accommodations:** 6 guest rooms (4 have private baths) **Meals:** full breakfast included; complimentary refreshments; dinner available three nights a week in winter; restaurants nearby **Rates:** $72 to $96; 10% discount offered to National Trust members and National Trust Visa cardholders **Payment:** Visa, MC, personal and traveler's checks **Restrictions:** children over 6 welcome; smoking limited; no pets (resident pets) **Activities:** Sugarbush Golf Course, cross-country skiing, hiking, biking, trout fishing

---

WEATHERSFIELD

Nearby attractions: Calvin Coolidge home, Augustus Saint-Gaudens home and studio, Hildene (Robert Todd Lincoln home), Billings Farm and Museum, antiques hunting, covered bridges, cross-country and downhill skiing, golfing, horseback riding

INN AT WEATHERSFIELD
Route 106
P.O. Box 165
Weathersfield, Vermont 05151
802/263-9217 or 800/477-4828 (reservations)
Proprietors: Mary Louise and Ron Thorburn
Location: 5 miles north of Springfield, near Perkinsville

In 1795, Revolutionary War veteran Thomas Prentis built a four-room farm-house in the Vermont wilderness, and over the years the house was enlarged as needs changed. Around 1900 a homesick minister from the South gave the house its southern antebellum-style dormers and front veranda. Sitting on 21 scenic acres at the end of a maple-lined drive, the inn today provides warmth and comfort against an early American backdrop. Twelve guest rooms—nine with working fireplaces—and seven public rooms are furnished with antiques from the colonial, Empire, and Victorian eras. The library offers 4000 books, many rare, and a collection of antique bottles. An original open-hearth fireplace, with beehive bake oven and other authentic accoutrements, is used frequently to create period recipes on winter holidays. The inn earns four stars from Mobil and three diamonds from Mobil AAA.

Open: year round **Accommodations:** 12 guest rooms with private baths; 3 are suites **Meals:** full breakfast, high tea, and 5-course creative Vermont-style dinner included; restaurant on premises **Wheelchair access:** 1 guest room and dining facilities **Rates:** $175 to $220; 10% discount offered to National Trust members and National Trust Visa cardholders **Payment:** AmEx, Visa, MC, CB, DC, Discover, personal and traveler's checks **Restrictions:** children over 8 welcome; smoking limited; inquire about pets **Activities:** nightly duo-piano entertainment, sauna, aerobic equipment, pool table, hiking trails, sleigh and carriage rides, volleyball, badminton, croquet, pond swimming or ice skating, fishing

WILMINGTON

Nearby attractions: Mount Snow/Haystack skiing, golfing, Lake Whitingham, canoeing, fishing, ice skating, sleigh rides, snowmobile tours, cross-country skiing, bicycling, tennis, horseback riding, antiques hunting

THE WHITE HOUSE OF WILMINGTON
Route 9
P.O. Box 757
Wilmington, Vermont 05363
802/464-2135 or 800/541-2135
802/464-5222
Proprietor: Robert Grinold
Location: 1/4 mile east of Wilmington Center

Built in 1915 as a summer home for lumber baron Martin Brown, the White House of Wilmington, with its matching gable-fronted wings and double-decker porches, boasts 14 fireplaces, lustrous woodwork, original French wallpaper, and Victorian-style brass and crystal light fixtures. Guest rooms, each with private bath, are furnished with period pieces befitting a New England country inn.

Seven of the rooms are located in the adjacent guest house. Nine rooms have fireplaces, six have balconies or terraces, and four have whirlpool tubs. Three restaurants offer a creative collage of continental dishes. The lower level of the inn contains a spa, complete with indoor swimming pool. The inn is listed in the National Register of Historic Places and has been praised by the *Boston Herald*, *New York Times*, and *Boston Globe*.

Open: year round **Accommodations:** 16 guest rooms with private baths; 1 is a suite **Meals:** full breakfast included; restaurant on premises; restaurants nearby **Wheelchair access:** yes **Rates:** $128 to $195; 10% discount to National Trust members and National Trust Visa cardholders **Payment:** AmEx, Visa, MC, DC, personal and traveler's checks **Restrictions:** children over 10 welcome; smoking limited; no pets **Activities:** 43-kilometer groomed cross-country trail network, ski rentals, group and private ski lessons, snowmobile trails and tours, indoor and outdoor swimming pools, spa, whirlpool, sauna, suntan room, hiking

---

WOLCOTT VILLAGE

Nearby attractions: Cabot Cheese Creamery, Ben and Jerry's Ice Cream Factory, Bread and Puppet Museum, Mount Elmore State Park, Fisher Covered Railroad Bridge, Mount Mansfield, Stowe and Craftsbury villages, fly fishing, canoeing, skiing, bicycling

GOLDEN MAPLE INN
35 Main Street
Wolcott Village, Vermont 05680-0035
800/639-5234
802/888-6614 Fax
Proprietors: Dick and Jo Wall

The amiable ghost of original owner "Benjamin" Bundy continues to switch off lamps and close doors in this richly elaborated 1865 Greek Revival inn. Architectural details abound, including wide board floors, architrave trim, "bubbled" glass windows, board-and-bead ceilings, and Italianate doors. A superb example of Vermont's connected "big house, little house, back house, barn," the inn offers three spacious guest rooms, each furnished with a variety of antiques, quilts, and comforters. A full breakfast is served in the Victorian dining room on sterling silver, bone china, and crystal, and evening teas and sweets are served in the library and parlor. The inn is situated among century old maples on lawns rolling down to the Lamoille River, famous for fly fishing and quiet canoeing.

Open: year round **Accommodations:** 3 guest rooms with private baths; 1 is a suite **Meals:** full breakfast included; complimentary refreshments; dinner available by reservation; restaurants nearby **Rates:** $64 to $74; 10% discount to National Trust members and National Trust Visa cardholders except holidays and peak weekends **Payment:** AmEx, Visa, MC, Discover, personal and traveler's checks **Restrictions:** no smoking; no pets **Activities:** fly fishing, canoeing, bicycling, back-country skiing

WOODSTOCK

Nearby attractions: Billings Farm and Museum, Saint-Gaudens National Historic Site, Calvin Coolidge Homestead, walking tours, Quechee Gorge, Ascutney State Park, covered bridges, swimming, canoeing, golfing, tennis, horseback riding, downhill and cross-country skiing, antiques hunting, art galleries

BAILEY'S MILLS BED AND BREAKFAST
Bailey's Mills Road
RR 1, Box 117
Reading, Vermont 05062
802/484-7809 or 800/639-3437
Proprietors: Barbara Thaeder and Donald Whitaker
Location: 10 miles south of Woodstock

Built between 1815 and 1837 by entrepreneur Levi Bailey, this Federal-style brick building derives a southern feeling thanks to the tall white columns that support the double-decker front porch. The building housed four generations of Baileys and mill workers, plus an 1829 general store. The community socialized in the top-floor dance hall and a nearby secret room hid runaway slaves. There are eleven fireplaces with two original beehive ovens in the inn. A "good morning" staircase ascends to the guest rooms and their private baths. Two rooms have working fireplaces. All rooms are appointed with antiques and country furnishings. Guests enjoy the parlor, library, and sunporch overlooking Bailey Brook and the ruins of the old mill dam. Rocking chairs line the front porch.

Open: year round **Accommodations:** 3 guest rooms with private baths; 1 is a suite **Meals:** continental-plus breakfast included; complimentary refreshments; restaurants nearby **Rates:** $65 to $115; 10% discount to National Trust members and National Trust Visa cardholders except in peak season **Payment:** personal and traveler's checks **Restrictions:** no smoking; well-behaved pets by prior arrangement **Activities:** exploring historic cemetery, swimming in stream-fed pond, picnics, walking trails

KEDRON VALLEY INN
Route 106
South Woodstock, Vermont 05071
802/457-1473
802/457-4469 Fax
Proprietors: Max and Merrily Comins
Location: 5 miles south of Woodstock

This 1828 Federal brick building surrounded by graceful porches has had a lively history. Once it hosted cotillions and May balls; later, the house hid runaway slaves during the Civil War. Now it is a New England inn, featured in such publications as *Country Living*, *Country Home*, *Good Housekeeping*, and the *Los Angeles Times*. Guest rooms feature queen-size canopy or antique oak beds, and many have fireplaces or Franklin stoves. Two fascinating collections—one of antique clothing, the other of heirloom quilts—fill the inn. Guests are welcome in the fireplaced living room with hand-crafted oak bar, needlepoint rugs, and a family of antique rockers. In addition to full country breakfasts, the inn's restaurant serves innovative dinners prepared in a style the innkeepers call Nouvelle Vermont, in which the freshest seafoods and local products are used.

Open: May to March **Accommodations:** 27 guest rooms with private baths; 2 are suites **Meals:** full breakfast included; restaurant on premises **Wheelchair access:** yes **Rates:** $117 to $194 **Payment:** AmEx, Visa, MC, Discover, personal and traveler's checks **Restrictions:** smoking limited **Activities:** swimming lake with beach, ice skating, sledding, croquet, 15 acres of grounds, 50-horse stable for trail rides, sleigh and surry rides

LINCOLN INN AT THE COVERED BRIDGE
Route 4 West
Woodstock, Vermont 05091
802/457-3312
802/457-5808
Proprietors: Kurt and Lori Hildbrand

Charles Lincoln, Abraham Lincoln's cousin, once owned this farmhouse. Built in 1790, it sits on five acres of rolling lawn bordered by the Ottauquechee River and a historic covered bridge. (The bridge is the only remaining wooden bridge in America designed by T. Willis Pratt, founder of the Pratt Institute of Design in Brooklyn, New York.) Today at the inn, fireplaces warm the library with its exposed hand-hewn beams, the lounge, and one of the dining rooms. Canopied and brass beds adorn the guest rooms. A full country breakfast is served daily, and rates can also include delicious dinners. Outside, there is a gazebo for relaxing and reading, a swing hanging from the rock maple, an old stone fireplace for cookouts, and a picnic area under a willow tree at the river's edge. In winter, sleigh rides and skiing begin on the property.

Open: year round **Accommodations:** 6 guest rooms with private baths **Meals:** full breakfast included; restaurant on premises; restaurants nearby **Rates:** $99 to $199; 10% discount offered to National Trust members and National Trust Visa cardholders **Payment:** Visa, MC, traveler's check **Restrictions:** children over 2 welcome; no smoking; no pets **Activities:** cross-country skiing, fishing, river swimming, hiking, picnicking, bridge- and leaf-watching

VIRGINIA

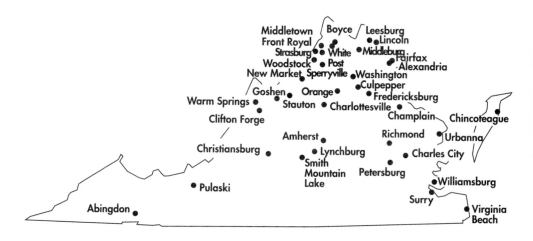

ABINGDON

Nearby attractions: Barter Theater, Virginia Creeper Trail, Mount Rogers National Recreation Area, Appalachian Trail, historic district, antiques hunting, arts and crafts festival in August, hiking, bicycling, boating

MARTHA WASHINGTON INN
150 West Main Street
Abingdon, Virginia 24210
703/628-3161 or 800/533-1014
General Manager: Charles Ingalsbee

Tucked away in Virginia's Southern Highlands is the award-winning Martha Washington Inn, constructed in 1832 as a residence for the large family of Colonel Francis Preston and his wife, Sara. The building has served as a women's college as well as a Civil War hospital. In 1935, "The Martha" opened as one of Virginia's finest hotels. The four historic buildings comprising the inn were painstakingly restored to their original elegance in 1985 at the cost of more than $8 million. Guest rooms and suites are furnished in Victorian antiques and reproductions. Some suites contain fireplaces. For dining, the Martha offers two restaurants serving continental cuisine and traditional southern dishes. Offering every amenity—including ghost stories—the inn's staff is dedicated to fine service and personal attention. The Martha Washington Inn is a charter member of Historic Hotels of America.

Open: year round **Accommodations:** 61 guest rooms with private baths; 10 are suites **Meals:** 2 restaurants on premises **Wheelchair access:** guest rooms, bathrooms, and dining facilities **Rates:** $79 to $250 **Payment:** AmEx, Visa, MC, CB, DC, Discover, personal and traveler's checks **Restrictions:** no pets **Activities:** live entertainment in The Pub and Act II lounges, bicycling, hiking

SUMMERFIELD INN
101 West Valley Street
Abingdon, Virginia 24210
540/628-5905 or 800/668-5905
540/628-5873 Fax
Proprietors: Champe and Don Hyatt

Built in 1923 by lumber dealer John Bradley, what is now the Summerfield Inn was occupied for more than 45 years by the Abingdon District Superintendent of the United Methodist Church. Restored in 1986, this hip-roofed, Colonial Revival house provides antique-and-chintz-furnished accommodations in the main house and cottage. The three cottage rooms have whirlpool bathtubs. Guests are invited to relax in rockers on the wraparound porch, in the spacious formal living room, or in the sunroom among wicker, ivy, and ferns. A guest pantry is stocked with refreshments. The inn is included in the local historical society's tour of notable homes. Abingdon, one of the first communities formed in western Virginia, offers lush mountain scenery at its 2300-foot elevation.

Open: March 1 through December 31 **Accommodations:** 7 guest rooms with private baths; 1 is a honeymoon suite **Meals:** full breakfast included; complimentary refreshments; restaurants nearby **Wheelchair access:** yes **Rates:** $70 to $125; 10% discount offered to National Trust members and National Trust Visa cardholders **Payment:** AmEx, Visa, MC, personal and traveler's checks **Restrictions:** children over 6 welcome; smoking limited; no pets **Activities:** library, television, card room, porch rocking, bicycling

ALEXANDRIA

Nearby attractions: Old Town historic walking tours, Masonic Temple, Mt. Vernon, Gunston Hall, National Trust's Woodlawn Plantation, all Washington, D.C. attractions

PRINCELY BED AND BREAKFAST, LTD.
819 Prince Street
Alexandria, Virginia 22314
804/725-9511
Proprietor: E. J. Mansmann

Twenty guest rooms are offered by Princely Bed and Breakfast in 18 historic houses, all located in the heart of historic Old Town Alexandria, across the Potomac River from the nation's capitol. These architecturally significant homes, dating from 1770 to 1879 range in styles from Georgian and Federal to Italianate and Queen Anne. All of the homes are furnished with antiques, many museum quality. Each house offers public rooms where guests can relax after a day of sightseeing, often before a warming fireplace. One guest room has a fireplace. All guests are provided continental-plus breakfasts. The houses are convenient to fast and efficient public transporation, including the Metrorail subway system, which transports guests to downtown Washington in 15 minutes.

Open: year round **Accommodations:** 20 guest rooms with private baths **Meals:** continental-plus breakfast included; restaurants nearby **Wheelchair access:** 1 suite **Rates:** $75 to $110 **Payment:** personal and traveler's checks **Restrictions:** no smoking; no pets

---

AMHERST

Nearby attractions: Washington and Jefferson National Forests, Blue Ridge Parkway, Lynchburg, Appomattox Courthouse, Monticello, Poplar Forest, Fort Early, Crabtree Falls, Natural Bridge and Caverns, Virginia Horse Center, hiking, golfing, fishing, skiing, canoeing, swimming, antiques hunting, crafts shops, eight colleges

DULWICH MANOR BED AND BREAKFAST
Route 5, Box 173A
Amherst, Virginia 24521
804/946-7207
Proprietors: Bob and Judy Reilly
Location: 14 miles north of Lynchburg

In the shadow of the Blue Ridge Mountains lies Dulwich Manor, a stately 1912

Colonial Revival home of Flemish-bond brickwork. The overhanging front gable, containing a small Palladian window, is supported by fluted Ionic columns. Inside, the decor recalls an English country home, and guest rooms contain canopied, brass, or antique beds. Some guest rooms feature fireplaces or whirlpool tubs in the private bathrooms, others may have bay windows or cozy window seats. Breakfast, served in the formal dining room or on the veranda, includes specially prepared entrees. Located at the end of a winding country lane on a hill in five secluded acres, Dulwich Manor offers a beautiful setting for strolling and watching the sun set over the mountains.

Open: year round **Accommodations:** 6 guest rooms (4 have private baths) **Meals:** full breakfast included; complimentary refreshments; restaurants nearby **Rates:** $64 to $89; 10% discount to National Trust members and National Trust Visa cardholders **Payment:** personal and traveler's checks **Restrictions:** smoking limited; no pets **Activities:** outdoor hot tub, badminton, woodland trails

BOYCE

Nearby attractions: historic sites, antiques hunting, wineries, hiking, bicycling, river activities

RIVER HOUSE
Route 1, Box 135
Boyce, Virginia 22620
703/837-1476
703/837-2399 Fax
Proprietor: Cornelia S. Niemann
Location: 14 miles east of Winchester; on southwestern corner of U.S. Route 50 and Shenandoah River

Commanding a strategic point on the Shenandoah River, River House sits on property surveyed by a young George Washington. In 1780 the property, known as Ferry Farm, was part of the huge Carter Hall estate. At that time the building was a one-story stone slave quarters. After a major expansion in 1820 that transformed the building into its present three-story configuration, River House was pressed into service as a military hospital during the Civil War. Later, its slave quarters served as tollhouse for the bridge that replaced the old ferry and as a waystation for bridge travelers. Further renovations were made in the early 1940s. Now River House offers five diverse guest rooms, from the original 1780 kitchen with its walk-in fireplace and intriguing theater collection, to the spacious master bedroom with its wide-planked pine flooring and romantic atmosphere. Heirlooms, books, and personal memorabilia fill all corners of the house.

Open: year round **Accommodations:** 5 guest rooms with private baths, fireplaces, and air conditioning **Meals:** full breakfast/brunch included; complimentary refreshments; restaurants nearby **Wheelchair access:** limited **Rates:** $80 to $115; 25% surcharge on Saturday-only bookings; 10% discount offered to National Trust members and National Trust Visa cardholders on 2-night bookings **Payment:** Visa, MC, personal and traveler's checks **Activities:** 17 acres of woodlands and riverfront for walking and picnicking, reading, relaxing, games, special theatrical weekend packages and house parties

CHAMPLAIN

Nearby attractions: historic Tappahannock, Stratford Hall, Wakefield, Saunders Wharf Steamboat Museum, Rappahannock River, river cruises, boating, fishing, golfing, Ingleside Winery

LINDEN HOUSE BED AND BREAKFAST
Route 17 South
P.O. Box 23
Champlain, Virginia 22438
804/443-1170 or 800/622-1202
Proprietors: Kenneth and Sandra Pounsberry
Location: 40 miles south of Fredericksburg

Listed in the National Register of Historic Places and a designated Virginia Landmark, Linden House is the 1750 home of planter Nicholas Faulkner. The stately three-story brick house and adjacent carriage house, joined by a courtyard, offer eight guest rooms, most with queen-size beds (two rooms offer antique high-backed beds). Some guest rooms have fireplaces and sitting areas. The house is furnished with eighteenth-century antiques. A full plantation breakfast is served each morning and guests can help them-selves to lemonade, tea, and coffee all day long. The sunroom at the rear of the house overlooks the terraced lawn, where a boxwood-lined path leads to an arbor. The herb garden is surrounded by a white picket fence and a rose-

laden trellis. The front of the house looks onto gently rolling pastures populated by grazing cattle and horses.

Open: year round **Accommodations:** 8 guest rooms (5 have private baths); 1 is a suite **Meals:** full breakfast included; complimentary refreshments; dinners for groups by reservation; restaurants nearby **Wheelchair access:** 1 suite **Rates:** $75 to $135; 10% discount to National Trust members and National Trust Visa cardholders **Payment:** Visa, MC, personal and traveler's checks **Restrictions:** children over 12 welcome; no smoking; no pets **Activities:** walking trails, croquet, lawn bowling, gazebo

CHARLES CITY

Nearby attractions: Colonial Williamsburg, James River Plantation tours, Civil War battlefields, Busch Gardens, antiques hunting, outlet shops, fish hatchery tours, golfing, tennis, bicycling

EDGEWOOD PLANTATION
4800 John Tyler Highway (historic Route 5)
Charles City, Virginia 23030
804/829-2962 or 6908
804/829-2962 Fax
Proprietors: Julian and Dot Boulware
Location: 28 miles west of Williamsburg, 24 miles east of Richmond in the James River plantation country

Edgewood, a Carpenter Gothic home, was built in 1849 by Spencer Rowland. Once part of nearby Berkely Plantation, it has seen use as a church, post office, and telephone exchange. Completely restored, Edgewood contains 14 large rooms, 10 fireplaces, five chimneys, and a spiral, three-story staircase. Romance is literally etched in this house; in an upstairs bedroom window is scratched the name Lizzie Rowland, who died waiting for her lover to return from the Civil War. Many believe she still waits for him, watching from the upstairs front windows. Guest accommodations are filled with antiques, canopied beds, and old-fashioned country artifacts. Breakfast is served in the country kitchen or by candlelight in the formal dining room. Edgewood, a National Register house, has been featured in *Country Home* and *Southern Living*.

Open: year round **Accommodations:** 4 guest rooms with private baths; 2 are suites **Meals:** full breakfast included; complimentary refreshments; restaurants nearby **Rates:** $110 to $178 **Payment:** Visa, MC, personal and traveler's checks **Restrictions:** children over 12 welcome; smoking limited; no pets **Activities:** swimming pool, picnic area, creek fishing, walking trails, English gardens

NORTH BEND PLANTATION BED AND BREAKFAST
12200 Weyanoke Road
Charles City, Virginia 23030
804/829-5176 or 800/841-1479
Proprietors: George F. and Ridgely Copland
Location: 25 miles west of Williamsburg

This history-steeped house survives as the best preserved expression of the Greek Revival style in the James River plantation country. Federal-style mantels and stair carvings survive from the oldest portion of the house (ca. 1819), as do all of the Greek Revival features from the 1853 remodeling. The house was built for Sarah Harrison, sister of the ninth president of the United States, William Henry Harrison, and was used during the Civil War as the headquarters of Union General Philip Sheridan while his army occupied the area. The house's current owners are members of one of Virginia's oldest families—the innkeeper is a great-great-grandson of Edmund Ruffin, who fired the first shot of the Civil War at Fort Sumter. They have filled North Bend and its spacious guest rooms with family antiques and heirlooms, including collections of rare books and antique dolls. A full country breakfast is served in the formal dining room. North Bend, listed in the National Register, is still an active farm on 850 acres.

Open: year round **Accommodations:** 4 guest rooms with private baths; 1 is a suite **Meals:** full breakfast included; complimentary refreshments; nearby restaurants offer complimentary desserts to North Bend guests **Rates:** $95 to $130; 10% discount to National Trust members and National Trust Visa cardholders **Payment:** Visa, MC, personal and traveler's checks **Restrictions:** children over 6 welcome; no smoking; no pets **Activities:** swimming pool, croquet, badminton, horseshoes, volleyball, nature trails, tandem bicycle, nature walks, fox hunts in season

CHARLOTTESVILLE

Nearby attractions: Monticello; University of Virginia; Ashlawn; Michie Tavern; National Trust's Montpelier; Blue Ridge Parkway; Skyline Drive; Appomattox; winery tours; antiques hunting; bicycling; golfing; horseback riding; hiking; tennis; James River fishing, canoeing, fishing, rafting, and swimming

CLIFTON COUNTRY INN
Route 13, Box 26
Charlottesville, Virginia 22901
804/971-1800
Proprietors: Craig and Donna Hartman
Location: 5 miles east of Charlottesville

Clifton was originally the property of Thomas Mann Randolph, husband of Thomas Jefferson's daughter Martha and an early governor of Virginia. Perched on a cliff overlooking the Rivanna River, the home was built in 1799. Its appearance is dominated by a full-facade columned portico. The same pine floors, paneled walls, and fireplaces (one in every room) that warmed Randolph family visits still welcome guests. Clifton's guest rooms are large, private, and comfortable, with luxurious baths and air conditioning. All have wood-burning fireplaces and elegant period furnishings combined with tasteful contemporary pieces in a spectacular country setting.

Open: year round **Accommodations:** 14 guest rooms with private baths; 5 are suites **Meals:** full breakfast and afternoon tea included; dinners by reservation; restaurants nearby **Rates:** $165 to $225; ask about winter discount **Payment:** AmEx, Visa, MC, DC, personal and traveler's checks **Restrictions:** no smoking; no pets **Activities:** tennis, croquet, horseshoes, lake, fishing, swimming pool, spa

HIGH MEADOWS INN
Route 20 South
Route 4, Box 6
Scottsville, Virginia 24590
804/286-2218 or 800/232-1832
Proprietors: Peter Sushka and Mary Jae Abbitt
Location: 17 miles south of Charlottesville

The only structure of its kind in the state of Virginia, High Meadows Inn is actually two dwellings, built in 1832 and 1882 and connected by a bilevel hall. The early half of the house is built of brick with Federal detailing, while the other half is a Victorian design covered in stucco. Located on a 50-acre estate, the unique home with its 17 rooms, nine fireplaces, and original grained woodwork is listed in the National Register of Historic Places. Five guest rooms are furnished in Victorian style, while two suites reflect the Federal period. The rest are in the late nineteenth-century Queen Anne style. All have original and antique art, sitting and writing areas, and garden or vineyard views, and are furnished with a decanter of port or sherry, fresh flowers, and fruit and candy. Guests are invited to enjoy the Federal parlor, Victorian music room, grand hall, west terrace, and teahouse.

Open: year round **Accommodations:** 12 guest rooms with private baths; 5 are suites **Meals:** full breakfast included; complimentary wine tasting and cheese; four- to six-course candlelight dinners served nightly by reservation **Rates:** $85 to $155; 10% discount offered to National Trust members and National Trust Visa cardholders **Payment:** AmEx, Visa, MC, personal and traveler's checks **Restrictions:** children over 8 welcome; no smoking; pets allowed with notice **Activities:** wine tasting, vineyard tours, horseshoes, croquet, bicycling, badminton, ponds and creeks, picnicking, bird sanctuary, mountain views, nature trails

INN AT MONTICELLO
Route 19, Box 112
Charlottesville, Virginia 22902
804/979-3593
804/296-1344 Fax
Proprietors: Carol and Larry Engel

Located just two miles from Monticello, Thomas Jefferson's beloved home, and the Michie Tavern, one of Virginia's oldest homesteads, the Inn at Monticello offers a perfect resting spot for visitors to these historic sites. This country manor house, built in 1850, is surrounded by dogwoods, boxwoods, and azaleas. Inside are five guest rooms, each uniquely decorated in period antiques and fine reproductions. Different rooms offer special features, such as a working fireplace, a private porch, or a canopy bed. The breakfast menu is designed to make the most of seasonally available specialties. A crackling fire in the living-room fireplace draws guests in cold weather, while the rocking chair-filled porch awaits on breezy summer days. The inn contains an exhibit about Thomas Jefferson's home life and a gift shop.

Open: year round, except Christmas week **Accommodations:** 5 guest rooms with private baths **Meals:** full breakfast included; complimentary refreshments; restaurants nearby **Rates:** $110 to $145; 10% discount to National Trust members and National Trust Visa cardholders, December through March **Payment:** Visa, MC, personal and traveler's checks **Restrictions:** children over 12 welcome; no smoking; no pets **Activities:** porch rocking, hammock, croquet, picnicking, bird-watching, fishing on adjacent pond

INN AT THE CROSSROADS
Plank Road
Route 2, Box 6
North Garden, Virginia 22959
804/979-6452
Proprietors: Lyn Neville and Christine Garrison
Location: 9 miles south of Charlottesville

Built as a tavern in 1820 to serve travelers on the Staunton–James River Turnpike, this four-story brick building with timber framing retains many of the features of ordinaries, or inns, of its time, including a long front porch. Serving travelers continuously over the years, the inn has been the local community's place to exchange goods and news, as well. Guest rooms pique the imagination with decor and piles of books centered on various themes. Guests may choose from the Country Garden Room, the Storybook Room, the International Room, the Ships and Shells Room, or the Country Squire Room. Breakfast is served in the keeping room on the lower level. Entrees are complemented by homemade muffins and specialty butters. Fresh vegetables and fruits are featured in season. The inn's grounds open to vistas of the foothills of the Blue Ridge Mountains.

Open: year round **Accommodations:** 5 guest rooms with shared baths **Meals:** full breakfast included; restaurants nearby **Rates:** $65 to $75 **Payment:** Visa, MC, personal and traveler's checks **Restrictions:** children over 8 welcome; no smoking; no pets **Activities:** swinging, hammock, walking, reading

---

CHINCOTEAGUE

Nearby attractions: Chincoteague Wildlife Refuge, Assateague Seashore, ocean beach, swimming, sailing, fishing, tennis, bicycling, bird-watching, kayaking, canoeing, fine seafood restaurants

ISLAND MANOR HOUSE
4160 Main Street
Chincoteague, Virginia 23336
804/336-5436 or 800/852-1505 (reservations)
Proprietors: Charles D. Kalmykow, Carol W. Rogers

In 1848 two young men on Chincoteague Island pooled their resources and built a large, two-story, T-shaped house. The young men married two sisters and lived together in the house until the sisters decided they did not enjoy living under the same roof. The house was split in two, and the front half set a short distance from the back. Today, the houses have been rejoined by a large garden room with a fireplace. The house has been restored and furnished in the Federal style. The hosts have gathered a collection of seventeenth-, eighteenth-, and early nineteenth-century furniture and art, which gives the inn a rich ambience. Guests may relax by the fireplace in autumn or enjoy the brick courtyard in summer. The inn is especially suitable for small wedding receptions and corporate conferences.

Open: year round **Accommodations:** 8 guest rooms (6 have private baths) **Meals:** full breakfast included; complimentary afternoon tea; restaurants nearby **Rates:** $65 to $120; 10% discount offered to National Trust members and National Trust Visa cardholders off season only **Payment:** Visa, MC, personal and traveler's checks **Restrictions:** children over 12 welcome; no smoking; no pets

MISS MOLLY'S INN

4141 Main Street
Chincoteague,
Virginia 23336
804/336-6686 or
800/221-5620
Proprietors: David
and Barbara
Wiedenheft

In 1886, fisherman J. T. Rowley, then known as the "clam king of the world," built a charming Victorian home on Chincoteague Island. His daughter, Molly, lived in this house until the age of 84, becoming one of the island's best-loved citizens. Her house has been carefully restored and now offers accommodations and island hospitality to visitors. Guest and common rooms are furnished with period antiques, and all enjoy gentle sea breezes. While writing the book *Misty of Chincoteague*, Marguerite Henry stayed in this grand house. In fact, she reputedly worked out the book's plot while rocking on the front porch with Miss Molly. In keeping with Miss Molly's heritage, the inn serves a traditional English tea each afternoon. The inn is available for wedding receptions and small corporate conferences.

Open: March 1 through New Year's Eve **Accommodations:** 7 guest rooms (5 have private baths) **Meals:** full breakfast included; complimentary afternoon tea; restaurants nearby **Rates:** $69 to $145; 10% discount to National Trust members **Payment:** personal check **Restrictions:** children over 8 welcome; no smoking; no pets

---

CHRISTIANSBURG

Nearby attractions: Virginia Polytechnic Institute and State University, Radford University, Historic Newbern Museum, New River State Park Bike Trail, Smithfield Plantation, antiques hunting, wineries, Blue Ridge Parkway, caverns, lakes, hiking, Appalachian Trail, boating, fishing, outlet shops

THE OAKS VICTORIAN INN

311 East Main Street
Christiansburg, Virginia 24073
540/381-1500
Proprietors: Margaret and Tom Ray

Three-hundred-year-old oak trees surround this elegant yellow and white Queen Anne home. Built ca. 1890 by Major W. L. Pierce for his family, the house is distinguished by turrets and a wide wraparound porch. Original features, including pine woodwork, ornate mantels, stained-glass windows, and tall windows, have been restored. Guest rooms combine fine antiques and contemporary furnishings with special features such as queen or king canopy beds, fireplaces, and refrigerators. Private bathrooms are stocked with plush towels, terry robes, and toiletries. Guests are invited to use the sun room, study, parlor, and garden, where a gazebo houses a hot tub. Full breakfasts, featuring entrees such as shirred eggs in spinach nests, are served by candlelight in the dining room. The Oaks has been named one of the top 12 inns of 1991 by *Country Inns* magazine. Listed in the National Register, the Oaks holds Mobil three-star and AAA four-diamond ratings.

Open: year round **Accommodations:** 5 guest rooms with private baths **Meals:** full breakfast included; complimentary refreshments; restaurants nearby **Rates:** $115 to $135 **Payment:** AmEx, Visa, MC, Discover, personal and traveler's checks **Restrictions:** children over 12 welcome; no smoking; no pets **Activities:** hot tub, sauna, library, videotapes

CLIFTON FORGE

Nearby attractions: Natural Bridge, Lucy–Selina Furnaces, C&O Railroad Museum, Virginia Horse Center, Virginia Military Institute, Civil War sites, Lime Kiln Theater, Longdale National Recreation Area, hiking, sandy beach lake, swimming, mountain biking, cross-country skiing, boating, fishing, golfing

LONGDALE INN
6209 Longdale Furnace Road
Clifton Forge, Virginia 24422
504/862-0892
504/862-3554 Fax
Proprietors: Kate and Bob Cormier

Built in 1873, Longdale Inn was once the manor home of Harry Firmstone, owner and ironmaster of the Longdale Iron Works. The 23-room mansion, complete with cupola and gazebo, features floor-to-ceiling windows, 11-foot ceilings, original embossed iron door hinges, and brass carbide chandeliers with etched-glass globes. Hand-painted marble mantles decorate each of the inn's eight fireplaces. The entire house has been restored and uniquely decorated with many items that originally belonged to the Firmstones. Guests may choose from 10 bedrooms furnished in Victorian, European, or southwestern decor. A country breakfast is offered in the dining room or in the privacy of guest rooms. The inn is surrounded by 12 acres of lawns, gardens, and woods.

Open: year round **Accommodations:** 10 guest rooms (6 have private baths); 3 are suites **Meals:** full breakfast included; complimentary refreshments; restaurants nearby **Wheelchair access:** 1 room **Rates:** $65 to $120; 10% discount to National Trust members and National Trust Visa cardholders **Payment:** AmEx, Visa, MC, Discover, personal check **Restrictions:** children over 12 welcome; no smoking; no pets **Activities:** croquet, bicycling, walking, horseshoe pitching

---

CULPEPER

Nearby attractions: Skyline Drive, wineries, walking tours, tennis, hiking, bicycling, golfing, National Trust's Montpelier, Civil War battlefields, museums, antiques hunting

FOUNTAIN HALL

609 South East Street
Culpeper, Virginia 22701
703/825-8200 or 800/29-VISIT (800/298-4748)
Proprietors: Steven and Kathi Walker

Fountain Hall, nestled in the heart of historic Culpeper County, was built in 1859 in a simple Victorian style. In 1923 it was remodeled to produce the existing Colonial Revival structure. A brick herringbone walkway leads to the columned front porch with balcony. Inside, the house has been completely renovated and appointed with period antiques and complementary furnishings. Guest rooms are individually decorated and offer various extras, such as balconies or whirlpool tubs. A generous breakfast is served in the morning room. Indoor common rooms include a library of old and new books and two parlors, one with a fireplace. Outside, guests enjoy formal gardens and comfortable lawn furniture. Situated on

one of Culpeper's oldest residential streets, Fountain Hall is an easy six-block stroll to the historic downtown.

Open: year round **Accommodations:** 5 guest rooms with private baths **Meals:** continental-plus breakfast included; complimentary refreshments; restaurants nearby **Wheelchair access:** yes **Rates:** $70 to $125; 10% discount to National Trust members and National Trust Visa cardholders **Payment:** AmEx, Visa, MC, CB, DC, Discover, personal and traveler's checks **Restrictions:** no smoking; no pets **Activities:** lawn games, board games, reading materials, golf packages, tennis, hiking, biking, and swimming nearby

---

FAIRFAX

Nearby attractions: George Mason University; Manassas Civil War Park; Center for the Arts; Washington, D.C.; historical walking tours; Mount Vernon; Gunston Hall; National Trust's Woodlawn; golfing; tennis; bicycling; wineries; horseback riding

BAILIWICK INN
4023 Chain Bridge Road
Fairfax, Virginia 22030
703/691-2266 or 800/366-7666
Proprietors: Annette and Bob Bradley

The first guests slept in this house nearly 200 years ago. One, former governor William Smith, was here on June 1, 1861, when he was called on to assume command of the Warrenton Rifles and defend the village against a U.S. Cavalry raiding party. This Federal brick house in the heart of historic Fairfax City was built in 1800 by Joshua Gunnel. With all of its historic features intact, the National

Register house now offers 14 antique-laden guest rooms designed to honor famous Virginians. The Thomas Jefferson Room, done in his favorite red and gold, is modeled after the president's own bedroom at Monticello; the George Mason Room duplicates the orignal colors and furnishings of this Virginia stateman's nearby mansion. Some rooms have fireplaces, others have whirlpool baths. In addition to a full breakfast, the dining room also serves a five-course, fixed-price dinner of Nouvelle American cuisine.

Open: year round **Accommodations:** 14 guest rooms with private baths **Meals:** full breakfast included; complimentary refreshments; restaurant on premises; restaurants nearby **Wheelchair access:** 1 room **Rates:** $130 to $300; 10% discount to National Trust members and National Trust Visa cardholders **Payment:** AmEx, Visa, MC, personal and traveler's checks **Restrictions:** no smoking; no pets **Activities:** brick-walled courtyard

FREDERICKSBURG

Nearby attractions: Mary Washington College, Rising Sun Tavern, historic plantations and estates (Belmont, Kenmore), Civil War battlefields (Chancellorsville, Fredericksburg, Spotsylvania, Wilderness), James Monroe Museum, Mary Washington House, Stonewall Jackson shrine, Hugh Mercer Apothecary Shop, antiques hunting, National Trust's Montpelier

LA VISTA PLANTATION
4420 Guinea Station Road
Fredericksburg, Virginia 22408
540/898-8444 or 800/529-2823
540/898-1041 Fax
Proprietors: Michele and Edward Schiesser

Built in 1838 by the Boulware family, this was later the home of Anne Tripp Boulware, first president of the Ladies Memorial Association of Spotsylvania County. LaVista has a past rich in Civil War history, as both armies of the war encamped here. The house reflects the Early Classical Revival style with its two-story front portico. Inside are high ceilings, wide pine floors, and acorn-and-oak leaf moldings. A guest suite, located in the sunny English basement, features a living room with fireplace, sitting room, bedroom, bathroom, and kitchen, all furnished in period antiques. The other guest accommodation is a large room on the main floor furnished with Empire furniture and a mahogany rice-carved four-poster bed. A full breakfast includes fresh farm eggs and homemade jams. The 10-acre grounds are filled with mature tres, shrubs, pastures, woods, gardens, and a stocked pond.

Open: year round **Accommodations:** 2 guest rooms with private baths; 1 is a complete apartment **Meals:** full breakfast included; complimentary refreshments; restaurants nearby **Rates:** $75 single to $95 double **Payment:** Visa, MC, personal and traveler's checks **Restrictions:** no smoking; no pets **Activities:** fishing, rowboat, tree swing, bird-watching, country walks, gardens, pick-your-own Christmas tree in December

SPOONER HOUSE BED AND BREAKFAST
1300 Caroline Street
Fredericksburg, Virginia 22401-3704
540/371-1267
Proprietors: Peggy and John Roethel

Spooner House, located in Fredericksburg's historic district, was built on land once owned by George Washington's youngest brother, Charles. In 1794, George W. B. Spooner built his home on this site. Spooner operated a general store from the first floor, and a later owner was licensed to sell "spiritous liquors." The property escaped the Great Fredericksburg Fire of 1807, which began one block away, and withstood shelling during the Civil War's Battle of Fredericksburg. Today, the house appears essentially as it did when it was built. Spooner House offers a spacious two-room suite with a private entrance. Amenities include a private bath, queen bed, television, wet bar, refrigerator, and morning newspaper. Full breakfast is served in the suite. The innkeepers offer a complimentary guided tour of the adjacent Rising Sun Tavern (1760), a National Historic Landmark.

Open: year round **Accommodations:** 2-room suite with private bath **Meals:** full breakfast included; complimentary refreshments; restaurants nearby **Rates:** $95 **Payment:** personal and traveler's checks **Restrictions:** no smoking; no pets

FRONT ROYAL

Nearby attractions: Skyline Drive, Shenandoah National Park, Luray Caverns, National Trust's Belle Grove Plantation, Civil War reenactments, antiques hunting, horseback riding, wineries, golfing, hiking, canoeing, tennis, fine dining, live theater

CHESTER HOUSE
43 Chester Street
Front Royal, Virginia 22630
703/635-3937 or 800/621-0441
Proprietors: Bill and Ann Wilson

This stately Georgian-style Colonial Revival mansion is situated on two acres in Front Royal's historic district. Built in 1905 by international lawyer Charles Samuels, the house exhibits much attention to detail. Local artisans designed the dentil molding, intricate woodwork, and hand-molded decorative ceilings; handsome marble mantels, fountains, and statuary were imported from Europe. Crystal chandeliers, oriental rugs, art, and family antiques blend the old with the new in today's elegant inn. Spacious bedrooms look out on the century-old gardens. In-room amenities include hand-ironed sheets, thick terrycloth robes, personal toiletries, fresh flowers, bedside mints, and homemade cookies. Two rooms have working fireplaces. Refreshments are offered in the fireplaced parlor or on the shaded portico. Shops, restaurants, and historic attractions are a short walk from the inn.

Open: year round **Accommodations:** 6 guest rooms (5 have private baths); 1 is a suite **Meals:** continental-plus breakfast included; complimentary refreshments; restaurants nearby **Rates:** $65 to $110 **Payment:** AmEx, Visa, MC, personal and traveler's checks **Restrictions:** children over 12 welcome; smoking limited; no pets **Activities:** television lounge, hammock for two, terraced gardens, boxwood mazes

KILLAHEVLIN
1401 North Royal Avenue
Front Royal, Virginia 22630
703/636-7335 or 800/847-6132
703/636-8694 Fax
Proprietors: John and Susan Lang

Killahevlin, on one of the highest spots in Front Royal, was built in 1905 for William E. Carson, first chairman of the Virginia Conservation Commission. He is known as the "Father of the Skyline Drive," because of his close involvement with the project. Historical markers found throughout the Virginia countryside are also attributed to Carson. The house, a massive square building with hipped roof and rows of windows, was designed by the Washington, D.C., firm of A. B. Mullet, whose founder built the Old Executive Office Building next door to the White House. On grounds that once served as a Civil War encampment for Union troops, Killahevlin offers professionally restored and designed guest rooms with working fireplaces and whirlpool tubs. The Tower House, adjacent to the mansion, has also been renovated and offers two suites.

Open: year round **Accommodations:** 6 guest rooms with private baths; 2 are 3-room suites **Meals:** full breakfast included; private Irish Pub with complimentary refreshments; restaurants nearby **Rates:** $95 to $160; 10% discount to National Trust members and National Trust Visa cardholders **Payment:** AmEx, Visa, MC, Discover, personal and traveler's checks **Restrictions:** not suitable for children, no smoking; no pets **Activities:** boccie, horseshoes, croquet, nature walks

GOSHEN

Nearby attractions: historic Lexington, Goshen Pass, George Washington National Forest, Lime Kiln Theater, Garth Newel Music Center, Warm Springs, Hot Springs, Blue Ridge Parkway, Skyline Drive, Staunton, Virginia Military Institute, Washington and Lee University, Civil War battlefields, George C. Marshall Museum, Virginia Horse Center, golfing, swimming, hiking, skiing, canoeing, fishing, hunting, kayaking

HUMMINGBIRD INN
Wood Lane
P.O. Box 147
Goshen, Virginia 24439
703/997-9065 or 800/397-3214
Proprietors: Diana and Jeremy Robinson
Location: 23 miles northwest of Lexington

At the core of the Hummingbird Inn is a 1780 two-room post-and-beam house. The remainder of the inn is the Gothic Revival house that enveloped the older house in 1853. It is adorned with pointed-arch windows, a steeply pitched cross-gabled roof, and decorative cresting along the front porch roof. The house has been operated as an inn for decades, and counts Eleanor Roosevelt among its many guests. One of the guest rooms, named in her honor, looks almost exactly as it did when she slept here in 1935, with its antique bird's-eye maple bedroom set. One guest room, in the 1780 portion of the house, holds a pencil-post canopy bed. All rooms have ceiling fans, natural-fiber linens, down comforters, and Caswell and Massey toiletries. Breakfast, served on antique china, includes the innkeeper's raisin-filled scones from a family recipe.

Open: year round **Accommodations:** 5 guest rooms with private baths **Meals:** full breakfast included; complimentary refreshments; dinner by reservation; restaurants nearby **Wheelchair access:** 1 room **Rates:** $80 to $105; 10% discount to National Trust members and National Trust Visa cardholders **Payment:** AmEx, Visa, MC, personal and traveler's checks **Restrictions:** children over 12 welcome; no smoking; no pets **Activities:** lawn games, trout stream

LEESBURG

Nearby attractions: historic Leesburg, hunt country, point-to-point and steeplechase races, horseback riding, historic house tours, National Trust's Oatlands, antiques hunting, Civil War battlefields, parks, wineries, Wolftrap Farm Park, golfing

FLEETWOOD FARM BED AND BREAKFAST
Route 1, Box 306A
Leesburg, Virginia 22075
703/327–4325 or 800/808–5988
703/327–4325 Fax
Proprietors: Carol and Bill Chamberlin
Location: 8 miles south of Leesburg; 11 miles east of Middleburg

Fleetwood Farm manor house was built in 1745 by the Reverend Doctor Charles Green, friend and doctor to George and Martha Washington, on a 1400-acre land grant received from Lord Fairfax in 1741. Revolutionary War Colonel Albert Russel owned the farm in the late 1700s, and John Singleton Mosby, the Gray Ghost, visited Fleetwood several times during the Civil War. The innkeepers have fully restored the property, now listed in the National Register, and offer two unique guest rooms, each with fireplace and private bath (one a whirlpool). Each room is decorated with fresh flowers, antiques, and quilts. An abundant country breakfast is served family style in the dining room. Guests have the use of the living room with television, books, games, and fireplace. Fleetwood Farm has been featured in *Country Magazine*, the *Washington Post*, *Washingtonian*, and *National Geographic Traveler*.

Open: year round **Accommodations:** 2 guest rooms with private baths **Meals:** full breakfast included; complimentary refreshments always available; cook-out facilities; restaurants nearby **Rates:** $110 to $135 **Payment:** personal and traveler's checks **Restrictions:** children over 12 welcome; no smoking; no pets (heated kennels nearby) **Activities:** croquet; horseshoe pitching; hammock; vegetable and herb gardens; flocks of sheep, cats, and a llama; canoe and fishing equipment for nearby reservoir

NORRIS HOUSE INN
108 Loudoun Street
Leesburg, Virginia 22075
703/777-1806 or 800/644-1806
703/771-8051 Fax
Proprietors: Pam and Don McMurray

This handsome brick house with green shutters, dentil molding, and roof dormers, was built in 1760 in the heart of Leesburg. It was owned by the Norris family from 1850 until its conversion to an inn in 1983. Built-in cherry bookcases in the library typify the exceptionally fine woodwork found throughout the inn. In addition to the library, guests have full use of the dining room, parlor, sunroom, and veranda overlooking the gardens. Guest rooms are tastefully appointed with antiques and canopy or brass beds. All rooms have comfortable sitting areas and three have working fireplaces. A tearoom, offering weekend service and special event space, is in the adjacent Old Stone House, purported to have been British headquarters in 1754 during the French and Indian War.

Open: year round **Accommodations:** 6 guest rooms share 3 baths; private bath available with 15% surcharge **Meals:** full breakfast included; complimentary refreshments; restaurants nearby **Rates:** $85 to $140; 10% discount to National Trust members and National Trust Visa cardholders **Payment:** AmEx, Visa, MC, DC, Discover, personal and traveler's checks **Restrictions:** children over 12 welcome; no smoking; no pets

OAKLAND GREEN FARM BED AND BREAKFAST
Route 2, Box 147
Leesburg, Virginia 22075
703/338-7628
703/338-5922 Fax
Proprietors: Bill and Jean Brown
Location: 6 miles south of Purcellville

On 206 rolling acres outside the rural community of Lincoln—a town settled by Pennsylvania Quakers—is Oakland Green Farm Bed and Breakfast. Built in 1740 by Quaker farmer Richard Brown, the house is owned today by Bill Brown, the builder's seven-times-great-grandson and parliamentarian of the U.S. House of Representatives. Built of stone, log, and brick, the farmhouse offers one guest suite, which occupies the earliest log portion of the house and includes a sitting room with stone fireplace and piano on the ground floor and two bedrooms and a bath upstairs. In warm weather the house is cooled by air conditioning, and guests enjoy swimming in the pool. All seasons are fine times for strolling down quiet country lanes and across the farm's fields.

Open: year round **Accommodations:** 1 guest suite with 2 bedrooms and 1 bath **Meals:** full breakfast included; complimentary refreshments; restaurants nearby **Rate:** $95; 10% discount to National Trust members and National Trust Visa cardholders, except Saturday night **Payment:** personal check **Restrictions:** children over 5 welcome; no smoking; no pets **Activities:** swimming pool, hiking, nearby tennis and horseback riding

LINCOLN

Nearby attractions: Civil War battlefields, Shenandoah River, Appalachian Trail, wineries, antiques hunting, bicycling, hiking, boating

SPRINGDALE COUNTRY INN
Lincoln, Virginia 22078
703/338-1832 or 800/388-1832
703/338-1839 Fax
Proprietors: Nancy and Roger Fones
Location: 45 minutes west of Washington, D.C.

Springdale was built in 1832 as a Quaker girls' boarding school. It is a stone-and-frame Federal structure of central passage plan. Front double doors are flanked by Tuscan columns; sidelights and a nine-light transom frame the entrance. A Victorian front porch has turned posts and a hipped roof. Inside, original six-panel doors have reeded trim and bull's-eye corner blocks. Nine fireplaces, with original mantels, are found throughout the building. Guest rooms are meticulously furnished with antiques from the Regency, Federal, and Victorian periods. Lupton's Loft Room on the top floor offers office space and equipment for business travelers. From meetings to weddings, groups can rent a portion or all of the inn.

Open: year round **Accommodations:** 9 guest rooms (6 have private baths) **Meals:** full breakfast included; full meal service available for groups; restaurants nearby **Wheelchair access:** yes **Rates:** $95 to $125; 10% discount to National Trust members and National Trust Visa cardholders **Payment:** Visa, MC, Discover, personal and traveler's checks **Restrictions:** no smoking; no pets **Activities:** walking paths, croquet

LYNCHBURG

Nearby attractions: Appomattox, Fort Early, Red Hill (home of Patrick Henry), Poplar Forest (home of Thomas Jefferson), City Cemetery, South River Meeting House, historic district walking tours, Blue Ridge Mountains and Parkway, Natural Bridge, Crabtree Falls, Lynchburg Symphony, galleries, colleges and universities, antiques hunting, outlet shops

LYNCHBURG MANSION INN BED AND BREAKFAST
405 Madison Street
Lynchburg, Virginia 24504
804/528-5400 or 800/352-1199
Proprietors: Bob and Mauranna Sherman

The Lynchburg Mansion Inn was built in 1914 for James R. Gilliam, Sr., president of five coal companies, the Lynchburg Shoe Company, and six banks throughout the state. The house, with its 9000 square feet of living space, is located in the Garland Hill Historic District, one of five National Register districts in the city. Neoclassical styling is evident in the huge columns that support the front portico and the paired columns of the porte cochere on side of the building. The front door opens to a 50-foot grand hall with soaring ceilings and cherrywood columns and wainscoting. Lavishly decorated guest rooms contain deluxe linens, padded satin clothing hangers, lace sachets, color cable television, a telephone, and a clock-radio. A full breakfast is served in the formal dining room with fine china, crystal, and silver. The inn has received a three-diamond rating from AAA.

Open: year round **Accommodations:** 5 guest rooms with private baths; 2 are suites **Meals:** full breakfast included; restaurants nearby **Rates:** $84 to $119; 10% discount offered to National Trust members and National Trust Visa cardholders **Payment:** AmEx, Visa, MC, CB, DC, personal and traveler's checks **Restrictions:** no smoking; no pets **Activities:** hot tub, library

MADISON HOUSE BED AND BREAKFAST
413 Madison Street
Lynchburg, Virginia 24504
804/528-1503 or 800/828-6422
Proprietors: Irene and Dale Smith

The architecture of the 1880 Madison House combines Italianate styling with Eastlake, or spindlework, detailing. The house, built for a tobacco baron, features original bathroom fixtures from the turn of the century, crystal chandeliers, a peacock stained-glass window in one of the parlors, and an enormous gold-leaf overmantel mirror in another parlor. The focal point of the dining room is an 1850s English banquet table, where a full breakfast is served on antique Limoges and Wedgwood china. Guest rooms are individually decorated in Victorian motifs and feature modern comforts such as telephone, cable television, and clock radio. Each private bath is equipped with toiletries and hair dryers. Listed in the National Register of Historic Places and located in the Garland Hill Historic District, Madison House is close to shopping, colleges, antiques shops, restaurants, and Civil War sites.

Open: year round **Accommodations:** 4 guest rooms with private baths; 1 is a suite **Meals:** full breakfast included; complimentary afternoon English tea; restaurants nearby **Rates:** $79 to $109; 10% discount to National Trust members and National Trust Visa cardholders **Payment:** AmEx, Visa, MC, personal and traveler's checks **Restrictions:** not suitable for young children; no smoking; no pets **Activities:** Civil War library, music room, afternoon tea

MIDDLEBURG

Nearby attractions: walking tour of historic town, antiques hunting, Civil War battlefields, horseback riding, biking, winery tours, hot-air ballooning, horse racing, Skyline Drive

WELBOURNE
Route 1, Box 300
Middleburg, Virginia 22117
540/687-3201
Proprietors: Nat and Sherry Morison
Location: 6 miles west of Middleburg

In 1830, the Dulany family bought a 1775 stone house that they named Welbourne, then added a brick and stucco front, several rooms, and a porch. Seven generations of that family have lived here ever since. Today, Welbourne is the manor house of a 600-acre farm in the middle of Virginia's hunt country. Its dependencies (a greenhouse, a billiards house, and servants' quarters) circle the main dwelling and have been converted to guest cottages. The proprietors refer to the property's ambience as "faded elegance." Many Civil War stories center on Welbourne, and in the 1930s, Thomas Wolfe and F. Scott Fitzgerald were visitors here, each writing a story using Welbourne as a setting. A National Register property and a Virginia Historic Landmark, the farm is a short distance to the Blue Ridge Mountains and Skyline Drive.

Open: year round **Accommodations:** 8 guest rooms with private baths; 3 are suites **Meals:** full breakfast included; complimentary refreshments; restaurants nearby **Rates:** $85.20 to $95.85; 10% discount offered to National Trust members and National Trust Visa cardholders **Payment:** personal and traveler's checks

---

MIDDLETOWN

Nearby attractions: Belle Grove Plantation, Cedar Creek Battlefield, Skyline Drive, Shenandoah National Park, historic Winchester, museums, galleries, antiques hunting, fishing, hiking, picnicking, downhill skiing

WAYSIDE INN
7783 Main Street
Middletown, Virginia 22645
703/869-1797
Proprietor: William Hammack

Guests have been visiting this quaint country inn—known variously as Wilkinson's

Tavern, Larrick's Hotel, and now, the Wayside Inn—since 1797. Steeped in history, the inn witnessed the Battle of Cedar Creek during the Civil War. With the introduction of the automobile, and Wayside's convenient location on the Valley Pike, it became known as "America's First Motor Inn." Guest rooms are decorated with rare antiques, fine art, and a potpourri of memorabilia. Furnishings reflect many periods—early American, Victorian, Empire, French Provincial, and Greek Revival. The Wayside Inn, a member of Historic Hotels of America, is also famous for its restaurant (with seven antique- and pewter-filled dining rooms) serving authentic regional cuisine, including peanut soup, spoon bread, and Virginia ham.

Open: year round **Accommodations:** 24 guest rooms with private baths; 2 are suites **Meals:** restaurant on premises **Wheelchair access:** limited **Rates:** $70 to $125; 10% discount offered to National Trust members and National Trust Visa cardholders **Payment:** AmEx, Visa, MC, CB, DC, Discover, traveler's check **Restrictions:** no pets

---

NEW MARKET

Nearby attractions: Skyline Drive, golfing, skiing, vineyards, caverns, antiques hunting, battlefields

RED SHUTTER FARMHOUSE BED AND BREAKFAST
Route 1, Box 376
New Market, Virginia 22844
540/740-4281 or 800/738-8BNB (800/738-8262)
Proprietors: George and Juanita Miller

The oldest part of this farmhouse was built of logs in 1790 by George Rosenberger. Although the outside is covered with clapboard, the interior has exposed logs with stone-and-mortar chinking and exposed-beam ceilings. The dining room is in this old section, with a guest suite on the second floor. In 1870, a large house, with high ceilings and a center entrance hall, was added to the log cabin. Owners in the 1920s added a library and bedrooms. Major Edward M. Brown, who owned the house in the 1930s, entertained extensively in political circles, his guests including Franklin D. Roosevelt, Mrs. Woodrow Wilson, and numerous ambassadors, governors, and other notables. Today's guests enjoy spacious bedrooms, a veranda with rocking chairs, a library, and 20 acres in the beautiful pastoral valley of Smith Creek.

Open: year round **Accommodations:** 5 guest rooms (3 have private baths); 1 is a suite **Meals:** full breakfast included; restaurants nearby **Rates:** $55 to $70; 10% discount offered to National Trust members and National Trust Visa cardholders **Payment:** Visa, MC, personal and traveler's checks **Restrictions:** no smoking; no pets **Activities:** library, board games, cards, children's toys

ORANGE

Nearby attractions: historic sites, Blue Ridge Mountains, National Trust's Montpelier, antiques hunting, hiking, bicycling, lakes, boating, swimming

WILLOW GROVE INN
14079 Plantation Way
Orange, Virginia 22960
703/672-5982
703/672-3674 Fax
Proprietor: Angela Molloy

Willow Grove was first a modest frame structure built by Joseph Clark in 1778. In 1820, Clark's son William added the brick portion, built by the same workmen who had recently finished work on Thomas Jefferson's University of Virginia. Today, Willow Grove is an impressive example of Jefferson's Classical Revival style. Guest rooms, named for Virginia-born presidents, showcase a 30-year collection of period furnishings, heirloom linens, hand-hooked rugs, vintage prints, and antique watercolors. Wide pine flooring and original fireplace mantels preserve the traditional character of the rooms. A plantation breakfast includes local and traditional southern specialties. The inn, listed in the National Register and designated a Virginia Historic Landmark, has been praised by the *Washington Post*, *Washingtonian*, *Washington Times*, *Town and Country*, and *Country Accents*.

Open: year round **Accommodations:** 5 guest rooms with private baths; 2 are suites **Meals:** full breakfast included; restaurant on premises also serves dinner and Sunday brunch; restaurants nearby **Rates:** $95 to $165; 10% discount to National Trust members and National Trust Visa cardholders **Payment:** personal and traveler's checks **Restrictions:** well-behaved children welcome; smoking limited; no pets **Activities:** tree-shaded lawns, gardens, stone barns, picnicking, hammock

---

PETERSBURG

Nearby attractions: Petersburg historic district, Petersburg National Battlefield, James River plantations, antiques hunting

MAYFIELD INN
3348 West Washington Street
P.O. Box 2265
Petersburg, Virginia 23804
804/733-0866 or 804/861-6775
Proprietors: Jamie and Dot Caudle **Manager:** Cherry Turner
Location: 2 miles west of Petersburg historic district

Listed in the National Register of Historic Places and designated a Virginia landmark, Mayfield Inn is one of the finest mid-eighteenth-century residences in the state. Built in 1750, the house is a one-and-a-half-story brick structure built over a raised basement. Two defense lines were maintained on Mayfield property, giving it an important role in General Robert E. Lee's final attempts to defend Petersburg in 1865. After numerous changes in ownership, and a stint as part of a hospital complex, the 300-ton house was saved from demolition and moved one mile to its present location. The current owners received the Association for the Preservation of Virginia Antiquities award for restoration of this house in 1987. Completely furnished with antiques and period reproductions, the inn offers elegantly decorated rooms with canopied beds, original rugs on pine floors, private baths, and fireplaces. A country breakfast is served in the fully paneled dining room. Four acres of landscaped and natural grounds include an outdoor swimming pool.

Open: year round **Accommodations:** 4 guest rooms with private baths; 2 are suites **Meals:** full breakfast included; restaurants nearby **Rates:** $69 to $95; 10% discount to National Trust members and National Trust Visa cardholders **Payment:** Visa, MC, personal and traveler's checks **Restrictions:** smoking limited; no pets **Activities:** swimming in a 40-foot-long pool, strolling grounds to enjoy gazebo and herb garden

---

PULASKI

Nearby attractions: train station museum, historic downtown, Blue Ridge Parkway, hiking and bicycling trails, lake boating and swimming, national and state parks, golfing, tennis, antiques hunting, art galleries

COUNT PULASKI BED AND BREAKFAST AND GARDENS
821 North Jefferson Avenue
Pulaski, Virginia 24301
540/980-1163 or 800/980-1163
Proprietors: Florence Byrd Stevenson

The Count Pulaski Bed and Breakfast is in a 1910 Prairie-style home in Pulaski's National Register historic district. The house is a fine example of a vernacular plan often called American Foursquare, with its square floor plan, low-pitched hipped roof, hipped dormers, one-story wraparound porch, and symmetrical facade. This brick house is further stylized by Italian Renaissance–inspired quoins at all four corners. Today, as a bed and breakfast, the home is filled with furnishings from the innkeeper's life in Europe and Asia, as well as with family antiques. Guest rooms (offering twin or queen- or king-size beds) have ceiling fans, individually controlled air conditioning, and private baths. A full breakfast is provided. Count Pulaski Bed and Breakfast has earned three diamonds from AAA.

Open: year round **Accommodations:** 3 guest rooms with private baths; 1 is a suite **Meals:** full breakfast included; complimentary refreshments; restaurants nearby **Rates:** $75 ($20 extra for third person in suite); 10% discount to National Trust members and National Trust Visa cardholders **Payment:** Visa, MC, personal check **Restrictions:** not suitable for children; no smoking; no pets **Activities:** gardens, television, Steinway baby grand piano, books, table games

---

RICHMOND

Nearby attractions: state capitol, Shockoe Slip, financial district, Sixth Street Marketplace, Richmond Center, the Coliseum, Valentine Museum, White House of the Confederacy, Carpenter Center for the Performing Arts, Virginia Museum of Fine Arts, Edgar Allan Poe house, Virginia Commonwealth University, James River plantations

WEST–BOCOCK HOUSE
1107 Grove Avenue
Richmond, Virginia 23220
804/358-6174
Proprietor: Mrs. James B. West, Jr.

The West–Bocock House was built in 1871 in the Greek Revival style as a suburban retreat for a wealthy family. In the 1930s and 1940s it belonged to the noted preservationist Elizabeth S. Bocock, who restored the attractive home on fashionable Grove Avenue. This street is now part of the Fan Area Historic District, listed in the National Register of Historic Places. The innkeepers have lived here for more than 20 years, collecting American and English antiques to complement an eclectic art collection. One notable find, now in a guest room, is a bed formerly owned by Lady Astor. One guest room has a sunporch overlooking the back garden, another overlooks the courtyard, and the third has a vista of the nearby cathedral and the city skyline. A plantation breakfast is served in the dining room or on the veranda.

Open: year round **Accommodations:** 3 guest rooms with private baths; 1 is a suite **Meals:** full breakfast included; restaurants nearby **Rates:** $65 to $75 **Payment:** personal check **Restrictions:** smoking limited; no pets

SMITH MOUNTAIN LAKE

Nearby attractions: Smith Mountain Lake, Booker T. Washington National Monument, Blue Ridge Parkway, Roanoke, Peaks of Otter, Mill Mountain Zoo, farmers' market, boating, fishing, golfing, swimming, tennis, antiques hunting

THE MANOR AT TAYLOR'S STORE, A BED AND BREAKFAST COUNTRY INN

Route 1, Box 533
Smith Mountain Lake,
Virginia 24184
703/721-3951
Proprietors: Lee and Mary Lynn Tucker
Location: 20 miles southeast of Roanoke

Skelton Taylor, a lieutenant in Virginia's Bedford Militia, established Taylor's Store as a general merchandise trading post at this site in 1799. The Manor at Taylor's Store is a Greek Revival house, built in 1820 as the focus of a prosperous tobacco plantation. The manor, situated on a 120-acre estate next to Smith Mountain Lake, offers six guest rooms, each containing a special feature such as a fireplace, balcony, or porch. Guests also enjoy the formal parlor with its grand piano, a sunroom, a great room, an exercise room, a guest kitchen, and a hot tub. Breakfast features heart-healthy recipes. A separate cottage with a stone fireplace, three bedrooms, two baths, and a fully equipped kitchen is ideal for families. The estate invites hiking or swimming, canoeing, and fishing in one of six, private, spring-fed ponds.

Open: year round **Accommodations:** 6 guest rooms (4 have private baths); 2 are suites **Meals:** full breakfast included; complimentary refreshments; restaurants nearby **Rates:** $90 to $150; 10% discount to National Trust members and National Trust Visa cardholders **Payment:** Visa, MC, personal and traveler's checks **Restrictions:** children welcome in cottage; no smoking except in cottage; no pets **Activities:** swimming, fishing, canoeing, hiking, volleyball, badminton, croquet, billiards, videotapes, hot tub, exercise room

SPERRYVILLE

Nearby attractions: Monticello, James Madison's Montpelier, Skyline Drive, Old Rag Mountain, Luray Caverns, Shenandoah National Park, fishing, canoeing, fruit picking, furniture making, golfing, tennis, wineries, dinner at world-famous Inn at Little Washington

BELLE MEADE BED AND BREAKFAST
353 F.T. Valley Road
Sperryville, Virginia 22740
540/987-9748
Proprietors: Susan Hoffman, Michael Biniek, Tobey Wheelock, and Jennifer Simmons
Location: 6 1/2 miles south of Sperryville

Belle Meade Bed and Breakfast is located on a 137-acre farm in Rappahannock County along the eastern slope of the Blue Ridge Mountains. The newly renovated, spacious Victorian farmhouse is on Route 231, a scenic Virginia byway. Large guest rooms with private baths offer views of the surrounding mountains. One guest accommodation is a cottage. Belle Meade offers a peaceful retreat where guests are invited to soak in the hot tub in view of Old Rag Mountain, explore the fields, small streams, and mountains, and swim in the pool. Guests of all ages are welcome at this family-run establishment.

Open: year round **Accommodations:** 5 guest rooms with private baths; 1 is a cottage **Meals:** full breakfast included; restaurants nearby **Rates:** $80 to $200; 10% discount to National Trust members and National Trust Visa cardholders for stays longer than 3 days **Payment:** personal and traveler's checks **Restrictions:** no smoking **Activities:** hot tub, hiking, swimming

CONYERS HOUSE INN AND STABLE
3131 Slate Mills Road
Sperryville, Virginia 22740
540/987-8025
540/987-8709 Fax
Proprietors: Sandra and Norman Cartwright-Brown
Location: 8 miles south of Sperryville on Route 231

Conyers House comprises two old buildings: the one Bartholomew Conyers built here in 1810 (known as Conyers' Old Store) and the ca. 1790 building he moved to this location in 1815, attaching it to his house. Serving as Fink's General Store in 1850 and as a hippie commune in 1970, Conyers House—with its four stories, nine levels, and tin roof—has been serving as a bed-and-breakfast inn since

1981. A variety of accommodations are complemented by eighteenth- and nineteenth-century antique furniture, cozy fireplaces, private baths, and beautiful vistas. A full breakfast is served and candlelit dinners are available. The innkeepers share with guests their interests in old cars, foxhunting, antiques, and gardening. They also claim that a "presence" is in residence with them, their horses, and their dogs at Conyers House.

Open: year round **Accommodations:** 6 guest rooms with private baths **Meals:** full breakfast included; complimentary refreshments; restaurant on premises; restaurants nearby **Rates:** $100 to $195 **Payment:** Visa, MC, Discover, personal and traveler's checks **Restrictions:** no smoking; pets boarded at $30 per night **Activities:** horses, dogs, foxhunting, hiking, walking

STAUNTON

Nearby attractions: Woodrow Wilson Birthplace and Museum, Museum of American Frontier Culture, Blue Ridge Parkway, Skyline Drive, Mary Baldwin College, Stuart Hall, Harrisonburg, James Madison University, Lexington, Washington and Lee University, Virginia Horse Center, Virginia Military Institute, Charlottesville, Monticello, University of Virginia, Michie Tavern, Ash Lawn, hiking, skiing

FREDERICK HOUSE
28 North New Street
P.O. Box 1387
Staunton, Virginia 24401
703/885-4220 or
800/334-5575
Proprietors: Joe and Evy Harman

Frederick House is actually five elegant row houses built between 1810 and 1910, all restored and furnished with American antiques and paintings by Virginia artists. The 1810 Young House, an early Classical Revival structure with a portico, was most likely the work of builders who worked for Thomas Jefferson—the house is similar to a building designed by Jefferson on the campus of the University of Virginia. The building even includes nails from the Jefferson forge. Frederick House guests enjoy oversized beds, ceiling fans, remote cable television, air conditioning, telephone, and private baths. Some rooms have balconies and all have private entrances. A full breakfast is served in Chumley's Tea Room. Frederick House is across from Mary Baldwin College in the heart of Staunton, the oldest city in Virginia west of the Blue Ridge Mountains.

Open: year round **Accommodations:** 14 guest rooms with private baths; 6 are suites **Meals:** full breakfast included; inn-owned McCormick's Restaurant adjacent to property **Rates:** $65 to 110; 10% discount offered to National Trust members and National Trust Visa cardholders **Payment:** AmEx, Visa, MC, DC, Discover, personal and traveler's checks **Restrictions:** no smoking; no pets

KENWOOD
235 East Beverley Street
Staunton, Virginia 24401
703/886-0524
Proprietors: Liz and Ed
Kennedy

This 1910 Colonial Revival home is located in historic Staunton, next door to the Woodrow Wilson Birthplace. Kenwood's brickwork has been embellished with corner quoins, decorative window lintels with keystones, and a full-width entry porch. Three gabled roof dormers contain round-arched windows. The house is filled with period furniture and antiques, providing a comfortable and relaxed atmosphere. Guest rooms contain queen-size beds and offer private baths. A full Shenandoah Valley breakfast is served. Kenwood is conveniently located in the Gospel Hill historic district and provides both on- and off-street parking for its guests.

Open: year round **Accommodations:** 3 guest rooms with private baths **Meals:** full breakfast included; restaurants nearby **Rates:** $70 to $80; 10% discount to National Trust members and National Trust Visa cardholders **Payment:** Visa, MC, personal and traveler's checks **Restrictions:** children over 5 welcome; no smoking; no pets **Activities:** reading, television, front-porch sitting

LAMBSGATE BED AND BREAKFAST
Route 1, Box 63
Swoope, Virginia 24479
540/337-6929
Proprietors: Elizabeth and Daniel Fannon
Location: 6 miles west of Staunton

Lambsgate Bed and Breakfast accommodates guests in an 1816 brick farmhouse on the Middle River in the historic Shenandoah Valley. The house is vernacular, an example of the I-house common in rural Virginia. A one-story frame addition at the back of the house dates to the late nineteenth century, and a porch, extending from the addition, together with the front porch, creates a wraparound veranda. Modernization provides comfort, yet the house retains its historic character in woodwork, doors, mantels, and heart-pine random-width floors. Three cozy guest rooms are furnished with a blend of antiques and collectibles. A bountiful southern breakfast is served in the dining room. Lambsgate is surrounded by a working sheep farm on which lambs are born each spring.

Open: year round **Accommodations:** 3 guest rooms share a bath **Meals:** full breakfast included; restaurants nearby **Rates:** $40 single to $50 double **Payment:** personal and traveler's checks **Restrictions:** no smoking; no pets **Activities:** viewing Allegheny Mountains from veranda, flower and vegetable gardens

SAMPSON EAGON INN
238 East Beverley Street
Staunton, Virginia 24401
703/886-8200 or 800/597-9722
Proprietors: Laura and Frank Mattingly

The Sampson Eagon Inn, an 1840 residence, shows an Italianate influence in its low-pitched hipped roof and tall, narrow windows, set in pairs. Several Victorian additions at the rear and sides were made by the house's various owners through the years. Now fully restored, the inn offers five distinctive accommodations, each with period decor. Every air-conditioned guest room has a canopied queen-size bed, a cozy sitting area, cable television with VCR, and a private bath. The innkeepers place chocolates on bedside tables, provide personal baskets of toiletries, and offer a refrigerator for guest use, which is stocked with mineral water, soft drinks, fruit juices, and ice. Bone china, cut crystal, and sterling silver are used to serve a full breakfast that may include such specialties as Grand Marnier souffle pancakes or gourmet egg dishes. Sampson Eagon Inn has been lauded by *Gourmet*, the *Baltimore Sun*, and *Country Inns*.

Open: year round **Accommodations:** 5 guest rooms with private baths; 2 are suites **Meals:** full breakfast included; complimentary refreshments; restaurants nearby **Rates:** $85 to $99 **Payment:** personal and traveler's checks **Restrictions:** children over 12 welcome; no smoking **Activities:** book and video library

STRASBURG

Nearby attractions: Strasburg Museum, Strasburg Emporium for antiques hunting, walking tours, Hupp's Hill Battlefield Park and Study Center, National Trust's Belle Grove, New Market Battlefield Historical Park

HOTEL STRASBURG
201 South Holliday
Strasburg, Virginia 22657
703/465-9191 or 800/348-8327
703/465-4788 Fax
Proprietors: Gary and Carol Rutherford

The Hotel Strasburg originated as Dr. Mackall R. Bruin's private hospital in 1895. It was converted to a hotel in 1915, accepting overnight and long-term guests. Today, the three-story white clapboard building and two adjacent Victorian houses provide a strong dose of Victoriana in their common areas and guest rooms. Furnishings are an eclectic mix of antiques in Queen Anne, Renaissance Revival, and Eastlake styles. Beds are made of brass, painted iron, or elaborately carved wood. The inn's antiques also are for sale. The dining room, overseen by a framed print of Queen Victoria, displays that era's penchant for indoor plants. Chef-prepared meals may include such items as chicken breast with sauteed Virginia peanuts, apples, and Smithfield ham in apple brandy and cream. Local wines are served. Overnight guests receive a complimentary continental breakfast.

Open: year round **Accommodations:** 29 guest rooms with private baths; 9 are suites with whirlpool tubs **Meals:** continental breakfast included; restaurant and pub on premises **Rates:** $69 to $149; 10% discount to National Trust members and National Trust Visa cardholders **Payment:** AmEx, Visa, MC, CB, DC, personal and traveler's checks **Restrictions:** inquire about pets **Activities:** antiques shopping, fine dining

SURRY

Nearby attractions: Williamsburg, Bacon's Castle, Smith's Fort Plantation, James River plantations, Chippokes Plantation State Park, Hog Island State Waterfowl Refuge, bicycling, boating

SEWARD HOUSE INN
193 Colonial Trail East
Surry, Virginia 23883
804/294-3810
Proprietors: Jacqueline G. Bayer and Cynthia H. Erskine

Dr. William W. Seward, town physician until 1940, built this spacious white frame house in 1902. The house, with its spindlework front porch, is located in the one-traffic-light town of Surry, with working farms all around. A grove of pecan trees stretches behind the inn's 1.7-acre grounds. High-ceilinged rooms are furnished for guest comfort and hold the treasured momentos of three generations of two families: hand-carved beds, old toys, photographs, and favorite bits of needlework and china. A full breakfast, including homemade breads and sausages, is served. A two-room cottage wtih private bath and entrance is also available.

Open: year round **Accommodations:** 4 guest rooms (2 have private baths); 1 is a suite **Meals:** full breakfast included; complimentary refreshments; dinners and packed lunches by reservation; restaurants nearby **Rates:** $65 to $80; 10% discount to National Trust members and National Trust Visa cardholders **Payment:** AmEx, Discover **Restrictions:** smoking limited; no pets **Activities:** bicycles, croquet

URBANNA

Nearby attractions: historic Urbanna, seventeenth- and eighteenth-century plantations, Old Court House, Old Tobacco Warehouse, Old Custom House, Yorktown, Williamsburg, Mary Ball Museum

HEWICK PLANTATION
VSH 602/615
P.O. Box 82
Urbanna, Virginia 23175-0082
804/758-4214
804/758-4214 Fax
Proprietors: Helen and Ed Battleson
Location: 1 mile north of Urbanna on Route 602

Christopher Robinson arrived in Virginia from Yorkshire, England, in 1666. In 1678 he built this brick manor home along an offshoot of the Rappahannock River. Robinson was a member of the House of Burgesses, President of the King's Council, Secretary to the Foreign Plantations, and was an original trustee of the College of William and Mary. His house sits amid 66 acres, which include an ongoing archeological dig that has been conducted by the College of William and Mary since 1989. Today's bed-and-breakfast guests are invited to visit the site during the school year. Guests will also find interesting the ongoing restoration of this very early colonial home, which is filled with period antiques. Listed in the National Register, Hewick Plantation is currently owned by tenth-generation descendents of Christopher Robinson.

Open: year round **Accommodations:** 2 guest rooms with private baths **Meals:** continental-plus breakfast included; restaurants nearby **Rates:** $95 to $105; 10% discount to National Trust members and National Trust Visa cardholders **Payment:** Visa, MC, personal and traveler's checks **Restrictions:** children over 6 welcome; no smoking; no pets **Activities:** house tours, croquet, bird-watching, on-site archeological dig

---

VIRGINIA BEACH

Nearby attractions: beach, water sports, state parks for hiking and cycling, Back Bay Wildlife Refuge, Marine Science and Life Saving museums, golfing, tennis

ANGIE'S GUEST COTTAGE
302 24th Street
Virginia Beach, Virginia 23451
804/428-4690
Proprietor: Barbara G. Yates

The first aerial photograph of Virginia Beach, taken from a Navy balloon sometime in the 1920s, shows Angie's Guest Cottage. It was built in 1915 in a typical beach-bungalow style and retains that style today with porches and sundecks. In the early days, Angie's housed the families of men who worked at the local Coast Guard station. Today, the Guest Cottage hosts travelers from around the world; it also runs an American Youth Hostel behind the cottage. Rooms are decorated in a casual, beach style with wicker, fresh flowers, and lots of seashells. Some rooms have private entrances, porches, and refrigerators. All guests are welcome to use the community kitchen. Angie's is one block from the beach in the heart of the resort area.

Open: April 1 to October 1 **Accommodations:** 6 guest rooms; 1 with private bath **Meals:** continental-plus breakfast included in season (Memorial Day to Labor Day); restaurants nearby **Rates:** $44 single to $72 double (rates drop by a third in off-season) **Payment:** personal and traveler's checks **Restrictions:** no smoking; inquire about pets; 2-night minimum **Activities:** barbecue, picnic tables, table tennis, library, sundeck and front porch for relaxing and people watching

BARCLAY
COTTAGE BED
AND BREAKFAST
400 16th Street
Virginia Beach,
Virginia 23451
804/422-1956
Proprietor:
Peter Catanese

Located in the
heart of the Virginia Beach recreational area, Barclay Cottage is named for its
former owner, Lillian S. Barclay. Used as a schoolhouse for many years, the
charming two-story, clapboard house has a pyramidal hipped roof and porches
fully surrounding its two floors. While fully modernized, the inn's historical
ambience is maintained through antiques and collectibles in every room. A full
breakfast is served. Guests enjoy backgammon and other table games in the living
room and a putting green outside. Just two blocks from the beach, Barclay
Cottage provides beach chairs for its guests.

Open: March to October **Accommodations:** 6 guest rooms (2 have private baths)
Meals: full breakfast included; complimentary refreshments; restaurants nearby **Rates:**
$65 to $90; 10% discount to National Trust members and National Trust Visa cardholders
Payment: AmEx, Visa, MC, traveler's check **Restrictions:** children over 12 welcome;
no smoking; no pets **Activities:** veranda sitting, reading, backgammon, cable television,
putting green

WARM SPRINGS
Nearby attractions: Warm Springs Pools; Garth Newel Chamber Music; scenic
drives; hiking trails; swimming in mountain lakes; the Homestead in Hot Springs
for dining, shops, golfing, horseback riding, and trap shooting

ANDERSON COTTAGE BED AND BREAKFAST
Old Germantown Road (Route 692)
Box 176
Warm Springs, Virginia 24484
703/839-2975
Proprietor: Jean Randolph Bruns

The original four rooms of this rambling old house were an eighteenth-century
log tavern. The building was joined to a four-room cottage in the early nineteenth

century, then gained further additions to reach its current shape in about 1840. There are 12 fireplaces with original mantels, authentic rough-plastered crooked walls, and old wood floors. More than a century of ownership by one family has provided a continuity evident in the furnishings, the library, and the innkeeper's knowledge of the area. Guest rooms range from spacious suites to single rooms, all with electric baseboard heat. Two parlors are available for guests, and spacious porches are ideal for rocking and reading. Behind the main house, an 1820 brick kitchen has been expanded to make a two-bedroom, two-bath cottage with living room and kitchen. A warm stream from the nearby Warm Springs pools flows through the two-acre property.

Open: Main House early spring to mid-fall; Kitchen Cottage year round **Accommodations:** 5 guest rooms (4 have private baths); 2 are suites; 1 cottage with kitchen **Meals:** full breakfast included; restaurants nearby **Rates:** $60 to $110 **Payment:** personal and traveler's checks **Restrictions:** Main House not recommended for small children; no smoking; no dogs **Activities:** reading, rocking, croquet, badminton, volleyball, soccer, cards, board games, unhurried conversation

---

WASHINGTON

Nearby attractions: Shenandoah National Park, Skyline Drive, Civil War battlefields, antiques hunting, wineries, stables, caverns, museums, waterfall watching, swimming, tennis, canoeing, golfing, climbing, fine dining

CALEDONIA FARM–1812 BED AND BREAKFAST
47 Dearing Road
Flint Hill, Virginia 22627
540/675-3693 or 800/BNB-1812 (800/262-1812)
Proprietor: Phil Irwin
Location: 4 miles north of Washington, Virginia; 68 miles west of Washington, D.C.

This Federal house and companion summer kitchen have the same two-foot-thick stone walls, 32-foot-long beams, mantels, paneled windows, and wide pine floorboards that were installed when it was built in 1812. The house was constructed of local fieldstone by Captain John Dearing, and the interior woodwork is attributed to Hessian soldiers who stayed in the area and found work as carpenters following the Revolutionary War. The winter kitchen's huge fireplace provides a delightful atmosphere during cold seasons, and three porches and a patio offer views of fields, mountains, and woods. The elegant decor is enhanced by working fireplaces in public rooms as well as in each antique-appointed bedroom. All guest rooms have individual climate controls and enjoy spectacular views of Skyline Drive. Listed in the National Register, Caledonia is a working cattle farm. Caledonia Farm was selected in 1992 by INNovations, a

B&B marketing company, as the only bed and breakfast in Virginia, and one of only 23 nationally, to receive "four ovations," designating it as "exceptional" and "significantly exceeding requirements in physical and operational categories." AAA has given Caledonia Farm a three-diamond rating.

Open: year round **Accommodations:** 2 guest rooms with semiprivate bath; 2 suites with private baths **Wheelchair access:** limited **Meals:** full breakfast included; complimentary refreshments; superb restaurants nearby (including the world-famous Inn at Little Washington) **Rates:** $80 to $140; 10% discount to National Trust members **Payment:** Visa, MC, Discover, personal and traveler's checks **Restrictions:** children over 12 welcome; no smoking; no pets **Activities:** lawn games, bicycles, hayrides, hiking, piano, television and VCR; other on-site extras include balloon flights, carriage rides, limousine service, custom photography, guided battlefield tours

WHITE POST

Nearby attractions: Blue Ridge Mountains, horseback riding, horse races, golfing, hiking, backpacking, tennis, health-club facilities, antiques hunting, vineyards

L'AUBERGE PROVENCALE
P.O. Box 119
White Post, Virginia 22663
703/837-1375 or 800/638-1702
703/837-2004 Fax
Proprietors: Alain and Celeste Borel
Location: 1 mile south of Route 50 on Route 340

Guests who travel to rural White Post will discover that they have arrived in the south of France, for here, at L'Augerge Provencale, the innkeepers have created a country inn in the spirit of Provence, offering elegant accommodations and nationally acclaimed French cuisine. The main house, Mt. Airy, is a large fieldstone structure with a columned portico, built in 1753. Guest rooms, some with working fireplaces, are individually decorated with Victorian antiques and furnishings. Mornings begin wtih a gourmet breakfast prepared by fourth-generation chef Alain Borel and described by a *Washington Post* critic as "a breakfast on one's dreams." While staying at L'Auberge Provencale, guests can travel the back roads of Clarke county, nestled beside the Shenandoah River and framed by the gently rolling Blue Ridge Mountains.

Open: February to December **Accommodations:** 10 guest rooms with private baths; 2 are suites **Meals:** full breakfast included; restaurant on premises **Rates:** $145 to $195 **Payment:** AmEx, Visa, MC, DC, Discover, personal and traveler's checks **Restrictions:** children over 10 welcome; smoking limited; no pets

WILLIAMSBURG

Nearby attractions: Colonial Williamsburg, James River plantation tours, Civil War battlefields, Busch Gardens, antiques hunting, outlet shops, fish hatchery tours, golfing, tennis, bicycling

APPLEWOOD COLONIAL BED AND BREAKFAST
605 Richmond Road
Williamsburg, Virginia 23185
804/229-0205 or 800/899-2753
Proprietors: Fred Strout and Marty Jones

Built by Colonial Williamsburg's construction manager in 1929, Applewood's architecture and Flemish-bond brick pattern recall the Georgian style. The inn is located four blocks from the restored area and across the street from the College of William and Mary. The current innkeepers have restored the house's elegant colonial decor, including the parlor's eighteenth-century-style dentil crown molding and fireplace and the dining room's built-in corner cupboard. An apple collection, scattered throughout the house, inspired the inn's name and the names of the guest rooms. These are filled with queen-size beds (some with canopies), oriental rugs, and antiques; all have private baths. Guests are served a full candlelight breakfast.

Open: year round **Accommodations:** 4 guest rooms with private baths; 1 is a suite **Meals:** full breakfast included; complimentary refreshments; restaurants nearby **Rates:** $75 to $120; 10% discount offered to National Trust members **Payment:** Visa, MC, personal and traveler's checks **Restrictions:** no smoking; no pets **Activities:** games, television

THE CEDARS BED AND BREAKFAST
616 Jamestown Road
Williamsburg, Virginia 23185
804/229-3591 or 800/296-3591
Proprietors: Carol, Jim, and Brona Malecha

The Cedars is the oldest and largest bed and breakfast in Williamsburg. Built by a doctor in the early 1930s, this three-story brick Georgian Revival home was constructed by Colonial Williamsburg restoration craftsmen of 200-year-old brick from a nearby plantation house. Less than a 10-minute walk to the restored area of Williamsburg, and across the street from the College of William and Mary, The Cedars offers candlelight and fresh flowers to enhance the full breakfasts, which are served from a hand-hewn huntboard on the tavern porch. The menu includes such inn specialties as oatmeal pudding with brandied raisins and smoked salmon flan. After breakfast, the porch serves as a meeting place for cards, chess, or other diversions. On cool evenings, the fireplace in the elegant sitting room invites relaxation and conversation. The eight guest rooms and the two-story cottage are graciously appointed, each with a unique style that reflects the romance of the colonial era. Four-poster and canopy beds abound. Each of the two suites in the cottage has a fireplace.

Open: year round **Accommodations:** 10 guest rooms with private baths; 2 are suites **Meals:** full breakfast included; restaurants nearby **Rates:** $95 to $165 **Payment:** Visa, MC, personal and traveler's checks **Restrictions:** no smoking; no pets

GOVERNOR'S TRACE BED AND BREAKFAST
303 Capitol Landing Road
Williamsburg, Virginia 23185
804/229-7552 or 800/303-7552
Proprietors: Sue and Dick Lake

Governor's Trace derives its name from the fact that it is adjacent to land purchased for the royal governors of Virginia. Built in 1930 during the restoration of Colonial Williamsburg, it is a replica of a Georgian, Flemish-bond brick manor house. Situated on a former peanut plantation, it fronts historic Capitol Landing Road, the route of commerce for goods unloaded from English ships. (Nearby is a recently discovered gallows site where 13 of Blackbeard's pirates were hanged.) Governor's Trace, the closest bed and breakfast to the restored area of Williamsburg, less than one block away, contains three spacious bedrooms with private baths. They are furnished with elegant four-poster beds, family antiques, and collectibles. One room connects to a private screened porch furnished in wicker. Another room sets an eighteenth-century tone with brass candlelighted lanterns, shuttered windows, and a working fireplace.

Open: year round **Accommodations:** 3 guest rooms with private baths **Meals:** continental-plus breakfast included; restaurants nearby **Rates:** $95 to $115; 10% discount to National Trust members and National Trust Visa cardholders **Payment:** Visa, MC, personal and traveler's checks **Restrictions:** no smoking; no pets

LIBERTY ROSE BED AND BREAKFAST INN
1022 Jamestown Road
Williamsburg, Virginia 23185
804/253-1260
Proprietors: Brad and Sandi Hirz

White beaded clapboard, a dormered slate roof flanked by twin chimneys, and brick gathered from the old Jamestown colony before it became a historic landmark, distinguish this house built in 1926 by the then-owner of Jamestown

Island. A complete renovation beginning in 1986 has transformed what was a vacant house into a romantic bed and breakfast, filled with an eclectic mix of English, Victorian, French country, and eighteenth-century antiques. Guest rooms are lavishly decorated with damask wallcoverings, silk, fine linen, and yards of lace. Private baths are luxurious, with marble walls and claw-foot tubs. Guests are invited to relax by the fireplace in the parlor, play a favorite tune on the grand piano, enjoy breakfast on the morning porch, and browse the tiny gift shop. The inn has received accolades from *Country Inns* and *Rural Living*.

Open: year round **Accommodations:** 4 guest rooms with private baths; 2 are suites **Meals:** full breakfast included; complimentary refreshments; restaurants nearby **Rates:** $110 to $185; 10% discount to National Trust members and National Trust Visa cardholders **Payment:** AmEx, Visa, MC, personal and traveler's checks **Restrictions:** children over 12 welcome; no smoking; no pets **Activities:** courtyard and gardens, gift shop

PINEY GROVE AT SOUTHALL'S PLANTATION
P.O. Box 1359
Williamsburg, Virginia 23187-1359
804/829-2480
Proprietors: Brian, Cindy Rae, Joseph, and Joan Gordineer
Location: 20 miles west of Williamsburg, 35 miles east of Richmond in the James River plantation country

Piney Grove (1800), a rare Tidewater log building, and the modest Greek Revival–style Ladysmith House (1857) are situated on property that includes flower gardens, fruit trees, farm animals, and a nature trail. Archeological digs on the grounds have unearthed an ancient Indian site and a deposit of three-million-year-old fossils. The inn includes a unique collection of antiques and artifacts that illustrates the history of the Southall Plantation, Piney Grove, and its residents, who have included planters, tavern keepers, merchants, farmers, and Confederate soldiers. The houses have been restored using original color schemes and furnishings, and all guest rooms contain working fireplaces. Listed in the National Register of Historic Places, the inn contains an impressive library of Virginia history and architecture. The grounds also include Ashland (1835) and the Duck Church (1900).

Open: year round **Accommodations:** 5 guest rooms with private baths **Meals:** full breakfast included; complimentary arrival refreshments; bottle of Virginia wine or cider; brandy nightcaps; restaurants nearby offer complimentary desserts to Piney Grove guests **Rates:** $125 to $150; 10% discount to National Trust members and National Trust Visa cardholders for stays of two nights or more **Payment:** personal and traveler's checks **Restrictions:** no smoking; no pets **Activities:** nature trails, swimming pool, library, croquet, badminton, bird-watching

WOODSTOCK

Nearby attractions: Civil War sites, National Trust's Belle Grove Plantation, hiking in national forests, canoeing, horseback riding, caverns, museums, shopping, antiques hunting, winery tours, skiing, wineries

AZALEA HOUSE

551 South Main Street
Woodstock, Virginia 22664
703/459-3500
Proprietors: Margaret and Price McDonald

Azalea House was built in 1892 as a manse by the United Church of Christ and was used for many years by pastors and their families. The most unique features of the large Victorian house are the almost square bay windows extending from ground to roofline and the adjoining first- and second-floor porches. The house, located near the Massanutten Academy, has unique stenciled ceilings and is decorated with many family antiques. Guests enjoy a full country breakfast. Breathtaking views from the balcony are topped only by the brilliant display of more than 100 azalea bushes blooming in the spring.

Open: year round **Accommodations:** 3 guest rooms with private baths; 1 is a suite **Meals:** full breakfast included; complimentary refreshments; restaurants nearby **Rates:** $50 to $70; 10% discount offered to National Trust members except in October and on weekends **Payment:** Visa, MC, personal and traveler's checks **Restrictions:** children over 6 welcome; no smoking; no pets **Activities:** bicycling and hiking

COUNTRY FARE BED AND BREAKFAST

402 North Main Street
Woodstock, Virginia 22664
703/459-4828
Proprietor: Elizabeth B. Hallgren

One of the oldest homes still in use in the region, the former Ott house was built in 1772 and added on to in 1840. This colonial-era dwelling features nine-over-nine double-hung windows and a center chimney. During the Civil War the house was used as a field hospital, one of many in the valley. Today, the Country Fare is furnished with the innkeeper's family antiques and heirlooms together with antiques collected in the area. Three guest rooms are decorated with stenciled wall designs and country collectibles. Breakfasts feature the inn's own home-baked breads. For relaxing, the inn offers a second-floor sitting porch and a patio. The Country Fare is the nearest lodging to the breathtaking summit view of the Seven Bends of the Shenandoah River.

Open: year round **Accommodations:** 3 guest rooms share 1 bath **Meals:** continental-plus breakfast included; restaurants nearby **Rates:** $45 to $65; 10% discount to National Trust members and National Trust Visa cardholders **Payment:** Visa, MC, personal and traveler's checks **Restrictions:** smoking limited; no pets

INN AT NARROW PASSAGE

U.S. Route 11 South
P.O. Box 608
Woodstock, Virginia 22664
703/459-8000
Proprietors: Ellen and Ed Markel
Location: 2 miles south of Woodstock

This log inn overlooking the Shenandoah River has been welcoming travelers since the early 1740s, when it was a haven against Indians for settlers on the Virginia frontier. Later it was a stagecoach inn on the old Valley Turnpike, and in 1862 Stonewall Jackson made it his headquarters during the Valley Campaign. Restored to its eighteenth-century character, the inn has its original fireplaces working once again and its pine floors gleaming. The massive limestone fireplace in the living room warms a cozy common area. Furnished in antiques and handmade colonial reproductions, the Inn at Narrow Passage offers comfortable guest rooms, some with wood-burning fireplaces and canopy beds. The back porches and five acres surrounding the inn provide relaxing places to unwind and view the river.

Open: year round **Accommodations:** 12 guest rooms (10 have private baths) **Meals:** full breakfast included; restaurants nearby **Rates:** $85 to $110; 10% discount offered to National Trust members and National Trust Visa cardholders **Payment:** Visa, MC, personal and traveler's checks
Restrictions: smoking lim-
ited; no pets **Activities:**
hiking, canoeing, fishing,
bird-watching, horse-
back riding, historic sites

WASHINGTON

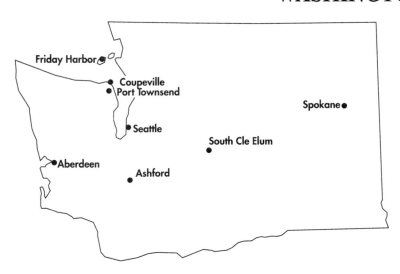

ABERDEEN

Nearby attractions: ocean beaches, oyster farms, cranberry bogs, rain forests, historic seaport, antiques hunting, nautical museum, farmers' market, whale-watching, clamming, festivals, kayaking, golfing, bird-watching

COONEY MANSION BED AND BREAKFAST INN
1705 Fifth Street
Box 54
Cosmopolis, Washington 98537
360/533-0602
Proprietors: Judi and Jim Lohr
Location: 2 miles south of Aberdeen

A circular driveway leads to the porte cochere of this 1908 mansion, built by lumber baron Neil Cooney. This National Register house, with its abundance of fine woodwork and many original Arts and Crafts furnishings and fixtures, has been fully restored. Built to showcase the mill's timber, the beamed and paneled first floor includes a living room, dining room, two parlors, and a sunroom. Spacious guest rooms have private baths with claw-foot tubs and access to a sundeck. An exercise room, sauna, and whirlpool offer one way to unwind. A library and video collection offer another. A three-course "lumber baron's" breakfast is served at the massive dining table. Golf, tennis, and a trout-stocked lake are available at adjacent Mill Creek Park. Rated with three diamonds by

AAA, Cooney Mansion has been featured in numerous publications, including *Sunset, Travel and Leisure*, and the *Seattle Post Intelligencer*.

Open: year round **Accommodations:** 6 guest rooms (5 have private baths); 1 is a suite **Meals:** full breakfast included; restaurants nearby **Rates:** $65 to $130; 10% discount to National Trust members and National Trust Visa cardholders **Payment:** AmEx, Visa, MC, CB, DC, Discover, traveler's check **Restrictions:** children over 10 welcome; no smoking; no pets **Activities:** sauna, whirlpool, exercise room, library, player piano, board games, rose garden, Christmas package

ASHFORD

Nearby attractions: Mount Rainier National Park, Northwest Trek Animal Park, Mount Rainier Scenic Railroad, Pioneer Farm Museum, hiking, skiing, lakes for swimming and boating

MOUNTAIN MEADOWS INN BED AND BREAKFAST
28912 SR 706 E
Ashford, Washington 98304
206/569-2788
Proprietor: Chad Darrah

The view in 1910 from the front porch of this mill superintendent's house would have taken in the activity at the booming sawmill town of National, Washington. National was located near Ashford on the Tacoma Eastern Railroad line and contained the biggest sawmill west of the Mississippi River. Unionization of labor and its subsequent demands caused the sawmill to close before World War II and the company town became a ghost town. Now the nearby superintendent's home provides lodging for travelers. Throughout the house an extensive model railroad collection and other memorabilia encourage guests to relive the glory days of logging, sawmilling, and railroading. The inn serves a hearty country breakfast. From the inn's front door guests can walk the trails to old National and reap the pleasures of untouched nature and wildlife.

Open: year round **Accommodations:** 5 guest rooms with private baths **Meals:** full breakfast included; popcorn and juice with movies; campfire evenings with marshmallow roasts **Rates:** $55 to $95; 10% discount offered to National Trust members and National Trust Visa cardholders **Payment:** Visa, MC, personal check **Restrictions:** children over 10 welcome; no smoking; inquire about pets **Activities:** model railroading, railroad museum, player piano, historical movies about the area, yard games, nature trails, fishing

COUPEVILLE

Nearby attractions: Fort Casey State Park, Ebby's Landing National Reserve, historic Port Townsend (via ferry), swimming, skin diving, bird-watching

FORT CASEY INN
1124 South Engle Road
Whidbey Island
Coupeville, Washington 98239
360/678-8792
Proprietors: Gordon and Victoria Hoenig
Location: $1^1/2$ hours from Seattle

Fort Casey Inn is a 1909 Colonial Revival structure built as officers' quarters for the then-active defense installation of Fort Casey on Whidbey Island. The restored National Register inn is located next door to Fort Casey State Park, with its bunkers, lighthouse, 10-inch disappearing guns, public beaches, and trails. Built to withstand attacks on Fort Casey, the house has a reinforced basement, which was intended for use as a bomb shelter. All guest accommodations are two-bedroom suites complete with bath, living room, and kitchen. The beautifully appointed Garrison Hall is available for seminars and retreats. Whidbey Island offers countless attractions, from sites of early frontier living to spectacular Deception Pass.

Open: year round **Accommodations:** 10 2-bedroom guest suites with private baths **Meals:** continental-plus breakfast included; restaurants nearby **Rates:** $75 to $110 **Payment:** Visa, MC, personal and traveler's checks **Restrictions:** no smoking; no pets **Activities:** bicycles

---

FRIDAY HARBOR

Nearby attractions: Whale Museum, whale and eagle watching, kayaking, boating, scuba diving, charter fishing and sailing, hiking and bicycling trails, island ferries, art galleries, beachcombing, picnicking

TUCKER HOUSE BED AND BREAKFAST
260 B Street
Friday Harbor, Washington 98250
360/378-2783 or 800/965-0123
360/378-6437 Fax
Proprietors: Skip and Annette Metzger

The Victorian-styled Tucker House, with spindlework front porch, is named for the vice-president of San Juan County Bank, who built it in 1898. The house contains two guest rooms upstairs—reached through a private entrance—that share a bath. The inn also offers three separate cottages with queen-size beds, wood-burning stoves, kitchenettes, television, and private baths. A full breakfast, featuring the inn's homemade cinnamon bread, is served in the solarium at the main house. Tucker House offers a picket-fenced yard full of flowers, decks to lounge on, and a hot tub for guests' relaxation. The inn is conveniently located only two blocks from the ferry landing and Spring Street, Friday Harbor's center of commerce.

Open: year round **Accommodations:** 2 guest rooms with shared bath; 3 separate cottages with private baths **Meals:** full breakfast included; restaurants nearby **Rates:** $75 to $135; 10% discount offered to National Trust members and National Trust Visa cardholders **Payment:** AmEx, Visa, MC, Discover, personal and traveler's checks **Restrictions:** no smoking; small pets welcome **Activities:** reading, television and VCR, outdoor hot tub

---

PORT TOWNSEND

Nearby attractions: museums, art galleries, home tours, state parks, marine science center, boating, golfing, tennis, windsurfing, kayaking, hiking, bicycling, swimming, fishing, beachcombing, clam digging, seasonal festivals

ANN STARRETT MANSION
744 Clay Street
Port Townsend, Washington 98368
206/385-3205 or 800/321-0644
Proprietors: Edel and Bob Sokol

George Starrett built this elaborate Queen Anne mansion as a wedding present for his wife, Ann, in 1889. The mansion is internationally renowned for its outstanding architecture, frescoed ceilings, and free-hanging three-story spiral staircase. The stairs lead to an eight-sided domed ceiling that is actually a solar calendar with frescoes that depict the Four Seasons and Four Virtues. Small dormer windows are situated so that on the first day of each new season the sun shines on a ruby red glass, causing a red beam to point toward the appropriate seasonal panel. Elsewhere in the house elaborate moldings feature carved lions, doves, and ferns. Guest rooms are furnished with antiques carefully selected to recreate the Victorian era of a century ago. The Ann Starrett Mansion has received praise from many publications, including the *New York Times* and the *London Times*.

Open: year round **Accommodations:** 11 guest rooms with private baths; 6 are suites **Meals:** full breakfast included; restaurants nearby **Rates:** $79 to $225; 10% discount offered to National Trust members and National Trust Visa cardholders midweek November through April **Payment:** AmEx, Visa, MC, Discover, personal and traveler's checks **Restrictions:** children over 12 welcome; no smoking; no pets

QUIMPER INN BED AND BREAKFAST
1306 Franklin Street
Port Townsend, Washington 98368
360/385-1060 or 800/557-1060
Proprietors: Sue and Ron Ramage

In 1888, Henry Morgan built a two-story house with hipped roof. A remodeling in 1904 by Harry and Gertrude Barthrop gave the house a third story through the addition of gables and dormers, and a dramatic presence through the further addition of a double front porch. After decades of neglect, the house was restored in the late 1980s and converted to an inn. Workers renewed such features as pocket doors, bay windows, Victorian lighting fixtures, and built-in shelves and cabinets. Guest rooms have been decorated with antiques and individual style. An easy walk takes guests downtown or to uptown districts amid cafes, shops, theaters, and festivities.

Open: year round **Accommodations:** 5 guest rooms (3 have private baths); 1 is a suite **Meals:** full breakfast included; restaurants nearby **Rates:** $70 to $140 **Payment:** Visa, MC, personal and traveler's checks **Restrictions:** children over 12 welcome; no smoking; no pets **Activities:** bicycles

SEATTLE

Nearby attractions: financial, retail, and historic districts of Seattle; Rose Gardens; Volunteer Park; Seattle Art Museum and Conservatory; University of Washington; Pike Place Market; convention center; parks; bicycling; swimming; tennis; zoo

CHELSEA STATION ON THE PARK—A BED AND BREAKFAST INN
4915 Linden Avenue North
Seattle, Washington 98103
206/547-6077 or 800/400-6077
Proprietor: John Griffin **Innkeeper:** Karen Carbonneau

After the Great Fire of 1896 and a second fire in 1899, brick became the building material of choice in Seattle. Chelsea Station, a Federal-style home built in 1929, displays decorative brickwork in an asymmetrical diamond pattern laid vertically on either side of the entrance. Largely decorated in Mission style, the house features antiques throughout. Guest rooms feature king- and queen-size beds with down comforters, and second-floor suites offer peek-a-boo views of the Cascade Mountains. Guests feel refreshed by the warm and casual mood at Chelsea Station. The property was originally part of the 1896 grant that established the Seattle Zoo and is located directly across from the Rose Gardens. The inn is also convenient to Woodland Park, Greenlake, and downtown.

Open: year round **Accommodations:** 6 guest rooms with private baths; 3 are suites **Meals:** full breakfast included; complimentary refreshments; restaurants nearby **Rates:** $69 to $114; 10% discount offered to National Trust members and National Trust Visa cardholders low season only **Payment:** AmEx, Visa, MC, CB, DC, Discover, personal and traveler's checks **Restrictions:** children over 12 welcome; no smoking; no pets **Activities:** neighborhood strolls

SOUTH CLE ELUM

Nearby attractions: Iron Horse State Park; Alpine Lakes Wilderness Area; hiking; bicycling; golfing; river rafting; fishing; skiing; rodeo; museums in Roslyn, Cle Elum, and Ellensburg; gold panning in Liberty Townsite, oldest gold mining town site in Washington

MOORE HOUSE BED AND BREAKFAST COUNTRY INN
526 Marie Avenue
P.O. Box 629
South Cle Elum, Washington 98943
509/674-5939
Proprietors: Eric and Cindy Sherwood

Moore House was built in 1909 by the Chicago, Milwaukee, St. Paul and Pacific Railroad to house workers who had the job of getting trains over some of the most hazardous track in the country. Now restored and placed in the National Register of Historic Places, Moore House offers bright and airy guest rooms, each named after a railroad crewman who stayed here. Old print wallpaper, oak antiques, and artifacts combine to create bedrooms ranging from economical to exquisite. Two authentic cabooses, each with queen-size bed, bathroom, television, and refrigerator, sleep up to five people. Guests are invited to examine the model trains, early railroading photographs, and collection of railroad lanterns as they enjoy breakfast.

Open: year round **Accommodations:** 12 guest rooms (6 have private baths); 3 are suites **Meals:** full breakfast included; restaurants nearby **Rates:** $45 to $115 **Payment:** AmEx, Visa, MC, personal and traveler's checks **Restrictions:** smoking limited; no pets **Activities:** outdoor hot tub, extensive railroad memorabilia collection

SPOKANE

Nearby attractions: Coeur d'Alene Park, Eastern Washington Historical Society, walking tours, Riverfront Park, golfing, Mt. Spokane, skiing, lakes, fishing

FOTHERINGHAM HOUSE

2128 West Second Avenue
Spokane, Washington 99204
509/838-1891
509/838-1807 Fax
Proprietors: Jackie and Graham Johnson

This late Queen Anne–style house is a primary site in the Browne's Addition National Register historic district. It was built in 1891 by Mayor David B. Fotheringham. Tin ceilings, wood floors, a curved-glass window in the entryway, the first-floor carved and tiled fireplace, intricate ball-and-spindle fretwork separating the entry and living room, and open, carved staircase are all original to the house. Guest rooms are furnished with Victorian-era pieces from England, Ireland, France, and the United States. Each room is decorated differently, from the four-poster bed in the Mayor's Room to the armoire and matching rose-carved bed in the Mansion Room. Evening tea and truffles and morning coffee and juice are set outside guest room doors. Full breakfasts feature a daily changing menu.

Open: year round **Accommodations:** 3 guest rooms (1 with private bath) **Meals:** full breakfast included; complimentary refreshments; restaurants nearby **Rates:** $70 to $85; 10% discount to National Trust members and National Trust Visa cardholders **Payment:** Visa, MC, personal and traveler's checks **Restrictions:** children over 12 welcome; no smoking; no pets

WEST VIRGINIA

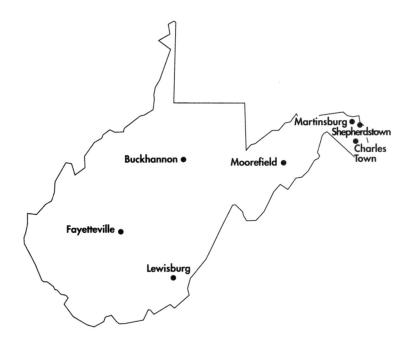

BUCKHANNON

Nearby attractions: West Virginia Wesleyan College, West Virginia State Wildlife Center, skiing, hiking

POST MANSION INN
8 Island Avenue
Buckhannon, West Virginia 26201
304/472-8959 or 800/301-9309
Proprietor: Juanita Reger

Originally built of brick in 1860, this mansion was purchased by State Senator William Post in 1891. Post made extensive alterations to both the exterior and interior of the house, based on designs by Draper Hughes. The resulting stone-faced style was Neoclassical, and the house became known locally as the castle, thanks to its castellated tower. After some years of decline and decay, the property was purchased by Mrs. Reger, who restored the 25-room house so that it is now listed in the National Register of Historic Places. The inn is fully furnished in late Victorian period furniture. Six acres of renovated grounds are bordered on two sides by the Buckhannon River.

Open: year round **Accommodations:** 6 guest rooms (4 have private baths); 1 is a suite **Meals:** full breakfast included; complimentary refreshments; restaurants nearby **Rates:** $50 to $100; 10% discount to National Trust members and National Trust Visa cardholders **Payment:** personal and traveler's checks **Restrictions:** children over 6 welcome; no smoking; no pets

---

CHARLES TOWN

Nearby attractions: Charles Town Races, Jefferson County Museum, John Brown Gallows site, walking tours, George Washington family homes, Antietam Battlefield, Harpers Ferry National Historic Park, Blue Ridge Outlet Mall, Bunker Hill Antique Mall and Mills, gift shops, antiques hunting, golfing, tennis, hiking, Shenandoah River rafting and canoeing

GILBERT HOUSE BED AND BREAKFAST
Middleway Historic District
P.O. Box 1104
Charles Town, West Virginia 25414
304/725-0637
Proprietor: Bernard F. Heiler
Location: 5 miles west of Charles Town, 11 miles southeast of Harpers Ferry, 60 miles west of Washington, D.C.

Gilbert House is an imposing Georgian structure located in the eighteenth-century village of Middleway, originally a mill site on the European settlers' trail into the Shenandoah Valley. Built in 1760, with additions in 1830, and included in the Historic American Building Survey in 1938, this National Register house has 20-inch-thick gray stone walls and six working fireplaces with original mantels. Some walls bear graffiti from long ago including a child's growth chart begun in 1839 and an 1832 drawing of James K. Polk. Guest rooms are filled with tapestries, antiques, oriental rugs, and oil paintings. Rooms on the second floor have fireplaces, and third-floor guests can enjoy the sound of rain on the metal roof. Sumptuous breakfasts begin with freshly ground coffee from beans regularly brought by the innkeeper from Mexico. The innkeeper also gives tours of a reconstructed eighteenth-century log house in the back yard.

Open: year round **Accommodations:** 3 guest rooms with private baths; 1 is a suite **Meals:** full breakfast included; complimentary refreshments; restaurants nearby **Rates:** $80 to $140; 10% discount offered to National Trust members **Payment:** AmEx, Visa, MC, personal and traveler's checks **Restrictions:** inquire about small children; no smoking; no pets **Activities:** investigating garden and restored log house; reading; piano; porch with rocking chairs

FAYETTEVILLE

Nearby attractions: New River Gorge National Park, historic district walking tours, museums, white-water rafting

MORRIS HARVEY HOUSE
BED AND BREAKFAST
201 West Maple Avenue
Fayetteville, West Virginia
25840
304/574-1179 or
800/CALLWVA
(800/225-5982)
Proprietors: George and
Elizabeth Soros

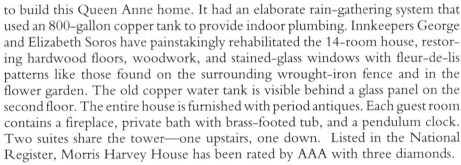

Morris Harvey was a Civil War
veteran, banker, county sheriff,
and generous contributor to the
failing Barboursville College, now
known as Morris Harvey College. In
1902 he commissioned R. H. Dickinson
to build this Queen Anne home. It had an elaborate rain-gathering system that used an 800-gallon copper tank to provide indoor plumbing. Innkeepers George and Elizabeth Soros have painstakingly rehabilitated the 14-room house, restoring hardwood floors, woodwork, and stained-glass windows with fleur-de-lis patterns like those found on the surrounding wrought-iron fence and in the flower garden. The old copper water tank is visible behind a glass panel on the second floor. The entire house is furnished with period antiques. Each guest room contains a fireplace, private bath with brass-footed tub, and a pendulum clock. Two suites share the tower—one upstairs, one down. Listed in the National Register, Morris Harvey House has been rated by AAA with three diamonds.

Open: April to December **Accommodations:** 4 guest rooms with private baths; 2 are suites **Meals:** full breakfast included; restaurants nearby **Rates:** $75 to $85; 10% discount to National Trust members and National Trust Visa cardholders **Payment:** Visa, MC, personal and traveler's checks **Restrictions:** inquire about children; no smoking; no pets **Activities:** flower garden, Victrola

LEWISBURG

Nearby attractions: historic Lewisburg walking tours, Revolutionary and Civil War sites, Pearl Buck's birthplace, Greenbrier Valley Theater, state parks, lakes, fishing, hunting, cross-crountry skiing, swimming pools, tennis, golfing, hiking and biking trails, Organ Cave, Lost World Caverns

GENERAL LEWIS INN
301 East Washington Street
Lewisburg, West Virginia 24901
304/645-2600
Proprietors: Mary Noel and Jim Morgan

History permeates every room of the General Lewis Inn. The original 1834 home and its larger 1929 addition contain numerous cupboards filled with early glass, pottery, china, and curios. The front desk was built in 1760. Patrick Henry and Thomas Jefferson registered at this desk when it was in the Sweet Chalybeate Springs Hotel, at one of the many springs in the area visited by Virginia's early aristocrats. The dining room, serving old-fashioned country cooking, is in the first floor of the original 1834 home. Memory Hall, a small museum contained within the inn, pays tribute to the resourcefulness of mountain pioneers in vast collections of tools, guns, household utensils, and musical instruments. Two bedrooms and two suites are in the oldest part of the house and feature original fireplaces and mantels. Every room in the inn is furnished with antiques that highlight the craftsmanship of early settlers.

Open: year round **Accommodations:** 25 guest rooms with private baths; 2 are suites **Meals:** restaurant on premises **Rates:** $60 to $95 **Payment:** AmEx, Visa, MC, personal and traveler's checks **Restrictions:** no smoking **Activities:** pioneer memorabilia display, porch rocking, gardens

---

MARTINSBURG

Nearby attractions: Antietam Battlefield National Park, Harpers Ferry National Park, Berkeley Springs mineral baths, C&O Canal and bicycle trail, Charles Town Thoroughbred Race Track, white-water rafting, auctions, golfing, antiques hunting, outlet shops

ASPEN HALL INN
405 Boyd Avenue
Martinsburg, West Virginia 25401
304/263-4385
Proprietors: Gordon and Lou Anne Claucherty

Aspen Hall is a limestone mansion situated on several acres under a canopy of giant locust trees. Built ca. 1750 by Quakers, the house was first a small fortified stone structure. George Washington noted in his journal that he sent troops to protect the inhabitants here during the French and Indian War. The Georgian section of the house was built in 1788. It was enlarged in the 1790s and again in 1905. The house has been restored to this Edwardian period. Each large guest room, furnished with antiques, has a sitting area and private bath. Some rooms have canopied beds; one has a fireplace. One parlor contains a grand piano, the other is a library. The dining room, showplace for antique china, is where a full country breakfast is served. Afternoon tea is enjoyed in the library or the streamside gazebo at this National Register property.

Open: February 10 through December 24 **Meals:** full breakfast included; complimentary refreshments; restaurants nearby **Rates:** $95 to $110; 10% discount to National Trust members and National Trust Visa cardholders **Payment:** Visa, MC, personal check **Restrictions:** children over 12 welcome; no smoking; no pets **Activities:** trout fishing, hammock, rocking chairs, croquet, horseshoes, gazebo, stream

BOYDVILLE, THE INN AT MARTINSBURG

601 South Queen Street
Martinsburg, West Virginia 25401
304/263-1448 or 202/626-2709
Proprietors: La Rue Frye, Bob Boege, Carolyn Snyder, and Pete Bailey

The 10 acres on which Boydville sits was once part of a large plantation purchased by General Elisha Boyd in the 1790s. Boyd built his stone mansion in 1812, and the house has changed hands only three times since then, leaving original woodwork, wallpaper, window glass, and mantels intact. Foyer wallpaper was handpainted in England in 1812 especially for Boydville. A mural, handpainted in France in the 1830s, graces a bedroom wall. All guest rooms are furnished with functional American and English antiques. Breakfast features native West Virginia products in season. Rocking on the long porch overlooking century-old boxwoods and trees in rockers original to Boydville is a favorite pastime. Guests also enjoy strolling the grounds and the ivy-covered brick-walled courtyard and garden.

Open: year round **Accommodations:** 6 guest rooms (4 have private baths) **Meals:** continental-plus breakfast included; complimentary refreshments; restaurants nearby **Rates:** $100 to $125; 10% discount to National Trust members and National Trust Visa cardholders **Payment:** Visa, MC, personal and traveler's checks **Restrictions:** children over 12 welcome; no smoking; no pets **Activities:** 10 acres for walking and jogging

---

MOOREFIELD

Nearby attractions: fishing, white-water rafting, golfing, hiking, canoeing, train excursions, wineries

McMECHEN HOUSE INN BED AND BREAKFAST
109 North Main Street
Moorefield, West Virginia 26836
304/538-7173 or 800/2WVA-INN (800/298-2466)
304/538-7841 Fax
Proprietors: Linda, Bob, and Larry Curtis

S. A. McMechen was a merchant and political activist. He built this three-story Greek Revival brick home in 1853 in what is now the Moorefield historic district. During the Civil War the house served alternately as headquarters to both the Union and Confederate forces as military control of the South Branch Valley changed hands. Listed in the National Register of Historic Place, the inn offers

seven graciously appointed guest rooms. The atmosphere is romantic, enhanced by the many antiques found throughout. An antiques and gift shop is also on the premises. A full breakfast and afternoon tea are served. Casual lunches are offered at the inn's Green Shutters Garden Cafe on weekends. The inn is within walking distance of shops and restaurants.

Open: year round **Accommodations:** 7 guest rooms (4 have private baths); 1 is a suite **Meals:** full breakfast included; complimentary refreshments; restaurant on premises; restaurants nearby **Rates:** $50 to $85; 10% discount to National Trust members and National Trust Visa cardholders **Payment:** AmEx, Visa, MC, CB, DC, personal and traveler's checks **Restrictions:** smoking limited; no pets **Activities:** books, games, antiques shop, live music in outdoor cafe, annual art show and one-man show

SHEPHERDSTOWN

Nearby attractions: historic Shepherdstown Museum, C&O Canal and Towpath, Antietam Battlefield, Charles Town Races, Harpers Ferry, Appalachian Trail, Morgan's Grove Park, Thomas Shepherd Grist Mill, Blue Ridge Outlet Center, Berkeley Springs Mineral Baths, golfing, fishing, boating, rafting, hiking, bicycling

THOMAS SHEPHERD INN
300 West German Street
P.O. Box 1162
Shepherdstown, West Virginia 25443
304/876–3715
Proprietor: Margaret Perry

In the heart of historic Shepherdstown, West Virginia's oldest town, the inn, a mid-nineteenth-century Federal structure, originated as the Lutheran Church's parsonage on land once owned by Thomas Shepherd. Later the home and office of a local physician, the house was restored in 1984. Today, it is the Thomas Shepherd Inn with six spacious guest rooms furnished appropriately for the period. Fresh flowers, thick towels, and scented soaps are stocked in private bathrooms. A living room, two formal dining rooms, a library, and a porch are shared and enjoyed by guests. Specially prepared dinners and picnic lunches are available. The inn offers bicycles to guests for taking in the many local sights.

Open: year round **Accommodations:** 7 guest rooms with private baths **Meals:** full breakfast included; restaurants nearby **Rates:** $85 to $135; 10% discount to National Trust members and National Trust Visa cardholders; business rates available **Payment:** AmEx, Visa, MC, Discover, personal and traveler's checks **Restrictions:** children over 8 welcome; no smoking; no pets

WISCONSIN

CEDARBURG

Nearby attractions: Cedarburg historic district, Cedarburg Cultural Center, Cedar Creek Settlement, Kuhefuss House, Covered Bridge Park, Pioneer Village, Cedar Creek Winery, Riveredge Nature Center, art galleries, horseback riding, tennis, bicycling, hiking, cross-country skiing, lake Michigan fishing and boating, antiques hunting

STAGECOACH INN
W61 N520 Washington Avenue
Cedarburg, Wisconsin 53012
414/375-0208
414/375-6170 Fax
Proprietors: Liz and Brook Brown

When city travelers journeyed by horse and coach up the Lake Michigan shoreline in the 1850s, they rested in Cedarburg at this country inn, known then as the Central House Hotel. It boasted "first class accommodations, choice wines, liquors, and beers. Good stabling and large stock." Restored in 1984 by the innkeepers, the 1853 Greek Revival stone building, now the Stagecoach Inn, continues its tradition of welcoming guests. Nine guest rooms are offered in the stone building and three are in the 1847 frame Weber Haus across the street. Guest rooms are furnished with antique wardrobes and canopy or sleigh beds. Six suites have two-person whirlpool tubs. The Stagecoach Pub and Beerntsen's Chocolate Shop are on the first floor of the main building. The pub features a 100-year-old bar, oak tavern tables, and the original tin ceiling. Stagecoach Inn is located in Cedarburg's historic district, within walking distance of shops, restaurants, parks, and the Cultural Center.

Open: year round **Accommodations:** 12 guest rooms with private baths; 6 are suites **Meals:** continental-plus breakfast included; restaurants nearby **Rates:** $70 to $105; 10% discount to National Trust members and National Trust Visa cardholders weekdays, January through April **Payment:** AmEx, Visa, MC, Discover, personal and traveler's checks **Restrictions:** children over 10 welcome; no smoking; no pets **Activities:** pub, garden

WASHINGTON HOUSE INN
W62 N573 Washington Avenue
Cedarburg, Wisconsin 53012
414/375-3550 or
800/554-4717
414/375-9422 Fax
Proprietor: James Pape

Washington House was Cedarburg's first inn, built in 1846 on this site. Forty years later the original structure was replaced by the present three-story brick hotel with decorative cornices and parapets. In the 1920s, the building remained but its use changed: the hotel was converted into offices and apartments. But when the building was sold in 1983, restoration began and Washington House was returned to its original use as an inn. Guests find themselves surrounded by a collection of antique Victorian furniture, marble-trimmed fireplaces, and freshly cut flowers. Tasteful guest rooms decorated in country-Victorian style feature antiques, down quilts, whirlpool baths, and fireplaces. Designer fabrics, bed linens, and wallpapers add elegance. Listed in the National Register of Historic Places, the inn has been praised by *Country Home*, *Innsider*, *Milwaukee Journal*, and *Milwaukee Magazine*.

Open: year round **Accommodations:** 34 guest rooms with private baths **Meals:** continental-plus breakfast included; complimentary wine and cheese; restaurants nearby **Wheelchair access:** yes **Rates:** $59 to $159; 10% discount offered to National Trust members and National Trust Visa cardholders **Payment:** AmEx, Visa, MC, DC, Discover, personal and traveler's checks **Restrictions:** smoking limited; no pets **Activities:** sauna, board games, cards, reading

EAST TROY

Nearby attractions: Old World Wisconsin, Kettle Moraine State Forest, horseback riding, Alpine Valley Music Theater and Ski Resort, hiking, bicycling, boating, fishing, swimming, canoeing, golfing, antiques hunting

GREYSTONE FARM BED AND BREAKFAST
N9391 Adams Church Road
East Troy, Wisconsin 53120
414/495-8485
Proprietors: Ruth and Alane Leibner
Location: 9 miles northwest of East Troy

The land at Greystone Farm, originally purchased in 1839 from the U.S. government, still holds the original structure built there in 1840. This building now serves as the kitchen of the present home, a house built by a gentleman farmer in 1885, its leaded-glass windows and gleaming maple floors intact. One guest room offers an 1860 Eastlake black walnut bed and matching dresser. Another has an Eastlake oak and bird's-eye maple bed. One room has a brass and white-iron bed, another contains an ivory-colored four-poster bed. A full breakfast is served at a time arranged the night before, for guests' convenience. The farm includes 17 acres of fields and woods. Guests are invited to stop by the barn to say hello to the miniature horses. For complete relaxation there is the fieldstone porch or the swing hanging from the old oak tree.

Open: year round **Accommodations:** 4 guest rooms (2 have private baths) **Meals:** full breakfast included; restaurants nearby **Rates:** $50 to $80; 10% discount to National Trust members and National Trust Visa cardholders **Payment:** AmEx, Visa, MC, personal and traveler's checks **Restrictions:** smoking limited; no pets **Activities:** murder-mystery weekends, farm walks, miniature horses

LA FARGE

Nearby attractions: Amish neighbor's furniture-making shop and maple syrup camp (in spring), largest Amish community in Wisconsin, local and state historic sites, three major rivers with related water activities, two state parks, bike trails

TRILLIUM COUNTRY COTTAGE
Route 2, Box 121
La Farge, Wisconsin 54639
608/625-4492
Proprietor: Rosanne Boyett
Location: 7 miles east of Westby, on East Salem Ridge Road

Trillium Country Cottage is a 1929 cedar-shake cottage with a timber-framed porch. It was moved to the innkeeper's farm in 1942 for her grandmother to live in, and today offers travelers a cozy, private refuge tucked into the hills of the Kickapoo Valley. The cottage contains original wood floors, original kitchen fixtures including a wood-burning stove, and a fireplace built with stone from the nearby Kickapoo River. Nearly every item in the cottage is a family heirloom, including the double-wedding-ring quilt, the oak Hoosier kitchen cupboard, and grandma's rocker in the living room. A fresh farm breakfast is brought to the cottage each morning, and guests are free to prepare all other meals in the cottage kitchen. Trillium is surrounded by woods, fields, orchards, and organic gardens.

Open: year round **Accommodations:** 1 cottage sleeps 6 in 2 double and 2 twin beds (plus portable crib) **Meals:** full breakfast included; complimentary refreshments; restaurants nearby **Rates:** $55 single, $75 double, $25 each additional guest over 12 years old **Payment:** personal and traveler's checks **Restrictions:** no smoking; no pets **Activities:** hiking, swimming in pond, bird watching, bicycling, porch swing and hammock, livestock chores and farm and field work in season

---

LAKE GENEVA

Nearby attractions: Geneva Lake Kennel Club dog racing, tennis, boating, swimming, golfing, museums, dining, shopping

T. C. SMITH HISTORIC INN BED AND BREAKFAST
865 Main Street
Lake Geneva, Wisconsin 53147
414/248-1097 or 800/423-0233
Proprietors: Marks family

Built in 1845 in downtown Lake Geneva, the T. C. Smith Inn is a blend of Greek Revival and Italianate architecture, a Victorian style typical of the pre–Civil War era. It is listed in the National Register as being of outstanding architectural, historical, and artistic significance. Victorian light fixtures illuminate a spacious foyer containing a parquet floor, original trompe l'oeil and miniature oil paintings on the walls, and a staircase bounded by a hand-tooled black walnut bannister. Fireplaces and hand-painted moldings and woodwork have been preserved, as well as all the pocket doors and cabinetry. Some spacious guest rooms offer fireplaces and whirlpool bathtubs. T. C. Smith Inn is surrounded by landscaped grounds and brilliant floral gardens, neoclassical statues, goldfish pools, and quiet benches.

Open: year round **Accommodations:** 8 guest rooms with private baths; 1 suite with private bath **Meals:** full breakfast included; complimentary refreshments; restaurants nearby **Rates:** $95 to $295; 10% discount offered to National Trust members and National Trust Visa cardholders **Payment:** AmEx, Visa, MC, Discover, DC, personal and traveler's checks **Activities:** bicycle rentals, gift shop

LEWIS
Nearby attractions: St. Croix River Valley, boating, fishing, state parks

SEVEN PINES LODGE
P.O. Box 137
Lewis, Wisconsin 54851
715/653-2323
715/653-2236 Fax
Proprietor: Lee Gohlike

In 1903, self-made millionaire Charles Lewis purchased 680 acres of virgin white pine forest with the aim of preserving it from logging. Careful not to disrupt the uncommon beauty of the region, Lewis had a lodge built completely by hand. The entire structure was put together with square wooden pegs, except for the nails used in the wood flooring. This was a grand fly-fishing lodge, with game trophies on the walls, a moose head over the fireplace, Native American handiwork, and sturdy Mission oak furniture. Although rustic, Seven Pines offered every convenience of the day, including indoor bathrooms and an enclosed mosaic-tiled swimming pool. The lodge remains virtually the same today, with its original furnishings intact and well maintained. Only six acres of the original tract remain, but they include a spring-fed stream and pond for trout fishing. Guests rooms are in the Main Lodge, the Carriage House, the Gate House, and the Stream House.

Open: year round **Accommodations:** 9 guest rooms (4 have full private baths; 4 have partial private baths) **Meals:** continental breakfast included; complimentary refreshments; restaurant on premises **Rates:** $84 to $170; 10% discount to National Trust members and National Trust Visa cardholders **Payment:** Visa, MC, personal and traveler's checks **Restrictions:** no smoking; no pets **Activities:** fly fishing, bird-watching, hiking woodland trails, bicycling

MADISON

Nearby attractions: University of Wisconsin and its Arboretum, Lake Mendota swimming and boating, state capitol, bicycling, antiques hunting, cross-country skiing, swimming, sailing, tennis, golfing, shopping

ARBOR HOUSE, AN ENVIRONMENTAL INN
3402 Monroe Street
Madison, Wisconsin 53711
608/238-2981
Proprietors: John and Cathie Imes

Arbor House, previously the Plough Inn, has been a Madison landmark since the mid-nineteenth century. Possibly built as early as 1834 as a private home, it was converted to a tavern and inn by 1853. It is a Greek Revival building, having been built in three stages of sandstone and brick. Later the building was covered in stucco. Arbor House blends historic features—original wood floors and natural stone fireplaces—with modern amenities that have an environmental emphasis—natural fabrics, energy-saving climate controls, and water-saving bathroom fixtures. Guest rooms are individually decorated with contemporary and antique furnishings and unique themes. Some rooms have televisions, fireplaces, and whirlpool tubs. The inn sits on a large landscaped lot with native gardens and mature trees across from the University of Wisconsin Arboretum.

Open: year round **Accommodations:** 5 guest rooms with private baths; 1 is a suite **Meals:** continental-plus breakfast included on weekdays; full breakfast included on weekends; complimentary refreshments; restaurants nearby **Wheelchair access:** yes **Rates:** $84 to $115; 10% discount to National Trust members and National Trust Visa cardholders, weekdays only excluding holidays **Payment:** AmEx, Visa, MC, personal and traveler's checks **Restrictions:** no smoking; no pets **Activities:** hiking, bicycling, cross-country skiing, canoeing

COLLINS HOUSE BED AND BREAKFAST
704 East Gorham Street
Madison, Wisconsin 53703
608/255-4230
Proprietors: Barb and Mike Pratzel

On the shores of Lake Mendota in one of Madison's oldest downtown neighborhoods, the Collins House was built in 1911 for lumber executive William H. Collins. It is listed in the National Register of Historic Places as a classic example of the Prairie Style of architecture, founded by Frank Lloyd Wright. The Prairie Style was considered an innovative form that embodied the heart and spirit of the Midwest; homes are characterized by open, light-filled interiors that reflect the peacefulness and beauty of their natural surroundings. At the Collins House, original details are still intact, including mahogany ceiling beams, leaded-glass windows, and wall stenciling. Guest rooms are furnished with antiques and handmade quilts. Furnishings from the Arts and Crafts Movement are found throughout the home.

Open: year round **Accommodations:** 5 guest rooms with private baths (some have double whirlpool tubs) **Meals:** full breakfast included; complimentary refreshments; restaurants nearby **Rates:** $80 to $140 **Payment:** Visa, MC, personal and traveler's checks **Restrictions:** no smoking; inquire about pets **Activities:** video and reading libraries

MANSION HILL INN
424 North Pinckney Street
Madison, Wisconsin 53703
608/255-3999 or
800/798-9070
Proprietor: Janna Wojtal

This elegant Italianate mansion was built in 1858 for Alexander A. McDonnell. Lacy wrought-iron balconies encircle carved sandstone facades and a belvedere crowns the roof of the National Register house.

Tall, gracefully arched windows fill rooms with light, ornate cornices and medallions crown spacious halls, and hand-carved marble and hardwoods enhance the many fireplaces. A four-story spiral staircase leads to a rooftop belvedere. Bedrooms are elaborately decorated with silks, lace, damask, and chintz. All rooms contain fine antiques. Private bathrooms are outfitted in brightly colored tiles and whirlpool tubs, marble, and skylights. Rooms feature fireplaces, minibars, and access to a veranda or balcony. A parlor, private wine cellar, Victorian garden, and entertainment center are offered for guests' use.

Open: year round **Accommodations:** 11 guest rooms with private baths; 9 are suites **Meals:** continental-plus breakfast included; complimentary refreshments; restaurants nearby **Rates:** $80 to $270 **Payment:** AmEx, Visa, MC, personal and traveler's checks **Restrictions:** children over 12 welcome; no pets **Activities:** gardens, television and VCR, stereo system, access to health spa and private dining club

---

STURGEON BAY

Nearby attractions: Door County Museum and Library, Miller Art Center, walking tours of historic district, shipyards, lighthouses, shops, boating, swimming, fishing, golfing, tennis, five state parks for bicycling and hiking, cross-country and downhill skiing

GRAY GOOSE BED AND BREAKFAST
4258 Bay Shore Drive
Sturgeon Bay, Wisconsin 54235
414/743-9100
Proprietors: Jack and Jessie Burkhardt
Location: in Door County, 2 miles north of city

Built on the shore of Sturgeon Bay by an ambitious Scotsman named Alexander Templeton, this 1862 farmstead was moved 100 yards inland in 1979 but still offers a water view. It is a nearly square, two-story red frame house with steep dormers and a full-facade porch (filled with comfortable old wicker and a wooden swing). In the dining room an heirloom table of solid oak, with matching ladderback chairs, is set with fine china from one of many cabinets; the room is lit only by soft lamplight and candles. Here, a gourmet "skip-lunch" breakfast is served. Four large antique-filled guest rooms are decorated to show off collections indicated by their names: the Pewter Room, Wicker Room, Flow Blue Room, and Advertising Room; the latter is loaded with nostalgic, colorful signs, food tins, and other advertising pieces.

Open: year round **Accommodations:** 4 guest rooms share 2 baths **Meals:** full breakfast included; complimentary refreshments; restaurants nearby **Rates:** $70 to $80 (winter and single rates slightly less) **Payment:** AmEx, Visa, MC, personal and traveler's checks **Restrictions:** children over 12 welcome; smoking limited; no pets **Activities:** hiking, snowshoeing, picnicking, croquet, bicycling, porch sitting, games, piano, books and binoculars for bird- and bay-watching

INN AT CEDAR CROSSING
336 Louisiana Street
Sturgeon Bay, Wisconsin 54235
414/743-4200
Proprietor: Terry Wulf

Built in 1884 at the corner of what were then called Cedar and Cottage streets, the brick vernacular-style building was originally a street-level drugstore with living quarters above. Over time, the building has been used as a tailor's shop, a soda fountain, doctors' offices, and a clothing store. After a thorough restoration in 1985, the Inn at Cedar Crossing opened as a bed and breakfast. The lobby features a pressed-tin ceiling, fireplace, and curved staircase. The Gathering Room offers another fireplace and a place for comfortable reading or games. Guest rooms are furnished with four-poster, canopy, brass, or cottage beds. Careful use of painting finishes, stenciling, wallpapers, and fabrics complements fine antiques. Down-filled comforters and private baths (some with double whirlpool tubs) add to the comfort of each room. Fireplaces with antique mantels grace many guest rooms. The Inn at Cedar Crossing is listed in the National Register of Historic Places.

Open: year round **Accommodations:** 9 guest rooms with private baths **Meals:** continental-plus breakfast included; complimentary refreshments; restaurant on premises serving full breakfast, lunch, and dinner **Wheelchair access:** dining room **Rates:** $79 to $135 **Payment:** Visa, MC, personal and traveler's checks **Restrictions:** supervised children welcome; no smoking; no pets **Activities:** pub on premises, television and telephone in all guest rooms

WYOMING

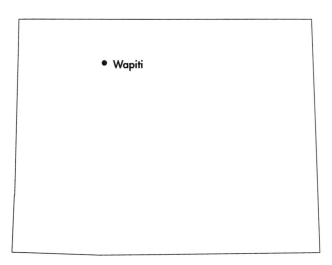

WAPITI

Nearby attractions: Yellowstone National Park, Buffalo Bill Historical Center, Cody Rodeo, Sunlight Basin, Beartooth Wilderness, river float trips

ELEPHANT HEAD LODGE
1170 Yellowstone Highway
Wapiti, Wyoming 82450
307/587-3980
Proprietors: Phil and Joan Lamb and daughters Gretchen and Nicole
Location: 11 miles east of Yellowstone National Park, 40 miles west of Cody

Buffalo Bill Cody's niece built this small log-cabin mountain resort in the Shoshone National Forest in 1910, naming it after a prominent rock formation nearby. She started with a canvas lean-to and tents, replacing these quickly with the main lodge and dining hall, and later adding individual cabins. The lodge has its original peeled-log interior and exterior, with a large stone fireplace. The dining room still serves freshly made meals. Each cabin has a log exterior and is furnished with antiques as well as handmade pine-log beds and tables assembled without nails. Flanked by rock cliffs on two sides and surrounded by pine trees, the lodge is but a few feet from the trout-filled Shoshone River. The lodge's mountain-wise saddle horses take riders into the solitude of pine forest trails.

Open: May 20 to October 15 **Accommodations:** 10 guest cabins with private baths; 2 are suites **Meals:** restaurant on premises serves three meals daily **Rates:** $66 to $80 European Plan—cabins only—excludes meals; $100 per person American Plan includes 3 meals daily and trail rides **Payment:** AmEx, Visa, MC, personal and traveler's checks **Activities:** horseback wilderness rides, river fishing, campfire cookouts, hiking, tubing, western movies